HUNGARY

PECS

SZEGED

DRAVA R.

TIMISOARA

VOJVODINA

RUMANIA

DANUBE R.

SAVA R.

MITROVICA

ZEMUN

BELGRADE

BOSNA R.

POZAREVAC

S

LOZNICA
KRUPANJ

SMEDEREVSKA
PALANKA

DRINA R.

E

VALJEVO

R

SARAJEVO

UZICE

B

KLALJEVO

ZAP. MORAVA

DANUBE R.

FOCA

DRINA

IVANICA

L

TIMOK R

EGOVINA

NOVI VAROS

Mt. Durmitor

ZABLJAK

A

IBAR

JUZ. MORAVA

MONTENEGRO

TREPCA

V

DUBROVNIK

NIKSIC

SOFIA

CETINJE
TITOGRAD

I

KOTARSKA

DRIN

VARDARSKA

BULGARIA

A

SKOPLJE

A

L

VARDAR

TRESNA R.

TITOV
VELES

MAVROVO

B

BREGALNICA R.

L

MACEDONIA

A

TIRANA

A

N

OCHRID

VARDAR R.

RESEN

I

BITOLJ

GREECE

palacios

(52-6359) 4-2-65

THE EAGLE AND THE ROOTS

The eagles are gone: crows and daws, crows and daws . . .
—WILLIAM SHAKESPEARE *Troilus and Cressida,* I, ii

OTHER BOOKS
BY THE SAME AUTHOR

BY LOUIS ADAMIC

THE EAGLE AND THE ROOTS

DOUBLEDAY & COMPANY, INC., GARDEN CITY, N. Y., 1952

LIBRARY OF CONGRESS
CATALOG CARD NUMBER 52–6359

COPYRIGHT, 1952, BY DOUBLEDAY & COMPANY, INC.
ALL RIGHTS RESERVED
PRINTED AT THE COUNTRY LIFE PRESS, GARDEN CITY, N.Y., U.S.A.
FIRST EDITION

Because of the author's death, the final work on this book was done by the undersigned. The editing consisted of cutting about a third of the text, along lines the author had suggested or we were reasonably certain he would have followed. No other changes were made. The body of the work is as the author wrote it, except for the following cuts:

one long chapter describing the world situation. It had grown to such proportions that the author came to the reluctant conclusion that it would have to be published separately;

a chapter about Old Yugoslavia, describing conditions that led to the revolution. This material is covered implicitly and explicitly in the rest of the book and in two of the author's earlier works on Yugoslavia —*The Native's Return* and *My Native Land;*

a final chapter which repeated ground already covered and which would not have appeared in its original form in any event;

routine tightening and minor deletions: footnotes, asides, references, and restatements that impeded the flow of the story.

The author often mentioned how much he appreciated the sympathetic patience and encouragement of Bucklin Moon, his first editor, at Doubleday.

STELLA ADAMIC
TIMOTHY SELDES

v

CONTENTS

vii

To begin with——

A TRIP WITHOUT ITINERARY . . . BUT OF COURSE
I MEANT TO GO TO YUGOSLAVIA

I think there is fatality in it—
I seldom go to a place I set out for.
—LAURENCE STERNE *A Sentimental Journey*

BOOK ONE

CHAPTER ONE: *I really wanted
to go to Russia first,
but——*

IN MID-AUTUMN OF 1948, as the Truman-Wallace-Dewey contest for the Presidency of the United States whirled to a startling climax, I found myself free to decide that I would spend as much of 1949 abroad as my exchequer and other circumstances allowed: five to ten months. I was not thinking of writing a book directly on the trip.

For a decade, off and on, I had been tossing about in my mind the idea for a narrative to be entitled "The Education of Michael Novak" (with apologies to Henry Adams) in which I would deal with aspects of the American and the world scene during the first half of the twentieth century from the point of view of a "successful" American who came to the United States in the 1890's as an immigrant from tiny Slovenia, then a part of Austria, later of Yugoslavia. And, beginning in 1946, I occasionally felt that I was about ready to settle down to the two- or three-year work—but I kept postponing it.

In a talk at the Unitarian Church in Orange, New Jersey, in January 1947, I said: "Whether or not we can avoid World War III, I don't know; but I feel that if we don't at least try to avoid it, nothing else is worth doing. If we don't try to avoid it, it is vain to wonder about the kind of curtains you will hang up in the spring. It may be pointless to write books or to read those already in print, except perhaps Herman Melville's *Moby Dick,* which I lately re-read and found to be a prophecy of the present moment. In that book, a character called Father Mapple says in the course of a thundering sermon: '. . . Woe to him who, in this world, courts not dishonor! Woe to him who would not be true, even though to be false were salvation. . . .' If we don't try to avoid World War III, it is ludicrous to worry about being called a Red, a Communist, or whatever; or about being hauled up before the Committee on Un-American Activities. If you're not doing anything to try to prevent another war, it may be futile to work at your job and worry about keeping on the good side of whoever can take the job away from you. . . ."

Now, late in 1948, when a majority of less than 49 per cent of the total of qualified American voters who went to the trouble of going to the polls decided—tentatively, at least—*in favor of a "Welfare State" domestic program which called for full employment, good wages, and price supports for farm products, but which was rabidly anti-communistic, anti-socialistic, and which, as such, I thought, could be partly and temporarily realized only in conjunction with a war crisis;* when a preponderance of Americans were said to believe that World War III was inevitable sooner or later; and when most of the "experts" scheduled it to break out sometime between 1952 and '55; now, it seemed to me that before I did anything else I wanted a look around to see if I could determine for myself, from direct contacts and impressions, where we were.

Not naturally a defeatist, I wished to get rid of my growing disposition to say "Yes" to the question John Dos Passos asked in 1916: "Are we not men crouching on a runaway engine?"

Naturally an optimist, I found no satisfaction in regarding as near-accurate Henry Adams' prevision in 1901 of events at the midpoint of the twentieth century: "All we can say is that, at the rate of increase of speed and momentum, as calculated on the [basis of Industrial-Revolutionary developments of the] last fifty years, the present society must break its damn neck in . . . not exceeding fifty years more. . . . If anyone told me that there is going to be Hell to pay all around, I should not care to contradict him."

However, if I understood my state of mind and feelings, it was not so much fear of our using the A-bomb or being devastated by it at some darkly hovering date, as revulsion at the cowardice, the informing, the fear, the telephone-tapping, the knuckling-under to intimidation, the hoodlum mentality, "the fix," that evidently had begun to creep into, if not to dominate, American life. For example: in the spring of 1948 I learned that the twenty-year-old son of a friend of mine, a university student whom I had considered a fine, intelligent young man, was spending much of his spare time in the campus bookstore, not really browsing but keeping tabs on professors and students who tended to pick up a "leftist" book or magazine before a "rightist" one.

When I decided on the trip, I had no itinerary—only some ideas of where I wished to go and what I wished to do.

Of course I meant to go to Yugoslavia if the State Department permitted it. (With few exceptions, American passports issued during 1947–49 contained a rubber-stamped invalidation for entry into Yugoslavia on the grounds that the country was unsafe for United States citizens.)

My mother had written me. She was seventy-three and not likely to get younger: When was I coming? I wanted to see, too, what war and revolution had done to my native land. I expected to meet Tito and some of the other new leaders there. I was more curious about than interested in the Cominform-Tito "rift," as it was called then. Late in 1948, four or five months after it burst into the headlines, it did not seem the most weighty business under the sun. I thought it was a mix-up of some kind, a stupid mistake or a piece of rascality, or a combination of the two: one of many such combinations rattling about the globe, each justifying itself with the others. But I wouldn't spend more than six or seven weeks in Yugoslavia, and I didn't care very much if they came at the start or at the end of my trip—except that, pushing fifty, I was a bit tired and I figured that a short rest in a skiers' or mountain-climbers' lodge *na Gorenjskem,* in the Slovenian Upland, might be pleasant to start with.

India interested me and Israel. Italy drew me too. But more than at any other place I wanted a peek at the "one-sixth of the globe" generally regarded as the second greatest power in the world.

In mid-December 1948—when my visa-seeking letter to Ambassador Alexander Panyushkin of two weeks earlier was still unanswered—I went to the Soviet Embassy in Washington. Two men in their late thirties received me and for an hour and a half exerted their talents to find out my political coloring and particularly my attitude toward the Soviet Union and the Cominform-Tito split, then in its sixth month but outwardly still fairly quiescent if compared to what it became in 1949–50.

In reply to their first question about my thoughts on the split, I told the Soviet attachés that I was more puzzled by it now than I had been by the first headlines at the end of June and early in July 1948—an article I had written in the New York *Star* then did not make sense to me any more. Lately I had tried to pry loose information from Yugoslav representatives in the United States, but they either couldn't or didn't wish to give it. And I had no idea how much I would learn from Tito or anyone else in Yugoslavia when I got there. Maybe no one in Yugoslavia would talk about it either.

Several times during the conversation I said that to satisfy my curiosity about the Cominform-Tito disagreement was only a fraction of my pursuit. The over-all purpose of my trip was to see if a non-official person could do anything, if *I* could presume to think I could do anything as a writer, to help prevent another war. *Peace,* I emphasized, was my chief concern; everything else I considered worthwhile pivoted on it. If the Cominform-Tito break was a digit in the war-or-peace calculation, I wanted to learn all I could about it. Was it? No answer. Was it a by-product of the "cold war"? No answer.

One of the attachés asked pointedly *why* I wished to go to the Soviet Union *first.* I said because in the making of peace the USSR's responsibility was about equal to America's. How long did I wish to stay? Six, seven weeks, or longer; I had no schedule. What did I wish to see? Moscow, Leningrad, Stalingrad, the Volga; a collective farm, a village or two, a factory or two; and one of the Asian republics, say Uzbek or Tajik. Why Uzbek or Tajik? I wanted a first-hand impression of the Soviet federal system: how it handled the nationality or minority problem.

Apropos of war-or-peace, I said, what interested me very much was the idea, which cropped up every once in a while between blasts of the "cold war," that the American and the Soviet systems could coexist peaceably until one or the other gradually won out in the practical side of the mind of the world; or, more likely, until the churning of forces within these systems and the passage of time rubbed them both to a compromise. Was anyone of consequence in Russia mulling over if and how coexistence could become a basis of relations, at least of a *modus vivendi*, between the United States and the Soviet Union? If so, could we discuss it?

One attaché smiled briefly, the other remained deadpan. Every now and then in the course of the increasingly unpleasant interview they exchanged remarks in very rapid Russian which I understood imperfectly. One such exchange had to do with "Marxism-Leninism"—that I evidently was unversed in it.

Suddenly—Did I not wish to go to China also? Of course, but, with the revolution in full swing there, how could I get in? Who gave visas to the Communist territory? Or wasn't a regular visa required? No answer.

If I got the Soviet visa, I said, would someone in Moscow confirm or reject, partly or wholly, my tentative notion that the difficulties between the USA and the USSR were less ideological than big-power? Would anyone in Moscow care to discuss the idea which I shared with a number of other Americans, that the center of the trouble between the two great powers and in the world generally was not so much the Russian Revolution *versus* the American Way of Life as the whole vast Unbalance brought on by the Industrial Revolution—backwardness versus modern technology?[1] The attachés stared at me with wooden

[1] As I begin to shape the final draft of this book, the first issue of a new magazine called *trans/formation* (New York) comes to my attention. It contains a too-esoterically written article on "World Energy"—on the unequal distribution of "energy slaves." The latter are "units of non-human, mostly mechanical or technologically created and

uninterest, or so it seemed to me. By-and-by one of them looked at the other, smiling uncertainly.

For Christmas in 1944, when the end of World War II was in sight, I received a book—*The Superpowers* by W. T. R. Fox, a conservative political scientist at Columbia University—in which I marked the passages on the possibilities of friendly, or at least warless, relations between America and Russia after their mutual military victory against the Fascist Axis, and on how the USA might act to make those possibilities a basis of its policies toward the USSR: "As between the risk of acting as if the Soviet Union will be a trustworthy partner in maintaining peace and the risk of acting as if it will not," wrote Dr. Fox, "the lesser risk is clearly that based on expectation of Soviet good faith. . . . If we assume faith in the motives and integrity of the Soviet government there is a good chance of agreement upon a common program of Soviet-Anglo-American leadership in peace as in war." Without attempting to give the attachés the gist of these and similar sentences, I inquired if they knew the book. One of them asked if it was an anti-Soviet book. I said no; it was, rather, a typical American scholarly study, aiming to be objective, fair, constructive.

Whom did I represent? Nobody. With whom was I connected? Nobody. Along with such people as Eleanor Roosevelt, Jo Davidson, Harlow Shapley, Lillian Hellman, Bartley Crum, and Corliss Lamont I was—or had been—on the sponsor lists of numerous transient committees but I was not actively "connected" with any of them; in fact, I partly or largely disapproved of many of them as they showed themselves in practice. I was making the trip on my own behalf as a free-lance writer bent on clarifying my thinking if I could.

Silence. Then, a bit hesitantly: What was I politically? I laughed; then, sloughing off a reaction that it was none of their business, I de-

---

used, energy serving man [which in 1950] outnumber 38 times the man population which they serve" and each of which is equivalent to "approximately 150,000 foot-pounds of work. A foot-pound of work equals the amount of energy required to lift one pound one foot vertically." These "energy slaves" are man's "net advantage in dealing with environment."

In other words, in 1950 the world's 2,250,000,000 people have 85,500,000,000 "energy slaves." But here is the rub. *While the average number of "energy slaves" per man throughout the world is 38, the average inhabitant of North America, with 180,000,000 population, has 347 of them, the average inhabitant of Europe with a population of 540,000,000 has only 27 and the average inhabitant of Asia, with 1,125,000,000 people, has only 2.* These figures are said to be within ten percent accurate.

cided to give them as detailed an answer as their side of the conversation would take. I said I had voted for Bob LaFollette in 1924, for Al Smith in '28, for nobody in '32 because I was out of the country, then for Franklin Roosevelt three times, but I would have voted for Wendell Willkie in '44, had he lived and been a candidate. In '46 I had voted for H. Alexander Smith, a Republican, for United States Senator from New Jersey, because I thought Mr. Smith was a better man than his Democratic opponent. In '48, I went on, I joined Henry Wallace's movement because now, after Willkie's death, he alone among prominent American political figures appeared to know, and was saying out loud, that lasting peace could be achieved by attending to the inequalities among the peoples owing to the Industrial Revolution; and that at least half of the responsibility for initiative in that direction was America's. But this too, I put in after a pause, was a temporary affiliation.

What did I think of Mr. Wallace? Somewhat evasively, I said he was a well-meaning man, in many respects a typical American: independent, unpredictable, incongruous in his ideas, apt to produce effects other than he and his supporters desired. Why did he come out so poorly in the election? I said I didn't think he came out so poorly, but unless they had an hour or so to spare I'd rather not go into it.

Was I a liberal? Overcoming another twinge of resentment at this interrogation, I said I had been called that, but I disliked labels which had various meanings for various people. I objected least to being called a radical in the classical sense of going to the root of issues, or a leftist in the classical sense of favoring general welfare, as the American and Soviet constitutions favored it. I had been labeled an American nationalist. I might, with some justice, also be called a conservative in the sense that I believed steps on the path of progress, or the desire for change, must include a concern and a plan for the preservation of human gains up to now; otherwise, as someone had said, "progress" was only an exchange of one nuisance for another. None of this evoked any comment from the Soviet officials. But, while vocally unresponsive, they looked very much interested.

As for Communism, that was a vast subject; but, briefly and roughly, my views on it at this time (in 1948) were as follows: Aspiration to a system called Communism was a massive fact in the twentieth century. The stimulus for this aspiration derived in large part and most immediately from the Industrial Revolution, from capitalism. Like everything else under the sun, as an ideology and a practice, as a way of life, Communism was evolving under the influence of its environment. Capitalism—in so far as it still existed and enjoyed popular support (mainly in the United States)—was an important phase of that environment. If capitalist America continued to fight the aspiration to Communism of large numbers of people in some of the little-developed and crowded regions and continents, it would be one kind of Communism; *if,* on the other hand, the American people recognized that aspiration as a groping drive to catch up with and share the benefits of the Industrial Revolution, and worked out a policy to help it along, it would be another kind of Communism. Conversely, I said, the American system and the American people were under the influence of *their* environment, in which the upsurge of the World Communist Movement was a paramount factor; and the formation in the years ahead of the American political mood and character would depend, to no slight extent, on the manner and methods of the World Communist Movement. Did they agree? Disagree? Their wordless smiles lamed the rest of my thought: that the Russians could help develop a favorable mood in America, thus helping her to understand them, by recognizing *her* special background and aspirations.

I broke the long pause by expressing a wish to see Ambassador Panyushkin. Sorry, the Ambassador was ill. I could return in a week or ten days: Could I hope to see the Ambassador then? No answer.

One attaché asked if I had ever written anything about the Soviet Union. No, not about the Soviet Union as a scene, a state, or a social system. How could I? I had never been there. But occasionally I had referred to Soviet Russia, basing what I wrote on what I had read. Favorably or unfavorably? Both, I said, but of late mostly favorably: this, in part, because nearly everybody else in America was riding Russia as the source of all evil. The last two or three years I had written and lectured on Soviet-American tension, maintaining that if we were to avoid a new military war we ought to cease the "cold war." I had been stressing the need for continual friendly *reciprocity*. I agreed with E. C. Ropes, former chief of the USSR Division, Office of International Trade, United States Department of Commerce, that the two great countries, with their tremendous resources, needed each other. Were they aware of Mr. Ropes' views? That he had published them in a Wall Street magazine (*Dun's Review,* May, 1947)? They looked at me wide-eyed. No answer.

Then another question: What did I think, *whose* fault was the tension, as I called it, between the Soviet Union and the United States? I replied that efforts to fix the blame could only lead to greater tension. An attempt to press me to say who I thought was at fault in the "cold war" led me to remark that, of course, if I thought the "fault" was America's, I wouldn't say so in a Soviet embassy any more than I would expect them to say the opposite in an American embassy. The attachés stiffened.

Trying to provoke them into some kind of spontaneous remark, I continued that as a writer and lecturer I believed Americans and Russians should cease writing and talking mostly of their own best qualities and the others' worst. From the Marxian vantage point, I admitted, this might be sheer utopianism, but I felt we should begin to notice each other's virtues and give our minds a chance to come to grips with the core of the human problem, a big part of which was in the unequal distribution of technological equipment and know-how, in the disparity of our production abilities, in the fact that between half and two-thirds of the world's population had no idea how it felt to have a full stomach, and in the possibility that the future lay not in rivalry between drives to domination and uniformity but in mutual help for aspirations to freedom and the tendency to diversity in economics and culture. If they wished, I would gladly send them copies of my articles and lectures in which I had tried to develop these views. No answer.

Early in 1947 the *Bolshevik,* the theoretical organ of the Communist Party of the Soviet Union, had published an eight-page review of my book *Dinner at the White House,* summarizing its contents, praising it mildly, and disagreeing in restrained language with its implication that the United States was not naturally and inevitably imperialist, certainly not in the British, Dutch, Belgian, and French or German and Japanese sense. Would the *Bolshevik* review weigh in favor of my receiving a visa? No answer.

"I'm not getting anywhere," I thought.

By-and-by one of the attachés smiled. Wasn't I afraid of being summoned before the Committee on Un-American Activities if I went to the USSR? No. Why should I be afraid? That committee—then headed by Congressman J. Parnell Thomas, representing the New Jersey district where I lived, but about to go to prison for defrauding the United States Government—already had me down as a subversive. Didn't that worry me? Not especially, I said; "subversion" was a rela-

tive matter; in the United States—and, it wouldn't surprise me, elsewhere—everybody who was at least half alive was subversive in one
way or another. Didn't I think the Committee on Un-American Activities was very powerful? Seemingly, right now, yes; actually, in the
long run, no; or at least I hoped not alongside of America's sound
qualities, traditions, and institutions, most of which derived from past
"subversion" but were now obscured by the hysteria which the Un-
American Activities Committee, aided by events abroad (I almost
said "aided by Soviet behavior, especially by Mr. Vishinky's speeches"),
was helping to generate.

Partly to crack the ensuing pause but mostly for the hell of it, I
added that my ambition was to be a free man, and I was coming to the
realization that, in a period like the present, one could enjoy freedom—
in relation to his environment and within himself—only if one did
not give a hoot what anybody thought of him, or what happened to
him. This, I hastened to explain, was not intellectual heroics. It was
simply that I felt I could not afford to be afraid or to worry about Congressman Thomas' notions of me, or what might become of me pro-
fessionally. No comment. In the following silence Thoreau popped into
my mind, as did my top-sergeant in the United States Army during
the First World War whose motto was "To hell with 'em all but six—
save 'em for pallbearers."

But the strange and pressing importance of Tito! Time and again,
one or the other attaché swung the conversation back to him. Had I
read the Cominform resolution condemning him and his clique? Yes,
also the Yugoslav retorts. Which did I believe? Suppressing the thought
which had occurred to me months before, that neither the resolution
nor the retorts were convincing, I answered that I didn't know enough
to say.

What did I think, asked one of the attachés, why was the State Department suddenly ready to unfreeze the Yugoslav gold and eager to
give Tito a loan? I recalled a recent news item that, according to a
State Department spokesman, an old Yugoslav application for a loan
was being dusted off by the Export-Import Bank. Well, why not?
Hadn't Czechoslovakia asked for American loans too? Hadn't Poland
obtained a loan of ninety millions (with the aid of a big Washington
law firm which had close State Department connections and was paid
a fee of fifty thousand dollars)? Hadn't Moscow itself sought, or was

it not still seeking, a two-billion-dollar credit arrangement with Washington? Why shouldn't America unfreeze the gold which belonged to Yugoslavia? It should have been unfrozen long ago.

That, averred the Soviet interrogator sternly, was not the point. The point was: Why was the State Department *now—suddenly—*anxious to improve relations with Tito, to do business with him?

I quoted a remark by Disraeli before he became Prime Minister: that international affairs were seldom what they seemed to be; he never believed anything about them until the Foreign Office denied it twice. I thought this was mildly funny but the attachés didn't think so. Neither cracked a smile, and I was stabbed by an odd feeling—a mixture of disappointment and resentment.

After a pause, deciding to answer the question, I said I could guess the State Department's motive to improve relations with Tito had to do with the "cold war," taking advantage of the Cominform rift. And I was sorry about that. I favored good relations among all countries and peoples: between the Soviet Union and Yugoslavia, between the United States and the Soviet Union, between the United States and Yugoslavia, between Yugoslavia and Guatemala. I had long felt that, with or without ideological admixtures, power politics would play havoc with the world someday. But now, trying to think within the jagged frame of things-as-they-looked-to-me, I couldn't bemoan the prospect of a bettering of American-Yugoslav relations, or of a loan to Yugoslavia—"we're throwing billions around anyway." I said the loan idea was all to the good even if it came in the wake of the Cominform break. I knew how greatly the break disturbed the Yugoslavs. The ones I saw recently in New York and Washington were deeply pained: I could tell by the way they looked when I pressed them with questions.

I was going to add my impression that Tito's representatives at Lake Success and in Washington probably had instructions from Belgrade to say as little about the rift as possible, lest they help make it worse, but I didn't. Righteous pleasure radiating from their faces, the Soviet attachés looked like a couple of simultaneously fanatical and smug religionists hearing about sinners hurtling to hell.

For a moment I wasn't sure I wanted to go to Russia. Then I thought of course I did—more than ever. Was Tito a part of the x in the peace-war equation? Maybe the Cominform story needed looking into more than I was able to imagine, and a part of it doubtless was to be learned only in Russia—if someone there would talk to me.

I had talked too much, too frankly, too naïvely. To get a visa, I should have tried to make these fellows think I was anti-Tito and opposed to the State Department's current inclination to improve American-Yugoslav relations. Too late now, though. I should have tried to cash in on my crimson reputation with the Committee on Un-American Activities. But that might not have worked either.

I was glad when the attachés rose. One of them said my visa request would be referred to Moscow; when they received a reply, they would inform me. When did they think a reply might come? The attaché's shoulders went up in a slow, heavy shrug. Would they cable Moscow? No answer. I picked up my hat and coat, and said I would be glad to pay for any cables. I meant to be off on my trip in about a month; if I heard from them within three weeks, it would give me time to arrange my transportation to Russia first.

We stood in silence awhile. . . . Well, thank you. Goodbye.

"What a hell of a way to make friends and influence people," I thought, walking back to my hotel. "The damfools! But maybe they can't help themselves. Or don't the Russians want to make friends as a matter of policy? Maybe the Kremlin feels it thrives on animosity, even on the danger of another war. Is the Kremlin crazy enough to *want* World War III? Or does it really think it inevitable according to the Marxian analysis as Jehovah Witnesses believe it is inevitable according to the Old Testament, or as the capitalistic Marxians-in-reverse hold it is inevitable simply because they want to see Communism destroyed?

"I probably handled myself even worse than I think I did. I should have lied."

Thinking over the interview, I went back five weeks, to November 7, 1948. In response to an engraved black-and-gold invitation, I had gone to Washington to attend the reception at the Soviet Embassy celebrating the thirty-first anniversary of the Russian Revolution. There were a half-dozen or so high-ranking American generals and admirals I recognized, and perhaps a dozen leftists, three or four who I was next to certain were card-carrying Communists; and I was vaguely uneasy. I stayed at the reception celebrating the Russian Revolution less than an hour, partook of none of the food and drink on the endless tables (partly because I didn't care to push my way through the great crowd to them), and caught an early evening train back to Trenton. In the car I entered was Henry Wallace with two New York leaders of the Progressive Party who I knew were non-Communist verging on anti-Communist. They invited me to sit with them. As the press and radio reported it the next day, Wallace and several of his prominent campaign workers had attended the affair as an anti-war gesture. Now the man next to Wallace, opposite me, was voicing a complaint against the Russian manner. Why were all the officials, from the Ambassador on down, so stiff, so cold? Who wanted all that damn caviar and sturgeon, champagne and vodka, if you couldn't get a smile and a genuinely open remark from the hosts? And come to think of it, said the man by the window directly opposite Wallace, why did they bar a man like George Seldes[2] from the Soviet Union? How were we to find out what was going on there? What *was* going on there? Did they expect us (American liberals or progressives) to be friends of the Soviet Union sight unseen and no questions asked? What did they take us for? . . .

Wallace was looking out at the lights along the way, and I couldn't tell whether he was listening or not. When the complainants fell silent, he turned and remarked, slowly, with the curiously unnatural smile I had noticed a few times before, that it wasn't easy to be a friend of the Soviet Union: official Russians did very little to help one understand their country, to make one feel they really wanted good relations or believed lasting peace possible. . . .

This was a factor in my wanting to visit the USSR first and foremost, even before Yugoslavia.

I got a passport with which I could enter any country that would give me a visa, including Yugoslavia.

On January 5, 1949, I telephoned the Soviet Embassy in Washington. A gritty voice, which I thought belonged to neither of the two attachés, clipped off the information that there was no word for me yet. What were the chances of my getting a visa? I was asked to hold the line a moment. I held it for three or four minutes. Then I was told again that there was no word for me yet. If word came in the near future, I said, would they please write me, or telegraph? They had my home address; their message would be forwarded.

[2] Editor of the weekly *In Fact* (discontinued in 1950).

On January eleventh I boarded a plane at LaGuardia Field and reached Belgrade *via* London and Prague in twenty-one flying hours. The smooth above-the-weather, non-stop flight over the Atlantic was a triumph of the Industrial Revolution, a miracle of the Machine Age: a sharp contrast to my first impression of Belgrade, where "brigades" of citizens, young and old, many of them ill clad and ill shod in near zero weather, equipped only with hand shovels—with not a single snow-removing machine in sight—were beginning to "attack" the three-foot snow that had fallen on northeastern Yugoslavia the preceding two days.

While in Yugoslavia in 1932–33, I had met a couple of Slovenian students in their earliest twenties: Edvard Kardelj and Boris Kidric. Now, in New Yugoslavia, Kardelj was Vice-Premier and Foreign Minister; and Kidric, as Chairman of the Federal Economic Council and the State Planning Commission, was in direct charge of the Five-Year Plan, of the whole national economy. Still in their thirties, both were members of the Politburo, the nine-man directorate of the Communist Party of Yugoslavia—the CPY—the revolutionary party in power.

Back in 1932–33, Kidric, whom I met several times, made more of an impression on me than Kardelj, whom I saw only twice, briefly. Unlike the ultra-dynamic Kidric, with his almost Da Vincian range of interests, Kardelj was a slight, frail chap with a subdued manner. He was just out of prison. Before he was sentenced to a two-year term for revolutionary activity against King Alexander's dictatorship, he had been beaten and tortured in the royal secret-political-police headquarters both in his native city of Ljubljana, the capital of Slovenia, and in Belgrade. Except for a letter from Kidric in 1934, about a year after my return to the United States, I had had no contact with either of the young men. Neither is mentioned in *The Native's Return,* published in 1934, for I never thought they would play leading roles in the Yugoslav revolution which appeared to me likely if not inevitable. But in *My Native Land,* published in 1943, Kidric occupies a good deal of space, because his name kept recurring in the information I was receiving from embattled Yugoslavia. Kardelj had just about slipped from my memory.

Early in 1945 Yugoslav representatives began to come to America for the United Nations meetings. Several were dogmatic, omniscient, smug

"Marxians" whose notions of America stemmed from *The Daily Worker*. Their minds and feelings were pinned to a fixed idea. They wore blinders. They were appalled when I suggested they read *The Wall Street Journal,* and shook their heads at my unawareness that a new depression, which would kick off a revolution, was imminent. Others I liked a lot.

Among the latter was a young Serbian giant named Vlado Dedijer. He had lived in the United States briefly in 1931—long enough to learn English and win the ping-pong championship at the Lynn, Mass., Y.M.C.A.—and then been a correspondent of a Belgrade newspaper in London for a while. I had heard of him before. In March 1945 he came to America as a Yugoslav delegate to the First United Nations Conference in San Francisco. He told me about his brother, Stevo Dedijer, a Princeton graduate who had been a paratrooper in the United States Army. Before Vlado went to the Coast, I showed him around New York and Washington a little. He was impressed by the Jefferson Memorial, especially by the text of the four panels inside. (One panel reads: "I am not an advocate for frequent changes in laws and constitutions, but laws and institutions must go hand in hand with the progress of the human mind. As that becomes more developed, more enlightened, as new discoveries are made, new truths discovered and manners and opinions change, with the change of circumstances, institutions must advance also to keep pace with the times. We might as well require a man to wear still the coat which fitted him when a boy as civilized society to remain ever under the regimen of their barbarous ancestors.") "Why, that's good historic dialectic!" Vlado exclaimed.

There was another young colossus, Vladimir Popovic, a Montenegrin with an open-faced smile. He was a veteran of the Spanish Civil War and Tito's first ambassador to Moscow. He asked searching questions about America.

There was Ales Bebler, a slim, young Slovenian who had learned English while he was a captain attached to the headquarters unit of the Lincoln Brigade in the Spanish Civil War. Like Popovic and like Dedijer, he openly admired many phases of American life which somehow existed despite the lamentable fact that the United States was professedly as unsocialistic as any country in the world.

All three were Communists from their early youth, figures in the Yugoslav Revolution, personal friends of Tito's and Kardelj's. (They became well known to those following the United Nations meetings.

In January 1950 Ales Bebler was made Yugoslavia's delegate to the United Nations Security Council at Lake Success. In May 1950 Vladimir Popovic came to Washington as the Yugoslav Ambassador to the United States.)

Every once in a while during 1945–47 Dedijer, Bebler, Popovic, and others whom I met asked me when I would revisit Yugoslavia. I said I did not know, but I would eventually, of course. Early in 1946 my brother France wrote me that people in Yugoslavia were wondering why I didn't come: Was I angry? I didn't explain that I was afraid the new setup there might tempt me to write another book on Yugoslavia: I felt two were enough. Nor did I explain that my heart and mind were riveted on the United States, the chief base of the Industrial Revolution and, as such, the world's greatest power, just beginning to assume its role and apt to bungle it. Traditionally isolationist, inexperienced in international affairs, inclined to be self-righteous, America might blunder more than was safe for world peace and her security. At times during 1945–46, as well as later, I hardly knew what I meant by "America" in this context. Clearly, while events moved at supersonic speed, the American people had little if anything to do with shaping the foreign policy of the United States. That was the function of small groups in strategic positions and of purposeful individuals with easy access to those groups. Propaganda, whose main ingredient was real or make-believe fear of Communism in Russia, was the chief means used by these policymakers. The military were coming to the top in domestic and foreign affairs. Some of the big financial interests, particularly those based on adventurous, unstable "new capital" and bedeviled by day-to-day urgencies, were out for a quick killing at home and abroad, and to blazes with the consequences. Leaders of organized labor tended more and more to follow the propaganda line and go along with the big interests. With their day-to-day mentality, intimately linked to the financial-industrial superstructure of American culture, they could do nothing else. Subversive elements were in control of government departments. They disguised their aims and maintained their position, in part, by branding harmless individuals and groups subversive. Some of the State Department personnel was homosexual; much of it was under subtle British and Vatican influence if not control. And there, like the great white whale in *Moby Dick,* loomed Red Russia! Was she really Red? Or primarily a great power, as inexperienced as America, and undeveloped and primitive to boot? Was it intelligent for Americans to attribute to her, to the Kremlin, everything that was bad under the sun, as the monomaniacal Captain Ahab attributes all evil to the whale ("that inscrutable thing") he hates and madly pursues to his own destruction? Wasn't Russia "white" too? Was D. H. Lawrence's analysis of *Moby Dick* right? That the strange voyage of the whaling ship was symbolic of the disasterward impulse of "the Great White Soul" at odds with itself? I was not indifferent to Yugoslavia, I could hardly be, but her future, also, depended on a lasting peace, which to me was largely a matter between America and Russia.

Much as I wanted to go to Russia first, there were moments early in January 1949, just before I left the United States, when I was almost glad the Soviet visa hadn't come through yet. I hoped it wouldn't until some time late in February, or until after I reapplied for it in March or April when I reached Czechoslovakia or Poland. As I say, I was tired, and I cabled my brother France in Ljubljana, who was director of *Slovenija Vino* (the wine trust of the People's Republic of Slovenia), to reserve a room for me for two or three weeks at a lodge in the Slovenian Upland, and to meet me at the Zemun (Belgrade) airport if he could. I thought he might help me get oriented and expedite my proceeding to Slovenia, for I had heard transportation was extremely tight in Yugoslavia.

France came to the airport, but I didn't see him at once. A crowd of men stood against a high bank of snow, waiting, their faces partly obscured by their breath in the cold air. I recognized three: Vlado Dedijer, Ales Bebler, and Boris Kidric. They grinned broadly, pressed my hand and pumped my arm, speaking words of welcome I couldn't hear for the propeller whir still in my ears. Others in the group were representatives of writers', journalists', and artists' organizations.

There were reporters and a photographer. To Vlado Dedijer, then Director of Information in the federal government, I said I wished the papers wouldn't report my arrival. He turned to Kidric and the rest of the crowd: "Look what this *Amerikanac* is trying to do—censor our free press! He's four years late in coming, now he wants to suppress the fact that he has arrived!"

Laughter. . . . I wanted to explain that I was trying to get into the Soviet Union, and that I was afraid publicity in Yugoslavia would not help. But Kidric steered me into the unheated airport restaurant. On the rough, coverless table were *slivovica* (plum brandy) and "coffee" (chicory, really, and roasted barley). There were questions about my trip. And I forgot what might get into the papers.

Two weeks later I read a New York *Times* clipping:

BELGRADE GREETS ADAMIC
GIVES AUTHOR BIGGER WELCOME THAN IT DID VISHINSKY

It was a Belgrade dispatch based on items in the Yugoslav press. The gist of the "story" was that Boris Kidric came to the airport to greet me, whereas no member of the Yugoslav Politburo met Vishinsky, then Soviet Deputy Commissar of Foreign Affairs, when he came to Belgrade as head of the Soviet delegation to the Danube Conference in the summer of 1948, about a month after the Cominform outburst against Tito.

"If this does not finish my chance of getting a Soviet visa," I thought, "it certainly reduces it."

In the next three weeks, however, the realization that I had never had a chance began to form under my thick cortex. I was born in Yugoslavia. Worse yet, I had written approvingly of the Tito-led social revolution. I had not recanted during the cross-examination by the two Soviet attachés in Washington. To have ever had a good word about Tito was after the Cominform's anti-Tito resolution as goading to Soviet officialdom as it had long been to the Chicago *Tribune* and the Brooklyn *Tablet,* to Westbrook Pegler and other columnists using the Un-American Activities Committee's "protected" or libel-proof materials originated by turncoat Communists and self-confessed spies. The difference was that the "Un-Americans" branded you a Stalin stooge and Tito-tooter, a Communist, pro-Communist, or fellow-traveler, which they beforehand made synonymous with son-of-a-bitch and equivalent to their own definitions of un-American and subversive; while in the Soviet or Cominform book now—in 1949—you were suddenly a fascist beast, reactionary shark, American spy, Wall Street warmonger, or imperialist cannibal.

In mid-February, near the end of my vacation in the beautiful Slovenian Upland, my youngest brother Joze—who had a job in Zone B, the Yugoslav-occupied part of the so-called Free Territory of Trieste— sent me a copy of a Slovenian anti-Tito paper called *Demokracija,* allegedly financed by the Anglo-American Intelligence Services and published in the "Anglo-American" Zone A, which reported that I had lately come to Yugoslavia to write another book in support of Tito's police state, or perhaps to induce the Belgrade dictator to knuckle under to the Kremlin again: for, according to unnamed sources in the USA, to which the editor had a pipeline, I was a long-time Soviet agent or spy.[3]

One evening a while later I was turning the shortwave knob on the radio set in my brother France's apartment in Ljubljana, and happened to get the tail end of an American newscast from Frankfort, bits of a BBC commentary, and a Radio Budapest attack on Tito. The attack, in the Serbo-Croatian language, was a paraphrase of numerous violent Cominform broadcasts on the same subject I had listened to, with waning interest, during my stay at the mountain lodge; and, bored after a few minutes, I was about to give the knob another twirl to see what else the East European air-wave had to offer, when lo! I heard my name in the Yugoslav pronunciation: Luj Adamic. The Budapest speaker said that I, a well-known White House lounge-lizard, State Department agent, and Wall Street pimp, had lately reached Yugoslavia to propel Tito and his gang deeper into the imperialist camp, then (before the Atlantic Treaty) in the process of being organized by Western warmongers aiming to attack the Soviet Union and the people's democracies. Why this action by me should be necessary, Radio Budapest neglected to explain: for in recent weeks Radios Moscow, Prague, and Budapest had said again and again that the nefarious,

[3] On September 15, 1950, the Pittsburgh *Press* published a "story" by its special Washington correspondent that while in the office of Strategic Services (the cloak-and-dagger OSS) during World War II I was a Russian spy. I could not sue the paper and prove at least that I had never been an OSS official or officer, for the "story" was based on some vague chatter in the summer of 1948 by an ex-Communist and self-confessed member of a Soviet spy ring in Washington, named Elizabeth Bentley, who then entered a Catholic retreat. Her chatter was libel-proof because she had engaged in it before a Congressional subcommittee. At the same time a rumor reached me that a group in Congress was planning to do with me in reference to the State Department's 1950 policy toward Yugoslavia what Senator McCarthy had done with Owen Lattimore in respect to China. This plan was to be executed soon after Congress reconvened in November. It was abandoned, presumably, because of the sudden very great crisis in American foreign policy brought on by the military debacle in Korea. This crisis—"a shocking and bruising fact," as General Omar Bradley called it—prompted even some of the fiercest anti-Communists and most loyal Vatican fellow-travelers in Congress to cast a pitying eye on "drought-stricken Yugoslavia," take a "calculated risk" with Tito, and vote for the $38,000,000 aid to him, lest "subversive forces" (President Truman's phrase) undermine his regime.

terroristic Tito clique had maneuvered Yugoslavia all the way into the Western imperialist camp months before.

What influences or what finally determines one's actions is not always clear. My decision to write and then my need to rewrite and rewrite this book under various working titles, finally settling on *The Eagle and the Roots,* may have been determined by an unusual experience I tell about later.

BOOK ONE

CHAPTER TWO: THE NATIVE RETURNS AGAIN

First impressions amid fortuitous circumstances
The White city is really white, also
very red and somewhat blue

> *The exact contrary of what is generally believed*
> *is often the truth.*
> —JEAN DE LA BRUYÈRE, Caractères, *1688*

> *You have no business with consequences;*
> *you are to tell the truth.*
> —SAMUEL JOHNSON, Boswell's Life, *1784*

> *Tell the truth and run.*
> —YUGOSLAV PROVERB

AT THE PRAGUE AIRPORT, the official in charge of the Belgrade-bound Yugoslav plane introduced me to the pilot, who shook my hand with great energy. He was a short, well-set Dalmatian in his early middle years. A beaked nose jutted out from a seamed dark face, and bushy brows from over deep-sunken blue eyes. His head had the immutability of a piece of sculpture, till he smiled; then all of him burst into life.

"The captain has just become a millionaire," said the official, and both of them smiled and waited for me to react to the information.

"A millionaire? In dollars, pounds, francs, kronen, zloty, dinars, or what?"

They laughed. It was a joke that needed further help from me to bring it out.

"I thought Yugoslavia was a socialist country," I said. "If you still have millionaires, then the Cominform accusation that you're back-sliding into capitalism is true."

They roared. "No, no," said the official when his laughter subsided enough so he could talk. "The captain is a *socialist* millionaire, a *Tito* millionaire. Yesterday, between Belgrade and Prague, he completed his millionth kilometer in the air."

I congratulated the captain, and said, "In America there's a saying that the first million is the hardest to make—meaning capitalistic dollars, of course. I hope this also applies to socialistic kilometers."

After we left Prague, looking out of the little window by my seat, I noticed *TITO* scrawled big on the wing; and a couple of hours later, over southern Hungary, when the captain popped out of the cockpit and sat down beside me, I asked, "Who did that?"

"Oh, some groundman at Zemun, no doubt."

"Why?"

The captain looked as if my question struck him as a bit foolish or ignorant. "Marshal Tito's name," he said, "is lettered all over Yugoslavia."

"Why?"

"Because . . . because—I find it hard to say why. I'm a flyer, a mechanic, a simple man. To me, to many of us Yugoslavs, Tito is everything. Especially of late."

"Since the Cominform hit you?"

"Yes"—dismally.

I said: "I read that before the war, the names of Hitler and Mussolini were painted on walls all over Germany and Italy."

The captain looked at me sharply, unhappily. Then he decided to calm down and rearrange his expression before he said: "If I didn't know you were a friend of Yugoslavia, I'd resent that. My dear *gospodine Adamicu,* there's a great difference between those signs in Hitler's Germany and Mussolini's Italy and the sign on the wing of this plane." He rubbed his chin, trying to find words for the rest of his thought. "It's no use," he said after a while. "I'm a simple man——"

"Forgive me," I said, "I didn't mean to offend you."

"I know, I know," he said, reaching for my hand and pressing it, with bitter solemnity. "The world is poured over with anti-Yugoslav propaganda. But you'll stay in Yugoslavia awhile, won't you? . . . Only a few weeks? Even so, you will see for yourself that the comparison you made—perhaps just to tease me, to see what I would say—is unjust. I'm not the man to explain; all I know is airplanes, and not too much about them; everything else I feel in my heart. I love my country and all I can say is: Tito is everything to us. *Everything.*"
He fell still, looking at his clasped hands. Then he glanced at his wristwatch and rose abruptly and looked down through the window. "We crossed the Yugoslav-Hungarian border a few minutes ago." He beamed. "Welcome to New Yugoslavia!"

"Thank you, Captain." We shook hands again. "How are things in New Yugoslavia?" I asked.

"Hard but wonderful, or I could say, wonderful but hard."

"What do you mean?"

The captain rubbed his chin again. "We're in a wonderful moment, making a new beginning in our history. This is difficult, very difficult. But as Marshal Tito said in his New Year's radio address two weeks ago, when did we Yugoslavs ever have it easy? However, this snow which fell in recent days is good. It may mean a big harvest for a change." He looked at his watch again, and smiled embarrassedly. "I came out of the cockpit to ask you about American airplanes, for I was informed you flew all the way from New York. Instead, we started a political discussion!"

"From New York to London," I said, "I came in a huge four-motored Constellation, non-stop in slightly over fourteen hours. Not a bump all the way; we flew above the weather."

The captain's dark face glowed. *"Boga ti!* Someday Yugoslavia will have such planes." Again he gripped my hand. "I must go back in now."

"Congratulations again on your first million, Captain, and the best of luck on your second."

The "Tito millionaire"—who, I thought, was not a simple man at all—smiled broadly, bowed and saluted, and disappeared into the cockpit. Fifteen minutes later he brought the plane down in a swirl of snow.

At the long, rough table in the chill, bare restaurant in the Zemun airport (we sat in our overcoats) I was wedged between the irrepressible Brobdingnagian, Vlado Dedijer—nearly seven feet tall, weighing about three hundred pounds—and my quiet, smiling thirty-nine-year-old brother France.

"How is everybody at home?" I asked France. "What are they doing? How's Mother?"

"Mother works hard as ever," replied France. "We keep telling her to slow down but she won't. Everybody else is fine too. Their main occupation right now is waiting for the prodigal. Only this time," he chuckled, "there won't be a fatted calf."

"Why not?"

When I returned to my birthplace in 1932, after nineteen years in the United States, my family killed a calf and gave a feast.

"Well," smiled France, "this time you took only sixteen years to come home." Then, earnestly: "So much was destroyed in wartime; we're trying to build up the animal stock again, and there's a tight control: every head must be accounted for."

Boris Kidric—"the economic dictator" in the Western press during 1947–49—was grinning at me across the table.

"You've grown older, Lojze," he said, using the Slovenian form of my first name. His voice was as I remembered it from sixteen years back: vibrant and emphatic even when he was not saying anything very special. One of his feet, close to mine, tapped in nervous rhythm under the table. His whole body seemed to vibrate, except the square face with the strong chin and the intent, amused eyes.

"I'm a bit tired," I said, "and I'll be fifty in a couple of months. But why bring that up? You aren't the youngster yourself I once knew, though you look like the same volcano of energy."

"Only now," mumbled Vlado Dedijer, "the volcano is in a state of eruption."

Laughter. "In a state of constant eruption," someone else suggested, "constant but planned and controlled." This was a gibe at Boris' official title: Chairman of the State Planning Commission.

"Let's change the subject," said Boris. He turned to France: "What about the prodigal and the calf?"

Vlado Dedijer broke in to tell about the feast my family gave when I returned in 1932, and that I described it in *The Native's Return.*

"Then there ought to be a calf this time," said Boris.

"Oh no," I said, uncertain for a moment whether he was joking or not. "I don't like veal any more."

Boris looked at Vlado, mischief leaping in his eyes. "If a calf was slaughtered in Old Yugoslavia," he said, ignoring me, "and is not in New, he'll write about *that*. Then the West will have further 'proof' that socialism is a failure and a misfortune, and the Cominform will seize on it as fresh 'documentation' that Yugoslavia is about to collapse because she went into the imperialist-capitalist camp."

"Don't worry," I said, "I have no intention of writing anything about Yugoslavia."

"He has no intention of writing anything about Yugoslavia," said Boris mock seriously, looking around the table. "Just the same, we ought to be on the safe side, no?" To France: "If your family has a calf, do you think the people's committee would issue them a permit to slaughter it?"

"We can ask for it and see," said France.

"No, you won't," said I. "No special favors."

Vlado Dedijer announced he was on my side: the calf should be allowed to grow up into a bull.

"What are your plans?" Boris Kidric asked.

"Nothing definite. If I get a Soviet visa, I'll go to Russia right away. If I don't fairly soon, I'll stay in Yugoslavia six or seven weeks."

They waited for me to continue.

"First I want to see my family, then stow myself away somewhere for a couple of weeks and catch up on sleep. Until I do, I'm not much interested in anything, in Yugoslavia, the Cominform, anything——"

A somewhat awkward pause. Then one of the men—Dr. Ivo Andric, president of the Yugoslav Writers' Union—raised his *slivovica* glass, giving a toast welcoming me in the name of the organizations represented around the table. Unable to think of an appropriate response, and vexed with myself, I said merely, *"Hvala liepa*—thank you very much."

Boris said, "Kardelj intended to come with us but was held up the last minute."

"I'm glad someone in Belgrade has something better to do than meet me. How's Tito? Why didn't he come?"

No one laughed and the moment turned stiff. Had I offended them? Their silence felt like a rebuff to me. Hours later, mulling over this, I

wondered what kind of man I would find Tito to be. His name seemed
to have acquired an exalted meaning. Apparently, it wasn't good form
to crack jokes about him.

After a while, in a (for him) flat voice, Boris said Tito was fine,
and added: "He hopes to see you before you leave for Slovenia."

I asked France when we were going. Did he have the railroad
tickets? He said he had just returned from a wine-selling trip to
England, Belgium, Holland, and Switzerland, and was obliged to take
care of some business at the federal Ministry of Foreign Trade during
the next several days. Would I mind waiting for him so we could go
to Slovenia together? He would hurry his affairs.

I was asked about my flight from New York to London, how conditions were in America, whether I knew Dean Acheson, the new
Secretary of State—and the talk flowed naturally again.

There was something very refreshing about "these guys," as I called
them in my mind. Their humor was warm, genuine. I knew and liked
Vlado Dedijer and Ales Bebler. I thought I would like Boris Kidric.
Suddenly, my memory of him in 1932–33 was very vivid. I wanted to
have a long talk with him and learn what generated that tense restlessness, how he felt about Russia now, how the Cominform split affected
the Five-Year Plan, how he saw Yugoslavia's perspectives——

All at once my weariness lifted; the prospect of staying in Belgrade
for a few days was exciting.

"Beograd"—the Yugoslav form for "Belgrade"—means White City,
and it really was white. The previous two days a heavy snow had
fallen in northeastern Yugoslavia.

"White manure," said Vlado Dedijer, in whose car—a 1942 Plymouth
—France and I rode from the airport to the city, across the Danube.
"Worth two, three billion dinars. It means the promise of a very
good harvest this year, the first since Liberation; I should say, the first
since before the war. In wartime much of the land lay fallow."

The snow and cold had brought to a standstill the huge "New
Belgrade" project at the confluence of the Danube and Sava rivers.
The uncompleted buildings, some barely started, looked desolate in
the midday winter sunlight.

"This," said Vlado, as we passed one of the largest and farthest advanced structures, "will be *Predsjednistvo* [the Presidency, or the main

government building]. That's the principal hotel, about half finished. Over there is a section of the new university."

"Isn't this project one of the grounds for the Cominform charge that 'the Tito clique' is smitten with megalomania?" I asked.

"Yes," said Vlado. "But we need these buildings and hundreds more. We're terribly overcrowded. In Belgrade alone we could use four, five new hotels and hundreds of apartment houses. A large part of the town was destroyed by Stukas on April 6, 1941, the first day Hitler attacked Yugoslavia. More was demolished in '44 as the city was liberated. Since then over a hundred thousand people have poured in, and more come daily. In a few years, according to present indications, Belgrade will be a city of half a million."

Among the skeleton buildings were rows of wooden barracks. "For voluntary labor brigades," Vlado explained. "Young people come from all over the country and donate their labor; all they get while on the job is food, workclothes, and a place to sleep. But in wintertime only a few thousand are here, mostly peasant boys. By spring the site will be an ant-heap of activity with twenty or thirty thousand volunteer workers."

On barrack walls, on unfinished buildings, on scaffoldings were slogans: *People, Party, Tito: We Are One . . . Tito Is All of Us . . . Hard, Conscientious Work Is the Best Answer to Slanders . . . The More They Slander Tito, the More We Love Him . . . Our Future Lies in the Successful Building of Socialism . . . Long Live Tito! . . . Hero Tito . . . Tito Is Everything . . .* or, as on the wing of the plane, just *Tito*.

I wondered what these signs meant: perhaps the same as the *Jesus Saves* inscriptions along the American roadsides: or that, as someone (was it Robert Louis Stevenson?) said somewhere, man subsisted not by food alone but chiefly by catchwords. My interpretation, I soon discovered, was wrong. As I subsequently wrote in my diary, I really knew almost nothing about "Tito's Yugoslavia."

With skid-chains on the tires, the squeaky old Plymouth bumped along over the hard-packed snow behind an overloaded truck. Here and there straggly groups of men and women, bundled in frayed shawls, with rags wrapped around their feet, shoveled or stood resting, their breath visible in the cold air.

"What a few dozen modern American snow-removing machines could do with this mess by tomorrow morning," I thought.

On the Zemun side of the restored Danube Bridge a large inscription was lettered neatly in Cyrillic: *We Are Tito's, Tito Is Ours.*

Who are "we"? . . . But the silent treatment accorded my jocular inquiry why Tito had not come to the airport, not to mention my experience with the "Tito millionaire" on the plane, inhibited me temporarily, and I kept the question to myself. I continued to wonder about the slogans. Many were newly painted. Were they a reaction to the Cominform—Yugoslavs talking back to Stalin? Also encouraging themselves? And a manifestation of pride? Did the people paint them spontaneously? (And *who* are "the people," and *who* are not?) Or were the signs inspired and engineered by the Communist Party's propaganda apparatus?

France, who sat in front, showed me the title of a book he picked up from the seat between him and the chauffeur. It was Theodore Dreiser's *The Titan* in Serbian translation. Vlado remarked that Bosko (the chauffeur) was a great Dreiser fan. I asked Bosko how he liked *The Titan.* He said he was only about half through: Was it a true portrayal of an American capitalist? I said I thought it was—"of one type of American capitalist of about fifty years ago."

Vlado told Bosko—a thin, sharp-featured Serbian; a good driver (whom I was to see often in the ensuing months)—that I had known Dreiser. After a while Bosko asked me if I knew Duke Ellington. He was disappointed that I had never met the jazz-maestro or heard his music, so far as I recalled. All I could tell him about Ellington was that he had a band which played in night clubs and on the radio, and that he was popular. A relative in Butte, Montana, had sent Bosko a collection of Ellington records and he played them over and over. He liked American jazz. No, not better than Dreiser; but he thought America must be quite a place to produce both Dreiser and Ellington.

In Belgrade proper, vehicles were stalled in the snow, and shovel gangs were out everywhere. I caught a glimpse of one small tractor with a snow-plow attached. It was stalled too.

Vlado reminded me that in 1945, when he came to the United Nations Conference in San Francisco, he stayed at my farm in the Delaware Valley for a few days.

"Now you should be my guest," he said, "but we have no room."

"I want to go to a hotel."

"All filled up. They'd have to put someone out, and you wouldn't want that. I'm taking you to Krleza's. Remember him?"

A Croatian, Miroslav Krleza was already the foremost Yugoslav writer when we met in Zagreb, the capital of Croatia, in 1933.

"He lives in Belgrade now, temporarily," said Vlado. "He's working on an idea for an international exhibition of our medieval art. [The Yugoslav Medieval Art Exhibition was held in Paris through most of the spring of 1950.] You know, between the ninth and thirteenth centuries, the South Slavs had an artistic flowering—hundreds of years ahead of the Italian Renaissance. . . . Last night Krleza had to leave on a trip, and he telephoned me to tell you he was sorry he couldn't be here to welcome you. He said to make yourself at home. Marija will take care of you, and of France too."

I talked with Marija Maricic, the elderly housekeeper, whose mild, calm face, framed in a faded kerchief, shone with a curious steady light. Her dignity issued out of her innate goodness and simplicity. Born on a barren island off Istria into a big family whose chief bread-winner died when she was a baby, she hired out as a servant at twelve. She told me briefly of her wartime experiences, without complaint or any thought of evoking sympathy. Hardship, struggle, and caring for others was her natural lot.

She was not a Communist, but she was the first to call me *"drug* Adamic." *Drug* (pronounced droog) is the Serbo-Croatian word for "comrade." I would wince if someone in America called me "comrade," but I didn't mind when Marija did, or when some of the others did, later. Tito, Kardelj, and most of the other top-level people called me *gospodin* (Mister). I don't think they liked to; the word had connotations for them that went against their revolutionary grain. Most of the men in New Yugoslavia, whether Communist or non-Communist, are called *drug* or *druze* in Serbo-Croatian, or *tovaris* in Slovenian; and most of the women, *drugarica* or *tovarisica*. . . .

During the next eight months I stayed in Krleza's house whenever I was in Belgrade, and I came to know Marija well. In June I wrote in my diary: "I think she's good all the way through."

A few other entries in my diary: "A young railroadman and his wife and mother-in-law occupy part of this house; Krleza has the rest. I have a small, clean, high-ceilinged room with a big french window. A good stoneshot up the street is Tito's house. It's on Rumunska

Ulica which curves over a ground-swell called Dedinje, on the right
bank of the Sava River. Parallel to Rumunska, on one side is Tolstojeva Ulica; on the other, Sekspirova (Shakespeare) Ulica; and on the
far end from Krleza's, Rumunska runs into a junction of Marsal Tito
Bulvar and Teodor Drajserova (Theodore Dreiser) Ulica. Somewhere
nearby is Carli Ceplinova (Charlie Chaplin) Ulica. . . ."

Complying with Krleza's message to make myself at home, I wan-
dered around his study. In a big folder on the desk were enlarged
photographs of Old South Slavic art, which Vlado Dedijer had mentioned and of which I had heard in 1932–33. The blowups showed details of frescoes in Orthodox monastery-churches in Macedonia and
in the southern regions of Serbia, some dating back to the ninth and
tenth centuries.

Obviously, these frescoes were part of the Byzantine artistic stream
which, flowing in the same bed as the Orthodox Church dogma, had
inundated the eastern and central Balkans and western Russia. But,
obviously too, they were very unlike the Byzantine frescoes, which
were one-dimensional design without expression and mood. These Old
South Slavic portraits, most of them predating the Italian Renaissance
by between three and five hundred years, were full of life and individual expression. They not only presented "humanity" in its various
pursuits, as formalistic Byzantine art did; they presented human beings
whose faces showed suffering or joy, intelligence or stupidity, goodness
or cupidity, passion or repose.

In the evening I let France talk me into going to the apartment of
a couple of friends of his who had come to Belgrade from Slovenia a
few years before—separately: the man to teach at the university, the
woman to work in an administrative position in a federal ministry.
Today was their second marriage anniversary, and they had asked
France to bring me along.

Vlado had put Bosko and the Plymouth at my disposal for as long
as I was in Belgrade, and at eight we drove to the party. On the way
Bosko wished to know what a New York night club was like, and if
Duke Ellington owned the one he played in; if I had a car, and what
make and year it was (he thought as highly of American automobiles
as he did of Ellington records); and if the traffic problem in New York

was really so serious, and what happened there when a heavy snow like this fell.

France thought we couldn't very well leave the party before eleven, probably not until after twelve; and Bosko said that was all right, he would wait for us. Not in this cold, I protested; he should either come in with us or go home and read Dreiser or listen to Ellington until it was time to pick us up, say at eleven-thirty. Bosko said he wasn't invited to the party and he thought he might go to the nearby *kafana,* or coffee-house, where the light was fairly bright, and continue *The Titan* if he got a seat or a spot to stand and lean against a wall. (Later I discovered that all *kafane* in Belgrade, in every city in New Yugoslavia, in fact, are jammed full evenings.) What Bosko did with himself until France and I came out at twelve-thirty, I don't know.

The celebrants had invited twenty people, but owing to the snow and near-zero cold only about a dozen came, Slovenians mostly. Even so, for three hours we sat in the small living-room—which probably was also the bedroom—as tightly packed as customers in a New York night club. There was no other basis for the comparison, which occurred to me because of Bosko's questions and because at first I was as sharply uncomfortable here as I had been every time I let someone drag me to a New York night club. There was no "glamor" at this party; no "gaiety," no posturing, no competition of outward symbols of well-being. No one's clothes were as good as mine, and for a while I was self-conscious about this and also because I was the only one who had galoshes, and because the hostess insisted that I take the only upholstered armchair in the room.

One of the people asked me why Henry Wallace received "so few votes instead of the expected ten or twelve million." Some of the other questions fired at me were: How many unemployed workers in a city like New York starved and froze in the winter? How many Negroes were lynched in 1948? Was the wave of terror signalized by the arrest and the impending trial of the eleven Communist Party leaders mounting?

I was taken aback by the picture of the United States implied in their questions and the tone in which they were asked, and I felt obliged to protest that I thought they knew as little about the current American scene as Americans knew about New Yugoslavia—and for the same reason, apparently: what they read in the Yugoslav press about America was as one-sided as what Americans read about Yugoslavia

in their papers. This brought a tense silence. But after a while we un-
limbered again. They poured out their resentment at America's attitude toward Yugoslavia during 1945–49, at the lies in the American
press. I tried to explain America: that her postwar attitude toward
revolutionary developments in Eastern Europe and Asia wasn't merely
a manifestation of the warmongers' purposes and the dynamics of
American capitalism. The American people, just emerging from their
traditional isolation, were frightened by their country's new position
in the world and at having their whole system of values confronted by
values and drives they could not easily understand. I added that in this
lack of understanding of other peoples Americans were not unique.

Several persons in the room gave vent to their bitterness at Russia
and at Yugoslavia's recent allies in Eastern Europe who, as one of them
phrased it, "overnight are revealed to be much worse than the West
ever was." Perhaps to lighten the mood, the host told the latest Cominform joke circulating in Belgrade.

"We Yugoslavs," he said, "have discovered a new proof that the
earth is round."

"What is this new proof?" someone asked.

"For five years we hurled mud at the West, now it comes flying back
at us from the East."

For a moment everyone sat still, as if thinking: "How true! How
awful!" Then everyone laughed. It turned out to be a pleasant evening
after all.

I persuaded some of the other guests and the hosts to talk of their
individual circumstances and of conditions in Belgrade and Yugoslavia,
and I gathered that even on the level of university professors and fairly
high government officials life wasn't all beer and skittles. Nearly everything was rationed. The "free market" prices were fantastically high.
No one was "really hungry" but many people didn't have "quite
enough" to eat and some were "hungry for particular foods and articles
and conveniences."

One man said: "I quit the office at six, by six-fifteen I'm usually in
line at the bus-stop, and I do well if I get into a bus by seven or seven-
thirty. It isn't the waiting I mind so much, or even the cold at this time
of the year—but oh, the waste of time! Sometimes I go to a distant bus-
stop, where there's an overhead light and I can read."

"Belgrade needs a minimum of five hundred more buses," another
guest said. "We had them on order from Czechoslovakia, and one or

two hundred of them were supposed to be delivered over a year ago. But they were not delivered before the Cominform threw the book at us, and of course they have not been delivered since. In Czechoslovakia and Hungary they were sabotaging our orders for busses and machinery—violating our trade agreements—months, perhaps a year, before the Cominform crisis came into the open; but it wasn't until much later that we found out what was going on. That's one reason we're so short of buses."

A woman said: "But the worst lacks are in little things. Shoestrings, for instance, and needles and bobby pins and combs. I'd give anything if I didn't have to go to my neighbor's for her broom. My sister would give anything for a rubber nipple for her baby."

"This is my first day in New Yugoslavia," I said, partly to end a long moment's silence in the tight room. "I'd like to ask a question. What is the gist of the situation in Yugoslavia?" After getting no response for perhaps half a minute, I admitted my question was so broad it might be unanswerable, and I tried to make it more specific.

"Are the present hardships and lacks and sacrifices justified in terms of perspectives, of outlook? Where are you? I mean as a country. I'd like a brief, simple answer—the whole picture in a nutshell—that the world outside of Yugoslavia could understand: a picture that would penetrate to my neighbor in America and jolt him a little. His farm is half a mile from mine—my nearest neighbor. He works as a house painter sometimes. He's not highly educated, but he's not unintelligent or indifferent. He's not a vicious warmonger, or anything like that. He's not a peasant in the European sense, or a worker-proletarian. Nothing so simple. He's a farmer, which is to say he's an agriculturist, a mechanic, a businessman——"

"A kulak?" someone asked.

"No—not if I know the meaning of that word. He owns a car, a truck, a tractor, and a half-dozen other farm machines but he's *not* rich by American standards.

"Sociologists might label him 'lower middle class.' I think there's no such animal as 'the average American,' but he could be called that. His home has many of the so-called conveniences and comforts which you may have heard about, but not all of them by a long stretch. His wife works hard in the house, keeps the accounts, helps with the milking, tends the chickens, worries about her oldest son who's a war hero and trying to get into the television business, and she's kind to a couple of another neighbor's boys who like to hang around her house. This farmer and his wife, well-off as they may seem to someone in the Balkans, are harried by troubles big and little. The machines break down; a cow gets sick; milk doesn't bring the price it should; it doesn't rain for weeks, or it rains too much, especially at haying time; and now and then he's sick and tired of it all. He likes to take his shoes off and listen to the radio in the living-room. He has a radio in the kitchen too, and in the barn and in his car. He listens to newscasts during lunch or supper or while they're milking or as he drives to pick up a load of feed at the feed-mill; and the reports of events at home and abroad, but especially in Europe, bother him. He fought in France in the First World War; his oldest son is in the reserves; his youngest is approaching draft age.

"'Will there be another war?' he asks me every time we meet.

"He calls me Louis, I call him Howard; his last name is Lippincott. And what about this Tito? Am I still for him? He tells me what he's just heard about Tito on the radio. Tito is against Stalin; that's okay as far as it goes—but is it on the level? Are Tito and Stalin really at loggerheads? And so what? Tito shot down American planes, didn't he? My neighbor knows next to nothing about Yugoslavia, but Yugoslavia worries him. Your point of view, the picture of New Yugoslavia that I sense here, doesn't reach him. He doesn't know what you're doing, or why. Revolution? That's a safe, respectable word if you're talking about the American Revolution; in any other connection, it makes my neighbor bristle with suspicion. He likes me, I believe, but he hears rumors that I'm a Red and he doesn't quite trust me, partly because I don't condemn Tito. I can't blame him. What does he know? True, I haven't tried very hard to overcome the propaganda to which he's exposed—what's the use? He'll only get another earful tomorrow, and I can't make a career of explaining Yugoslavia to Howard Lippincott. Why should I? New Yugoslavia isn't explaining herself. She's made no effort at all to present herself to people like my neighbor. Not that the effort would be easy; it wouldn't, for, as I say, his life is full anyhow. But I insist he'd be interested, *if* . . . and *if*—— What would you say to him? Where are you heading? What are you doing?"

A long silence.

"We're building socialism," a young man said in a taut voice.

"I'm afraid," I said, "that 'building socialism' wouldn't mean the same thing to my neighbor that it means to you. It wouldn't stimulate his faculties for sympathetic understanding, which is about the only kind of understanding that amounts to anything. My neighbor isn't a socialist; he doesn't know what socialism is; but he's heard over and over again that it's bad—a sin. This may brand him a political illiterate in some minds, but that doesn't dispose of him—it reveals those minds are relatively just a little more illiterate than his. There he is: an American, practical, stubborn, conditioned by his experiences, but ready to listen, eager to get hold of a new twist on something, then roll it about in his hard head and repeat it to others."

A man (who earlier in the evening had asked France where I was staying) said, slowly: "I was a member of a trade mission to England recently, and I think I know what you mean by 'the whole picture in a nutshell.' Such a 'picture' is certainly needed if the so-called West, if your neighbor, is to understand us. But it will take a genius to draw it in a few, simple lines. . . . I'm told you know Miroslav Krleza, or met him when you were in Yugoslavia last time. In a speech a few months ago, Krleza declared that but for Marshal Tito, but for the Communist Party's wartime leadership, we Yugoslavs wouldn't now exist as a country or as an entity in the world; and that now (I'm paraphrasing Krleza, and poorly) we're boring tunnels through our Middle Ages: through the mountains of muck and debris piled in the South Slavic regions, in the Balkans generally, by our protracted Middle Ages. Would *boring tunnels through Balkan medievalism* be a picture-in-a-nutshell your neighbor would understand?"

"Not easily," I said. "He'd get *boring tunnels,* all right; *Balkan medievalism,* however, would stump him as well as many Americans with more schooling than his. I'm sure President Truman, for instance, wouldn't come anywhere near sharing your intellectual and emotional meaning of the phrase. You see, American history has no Middle Ages, no Reformation."

But I was too tired to develop this thought; also, it had occurred to me if someone asked me to give them "the whole picture in a nutshell" of America which *they* could grasp, I would be at a loss; and I was glad that a moment before some people had risen. Now one of them said apologetically that it was nearly midnight: they had to be up at five in the morning in order to be at the office by seven, when the working day began for government officials, from ministers on down.

Sunday forenoon, and again after lunch, France and I walked in downtown Belgrade. The snow was packed hard in the shade, melting to slush in the sun. "Brigades" of university students and other young people were out shoveling it from the middle of the main streets and piling it along the sidewalks. Few wore gloves; fewer, overshoes; none had both.

Near one of the hotels a gaunt middle-aged woman, with sacking around her feet, worked alone. When we came by hours later, she was still shoveling. Had she had anything to eat? I wanted to ask her, but didn't. France thought she might be one of the volunteer workers who chose this way of honoring someone fallen in the war on or near this date, by donating toil to the *skupnost,* "the common good, the commonwealth." Many people were sublimating their personal sorrow in this way. For days afterward the picture of this woman came back to me.

I noticed all stages of poverty and well-being; only luxury as displayed by the very few in Old Yugoslavia—Thornstein Veblen's "conspicuous waste"—was not evident. By my standard, perhaps one-third of the people I saw were adequately dressed and looked well fed. A considerable proportion were too thin and had a sickly pallor. But when I remarked about them, France said that didn't necessarily mean their present diet was deficient. They might not have recovered from their wartime sufferings. Some were evidently tubercular—the incidence of tuberculosis in the country was high, but a systematic fight against the disease was being waged, in part under the auspices of WHO, the World Health Organization. Some men and women appeared depressed, down-at-the-mouth. Many of these, France thought, were probably of the prewar well-to-do class who found adjustment to the new life rough going. Others were simply overworked; there was so much to do and there were not enough people to do it.

Within twenty minutes, walking up and down two thoroughfares, I counted eighteen people who had an arm or a leg off, or both arms off, or an eye out, or a scarred face. Some of these veterans were delegates from outside of Belgrade to the Second Congress of the Communist Party of Serbia which opened tomorrow.

Small Serbian flags (red, white, and blue with a red star in the middle) and great crimson banners with the hammer-and-sickle in the upper left corner were being hung from windows and roofs all over town—"in honor of the congress," France explained. The red of the banners was the more striking for the sun-lit snow covering the roofs and filling the streets. Stretched across the façade of the hall where the congress was to be held were immense sheets of canvas with crude, unattractive paintings of Marx, Engels, Lenin, Stalin, and Tito.

Stores were closed. In every fourth or fifth show window the most prominent object displayed was a picture of Tito, occasionally beside one of Lenin or Stalin. (A few months later—by July 1949—the Stalin image was nowhere to be seen in Yugoslavia.)

Posted on a board between two ground-floor windows was a quotation from Tito: *If we are to lead, we must know how; to know how, we must study.* The front wall of the large building was pockmarked with rifle and machine-gun fire, dating back to 1944. It was one of several Communist Party schools in Belgrade. Students hurried in. The majority were under thirty, many not yet twenty. Some came in formation, sloshing through the snow, singing their determination to never let the Party, now "pure as sun, pure as the blood of the fallen proletarians," veer from the trail *druzhe* Tito had blazed for them.

One group sang about *"druzhe* Tito the white violet . . .";* I couldn't make out the rest of the words. " 'Tito the white violet'—what the devil does *that* mean?" I asked France.

"It's one of the most popular of the Tito songs," smiled France. "It originated during the war. Partisans sang it in Bosnia and Montenegro. I've heard it so often I take it for granted. 'White violet' means tenderness and that Tito is a rare one—like a white violet."

In St. Mark's, the large Serbian Orthodox church, Sunday services were being held for about forty or fifty people, most of them old or middle-aged. France thought the majority were of the former rich class. The fur coats some of them wore had been new a decade ago. The probability was, France went on, that before the war few of these people attended church oftener than twice a year; now they came every Sunday, as a political gesture. Among the half-dozen younger worshipers were two officers of Tito's new army. How to account for them? France didn't know.

As we came out of the church, my eye caught the words *Brotherhood and Unity* and *Truth Shall Prevail* on a near-by fence. Slogans were on walls almost everywhere, some freshly painted for the occasion of the Serbian CP Congress: *Long Live the Central Committee of the*

CP of Yugoslavia, Headed by Drug *Tito . . . Are You Doing Everything in Your Power to Help the Five-Year Plan Succeed? . . . With Tito in War Until Victory, With Tito in Peace Toward a Better Future . . . We Have Everything We Need to Build Socialism, But Our Chief Resources Are Our Working Class, a People Striving for the Best While Ready for the Worst, a Party Tested Under Fire, and Tito*——

France called my attention to a small sign on the wall of a private house: *They Can Only Spit Beneath Our Window.*

"What does that mean?"

"That the people inside are united, and the worst the world outside can do them is to spit beneath their window. It's a famous Serbian proverb, currently a popular retort to the Cominform attack."

"What about the Cominform attack?" I asked France. I knew he wasn't a CP member. During the war he had worked with the Liberation Front organization in Slovenia.

"I don't know much about it," he said after a moment's hesitation. "In this respect, I'm like most people, even most Party members—or else the CPers aren't telling non-Communists the little they do know. Tito and Kardelj, of course, and other top men in the Party and the government know all about it, but they haven't spoken out yet so the average citizen can grasp it. All they have said up to now—in effect—is that the Cominform resolution and the subsequent accusations are false and unjust."

France interrupted himself to remark that the tall, thin-faced young man entering that building over there (a ministry of the People's Republic of Serbia), was Branko Mihailovic.

I didn't make the connection. Mihailovic is a common name in Serbia, as common as Wilson or Harrison in the United States.

"Branko Mihailovic," repeated France, "son of Draza"—Draza Mihailovic, the Cetnik leader whom the Tito regime tried and executed for high treason in 1946. "His older brother (I don't know his name) was killed while he was a Cetnik officer on Draza's staff. The story in Belgrade which is true, I believe, is that Branko and his sister Gordana, who is a few years younger, never liked their father. He caroused and philandered, which made their mother unhappy. That was in the '30's. Later, around 1940, both Branko and Gordana were swept into the Communist-led student movement in Belgrade. During the war the Mihailovic family was under close German and Nedic [quislingist] surveillance, but in 1943 Branko and Gordana slipped out of Belgrade and joined the Partisan forces in Serbia and fought the Germans and the Cetniki."

"What a strange story!" I thought.

"When Draza was up for trial," France continued, "both Branko and Gordana declared themselves in favor of their father's execution as a traitor: not because the Party urged them to, or anyone else, mind you, but on their own initiative, for their own political reasons which jibed with the Party's and the government's. The story goes that their only complaint about this, which Branko is said to have expressed privately, is that he and Gordana are not a special case that calls for special attention in the world press because Draza was their father. Hundreds of thousands of Yugoslavs were Partisans whose fathers and brothers, uncles and cousins, were Cetniki, Ustasi, White Guards, or collaborationists of some other kind. Draza was simply blown up into a big name by Western propaganda during 1941–44; they, his son and daughter, had nothing to do with it; and they wished foreign correspondents wouldn't single them out. Branko is very shy. He's a minor official in a ministry, a member of the CP of Serbia, and decidedly pro-Tito and anti-Cominform. Gordana, whom I don't know, is a medical student and receives a government stipend. She also regards herself as a Communist but isn't yet a Party member and right now, according to reliable talk, is veering toward the pro-Cominform line."

France resumed talking of the general situation in Yugoslavia. From the drift of my questions, he gathered what interested me; the highlights of his answers follow:

"At intervals in the last two years, as a member of different trade missions, I spent two, three weeks at a time in Italy, Switzerland, Belgium, Holland, and England. I was also in Czechoslovakia and Austria, and traveled through Hungary, Denmark, and France. I like many features of life abroad, but each time I return home I'm impressed by what is commonplace in Yugoslavia. Nowhere do so many people work so hard, sing so much, complain so persistently, and believe so strongly in the future. Behind the bleak exterior, though, behind the pleated brows and the mutterings, behind the poverty and the hardships, there's—how shall I say?—plenty of tough fiber which I notice, perhaps, because I've been abroad. Meshed together in that fiber are patriotism, devotion to the government and the Communist Party, fear of foreign designs on our natural resources, love of country, love for Tito——

"Yes, there is love for Tito, and not only personally. There's a suprapersonal element in it; but if 'love' isn't the word for it, I don't know what is. Some of these inscriptions which impress and baffle you so much (and annoy you a little?) *are* the work of specially dedicated Communists, or may be a result of instructions from the Central Committee, but many of them were written spontaneously by people who may or may not be Party members. . . . No, I never met Tito; I saw him close up a few times, and he's quite a man, quite a man. As the pilot on the plane said to you, he's 'everything.' "

" 'Everything'—can you break it down?" I said.

France laughed. "You and your questions! Of course some of them have occurred to me too in recent years, but I haven't had the time or data to figure out the answers. Offhand, I can't recite what 'everything' means."

"Try some other way, then," I said. We laughed.

"I suppose," said France, "you're still after the 'whole picture in a nutshell.' "

"No," I said. "I've given that up as premature. My eyes are still bulging, and I'm ready to settle for mere glimpses of the broad canvas still being painted."

"Well, to a great many of us, on the broad canvas, Tito represents Liberation," my brother said after a pause, thinking things out under the stimulus if not the pressure of my interest. "But, you understand, *'osvobojenje'* or *'svoboda'* doesn't have the same shades of meaning that 'freedom' has, or *'liberté,'* whose nuances come out of a past unlike ours. Tito represents Liberation in the Yugoslav sense.

" 'What's the Yugoslav sense?' I knew that question was coming too. As I say, I haven't had the time, the information, or the mental energy to elucidate these matters, to define in my own words what the masses of people feel and know. But I can tell you that 'Tito' and 'Liberation' *are* synonymous. They mean specific, concrete, every-day things. Already now, a few years after the end of the incredibly destructive war, there are more schools, theaters, and cinemas in Yugoslavia than there were before, and many more books and newspapers, more electric lights, highways, railroad trackage, and so on. To thousands of families,

'Tito' means a new home with a separate kitchen and a bathroom—conveniences they didn't even dream of before Tito.

" 'Tito' means a three months' vacation for the factory worker when she bears a child—a pension for the war widow fourteen times higher than the pension a woman widowed in the First World War received in Old Yugoslavia—a stipend for any boy or girl anywhere in the country, regardless of his nationality, who wants an education——"

I asked France if he had heard of Gertrude Stein; he said he hadn't; and I told him a little about her, and that she might have summarized his words with some such sentence as "Tito is 'Tito' is Tito."

After a moment's thought, France laughed, remarking, "And lots of Yugoslavs would have said, 'Exactly'! That's our whole story in a nutshell. Maybe that *is* your nutshell."

"No, I'm afraid not," I said. "Go on; I'll try not to interrupt you again."

"To others, of course," France continued, " 'Tito' means the direct opposite. To one man I have in mind, it means the execution of his oldest son as a war criminal, and the loss, the complete loss also, of his younger son and daughter who turned Communist and moved out of the family mansion. He was once a man of consequence or so he regarded himself; now he is regarded with suspicion, even hostility, by his own flesh and blood. In the summer his son and daughter push wheelbarrows and swing picks and shovels as volunteer laborers on construction jobs; whereas 'in the good old days' they would have belonged to the Yacht Club and gone to Oxford or the Sorbonne. The girl might have aspired to marry an Englishman; now she's in love with a Yugoslav, a fellow-Communist, who was a worker before the war and now is a foreman in the new Zelezniki factory, which of course is a state enterprise.

" 'Tito' means that the tiny factory this man once partly owned is government property, managed by a worker he hired in 1937. He gets sick every time he thinks of it, every time somebody tells him that production in 'his' plant is now three, five, seven times higher than it was in '39, and that it continues to increase. How can that be? It's a Communist lie, but he can't rid himself of the suspicion that it's true.

"To him 'Tito' means the eclipse and vanishing of many of the old values and customs, the old opportunities for people 'close to the throne,' the old loyalties and prejudices and hates, the old royalties and schemes and deals, which but a few years ago were the warp and woof of his life, all legitimate or even patriotic. It means that most Serbians no longer despise the Croatians, and the other way about; that it's against the law to defame the minorities. Who ever heard of such a thing 'in the good old days'?

"Once upon a time he and the others thrived behind the screen of politics spinning around the 'Serbo-Croatian problem.' Now when he takes a walk, he keeps his eyes straight ahead so as not to see the *Brotherhood and Unity* slogans on the walls. He's sure, but not altogether sure, that all this 'brotherhood and unity' stuff is politics also, the old politics in reverse, and completely wrong.

" 'Tito' means that the Church—Orthodox, Catholic, and Moslem— is backed into a corner. It's free—unmolested; but it's no longer privileged, no longer tied up with the State apparatus, so it considers itself menaced and desperately unfree. The Church doesn't realize that it's weighed down by itself, by medievalism, by the atrocities people saw many priests commit during the war. It doesn't know how to reorient itself to meet the new competition.

"These people who suddenly find themselves on the peripheries of society brood over the changes and are chewing themselves up alive. Some actually are ill, although their doctors can't discover anything organically wrong with them. Their sole prospect is another war, which will come as a personal favor to them, to crush 'Tito' along with Tito the man, the Communist. But now the Cominform crisis has some of them completely bewildered. Now, suddenly, even in America someone occasionally has a good word for Tito. So they don't know if they should think less harshly of Tito or more generously of Stalin. They wander around at the edge of sanity like so many King Lears, not knowing whom to hate, whom to clasp to their bosom."

About noontime France and I climbed five flights to the tight, sparsely furnished flat of his brother-in-law, Stane Valentincic, and his wife. Stane is a Slovenian, a Communist, in his late thirties, with a good education and an outstanding Partisan record; a lieutenant colonel in the inspector general's division of the Yugoslav People's Army who travels continually to all sections of the country. This morning he was just back from a tour of Macedonia.

France remarked to his brother-in-law that I was struck and puzzled by the use of Tito's name all over town.

Stane looked at me, musing.

Through the uncurtained window, facing the snow-covered roof of the adjoining house, I saw

T
I
T
O

on the side of a chimney. "*That,* for instance," I said. "What impelled someone to paint those four letters up there?"

Stane looked out. "I didn't notice it. Did you?" he asked his wife.

She shook her head. "We're so used to these signs, we don't read them any more, scarcely see them."

"No," he intercepted the thought behind my smile, "the profusion of them isn't defeating their purpose. Whoever painted that one up there did it to express himself politically, not to propagandize others, for there may not be a dozen people who live high enough up and down the street to see it. Even though what he had in mind has already been expressed many times all around him and everywhere in the country, he had to do it over again, himself. Why? For the same reason that some people write poetry and books. He painted 'Tito' because something hurts him."

"What hurts him?"

"The same thing that hurts the rest of us—my wife, me, the family next door."

I asked other questions.

"Where can I begin?" Stane looked at his wife, then at France, then at me.

"Before the last war, Yugoslavia was one of several small semi-colonial states in the Balkans, a football for the big powers to kick around as they wished, depending on the vicissitudes of the game. Our principal resources were under the control of foreign capital, while our home-grown exploiters—the King at their head, and their prime model —cheated the government and robbed the people right and left, depositing their loot in Swiss, British, French, American, and Brazilian banks. Our investigators, now beginning to dig into the archives of Old Yugoslavia, are uncovering the facts. One prime minister, in intimate partnership with foreign-imperialist capital, 'made' eight hundred million dinars [forty million dollars] in a few years, and probably saw nothing discreditable in it."

"Except, possibly, in the privacy of his soul," said Stane's wife.

"Possibly," Stane said. "Throughout the career of Old Yugoslavia, while such commerce was going on, from the early 1920's to 1941, there were no public works to speak of, no honest attempts to lift up the country, to raise the living standards, to make education worthy of the name. The politics of the dominant Serbian clique (not the Serbian people) were spun to enrich the clique and to keep the national minorities down, the Croatians and Macedonians especially.

"In international affairs Old Yugoslavia was of no account. One explanation for this—advanced by people who considered themselves intellectuals and were more or less dissatisfied with it—was that we were a small country—worse, Balkanites and, still worse, Yugoslavs— a heterogeneous, unsubdued mess, our own worst enemies. 'What can you expect?' This was the theme song. The press, the Church, the politicians drummed it in all the time. The French and British managers of our mines encouraged the lament and added new lines to the old theme and cooked up new variations. They were, of course, diplomatic and military intelligence agents in disguise.

"The sons of our 'best families' returned from universities in Berne, Paris, and London their custom-made collaborators. A pack of snobs. Yugoslavia, alas! was a concentration of inferiorities impossible to overcome. One *could* help oneself, however, and one's brothers and brothers-in-law and cousins, and one's cousins' cousins, and their in-laws, by taking the post of a minister of the royal government when the King saw fit to reshuffle the cabinet. A minister could 'make' ten million dinars in a few years. So could an ambassador if he was lucky enough to be sent to Switzerland, France, or Britain, Brazil or the United States, where he also handled the King's private interests, and the prime minister's and the foreign minister's as well. This was an ideal way of getting in on the enterprises of the British and French investment syndicates. Then, although a Yugoslav, although a Balkanite, he could live bearably as a 'cultured' individual or family should live. In the winter he went to the Riviera, or to Egypt to marvel at the Sphinx and the pyramids; in the summer he *ah-ah*-ed at the fjords of Norway——

"Yes, there were exceptions, many exceptions. Repelled by the role of our bourgeoisie, many sons and daughters of the 'best families' swung left and, step by step, became Communists. By 1941 some of the 'finest' homes in Belgrade, as well as in other cities, were headquarters for some of the most important Communist activities, and *drug* Tito's personal hideouts.

"The average Yugoslav somehow knew or felt what was going on, and when he turned it over in his thoughts, he did not like it. He *did* like being a Serbian, a Croatian, a Slovenian, a Dalmatian, a Bosnian, a Macedonian—in a way that seemed odd even to the sympathetic outsider. To the unsympathetic outsider who saw only evil in every nationalism but his own, he was a rank nationalist, a dangerous chauvinist. And there *were* crazed creatures living on hate, or cunning ones who stimulated hate among the nationalities to advance themselves politically. The run-of-the-mill Yugoslav, however, was guilty only of being attached to his customs, traditions, and values. They were the ones he knew, and he thought they were all right. Liberty. Justice. Truth. He was familiar with and, in many instances, proud of his national history: of the wars of liberation his forefathers had fought and lost or but half won, and the various movements between the wars which appeared to aim at benefiting the people. Gradually, though, it began to dawn on him that foreign and domestic capitalists were sucking the state white—that the nationality problem and the standard of living were worsening year by year—that poor economic conditions in the 1930's weren't due to the American depression alone, as the papers and the King and his *politikasi* would have him believe—and that his national pride and personal self-respect were actually more than a little threadbare.

"Into this soil Josip Broz Tito sowed the seed of revolution. As Secretary-General of the Communist Party of Yugoslavia, he offered the Marxist-Leninist way as the only possible way out and ahead for Yugoslavia. In 1941 he called the people into *borba*. [*Borba* is an old all-Yugoslav word meaning "struggle," "fight," "contest." To its original content, Yugoslav history since 1941 has added new, not easily translatable, meanings, which will emerge in the following pages.]

"What happened then, what happened in the *borba,* is beyond telling—at least by me, because I saw too much of it and my language is inadequate. Someday we'll have a Tolstoy to write our *War and Peace*. Under the direct leadership of Tito, whom the Central Committee of the Communist Party of Yugoslavia appointed supreme commander of the country's revolutionary forces, the people won the simultaneous war against the invader, the civil war against domestic reaction, and the social revolution. In the November 1945 elections, the people abolished the monarchy, which had served to screen so much corruption and chicanery in Old Yugoslavia, and they declared New Yugoslavia a republic. They threw off the yoke of foreign capital and of the domestic exploiters. They took the country's resources and means of production into their own hands. And they declared that work was *the* condition for membership in the new society.

"After the reconstruction period, in which UNRA helped us greatly, we threw our energies into transforming Yugoslavia from a backward peasant land into a progressive agricultural-industrial one—and already the results are visible. There are hundreds of new factories, large and small. Scores of hydroelectric works are in operation, scores of others are being completed or started. Thousands of articles formerly imported, or unknown to us, we now manufacture ourselves or will soon begin to manufacture, some of them with homemade machinery. The over-all living standard appears low to a visitor from a technically advanced country, but it is already 28 per cent higher than it was before the war. The old 'Serbo-Croatian problem' and the 'Serbo-Macedonian problem' are dead and gone down the ditch along the highroad of history. Unemployment is only an uneasy memory—the older people alone still mention it. Yugoslavia is an independent, sovereign state which other states, the great powers too, must take into account. We have a wonderful new army.

"The average citizen nowadays knows this. Shabby and tired as he is, he assesses the picture for what it is worth to him and to our new society either right now or potentially. He is living it, and this large, compelling experience lives in him. He works dreadfully hard, often he's dog-tired; he grumbles, he curses; but he doesn't forget for much more than a minute of his waking hours that he's caught up in a new promise of the good life; and, asleep, he dreams of it.

"Poor as they may look to someone from America, our people feel and some know consciously, intellectually, that we're being drawn into a creative life, personally and nationally; into a rounded-out culture. We're confident of a good life eventually because the means for making it good are in our grasp. Those means are very considerable. Our country is rich; we're just beginning to discover how rich.

"Under the leadership of Tito, Yugoslavia entered the ranks of the progressive countries. Regression is inconceivable. Within us burn pride, zeal, resolution, *borbenost* [the spirit of do-or-die] and all these qualities are tightly linked with 'Tito.' Tito isn't so much the man as the symbol: and, more than the symbol, a surging idea. Most of us can't articulate it, so we say 'Tito,' or paint the word on a chimney, a telegraph pole, or a cement mixer.

"It can be said that the people, the country, gave birth to Tito, to lead us into a better future, and that he did not disappoint us. To write *Tito Is Ours and We Are Tito's* is to write the truth. To attack and slander Tito is to attack Yugoslavia, to slander our essence. To try to destroy him is to try to destroy our country as we will have it. We can easily understand the lies about Tito and our *borba* which originate in the West. We resent them, naturally, but we are not surprised. What can you expect? Coming from the Cominform, they are monstrous!

"As yet, people outside the Party don't know very much about the crisis. But multitudes of them *feel* what it's about. They haven't yet demanded that they be told the whole truth, as though they sense it is very bad, maybe so bad that it's best not to talk about it openly. They feel *drug* Tito knows how to handle it, but they're hurt and they wonder, and of course they're anxious. They worry about Tito. Is he well guarded? Is he well? I understand he receives hundreds of letters daily from individuals who think it will help him to know that they're with him in this crisis: that they worry too.

"Our critics—our antagonists in the Soviet Union—know this, or at least they suspect it. They're beginning to realize what 'Tito' means. They don't want a Tito kind of Yugoslavia. They can't kick it around as they wish to in their game with Britain and America. So the Cominform meets and issues a long resolution which says: 'Break it up.' Tito is the center of Yugoslavia, 'Tito' means Yugoslavia: so 'he must be removed'—a bullet or exile for him. But we say *No!*

"I go around. I'm a Communist and an army officer, open to the suspicion that I see things which don't exist, or which are not as I see them. Just the same, this is what I think. Of the sixteen million of us citizens of New Yugoslavia, at least eight million are ready to die to back up that *No!* and to give ever stronger meaning to the tremendous *Yes!* in our hearts, and minds. This is what 'Tito' on that chimney means. I know intimately hundreds of our officers and many of the men in the ranks who resent the fate that they have only one life to give."

I asked Stane Valentincic if he had ever heard of Nathan Hale. He hadn't. Nor had his wife and France. I enjoyed telling them.

France repeated what I had told him about Gertrude Stein, and how I thought she would have summed up the current Yugoslav story.

"Tito is 'Tito' is Tito," repeated Stane. "Yes, that's perfect."

In the evening I went to a reception given by the Union of Yugoslav Writers. It turned into a three-hour *diskusija* with about thirty literati. The majority were Serbians and CP members. Perhaps half of them had participated in the War of Liberation with gun or pen, or both. Some had been recognized novelists, essayists, poets, and playwrights in Old Yugoslavia; others found their voice during the *borba*.

Ivo Andric, president of the Union, who had been at the airport on Friday—a novelist and short story writer of high skill, as I discovered months later when I read two of his books—was the host. The rounded, subtle grace of his little speech made my response to it, in my limited, unpracticed Serbo-Croatian, sound all the more awkward to me. And no sooner were the formalities over than my head reeled in a flurry of questions.

Why were American books so expensive? Were they published only for the rich? What was the standing of the "genuinely progressive, anti-fascist writers" in the United States? Could they publish their writings in spite of the "Un-American terror"? What was the political-cultural content of American progressivism? How firmly anti-fascist and anti-war was it? Henry Wallace? Did many American progressives believe the accusations in the Cominform resolution? Or what did they think? Did Wallace really believe, as reported, that the Cominform crisis was only a result of Soviet-Yugoslav differences over the peasant problem? Why didn't he come to Yugoslavia himself and see what was happening? Did I know him to talk to? Jo Davidson, Harlow Shapley, Paul Robeson? Would the Un-American Activities Committee, Wall Street, and the reactionary press succeed in hounding Charlie Chaplin out of Hollywood and the United States? And (in the same breath) did I think Chaplin would consider making movies in Yugoslavia? Why was news about Yugoslavia in the capitalist press of the United States so much worse even than in France, Italy, and England?

These and similar questions were asked by honest, intelligent people. The tone—the whole atmosphere—in which they were asked disturbed me no end. Here was another batch of victims of the tidal waves of lies, distortions, half-truths, oversimplifications, ideological complexity, and fear beating on the consciousness of the Soviet orbit, that were having much the same effect as the tidal waves of misinformation, misconceptions, and hysteria beating on the American mind. I couldn't dispose of the questions briefly, and I talked until my voice grew hoarse.

I had meant to ask the writers how *they* saw the Cominform crisis, what they thought of the "Tito" signs, but I didn't get to either subject.

We scarcely touched on their circumstances as writers in a revolutionary environ. When I asked whether or not they were free writers, several of them laughed or smiled. One or two declared that they were, and no one said they were not.

I hadn't heard most of their names before. But for about a year I had received the four-page weekly organ of the Union of Yugoslav Writers, *Knjizevne Novine* (Literary Gazette), and lately I had read stories, poems, and *reportaze* by a few of them, including a poem by Gvido Tartalja, a Dalmatian:

PEASANT TO FOREIGN CORRESPONDENT

You say you're a foreign correspondent?
Then quote me thus: "For years we lived . . . no, we barely existed here;
For centuries we shivered in the cold, in the driving rain.
At long last, for us too the sun is overhead."

If your editor allows, write thus in your dispatch:
"Our faith is in our land—in the vineyards on the sunward slope,
In the grain in our fields, waving in the breeze, glistening like gold;
In the old oak and pine forests, in the newly planted plum and apple orchards."

Say this: "Our purpose now throbs in the veins of our workers' hands,
It flowers out of our calluses as we toil long days that pass too soon."
And try not to overlook the proud manner of our shepherd and our student,
For in this youth—in these our children—we believe, we believe.

Write of our rebuilt villages and towns, our new factories,
And maybe mention the streams of our blood and sweat in wartime and since,
And give, perhaps, a line or paragraph to our women, our mothers—
Their faces still are caked with the salt of tears after battles.

You might write of our art, our dance and music, our battleborn songs.
Tell of laughter mingled with the groans of strain on our projects.
Say what you see in our eyes, say what we ourselves cannot yet utter
About the centuries-old longing—the dream now coming true.

Write that I, a common man, said this to you: "We know what we are doing.
We now are masters of our homeland, shaping our prospects, our destiny."
And, in conclusion, quote me: "Clean winds will blow and rivers will flow,
No matter how the beasts of prey yelp and bellow and growl."

When I first read the poem, early in 1948, a few months before the outbreak of the Cominform crisis, it struck me as an effective protest against the treatment accorded Yugoslavia by the American press. Now, meeting the author and recalling the poem, I thought it summed up France's and Stane's answers to me earlier in the day and, mindful of the Cominform crisis, I felt that it was addressed to the "East" no less than to the "West."

BOOK ONE
CHAPTER THREE: *Figures in a taut moment . . .
and the question:* What is America?

AT NINE on Saturday morning (January 15, 1949)—as arranged the day before—Boris Kidric picked me up at Miroslav Krleza's house to go to Edvard Kardelj's about half a kilometer up the Dedinje hill. I was waiting for him and he probably surmised I was impatient—a stickler for punctuality, American style—for he pointed to his watch and said he was right on the dot, and laughed. Once upon a time Yugoslavs were notorious for their inexactitude in keeping appointments. Suddenly, too, I recalled that on an occasion in 1932 or '33 Boris had kept me waiting somewhere, and then been very apologetic.

"Your handshake, Boris," I observed, "is the same two jerks it was sixteen years ago."

"I've spotted a mannerism or two which show you haven't changed much either." He wouldn't say what they were. Instead, after a moment, he remarked, "The damnedest things you notice—after sixteen years. You may be a dangerous man to have around."

"Don't worry," I laughed. "I really don't intend to write anything about Yugoslavia this time. By the way, how's your father? I forgot to ask you at the airport yesterday." I had met Professor Franc Kidric during my first visit to Yugoslavia. He was then a leading member of the faculty of the University of Ljubljana. In the summer of 1932 I spent an afternoon on his farm in Styria and heard him object to Boris being a Communist. It wasn't the ideology he minded so much, it was the danger of trying to put it over.

"He's quite well," Boris said. "You know, he's president of the Slovenian Academy of Art and Science."

"Yes, I recall reading that in the papers," I said. "How does he feel about you now?"

"Oh, much better than he used to," smiled Boris. "When you met us in 1932–33, I was always asking him and Mother for money for the movement, and he was forever getting me out of prison or some minor jam with the police. Now, it's just the other way around: he's always after me for this or that for the Academy. Right now he wants printing equipment with high-mathematical symbols, so the Academy can publish scientific papers. We haven't got that kind of type-setting machines, and the old man and the Academy will have to wait till we can buy such equipment abroad. . . . Incidentally, do you remember my asking you for a contribution—in the winter of 1933, I think it was —to help a fellow escape across the Austrian border?"

"No," I said after a moment. "I hope I turned you down."

"You didn't," chuckled Boris. "You gave me ten dollars in American currency."

"I hereby deny any such thing," I said. "The only money I had while I was here was the fellowship award given me by the Guggenheim Foundation—one-hundred-percent capitalistic money. If the Committee

on Un-American Activities hears of it, I'll be branded an operator of
International Communism, and the Guggenheim Foundation and I
will be accused of underwriting the whole awful un-American revolution in Yugoslavia."

Boris laughed. "I won't tell a soul."

"Did the fellow, whoever he was, get across the border, and what
happened to him afterward?"

"He got across all right," Boris said, seriously. "Then, in 1944, he
fell in battle. If I'm not mistaken, it was in a minor scrimmage, an
effort by our Partisan boys to get to some American flyers who had
bailed out of their damaged bomber."

"Did your boys get to them?"

"I'm not sure—there were dozens of such battles; we can have the
details checked if you wish, to make sure—but I think they did get to
them and the two or three flyers were escorted to Italy and turned over
to the American Air Force Rescue Mission, with whom we had liaison."

As we passed Tito's place at Rumunska 15, Boris remarked that most
of that day and the next Tito would be receiving groups of delegates
to the CP of Serbia Congress who were converging on Belgrade during
the weekend for the opening session on Monday. The marshal planned
to have me to lunch on Tuesday. Would that be convenient?

At Kardelj's gate—Rumunska 29—the guard saluted and motioned
us in. The walled-in villa was national property assigned to the Foreign Minister of the federal government who, in the person of Edvard
Kardelj, was also the First Deputy Premier and one of the chief architects of the new state. Like many of the other houses on Dedinje formerly owned by the "best" (richest) Belgrade families, the villa was
mediocre architecture, about what you would find in a 1925 development in Shaker Heights, Ohio, inhabited by bank tellers, insurance
agents, and small manufacturers.

The over-all effect of the interior was in keeping with Kardelj's personality, which weeks later I characterized in my diary as "quiet, har-
monious, outwardly shy—but also very alert and obliquely forceful.
His reticence is a protective covering, a tactic with the environment.
He's quite unlike Kidric, but the two have a lot in common. Every
once in a while I sensed they were communicating with each other
without speaking."

The paintings in the spacious reception-room were unexceptional, the furnishings conservative and ordinary. In the small study to which Kardelj led Boris and me, the one tall window was shaded so that most of the light fell on the neatly arranged papers, books, telephones, and inkwell on the desk. Ceiling-high bookcases occupied two sides of the room. On my eye level, near the door, were sets of the collected works of Marx, Engels, Lenin and Stalin, in Russian. On the other two walls hung pictures of Marx, Engels, Lenin, and Tito. Adjoining the study was a larger room with a big conference table and lined with more books. Both rooms were tidiness itself, giving the impression that every object was in place, exactly where its occupant wanted it to be. In the opinion of other Yugoslavs, Slovenians have a reputation for orderliness, punctiliousness, and self-discipline.

The press in the "West" often pointed out that Kardelj's personality and manner are professorial, and that he resembles Molotov. Both observations are accurate—the last, especially if one looks at profile photographs. But Kardelj is much younger (not yet forty in 1949) and his face—with its red cheeks, small mustache, lively eyes behind spectacles, and trim, slightly curly black hair—and his manner have a subdued eagerness and natural cordiality I didn't perceive in Molotov's the one time I saw him at a reception in New York.

"It's been a long time," said Kardelj, greeting me in the doorway, "but it seems like yesterday too, doesn't it, Peter?" Peter was Kidric's Partisan or underground *nom de guerre*. (Kardelj's pseudonyms were Kristof in Slovenia and Bevc elsewhere in embattled Yugoslavia; before that, during 1935–36, he lived in Moscow under the name of Birc.)

Boris—always emphatic—nodded vigorously.

We spoke in Slovenian; early in 1949 Kardelj and Boris knew no English. Since then (as I work on the final draft of this book) Kardelj attended the 1949 and 1950 General Assemblies of the United Nations and began to learn the language.

"Perhaps I should apologize," I said to Kardelj; "I know we met in 1932 or '33, but when I first saw your name under your picture in an American paper early in 1945, I didn't recognize either your name or your face."

"No reason why you should," smiled Kardelj. "When we first met, I was *v ilegali* [of illegal status: a political outlaw] and Boris may have introduced me to you by my underground name, which was Levc in those days, I think. I was about twenty, just out of prison, and perhaps a bit starved-looking. Someone dug up a photograph of me lately from the police records of 1930, when I was arrested, and"— his held-in smile widened—"I scarcely recognized myself."

For a long moment, sitting around a low round table—on which an attendant placed tiny cups of coffee and a decanter of *slivovica* and tiny glasses—the three of us grinned at one another. Then, after Kardelj and Kidric exchanged glances which may have had a special content, Kardelj said my writing on Yugoslavia had helped them. In 1934 and later, translations of sections of *The Native's Return* were printed on cigarette paper and circulated through the Yugoslav underground. Late in 1942 the hard-pressed Liberation forces received a lift when they learned from a New York shortwave broadcast that their struggle was becoming known outside their country through an article of mine in an American magazine.[1]

I said I appreciated his saying so, and I was glad the article helped; but I had to admit that when I wrote it—and later *My Native Land*— I wasn't thinking of that. It didn't occur to me I could help at such a distance, or that they, deep in *Festung Europa,* would hear of what I was doing.

"I wrote for Americans," I continued. "Under Franklin Roosevelt, for a while, there was hope—perhaps only an illusion—that the United States might formulate a sound foreign policy toward countries going through their revolutionary phase. I wrote on Yugoslavia as a case in point because I was born here and visited the country in 1932-33, and thought I knew enough about it to try to guess what was going on here."

"I understand," said Boris. "You're an American."

"*Da, da, da*—yes, yes, yes," said Kardelj in his quick, responsive way.

"I don't underrate Yugoslavia because she's small," I said. "For all I know, her importance may be large, especially now, with this Comin-

---

[1] *The Saturday Evening Post,* December 19, 1942. . . . Early in 1950 this magazine published an anti-Tito article by a former official in the Tito regime who took a sideswipe at me as a persistent pro-Titoist and, *ergo,* subversive vis-à-vis American national interests. I wrote to Editor Ben Hibbs reminding him that it was he who published the first pro-Partisan piece on wartime Yugoslavia: and didn't that make him my fellow-subversive—then or now? One of his assistants replied that when the *Satevepost* ran my article even Winston Churchill was pro-Tito. Actually, Churchill didn't condemn Draza Mihailovic and his Cetniki, and come out in favor of Tito and "his gallant bands," until February 22, 1943, thereby joining Ben Hibbs and me in subversion against Western civilization.

form crisis; but I feel the big peace-or-war decisions are being made within American-Soviet relations."

Kardelj's face turned blank. He looked away. Boris tilted his head and glanced at me as if disagreeing, and I expected he would burst out, but he didn't. He smiled and asked if I had heard that there were only three really sovereign powers: the Soviet Union, the United States, and Yugoslavia. The first two, he said, were great powers; they had within their orbits all the other lands—except Yugoslavia, which differed from the USA and the USSR in size and also in having no satellites and wanting none.

I said that in London three days before I had read this was a joke circulating in Yugoslavia.

"But how much of a joke is it? Last night at a party my brother took me to, I heard that your former fellow-members of the Soviet sphere ceased deliveries on your orders for buses, machinery, oil, gasoline, and other necessities. Isn't that putting a kink in your Five-Year Plan?"

"*That* part of it is no joke," said Boris; "it's giving us serious trouble. But this is strictly off-the-record; we're not admitting it publicly. However, don't get the impression that the Plan isn't going ahead. It *is*—so far, with only minor changes and very few dislocations. We've had to make some adjustments, and we'll have to make more—many more, perhaps—but no essential changes, at least none I can foresee at this time. Our differences with the Soviet Union and our former fellow-members of the Soviet sphere didn't begin in June 1948; they began a good while before, and the Cominform crisis, as it's now called, didn't take us entirely by surprise. Some of the machinery not delivered to us, say, by Czechoslovakia, already is in the works, or has even been completed, in our own plants. Some of the items which we can't tackle yet ourselves are on order in Western countries, and deliveries are being made. We have no chance of overlooking the fact that it's a struggle. But we're not worried. All this is bound to be to the good in the long pull ahead, no matter what other roadblocks we encounter between here and our ultimate goals. Now we *know* that we must depend mostly on ourselves, on our own resources. We need about three good harvests, so our people can get enough calories to build up their health, which was impaired during the war."

After a slight pause I said: "More and more, in recent years, I've been thinking that events like this Cominform crisis are culminations of stupidity, of blunders, on one side or the other, or both. A minute ago, Boris, you said that the Cominform crisis didn't take you entirely by surprise. Does that mean that you—the Party leaders—saw it coming a good while before it hit you? That you didn't stumble into the dispute with the Cominform, which must mean the Kremlin, which means Stalin, but that you assumed a posture and met the crisis with your eyes open?"

Kidric nodded emphatically and looked at Kardelj.

Kardelj thought a moment. "The differences that converged in the crisis were long in coming. We assumed the attitudes and took the steps to meet the crisis with our eyes wide open." He didn't elaborate.

Deciding not to press Kardelj and Kidric on this point, I almost asked if they felt they—the CP and the Government of Yugoslavia—had made any serious mistakes; instead, I remarked that I was aware Yugoslavia wasn't doing any business worth mentioning with the United States. Kardelj and Kidric said that wasn't Yugoslavia's fault; the United States had long been intensely hostile to their country, refusing even to unfreeze her fifty-million-dollar gold deposit.

"That might be so," I said; "but was Yugoslavia entirely blameless?" They didn't reply.

"For years," I said, "while Poland and Czechoslovakia were doing business with the United States, playing the game the capitalist way, getting substantial loans (Poland paid fifty thousand dollars to a Washington law firm 'with good connections' for arranging one such loan), Yugoslavia was virtuously one-hundred-percent in the Soviet orbit. Off and on, I wondered if that wasn't partly because Yugoslavs have a tendency to take an idealistic one-hundred-percent position on whatever they venture into. You put all your eggs in one basket."

"Da, da, da," said Kardelj in a way that I couldn't tell whether he agreed or merely acknowledged my statement. He rose to answer the buzz of one of the two telephones on his desk.

Boris' foot tapped in a quick rhythm. " 'All the eggs in one basket,' " he said, "is that an American saying?" I nodded. We sat silent until Kardelj finished talking on the telephone.

"To comment fully on that," he said, returning to the table, "would require going over the whole history of Yugoslav-American relations in the last five years." A pause implied that was too long a story to go into this morning. Four days later, after a long confabulation at Tito's, it began to dawn on me that during 1945–48 New Yugoslavia's sharp attitude toward the "West," in so far as it wasn't a reaction to the "West's" sharp attitude toward New Yugoslavia, was a futile tactic to keep out of deeper trouble with the Kremlin.

I tried to get Kardelj and Kidric to talk about the Cominform break, but they evidently had agreed beforehand to have me talk about America. They only said the break occurred because Yugoslavia wanted relations among socialist states to be socialistic, democratic, equable, just; and the Soviet Union, Czechoslovakia, Poland, and Hungary took advantage of their size and superior industrial plants, to exploit the less developed states within the Soviet orbit—a pattern of behavior tantamount to capitalist imperialism, but in some respects even worse. Yugoslavia decided to stand up against it.

Followed a remark by Kidric (which I couldn't recapture verbatim in my Belgrade notes, written weeks later) that soon after the war Yugoslav CP and government leaders had begun to feel that New Yugoslavia needed more freedom internally than the rigid Soviet system allowed: but, having copied the Soviet system, they didn't know how to loosen it up.

The rest of the morning I spoke about America, whatever came to my mind under the stimulus of Kardelj's and Kidric's remarks and questions. My hastily written January 15 diary entry reads, in part: "Judging from the persistence of their questions—which were really one question, *What is America?*—their interest in the United States is very great and disposed to be sympathetic.

"They took my words with good grace but, I suspect, more than a pinch of salt. Possibly they framed their questions to provoke me and draw me out. But, obviously, they know almost as little about America as the people at the party France took me to last night. I said so, and they didn't mind. Intelligent as they are, they're victims of gobbledygook, of Marxist jargonization, of the wave upon wave of Soviet-oriented propaganda in which they have been doused these past years —and, in turn, have helped douse Yugoslavia. But this doesn't come anywhere near covering them, or even their interest in and lack of knowledge about the USA. I felt that each in his own way Kardelj and Kidric are extraordinary: still young and growing: politicians, of course, but *honest men.*"

I urged them to visit America soon.

"*Da, da, da,*" said Kardelj.

Kidric said, "I wish I could."

I gathered he was pinned down by the immense problems of industrializing an undeveloped country in the Middle of Nowhere.

When I mentioned that in 1948 the United States turned out seven million motor vehicles, twenty or thirty million radio and television sets, enough textile material to wind around the earth I didn't remember how many times, and three or four hundred million little electric bulbs for Christmas trees, Kardelj and Kidric sat expressionless for perhaps a quarter of a minute. I explained that I chanced to have these figures at the tip of my tongue because I saw them in a news-magazine I picked up on the plane between London and Prague, and I continued:

"There's lots wrong with the United States' current behavior toward the revolutions going on in the industrially backward countries. Recently a critic of American foreign policy said that our State Department was trying to ride a capitalistic horse in a predominantly socialistic circus. When that is said, however, America remains a terrific place, full of promises and dangers—to herself and the world. One has to see the country to realize what it is."

Between two and three-thirty on Saturday, I lunched at the Dedijers' and met Vlado's second wife, Vera, a pretty, quiet young woman from Slovenia, where she played a part in the resistance and the revolution. Vlado's first wife, Olga, a physician, died a heroine in the mountains of western Yugoslavia in 1943.

"Vera and I had a fight last night because of you," Vlado said in English when Vera went into the kitchen. "Well, not really a fight—a squabble. She wanted to go out and beg, borrow, and steal to give you the kind of lunch she imagines you're accustomed to in America. My argument was: 'To hell with him! If he doesn't like what we have here, he can go back where he came from.'"

Vera didn't understand why Vlado and I laughed so heartily. I explained to her that the phrase "go back where you came from" is used by super-patriots in the United States to put "furriners" like me in their place.

"I told Vera," Vlado went on, "that at your home in New Jersey we ate in the kitchen and I helped myself from the refrigerator. Unless she went back on her word, you won't get anything special."

I said I was grateful for that.

"I agreed to only one extravagance," Vlado continued, "that this room be heated," and he put a hand on the tall green tile stove in the corner. "Usually in winter the kitchen is the only warm room in the house. The children stay there most of the day."

"Why don't we eat in there?"

"Too small. Also, no refrigerator full of milk, butter, eggs, fruit, ginger ale, Coca-Cola, and ice cubes. Come, look"—and, to Vera's distress, Vlado ushered me into the kitchen. The children's toys and the crib of the youngest were there.

As Director of Information, Vlado's rank was about equal to a deputy minister's and, under the system of privileges then in effect, he was entitled to extra food allowances. These were accorded officials primarily so they could entertain foreign visitors. Vlado said he left the house at seven in the morning, returned at two for half an hour, when he could, for lunch; and when he came home again, it was late evening and he had no time or taste for social life—a disqualification for his job.

"What's that American gag? Oh yes, I say it's spinach and to hell with it! Anyhow, like a good many others, Vera and I don't need or want the privileges."

I asked if the privileges were abused.

"By a few," said Vlado, "and there's plenty of talk which makes it unpleasant for the many who live modestly and isn't helpful generally. There's quite a struggle going on inside the Party against the privileges. It's not a simple matter, though. Some of the *drugovi,* like Tito, Kardelj, Kidric and Bebler, have nice homes—by our standards—and enough fuel and food: they must; for they have foreign visitors all the time. If Tito didn't have all that the No. 1 man in a country should have when guests come, even the people who now prattle about the 'luxurious living of the higher-ups' would protest because he permitted strangers to see our backwardness and poverty."

I mentioned the story told—and enjoyed—in the United States about the hot-dog picnic lunch President and Mrs. Roosevelt gave the King and Queen of England at Hyde Park when they were on a state visit in America in 1939.

"The Roosevelts could do that with the King and Queen of England," said Vlado. "Both America and Britain are great powers."

"And apart from the King and the Queen," I said, "the Roosevelts were the Roosevelts. Not every American President and his wife could give hot dogs to a visiting monarch."

Vlado smiled, nodding he understood. "I'm not sure this is authentic, but I heard that King George of Greece very much resented a similar lunch at Hyde Park—maybe because he was a cheap, upstart character, or possibly because he didn't like hot dogs, or whatever ordinary fare the Roosevelts served on that auspicious occasion; but also, I wouldn't be surprised, because Greece is a small country and its representatives, for that reason, are very touchy and want to be doubly, triply certain they're not being slighted by a big power. Very complex, this business of being a small country. Ugh! . . . Incidentally, I like hot dogs very much. At the United Nations Conference in San Francisco, there was a hot-dog stand near the auditorium; I ate them all the time."

Lunch at the Dedijers consisted of *ricet,* a Slovenian dish of barley and beans and pieces of pork, potatoes, dark bread, substitute "coffee," and *palacinke*—rolled pancakes with fruit jelly.

"This is the only special," was Vera's aside to her scowling husband as she brought in the pancakes.

"Where did you get the butter and eggs?" asked Vlado, giving a good imitation of the "Western" conception of a Balkanite bullying his wife.

Vera smiled and placed her forefinger on her lips.

After lunch, Vlado and I sat alone awhile.

"I forgot to ask you," I said, "how's your head?" At the time he buried his first wife in a Bosnian forest he was severely wounded, and I knew he had a hole in his skull, about the size of an American nickel, covered by his thick dark hair. When he was in the United States in 1945, his head often ached terribly. I urged him to go to the Mayo Clinic. He said he expected to go to the Soviet Union soon and would have his head looked at there.

Now he told me: "In '46 I went to a hospital near Moscow. A committee of doctors had me under observation for a week, then they said I had to be very, very careful—work only two hours a day, avoid alcohol, smoking, sports, anything strenuous. I never drank or smoked anyway; the rest of that regimen, however, would be intolerable to me. Besides my own writing, which I do nights, I have two jobs—one in the Government Information Office, another in the propaganda division of the Central Committee of the CPY. Each takes five to eight hours; so I work, like nearly everybody else, fourteen to eighteen hours a day. I play tennis and basketball, and I like nothing better than a three-, four-hour tramp in the woods, preferably uphill. . . . Slivers of metal are still in my head, moving around, and I feel pain occasionally, in different spots, but——" He shrugged.

"You should have it looked at again."

"That's what *Stari* harps on," said Vlado, meaning Tito. *Stari* is the equivalent of "the Old Man," used the way members of a ship's crew refer to the captain they like. It is used by some of Tito's closest wartime and peacetime *drugovi*.

"Don't you listen to him?"

"Hell no!" said Vlado, lapsing into one of his favorite Americanisms. "What kind of dictator is he?"

Vlado laughed. "Ask *him* that. . . . Maybe next time I go to the United States I'll have it looked at again. There's a specialist on head wounds in Detroit."

Before I left, Vlado took me into his small, unheated study to show me his library. He pointed to a collection of anti-Tito literature which appeared in the United States during 1946–48.

"Fantastic stuff," he said. "Some of it is hilarious. Do you know how many copies any of these books sold?"

I was sure the sales figures were very low.

"Since you brought down those planes in '46," I said, "Yugoslavia and Tito have been so unpopular in America that even anti-Yugoslav, anti-Tito books don't sell."

Vlado's face was deeply serious for an instant, then he laughed briefly. "Tell that to *Stari* when you see him, won't you?"

Vlado had to return to one of his two offices in the heart of town, and drove me back to Rumunska.

"Boris Kidric told me," I said, "that a congress of the Communist Party of Serbia starts on Monday. Any chance of my getting in?"

"It would be a little irregular," said Vlado after a moment's thought, "but I'll get you a pass. I'm a delegate."

As we reached the house, Marija, widening a path in the snow, said that a *drug* from the *marsalat*—Marshal Tito's office—was waiting inside. "I'll see who it is," said Vlado and came in with me.

It was Tito's personal secretary, a handsome young lieutenant colonel with a snappy manner and a pleasant voice. He said the marshal hoped I would call on him at twelve o'clock on Tuesday, January the eighteenth, and stay for lunch.

"Why all this formality?" I asked Vlado after the officer left.

"I think *Stari* wants to rub it in a little."

"Rub what in?"

"Perhaps I didn't express myself correctly," said Vlado. "The last three, four years, several of us who know something of what you did (whether or not you intended to do it) for Yugoslavia during the war have been a little sore . . . not really sore at you, you understand . . . but, well, we wondered, off and on, why you didn't come. Were you sore? Disappointed with us? I tried to explain to myself and to others: you're an American, you have your responsibilities in the United States, and so on. After those airplanes in '46 we heard you *were* angry, that you thought we were a pack of dopes completely under the Russian thumb, and so on. . . . Then, about a year ago, we got a memo from someone on the Yugoslav Embassy staff in Washington, I forget who, that you asked him to tell Tito his uniform was awful and you didn't blame the reactionary press for comparing it to Goering's."

I had almost forgotten. "Did Tito resent it?" .

"No, no," answered Vlado, "not at all. But some of us felt you didn't quite understand the subtler problems here."

We stood quiet for a spell.

"What subtler problems?" I thought. Vlado was rebuttoning his immense mackinaw, which I recalled he had bought in the Store for Big Men on Sixth Avenue in New York, where I took him in 1945.

"Don't let it bother you, though," said Vlado, leaving. "I think you'll like *Stari*. I must run now."

France was out. I went to my room, and to bed. I slept till Marija rapped on my door at six-thirty, when I had asked her to wake me.

At seven-thirty I rang the doorbell of the small, unguarded Bebler villa on Tolstojeva Street. Waiting to be let in, I had a wide view of the Belgrade lights below.

Vera Bebler—whom I hadn't met before: an attractive young woman with an open manner, an actress, speaking a melodious Slovenian— welcomed me. Ales would be down presently, she said; he was trying to talk Jasna—his little daughter—into going to bed.

From a cupboard in the living-room she lifted a beautifully shaped, sea-green wine glass and held it up against the light.

"Just as you rang, Ales called down to me to put this goblet at your place on the table. It was Ivan Prijatelj's."

The name sounded familiar. "Oh yes, I remember!" . . . During the first quarter of the twentieth century Ivan Prijatelj was a Slovenian cultural historian and social critic whose somewhat pedantic essays, like those of Dr. Franc Kidric, helped the tiny Slovenian nation to awaken politically.

"When I was about thirteen, going to the Gymnasium in Ljubljana, not long before I went to America," I told my hostess, "an older student living in the same boarding-house made me read an article of his. I don't think I understood it. Could it have been something on Reformation and Counter-Reformation in Slovenia?"

"Yes," said Vera Bebler; "he wrote on that. We must tell Ales, he'll be pleased."

"Tell me what?" asked Ales Bebler, coming down the stairs—a tall, thin man in his mid-thirties, with a limp from a wound he received in the Spanish Civil War: his diplomat's face, a mask one minute and a vivid graph of his feelings and thoughts the next. It melted with pleasure when Vera told him I recalled reading something as a boy by Ivan Prijatelj.

"He was my uncle, you know, and in a way, my spiritual father. He wasn't a radical consciously, but he had a lot to do with my becoming a Communist. His work influenced my generation. . . . Like most Slovenians, he loved wine, and that goblet was one of his most prized possessions. For some reason, he willed it to me; it survived the war; and tonight, although I remember that you're even less of a drinker than I am, you'll have to take at least a few sips from it."

Then I remembered that in 1938 or '39 my next-to-the-youngest sister, Polda, married a man named Prijatelj—Anton (or Tone) Prijatelj —a peasant who had been an industrial worker in Cleveland for ten or a dozen years, and who, according to a letter from my family, was a second or third cousin of the late Ivan Prijatelj.

"That practically makes us relatives," said Vera.

"Better yet, friends," smiled Ales. *Prijatelj* is the Slovenian word for friend.

"Why don't you sit down?" said Vera. "I must take a look at Jasna."

"I hope you won't mind," said Ales, "you're in for a big party tonight. I remembered at the airport you said you were tired, and I thought we'd have you to ourselves; but when the gang at the [foreign] office heard you were to be here, several of them wanted to come too. And we asked a few writers, artists, actors, and doctors to drop in after dinner."

As a deputy foreign minister, knowing half a dozen languages and being in closer touch with the diplomatic corps than anyone else in Belgrade, Ales Bebler had to entertain a great deal, and his house was staffed and equipped for large parties. The modest four-course dinner was wonderfully prepared and served.

The other guests, I found, had wanted to come because Yugoslavia's new position in the world picture was forcing them to take an intense interest in America. I had met three of them in New York during United Nations meetings. Four or five of them were division chiefs in the Foreign Office and assistants to Foreign Minister Kardelj.

There were, on a rough count, a half-dozen people called Popovic—meaning "priest's son"—a name as common in Serbia as Smith is in the United States. One of these was Vladimir Popovic, lately returned from the ambassadorship to Moscow to become Deputy Foreign Minister in charge of the increasingly tough relations with the Soviet Union and the countries in its orbit. Another was Dr. Djoni (Johnny) Popovic who, along with two-thirds of the men in the gathering, spoke English. He asked me if I had ever been to Jerome, Arizona, his home town. Yes, he was born there; his parents returned to Montenegro early in the 1920's, when he was six years old. I saw the boyish-looking *"druze doktor* Djoni," as everyone called Tito's personal physician, often, months later.

All the men and some of their wives or *drugarice,* I surmised, were Communists. Several of them, including Ales Bebler, had been Party members from early youth. All had participated in the War of Liberation. Most of them were in their thirties; a few of the women were still in their twenties—two of them were beautiful. All the men had attended universities in Yugoslavia; some had also studied in Paris, Prague, and Moscow. Among them they spoke a dozen languages and read or partly understood as many more.

A good part of the conversation was in English; all of it was characterized by a high degree of frankness both at the dinner table and later with the larger group in the living-room. It started when one of the guests remarked to me, "We heard you had a session with *drugovi* Kardelj and Kidric this morning."

Two of the men besides Ales Bebler and Vladimir Popovic had had close personal contact, at United Nations meetings and during the Paris peace conference in 1946, with James F. Byrnes, Arthur H. Vandenberg, Tom Connally, John Foster Dulles, Bernard Baruch, George C. Marshall, and Eleanor Roosevelt, as well as with lesser American representatives. As the conversation livened, their chagrin over the United States' official attitude toward their country during 1945–48 emerged sharply. Where was that wonderful anti-imperialist, progressive tradition I talked about?

I wondered how much of what we discussed in the morning Kardelj had told them.

I was able to defend American behavior in some instances; in others, not. "You were in the Russian bloc," I said. "What about *their* behavior? And your own? What about the American planes *you* shot down?"

"Look here, *gospodine Adamicu,*" said one of the young men. He paused to soften his voice and relax the tense lines on his face. "We know the plane incident upset you. If you allow me to say so, however, there's much you don't know."

"No doubt," I admitted, "but my ignorance isn't entirely my fault."

"For months before the incident," the young man said, "British and American planes flew over our territory, not only over the narrow corner bordering on Italy and Austria, which we might have overlooked on the ground that the flyers wished to take the easiest course or a short cut, but often fifty, a hundred kilometers deep, sometimes even deeper, inside our borders, frequently very low. They came every few days, on some days by the dozen, by the score—transports, bombers, fighters, mostly American. All without permission required by international law. They never thought of asking for it. We made one protest after another, to no avail. We were sure the planes were photographing our terrain. What else could we believe when Mr. Richard Patterson, your ambassador here, continually bristled with antagonism toward our government . . . when [on Decoration Day, 1946] an American military attaché in Belgrade publicly insulted Marshal Tito . . . when several American soldiers, under that attaché, stuck out their tongues [in a "Bronx cheer"] at our flag as a unit of our army marched by a building housing the United States Army Graves Mission . . . when almost the entire American and Western press screamed for war . . . when our border guards were capturing numerous *Ustasi* [Croatian quislingist] war criminals who had escaped to Austria in 1945 and who now, in the spring and summer of '46, were being sent back to Yugoslavia, as they confessed, by the Anglo-American intelligence officers to join the new *Krizari* [Crusader] forces being formed in the woods of Croatia under flags specially blessed by Archbishop Stepinac . . . and when a rumor-whispering campaign, indubitably inspired by Anglo-American Intelligence in Austria, was started in various parts of the country that American planes were dropping supplies to the *Krizari?* Were we supposed to enjoy the sight and sound of those planes thundering across our sky? . . . We're a small country, true; but haven't we shown we're worthy of respect? What does America think we are—Honduras, Venezuela, the Congo? Yugoslavia couldn't possibly allow those violations of her air space and of international law to continue indefinitely, particularly in the face of Churchill's speech [at Fulton, Missouri, February 1946], of the Truman Doctrine, of the war hysteria being generated in the United States."

I nodded, partly agreeing. "But before you sent up your fighters to stop the violations, certainly before your fighters started shooting, you should have first exhausted all the diplomatic and propagandistic means."

"*What* more could we do? We sent eleven protests to the British and to the Americans. Marshal Tito warned in a speech in parliament that Yugoslavia wouldn't tolerate the violations indefinitely. Did the American and British authorities think he was talking to himself? . . . Intolerable as the flights were, Yugoslavia did no more than protest until the summer. Then, after the eleventh unheeded protest, our fighters went up to insist the planes come down. No more. The first plane obeyed the summons. The second plane ignored it. There was no intention of destroying the plane and killing the crew."

"I don't doubt it," I said. "The trouble was that not a hundred people in the United States knew—or know now—what you're saying. I read practically everything published about Yugoslavia in that period, and I knew nothing of what was going on."

"Is it *our* fault," asked the young man, "if the American Ambassador and his military attachés in Belgrade and the State Department and the military in Washington suppressed our protests? Are *we* to blame if your American press and radio didn't report *drug* Tito's warning?"

"Look," I said, "I make no apology for official America, or for the American press and radio. I wrote a couple of articles condemning their share in the matter as I saw it dimly a few weeks after the incident. My point is that the American people—not all but many, not always but usually—want to do the right thing. *If* they knew of the continual violations by American planes of international law and Yugoslav air space, quite a few would have objected. That they didn't know was partly, if not largely, your fault."

"Why? *Why?*"

"You should have prepared a near-ultimatum to the United States Government giving the exact numbers and dates of illegal flights, and the identifications on the planes. And you should have instructed your Ambassador in Washington to call a press conference just before he took the note to the State Department and to hand out copies and declare as dramatically as possible that Yugoslavia would no longer tolerate unauthorized flights over her territory which in effect, or in your eyes, flaunted her sovereignty. I assure you that something unusual like that would have cracked the conspiracy of silence, would have landed the story, however garbled, on the front page of many big newspapers in the United States, and many Americans (some for the wrong reasons, perhaps) would have been on your side, and public opinion would have forced the flights to cease."

"Perhaps, to be adequately 'dramatic,'" said the young diplomat, "our Ambassador should have stood on his head while declaiming to the press."

"I'm sounding off too much," I thought. "But I can't stop now. . . ."

"Well," I said, "even such a stunt would have been preferable to the action you took and the result it produced. But let me say that my outline of a procedure is born of hindsight, which I know is a lot easier than foresight. . . . Another thing. After I read a letter the pilot of the second plane wrote from Italy to his sister in Illinois,[2] I was

[2] The second plane incident occurred on August 19, 1946. On the seventeenth, its pilot, Captain Richard H. Claeys, wrote an airmail letter to his sister, Mary Claeys, in St. Charles, Illinois, who received it about a week later, four or five days after her brother had been killed. She showed it to a Hearst reporter and the Chicago *Herald* published it on August 26 as a scoop—but only in one edition. Apparently, the editor pulled it out when he realized the significance of this sentence by the dead flyer: *"I'm flying tomorrow over the same area where others of our planes have been forced down."* His plane did not take off "tomorrow," which would have been the eighteenth. It took off on the nineteenth. What delayed it? Perhaps nothing that had any bearing on the incident of the nineteenth. But why was Captain Claeys made to fly "over the same area where others of our planes have been forced down"? By whom? Who issued the orders? Why did Captain Claeys circle twice low over Ljubljana (as the Yugoslavs claimed he did) before the Yugoslav fighter went up and signalled him to land? Why

nearly sure that those long-drawn-out violations of international law were a provocation of British origin carried on by Americans. *But were they, really?* I didn't raise this question when I wrote about the incident in the United States in September 1946, for then I was convinced that the 'Anglo-American' role in the affair was a dirty trick. However, I claim to know something about America and Americans; and on second and third thought, wasn't the whole affair too elaborate, too extended in time, to be a downright provocation, to be a stunt worked up with evil design? It could have been a blunder, maybe half-willful, or of studied negligence; or a blunder into which Americans were led by their British and Roman friends."

There followed a calmer discussion among the other guests as to whether any other procedure would have been effective.

"In any case," said one of them after a while, "we all readily admit that in the field of propaganda and public relations we Yugoslavs are nowhere." No one disagreed.

"Let's assume," I rubbed it in, "that most of those flights were a provocation—a tactic in the 'cold war' which cliques in America, Britain, Italy, and elsewhere wanted as a prelude to a possible 'preventive war,' then probably under consideration. Yugoslavia fell for it. Which is worse—working up a trick like that or falling for it? I mean, worse *in effect?*"

"A moral question is involved," said one of the Yugoslavs in a tensely subdued voice.

"Yes; and without knowing exactly how you see it, I'll say that in the main I sympathize with your viewpoint. However, if we found the persons responsible for the provocation for which you fell, they would make a moral claim too. What is going on in the world is a war between two forces—one good (they), the other bad (the Soviet power, and you were a part of it in 1946)—a war now called cold, but likely if not bound to get hot. And isn't everything fair in war?"

---

did he ignore the challenge and try to head for the Austrian border, thus compelling the Yugoslav fighter to open fire on him? Was he merely carrying out his orders? . . . Captain Claeys wrote *"others* of our planes," whereas it is definitely known that only *one* other American plane (on August 9) was challenged and forced to land in Yugoslavia. Any significance in that? . . . Both planes were supposed to be flying between Italy and Austria. Did the American commander in Italy investigate the matter? Did General Mark Clark, then the American High Commissioner in Austria, look into it? He doesn't so much as mention it in his book *Calculated Risk* (Harper, 1950), although he devotes pages to lesser incidents involving Tito and Yugoslavia.

"As a sidelight, this may interest you," said one of the men who until then had only listened. "A day or two after the airplane incident, the chief of our trade mission to several South American countries had an appointment with a minor official in the Foreign Ministry [in the capital of one of the republics]. When he got there, the official told him excitedly that the *Presidente* wished to see him. To his astonishment, the President rushed to greet him with outstretched hands, and said, 'Congratulations, congratulations! Please extend my compliments to Marshal Tito! What Yugoslavia did to those planes is the only language the *Yanquis* understand.' "

"That's interesting," I said, "and understandable; and awful, from my American point of view. And no good from yours either. You should have been in America that week! Suddenly many Americans were ready to A-bomb Yugoslavia and go to war, if need be, against the whole Soviet bloc. . . . Before the plane incident, as I remember, the anti-Communist and war hysteria in the United States wasn't very serious. Most Americans were ducking the issue, or trying to; they'd had a bellyful of the last war and they didn't want another. The feeling was: let the other fellow throw his weight around if he wants to, and make a big noise; we're not scaring easily, and we don't want to get really tough unless the other party, the Soviet orbit, insists on it. The Fulton speech didn't swell Churchill's popularity; rather the contrary. In March, the Truman Doctrine raised more eyebrows and arguments than applause. Then—you did it! And a great many normally sane Americans went wild. Then our American international adventurers (imperialist warmongers, to you), our very able manipulators of American public opinion who regard their dexterity as the quintessence of democracy, the shapers of our foreign policy, really had the 'cold war' blowing hot. At long last, with *your* help, they had the American people in the mood they wanted them in. From then on, the policymakers did almost anything they thought was necessary in foreign affairs, feeling quite certain the American people would go along.

"The incident occurred in the midst of the 1946 Congressional election. As presented in the American press (in exactly the way the manipulators of public opinion wanted it presented), 'Tito shooting down American planes' suddenly drove home the point of all the anti-Communist, anti-Soviet, anti-Slavic propaganda that had been directed at the internationally inexperienced mind and feelings of the average American since Churchill's Fulton and Truman's Doctrine speeches—

propaganda which, in its domestic focus, was anti-Roosevelt, anti-progressive, anti-labor.

"So Bill Jones and John Voynich and Sarah Bernstein, millions of Americans turned abruptly Right in both the primary and final elections. They voted for the most reactionary 'tough-policy' candidate in sight, Republican or Democrat. They voted, in other words, against Roosevelt, against 'Communism' (New Deal) in America, against Stalin and Tito in foreign relations. If there was no difference between opposing candidates, they voted Republican because Republicans were 'out' and not responsible for Roosevelt policies. Or else, confused and disgusted, they didn't vote, which also benefited the Republicans. So the Republicans won a powerful, too powerful, majority in the Eightieth Congress, and they and the reactionary Democrats thought they had a mandate from the people to swing the country Right and 'get tough' with Russia and her satellites and, indirectly, with the progressive impulses of the people from whom they claimed to have a mandate. The Taft-Hartley Act was made possible; the Committee on Un-American Activities went to town and painted it Red. . . . And I came to the hard conclusion that Yugoslavia, my native country, was instrumental—as a catch-all net, at least—in bouncing American reaction to the surface once more. An unpleasant conclusion."

"That's a terrible thing you're saying," said one of the Yugoslavs.

"I'm shooting off my mouth too much."

"Oh, no," said someone else—evidently not out of mere politeness.

"Oh, yes!" I said.

There was a ripple of laughter. Someone said, "We *want* you to talk."

"All right," I smiled. "But perhaps I should be less critical."

"No, no; go ahead in your own way."

"Well, if what I said a while ago sounded terrible, I can't say I'm really sorry. The world is an uncomfortable, sensitive One World now. Something goes off, *boom!* here and something collapses or springs up there. What I'm trying to say is that what America does affects Yugoslavia, and vice versa."

I looked around—no one seemed to resent me. Several people smiled. I took a sip from Ivan Prijatelj's goblet.

"I'm sure you mean to be helpful, Louis," said Ales Bebler, his brow corrugated, "and you may have a point, several points, *but* . . . aside from not liking to be jabbed at, we can't go along with all of your thesis. There *is* a lot you don't know."

"Of course, Ales. And I admit again it may be partly my fault, but it might help if New Yugoslavia made an effort to inform me and the rest of the world about her angle in the plane incident."

"Well," one of them cleared his throat, "the incident occurred: how could we have brought out the truth—from our angle? And don't forget our inexperience in public relations, and that our propaganda means were even more meager in 1946 than they are today."

"I don't know," I said, "but in the fall of '46 I hoped you would demand a full airing of the incident before the United Nations. Instead, you knuckled under to Richard Patterson, whom the American press then elevated into a great ambassador and a hero, because he made Tito pay indemnity for the loss of American lives."

There was a long silence, just as there had been at Kardelj's when I said this. I wondered if the Yugoslavs hadn't brought the matter up before the U.N. because they were in the Russian bloc and the Russians were afraid it might arouse the American people still more. Better pay up and drop the whole business. Perhaps, too, the Yugoslavs themselves felt it was futile to try to have the affair examined without prejudice by the preponderantly anti-Communist, anti-Soviet, and anti-Slavic U.N. . . . Months later Vlado Dedijer, who had been at the Paris peace conference when the plane incident occurred, told me that Molotov had had the entire Yugoslav delegation on the carpet. "What have you done?! What have you done?!" cried the chief of the Soviet delegation. This, while the American press and radio blared forth the theme that Tito was Stalin's "goon"! . . . Later still, I heard the suggestion (but couldn't get anyone to confirm or develop it) that the American flights had been continued despite the Yugoslavs' protests because "bull-headed Belgrade"—unlike Prague and Warsaw— persisted in refusing to allow American and British commercial airlines, then extending themselves over the world, the right to land their smaller craft in Yugoslavia and eventually enlarge the Zemun and other airports so they could receive great sky-cruisers. The Yugoslavs refused, presumably, because they suspected the airway expansion was related to the British and American foreign policies (the Truman Doctrine, etc.) which they believed had designs on the Balkans.

"Thanks in large part to the incident," I added, "the 'preventive-war' party in the United States—linked to the Vatican, to Rome gener-

ally, and to the old imperialist crowd in Britain and to reaction elsewhere—began to gather strength in the summer and fall of '46. I think
it's possible to argue that, were it not for Henry Wallace, who just then
took a stand against the Pacelli-Churchill-Baruch-Dulles-Byrnes-Van-
denberg-Spellman American foreign policy, and who broke with Truman and became the active leader of a peace movement soon after . . .
were it not for this, a 'preventive war' might well have occurred in
'47. For a while early in '48 the Wallace movement pulled together
what peace sentiment remained. If I know my mind, I joined it mainly
because of that."

Thus we came to discuss the reasons for Henry A. Wallace's small
vote in '48 . . . my reason for saying I wouldn't have been for Wallace
if I thought he had a chance of being elected, and for believing that
Thomas E. Dewey, backed by intelligent capitalists like Winthrop
Aldrich, might have been preferable to Harry S. Truman, whose financial support came from unstable, less responsible "new capital"
. . . the negative role of the American Communist Party in American
life . . . the "essence of America" which I said precluded any such
overturn as occurred in Russia and Yugoslavia and was taking place in
China . . . and American characteristics, practices, hallucinations, de-
lusions, and folkways which I suggested the Yugoslavs might bear
in mind if they reoriented themselves towards the "West" (as I began
to feel they would have to).

Monday morning I went to the National Bank (the only bank in
the country, with branches in all cities and larger towns) to get some
Yugoslav currency on my letter of credit. It took the better part of an
hour to surmount the red-tape entanglements. Going from window to
window, and sitting on the waiting-bench, I looked around the vast,
high-ceilinged room.

The interior was too ornate—as I vaguely remembered it from
1932–33. Overhead was the same flamboyant chandelier. Among the
obviously new fixtures was a marble column near the exit, dedicated
to the memory of the bank employees who fell in the Communist-led
borba during 1941–44. In the middle of one wall was the same big
clock, all but lost in the petty ornamentation around it. On another
wall, once occupied by a life-size portrait of King Alexander, was an
arrangement of pictures of Communist revolutionaries from Marx to
Tito. Around the room were slogans reading: *Hurrah for Workers*

Competing [among themselves] *for Higher Production! . . . Hurrah for the Five-Year Plan! . . . All for the Plan! All for Tito! . . . With* Drug *Tito to Victory in the Building of Socialism! . . . Workers of the World, Unite!*

Back at the house on Rumunska, a messenger from the Central Committee of the CP of Serbia gave me an invitation to the opening session of its Second Congress. Enclosed was a pass I was to sign for and present at the entrance. The congress opened at four.

Marija informed me that Vlado Dedijer had telephoned to ask if she was taking good care of me ("You know *drug* Vlado—how he likes to joke"). She had invited him to lunch, and hoped it was all right: he was coming at two.

Vlado Dedijer, whom I hadn't seen since Saturday afternoon, related he had spent the evening and all of Sunday talking with a number of *drugovi,* who were in town for the congress, as part of his job of research on the Communist Party in Serbia, particularly in Belgrade, since 1937. He had been working at it, on and off, during the last two years. A terrific story—of courage and martyrdom, he said; of patriotism and solidarity with the international working-class movement. He planned to put it into a book some day if he ever got the time. He fell silent for a spell, thinking of his material, perhaps. Then he remarked he had heard of my arguments at Bebler's and at the Writers' Club. What else had I been up to?

I told him . . . and said that everything I had seen and heard in the last few days was impressive and disturbing, and that I felt the current Yugoslav scene was at least mildly terrific too.

"During the last five or six years I've read possibly a couple of million words on Yugoslavia," I said; "now I discover I know almost nothing about it. And some of that may be your fault. You're sitting on the story, or somebody is. What kind of Director of Information are you, anyhow?"

"Lousy, to be exact," said Vlado. "I'm glad you agree, and when you see *Stari,* tell him so, will you? . . . Seriously, I'd like to be relieved of this job and do nothing but delve into our recent history and write as many volumes as it takes. Tito, Kardelj, and Djilas keep saying they need me on this job, and I stick to it. I'm supposed to be a disciplined Communist; also, poor as I am at it, there's probably no one better for the job right now. We're very short of qualified people.

"On the other hand, what *can* I do? What could any director of information do? For a while about two years ago I tried to work closely with the foreign correspondents, but the drivel they turned out, almost without exception, had so little contact with truth it made us sick. . . . The questions some of them asked were so hostile or stupid, or both, that the whole picture of what's going on here got out of focus before we answered them. 'Cold war' stuff. It bypassed, or even scoffed at, the heroism of our people. It magnified our shortcomings and, if it mentioned them at all, minimized the widespread and not inconspicuous evidences of our progress. . . . Gradually, along about in 1947, we got into a what's-the-use attitude, which led to the policy: the less we give out, the less we try to cooperate with these fellows, the better.

"You disapprove. Okay, I agree. . . . I heard how you bawled us out at Bebler's," he smiled; "I'm sorry I missed it. I grant we don't know the first thing about public-relations methods. We should learn. But I tell you, they go against our grain.

"Yes, since the Cominform hit us, the attitude of the Western press and radio has changed, at least superficially—*but!* How can I explain? . . . the New York *Times* man assigned here now [M. S. Handler] is evidently a nice chap. One can see he wants to be 'objective.' When Tito or Kardelj says something, he picks the key passages and quotes them accurately. But, for the life of me, I can't get over the feeling that the man-bites-dog system and spirit of the Western press and radio, the American press and radio especially, while not without merit, are slightly barbaric.

"No, by this I don't mean that *our* newspapers are ultra-civilized; we adopted the Russian form whole-hog, now we're stuck with it. We don't know how to change. We certainly don't want to copy the blatant, shrill ways of the Western press, which thrives on disaster and sentimentality, oddities and scandal. We'd like to emulate the good features of any country's press and find a form of our own. But that's another subject. . . .

"Right now, what really gets me down about the foreign correspondents, and that includes the few Russians and East Europeans who are still here, is that they don't give a damn about anything except the shot they hope will go off and make the headline of the year. How can anyone expect me to *want* to work with people like that? . . . All we try for now is to put out our releases in as good English or French as we can, and deliver them to the Hotels Majestic and Moskva," where the foreign correspondents live. "You're right, in a way," said Vlado in the car, on the way to the hall; "we *are* sitting on the story. But what *can* we do? What can *I* do?"

"Will foreign correspondents be admitted to the Serbian CP Congress?" I asked.

"Hell, no," said Vlado, lapsing into another Americanism he had picked up around the Lynn, Mass., Y.M.C.A. or during the United Nations Conference in San Francisco. "No Western correspondents, anyhow. They'd misunderstand or deliberately screw up the whole affair. The best of them see mostly the foam, the scum on the surface; the currents swirling underneath don't interest the 'trained' observers from abroad. . . . We sent passes to a Czech, who knows Serbian and we think is a decent fellow, and to the *Pravda* man."

"Is he 'decent' too?"

Vlado shrugged his huge shoulders. "He knows Serbian. At least it will do no harm for a Russian to see the congress, and it may do some good."

"Why?"

After some thought, Vlado answered: "*Stari* and a few others at the top of our Party and government feel there's still a chance, although more remote daily, that if the Russians realize they can't induce our people to throw over their leaders, the Cominform crisis may dissolve. We believe the Moscow man will report accurately that—like the Croatian, Slovenian, Montenegrin, Macedonian, and Bosnian-Herzegovinian CP's which had their congresses recently, since the big Fifth Congress of the CP of Yugoslavia, last July—the Serbian CP, too, continues to be solidly behind Tito. He won't write this report for *Pravda,* which wouldn't use it, but for some eyes, perhaps, in the Kremlin."

I said, "I don't understand why, when Yugoslavia is more or less at odds with both the 'West' and the 'East,' perhaps more with the 'East' than the 'West,' you admit two 'Eastern' correspondents—one because he is 'decent'—and not even one 'Western' correspondent. You said the *Times* man looks decent; why don't you admit him?"

"He doesn't know the language," said Vlado. "We can't undertake to translate and interpret for the Americans. They employ translators and legmen of their own; but we know these people too well to let them into a meeting like this. . . . You have a point, though. Our whole policy toward the foreign press needs rethinking."

As we left the car near the hall shortly after three (an hour before the congress opened), Vlado caught sight of a wartime comrade, a young man almost as large as he; they embraced and banged each other on the back, and walked on together, talking jovially, while I gawked at the scene around me, alive with people and with fluttering red banners.

At the entrance I discovered I had lost Vlado, and for a moment, this being my first Communist congress, I thought I might have trouble getting in. But one of the militiamen merely glanced at my pass and the surge of delegates behind me propelled me inside.

The large vestibule was full of cigarette smoke, hearty words, and laughter and Serbians—*Srbijanci:* from Serbia proper. Many were peasants, wearing their regional holiday dress, which gave the occasion a splash of color. Scores of soldiers, from generals to privates, stood or sauntered about. The greatest number of assembling delegates were in modern civilian clothes, most of it worn, faded and frayed.

A sprinkling of men and women were without a limb, an eye, a cheekbone, or part of a chin. One young woman was armless. Nearly all the delegates were veterans of the War of Liberation and the Revolution; a majority were Party members since before and during the war. Several were past their middle years, but the average age was between twenty-eight and thirty. They were the local leaders of the inner core of the CP of Serbia, its most dedicated and devoted *aktivisti*—or party whips, to use the British and American phrase.

People stood about, lighting one another's cigarettes, telling whom they had just seen—"and I thought he died in the Fifth Offensive: imagine my surprise and joy!" Some walked around looking for others. Names were called out; their owners replied. The congress was a Partisan reunion.

Making my way toward the *garderoba* counters, I saw a slight, dark, withdrawn young man who was at the Union of Yugoslav Writers' affair on Saturday evening. He seemed to be looking at me, or at least toward me but without any sign of recognition. I went up to him and said I didn't remember his name and hoped he would forgive me. He was Jovan Popovic, an editor of *Knjizevne Novine,* blind in one eye and barely able to see out of the other. Months later I learned he had lost the eye during a forced march at night through the Bosnian woods in 1943. He was too shy or reticent to tell the girl Partisan ahead of him in the tight column not to let the branches snap back. A twig hit him across the eyes. No medical attention was available for days, and——

Another writer—Oskar Davico, of Serbian-Jewish origin—appeared, and Jovan Popovic and Davico joked about my "misplacing" Vlado Dedijer, who towers seven feet high, as I say, and tips the scale at three hundred pounds. "Only an *Amerikanac* could achieve such a feat."

They knew many of the delegates and introduced me to some I had heard of before—young Colonel General Koca Popovic, a son of one of the leading prewar Belgrade banking families who had studied in Paris, become a surrealist writer, then a Communist and a fighter in Spain, then the first Commander of the First Proletarian Brigade which Tito created in Serbia late in 1941, and who was now Chief of Staff of the new Yugoslav Army; Lieutenant General Kosta Nadj, another young member of the General Staff; Vlado Zecevic, one-time Orthodox priest who quit Mihailovic's Cetnik forces late in 1941 when he saw they were collaborating with the enemy, and now was Federal Minister of Forests; Nikola Petrovic, Minister of Electrification; two or three university professors; an editor of *Borba,* the organ of the Central Committee of the Communist Party of Yugoslavia and the largest newspaper in the country; an editor of *Jez* [Porcupine], the humorous Belgrade weekly; and an elderly woman from a small town in central Serbia whose entire family—father, husband, and five sons and daughters—had died in the *borba*.

Part of her face, including one eye, was shot away. She said she had read of my arrival: she had a brother in Pittsburgh who was pro-Cetnik, she heard: how was that possible? I didn't catch her full name; the delegates passing by, many of whom knew her, called her *drugarica* Dusanka.

About twenty minutes after entering the vestibule, I found myself cornered both physically and intellectually by a Serbian writer whom I will call X. The following conversation was as frank as it was because there was no thought of publishing it—until much later, when I was asked to disguise his identity. The man had been at Bebler's on Saturday and at the Writers' Club on Sunday, but had taken no part in either discussion. He inquired how I was and what my impressions of New Yugoslavia were.

My impressions were restricted to Belgrade so far, I said, but they led me to think that New Yugoslavia was quite a place; and I felt all right, considering.

"I talked too much on Saturday and Sunday nights. This morning I woke up with the determination to improve my manners. It won't be easy, but hereafter my policy is to look and listen mostly."

"You didn't talk enough," said X. "There wasn't enough time, either at Bebler's or at the club, for us to get at you really, to dig into the subjects you or we brought up. It may interest you to know that some of us have been discussing them since, and that I was assigned to prepare a memo for possible circulation within the Central Committee. Just now I ran into *drug* Dedijer; I asked him if you were still in Belgrade and he said you were right here—he had lost you, but I might find you. He told me you accused him of sitting on our story, and he explained briefly what you meant by that."

"This just underlines my determination to look and listen from now on," I laughed. "Is Vlado angry?"

"No, no; on the contrary, he seems to agree with your criticism."

"And you don't?"

"I'm disturbed that even you—a friend of New Yugoslavia—haven't given any real study to our side. *Drug* Dedijer, I gather, likes your accusation that we're sitting on the story; I'm not sure I do. May I ask, what do you mean by the phrase?"

"Here goes my look-and-listen policy," I sighed self-mockingly, trying to conceal my annoyance, not so much at X as at the stir my jabber had roused and its being put into a memorandum. "Some of us in the United States think that what the world needs is information from all sides." I told him of Henry Wallace's remark on the train coming back from the Soviet reception in Washington: that it was hard to be a friend of the Soviet Union. "That goes for Yugoslavia. Many American progressives suddenly feel they have no idea of the truth 'Behind the Iron Curtain.' Our chief concern, my chief concern, is the persistent probability of another war. How to prevent it? At your club last night, I admitted that it might come because of America's attitude toward Russia and vice versa, or as a result of the compulsions in the American capitalist system intensified by its fear of Russia and Communism. But I want to say again that if anybody in this part of the world is interested in reducing the war danger in so far as it exists because of American policy, the way to reduce it," I emphasized, "is *through the American people*. At this moment so far as I can see, Yugoslavia still pretends to be part of the Soviet orbit in spite of the Cominform's behavior toward her; I think she's out of it, out in the

cold, between the devil and the deep blue sea; but Yugoslavia *is* going into socialism, and as such she is used—very successfully—to scare
the American people into accepting the probability of World War III.
I think it would be proper for New Yugoslavia to resent being used
for such propaganda purposes. She might at least attempt to find a
method of conveying to the American people, through their press and
over the head of their press, the kind of life she wants. She might admit
that she hasn't yet achieved what she wants, that she's only working
toward it. I know this is easier said than done. But if Yugoslavia even
just *tried* to tell the truth, it might reduce the danger of war."

X grinned. "Now I have you where I want you. Why should the
burden of preventing another war fall on Yugoslav shoulders? Or on
the far broader shoulders of the Soviet Union or the Soviet orbit?—
setting aside, for the moment, the question of whether Yugoslavia is
still part of the Soviet orbit or not."

"I didn't say the whole burden should fall on Yugoslavia. I said
Yugoslavia is permitting the world to lie about her. At the Writers'
Union Club, I tried to say that if you Yugoslavs didn't do anything
about this, you might help hatch something you didn't want."

"But why should you require us to learn public-relations methods
without delay and go to work on the American people? This may
sound exactly like the kind of carping question a loud-mouthed but
really inferiority-ridden nationalist in a small country would ask. But
I don't feel it is carping and nationalistic to ask it. Speaking for myself,
I believe we simply must not knuckle under to mere size, to paramountcy, to fear—even of war."

"I agree—but what are you driving at?"

"I'm coming to it in a roundabout way partly to give you a glimpse
of our thoughts and talk since you began to jab at us. . . . To *you,* we
freely admit all our inadequacies. To *you,* I'm personally eager to admit that we doubtless have additional flaws and lacks of which we
aren't even aware and which you, coming here like an explorer, may be
sighting at every turn. . . . You're an American. Very well. But how
about America as a country, a state, a civilization? Even before you
came," he smiled, "we had an inkling that American production was
phenomenal, that the United States was a 'terrific place.' We were impressed by your statistics: that last year America produced so many
million automobiles, and so on. Such facts make our mouths water.
But! . . . You did mention some of America's imperfections along-

side of her wonders, and no doubt if we had a chance to talk several
hours daily for a week or a month, we'd extract from you a fairly well
rounded-out picture of your adopted homeland. And we need it, we're
eager to have it. *But,* to repeat, why should you require us to address
ourselves to the American people strictly and only in the language *they*
understand, employing only the methods *they* understand because *they*
invented them to propagandize and persuade one another, and because
America is big and therefore is a big factor in the danger of another
war. Wouldn't it be reasonable to expect Americans to make a little
effort themselves to understand our ways and why we are the way we
are?

"Your emphasis, *gospodine Adamicu,* understandably is on America. But can we tell the truth to Americans? Two or three years ago,
as *drug* Dedijer may have told you, public-relations firms in New York
and Washington tried to sell themselves to our representatives for immense sums of dollars, in return for which they promised to 'sell Tito's
Yugoslavia' to the Americans by methods which they claimed were
effective in 'selling' other governments that had engaged their services.
So far as I could discover from the elaborate, neatly typed outlines of
their plans for our penetration into the friendly corners of the American mind and heart, these firms had no interest in the truth about the
Yugoslav experience. They told our officials in New York and Washington that *they* knew what 'went' in America. One of them spoke of
'creative publicity' and explained it need have no connection with
truth. Another firm intimated that if we engaged them, our government, our Politburo, would have to take their advice in matters of
policy! When our representatives rejected this proposition, the public-
relations magicians said they only meant to help us, they only meant to
create the sort of 'facts' or 'truth' that America would 'go for.'

"Occasionally I listen to the Serbo-Croatian 'Voice of America' which
originates in Washington and New York. It's intended to be propaganda but it's hollow—nobody of any intelligence or influence here
succumbs to it. Of course all 'The Voice' says may be factually so, but
it's one-sided, not the truth. I recall your criticism last night that our
press gives only the negative side of American life. My reply to you is
that we try to give the side of the American picture that 'The Voice'
implies doesn't exist.

"We're Marxists and as such we have our ideas about American
capitalism. You hinted that those ideas aren't strictly accurate: that

some are even obsolete. . . . We do believe in the possibility of capital-ism and socialism coexisting without war, at least the kind of socialism we're creating in Yugoslavia. But why should we open an information office in New York or Washington and pour out facts and figures about New Yugoslavia, about the Five-Year Plan, when on the evidence of our faint efforts in the past we know that the information would either be ignored or compared to American facts and figures and found laughable?

"And why should we try to tell the truth about ourselves to America whose 'Voice' clearly has no intention of telling us the truth about her-self, of coming anywhere near telling us what you told us about the progressive American tradition? Why doesn't 'The Voice' quote Lincoln and Jefferson as you quote them? We're a revolutionary country and we'd enjoy hearing words like that. They would give us a feeling of kinship with America. But 'The Voice' doesn't give them to us. Why? Because it's not the voice of your kind of America. . . . Very well, put it that way: 'It's limited by fear of attacks in Congress and by the whole cold war psychology.' What difference does it make? As I hear it, 'The Voice' isn't interested in reaching us *as we are*. It clearly implies it wishes we weren't this way. It implies we are wallow-ing in Communistic sin. It's uninformed. Worse, it implies that Amer-ica isn't interested in the truth about us. All 'The Voice' is interested in is counter-revolution. Do Americans at large know of these broad-casts? Are *they* interested? How many? What percentage of the popu-lation? If Yugoslavia opened an information office in New York, how much would it cost our government to run it in order to reach those people? We're short of *valuta* and the question arises: would we be smarter to spend our scarce dollars trying to tell the truth to those who more or less want to hear it or to spend the money for machinery which we desperately need to build socialism?

"Finally, like Pilate, what is truth? It's relative, for one thing, and elusive, difficult to grasp. Like colors on a canvas—one brings out the other or dims it. The greater the honesty, the greater the penumbra of doubt. We can work towards truth as an artist striving for beauty. . . . But how can you play fair with someone who you see has no active desire to play fair with you, no real interest in truth for truth's sake or for you or himself?

"Am I unfair? I don't want to be. But there are forces in the world that disturb us. As you probably gathered from the talk at Bebler's and at the Writers' Union Club, some of us are dismayed as we watch the whole amoral game among the big powers. . . . No, no; please don't misunderstand me. I'm not trying to dodge our share of the responsibility for the present world mess on the premise that we're a small country and helpless to do anything about it. We are a small country but we don't consider ourselves utterly helpless; we want responsibility; and I don't completely reject your criticism of our behavior and policies.

"Last night you expressed a suspicion that we didn't inform 'even the Soviet Union' about New Yugoslavia and that the Cominform split may have come about partly because of that. You didn't realize that you touched a very sore spot. I must tell you that by and large from 1945 on we consciously but very unwillingly and uneasily 'sat on the story' not only in reference to the West but also to the Soviet Union because of a mounting conviction that official Russia was almost less interested in the truth about our revolution and was more scornful of it than the West. But that's a story in itself. . . .

"I remember that at Bebler's and at the club, touching on Russia and America and the Cominform mess and the danger of another war, you asked us, 'What is the outlook?' Very well, what *is* the outlook? For Yugoslavia, for the world—for man? That question should also be asked in America. *Is* it? . . . The approach to truth, to good relations, is a two-way street."

Vlado Dedijer loomed up suddenly out of the thickening throng. He apologized for our getting separated. I was about to ask him if he had arranged for X to tackle me, but then a bell rang at a few minutes to four, and there was a rush into the auditorium.

I saw Vlado twice more before leaving Belgrade, and I came to the conclusion that he had nothing to do with X's talking to me as he did. In the main, without agreeing with him entirely, I liked what X had said. Two or three weeks later (in early February 1949), after I heard several Serbo-Croatian and Slovenian "Voice of America" broadcasts, I appreciated his views still more.

Vlado cracked a few jokes, said he would be sitting in back of the hall talking with a *drug,* indicated a spot in the vestibule where we would meet after the session, told Jovan Popovic, Oskar Davico, and X to continue to look after me, and put an arm around *drugarica* Dusanka and pressed her head against his enormous chest without saying a word or glancing at her, as we joined the rush into the hall whose capacity was eight hundred but now took in twelve hundred.

Jovan Popovic spoke to an usher, who led us to a section of unoccupied seats in the middle of the second row. I wanted Dusanka to sit next to me, and I took her right arm. It was limp, paralyzed by a wartime wound.

"You know Vlado Dedijer?" I asked.

"Everybody knows Vlado," she said. "He and two of my sons were friends before the war. They were students in Belgrade."

"You're a delegate?"

"*Da, da,*" she said proudly, "only delegates can attend. And you, of course: you're our guest. . . . I'm a Party member since 1938; my husband was too. We parents became the children of our sons and daughters; they made us Communists. My sons died in the Revolution; their cause is my cause, my whole life, now."

THE OUTER EDGE of the stage was only a few yards from where I sat. High up on the crimson backdrop, the motto *Workers of the World, Unite!* was emblazoned in Cyrillic letters. A little lower were gilded casts of the hammer-and-sickle and the emblems of the People's Republic of Serbia and the Federal People's Republic of Yugoslavia. On a pedestal draped in red cloth was a three-times-life-size plaster bust of Tito bearing no resemblance to any photograph of him I had seen. A spotlight accentuated the ultra-bold, challenging tilt of the head, reminiscent of Ivan Mestrovic's modelings of the legendary heroes of the Saga of Kossovo. To the left were small bronze heads of Marx and Engels; to the right, of Lenin and Stalin. In front was a lectern with voice amplifiers and radio microphones; behind it, a long, narrow curved table and about twenty chairs. The lectern and the table were also draped in red cloth. The whole set was heavy with ideology and innocent of aesthetics.

Slogans were all over the hall: *The Five Year Plan Shall Be Carried Out! . . . Long Live Tito! . . . We Follow the Marxist-Leninist Guideposts——*

From the second row on back and up in the balcony the chairs were the creaky, folding kind, placed tightly side by side. There weren't nearly enough of them; hundreds of delegates stood pressed against the walls.

The first row consisted of thirty-odd substantial armchairs placed a half-foot apart, except for two in the middle, directly in front of X, Dusanka, Jovan Popovic, Oskar Davico, and me. These were handsomely upholstered easy chairs, about a yard between them.

"Who's going to sit in those?" I asked Dusanka.

"*Drug* Marshal Tito," she whispered, "and *drug* Ribar"—Dr. Ivan Ribar, chairman of the 1920 Constituent Assembly which determined the unfortunate political form of the first Yugoslavia; now president of the Praesidium of the *Skupstina* (parliament) of the Federal People's Republic of Yugoslavia and, as such, head of the state, the personal symbol of its sovereignty, and nominally Tito's superior.

Vlado Dedijer hadn't mentioned that Tito would attend; he probably took it for granted that I assumed he would. I turned to ask Jovan Popovic if he really was coming; but just then, a few minutes past four, the twelve hundred persons in the hall exploded with enthusiasm . . . and there was Josip Broz Tito, secretary-general of the Central Committee of the CPY and head of its Politburo, Premier and Defense Minister of the Federal Government, one of about a dozen living Heroes of Yugoslavia, president of the People's Front of Yugoslavia, etc., etc. A handsome man in a dark civilian suit, a soft-collared white shirt with a conservative dark tie, and gleaming black shoes; a bit too portly for his five-feet-eight-inches, but well-proportioned and lithe, he strode from the door to his seat with a broad smile. He clapped his hands to the rhythm of everyone else.

Beside him walked Dr. Ribar, a short, rotund man in his late sixties with thick gray hair. Behind them came the rest of the Politburo of the CPY, in this order: Edvard Kardelj, Aleksandar Rankovic, Boris Kidric, Mosa Pijade, Blagoje Neskovic, Milovan Djilas, Ivan Gosnjak, and Franc Leskosek; and behind them, the Politburo of the CP of Serbia, headed by its titanic secretary-general, Petar Stambolic. Stopping at their seats, they faced Tito and Ribar, in the middle of the front row, and every so often turned to the various sections of the audience, and smiled and bowed slightly and clapped without joining in the uproar.

Unaccustomed to such a din in so limited a space, I couldn't make out the words the delegates were shouting rhythmically with indescribable gusto and at the top of their voices. I looked at Tito, barely four feet from me, and wondered whom he reminded me of. At the same time I was trying to concentrate on the sound spurting from the nearly toothless mouth of old Dusanka beside me. With one arm paralyzed, she couldn't clap; so, chanting with the rest of the crowd, she tapped her chest with the other hand. After a while I made out the words:

"Heroj Tito! *Heroj* Tito! *Heroj* Tito! . . . Hero Tito! Hero Tito! Hero Tito! . . ." on and on . . . and on . . . and *on*——

The chant was accompanied by the thunder of twelve hundred pairs of hands striking together simultaneously. So far as I know, there is no English word for an ovation of this kind; the Yugoslav word is *skandiranje*.

Tito took the acclaim with a businesslike, amused, genial matter-of-factness. His whole manner showed a flair for public life. It had an impersonal grace, direct and artless, free of any false modesty, and also free of braggadocio. Off and on, clapping his hands lightly to the pendular swing of the show, he swayed almost imperceptibly to the swaying of the compact mass of people in the hall.

The stage remained empty. I looked at the front ends of the balcony, on either side of the hall, for the equivalent of cheer leaders at an American football game or political rally. There weren't any. The assembly—"this inner core of the CP of Serbia," as I later characterized it in my journal—was like a giant American "jam session": it was "sent," although there wasn't any music either. The vast rhythm thundered out of the crowd. Tito and his co-leaders took it from there.

The practice of leaders applauding the audience while the audience applauds the leaders is Russian in origin. The Yugoslavs adopted it during the war and in the immediate postwar era when they were oriented toward the USSR. Later I saw it repeated many times on a larger or smaller scale throughout the country, and I think the Yugoslavs will retain it no matter how many other forms they drop or modify because of the Cominform schism. It is one of the good features they learned from the Russians. It is applause in dialogue instead of monologue, linking the people and the leaders.

On this basis, I liked the two-way applause right away, but the extremely loud chanting grated. What was the difference between *"Heroj* Tito! *Heroj* Tito! *Heroj* Tito!" and *"Duce! Duce! Duce!"* which I had once heard in a broadcast from Rome in the late 1930's, or the screeching in Charlie Chaplin's film *The Great Dictator?* I knew how the "Tito millionaire" pilot and Colonel Stane Valentincic would react to this question. . . . But how about the foreign correspondents in Belgrade who might be listening in on their radios if this part of the show was on the air. I could easily visualize the derisive comparisons those fellows were making, sitting in their rooms in the Majestic and Moskva hotels.

If you were in the hall, however, there was a difference, bigger each time you focused your attention on some element in the scene. For one thing, this handsome man with the captivating smile, free-wheeling manner and agile movements, nodding and waving to the wartime comrades he recognized, was no Mussolini. He looked decidedly undictatorlike. There was nothing cheaply theatrical about him, nothing fraudulent. He couldn't be a tyrant; rather, he was the most obvious, perhaps the most emphatic nod in a vast, well-nigh incredible consensus.

Wendell Willkie! Of course! That's who he reminds me of. The same personal glow. . . .

To be sure, the differences were strong. Tito's makeup, though unmistakably free, had almost too much form. None of Willkie's slouchiness which I liked even while half-suspecting it was partly put on. Could Tito wear a shapeless hat parked on the back of his head? Put his feet on the desk in his office while talking to a visitor, the way Willkie did? Hardly. His necktie was just so; his clothes were overneat: like Harry Truman's, too dapper, too carefully pressed—a haberdasher's dream. But Tito's face, posture, and movements took you in even when his eyes were not on you.

Soon to be fifty-seven, he was in his prime. His thick, curly light-brown hair had a gray overcast. Like Willkie—or, better, like that other Hoosier, Paul Dreiser, alias Dresser, the songwriter, whom his brother Theodore wrote about, he had "the stomach for life." Tito was almost too good-looking, with wide-apart, gray-blue eyes and symmetrical features. The word glamour fit him; women must go for him. His face changed expression continually, flashing with variations of pleasure and humor. He moved jauntily, with a fresh ease, a natural cockiness.

Then there were Dusanka, Jovan Popovic, Oskar Davico, X, Vlado Dedijer, Kardelj, Kidric, and the others I knew or had just met . . . *they* didn't look like the Fascists and the Nazis in the prewar news-reels. They didn't behave like them. I glanced about again, at the men and women in back of me and up in the balcony. Here and there they were so closely packed they could hardly negotiate their hands to applaud. When I found time for my diary, I described their expressions as a "curious fusion of revolutionary ecstasy and agony which, for some reason, found widening meaning in Tito being Tito, in that he breathed and smiled and returned their applause, and was with them, one of them. . . ."

Kardelj caught sight of me and waved a greeting. He stepped to Tito and said something into his ear. Tito's eyes sought me out. He bowed slightly, with a faintly different smile than a moment before, while his hands went on clapping. Then he swayed again dancer-like with the crowd.

After three or four minutes of *skandiranje,* Tito rose slightly on his toes and swung his arms high and down, accenting the down-beat, as if to say "Enough, enough! Let's stop this, now, and get to business." The look on his face mingled affection and mock displeasure. In quick succession, he repeated the gesture a few times, to no avail; the pitch of the performance by the Second Congress of the CP of Serbia only rose to a new high. Tito's arms fell to his side: he gave up. He smiled enigmatically and moved to his armchair. But before he sat down, a complex smile lit up his face, and he extended his hand to me and said under the pandemonium:

"*Dobro nam dosli!*—Welcome!"

"*Hvala liepa*—thank you very much." I didn't know if he heard me or not.

Old Dusanka stopped chanting abruptly. Her good hand left her chest and grasped mine. *"Dobro nam dosli!"* she said, either to follow Tito's suit or to touch the hand that Tito's had touched. Then she resumed chanting *"Heroj* Tito! *Heroj* Tito! *Heroj* Tito! . . ."* and continued tapping her chest.

The volume of the *skandiranje* increased.

Tito alone was seated. Kardelj and Kidric, whose eyes met mine now and then, went on applauding, beaming, facing the audience, glancing at Tito. So did Ribar, Rankovic, Djilas, Pijade, and Leskosek whom I recognized from their pictures, and all the others out front whose names and faces I didn't know.

With his elbows on the arm-rests, Tito sat comfortably relaxed, gazing at the empty stage. For a moment Dusanka's chest-tapping hand trembled as if she wanted to reach out and stroke his round head. It looked smaller than in the photographs, I thought—normal-sized and well-shaped, quite unlike the fantastic plaster-cast image of it up on the stage.

I was ready to sit down too; and noticing the difference in the chairs again, I was sure that even aside from the principle of equality (which I knew was an uncertain part of socialist idealism) it would have been better politics for the big-wheels to sit like the rest of us, pressed close together, on these rickety folding contraptions. I looked at X who, on the other side of Dusanka, was clapping too, and chanting *"Heroj* Tito! *Heroj* Tito!"* but not as vehemently as the other delegates; the intellectual in him moderated his enthusiasm. What would he say if he knew what I was thinking? . . . Of course my misgiving was a bit silly. The President of the United States drew the best of everything wherever he appeared too, as a matter of custom and courtesy: the best chair, the most dynaflowing Cadillac, the finest suite of rooms, the box behind the plate in a ball park. Thus the community or the group, honoring him, honored itself. Even a lecturer, as part of his ordeal, say, before the Women's Club of Ottumwa, Iowa, was likely to be installed in a throne-like affair while Madame Chairman made her introduction. Or take John L. Lewis and his sixteen-cylinder limousine and his six hundred thousand United Mine Workers of America, whose average wage was under $150 a month. Perhaps they drove his car vicariously, and he knew it.

One thing was fairly certain: from the looks of him alone, it was not Tito who demanded that he be set apart and above. It was, as in America (and elsewhere), partly custom, courtesy, form, something in human nature. That something also reveled in Tito's dapper civilian clothes and elaborate marshal's uniform. Here was one for "Marxism-Leninism" to figure out. So far as I knew, "Marxism-Leninism" hadn't begun to touch it. But it was the kind of thing that nudged the writer in me.[1]

"Marxism-Leninism" . . . *what is it?* Something like the Bible or

---

[1] Prior to 1949, my reading of "Marxist-Leninist" literature was sporadic and spotty, mostly what chanced to float up to my attention. My feeling about Marxism was approximately that of Nehru: "I am a revolutionary, but I do not say I am a Marxist. I think Marxism is very helpful. It helped me, certainly, in understanding the various processes of history but I assuredly do not accept all the Marxist theories, and I think that what has happened subsequent to Marx has disproved at least some of the things he stood for."

I relished, still relish, Marx' remark near the end of his life, "I am no Marxist." (If Christ re-appeared on earth, one of his first remarks might be, "I am no Christian." If Jefferson or Lincoln emerged from their lovely memorials on the Potomac in 1950, they might be subpoenaed by the Committee on Un-American Activities.)

I found it interesting that Marx was disturbed by the publication in Russia, in 1872, of the first translation of *Das Kapital* into any language. "It is an irony of fate," he wrote to his friend Kugelmann, "that [the Russian revolutionaries] whom I have fought for twenty-five years . . . have always been my 'patrons.'" It was the Russian habit, he explained, to "always run after the most extreme ideas the West has to offer." Another irony was that when the Czar's censor passed Marx' book thinking it was a purely scientific job, he confiscated the works of Adam Smith, whose *laissez-faire* idea had begun to liberate parts of the world from feudalism! . . .

I was aware that, in a letter published in the February 1947 *Bolshevik*, Stalin quoted Lenin: "We do not regard Marx' theory as something completed and untouchable; we are convinced, on the contrary, that it has merely laid the cornerstone of that science, which Socialists *must* move further in all directions unless they want to be left behind by life. . . ."

I knew, too, that Lenin had been democratic in his personal habits; he was apt to come to a hall where he was to speak ahead of time, wrap himself over any kind of chair almost anywhere in the place, and chat with the comrades; and that Stalin disapproved of such behavior as unbecoming a leader and politically unsound.

During 1949–51 I read about a ton of Marxist and anti-Marxist, Leninist and anti-Leninist, Stalinist and anti-Stalinist, pro- and anti-Communist, and pro- and anti-Russian material. . . . In *The Deadly Parallel* (Random House, 1950), George Backer's study of the similarities between the regimes and the imperialist designs of Czar Ivan the Terrible and of Stalin, I found (on p. 189) this quotation from Marx: "Will the giant Russian state ever halt in its march toward world power? Even if she wishes to do so, conditions would prevent it. The natural borders of Russia run from Danzig or even Stettin down to Trieste, and it is inevitable that the Russian leaders should do their utmost to swell out until they have reached this border. Russia has only one opponent: the explosive power of democratic ideas and the inborn urge of the human race in the direction of freedom."

Walt Whitman, Christianity or Jeffersonian democracy, depending on
who you are, and where and how you grew up. (In the middle of the
nineteenth century, a Know-Nothing candidate for the United States
Congress tried to present himself as an exponent of Jeffersonian democracy. His opponent flung a devastating quotation from Jefferson at him.
Whereupon the Know-Nothing remarked that the great political philosopher of Monticello "can be quoted every which-a-way: he writ so
much.")

What is "Marxism-Leninism" in Yugoslavia? *We Follow the Marxist-Leninist Guideposts*: what do they mean by that? That "Marxism-
Leninism" is *not* Stalinism here—*now,* although it was more or less
till recently? Then what is it now? "Titoism"? But "Titoism" is partly
Stalinism too. It derives from it (*via* heresy) as Christianity derives
from Judaism, Protestantism from Catholicism. socialism from capitalism.

"*Heroj* Tito! *Heroj* Tito . . ."[2]

Someone once said that heroes are bred where making a living comes
hard. That fits Yugoslavia, the Balkans, like a kid glove. People do
dream of God, of gods and demigods, of saviors, when they're poor and
afraid. It may well be that in Yugoslavia (and in Russia) "Marxism-
Leninism" has less to do with a set of precise but adjustable theories
like socialism or communism, and with a deliberate conscious lunge
into a new order, than with a people's plight in their environment and
within themselves, with their need to be proud of being Serbians, to
have an identity as Yugoslavs (or Russians). Setting up a demigod in
place of the old God of the Church, suddenly doubted or rejected.
Setting up a Here-and-Now, where eventually everybody may have a

---

[2] Late in 1950 the editors of *Naprijed,* organ of the CP of Croatia, published in Zagreb,
took time out to note that on the front page of the November 17, 1950, *Pravda* Stalin's
name appeared one hundred and one times—thirty-three times as "Comrade Stalin,"
seven times as "Dear and beloved Stalin," sixteen times as "Great [or great leader]
Stalin." Other variations were "Stalin the genius," "great leader of entire mankind,"
"great chief of all workers," "protagonist of our victories," "great fighter for peace,"
"Stalin, the hope of fighting for peace," "faithful fighter for the cause of peace," etc.

On the front page of an early-1949 issue of *Borba,* the daily organ of the Central
Committee, CPY, Tito's name appeared twenty-odd times.

The following paean appears in *Zemlya Russkaya,* a book published by the Soviet
Young Communist League in 1946: "Stalin! Always we hear in our souls his dear
name. And here, in the Kremlin, his presence touches us at every step. We walk on
stones which he may have trod only quite recently. Let us fall on our knees and kiss
those holy footprints."

chance, in place of the old Hereafter where the last were to be the first. . . .

As the chanting and clapping gained and mounted, Tito rose, faced the delegates again, smiled and clapped, again motioned the crowd to quiet down and flung himself into his chair.

It was a ritual. It went on for thirty minutes or longer. Tito got up, clapped, sat down, got up; clapped, sat down, and so on. After the first quarter of an hour the words of the chant changed every half-minute or so.

First to: *"Tse-kah,* Tito! *Tse-kah,* Tito! *Tse-kah,* Tito! . . ." linking Tito with the *Centralni Komitet* (CK) of the CPY.

Then to: *"Partija,* Tito! . . . Party, Tito!"

Then to: *"Narod, Partija,* Tito! . . . People, Party, Tito!"

Finally, the lusty voices joined the names of some of the other Politburo members to Tito's:

"Tito, *Kar*delj! Tito, *Kar*delj! . . ." It was like American students rah-rah-ing a star of their football team, then adding the names of the coach and the college to his; only here, as I say, there were no cheer leaders and no band music. The shouting was self-started, collectively impelled.

"Tito, *Kid*ric! Tito, *Kid*ric! . . ."

"Tito, *Mo*sa! Tito, *Mo*sa! . . ." Mosa being the sixty-year-old Pijade, a little man whose Jewish forebears fled to Serbia from the Spanish Inquisition centuries ago. As he stood, clapping lightly and looking nowhere in particular, his humor-crinkled face was like an intellectual Bronx tailor's when he comes upon a witty paragraph in a *Freiheit* editorial. . . .

"Tito, *Mar*ko! Tito, *Mar*ko!"

"Who's Marko?" I yelled into Jovan Popovic's ear.

"Rankovic—Aleksandar Rankovic," Popovic shouted back. "Marko is his Partisan *nom de guerre.* He's next to Kidric, over there."

I knew Rankovic, a Serbian, was Minister of the Interior and, as such, head of the security police; the CPY's organizing secretary and a colonel general in the army. "Is he blushing?" I asked, surprised.

Jovan Popovic nodded. "He always blushes on occasions like this. You know, he's that notorious *krvnik"*—killer, executioner, terrorist— "as the Western newspapers labeled him long ago and the Cominform press and radio are calling him now. He's the ogre, the sinister mastermind directing all the unspeakable atrocities. Tito, poor man, is his prisoner and puppet." Jovan Popovic laughed, talking into my cupped ear. "Actually, Marko is one of our most beloved *drugovi*. He's our conscience. Understand? I mean he's the conscience of the Party. If one of us realizes he did something unbecoming a Communist, a Party member, he goes to Marko; Marko listens, and the matter is resolved both inside the individual and inside the Party. I can't begin to tell you how we feel about him—not here at any rate."

While the others were cheered, Tito stood, flashing his swift smile at each one, and applauding more vigorously than when the *skandiranje* was only for him.

Then, again: "*Heroj* Tito! *Heroj* Tito! . . ." And: "We're Tito's, Tito is ours! We're Tito's, Tito is ours! . . ."

At the press table, near the door, the Yugoslav journalists were on their feet, clapping and chanting, throughout the *skandiranje* period. Two men sat still and stared glumly at the table-top. I guessed they were the Czech and the *Pravda* correspondents Vlado Dedijer had mentioned to me.

By-and-by, pointing emphatically at his wristwatch and looking really annoyed now, Tito gestured to Petar Stambolic to get up on the stage and stop the commotion. But the somber-faced colossus who is the secretary-general of the Serbian CP—a war hero, in his late thirties or early forties; son of a once prosperous peasant family; a leading member of the Central Committee of the CPY, and Prime Minister of the People's Republic of Serbia—was in no hurry. It was another five minutes before he heaved himself behind the lectern, and another eight or ten before his upraised arms stilled the din and he opened the congress with a formal greeting.

"The Internationale"—formerly the anthem of the Soviet Union—was sung, led by a professional singer who was also a delegate.

The chairman of the committee on procedure and nominations read a list of a score or so of *drugovi* and *drugarice* hailing from all regions of Serbia who were proposed and promptly elected to the *predsjednistvo*—the presidency—of the congress. They took their places behind the long, narrow curved table on the platform and chose Mosa Pijade chairman. All this was obviously arranged beforehand—perhaps no more so than at a party convention in the United States.

Pijade moved to the center seat, behind the lectern, while the congress chanted "Tito, Mosa! Tito, Mosa! . . ." for two or three minutes, then "Tito, *Cica!* Tito, *Cica!* . . ." Pijade's wartime name was *Cica* Janko (Uncle Johnny).

At long last, about three-quarters of an hour after Tito had entered the hall, the first session of the Second Congress of the CP of Serbia opened.

A dozen speeches, five to twenty minutes each, delivered in several languages, mostly Serbo-Croatian, took up three hours flat. The speakers were envoys from the CP's in the five other republics of the federation; a young general of the Army; and representatives—most of them in their thirties—of the executive committees of the Labor Unions' Council, the People's Front, People's Youth, Veterans of the War of Liberation, Anti-Fascist Women, and Peasant Cooperatives. These organizations are keystones of the shrewdly constructed "apparatus" I was to observe in the ensuing months, that integrates the various regions and the diverse elements of the population into a "people's democracy" within the revolutionary purposes and program of the Communist Party, and within the whole *vlast* or *oblast*—Serbo-Croatian and Slovenian forms of the same word which roughly means power or authority, the texture of policies and functions of the government, and the will and the security of the people.

With one or two exceptions, the speeches were too wordy. They had the same general pattern and often the same content. Each began with an effusive, ritualized "comradely" or "brotherly" greeting to the CP of Serbia from the organization the speaker represented. This was followed by vehement assurances of solidarity with the Serbian CP within the glorious frame of *Kah-Peh-Yot* (KPJ) or *Komunisticka Partija Jugoslavije,* "headed by our teacher and leader *drug* Tito" (a phrase I was to hear and read thousands of times in 1949) . . . by protests against the "infamous" or "incredible" Cominform resolution . . . by expressions of shock at the campaign of "lies and slanders" then just starting in earnest in the Communist press and on the radio outlets the world over, and of satisfaction at being Communists under a leadership that adhered to principles and dared to stand up to injustice and lies . . . by impassioned pledges to complete the Five-Year Plan, come what may . . . by vows of devotion to Marxist-Leninist principles, to the Central Committee of the CPY, to "our much loved *drug* Tito"—

Each reference to Tito or the Central Committee instantly set the delegates off on another round of *"Heroj* Tito! *Heroj* Tito! . . ."* or: *"Tse-kah,* Tito! *Tse-kah,* Tito! . . ."* or: "We're Tito's, Tito is ours!

. . ." which lasted until Tito rose, clapped awhile, scowled, then smiled, motioned the crowd to give the speaker a chance to go on, and sat down.

"*Drug* Stalin" and the "SKP(b)"—the Communist Party of the Soviet Union (Bolsheviks)—were mentioned with habitual respect, now suddenly a little constrained, and also with more than a touch of chagrin verging on dismay. A conflict was going on in the hearts and minds of Yugoslav Communists, revealing itself in a duality of expression, replete with *buts, whereases* and *howevers*.

Right then, early in 1949, the Yugoslav Communists' confusion over the Cominform crisis was probably at its worst. They began to know a good deal about the split, but didn't yet understand it. Offended beyond adequate utterance, they didn't want to be angry, much as a grown-up son doesn't want to be angry at his crotchety father, nagging mother, or pestiferous brothers and sisters. They didn't dare be angry, lest anger admit the quarrel and so deepen it, and make the action of severing themselves from "Mother Russia" imperative. They didn't want to be anti-Stalin, much less anti-Soviet, which wasn't the same, but almost. The "infamous" June 28, 1948 resolution was a blow between the eyes, which made them reel; but for months many felt it might have been just an awful blunder. What about these broadcasts, however, from Budapest, Prague, and Moscow, full of rotten phrases like "Tito's fascist clique" and "blood-thirsty butcher of the people, Rankovic"? So the second- and third-level people within the structure of the Yugoslav Party—war heroes, most of them—as yet unclear themselves, but veering sharply into an anti-Kremlin attitude, suffering guilt and anxiety—were caught in a taut, trembling fear of fear. They couldn't afford to be afraid. They were whirling in a maze of questions and doubts about Stalin and the USSR. Some found themselves close to hating nearly everything Russian, but feared to give in to that emotion. As Vlado Dedijer had told me a few hours earlier, many Yugoslavs (Vlado himself) could no longer sit through a Soviet motion picture. Up until seven months ago the spacious Soviet bookshop in Belgrade was jammed with customers, Communists mostly, buying the latest Moscow newspapers and magazines like *Bolshevik, Novoye Vremya* and *Krokodil;* now it was all but unpatronized.

I happened to come to New Yugoslavia when her Communists were edging toward the realization that a patch-up with the Cominform was doubtful and probably impossible, unless they gave in, unless they turned away from the "Marxist-Leninist guideposts," as they saw them; and that, if they didn't give in, they faced essentially the same problem on the other side, from the West—the problem of preserving their revolutionary integrity, their national independence, the meaning of their sacrifices, their country's natural resources, while reorienting themselves Westward commercially and culturally. They also faced the problem of thwarting the West's certain intention of using the Cominform split to check the building of socialism in the USSR (for they were still two years away from realizing that the USSR had almost no kinship with socialism) and in other states, including Yugoslavia. And, finally, they faced the problem of retaining their link with the international working-class movement and the progressives generally whose organizations and psychology were nearly all tied up with the Soviet Union.

There were pained, outspoken references to the "people's democracies"—Poland, Czechoslovakia, Hungary, Rumania, Bulgaria, Albania—and the "brotherly" parties in those countries which now behaved so unbrotherly, so outrageously, toward Yugoslavia and the CPY. Speaker after speaker declared that he and the comrades he represented couldn't imagine how the leaders of the "great SKP(b)" and the other "Com-parties" could abide themselves while they slandered *drug* Tito and the rest of the Yugoslav leadership—"really slandered Yugoslavia, our *borba,* our people!" cried one orator, tears in his voice. How *could* they? How could they be so grossly unfair? In some respects they were worse than the lackeys of Wall Street. "How can they so mock truth?" asked another speaker. "Are we in the presence of a collapse of morality, of the attachment to justice, not only in the capitalist world, which is essentially, inevitably corrupt, but also in the Soviet Union and the . . . people's democracies?" He stumbled on the last phrase, as though it struck him as inaccurate: but it was there, in his script, and he went through with it. "Why don't they accept *drug* Tito's invitation and send a commission, several commissions, to Yugoslavia to see and report that a social revolution *is* going on? . . ."

The speeches were too long. Thoughts were tangled up in never-ending sentences, replete with meandering clauses and quotations from the masters—Marxian jargon which may have been clear as a bell in Western Europe in the second half of the nineteenth century but which sounded cracked (to me) at the mid-point of the twentieth. Not many of the speakers were formally educated. Most of them were young not only in years; they were just edging toward their first disillusionment. Some found a momentary haven in not really knowing what they were saying. They overflowed with passionate vagueness. Redundancy abounded. So did the words *objektivnost* and *objektivno* which mirrored the speakers' deep subjectivity. But there were also natural eloquence and the instinctive ability to hit the nail on the head and hammer it in; this, especially when the speaker felt the need to depart from his prepared address.

No matter how poorly composed, each speech added to the drama of the meeting. "Our love of truth and justice," one young man said, "will not let us slump into spineless opportunism."

The Soviet Union was not only mentioned with respect and with awe but with the frequent implication, or the near-explication, that without the earlier "Great October Revolution" the Yugoslav Revolution could not have taken place, and also that the Yugoslav peoples could not have liberated their country if the "heroic Red Army, under the supreme command of *drug* Generalissimo Stalin," had not played "the decisive role in destroying the main body of Hitlerite might." No reference was made to the American and British contributions to victory.

But to give full credit to the Red Army, speaker after speaker hastened to add, was *not* to say that Yugoslav liberation forces under the supreme command of *drug* Marshal Tito——

"*Heroj* Tito! *Heroj* Tito! *Heroj* Tito! . . . Tito is ours, we're Tito's! . . ." for two, three minutes, until Tito rose, clapped briefly, smiled and scowled, pointed at his watch, and lifted his arms and brought them down in an insistent gesture.

. . . But to give full credit to the Red Army, the speaker resumed, was *not* to say, as the infamous Cominform resolution would have it, that Yugoslav liberation forces did not play a signal part in the antifascist war, or that the Yugoslav people did not sacrifice greatly. The very opposite was true! The loss of 1,700,000 men, women, and children out of a population of sixteen million, or eleven percent of the population—was that "a mere batch of 'trifles light as air' " (quoting from *Othello*)? Were Soviet losses as large, percentage-wise? Was the destruction of four thousand villages and towns in a country the size of Yugoslavia to be brushed aside? . . . Why did the Cominform belittle "our *borba*" so furiously by comparing it unfavorably to the rela-

tively minor resistance movements in France, Czechoslovakia, and
Italy which got nowhere politically? . . .

Such questions were not asked in any hostile-to-other-nations sense.
Nor were they "megalomania," as Cominform propagandists would
have it. One speaker described them as issuing "from our bafflement
and pain over the attitude and actions of the Soviet Union and the
people's democracies."

References to the Communist leaders of the "people's democracies"
of Poland, Czechoslovakia, Hungary, Albania, and Rumania evoked
laughter. Unlike the Yugoslav leaders who had fought at the head of
an aroused people in the war and the revolution, they each came home
from Moscow at the war's end in a Soviet automobile or plane, and
took over power . . . which, said one speaker, "rests on Soviet bayonets
and is nursed by the NKVD," the Soviet secret police. "And it is
Pauker, Gottwald, Beirut, Rakosi, and Enver Hoxa," another orator
said, "it is *they* of all people who now slander him who led our Revolution, who fought by our side—our beloved *druze,* Marshal Tito!"

"Heroj Tito! *Heroj* Tito! . . ."

Perhaps the best address was made by the emissary from the CP of
Bosnia-Herzegovina—a young man of Moslem parentage, Jovan
Popovic told me. He quoted Stalin's July 1941 appeal to all the peoples
of occupied Europe to rise in armed revolt against the invader. Then:
"Apparently we in Yugoslavia blundered by being the only people who
took *drug* Stalin's call to arms seriously enough to respond to it. It was
sheer foolhardiness to start a *borba* that engaged nearly thirty enemy
divisions at its peak, keeping them from the Eastern Front. It was
clear-cut megalomania to fancy that poor little insignificant Yugoslavia
could help the mighty Soviet Union at all when her Supreme Commander yelled for help."

A gale of laughter, Tito joining in.

Oskar Davico called my attention to the *Pravda* man at the press
table who held a hand over the lower part of his face, evidently to cover
up a smile. The Czech journalist, next to him, kept a poker face.

It was eight o'clock when Chairman Pijade banged the gavel, closing
the first session. The delegates remained in their places, clapping and
chanting "People, Party, Tito! People, Party, Tito! . . ." while Tito
and the rest of the Politburo withdrew.

Kardelj and Kidric picked me up on their way out, and led me to a
small reception-room adjoining the hall, and formally presented me to

Tito. He introduced me to Ribar, Neskovic, Djilas, Rankovic, and Stambolic, who sat at the table with him. One of them gave me his chair next to Tito.

Tito offered me a cigarette. How could I be a writer and not smoke? I pointed out that Vlado Dedijer was a writer and didn't smoke. Tito said that Vlado was a special case in more ways than one.

Sandwiches made of dark bread and Serbian salami were passed, and two or three kinds of drink.

"I didn't expect to see you until tomorrow, Marshal Tito," I said.

Tito said it hadn't occurred to him that I would be at the meeting either. "What did you think of it?"

"If I hadn't seen it, I wouldn't believe it," I said.

"Believe what—specifically?" Tito asked, intensely interested.

"The whole show—the shouting and clapping, the crowd and you——"

"We were through the struggle together, most of us," Tito said. "I know at least two-thirds of the delegates." For a moment his manner showed a trace of self-consciousness; just why, I wasn't sure. Perhaps he was trying to imagine how the form and spirit of the congress had struck me, a newcomer. He inserted a cigarette into a slim filigree holder shaped like a small pipe. Someone lit it for him.

"You don't smoke; you don't drink"; he smiled, his steel-blue eyes boring into me; "have you no vices?"

He laughed at my remark that having no vices might be the most serious vice of all, as witness the case of our friend, Vlado Dedijer; and that this shouldn't permit the megalomanic Yugoslav depravity to look down its nose at my American Puritanism.

"Well, if you won't have *slivovica,*" he said, "try this wine; it's very light—mere colored water. My drink nowadays." He poured us each a glassful. Later I heard he drank nothing stronger on Dr. Djoni Popovic's orders. He had just recovered from an attack of jaundice, brought on by an emotional disequilibrium caused by the Cominform crisis.

"I can well imagine," he said, returning to the subject of the meeting, "that to someone coming upon us all of a sudden from another country, even to someone born here but long away, we may look a little strange. Our people"—very gravely—"went through a profound experience, of which the world has no inkling as yet, but whose meanings continue to churn inside us and to demand expression and satisfaction."

A pause—a sip of wine.

"I am pleased to see you looking so well," I said.

Tito said nothing to this. He smiled at Vlado Dedijer who, not find-ing me at the appointed place in the vestibule, had come to look for me here, and stopped to talk with Djilas at the other end of the table.

"I thought the Cominform mess would have you down," I said, "all of you—but you seem to be having a good time."

"We laugh, yes," said Tito, unsmiling, "but we're not enjoying the 'mess.' It's endurable only because we can joke and laugh. What do the people in the United States think of it?"

"Of the rift? . . . For the general public it's just another newspaper sensation. An oddity. The average American has no idea what it's about, and doesn't give a damn. He sees the headlines and he thinks it's one of those barbaric goings-on behind the Iron Curtain, something weird like the Moscow Trials, and he shakes his head and turns to the sports or comics page. . . . Some of the intellectuals on the Right have explained it, to their own satisfaction at least, as a fraud cooked up by you and Stalin to delude the West—a mysterious 'cold war' move."

Tito grimaced. "Even here we have people who babble such non-sense. But what about the Left, the progressives, in America—what do they think?"

"The story goes that two minutes after the newsflash 'Cominform denounces Tito' reached the offices of the American Communist Party, the pictures of Josip Broz Tito were yanked off the walls; and I sup-pose the Communists simply are following the Soviet 'line'—you're a deviationist, a Trotskyite, a traitor, et cetera. The non-Communist Left, by and large, neither accepts nor rejects the Cominform or Krem-lin line. In general, it regrets that the split occurred, but having no facts to get its teeth into, it's confused. This was true of me when I left the United States a week ago. And it's still true."

Tito listened with utmost attention. He was about to say something but remained silent, looking at me.

"This may not be the time or the place to ask you," I said, "but—what's it all about?"

Tito changed his position and took a puff at his cigarette and a sip of wine, thinking. "Were you able to follow the speeches?" he asked.

"Yes."

"How did they strike you?"

"Offhand, I think everybody in Yugoslavia is obsessed with the injustice of the Cominform resolution. But I couldn't get to the *core* of the fracas. . . . This morning I reread your long speech before the Fifth Congress [of the CPY, late in July 1948] but I still have no clear idea *why* the schism came about. The CP of Yugoslavia demands democracy and equality among the Cominform states which are 'building socialism,' whereas the CP's in these states, as well as the CP's in other countries, spurn that demand. That's one issue, as I gather it. But my question is: why did it, or why was it allowed to, come up? The other issue is whether you or they are truly 'Marxist-Leninist.' But nowhere in your Fifth Congress speech, or in today's torrent of words, did I find a clear definition of 'Marxism-Leninism' or catch a hint of why the Cominform, the Kremlin, Stalin himself, permitted the break to occur. You say *you* didn't want it. You wanted to stay in the Soviet orbit; you even want to get back in. I think I faintly understand why. But why did they boot you out?" I spoke (less fluently than I quote here) in a mixture of Serbo-Croatian and English, which Tito understands fairly well but doesn't speak. "Are they crazy—is Stalin out of his head?"

The others around the table were not listening. They talked and chuckled among themselves. Tito paid no attention to them. He shifted his body to face me squarely.

"Do djavola—to the devil with it," he said, using this Serbian expletive denoting worry and exasperation, "in my opinion they're not 'crazy,'" quoting the English word. "But I'm afraid I can't answer your questions in a few minutes." He looked at his wristwatch, then nodded to an adjutant who had been trying to catch his eye. "How shall I put it briefly? . . . I saw Stalin a few times, I spoke with him; I thought I was getting to know him, to understand him, and I say, definitely, he's *not* 'crazy' or 'out of his head'. He's singularly intelligent. Resourceful. He has a vast amount of experience and information——"

Tito interrupted himself, checked the flow of his thought. He nodded to his adjutant again, who held his overcoat, and said he'd be ready to go in a moment or two.

"But something has happened in the Soviet Union," Tito went on, turning back to me, "in the Kremlin, in the SKP(b). . . . What happened? For one thing the Bolshevik revolutionary mind, which Lenin exemplified, was supplanted by the bureaucratic and police mind, if it can be called a mind. But this is a tremendous subject, perhaps not easy to grasp unless one has been in the Soviet Union. . . . I suppose her leaders' primacy in the International Communist Move-

ment, their being the rulers of a vast land and a great power, and winning a tremendous military victory, all this has blinded them, and
they've blundered into the rankest type of nationalism: into Great-
Russianism, which always had imperialistic overtones."

"But this didn't happen all of a sudden," I said. "According to certain papers in America and England, which I've seen, it began even
before the war. Why did you play along with Moscow, stay in the
Soviet bloc, as long as you did, until they pushed you out?"

Tito's answer came slowly: "Partly because we thought that our
trouble with Moscow wasn't irreconcilable, that eventually we would
win their respect, but also because we didn't see it as clearly as we're
beginning to see it now."

"Or, perhaps, because you didn't allow yourselves to see it clearly?"

"Perhaps. But, frankly, that's a difficult subject, and a long one. It
could engage us all night and all day tomorrow. . . . You used the
word 'crazy,' and I said it wasn't the right word; but, *do djavola* what
the Soviet leaders are up to of late certainly isn't the height of sanity.
Claiming all those inventions first—why?"

Tito shrugged his shoulders, gestured in puzzlement, and puffed at
the odd cigarette holder, a heavy expression spread over his face.

"I was in Russia and I *love* Russia—you understand?" he said. "All
of us, as you heard in the hall, have the deepest appreciation of the
Great October Revolution, of its meaning for us, for the world. We're
Communists, revolutionaries. In the war, thousands of our *drugovi*
died with the names of Stalin and the Soviet Union on their lips. We
Communists taught the Yugoslav people to love the Soviet Union. But
something there, in the Kremlin, within the SKP(b), has degenerated,
has become so distorted that as one ponders it and seeks high and low
for explanations, and at the same time can't stop loving Russia and
thinking of the Great October Revolution; one turns sick inside and
refuses to believe it's true. Yet it is true."

Tito took another sip of wine. "Now I must go. The session lasted
longer than I expected. Monday evenings I try to spend with my *mali*
[little son] and I'm late. As I say, I didn't know you were to be here.
We will have more time tomorrow." He rose and slipped into the overcoat his adjutant held for him.

Vlado Dedijer came to our end of the table. "Good evening, *druze*
Marshal."

"Good evening, *druze* Vlado." Tito smiled.

"How are you two getting along?" Vlado asked me.

"All right, I guess."

Tito noticed me watching him button his civilian overcoat. Suddenly, with a flash in his eyes that wasn't all humor, he said: "You know, *gospodine Adamicu,* I happen to be Commander-in-Chief of the Armed Forces."

So this is his retort to my criticism of his marshal's uniform.

Aloud I said: "I've heard a rumor to that effect, Marshal Tito."

. We were looking into each other's eyes. Then Tito smiled broadly and we shook hands.

"See you tomorrow," he said. *"Do vidjenja!—So long!"*

A ten-foot stone wall bars a view of the house from the street. On a marble slab embedded in the wall on one side of the heavy wooden gate, with its handsome wrought-iron frame, a legend in Cyrillic letters tells of a taut spell of time in the autumn of 1944. From here Lieutenant General Peko Dapcevic—a Montenegrin, then thirty-three—directed the operations of such-and-such units of the new Yugoslav People's Army in the liberation of Belgrade, while Soviet forces pressed against the enemy from across the Danube, below.

For four years prior to the liberation, the villa was the residence of the German commander of Belgrade. Who lived in it before the war, I don't know. Now government property, it is the home of the Marshal of Yugoslavia.

Here—at Rumunska 15—Tito attends to most of his office work and sees visitors who come individually and in small groups. He receives large delegations at Beli Dvor (the White Palace) on another side of the hill. Beli Dvor is somewhat of a showplace. It was the residence of Oxford-educated Prince-Regent Paul Karageorgevic during the 1930's and until '41, when the people of Yugoslavia—of Belgrade, principally —rose against the pro-Axis policies of his regime under the leadership of the Communist Party.

A stoneshot from Rumunska 15 is the villa that was Tito's hideout and headquarters in 1941. There he and the rest of "the general staff," appointed by the Central Committee of the Communist Party of Yugoslavia, organized the uprising of the Yugoslav peoples.

When I pushed the button, a tall young soldier, huge in a sheepskin greatcoat and fur-lined boots, opened a small door in the gate to admit me. He was apparently unarmed. He didn't inquire who I was. He saluted with a prodigious snap. And I followed the partly cleared driveway curving around the snow-covered grounds towards the large three-story house. Of no particular style, it brought to mind the Sewickley Heights home of a minor Pittsburgh industrialist whom I used to visit in the 1930's.

In front of the three-car garage—a sprawling stone building which is also the officer-of-the-day's office, about midway between the gate and the villa—a young captain and an even younger lieutenant, also in vast sheepskin coats and fur-lined boots, watched my approach. I thought *they* might want to see my passport and make sure it was me, but no —they saluted, smiled, and waved me on.

"Well," I thought, "he does *not* live in 'a fortress full of soldiers armed to the teeth'" . . . as a news-magazine recently had it.

Statuary protruded from the snow amid the leafless trees and shrubs. One figure was a wounded Partisan I would have liked to look at longer, from all around. But Tito's secretary—the same youthful lieutenant colonel who had brought me his invitation—appeared on the terrace, calling out greetings. Bareheaded and smiling, he hastened over and took my arm so I wouldn't slip on the icy walk and steps. To make conversation, I asked him if the snowfall wasn't even heavier up here on Dedinje than in the city as a whole, and he replied he believed it was—and altogether wonderful: almost a guarantee of a good grain harvest next summer.

Near the entrance, just inside the spacious reception-room, two small bronze statues of Partisans attracted my eye. There were doors on all sides, sofas and chairs along two of the walls, a stairway at the far end, a skylight in the high ceiling. My hat and coat were taken so unobtrusively I didn't notice by whom.

The secretary steered me toward the door ajar on the right.

I was face to face with Tigar, the large German police dog I had heard about. He gave a low, menacing growl; then, as I said his name, he squealed in a tentatively friendly tone but retained his vigilant stance. The ends of his tail and ears were snipped off in puphood, and he is no outstanding example of canine beauty; but he bristles with "personality," especially before Tito's words and manner convey to him that the newcomer is welcome.

*"Zdravo!—*Greetings!" said Tito, removing his glasses and rising

from his desk in the corner behind the door. The words he muttered to Tigar transformed the dog forthwith from a tense, strained animal to a tame, loose-limbed one, and Tito and I came together and shook hands. Someone photographed us, as I recalled with some annoyance a couple of days later when I saw the picture in *Borba* and other newspapers. I knew it wouldn't help me get a Soviet visa. . . .

Tito was in uniform—gray-blue tunic with the marshal's shoulder boards and the single crimson silk ribbon of the Order of the Hero of Yugoslavia, dark-blue breeches, and well-polished high black boots. He didn't look like Goering, but I still thought I preferred him in mufti.

The room was long and narrow and uncluttered: a man could walk up and down it when he was trying to argue something out with himself. The light in it was rather too bright for my eyes, partly because of the sun's reflection on the snow. On a pedestal beside a window was a dark-bronze bust of Lenin.

The secretary and the photographer withdrew and closed the door.

Tito led me to a low round table with several leather chairs in the farthest corner from his desk. There was a tray with bottles of Serbian *slivovica* and Dalmatian maraschino, and small glasses.

Tigar sidled up to me, wagged his stumpy tail, and squealed ingratiatingly. Tito smiled and told him to go lie down like a good dog. I said I had a dog at home, and roughed Tigar's head behind the ears. He let out a satisfied yowl; then, curiosity and friendliness abated, he plunked himself on the carpet between Tito and me.

I told Tito I had read that he and Tigar were "inseparable" but I didn't remember, if I ever knew, how they got together. "You had another dog before him, didn't you?"

Tito smiled when I inquired about Tigar; the last question, though, brought a grave, thoughtful expression to his face. "Early in the war I had a dog named Lux. One day the Germans were shelling us heavily, hour upon hour. It was in western Bosnia. We—several *drugovi* and *drugarice* of the Supreme Headquarters Staff, and I—were in an erosion ditch on the side of a canyon, trying to keep low. Missiles of all descriptions tore the air around us, spattered the dirt, and splintered the rocks.

"Lux"—Tito pronounced the name *Looks*—"lay by my head, the bulk of his body pressed close against one side of my face. He wasn't clean, he smelled to high heaven, and he was full of lice. Besides, he blocked my view. I had to lift my head to see what was going on. We were in a bad spot; many of the *drugovi* and *drugarice* near me were killed or wounded that day. I kept pushing Lux away. But it was no use; he settled himself almost on top of my head and wouldn't budge. He lay very still, unless I shoved him; and when I shoved him, his body simply fell back against my face, like a sack of grain, not quite full. I became impatient and angry, but there was no moving him; so I let him be. All at once, in the midst of that din, I felt a tremor ripple through Lux; then he was absolutely still. He stopped a piece of shrapnel that otherwise would have gone through my head."

Tito looked at his cigarette-holder for a while, then went on: "For several months after that I had no dog. I like animals, dogs and horses especially. . . . Toward the end of the Sixth Offensive, in which we crushed several German and Cetnik encirclements, we were moving our Supreme Headquarters, and we came on a camp abandoned by a German dog regiment.

"The Germans had entire battalions and regiments in Bosnia in which every second or third soldier had a specially trained bloodhound or police dog as the main item of his equipment. The bloodhounds, of course, were employed to track us down, to smell out our dugouts, caves, and other hiding places and special positions; and the police dogs, to creep up on us and attack us. The idea of bringing these dog units to Yugoslavia was Himmler's, I think, when Hitler assigned him the task of wiping us out. When Rommel took over the campaign against us, the emphasis on dogs became stronger still. The bloodhounds were bad enough; the police dogs were worse than wolves. They choked and tore up many a *drug*. Our people began to call them tigers. . . .

"Well, this abandoned German dog-regiment camp interested me. I went through it . . . and there, tied to the stump of a tree, was this fellow." Tito looked at Tigar, whose mouth was just closing on a yawn that was also a sigh. "He was full grown but evidently still a pup, and he was half dead. Whoever was in charge of him probably had overlooked him in the rush, or he may not have been up to Himmler's criterion, and so he was left behind. Anyhow, there he was: obviously he hadn't seen food or water for days, he'd been freezing, and he was barked out and lonely and terrified.

"I had a scrap of meat in my pocket, a crust of bread, and two or three lumps of sugar. I untied him and offered him the meat. He lifted his head, but he couldn't take it. He was barely able to move. He looked up at me and whimpered. Never, never have I seen a live creature in worse condition. So weak and hungry he couldn't eat. So forlorn. I poured a little water from my canteen into his mouth, just enough to wet his tongue. He rolled his eyes, and his tongue—which resembled the tongue of an old shoe—showed the first signs of interest. Another trickle of water laid him out flat—it was so good." Tito smiled. "His head, when I let it go, dropped to the ground like a lump of clay.

"One of the boys in the headquarters detachment had the good sense to start massaging the big pup's legs and paws and to knead his sides and the back of his neck, and slowly he began to come to life. Every now and then he yipped faintly.

"I poured some water into a pan but he couldn't go for it right away. We melted a lump of sugar and made him swallow it. The rubdown started his circulation and before long he could sit up if someone held his head. He gulped down a scrap of meat. . . . We stood him up. He was a sight, at once dreadful and funny: as large of frame as he is now, but under half his present weight—mere skin and bones. He staggered around the tree stump, lost his balance and looked at us, perplexed and ashamed because he couldn't handle himself better. The most miserable dog in existence. But he was wonderfully responsive to good treatment. He tried hard. Each time he rose we cheered him on. One of the *drugovi* called to him, 'Keep it up, Tigar, you're doing fine!'

"And he was doing fine, and here he is—'Tigar' ever since."

When Tito said his name, Tigar leapt vigilantly to his feet and growled until he was ordered to hush up and lie down; and, a bit abashed, he obeyed.

"To complete the story," Tito went on, "he attached himself to me, and that"—smiling—"was agreeable to me too. As I say, I love animals; and after Lux, I missed having a dog. The *drugovi* and *drugarice* around Headquarters spoke of the new dog as a 'good German,' then as Lux's successor. He must have been about a year old when we found him; and he evidently had had lots of training of the wrong kind, the Himmler kind, but it didn't take, for he adjusted himself to me very quickly. On my part, I found him endearing and funny.

"He still perks up when he hears German, but the *drugovi* in the house say he's a 'good Yugoslav' now: but"—Tito smiled—"this is strictly confidential. If the Cominform propagandists find out about it, they'll use it as a fresh proof of our nationalism. In any event," pointing at Tigar instead of saying his name, "he's a 'good Yugoslav' now. He understands Serbo-Croatian. When I really want to dress him down, however, I do it in German in what I have some basis for imagining are the Nazi tone and manner, and he suffers terribly. It's true, as foreign journalists have written, that we two are inseparable. It's one of the few facts correctly reported."

Telling me about Lux and Tigar, Tito's face went through a series of changes. Of Lux's death he told slowly, wonderingly, as if he had often pondered whether, "Marxism-Leninism" more or less to the contrary notwithstanding, there was such a thing as chance—luck—destiny.

When he remarked he had heard some of the comments I had made around town, Tito's expression mixed concern, resentment, and eager interest. He said he had asked "a few others" to lunch. "A frank, off-the-record exchange might not be amiss." He shot me a quizzical look.

I nodded calmly (at least I thought I was calm) and sat silent. Then I realized I was a bit uncomfortable.

Tito rose and walked to his desk, took a fresh cigarette and lit it, and returned and sat down again opposite me. He opened up rather stiffly, in an official manner, expressing his *zahvalnost i priznanje*—gratitude for and recognition of—"what you did for us during the war, especially with your book *My Native Land.*" He saw me grimace; he hesitated a moment, then continued:

"In January or February 1944, an American officer, who came to us with a mission, brought the book from Cairo, or perhaps it was from Bari, Italy. I found it on my table at headquarters one morning. . . . New Yugoslavia was just being born, and my *drugovi* and I were very conscious of the great problems still to be met. The publication of your book in America helped me to feel for a time that there were people in the United States who understood us or who wanted to understand us, and that New Yugoslavia and America, where so many of our people emigrated, *could* work together."

These words brought a pleasant thought to the forepart of his mind and he became a different man. He dropped his official manner, stirred in his seat, smiled vividly, and said: "You know, when I was about eighteen, I almost went to America."

"No—really? Why didn't you?"

"No money. Besides the train ticket to Hamburg and the boatfare,

I needed twenty-five dollars, or some such fabulous sum, before I could land in America. That was in 1910."

"Very interesting," I said. "Tell me more."

"What do you mean—'very interesting'?"

"Oh, one could speculate endlessly about what you would have become, had you gone to America. Also, about what would and what would not have happened in Yugoslavia in the 1940's, had you emigrated in 1910."

"Well, what would I have become in America?" said Tito. His face smiled, but his eyes were fixed on me with an oddly grave intentness, which may have been mostly self-consciousness.

"I don't know," I said, trying to be casual. "All such speculation is silly, of course; but offhand, looking at you, Marshal Tito, I doubt that you would have become a social revolutionary, a Communist leader, in America."

"What do you mean?"—with a touch of bemused resentment.

I laughed, perhaps with more than a touch of uneasiness. "Last night I jotted down some of my impressions of the show in the hall yesterday afternoon. In a week, a month, I'm apt to revise my notes under the impact of new experiences; as of now, though, the gist of my thinking is that this Revolution in Yugoslavia is probably an organic movement of great force, and that you're an organic and the most precise part of that force. In the hall yesterday, I noticed you were in absolute congruence with the mass of delegates, although most of them are obviously very unlike you."

By-passing his frown provoked by my last few words, I continued: "In America, the Communist Party is not organic; the kindest adjective that can be applied to it is eccentric. A revolution such as you achieved here is impossible in the United States, and will remain so—unless the USA suffers defeat and great destruction in the 'next war.' Any attempt to create such an upheaval in America today would be inorganic, stupid and unsuccessful, and I'd be opposed to it. By this I don't mean that, had you emigrated at eighteen, you wouldn't be a revolutionary in America; or that America is not revolutionary. On the contrary, in a way she is the *most* revolutionary country in the world: the supreme headquarters of the Industrial Revolution, of which your Revolution here, as I see it, is but an offshoot."

Still frowning, Tito curbed his need to set me straight.

"For some time," I said, "I've had the following idea: that in the last

few centuries some of the most resourceful and energetic Europeans
either went to America or plunged into socialism of one kind or another. Those who plunged into socialism, as you did, became *social*
revolutionaries in the Old World; many of those who emigrated
became *industrial* revolutionaries in the New World. In my mind, this
applies to many American capitalists as well as to many workers and
most technicians, to numerous housewives and farmers. My neighbor,
for instance, who is both a worker and a small farmer, improvises a
new contrivance every few days to improve a machine or replace a
broken part. He's an improviser, a tinkerer—a typical American. His
youngest son, about seventeen, is forever dismantling and re-assembling
his jalopy. He never went to a mechanical school. He's just a natural
mechanic, an innovator—an offspring of the Industrial Revolution."

Himself a mechanic by trade, Tito listened intently.

"My guess is," I went on, "if you had gone to America in 1910, and
remained an organic individual, true to your nature, you might have
become, in the period just behind us, an industrial rather than a social
revolutionary. But remember I said all such speculation is probably
silly. Which reminds me that since my arrival here I've talked too
much. My new policy is to look and listen. Before I follow it, however,
I'll come to the point of my theory about the two kinds of revolutionaries. It's a point that may strike a Marxist as utopian, as part of a
writer's itch for goals remote—but here goes.

"We seem to be in a preluding moment; a climax of some sort isn't
far off. The 'next war,' if it comes, is apt to play hell with both the
Industrial Revolution—whose chief base, as I say, is in America—and
with your social, would-be-industrial revolution here. I think there's
only one way to avoid that war. The two kinds of revolutionaries—
men like you, now coming up in the Old World, and our industrial
production men, now at their peak and uncertain which way to turn,
will have to get together, and soon."

Tito started pacing the room, Tigar at his heels, and during the
silence which followed the two struck me as a complex simultaneous-
ness of the myriad perils and quandaries bedeviling the world.

Tito sat down again, signaled Tigar to lie down, and asked in a,
for him, unusually dull voice: "Have you perchance any idea how these
'two kinds of revolutionaries' can get together?"

"No," I said, "no concrete idea. I'm a writer, not a politician: a
writer's job is to try to lay out the problem and take a chance the

politicians will see it and do something about it. Stalin and Wendell Willkie and Henry Wallace and a few other men in Russia and America have said that the capitalist and communist systems could coexist. I don't know if they can or not. One reason I'm on this trip is to try to find out if they can."

"Are you going to write a book?"

I told him of my plan to write "The Education of Michael Novak," in which I might incorporate my idea about the two kinds of revolutionaries. "In fact, writing my notes last night, it occurred to me I might use you as my protagonist of the social revolution in the Old World and make my protagonist of the industrial revolution—'Michael Novak,' a fictional Yugoslav immigrant who becomes a big American industrialist and is sympathetic to your revolution—a native of some village near Kumrovec, if that's where you were born."

"What do you mean—'if that's where I was born'?" Tito asked ruefully.

"Well, there's some dispute as to your birthplace—in fact, as to your whole background and even as to whether you're a man or a woman, or the same person who was Tito in 1942." I laughed.

Tito's expression wavered between amusement and dismay; then he gestured as if to say, "Let's drop that nonsense," and asked: "What did you really think of the meeting yesterday?" His voice was vivid again.

"A hundred years ago," I said, "an American wrote a novel called *Moby Dick*. In the hall yesterday, a phrase in that book occurred to me: '. . . those stage managers, the Fates.' Perhaps that tells you how the meeting struck me. You all looked a little bewitched. There was a dedication at once wonderful and terrifying. A fanaticism, a hallucination, if I may say so. Perhaps all human upheavals and processes are impelled by hallucinations. American industrial production, for instance. In America, those 'stage managers, the Fates' really are in full charge of the show. . . . In Yugoslavia, the spell appears to be breaking. Only in their references to the Communist Party and to Tito did the speakers convey an enduring faith. Is that a delusion too? Your responsibility is really inhuman." I had noticed that Tito was glaring at me, and I added, "But I talk too much."

"No, no," he said quickly. "Please go on."

"Oh to hell with it!" I said in English. I wasn't at all sure Tito wanted me to go on.

By-and-by the pause of silence struck us both funny. Tito smiled

and rose again, and he and Tigar walked the length of the room.
When he returned to the table, I gave in to his seeming insistence
that I talk:

"I'm glad you didn't go to America in 1910, Marshal Tito. I *did* go
[in 1913], partly because my family was able to scrape together the
twenty-five dollars I needed for entry in addition to the passage money;
which is what I'd like to get back to, if you don't mind. I want to
repeat what I said to Kardelj and Kidric. I didn't write *My Native
Land* to help you primarily or specifically."

Tito tried to break in; I reminded him that he wanted me to talk,
and I asked him to let me finish.

"You thanked me," I said, "but I just want to tell you, too, that I
wrote that book in '43 because I was trying to help the United States
hit on an open-minded policy toward countries with revolutionary
situations. And finally, if not first of all, I wrote it for myself because
I more or less had to, for much the same reason—so I'm told—that
some people in Yugoslavia write slogans or 'Tito' on the walls and
chimneys and wire-poles. As far as I am concerned, gratitude is out
both ways."

"I understand," said Tito. "But you know, in a way, you're almost as
difficult as some people think I am."

We laughed.

"A Yugoslav characteristic," I said. "Should we mourn or cheer?"

We laughed again.

"I think I understand you," Tito repeated, thoughtfully. "But you
must make an effort to see our side. If you refuse our hospitality, we'll
be offended."

"Look," I interrupted. "I'm half-dead already, and not only from the
weariness I brought with me. Last night, when I reached my room
after the meeting, I realized that all that emotion in the hall had just
about knocked me out. I couldn't go to sleep. For the first time in my
life my hands trembled. I noticed it unlacing my shoes."

"What of it? Your years are fewer than mine."

"This morning," I continued, "I didn't get up until eleven and,
reading the papers, I thought if I knew what was good for me I'd get
the hell out of Yugoslavia and not come back until I got a rest. . . .
If I had to be born in Europe, why wasn't I born in a country like
Norway or Denmark, where people are said to be cool, calm, and collected?"

Tito leaned back in his chair and laughed. His expression seemed to say—"Oh well, let him rave."

"This impulse to hospitality!" I raved. "This avidity! This effervescing, super-charged energy!"

"Nonsense," Tito cut in. "What about your American energy and all that turmoil we hear about? When our *drugovi* return from a few weeks of United Nations sessions in New York, they're so done in from the rush of traffic and the weight of skyscrapers that we have to send them away to the mountains or seashore. You should have stayed here—like me," he grinned, "and you'd be leading a nice, quiet life with nothing to do but help consolidate a revolution in the face of the world's opposition to it."

I liked his humor. "Even if your information service has already reported it to you," I said, "let me tell you the rest. I want to go to Russia, especially since what you told me last evening; and being in Yugoslavia right now, attending Party congresses, and all that, is *not* helping me to acquire a Soviet visa. I applied for it in Washington. If it doesn't come soon, I mean to re-apply for it in Prague or Warsaw."

"Maybe they'll give you a visa," said Tito. "You're an American citizen, you're not responsible for our sins."

"That won't help if I stay on," I said, "and if it leaks out that you had me to lunch——"

"Well," interrupted Tito, somewhat miffed but light-hearted still. "You don't expect me to cancel this lunch, do you, on the remote chance that it will help you procure a Soviet visa?" Then, solicitously: "What can we do? What is it you want? What are your plans?" The three questions tumbled out of him as one.

"Tonight I leave for Slovenia," I said. "Tomorrow I'll be seeing my mother. I counted on a two weeks' rest, and my brother made a reservation for me in the Slovenian Upland. But this morning I thought —quite seriously—that I'd go to Italy now and return to Yugoslavia later."

"You can't do that!" said Tito. "As I said before, you'd offend everyone, including me. . . . Very well, we are *not* 'grateful'—you can go to the devil! But you can't get away from the fact that you were born here. Nor can we. If the Russians hold it against you, you won't want their visa—if I'm beginning to know you correctly. If they do hold your Yugoslav origin against you—which is possible—then, of course, they'll not give you a visa—— Come in!"

The secretary announced that the other guests had arrived. Tito rose and, with an easy, fluent gesture, invited me to accompany him. Halfway to the door, however, he stopped and, squinting at the sun's midday glare through the unshaded windows, appeared to ponder something for ten or fifteen seconds.

"This is Tuesday," he said then. "Could you change your plans and be here next Saturday evening?"

I said I couldn't. "My brother and I are leaving for Ljubljana tonight. My mother is waiting for me; I haven't seen her for sixteen years."

Tito nodded. "It occurred to me to give a party, invite twenty or thirty of our writers ostensibly to welcome you but really to discuss things. Frankly, our writers are not producing anything substantial. *Drug* Kardelj is worried too. He and Djilas and I talked about it the other day. I don't know what the matter is. In Old Yugoslavia scarcely anybody made a living writing; I guess Krleza was the only serious writer who did. Now poets, novelists, and journalists are well paid for everything they do; in fact, they receive huge honoraria for books they wrote before the war which are being reprinted; *but*—— Is it too early to expect major literature? Don't the writers feel free? I want them to be free, to write anything they wish, so long as it's honest." He paused, musing again.

"Freedom—honesty," I said; "there's almost nothing more difficult for writers to achieve and practice than that. In America, too. Especially in a period like this. Especially freedom and honesty together. There are various definitions of each. But to hell with it!"—in English. "I'm in no shape to go into all that."

Tito's smile was half a scowl.

"I think I like this man," I thought.

BOOK ONE
CHAPTER FIVE: *Talking at the confluence
of unparalleled events*

THE GROUP OF MEN in the reception room included
Edvard Kardelj, Aleksandar Rankovic, Mosa Pijade, Milovan
Djilas and Boris Kidric—(with Tito) two-thirds of the Polit-
buro. There were a couple of other members of the Central Committee,
CPY, both Serbians; a Belgrade newspaper editor I hadn't met before;
and X, whose warm smile and bone-crushing handclasp I took to mean

he was glad I didn't resent the polishing-off he had given me the previous day.

In official Belgrade circles lunchtime is between two and two-thirty. Tito explained he was having us early because about half these *drugovi* were attending the second session of the Second Congress of the CP of Serbia, and he wanted us to have enough time to talk. He led us into the large dining-room, none too large for this party, and distributed us around the table. Pijade, the oldest, he put on his left; me, the visiting fireman, on his right; Kardelj beside me, Kidric next to Pijade, and so on.

But for minutes after we were seated none of us had anything to say. Tigar alone was uninhibited. He nuzzled Tito, Pijade, and me until his master muttered to him in German, whereupon he sank to the floor behind Tito's chair with a woebegone whine, followed by agonized little yips and moans each time a course was served.

Except for the many paintings on the walls, the dining-room could have been in an upper-middle-class home in the United States. The wide double door opposite me was open on a sun-room full of light, green plants, and the warbling of canaries. During the awkward silence I thought the birds made a lot of noise. Months later I learned that Tito enjoyed watering the plants and feeding the birds.

Two weeks later, writing my notes on the luncheon, I was uncertain what we had to eat. All I remembered was the beautifully embroidered white linen tablecloth and the dark bread. Several of us scarcely ate. After the meal we sat on in the dining-room and the "frank, off-the-record exchange" swung back and forth for nearly three hours. Tito steered the discussion into a serious vein by asking me what I knew, or thought I knew, of the Cominform split.

Not much, I said; mostly that the Yugoslavs wanted to fashion a system of equal relations among the states constituting the new socialist world, and got nowhere with the idea——

Had I read *The Memoirs of Cordell Hull?* In the second volume, said Tito, there were several pages on the secret Russo-British negotiations in 1944 over "spheres of influence" in the Balkans. According to Hull, when Churchill went to Moscow in mid-autumn, he and Stalin agreed on a division of the Balkans between them. The Soviet Union would extend her hegemony over Rumania and Bulgaria. Greece would remain one-hundred-percent in Britain's orbit.

In Yugoslavia, sportsmanlike, the Russians and the British would go "fifty-fifty."[1]

Tito used the English phrase, pronouncing it "feefty-feefty."

I was told that up until about three months after the appearance of Hull's book, when that work was somewhat belatedly called to their attention, they had lacked reliable information about the "fifty-fifty" deal. Off and on during 1945–48 one or the other among them had jokingly referred to a remark by Randolph Churchill, Prime Minister Winston Churchill's son, that the Yugoslavs need not worry their heads about their country's future: it was being nicely arranged for them by the two greatest living statesmen in the world, his Papa and Uncle Joe. For several months young Churchill was a member of the British Mission to Tito in the Liberated Territory of Yugoslavia. His remark was made late in April or in the first half of May 1944 to a couple of Yugoslavs who understood English and who promptly reported it to the Supreme Headquarters. But Tito and

---

[1] This point, discussed at length on pages 451–58 in *The Memoirs of Cordell Hull* (Macmillan, 1948), is succinctly covered by Edward R. Stettinius, Jr., who was Undersecretary of State in 1944, on pages 12 and 13 of his *Roosevelt and the Russians* (Doubleday, 1949) as follows:

"When Ambassador Gromyko asked the State Department on July 1 our views on the Balkans, he was informed that the United States had agreed to the arrangement for a three months' trial period, but we wanted it to be made clear that we did not favor the extension of the agreement into spheres of influence.

"*Churchill and Stalin at Moscow in October 1944 did, however extend the arrangement by reducing to percentages the degree of influence each would have in the Balkans. Our embassies in Moscow and Ankara informed us that the Soviet Union would have 75/25 or 80/20 predominance in Bulgaria, Hungary, and Rumania; Britain and Russia would share influence in Yugoslavia 50/50; and the British would have full responsibility in Greece.*" (My italics.—*L.A.*)

Late in 1949, while writing this book, I read a lengthy memorandum written in 1948 by Prince Peter of Greece, intended for private circulation among conservative Americans of Greek birth. In a passage toward the end of the document, Prince Peter tells of a discussion in the office of Sir Orme Sargeant, British Assistant Secretary of Foreign Affairs, one day early in December 1941. A full-scale war was going on in Greece against the Italian invaders, and at the same time the conflict between the regular Greek Army and the Communist-led EAM or Liberation Front guerrillas was growing in scope and intensity. Prince Peter wondered if the guerrillas might not become too strong if the British continued to send them supplies as well as the regular forces. The prince quotes Sir Orme as saying: "We will be strong enough to crush them, should they become a nuisance." "Yes," said Prince Peter, "but should the Russians be behind the Communists, what then?" "The Russians are our allies," said Sir Orme, "and we can arrange that with them."

his co-leaders didn't take it seriously because Randolph was apt to chatter idly.

The serving of a new course—by a couple of waiters in white jackets—brought a pause in the conversation. Then, to see what Tito would say, I repeated my remark to Kardelj and Kidric four days earlier: that Yugoslavia's rushing one-hundred-percent into the Soviet orbit and putting all her eggs in one basket had looked like a mistake to me.

"We're Communists, you know," said Tito quietly, as if he thought I was overlooking the most obvious fact about them.

As for pushing one-hundred-percent into the Soviet bloc, *that* was *not* a mistake. Yugoslavia had no alternative, even though, as eventually became apparent, Russia did not really want her in the shape she came in, with "the Tito clique" at the head of her Communist Party and her government. . . . No, the Kremlin did not want her until it perceived that London, with its Labour Government, was not interested in the "fifty-fifty" deal, and that Washington did not care anything about Yugoslavia (in 1945–48) except to use her as a bogey in the Voice of America broadcasts. Then (but exactly when was uncertain) Moscow decided to take Yugoslavia over and put her party and government under a subservient leadership. "Only it didn't work out that way," said Tito.

I was told, a bit ruefully, that of course if I wished I was free to think that in plunging into the Soviet camp they were half propelled by a delusion. But that "delusion" originated before the war and enabled the CPY to lead the Yugoslav peoples into a successful social revolution. Had they not plunged into it, they could not have projected the clear-cut wartime character of the revolution into the postwar period and given the people an unmistakable surge toward socialism. Besides, immediately after the war's end "Anglo-American" policy took so violent an anti-Yugoslav tack that, aside from all other Yugoslav considerations, they (Tito and his co-leaders) *had* no choice but to take the country completely into the Russian sphere.[2]

[2] In May–June, 1949, when I began to work toward having the off-the-record injunction on this and other conversations removed, I was asked by several of the men present at this luncheon at Tito's (on January 18, 1949) to keep their names out of anything I might write. I was reminded that had they known I would eventually quote or paraphrase them they wouldn't have talked so openly. Some of them wished to see my notes. I gave them copies of my diary entries and extracts from my letters to people in the United States. When they had them translated, two or three of them protested that they didn't recognize the words I put in their mouths. This rumpus.

"What about the Russian angles?" I asked.

Perhaps to keep the session from going off the deep end and becoming unmanageable within its time limit, or perhaps because at that juncture of his role as a heretic he could not go along with every detail of the argument and did not want to complicate it still further, Tito repeated his remark to me of the day before: that the Kremlin mind had somehow worked itself into a super-nationalism which, bordering on madness, distorted everything. Then he added that, in his view, the Soviet leadership had meandered into revisionism.

Little as I knew of "Marxist-Leninist" politics, I knew enough to realize that this was a serious charge. After a pause in the conversation, I asked Tito why he or one of the other Yugoslav leaders did not say so publicly.

"We all hope it may turn out to be unnecessary," he answered.

"But of course, even if you did," I said, "most of the non-Marxian world wouldn't know what you were talking about. I'm not sure I do myself, precisely. By revisionism, do you mean that the Soviet leadership has gone back on the Revolution—in other words, is counter-revolutionary?"

"Yes," said Tito.

"Counter-revolutionary in intent or in effect?"

"Perhaps both—certainly in effect."

The others didn't disagree, but most of them—maybe Tito particularly—were loath to believe that the Russian Revolution, which had

---

arose partly because my jottings were in a freehand English translation concerned with meaning rather than literalness of language, whereas their translators rendered my *non*-literal version literally back into Serbo-Croatian.

An even more interesting reason for their uneasiness over my notes was that in the intervening months—from mid-January, to, say, the end of July—when the possibility of my writing another book on Yugoslavia turned into a probability, many of the top Communist leaders in Belgrade, and such of their side-kicks as X, had substantially revised their thinking about the Yugoslav Revolution and its kinship to the Soviet Union. By midsummer 1949, just before I left Yugoslavia to return to the United States, the very texture of the minds and temperaments of some of them impressed me as being strikingly different from the way I remembered it as having been in the winter.

Another thing. Much that I learned during the luncheon at Tito's about the Cominform split is not included in this chapter. It is incorporated in Book Two, because really to understand the split, at least from the Yugoslav angle, one has to see its various elements in the light of an outline of the whole Yugoslav story, a big chapter of which, as I was to discover, is Tito's life story.

inspired such hopes in the working classes the world over, had become intentionally destructive of progressive impulses elsewhere.

Returning to a point which had been touched on before, one man argued that perhaps the weight and involutions of Russia's internal problems created tensions within the Politburo of the Central Committee of the Bolshevik Party that pulled everything askew.

"'Askew,'" said another man. "I think things inside the Kremlin have gone so far askew that the progressive movement all over the world is in danger of becoming an instrument of Russian imperialism."

I expected or hoped he would enlarge on this thought, or that someone else would take it up. But he didn't and no one else took it up.

Two of the men, who had been in Moscow a number of times during 1944–48, stressed that "fear, primitive fear," was a main cause of the whole convulsion.[3] But, aside from primitive fear whose psychological ins and outs we lacked time to discuss, it was an objective fact—*objektivan fakat*—that Russians were afraid of the rest of the world and particularly America, with her tremendous industrial capacity and her palpable drift into a state of mind which, according to all reports, considered World War III inevitable. Hadn't Mr. Harry Truman, soon after Hitler invaded the USSR, publicly declared that the USA ought to help Russia if Germany was winning, and if the Russians were too successful, America ought to help Germany so she could kill a lot of Russians? (The New York *Times* of June 24, 1941, quoted the then Senator from Missouri: "If we see that Germany is winning we ought to help Russia, and if Russia is winning we ought to help Germany, and that way let them kill as many as possible. . . .")

I said that America's drift into a state of mind accepting another war as likely or inevitable was a fact, sure enough, but one of its main causes —at least on the surface, in newspaper headlines—was her fear of Communism, or rather of the combination of Russia and Communism: for Russia (like America) had a long expansionist history and Marx, Lenin, and Stalin were on record as believing that the capitalist system

---

[3] As I work on the final revision of this book, my friend Carey McWilliams draws my attention to Chapter 10, "The Legend of Maxim Gorky's Youth," in Erik H. Erikson's *Childhood and Society* (W. W. Norton, 1950), with its brilliant insight into the "Russian soul" bent on adjusting itself to the new situation in the world brought on by the Reformation and the Industrial Revolution, by knuckling under to the ups and downs of the Marxist-Leninist-Stalinist ideology. Mr. Erikson holds that the Russian Revolution is the most obvious, the most massive lunge of a delayed "protestant" movement in industrially undeveloped Eastern Europe.

must and would be destroyed, and that wars were inevitable until that
happened. And all the reports which I inclined to trust left no doubt
that Moscow was preparing for the "next war" with greater shrewdness
and intensity, if less publicity, than Washington was. Also, while prominent Americans, among them outstanding industrialists, financiers,
and stock-exchange-gamblers-become-elder-statesmen, were on record
as favoring a war with Russia as soon as possible, there were capitalist
spokesmen in America who maintained that World War III was pre-
ventable[4] and that re-armament appropriations, especially those for
Western Europe, came under the heading of Operation: Rathole. I
strained the credulity of everyone present by saying that not long

[4] Wrote Robert R. Young, multi-millionaire board chairman of the Alleghany Corpora-
tion and the Chesapeake & Ohio Railroad, in the March 8, 1947, *Saturday Review of
Literature,* whose initial "angel" was the late Thomas Lamont, a Morgan partner:
"Those who say that war is inevitable between Russia and America because of clashes
rising out of ideological differences and economic competition, just do not know what
they are talking about. It is as if they said that the Russian system is so bad we must
fight to make it better; whereas, if it were better, they would demand that we fight to
make it worse.

"Of all nations, these two are the most independent of each other, the most self-
sustaining. Communist Russia and capitalist America, with their present ways of life,
can live just as peacefully in a world of constructive competition and commerce as
capitalist America and socialist Britain, or communist France. *Indeed we should welcome the competition of all, politically and economically. This is the way of progress.
If we cannot meet the competition of others peacefully, we do not deserve to meet it
at all.* [Italics added, here and below.]

"If we have a specific long-range policy as regards Russia [that makes sense in any
sort of constructive way], our policy makers must be afraid to declare it, for the common man has not been taken into their confidence. Russia is as weary of war as we are.
Stalin would have trembled at the thought of a new war. . . . Common sense tells us
that. He will sincerely welcome preservation of the *status quo* long enough to stop and
think, long enough to discuss disarmament, to arrange a sound solution in Europe,
*if our politicians will only stop edging up into his Mexico—with their hands at their
hips.*

". . . I must record my conviction that the atrocity of Hiroshima and Nagasaki
was not only one of history's grossest violations of morality, after our [American]
stand on poison gas, but also a political and strategic blunder of such dimensions as
to threaten the foundations of the world.

"This is a strong statement. I make is advisedly because I think the time has come
for us to Stop Kidding Ourselves. *We are kidding ourselves if we believe the atomic
bomb was dropped on Japan.* There is evidence that fully eight months earlier Japan
was ready to capitulate. If the purpose of the bomb was to save American lives, then
a fair warning before Okinawa would clearly have saved more. . . . *No, the atom
bomb was dropped [not militarily on Japan but diplomatically] upon Russia. . . .*"

ago the *Wall Street Journal* editorialized against the Atlantic Pact.

The conversation swung to the "cold war." Everyone agreed that the "cold war" wasn't unwelcome to the Kremlin; it helped to inhibit the Soviet peoples' demand for more consumer goods, to strengthen the Kremlin's hold on Eastern Europe, to make Mao Tse-tung realize that his future lay with the USSR. But the "cold war," with its prospect of a "hot war," had been spearheaded by the United States—by Churchill's Fulton speech, by the Truman Doctrine, by many other imperialistic, warlike declarations of prominent Americans, led by the (then) American monopoly of the A-bomb—there was no getting away from that—and it tightened the Russian leaders' fear. It further twisted their outlook. It impelled them to exploit the colonial and backward peoples' unrest for all it was worth. It riveted their minds to the classic Marxian prognosis that as long as classic capitalism held sway over any considerable part of the globe, wars were not only inevitable but desirable. So far as I know, this classic Marxian prognosis was best summarized by Leon Trotsky (whose name is anathema in Tito's Yugoslavia no less than in Stalin's Russia) in his book *Living Thoughts of Karl Marx* (Longmans, Green: 1938): "Plundering the natural wealth of the backward countries and deliberately restraining their independent industrial development, the monopolistic magnates and their governments simultaneously grant financial, political and military support to the most reactionary, parasitic, semi-feudal groups of native exploiters. . . . The fight of the colonial peoples for their liberation, passing over the intervening stages, transforms itself of necessity into a fight against imperialism, and thus aligns with the struggle of the proletariat in the mother countries. Colonial uprisings and wars in their turn rock the foundations of the capitalist world more than ever and render the miracle of its regeneration less than ever possible."

"Which of these circumstances," one man pondered, "is cause and which is effect, isn't easy to say. At times cause and effect are the same whirling dervish, but you can't be sure, for he whirls so furiously that now you see him as one, then as two. . . . This much is certain: there's a crisis within the USSR which is a large segment of the world crisis, and one of its manifestations is the tensions and factions within the Politburo of the Bolshevik Party that Stalin is finding ever more difficult to deal with."

"Stalin—what's he like?" I asked, looking at Tito, who did not reply. I said, "A few years ago a very acute, intensely anti-Communist American newspaperwoman who is a devout Catholic and specializes in international affairs"—Anne O'Hare McCormick of the New York *Times*—"told me that when she took part in interviewing Stalin shortly before the war she felt she had never seen a man more animal-like, or words to that effect."

"Well," said another Politburo member when Tito remained silent, "several of us here met Stalin in recent years, some of us more than once, and"—smiling—"until lately we felt we knew him. Personally, I still feel that my impression of him was correct. 'Animal-like'? I think it's a mistake to try to deprecate him with such characterizations whose meaning is relative, or to employ other methods to minimize his stature. Better not ignore the obvious (as I see it): that Stalin is a ruler less in the Marxian sense than in the tradition of Ivan the Terrible and Peter the Great. Significantly, in the Soviet Union it's forbidden to write or say anything unfavorable about those two czars. I believe Stalin's cardinal fault as a leader in this period is that, his speeches and writings to the contrary notwithstanding, he has no faith in the people, not even the Russians. This attitude endangers the progressive impulses around the world because they have been so closely associated with his name and the existence of the Soviet Union. In my personal view, *gospodine Adamicu,* there you have one of the main reasons for our expulsion from the Cominform. We challenged Stalin's attitude. Believing in our people and in other peoples, we got under the Kremlin's skin already during the war, though at the time we didn't realize that that was what was wrong with us. Live and learn."[5]

By about three o'clock, after I had been given numerous insights, from the Yugoslav point of view, into the seamy side of Soviet-Yugoslav relations prior to the Cominform outburst, the writer in me began to itch and I expressed regret that I was getting the information off-the-record.

Boris Kidric laughed. "So all of a sudden you're a writer! Only a few days ago, at the airport," he explained to Tito, "he said he had no intention of writing about Yugoslavia."

[5] Erik H. Erikson's (op. cit.) theory about the Russian soul is that the Russian people have no faith in themselves and that they are effectively encouraged not to trust themselves and to leave their future—at this stage of their would-be emergence from extreme primitiveness, from the whole complex of animalism and fear—to the elite, *i. e.,* the Central Committee of the Bolshevik Party.

"Well, I still haven't that I know of. Keep right on sitting on your story."

The conversation turned serious again. I was told with great emphasis that I was the only outsider in whom they had confided, but it was not yet time to publish the Cominform story.

"When will it be time?"

No answer.

"From Vlado Dedijer I gathered yesterday," I said, looking at Tito, "that some of you continue to hope for a reconciliation with the Cominform. A while ago, Marshal, you confirmed this indirectly by saying you're hoping it may not be necessary to accuse the Kremlin of revisionism or counter-revolution. But, if all that I've been told here is true, even if only from the Yugoslav angle, is a patch-up even remotely possible? Are you working toward it? Toward its possibility?"

No answer again. Tito was taking a turn around the room, Tigar at his heels.

"If you are," I said then, "it's beyond me why you should be."

No comment. But Tito and his co-leaders were not in a funk, as I thought at the moment—only in a betwixt-and-between predicament. For some time they had been treading the rough path to a decision; its end was not yet in sight.

"For all I know," I said in another attempt to get a clear statement out of one of them, "you may be thinking if you leave the Soviet orbit you're nowhere. On the other hand, in the light of what you've told me, where are you *in* it—if you are in it? At best, or worst, right now you're not more than about half in it. So where will Yugoslavia be if she stays half in or returns completely to the Soviet orbit without you, Marshal Tito? For my guess is she can stay in it or return to it only without you."

Tito said nothing. A few of the men exchanged glances agreeing with me.

"If I understand you," I added, "I believe the split was inevitable— if not over one set of issues and annoyances, then over another."

"As I told you, *drugovi,*" said Tito with a sudden chuckle, "our guest is capable of making interesting observations. Fortunately, his look-and-listen-only policy collapsed before he embarked on it."

The laughter which followed neatly disposed of the lead in the atmosphere. Tito's remark about my garrulity referred, I thought, not only to my probing into the Cominform story but also to some of my answers to their questions about America, in the course of which I repeated a good deal I had tried to get off my chest at Ales Bebler's.

"I really think you're out of the Soviet sphere, out in the cold," I persisted, "and will stay out. What's your outlook?"

"We mean to go on building socialism—if necessary, alone—with whatever foreign trade we can drum up with countries ready to do business with us."

"But suppose there's a general war in the near future?"

"Personally, I don't think 'a general war in the near future' is in the cards," said Tito.

"But suppose you are attacked and the war against you is localized?"

Tito didn't answer at once. Boris Kidric asked, "Attacked by whom?"

"By Russia or by a combination of your neighbors—Hungary, Rumania, and Bulgaria."

Several of the men shook their heads, grunting that was out of the question. "After all," said X, "the Soviet Union and Hungary, Rumania and Bulgaria *are* socialist countries."

"Are they really?" I was going to ask, when Tito said slowly, quietly, his glance circling the table:

"An attack upon us, *drugovi,* is not excluded."

During the ten or fifteen seconds' stillness which followed Tigar sighed deeply behind Tito's chair.

"If an attack is tried," Tito continued in a voice so low it strained my hearing, "it probably won't come before next summer [1949] and the Soviet Army won't participate. We'll repel it easily even if our neighbors use Soviet arms. The chances are their soldiers won't want to fight us; their hearts won't be in it. Those who may be thinking of such an adventure know this as we do, and so it may not materialize. On the other hand——" He paused. "Of course, if the Soviet Army itself attacks us, say, with a lot of Asian divisions, it won't be easy. But that's hardly conceivable."

"Why?"

"It would be stupid."

"More so than the Cominform action? Has stupidity any limits, once it gets started?"

"A military attack *would* be more stupid. And stupidity may not be unlimited. There are several reasons why the Soviet Army wouldn't be thrown against us; I'll give you two. First, it would deepen the disillusionment the progressives everywhere feel toward the Soviet Union because of the Cominform resolution; and, second, it would create an even greater disturbance in the world than, say, the *coup* in Czechoslovakia did early in '48."

"You'll still have to maintain an army," I said. "Most of your equipment is of Russian make, isn't it? How are you going to replace it when it wears out or becomes obsolete? Especially heavy and intricate matériel like tanks and planes?"

"We'll make them ourselves."

"Can you?"

"Yes. Also, it may be that we can buy some elsewhere."

"In the 'West'?"

Tito's shoulders rose in a noncommittal shrug and he fitted a new cigarette into his pipe-like holder. I repeated a question I had asked a few minutes before: "What's your outlook?"

The ensuing exchange revealed that the Yugoslav leaders considered the American Ambassador, Cavendish Cannon, a career diplomatist whom I had met in Washington a few times during 1942–44, a distinct improvement over Richard C. Patterson, Jr., whom he replaced in 1947, but they had almost no contact with him or anyone else at the American Embassy. They seemed reluctant to face the eventuality that they might have to reorient themselves "Westward" to some degree. Their position was like arguing which was better: to be hit by lightning or by a train going sixty miles an hour.

"We're really optimists," said one of the men at the far end of the table. "There were periods during the war when an outsider seeing our plight would have thought our cause was hopeless; yet, somehow, we knew we would win."

"During the war," I said, "you had a lot of allies, Russia and America among them, hammering at the Axis. You couldn't have won without them."

"True. Our allies now are less obvious and not nearly as well organized as our 'allies' (who weren't really for us) were during the war, but if the Kremlin's enmity persists, our allies will appear and organize."

As I realized writing my notes weeks later, some of the discussion sprawled outside my ability to give it coherence and continuity. It was bound by a quality I can't find a name for. The quality came through facial expressions and intonations of the voice. Some of the answers

my questions evoked were easily recordable but told little or nothing
unless one bore in mind the asides, the oblique and casual remarks,
the smiles and scowls which preceded or followed them.

I asked why Yugoslavia didn't join the Marshall Plan. "Because we
felt the Marshall Plan would try to interfere with our first Five-Year
Plan [begun in 1947]," Boris Kidric answered very emphatically, "and
we couldn't take any such risk." But this was little more than a rational-
ization. The real reason why Yugoslavia was the first of the several
countries in the Soviet bloc to spurn the Marshall Plan was her leaders'
paradoxical attitude toward the Soviet leadership: their deep-down
aversion to follow Stalin's "revisionism" and their ever-readiness to do
almost anything to mollify the Kremlin gremlin so long as it didn't
conflict frontally with their principles as Marxians and Yugoslav
patriots.

The Marshall Plan moved the conversation to America's over-all
"contain communism" policy. One man called it stupid and unfortunate.

"From whose angle?" I said. "If you say from the American angle,
I agree."

"From several angles—ours too."

"Why?" I pursued. "If the Soviet Union under Stalin is imperialistic,
bent on turning Yugoslavia into a colony with a stooge government
like Poland's, Czechoslovakia's, and Hungary's, and wants to keep
Yugoslavia from industrializing so she can exploit her raw resources
and manpower, isn't it a stroke of sheer good luck for Yugoslavia that
the United States *did* embark on her 'contain communism' policy? To
put it another way: if it were not for the partial success of that policy,
whose declared aim is to 'stabilize' Western Europe and 'save democracy' in Turkey and Greece, to say nothing of the Middle-Eastern oil
deposits, wouldn't all or most of Europe now be under a form of Moscow domination worse (at least for the French and Italian peoples)
than that now in effect in Poland, Czechoslovakia, Rumania, Bulgaria,
and Albania? And if so, where would you be?"

Tito waited impatiently for me to finish my question, then asked
the other man's leave to take up the argument, and said: "If the 'contain communism' policy hadn't interfered with the revolutionary process in Italy, France, and Greece, those countries would have had their
revolutions and would now be balking against Moscow domination

while building socialism. Italy and France would be balking even under such Communist leaders as they had immediately or soon after the war: Togliatti, Duclos, and so on. Italy and France would be bigger Yugoslavias. They would insist on building socialism in their own way, in line with their cultural precedents."

"And it wouldn't have cost the American people a cent," someone else said.

"And, by now, there would be a group of independent European states openly moving into socialism which would not be Soviet satellites. They wouldn't be anti-Soviet (unless, of course, the Kremlin insisted on being anti-them), but they wouldn't be pro-Soviet in the sense of being ready to fight on the Soviet side in a new war. These states would constitute an independent peace bloc making the possibility of a hot war between America and the Soviet Union extremely remote."

"I don't know France and Italy," I said, "but this last batch of remarks strikes me as too pat."

"That may be because some of us are looking at our watches and stating our ideas too hastily and too simply. Naturally, there would be complications."

I said, "How do you know that Italy under a Togliatti and France under a Duclos would stand up as you did? They're Moscow men as much as Bierut or Gottwald."

"They'd have to stand up," said Tito, "or they'd be replaced by men who would."[6]

I couldn't be sure of that. I repeated the question I had asked Kardelj and Kidric a few days before: Had they blundered into this fix or walked into it with their eyes open?

"With our eyes open," said Tito. "Of course, in repeatedly resenting

---

[6] Slightly less than two years later, some leading Americans began to approach Tito's thesis. Said Paul G. Hoffman, ex-chief of the Marshall Plan, on December 14, 1950, before the Bond Club in Los Angeles: "If the Russian leaders try to digest Western Europe, they'd lose their jobs in the process. Discontent and tensions in Russia and its satellites are terrific." The same idea rumbled in back of Joseph P. Kennedy's address on December 12, 1950, before the Virginia University Law School forum; Herbert Hoover's December 20, 1950, broadcast; and Robert A. Taft's long speech in the United States Senate early in January 1951. Explicitly or implicitly, all three urged the United States not to deprive the Kremlin leadership and the Moscow-controlled Communist Movement of the opportunity to ruin themselves by taking over Western Europe.

the Soviet attitude toward us and resisting Soviet tactics which evidently aimed to put Yugoslavia in the position of a colony—of Rumania, say—we knew the problem was bound to come to a head someday, but we didn't dream the showdown would take this form, or that they would make it so nasty. We knew, however, that socialism, the way of life we are interested in, had a rough road ahead unless the states going into it worked out political, commercial, and cultural relationships based on the principles of cooperation and solidarity, of mutual aid according to each state's needs and abilities rather than on secret-police domination and the exploitation of small and less developed states by the big or better developed ones. And we knew too, at least since early '48, that if worse came to worst we must make an issue of this and take the consequences. We felt it was the only honest and intelligently politic thing to do. We felt the chance for peace depended in part on somebody in the socialist world taking a stand."

"A generation or two ago," I said, "an American writer named Ambrose Bierce, a cynic, defined peace between nations as a period of swindling one another between two wars. I think he was right, and that Yugoslavia is in a spot. So I ask for the third time: What's the outlook?"

"Our position isn't the height of comfort," said Tito, "but had we given in to Soviet pressure, it would have been incalculably worse. And I don't mean worse for me personally, and for these *drugovi* here. I mean it would be worse for Yugoslavia and for progressive forces the world over. . . . Our outlook? As you've gathered, some of us keep thinking a reconciliation *on a decent basis* isn't excluded. It's very unlikely and some of us believe it's impossible and, like you, even undesirable. Those in the last group have agreed to give the rest of us an opportunity to prove ourselves right. That's our usual procedure when we differ about how to cope with our dilemmas. We shall see. Whatever happens, the worst can't be much worse than the peoples of Yugoslavia went through in the war. In one way or another, we here—I, personally—mean to do everything possible to preserve the integrity of our *borba,* our Revolution. We're Communists. We intend to go on building socialism in spite of anything any power can do to us, short of military conquest. And I don't doubt we'll win out, because we believe we're right and, believing that, although we're a small country, we have great strength. We have a great people. Many of them may be confused about numerous aspects of the problems facing Yugoslavia and the world, but most of them, Communists and non-Communists, feel they can achieve their personal integrity only through the program crystallized in the fire of our revolution, under the leadership of CPY: only in a culture with a real character, only in a socialist culture of our own creation. . . . There's another reason why we'll win. Forces all over the world will rally to our side; if not immediately, soon——"

The discussion might have gone on into the evening, but Pijade, Rankovic, X, and the three other leading members of the CP of Serbia had to be in the congress hall at four. Pijade invited me to come with them, but I begged to be excused.

"Enough is enough—*ne?*" smiled Tito.

"*Da,*" I said. "I'm going for a walk in the snow."

"I wish *I* could do that," said Tito in a pensive tone. Then: "Don't you want to change your mind about a party here on Saturday with some of our writers?"

"I'd like to, Marshal Tito, but I can't. I really must leave for Slovenia tonight."

"I'm told that the weather in Slovenia is strangely springlike," he said. "*Do vidjenja*—so long."

From a letter to a friend in California: slightly revised:

> Trzic, Slovenia,
> *February 4-7, 1949*

Well, Ben, I've been in Yugoslavia three weeks now. The first eight days were very crowded and strenuous. This country is so alive it wears you out. It did me anyhow. I thought I'd scoot down to Italy for a rest, but the people here talked me out of it.

The last twelve days I've slept long hours. Afternoons I walk miles in the woods of Upper Slovenia, near the Austrian border; occasionally on a highway the Romans built about two thousand years ago. It's still used—by horse- and ox-drawn carts and lorries, autos, trucks, and bicycles nowadays. Here and there the highway is cut into the granite mountainside. I wondered how the Romans did it without dynamite, so I asked and learned they built roaring wood fires under the great gray cliffs in freezing weather, making them split.

Between sleeping and walking I write letters and very extensive rough notes, though I doubt I'll be able to use them in the near future, if ever: first, because the heart of the Cominform story, which I picked up during a session at Tito's a few days after I reached Belgrade, beats with a hundred details that were given me off-the-record; and, second, because the "cold war" hysteria in the United States is rising by the minute, it appears.

Last night I went through a pile of middle- and late-January issues of the international edition of the New York *Times,* the Paris edition of the New York *Herald Tribune,* and two recent numbers each of the air-edition *Time* and *Newsweek.* Downright fascinating. I learned that the Brooklyn dock-wallopers refused to load the Yugoslav ship *Radnik* because pictures of Tito and Stalin hung on one of her walls, which made her a floating evil. I read that Elizabeth Bentley, the tabloids' "spy queen," the self-confessed traitor, a courier for a Russian spy, who now is said to be entering a Catholic convent to expiate her sins, testified once more before a Congressional subcommittee that I'm a Red mastermind, and, contradicting herself, corroborated the claim of Louis Budenz [*another ex-Communist converted to Catholicism*] that it was he who, by order of the CPUSA and Soviet agents, roused my interests in the Tito-led Communist movement in Yugoslavia, back in 1942–43. And there was the red-hot news of battles between "anti-Tito guerrillas" and Tito's forces raging in the woods and mountains of Yugoslavia, the very woods and mountains where I walk and encounter only deer and squirrels. . . . During my first week here, in Belgrade and in Slovenia, the absurd ideas many Yugoslavs have about the United States vexed me no end. I began to be annoyed with myself too, because, trying to change those ideas, I was turning into a geyser of American chauvinism. At first I ascribed their misconceptions to anti-American propaganda rampant in the Soviet orbit. Then I realized they can't be ascribed to that alone. If I lived in Yugoslavia and "knew" only what I read in American prints, heard on the Voice of America broadcasts, and saw of American movies, I'd probably think and feel about the USA as they do.

I have a bright, clean room in a quiet lodge on a hilltop, five or six kilometers from a small industrial town called Trzic (in two or three lessons I could teach you to say it), with great wooded mountainsides to be seen from the balcony. The weather in Slovenia has been wonderful—a false spring: sunny and warm, with just a little snap in the air.

Walking in the woods, I mull over what I've bumped into so far. I

can't give you a comprehensive picture. I can only flash you some highlights among my first impressions, all of them subject to revision or
discard.

When I came to Slovenia from Belgrade, I was very curious about
Tito. I asked two men about him, both writers I met back in 1932–33,
who I thought would have amassed a lot of details about him—one of
them, Josip Vidmar, in 1943 proposed that Tito be made Marshal of
Yugoslavia, and is now his friend. Oddly enough, my questions surprised and embarrassed them. They couldn't tell me anything concrete,
specific, or interesting. No biographical material worth reading is
available. No one has thought of compiling it. Apparently, it's not
needed domestically, and there's a great reluctance to release facts about
Tito and his co-leaders for publicity outside the country.

One explanation for their reticence to divulge facts about Tito, dig
into his beginnings, take apart his attributes and lacks, and balance his
dimples against his warts, is that the Communists don't believe in the
importance of individual leaders; this, at the same time that Tito is
tantamount to the Egyptian king-god, to a Messiah—but with a significant difference: he's not remote from the people but is synonymous
with them.

Another explanation is that during the Revolution which began in
1941—and is still in process in Yugoslavia, and accelerating—*konspiracija* was for so long the attitude and practice that the habit of it
lingers on. Searching or curiosity-motivated questions about Tito and
the other top leaders are not asked, which, from the American angle,
and especially if one happens to be a writer, is disconcerting. In the
United States people lapped up personal, intimate details about Franklin Roosevelt, but there was no great popular interest in what really
made him tick. In Yugoslavia the opposite prevails. Tito? There he *is*
—why ask how he arrived and how he got that way and what he likes
for breakfast and what kind of father he is to his little boy? He's all
right, *ne?* Isn't that as obvious as Cyrano's nose? So why pry? Everybody knows he "comes out of the people."

Phrases like "comes out of the people" have a definite, precise meaning here, but mostly within the subjective complexus of the country. I
think this goes for the leaders as well as the run-of-the-mill folk. They
don't realize that in the "West" scarcely anybody knows what "comes
out of the people" means.

At the risk of mystifying you further, there's Tito the man and "Tito" the word, the shorthand symbol for "everything," the abstraction of "everything" that was, is, and will be in Yugoslavia. Where the symbol ends and the man begins, or vice versa, is hard to say. Tito is the well-head of the future. Seeing him or his picture, or merely knowing he's around, gives a lot of people (not everybody) a strange satisfaction. It makes them feel they're part of something; not merely because "he's a somebody, so I'm a somebody too," but because *they* constitute his being a somebody, and they know it.

Tito doesn't know too much about the United States but he's greatly interested, as they all are, in American technology and the politically progressive forces in American life. As Marxians, they have lots of things analyzed in ways which, to my mind, don't always shape up to reality. But they didn't cavil about many of the points I tried to make: one of them, that Marxism is an oversimplification. Of course they went along with my saying that the American social-economic system, with its wonders, its dynamic, and its problems that tumble over one another endlessly, was expansionist—imperialistic, in the Marxian book; that the "cold war" was also an expansionist gimmick to be used now or later; and that if peace broke out, American economy would take a dive, which would make the world landscape fluid as a torrent cascading through a gorge.[7] . . . What the Yugoslav leaders couldn't understand was why organized labor in the United States supported the "cold war" policy. I'm afraid I didn't do a very good job of explaining. It's no easier to pit yourself against the pattern of Marxian reasoning in Yugoslavia than it is to contend with hysteria in America.

To reproduce a conversation in which eleven guys let off steam (as they did at Tito's luncheon), is a bit of a task. The gist of it was that the future is impaled on the stakes of "Western capitalism" and "Eastern communism," each operating under the slogan to contain the other,

---

[7] In the matter of incompatability between peace and the American system I was but slightly "premature." Wrote columnist David Lawrence in the April 5, 1949, New York *Sun:* "It makes one shudder to think what the sudden outbreak of peace might mean to American economy." . . . Said United States Senator Edwin C. Johnson of Colorado on May 4, 1949: "If Russia suddenly decided to be a good neighbor, there'd be hell to pay." . . . Said President William A. McDonnell of the First National Bank of St. Louis on June 16, 1950: "Have you ever stopped to think what would be the effect upon American industry if international tensions could be eased so that [the current twenty billions for armaments and European aid] could be reduced by even fifty percent, or ten billion dollars?"

having more in common than is generally supposed, yet likely to collide and produce a general cataclysm. When? Not right away, thinks Tito, maybe not for years—except by a fluke, not until the big powers are technically ready with their new weapons and counter-weapons. In Tito's estimation, this "next war" is not inevitable. The peoples of the world don't want it. They're sick of wars; they want a chance to live out their lives, to raise children who will have a chance to live out their lives. So the masses of the world are in a revolutionary ferment, full of contradictory dynamics which, according to both Karl Marx and Bernard Baruch, are bound to explode sooner or later. Listening to Tito and his co-leaders, looking at them, I felt they could not yield their central aim: to build socialism. This appears idealistic. They say it's also practical—the *only* practical policy.

Not that I think they're crystal-clear and overly precise as to what they're about. On the contrary. As we talked, the phrase "building socialism" popped out of one or the other of them at the least provocation. By socialism, as a beginning, they apparently mean electrification, industrialization, Yugoslavs becoming masters of their own country: talk that sounds logical in a one-two-three fashion. But I suspect there's little intellectual logic in the way things are or aren't shaping up. What I see most clearly is an elemental drive to better the lot of the people: and quite a number of former underdogs already are better off, while the relatively few former upper-dogs are worse off. Yugoslavia never had a sizable upper and middle class; so, lacking capital, she can achieve industrialization only through a revolution, socialism, collective action: taking over the resources, drawing up a plan, training cadres of technicians, organizing the present generation into work "brigades," into teams of shock-workers, and firing the youth with enthusiasm to work harder than people ever worked before.

In her deep-down and widespread motives, New Yugoslavia's industrialization-through-socialism is primarily anti-imperialism: a holding action—holding on to her natural resources and staving off the greed- and panic-driven jogs and jolts of the big powers. The emotions and thoughts, open and private, and the relationships that go with this action throb with a promise—not for everybody but for a great many, not for tomorrow but for a period a good many years hence. Many people engaged in this action are finding themselves, or so they think; which for the moment is a great deal—enough. They feel they're busy at something worthwhile, functioning in a big job. They're not comfortable or at ease, not by a long shot. Life is tough, work is excruciating; the "pursuit of happiness" as practiced individually by not a few in America is an unknown sport here. But some Yugoslavs, perhaps a majority of the youth, are catching glimpses of a frame which will someday contain a new picture. In that picture all the working, producing people will have a place as individuals and as members of a society, a chance for a life of integrity, purpose, creative freedom.

This is a mouthful, I know, but I think it describes the Yugoslav outlook (apart from the "next war"). And I think it also covers the hopes of people in China, in all of Asia, and maybe in all of Africa and much of Latin America, and in different ways and degrees in the USA and the USSR.

Both the "Western" press and the Cominform propaganda have characterized Tito as conceited and a megalomaniac. He *is* proud, perhaps too palpably so. But that may be only surface glint. It doesn't nearly describe him. He's multi-stranded. As for charm, when he turns it on full tilt, it brings the birds down. He's *not* a dictator in the sense it's meant in the American press; not the kind of dictator Stalin is supposed to be, or the Latin-American kind. He hasn't the nature for it—unless I'm utterly mistaken and all I've seen and heard so far simply isn't so.

At one point in the course of the long luncheon conversation, he listened with a vinegar aspect to an awkward attempt on my part to taunt him with being a dictator; then he smiled suddenly and said: "I'd just like to see anybody try to be a dictator in this country and hope to live to a ripe old age."

This doesn't mean that he's a democrat in the best American, Jeffersonian, sense. He definitely is not. Having come up in the Balkans and pulled off a revolution with the aid of the Soviet Union's existence, he couldn't very well be.

The men around Tito? They came up the hard way with him, with the Revolution, through torture chambers and prisons in Old Yugoslavia, through a four-year military struggle that America and Western Europe and most of the rest of the world can hardly imagine. Watching five of them in the same room with him, I felt that, if anything happened to him, they would carry on around "Tito" the symbol. But none of them would be anything much without him to begin with.

And without them he, in turn, would not be the "Tito" he is, if at all. They and he are what he calls the leadership *kolektiv,* or team.

No one who meets the team as I did—in such propitious circumstances, which made it possible for them and me to open up—can doubt their honesty, intelligence, and industry, or that they're driven by a great idea and purpose (as they see them) and a strong faith. By this I don't mean they're not inches, yards, or miles from perfection as individuals, politicians, executives, or what-have-you (as yet, I've no firm basis for saying anything about them on those scores except that some of them are simply loaded with personality). Their methods and procedures are open to debate; so is socialism as a philosophy and a program. There's no gainsaying, though, that they mean well by the people—to help infuse with self-respect the least of them, to make sound use of the country's great natural resources, to insist on respect for their state, to make it a player instead of a pawn in the terrific game ahead.

They're Communists and *patriots* (not a contradiction of terms here). They're bent on building a new society not because they're so perverse as to enjoy the immense task, its shocks and ravages, but because as patriots they see (and, I think, actually have) no other choice. I'm afraid none of them have a very keen, continually active sympathy for the many individuals and families all over the country who are going through personal agonies as part of the Big Change they're directing. The agony is too close and commonplace; one who felt for it constantly, if that were possible, and too acutely would be good for nothing else. The Yugoslav leaders know enough about it from their own lives and the lives of their families, if in no other way, to agree with Bernard Shaw that "there is nothing so revolting as revolution except capitalism."

Capitalism in prewar Yugoslavia, as I wrote in *The Native's Return* and then in *My Native Land,* was worse than revolution. All peoples are naturally conservative; they don't indulge in bloody uprisings for the fun of it. They heave up only in extremity when they *must* to survive as a cultural entity vis-à-vis the rest of the world.

I talked with my twenty-five-year-old nephew, Tine, who told me the biggest moment of his life arrived a year ago, about five months before the Cominform outburst, when he was inducted as a full-fledged member into the Communist Party of Slovenia. He'd been a candidate for eighteen months. Behind the sudden glow on his face (and he's no will-o'-the-wisp chaser, no idyll addict) was the absolute conviction that were it not for Tito, for the "Tito" concept and process, there would be no Yugoslavia, no People's Republic of Slovenia—perhaps no Slovenians, for Hitler planned to do away with them, as thoroughly as he almost did away with the European Jews.

To document fully that conviction would take a book (which I fear no American publisher in his right mind would publish as long as the present hysteria lasts). Let me just say that I think Tine is right. Efforts to weaken Yugoslavia, to bleed her white, or destroy her forever, or prevent her restoration were exerted at various times—often at the same time—not only by the Axis and its Serbian, Croatian, and Slovenian bootlickers, but by cliques in the Foreign Office and the State Department, by the Vatican and—last but not least, as we now see— by the Kremlin. As secretary-general of the patriotic and purposeful CPY, Tito thwarted them all. Therein is his virtue—and his sin.

"To put power into the hands of the people" is no empty demagogic phrase. Nor is "people's democracy." Walking through Upper Slovenia in recent days, I saw people's committees in operation in a few of the villages and in Trzic, a town of about five thousand. These committees are the foundation of the new system of government, still in the process of being formulated. The people are in charge, or they are taking over, to the extent that a majority are actively participating in the working-out of their future.

The question "Who are the people and who are *not* the people?" occurred to me the second day I was in Yugoslavia. I put it to Kardelj, who had used the expression *ljudstvo* (the people) three or four times at short intervals in the course of a morning's conversation. At first he looked as though my question struck him as strange, possibly even as a bit of a *podvala* (ill-intentioned trickery or innuendo) and he had to think awhile before he answered: "All those are *ljudstvo* who in any way with physical labor or mental effort make a positive contribution to the totality of the constructive process in the state."

"Even if they are opposed to the regime?" I asked.

"Even if they are opposed to the regime," said Kardelj after a brief hesitation which probably was due to his not knowing me well and not knowing what I might be driving at.

"Just so they work and contribute?" I said.

"Just so they work and contribute."

This didn't satisfy me, for it was obvious that Kardelj hadn't given the matter much thought, but I didn't want to press him too hard. When I got to Slovenia, I tossed the question at Josip Vidmar during a dinner party in his home. His mind seemed to me as incisive as it had been in 1932–33, but calmer.

" 'Who are the people and who are *not* the people?' " Vidmar repeated, thoughtfully. "To tell you the truth, we haven't given it much thought. Hardly any, in fact. The question was in the main resolved within us—subjectively—during the war and since, in the course of the Revolution. We know quite clearly who are the people and who are not the people." He added that he would think about it, however, and we could come back to the subject again later. But I imagine that he pretty well covered it—how the leaders feel about it.

Yesterday afternoon I went to get my mail at the post office in Trzic, and walking back to the lodge, I saw this sign on the wall of a small factory: *For the First Time in Our History We Are Working for Ourselves*. I suppose the "we" in that inscription are the people.

I haven't been everywhere of course, not even in Upper Slovenia, but where I've been I've seen no "terror." There's a security police, to be sure. It was known under the initials OZNA and is now called UDBa. (UDBa—*Uprava Drzavne Bezbednosti,* the Administration of State Security.) It goes about its business as unobtrusively as the FBI in the United States.

I saw Tito in a hall jammed with twelve hundred people; he walked through a long vestibule to his car outside without a bodyguard or any guard I could see. This doesn't mean there were no guards. The next day, when I expressed concern over his security and asked him how *he* felt about it, he said: "I feel safest when I am among the people."

During the lunch at Tito's I talked with Aleksandar Rankovic, federal head of UDBa, who according to the "Western" and "Eastern" press, is a sadist and terrorist. I found him gentle and thoughtful, which wouldn't preclude his being "bestial," as the Budapest radio described him night before last. But his ideas and values, like Tito's, Kardelj's, Kidric's, Djilas', and Pijade's, are just the opposite: and he couldn't fake them any more than he could fake his smile and the expression in his eyes which are possible only in a man of fine-grained sensibilities.

Much of what these men talked about had to do with humanism, morality . . . with what is right: why it would have been wrong for them to knuckle under to the political-police agents the Kremlin was sending to Yugoslavia in large numbers during 1945–47 . . . with the belief that man is man, or rather that *a* man is a man, loaded with human nature, and not a component of rabble, not a robot who must be steered and pushed this way and that, who must be dictated to. I think that difference of concept is one basic reason for the Soviet-Yugoslav split. But don't misunderstand: I'm not saying that Yugoslavia is imbued with a sense of personal liberty, welfare, and security to the extent that there is no pushing-around, or that the individual's rights are established and safeguarded beyond doubt or dispute.

The Yugoslav background takes in the Greek and Latin classics, Christianity, the Renaissance, Enlightenment, and other facets of "Western" culture. Tito, Kardelj, Pijade, *et al.,* grew up in a "Western" environment. They're Marxians, and Marxism is a "Western" criticism of Western civilization and Christianity. They all have read stacks of Russian literature, and some of it is distilled in their makeup. But they're steeped, too, in South Slavic lore and letters, and they're just naturally much more of the "West" than the "East"—or of neither, turning critical eyes at one and then at the other, seeing good and bad in both. Their essence may be something between the two with a core and a drive of its own.

I think this applies to the second-level leadership. When I was at Josip Vidmar's that first day after my arrival in Slovenia, I admired a painting in his living-room. It was by a Slovenian impressionist, now dead, who studied in Paris. Vidmar smiled; I asked what was amusing him.

"One evening four years ago," he said, "I had a guest who characterized that painting and others in this room as 'decadent.' He was the head of a Soviet cultural mission, and he all but told me to take them off the walls. I told him I thought I knew something about art: while these pictures might not be great works, they were rather good, they were by Slovenian artists, some of whom I knew personally, and they would stay where they were. We had no end of such experiences with Russian visitors."

When I asked him, as one writer to another, what he was working on, he replied he was preparing to write a book entitled "Communism—the New Humanism."

Vidmar wasn't formally a Communist before or during the war; as I had learned earlier in the evening, he joined the Communist Party of Slovenia only six months before—immediately after the Cominform split.

" 'New Humanism'?" I said. "I'm faintly familiar with a couple of humanist movements in America, through the magazines they publish —rather fuzzy-minded stuff, full of wordy concern about 'humanity,' which these humanists haven't yet defined in terms I understand. What do you mean by 'New Humanism'?"

"People," said Vidmar. "Human beings. A chance for them to grow as close as possible to their full stature and performance. In this country, I think, that's achievable only if there is an intelligently organized collective economy and a culture providing freedom for the individual and opportunities for his creative integration with society. Clear?"

I said I thought it was.

Someone else at the dinner table was reminded of a folk saying current in Macedonia and also known in Greece: "We do not live, we wear ourselves out one against the other."

"Will your new system, now being organized around this 'Tito' concept and symbol, tackle that?"

"Quite a few of us believe it will."

Ever read Joseph Conrad's *Nostromo?* I came on a battered old copy in the lodge where I am staying. A beautiful job. Using a subtle plot full of wonderfully drawn characters wearing themselves out one against the other, it deals with the pattern of big countries' exploitation of small countries and with its effect on everybody and everything involved—on human nature and on the whole circumambience of the earth. The story is laid in Castaguena, a fictitious Latin-American republic. There's a silver mine operated by an Englishman who needs more money for further development and to grease the palms of Castaguenan politicos. He approaches a San Francisco financier, who says to him:

"We [in the United States around the year 1900] know just about enough to keep indoors when it rains. We can sit and watch. Of course, some day we shall step in. We are bound to. But there's no hurry. Time itself has got to wait on the greatest country in the whole of God's Universe. We shall be giving the word for everything: industry, trade, law, journalism, art, politics and religion, from Cape Horn clear over to Smith's Sound, and beyond, too, if anything worth taking hold of turns up at the North Pole. And then we shall have the leisure to take in hand the outlying islands and continents of the earth. We shall run the world's business whether the world likes it or not. The world can't help it—and neither can we, I guess."

Perhaps *we* Americans can't help it. But the world doesn't like it. Here's Tito, here's Yugoslavia. . . . There's China, turning over to help herself.

On his title page Conrad quoted this line from Shakespeare: "So foul a sky clears not without a storm."

WHILE the northeastern parts of the country lay
under a great snow, the northwestern basked
(as had been reported to Tito) in a false spring.
France and I arrived in Ljubljana around noon on Wednesday,
January nineteenth. The *peron* of the old station teemed with people
hurrying through the sunshine. France led me off to one side where

a part of our big family that lived in the city was assembled. An apple-cheeked little girl called me "Uncle Lojze" and handed me a bouquet of crocuses and snowdrops. She was France's four-year-old daughter Maruska. Her brother Mihec, two years older and all excited, said they had gathered the flowers in the park. A thin, pale six-year-old boy, of whose existence I was also but dimly aware, recited a welcoming poem, composed by his mother, whom I had never met either. He was Riko, my youngest brother Joze's son. Still another nephew, Boris, the husky, curly-headed five-year-old of my youngest sister Anica, greeted me with a raised fist and the declaration: "I'm Tito's!" His father, a Partisan doctor, was captured and killed by the enemy two months before he was born, near the war's end.

A short distance from this scene, in the noontime glare, stood a group of men. I recognized several of them from 1932–33, when they had been writers mostly of unpublished or suppressed books and editors of frequently censored journals. Now some of them were widely published and edited leading magazines, and were high officials in the local state apparatus. One—Josip Vidmar, a prewar non-Communist (sometimes anti-Communist) polemicist on national and social-cultural issues—had been a foremost leader in the War of Liberation and now was President of the Praesidium (the center of sovereignty) of the PR (People's Republic) of Slovenia, a member of the Federal Parliament, and professor of the history of the theater in the new Academy of the Drama in Ljubljana. Would I come to his house for dinner that evening?

I spent the afternoon at my homeplace, twenty-odd kilometers south of Ljubljana.

Mother met me on the spot in front of the house where we had said good-by in 1933. "*Nu,* you came a few years sooner this time," she said. In '33 her parting remark had been that I probably wouldn't return for another nineteen years.

"It seems like yesterday, Mother."

"Like eternity," she disagreed. She was perceptibly older but, as I had anticipated from France's report, in good health for a woman past seventy, at least outwardly. Her eyes were sunken but bright.

Ante's suicide wasn't mentioned. Nor the death of my sister Paula's son in the war, or of Anica's husband. This was my second homecoming, and Mother and the rest of the family must have made a compact to present a cheerful front. But I couldn't help sensing a deep change in the family I described in *The Native's Return,* and not only because we were all sixteen years older. Things weren't the same. Mother, perhaps, was the only one who was essentially unchanged. She talked and acted as calm and commonsense as ever. Most of my eight brothers and sisters were a little tense. They smiled as our glances mingled, but behind their manner were the war and the Revolution and their aftermath.

The recent past hung on. The present was a rush of fragmentary day-to-day experiences—anxious, uneasy, almost unreal. There was so little time to think. Here was the task, and something in the air and within you made you attend to it. The Revolution: it was synonymous with the future. As the afternoon wore on, I received the impression that Mother had the sharpest, simplest, and also the most spacious perspective on its compulsions and goals of anyone in the family. Somehow, age and her natural intelligence had released her from clutching at the past and abstracted her from much that was mere *direndaj,* skimble-skamble, in the present. She was interested in the crux of events. Like her explosive little grandson Boris, she was on the threshold of tomorrow.

Anica tried to keep her boy quiet. At intervals he cried out "I'm Tito's!" and his grandmother smiled and said to her daughter, "Let him yell." Anica disappeared; when she returned, her eyes were red.

We sat around the table in the kitchen, which is the largest room in the house, the living-room really, and I pressed my question as to how it had been during the war. Mother's reply came with a hesitant effort:

"It's—beyond telling. You couldn't imagine it even if we had the words to tell you. Many of those who joined the Partisans and fought in the *borba* were killed or maimed, or no one ever heard of them again, but I often thought they had it simpler than we in the crossfire, though not easier. In the four years of war, this valley [because a railway goes through it] was always full of troops. We were occupied by eight different armies: the old Royal Yugoslav Army, the Italians, *Beli* [or the Whites, the enemy-equipped, priest-directed quislingists], the Partisans or the Reds, the Cetniki or the Blues, the Germans, the Vlasovci [bands of German-sponsored anti-Soviet Russians], and finally Tito's new Yugoslav Army. There were battles. One day an airplane crashed into our meadow right over there, between the railway track and the creek. If I had the gift of narration, I could tell you how it was; but years have gone by and we've all been trying to forget. Now you ask——"

Mother paused; all the rest of us were silent, till Boris exploded again. Mother smiled at him. "It's a wonder so many of us are still here," she went on in a faltering cadence. "I don't know what the explanation is, really. We couldn't all go into the woods. Some of us were too old to fight. In a way, life went on; somehow, it always does, *kaj ne?* Some of the people didn't understand what the *borba* was about. Maybe they couldn't. Some did. We left food for the Partisans in the fields or under a bush. They appeared at night, we told them where it was, and in the morning the sack was gone.

"Under the Italians and Germans, we couldn't go beyond the rim of the village without risking death. The enemy treated us like animals or, at best, like furniture; we weren't permitted to move from the house. The children who were away couldn't come home except if they took their lives in their hands and slipped in through the ring of guards and informers. The informers. The enemy was the least to worry about. The worst of it was that we couldn't trust all of our neighbors"—some of whom are our relatives.

Listening to Mother, I had a torn feeling: it would take me a while to grasp the story.

The *kozolec*—drying-shed, typical of Slovenia—was new; the old one had burned down. The six-hundred-year-old house had had a section of its roof and a corner blown off, but it looked better than I remembered it. My nephew Tine—my oldest sister Toncka's twenty-five-year-old son, a student of architecture at the University of Ljubljana—had supervised its repairs. The young man whom I recalled as a nine-year-old boy was tautly silent all afternoon—eager, as I discovered later, for a long talk.

Inside, the house was almost the same as before. It is a large house for Slovenia, and I found one-third of it occupied by a school for training typists, bookkeepers, and filing clerks. School closed for the afternoon, and I was invited into the old apple orchard to meet the students, about a score of teen-age girls, and their teacher, who was in her mid-twenties.

One of the students made a speech, probably written by the teacher.

The speech said it wasn't unusual for someone born in this part of Slovenia to become an author. It gave a roster of the novelists and poets born in the villages and hamlets within the jurisdiction of this *krajevni* or regional people's committee. I was grateful for the girl's delivery; it was nearly as awkward as mine when I replied to her address.

The teacher told me there were hundreds of such schools the country over, run by people's committees, preparing young peeople for jobs in the local government apparatus. The courses were part of the Five-Year Plan. The teacher herself was a former factory worker, a Communist since 1944. She had been a Partisan soldier for three and a half years. A shrapnel wound left a scar on her face. Before the war she had scarcely known how to read; between battles, during 1942–45, she had gone to school in the woods, where an education system was organized by the People's Liberation Front of Slovenia. Two years ago she had taken courses in typing, bookkeeping, and filing.

Two students giggled their way through a routine of jokes that raised gales of laughter. Example: "You know what?"—"No; what?" —"There won't be any flies this year."—"There won't?"—"No, all the flies are taking courses to become bees."

I asked Mother if she minded having the school in the house. She said, no, not really; why should she? During the war the house was always full of officers of one occupation army or another and the family was allowed only the use of the kitchen and two rooms. Now the school only took up the back part. The girls behaved very well. Wasn't it wonderful the way they were being trained? In no time at all they were pounding the typewriter. Mother knew the parents of many of them. Sometimes she wondered what it was all about. Was it good? And she couldn't help believing it was. A new world was being born.

On a ledge beside the woodstove in the kitchen was a paper-bound copy of a Slovenian translation of Stendahl's *La Chartreuse de Parme*. A pair of spectacles marked the place between the pages.

"Who's reading this?" I asked.

"I am," said Mother.

"Like it?"

"I'm not quite half through. I find it interesting."

Later my brothers and sisters told me that since Ante's suicide

Mother read voraciously. Once she remarked to Toncka: "I feel as though I'm opening windows I didn't know were there on vistas I never knew existed. Too bad I'm old. When we begin to know something, we're ready to die."

Paula, my second-oldest sister, eagerly helped Mother set before me more food than I could consume in a week—chicken soup, boiled chicken, fried chicken, pan-fried potatoes with onions ("the way you liked them sixteen years ago"), sausages, ham, horseradish, *potica* (cake), dark bread, apples, linden-blossom "tea," and I don't know what else. But otherwise she was rigidly restrained. Paula always was the shy one. I wondered if anyone knew her. She was locally famous as a hard, efficient worker and an expert on raising hogs. Her dark kerchief was tied tightly, framing her mild face with its subdued, unsure smile. Her hair was hidden: was it graying? She was fifteen, twenty years younger than Marija, the woman in the Rumunska Street house in Belgrade where I had stayed, but a good deal like her. Behind her sealed-in personality was an unfortunate love affair; an "illegitimate" child who grew up into an unusually talented youth. At fourteen he decided to study technology. At seventeen, attending school in Ljubljana, he joined the underground Communist Youth organization. He died in the war on the day of Liberation. Paula had accepted life's terms. It would have been futile and cruel to pry into her inmost being.

Here was Mimi, my next-to-the-youngest sister, with her husband and three children, still the beauty of the family. The last time I saw her she was a nun serving as a nurse in a Belgrade hospital. I remembered her silence when I asked, "Why are you here?" There was still something of the nun in her self-effacing manner. Her smile, Madonna-like sixteen years ago, had a Mona Lisa quality now. I was unable to find a common ground with her husband. He had been the engineer in charge of the heating system in the hospital, and had induced her to quit the Order. (In the summer of 1936 the affair was an international sensation for a week.) There was something crass, over-aggressive about him. He wanted to look at my wristwatch; he said he didn't have one. He appeared to resent me, perhaps because I lived in America. I don't know. We didn't meet again.

Another relative-in-law was bitter because she had to wear a coat made over from a favorite topcoat of mine I had sent in a bundle of clothing, used and new, in care of Mother soon after V-E day. Her pride and hidden reproaches of my favored circumstances annoyed me. Then I felt that I had no right to be annoyed.

One young woman living in the city complained how hard it was to shop for her household's daily needs. You got in the queue in front of the store at seven in the morning; even at five or six there was a line; and you waited; and when at last you inched your way in, you couldn't get this and there wasn't any more of that. It was enough to make you blow your top. Whose fault was it that distribution was so poorly organized? Conditions had been infinitely better six, eight months ago; were Cominform agents disorganizing distribution? Or was bureaucracy just at its usual tricks and a little more brazen? Was bureaucracy inevitable under socialism?

A heated discussion developed as to whether or not the *delavne zadruge,* or peasant cooperatives, then beginning to be organized all over Yugoslavia, were a good idea. My oldest brother Stan, the legal owner of the old homestead, was dead against it. He said he liked being his own boss, working for himself. If he worked hard in a *zadruga* and the other fellow didn't, he would feel like a fool. As for the promised leisure after you did your stint under the new system, who cared about that? What could he do with so much free time? He was used to rising before dawn and working past nightfall, eating and going to sleep. What more did a man want? When you came down to it, what else was there to life?

Mother listened calmly for a while, then she said: "Let me say a few words, please. There isn't enough manpower in the villages— right here, in this village, as we know. So many died in the war; afterward people fled to Austria, or to Italy, and went on to Brazil or God knows where. Now so many are going to work in the new factories and mines. Who can blame them?"

I saw she was telling this for my benefit, or her own peace of mind, so she could feel satisfied I understood the argument. She turned to her next-to-the-oldest son:

"We talked about this before, Stan, you and I. It's one thing how you think you'll feel working in a *zadruga,* and what you'll do with your spare time. Maybe you'll read or find something else to do that you'll like very much. But it's another thing how you'll work this place *alone* with your present tools, especially at harvest time. You know you couldn't acquire a tractor and other machinery for your own use even if it were available for you to buy. *Najmocnejsi kmet*"—the strongest or richest peasant—"is too poor for that. And, to begin with, no single peasant in Slovenia has enough soil to make any real use of a tractor. So where are you?"

Stan didn't answer; he smiled enigmatically.

"We all agree that the land must be cultivated," Mother continued. "But if we don't organize into *zadruge* and pool our working ability and the little we have, how are we going to cultivate the land and produce food? And if we don't produce food, how is Tito to going to feed the workers who are building the new industries? And if Tito and the workers don't succeed in creating strong industries, where will Yugoslavia be? I'm getting old, soon I'll depart; the rest of you, though—will you have to go through another war like the last, or even worse, under the circumstances we went through this war? What chance will you have?"

"Where does she get that?" I wondered. She's not a Communist— couldn't be a Communist, consciously. She might be upset if one called her a Communist. Later I was told that Mother had been talking in this vein for some time. She had figured things out for herself on the basis of reading and commonsense—except that she stated her ideas better, more simply, than the leaden-footed ideologists and their gobbledygookish echoists on some of the newspapers I used to glance at when they reached me in America, and which I had been reading carefully and with irritation the last few days.

Milka, Stan's wholesome-looking wife, whom I hadn't met before, took me into the pantry. Mother and Paula came along. There were a dozen hams, over a dozen slabs of bacon, a couple of hundred sausages strung out on smoke-blackened poles, baskets of eggs, sacks of beans, barrels of other staples. A picture of abundance.

"Why do you keep all this?" I asked. "You don't need it all, do you?"

Milka smiled embarrassedly and didn't answer. Paula was silent too.

"I've told them the same," Mother said in a low, wavering voice only half-agreeing and implying that it wasn't as simple as all that.

I gathered it was Stan, old-fashioned Stan—in his late forties, the conservative peasant—who wanted to hold on to more than they needed. This was a point of tension between the members of the family. But it seemed that Mother, too, who was the freest about the future, wasn't clear which was the right thing to do: hold on to food at the expense of the *skupnost,* the community, in this difficult transitional period, or sell it for money which, because of the shortage of manufactured consumer goods, had little purchasing value. Stan was the way he was because she had raised him so; now he couldn't change, couldn't see why he should, just because the world around him had gone awry. Also, many of the other peasants were holding on, or were eating up what they formerly would have sold; and people like my family felt: why should they sell when the others didn't? The new system wasn't well organized yet, was barely starting; and *reakcija*— notably the priests—were encouraging people to resist it.

In our family the tension was eased by Stan's readiness to listen to Mother and to sell to the government at its price more grain, beans, potatoes, and pigs than the minimum required; and to give from the surplus to France's, Joze's, Mimi's and Toncka's families, who lived away from home, in cities where fats, meats, eggs, and other food items were scarce. Many families did this. But there was a multitude of political and personal psychological complexities, of strains and stresses. Bonds were tightening and sundering. There were sharpening jealousies among members of the same family and between them and the community. There were affinities on new bases, integral with the *prelom,* the break, the Revolution, that I knew would take me a while to assemble and understand. All this was on a different level of life than the levels I had glimpsed in Belgrade.

Stan invited me *v stalo*—into the combined cow barn, horse stable, and hog pen—to show me his animals. "Of course they aren't really ours," he said. "We can't sell them without the written permission of the people's committee, and then only at a set price and, as a rule, only to the state. We can't slaughter a pig or a calf without leave. There's your calf," he smiled; "we can kill it for your homecoming if you like."

I shook my head.

"I didn't think you'd want us to," said Stan.

He and I took a long look at each other. I couldn't guess what he was thinking of me. I didn't know him and didn't think he could know me. Yet here we were, sons of the same mother; had we anything else in common? . . . I thought he must be an honest man, a good man, a hard worker, but within the Revolution his future as an individualist peasant was brief. The Revolution was re-defining "good," and Stan knew it.

Not that he was actively against the *prelom*. In his own way, he saw the menace threatening Slovenia and Yugoslavia. He felt at least remotely the coercions of the industrialized and being-industrialized world that forced the small peasant country into an upheaval, into industrialization. He wasn't actively against Mother's realistic siding with the Revolution. Although she no longer owned the place, she retained her authority in the family owing to the strength of her character and because in the past she had usually been right.

A great storm was on. Mother had looked up and out, and sized up the storm's direction, velocity and scope; and she felt she had found refuge for the family and herself in the new state, in "Tito." Stan was still peering at the clod of earth at his feet, at the rumps of his two horses and eleven cattle. Perhaps he couldn't look up and out. A pang made me put an arm around him as we turned to leave.

Some of the others came into the barn. Paula wanted to show me the hog pen, under the same roof. The twenty-odd pigs, counting a litter of sucklings, were in her charge. "They aren't really ours," she said. The people's committee—the new state—had control of them; in the spring they would be obliged to sell half at a price set by the government. But Paula was very proud of them. She wouldn't say whether the new system was good or bad; apparently she accepted it—perhaps because her son had died in the Revolution to bring it about.

Stan disappeared. I didn't see him again that afternoon. When I asked about him at departure, Mother said slowly: "He may have gone off somewhere." He might have gone to the woods to sit on a stump, or to the hayloft to bury himself in the hay, to be alone, to weep or to think.

Late in the afternoon scores of relatives came to the house to greet the *Amerikanec*. Many I didn't know at all. Some left soon, partly because there was a crowd, partly because they had been near-collaborationists in wartime or didn't like me anyhow, and just wanted a quick look. Several others—cousins, nephews, nieces, in-laws—wore the Liberation Front button signifying their substantial participation in the war. It was a strange intermingling: oil and vinegar in a container momentarily filled and stirred by my arrival.

The outright "Tito" people and those more or less reluctantly for

"Tito" were in the majority. They were full of questions about the United States, my trip, the planes on which I had traveled, my sensations when flying at a great altitude; my impressions of Tito, whom most of them had never seen—and what did I think of this feud between the Yugoslav CP and the Cominform?

There were two cousins, the sisters of a fanatic France had told me about on my first day in Belgrade. In wartime, under religious and anti-Communist slogans, he had butchered scores of men, women, and children whom he and his informers suspected of being pro-Liberation; and after the war he had escaped to Italy and thence, with Vatican help, to Brazil. His sisters did not mention him. There had been civil war in many families: its scars, I thought, would outlive many of the individuals bearing them.

Among the "Tito" people who came to the house was my sister Polda's husband, Anton Prijatelj, a second or third cousin of Ales Bebler's uncle, Ivan Prijatelj, the writer. The ten or twelve years midway between the two world wars when he lived in Cleveland had left their mark on him. His manner was quite American, direct, brash, but not offensively so. He spoke almost fluent if ungrammatical English. Polda, I was told, lay seriously ill in the Ljubljana hospital: in wartime she had gone through hell. In a low, anxious voice Mother urged me to visit her as soon as I could. I said I would the first thing tomorrow.

My father was an old man when I saw him in 1932–33; he died at eighty-four in '38. Now, it seemed, his last two brothers out of four were on their deathbeds in the village, one of them in the house across the road. Mother thought I should call on them even though they had both been anti-Liberation.

"*Revcka*—poor wretches," she said. "We shouldn't hold their politics against them when they're dying."

"The only reason they're still alive," said sister Toncka, "is because they were waiting for you to come back. Uncle Miha, especially. The talk through the valley is that he wants to give you a piece of his mind. Now that you're here, they'll die, and of course *reakcija* around here will blame you for their deaths. But don't let that worry you." Later her son Tine told me that Toncka was secretary of the Liberation Front organization in her neighborhood in Ljubljana and a candidate for membership in the CP of Slovenia. Politically, she was her son's child too—like old Dusanka, the Serbian woman I had met at the Serbian CP Congress.

First I called on eighty-one-year-old Uncle France, whose shrunken giant's frame was still over-long for the bed on which he lay motionless. He asked if I had ever seen his son who emigrated to the Argentine in 1928. He had asked me the same question in 1932. I explained again that the Argentine was farther from where I lived in the United States than Yugoslavia was, and that I had never been there. But I couldn't tell if the old man understood me or not, or really cared. He closed his eyes and said nothing more. He died three months later.

At eighty-six, Uncle Miha was a ghost of the man I had known and liked in my boyhood and also on my previous visit. He couldn't or didn't want to lift his hand to take mine. By then I knew he had been pro-quisling along with one of his sons, a "rich" peasant or *kulak,* and that he remained a bitter anti-Communist. A deep chasm lay between us, and not knowing what else to say, I asked my embittered uncle how his bees were, for I remembered him most pleasantly as an apiarist. But that had been long ago, perhaps longer for Miha than for me. He didn't reply. Instead, the skin-enveloped skeleton raised itself slightly and a cracked, weirdly distant voice spoke:

"I waited for you, Lojze . . . to tell you . . . to tell you myself . . . in my own words . . . that it's all your fault . . . all your fault, just like the priest said it was." He paused, breathing heavily. "The Communists wouldn't have come to power if . . . if you didn't know Roosevelt and make all that propaganda in America. . . . All your fault," he repeated, not looking at me. "If it weren't for you . . . the Anglo-Americans would have invaded here as Churchill wanted. . . . They would have come from Trieste and taken over . . . and the Communists would have lost. . . . All your fault."

The voice fell silent and the hate-pickled skeleton slumped back. Two weeks later Uncle Miha died.

No doubt he had rehearsed his fantastic speech. Perhaps his son, a man close to sixty, who didn't show his face on the afternoon of my first visit to the village, had coached him. To deny my responsibility, or rather to take credit, for the "Anglo-Americans'" failure to invade western Yugoslavia would have been pointless. The old man might not have understood, or would not have believed the whole story of Winston Churchill's long and futile struggle with the American war leaders for an invasion of Europe's "soft underbelly"—how Churchill originally wanted a Balkan push instead of an early second front in France, but was overruled by President Roosevelt at Cairo in November 1943: how Churchill continued to oppose a cross-Channel invasion even as late as mid-May 1944: and how in the summer of that year, after the Allied breakthrough in Normandy, Churchill demanded that troops allocated for the invasion of Southern France be transferred to Italy for operations in the Balkans, specifically for an Allied push into Yugoslavia from Trieste through the Ljubljana Gap, and that in this instance Washington (Roosevelt, Marshall, Leahy, the Joint Chiefs of Staffs) let General Eisenhower make the decision and overrule Churchill.[1]

It would have been vain, too, to argue with my uncle, trapped in a vise worse than death, that the strong Tito forces and the whole revolutionary impulse in Slovenia and throughout Yugoslavia had also had a share in precluding such an invasion, and that I hadn't had anything to do with building them up.

As I returned to Ljubljana toward evening, my mind was in a whirl. I kept thinking that all this I had plunged into would be endurable only by a deliberate effort at detachment, by seeing it against what I had learned in Belgrade; in short, that I, the relative of these people, would serve them, myself, and everybody else best if I managed to turn the maze of impressions and feelings over to the writer.

When I got back to Ljubljana from my homeplace, I thought I might have a chance to wash up and change and possibly stretch out for an hour before going to Josip Vidmar's for dinner, at eight. But in the guest-house where someone had taken my bags, and where I was informed I had a room, I was given a message from Polda's doctor that, even though it was long past visiting hours, I should go to her bedside at once.

Dr. Bozidar Lavric—who had been in New York and Boston a year and a half before, catching up with the latest advances in American medicine—was waiting for me in the hospital office. He said that the effects of my sister's wartime experience on her nervous system had converged into an acute internal goiter. An operation was necessary. But first she needed quiet and strength. Ever since she had read of my

---

[1] See pp. 194, 198, 245 and 281–84 of General Dwight Eisenhower's *Crusade in Europe* (Doubleday: 1948) . . . the middle of page 644 of *My Three Years With Eisenhower,* by Captain Harry C. Butcher, USNR (Simon & Schuster: 1946) . . . and pp. 368–72 and 408–409 of General Mark H. Clark's *Calculated Risk* (Harper: 1950).

arrival in Yugoslavia, four days ago, she had been intensely impatient to see me, and it hadn't helped her. Dr. Lavric said I could stay with her for an hour. I should let her talk, and it might help if I came to see her daily for a while.

I found my sister weeping. Unable to say a word for a long time, she gripped my hand. Then she asked if I knew, or had heard of, a priest named M. who in 1945 escaped from Slovenia into Austria and now lived, still a priest, in the United States.

I said I didn't know him, or of him; what about him?

"Well, he was the priest in the village near where Anton and I have our farm," Polda said. "We were for the Partisans from the start, although not actively in the daytime. At night men came from the woods and we gave them food, and Anton became one of their liaison-men in our valley. M. got wind of it, so he had the Italian-fascist occupation authorities grab Anton, and they sent him to the concentration camp on Rab"—an island off Dalmatia, where in two years over nine thousand died of thirst, hunger, exposure, and disease. "It is a miracle Anton stayed alive. While he was on Rab, M. came with his gunmen every few weeks and threatened me with death and hell. Eight times I looked into the muzzle of a rifle, revolver, or tommy-gun. Each time I thought it was the end. Each time M. was there, watching me to see if I were afraid; and I was, but I tried not to show it. He called me a Communist and names I can't repeat. He had lots of people killed or shipped off to concentration camps where they died. But he told his gunmen not to waste a bullet on me. Eight times he did this. Why? To break me? Because he knew I was your sister? He never mentioned you, but I felt he was thinking of you. Or was he persecuting Anton and me, to begin with, because I am your sister? Or is he simply a beast? A priest! How can I explain him? Why didn't he send me to Rab too? I don't know. I got to be a nervous wreck and sick otherwise. That was what M. wanted, I think. I asked him, but he wouldn't say. He just leered at me."

Polda lay quietly for a while, holding my hand. The light in the ward was dim, and I couldn't see her very well, but she looked at least ten years older than she was.

"I was too sick to be of any use to the Partisans," she continued; "I would have been a burden to them. So I went to the woods and lived by myself like an animal. Once a week or so, I dragged myself home at night to get some food and clothes. Most of the time I lay in the underbrush, wrapped in damp blankets. I worried about Mother. I thought if she were alive, the others must be all right too. They didn't know about Anton and me; they must be worrying about us. I myself had no idea if Anton were still alive.

"I tried to pray, as Mother had taught us when we were children, but I couldn't. Priest M. got between me and God, and other priests who I knew were worse than M. He, so far as I know, didn't kill anybody with his own two hands. I began to doubt there was a God, and I was scared of myself." Polda paused and sighed deeply. "If there is a God, I wondered, will He punish me? Is He punishing me now? But if there is a God, how can He allow all this to happen? Does the Pope know? . . .

"When you were home last time, we never spoke of such things, but I noticed you didn't go to church, and it seemed you didn't approve of Mimi being a nun. So when I thought M. would have them shoot me, and when I hid in the woods, I thought of you in far-away America all the time. Could you know about us? Could you know what was happening here, what we were going through, what M. and some of the other priests were doing in the name of God? . . . Oh, there were good priests too. Yes, there were wonderful men! *Real* priests. Like Father Leopold, the Prior of the Carthusian monastery in Pleterje. He was on the side of the Partisans all the way through and now he supports the Tito revolution. You should meet him. . . . And there were priests who weren't for the Partisans, but were good priests just the same, ministering to the people as usual. . . .

"After the war I tried to write to you, but I couldn't get it down. Once, I guess it was early in 1946, I scrawled on a piece of paper *Please come home at once. Your loving sister, Polda,* and I was going to mail it, but Anton wouldn't let me. He said you wouldn't understand: how could you? You might think I was hysterical, crazy: and maybe I was. . . . I forgot to tell you that Anton came back from Rab in '43 after Italy capitulated looking like a ghost, but, thank God, his health wasn't affected seriously. He was in America a long time and so I guess he knew you better than I did, although he never met you. Anyhow, that's what he told me: not to mail the letter."

She paused.

"Why does America give refuge to such a beast as M.? You say you never heard of him? . . . Anton would say: naturally. America is so big, and a creature like that just slips in. That's how Anton explained it to me, but it's hard for me to understand. . . ."

On my fourth visit to Polda she suddenly asked me: "You know about Ante?"

"I know he committed suicide."

She closed her eyes, and said after a while: "There was never a more wonderful human being than Ante. Always so happy, so good-natured; always kindly toward everybody, always the life of every gathering. He was *no* collaborationist!

"The Germans captured him and made him sweep streets in Ptuj" —a town in Styria. "He had no head for politics; maybe he was too good for politics, too good for war. I don't mean that those who fought in the *borba* were not good; they were, oh, so good, many of them. But I think the world needs people who are beyond and above some of the occurrences going on from day to day and from year to year; don't you? . . .

"Ante was unusual. I suppose he figured that, war or no war, under Germans or under anybody else, it was good to have clean streets. That's how he was. . . . He had only four years of schooling, but he wrote poetry. Often he spoke like a poet. We know that after his death Paula found a batch of his poems, but she won't show them to anybody. Even Mother hasn't seen them. Paula may not show them to you either. Don't ask her. God knows what's in them, and Paula may lie to you, too, that the poems are 'nothing' and she doesn't remember where she put them. That's what she said to me. That's how she is. If she shows them to you, it will be of her own accord."

(Paula didn't show me the poems. Others in the family also told me that she had a bundle of Ante's manuscripts.)

"He wasn't a collaborationist," Polda said. "Maybe he tried to escape from the Germans but couldn't. . . . After the war he came back to the village and he was arrested and put in prison and investigated, and in a few weeks he was released—*not* guilty of collaboration. And for a year or so that was that: everything was fine. Then the neighbors, our relatives mostly, began to gossip about him, and he must have suffered unspeakably. He said nothing to anyone. He was cheerful and worked hard as usual. He could fix anything, and he fixed everything for everybody, not only at home but wherever anyone asked him to.

He did most of the work repairing the damage to the house. . . .
Then, a year ago last autumn, after he helped nearly everybody in the
village to put in the harvest, they found him——"

Polda's hand tightened on mine.

"How old was he?" I asked.

"Thirty-six."

"Why do you think he did it?"

Polda answered after a while: "All that any of us know is that there
was a lot of talk behind his back that reached him, but he couldn't
pin it on anybody. One bit of gossip was that Ante had been let out only
because of you, because the new government wouldn't keep a brother
of yours in jail; and that when you returned again, you would give
him a piece of your mind. Of course you knew nothing about it. . . .
It was sheer malice or politics, or both. Anton believes it was politics
thought up by *reakcija* to hit our family after the war. Ante smiled at
all of it: but as it turned out, only outside. Inside, he suffered. I guess
he noticed people looking at him differently. I heard that once, a
couple of months before he hanged himself, when he entered an inn,
the people suddenly fell silent. Before the war, and even right after he
came out of prison all cleared, they used to greet him with shouts and
make him sit with them."

"Who were those people at the inn?" I asked.

Polda told me some of the names. I didn't recognize them. She told
me their stories, and characterized them. In all probability, none of
them made up the gossip. They repeated it. Some were "new Communists." Their part in the war of Liberation was questionable but in
1945, when the "Anglo-Americans" failed to even try to take over
Slovenia and Dalmatia, they vaulted on the Tito bandwagon; and in
'46 and '47 they had to reassure themselves and others that they supported the new regime.

"There were other such incidents," said Polda. "And gossip, gossip,
gossip——"

"Who, precisely, started it?" I asked. "And why?"

"*Reakcija*—that's all we know," said Polda. "If I told you who we
think is responsible for it in and around our village, that would be
gossip too, as Mother says. She told us not to engage in guesswork, not
even among ourselves. Anton is sure, though, that the whole business
was politics thought up by priests like M. You don't agree?" she asked
when I shook my head.

"It sounds a little far-fetched," I said, "but possible," I added on second thought. *"When* did the gossip start?"

"We don't know," said Polda, "but Anton and I figure it must have been in the second half of '46. Why do you ask?"

I shook my head. I was thinking of an "Open Letter to Louis Adamic" published in the pro-Clerical, anti-Tito Slovenian-language paper in Cleveland, *Ameriska Domovina* [The American Homeland], and signed by the war-criminal cousin who had escaped to Brazil: but I couldn't remember the approximate date of publication. At that time I had no idea the cousin was a war criminal or a refugee in South America. I knew he was uneducated and that he couldn't have composed this letter sprinkled with Latin phrases. The letter said "Communists" were persecuting my brother Ante, and asked: "How in God's name, my dear cousin [meaning me], can you go on supporting Tito's terrorist regime?" . . .

"It may sound far-fetched to you," said Polda after a pause, "because you didn't live in Slovenia during the war. If you did, you would believe that *reakcija* is capable of anything."

To my mind, I said, it was unlikely that Ante killed himself because of the gossip or the persecution, if that was what it was. The gossip may have caused something to snap in him, but the tension that snapped under the weight of the gossip was something else. "Was he in love?" I asked.

"Yes," said Polda; "but none of us knows much about that, either. The girl was too broken up to talk. She's gone to work in a factory somewhere. I can't believe love was the reason."

I am the oldest, and by law and custom Mother should have signed the old *domacija* (homestead) over to me; but I didn't want it, and I had written her so early in 1946 when the question arose. I suggested she sign it over to Stan or to anyone else she wished. I added it didn't matter greatly what she did with the property; for the way the winds were blowing, it wouldn't remain in private ownership long. Now, talking with Polda, it suddenly occurred to me: "Did Ante want the property?"

"No-o-o-o," said Polda, thoughtfully, "I don't think he did. There was some discussion of whether Stan or Ante should have it, but Ante said he didn't want it. Besides, Stan was the next oldest after you, and he had put in all his life working on the place, just like Ante. Ante laughed and said he agreed with you: that private ownership would soon be over, and it didn't matter who owned our *domacija* meantime."

"What Ante said and what he thought or felt," I said, "may be two different things."

"No, I believe he really wanted Stan to have the property. Early in '46 he spoke of going to Ljubljana by-and-by, or some other place, and getting a job in one of the new factories. That's where the future was, he used to say. He didn't go right away because he felt he was needed on the farm. He didn't want Mother to feel she had to work so hard in her old age. Also, part of the house was in ruins, and he liked rebuilding it according to nephew Tine's plans."

"He probably didn't want to leave," I thought aloud. "He may have been afraid of going into a factory, or of gossip pursuing him wherever he went."

"Maybe," said Polda, thinking. "Maybe, as you say, the gossip only snapped something inside him; but if that is so, *it* did snap it; and I would say it was meant to. . . . The war and Revolution brought out many wonderful qualities in some people, but also much horror, evil and meanness in others; and sometimes I think evil is much smarter than goodness. Maybe somebody on the *reakcija* side knew Ante better than we did."

"You blame it on *reakcija*," I interrupted. "That's a word. I can't say you're wrong, but it seems the 'new Communists' also contributed toward making life miserable for Ante. He may have felt he was caught in a riptide and couldn't see a way out for himself and into something where he would belong and be at ease. . . . But I interrupted you: what else were you going to say?"

"I wanted to say," said Polda after a moment, "that Anton and I are convinced the purpose of the gossip was to hit at our family because we had people in the Partisans while some of our relatives and others in the vicinity were anti-Liberation or tried to straddle the fence. Also, because you, one of us, were in America. And also, because France and Joze are educated and have fairly big jobs in the new state. Envy, envy.

"So many people were envious when—just before the war—Anica married a doctor. And she's almost positive that [one of our cousins] informed on her husband and is responsible for his death. Did she tell you? Well, maybe Mother told her not to. About a year ago, Anica suddenly said she wanted to stick a knife into [that cousin], and Mother seized her by the shoulders and told her to get the thought out of her head. 'He may have done what you suspect,' said Mother, 'but what good will it do for you to kill him? Killing must stop! The way to stop it is to stop. If we're ever to have a little peace of mind again, we must stop acting on mere suspicion. We must know what we're doing.' Of course Mother is right; suspicion is like poison: it destroys you. But there is Anica, a young woman and a widow. Every minute of the day her son reminds her of her dead husband. That Boris of hers, isn't he wonderful? Anica came to see me yesterday and she brought him along. The first thing he said to me was 'I'm Tito's!' and up went his tiny clenched fist. Oh, it gladdened my heart to look at him. I can't doubt that life will be better for him than it has been for us or for Mother.

"For a few months after Ante hanged himself we were afraid for Mother. She aged so. She seemed to be caving in before our eyes. She wanted to be alone; I guess she prayed and thought. For a while none of us could look one another in the eye. We drew apart. It was different when Anica's husband died, or Paula's Ivan. Then we grieved together. That was war, that was Revolution. Ante's death, though—after the war—was a terrible reproach to us all. We each felt lonely and cut off."

The large ward room, full of other patients, wasn't the best place to talk. But it didn't bother Polda; nor me by the third or fourth visit. The ward nurse said talking was doing my sister good. . . . A few months after the operation she was well again.

I learned more from Polda about our family than from any of the others. Between visits to her bedside, thinking over all that had happened to them, I felt as though I was pressed against Yugoslavia's heart, feeling its palpitations and its steady beat; and at times as though I was peering at an X-ray of Yugoslavia's insides.

Tito? And "Tito"? The questions kept popping into my writer's mind. What was the whole story? The total of all the stories like my family's? Was Tito's own story, which I didn't know, like them or different? Something special that threaded the others together? Or did Tito's story have meaning only in the light of the flashes of the others? . . .

Josip Vidmar is a Slovenian whose tough, honest, clearly expressive mind lurks behind a finely woven screen of irony, and whose face, at once vividly boyish and wearily middle-aged, is ready to crack into a smile at the least provocation. His wife, an opera singer, was Carmen that evening, so the dinner to which he had asked me on the day of my arrival in Slovenia was stag. Some of the others at the party were writers and editors whom I knew in 1932–33.

After we disposed of my air trip, of Truman and Dewey and Wallace, of Howard Fast, and of several other subjects related to these, America and I were set aside for a while, and Josip Vidmar and Ferdo Kozak fell into a wrangle over the next chapter in the careeer of France Preseren.

Preseren was a lesser Goethe, a contemporary and spiritual kin of Pushkin and of Adam Mickiewicz, the great Polish poet who also is largely unknown in Western Europe and America. In the second quarter of the nineteenth century, he composed a few hundred poems, some of them exquisite, with deep insights—and this in the Slovenian language, which until then scarcely anyone had used as a medium of literary expression. Preseren was the first major—and remains the foremost—Slovenian poet. His verse and biography are one of the firmest cultural bases of Slovenian nationhood. An heir of eighteenth-century Enlightenment, he wrote a few poems which are clearly political. During 1941–45 they were recited by Partisans going into battle. The Slovenian contingent of the Yugoslav revolutionary forces, under the direct leadership of such men as Edvard Kardelj, Boris Kidric and Josip Vidmar, was deftly geared to Preseren and to a handful of writers who came in his wake and further enriched the Slovenian language and strengthened the little nation's link with European culture.

Preseren died on February 8, 1849 . . . and now, on the eve of the centenary of his death, as I gathered from the Vidmar-Kozak exchange, all of Slovenia—in fact all of Yugoslavia—was busy with preparations for its *proslava* or commemoration, to be held in the second week in February. And Slovenians, notably the intelligentsia, were involved in a sizzling argument whether to leave his remains where they were, in the cemetery in the town of Kranj, where he died, or transfer them to his native village of Vrba, thirty-odd kilometers away. The transfer idea had a point in that annually tens of thousands of people visited both the poet's grave and his birthplace (a humble, curiously beautiful old peasant house, now a national shrine), and were the grave also in Vrba, it would save a lot of time and traveling.

Of course the town of Kranj was up in arms against the whole idea, and had sympathizers throughout Slovenia. Just then it was, in fact, the hottest surface issue in the land.

Vidmar was for the transfer, Kozak against it.

"I'd say," said Vidmar, "that if Preseren could put in his word on the question, he'd want to be back in Vrba."

"I'd say," Kozak said, "that he'd want to be left alone."

Preseren's grave remains in Kranj, and I visited it, as I did his old homeplace in Vrba. In fact, I participated in some of the week-long observance which was front-page material not only in the Republic of Slovenia but throughout Yugoslavia. The several radio stations had special Preseren programs. Tito issued a statement on the poet's significance. Edvard Kardelj and Boris Kidric each wrote an essay on the subject, as did Josip Vidmar, Ferdo Kozak, and many other writers in Ljubljana, Belgrade, and other centers. The university library in Ljubljana arranged an exhibit of Preseren manuscripts, letters, and early editions. Bookshops featured books by and about him. Pictures of him were displayed in the show-windows of most other stores. National flags with the red star in the middle and CP banners with the hammer and sickle were out everywhere.

Kardelj and Kidric came to Slovenia for Preseren Week. So did Rodoljub Colakovic, a long-time Bosnian Communist, who spent most of his early youth in prison, now Minister of *Prosveta* (enlightenment, education, culture, civilization) in the Federal Government. So did representatives of all the other five People's Republics—Serbia, Croatia, Montenegro, Bosnia-Herzegovina and Macedonia—and of writers' and artists' organizations. They made pilgrimages to the grave in Kranj and to the peasant hut in Vrba. Speakers eulogized aspects of the poet's life and work. Organizations and individuals placed wreaths and small bouquets around his monument—the biggest monument in Ljubljana—till the heap was halfway up the pedestal.

The climax of the commemoration was the *akademija* held before a capacity audience in the largest hall in Ljubljana. The symphony orchestra, conducted by an Italian from Trieste who likes to live in Yugoslavia, played Beethoven's *Eroica*. Actors recited Preseren's poems; I recalled having to know some of them by heart when I was a *gymnasium* student in Ljubljana long ago. And a young man, Boris Ziherl—he, too, served time in prison before the war: and now is Director of the Institute of Social Studies, started in Belgrade in 1948—delivered the commemorative address.

The newspapers published the full text the next day. The essay is evidently intended to establish poet Preseren forever as a main influence in the leftward process from way back to its culmination in the Slovenian and the all-Yugoslav Revolution. It elaborates on the progressive forces from before the Renaissance till after the Enlightenment that went into the poet's makeup. But it specially stresses the acceptance of justice and truth as basic values, and the habit of resistance to injustice, to brutality, and to the lie as ingrained characteristics of the Slovenian people—a small, stubborn breed which for a thousand years withstood all the efforts of powerful and aggressive neighbors to whittle it down and destroy it. Preseren, according to Ziherl, is the offspring and the summation of those values and that character, now at long last breathing full in the first Slovenian state, a people's republic within a family of people's republics. Slovenia found her true character in the heat of the War of Liberation and the Revolution, and is now demonstrating her fiber in building socialism and in facing, with the rest of Yugoslavia, the appalling behavior of the Cominform countries. (*"Long and thunderous applause,"* greeted this statement, as was noted parenthetically in the text.)

It was past midnight at a party at Miha Marinko's, in February 1949, when the main table got around to America and Russia. Then for the next two hours the theme of the conversation was gigantism: the simultaneously blind drive and cunning game of the big powers which, if not checked, can lead only to disaster. It was a somber subject. My contribution to it wasn't mine but William James'. I tried to give the gist of his aversion to great things and big things and his bent for stirrings within and among individuals; which, it occurred to me a while later, was not quite apropos—for what the rest of them had in mind, being convinced collectivists, was the good potential performance of small nations because they were small *versus* the actual bad performance of big powers because they were big. By-and-large it was Josip Vidmar who led the conversation.

In 1932 he published a little book, *Slovenia's Cultural Problems,* in which he dealt, rather cursorily and (not being a Communist then) nationalistically with the promise inherent in the plight of the tiny Slovenian nation. King Alexander's *diktatura* promptly suppressed it.

I read the book in 1932 or '33, and have it before me now. It contains references to Goethe and Preseren, and presents the idea that Slovenians have a mission too, perhaps largely a "cultural-artistic mission," as other small peoples have. The Ancient Greeks, a small nation, formulated the values that today's civilization goes by. The Israelites produced Christianity. The English produced Shakespeare soon after they overcame their fear of Spanish aggression and before they even thought of taking a fling at the big-power game. Dante appeared in tiny Tuscany; Goethe, when Germany was of scant account. In modern times the Norwegians, only a shade more numerous than the Slovenians, enriched the world with Ibsen, Bojer, Undset. And the Slovenians have France Preseren—

Within the human race [wrote Vidmar in *Kulturni problemi slovenstva*] *there is a great cultureward impulse, which is not marching to its goal in a compact formation. If it did, it could not get anywhere. To move on, it broke up into a multitude of clans, peoples, nations, and cultures; each is a plant, a vine, a tree by itself with its own roots, each growing stems, sprays, twigs, and blossoms according to its nature. Thus humanity enjoys the benefit of more light than it would, were it a single living structure. The human community is too great an organism to be warmed by one heart. So it separated into smaller units, each with a heart of its own. Therein is the real significance of nationhood.*

Nations which came into existence [in large part under the above-mentioned cultureward impulse] *are diverse not only in their initial characteristics but also in their numbers or size. We have big and small nations. The central purpose of the one and the other is the same—culture.*

Which attains it more readily?

One can say the spirit of a big nation is like a heartbeat's echo along an organism's peripheries. This, I know, is an imperfect analogy, but it suggests a touch of truth. The bigger a nation, the less agile it is, the harder it is for its spiritual center to spread its riches to all its spheres and the slower is its culture in getting around to caress and embrace the masses.

And, conversely, the smaller a nation the more intensively are its members drawn to the core of its cultural work and life, and the more vitally the central energy reverberates through the entire body. A small nation is like a peninsula barely linked to the mainland: waves wash against it on all sides and breezes play over it. The heavy fogs and ill-smelling fumes that as likely as not settle over a big nation only a hurricane can clear away.

Big nations have at their disposal great physical resources which a quick glance may regard as significantly advantageous. Sober thought, however, soon suggests that their very might encumbers them with inner perils and with "duties" which . . . *violate human nature. A nation's great physical might is a perpetual threat not only to others but also a menace to itself.*

This paradox is intolerable and needs to be masked with an aspect of congruency which politicians call balance. The creation and maintenance of that mask, however, is a dangerous and exhausting task which cannot but draw energy and talent away from cultural [the really important human] *activity. Indeed, in its ultimate sense the awful task which is the lot of big nations, of big powers, is quite sterile. . . .*

The so-called great nations persuade themselves that besides cultural duties they have urgent political "missions" in the world. Essentially, however, these "missions" are so much of nothing-at-all, for, to repeat, they draw upon human powers that ought to be going into cultural creativeness. . . .

Look at the First World War. All the big European countries were involved in the bloody mess induced by the need of rearranging the "balance," of devising a new mask, whereas a good many of the little countries stayed, or could easily have stayed, out of it. Those small countries which did stay out of it went on attending to man's real job, building culture, while the big nations had begun to slip culturally . . . [as witness] *such phenomena as Nazism in Germany.* [Freely translated by L.A.]

Thus Vidmar in 1932. Now a Communist, he retains a large portion of that thesis, but his emphases have shifted. In 1941–45 he helped to lead the small Slovenian nation in an uprising because Communists Kardelj and Kidric had convinced him, as he told me, that to try to stay out of war would mean the end of the Slovenians. Now he and many other Yugoslav leaders feel that the "gigantisms" of America and Russia are both bad, although one is capitalistic and the other supposedly socialistic.

Both colossi, the Vidmar thesis continues, are out to "solve" their problems by becoming still bigger—through expansionism, through imperialism, such as history hasn't witnessed before. And of course this means a third world war, which, the chances are, will solve nothing. This war might be prevented if somebody somewhere takes a stand against it and reveals the real problem and begins to create an anti-"gigantism" attitude in a considerable number of people around the world—in America and Russia, too. Here it occurred to me that my reference to William James hadn't been inapposite; so I repeated it, and Vidmar asked me to get him the exact quotation. ("I am done with great things and big things, great institutions and big success, and I am for those tiny invisible molecular moral forces that work from individual to individual, creeping through the crannies of the world like so many rootlets, or like the capillary oozing of water, yet which, if you give them time, will rend the hardest monuments of man's pride.")

When the other guests got wind of what the discussion was about, they rose from their corners and crowded around our table and listened.

No one said this outright but I couldn't help sensing that anti-"gigantism" was an oblique factor in the Yugoslav side of the American airplane incident, and that their insight into Russia as a "giant" is a fundamental reason for the Cominform-Tito split.

Since the Marinko party I've been asking questions about all this at other sessions and while talking with individuals. And I find that a number of people in Ljubljana—perhaps because they're members of one of the smallest nations in Europe—are aware of a good deal of literature pertaining to "gigantism."

The pro-"gigantism" literature is immense and familiar. It was produced by the "giants" themselves. To disguise its mad drives, it emanates messianism. Dostoievski, with his terrible insight into man, into the Russian makeup particularly, wrote as though he foresaw Stalin's USSR in detail: "Every great people believes and must believe that in itself and itself alone lies the salvation of the world, that it lives only to lead all other peoples and is predestined to exercise such leadership." In the United States we have Henry R. Luce, with his messianic "American Century" idea, whose *Time, Life,* and *Fortune* are the principal megaphones of the successors of the American financier in Joseph Conrad's *Nostromo.* In Britain some of the most talented writers (Kipling, *et al.*) were ideologists of "the White Man's Burden" and mere soldiers in the struggle for expansion and power.

Anti-"gigantism"—in keeping with itself—has a less voluminous literature, but it is no less interesting. "There is a point," wrote Guglielmo Ferrero, "beyond which might tends to devour itself." (I am translating from the Slovenian translation of the essay entitled "Address to the Deaf.") "Reality is nothing but a scheme of limitations."

There was a Frenchman, André Suarès, who apparently commanded some respect as a thinker. I never heard of him before; he died in 1948. A few excerpts translated, also *via* a Slovenian translation, from his book *Vues sur l'Europe* (Paris: Grassett. 1939):

I stress the greatness of little nations. They . . . are of the scale to fit the human being. . . . The small countries . . . have the atmosphere in which the [sound? worthwhile?] *modern individual has developed. The big empires have not even begun to understand the laws essential to human dignity. Big empires have quantity; small nations cultivate quality.*

All that makes us humans we owe to [values evolved within] *small political units. . . . All the vast empires . . . have worked against the spirit . . . have dulled the conscience . . . have wanted unity through uniformity . . . have scorned the unique . . .* [have suppressed] *the longing for justice that ever turns against the destructive pressures of utilitarianism. . . .*

The big nations . . . have slavish numbers. The small nations have ideas, originality . . .

The Amsterdam of Rembrandt, Huyghens, and Spinoza was greatly preferable to the Turkey which dominated large sections of Europe and Asia for nine centuries. The Spain of Cervantes . . . will live for ever; the "great" realm of Phillip II is naught but a remembrance of disaster.

Always the barbarians are empires, never [little] *nations. . . .* [Big nations] *degenerate into bee-hives and ant-heaps. A small nation's affinity is with Pascal in his garret, with lonely Shakespeare at Stratford, with aging Goethe in Weimar, ever with the poet, ever creative. Empires are built with the cement of servitude: they live in the belly. Little nations move with heart, reason, consciousness.*

. . . Great empires are great mainly in that they have great cannon factories. They excel in destruction. The little nations are the salt of the earth.

Of course this is as objectionable as a big nation's chauvinism based on physical paramountcy and disguised as messianism. If the giant has a global complex, looking down, the dwarf obviously has a distorted perspective, looking up. Neither can see much good about the other. In this juxtaposition, the small-nation personality—like the personality of Vidmar's Russian guest who wanted him to take the impressionist pictures off his walls, like the personality of some of the American Marshall Planners in Europe—is also problematical, even to itself. To free themselves of fear, to preserve their identity, to survive, many Slovenians have taken to "Marxism-Leninism" like a fish to water and are mainly unaware of such contradictions as, *one,* that "M-L-ism" is itself a gigantism, a vast and complex reaction to the Industrial Revolution, to the Machine Age, aiming to overcome its evils; *two,* that as it has worked out in Russia "M-L-ism" is as full of unbalances and incongruities as the gigantism it aims to displace, "free-enterprise" capitalism; and *three,* that either "M-L-ism" is driving the Soviet Union into ever greater gigantism (as "democratic capitalism" is the

United States) or that "M-L-ism" may be the gigantic means for the Russian Empire to grow bigger. (Of course, if the Slovenians and other Yugoslavs had been aware of these contradictions, "M-L-ism" would not have served them as it has up to now. When you embrace an idea in a moment of crisis, it's no good to you; it doesn't infuse you with the necessary fervor and resolution, unless you believe in it utterly and tumble to none of the *buts* which begin to plague you later.)

Boiled down, as I see it, anti-"gigantism" is the clenched fist of a small nation that finds itself in the most-traveled crossroads of world imperialisms and messianisms and wants to survive.

BOOK ONE

CHAPTER SEVEN: *The false spring . . .*
and the eagle in a plight

> *I remember the first albatross I ever saw. It was*
> *during a prolonged gale, in waters hard upon*
> *the Antarctic seas. From my forenoon watch be-*
> *low, I ascended to the over-clouded deck; and*
> *there, dashed upon the main hatches, I saw a re-*
> *gal, feathery thing of unspotted whiteness, and*
> *with a hooked, Roman bill sublime. . . . Though*
> *bodily unharmed, it uttered cries, as some king's*
> *ghost in supernatural distress. Through its inex-*
> *pressible, strange eyes, methought I peeped to*
> *secrets which took hold of God.*
> —HERMAN MELVILLE: *Moby Dick*

THE BRIGHT GENTLE DAYS I found in Slovenia when I
arrived there continued through the rest of January and
throughout February. The infrequent rain squall, snow
flurry, or dry blow only accented the unusual weather.

Out walking in the wooded Upland—ten or twelve kilometers from
Yugoslavia's uneasy Carinthian boundary with Austria—it was sheer

delight to come upon splashes of white, yellow, and purple wildflowers in the sheltered corners of clearings on sunward slopes. It was a keener, more complex sensation than delight to round a trail's bend and have my sight filled with a pair of deer not ten yards away.

A light breeze was blowing toward me and my steps must have been soundless on the path's mossy shoulder from which winds earlier in the winter had swept the dry leaves. I stopped dead, holding my breath. The doe nuzzled at a patch of newly sprung-up shoots of a forest plant. The buck was on the alert but his nose and ears were momentarily into the breeze, away from me, and my nearness didn't register for perhaps five seconds.

It flashed on them both simultaneously. The male emitted an ultra-urgent sound, and, with a bound so swift and lithe I barely perceived it, they vanished in the close-by undergrowth.

In the New York office of the United States Department of State, where I applied for a passport without the rubber-stamped injunction barring me from Yugoslavia, I had been warned that my native country wasn't safe for American citizens.

Now in Slovenia I carried no identification papers, and my pockets bulged with enough notebooks, scratch-pads, and pencils to give me every appearance of a hard-working Cominform agent disguised as an imperialist spy, or the other way about. I wanted a taste of the "Tito terror." But no one stopped me to inquire about my identity or anything else. I moved about as I chose, going wherever I wished; at the end of January and the beginning of February by myself, later sometimes with others. Now and then I came to a remote mountain hamlet whose name I didn't know or bother to find out. With tiny bare fields and great woods about them, these settlements spelled Peace itself.

One afternoon, wandering on and off a trail in a thinned-out forest, I heard a thrashing ahead. It came sporadically. Going toward it during a quiet interval, I thought for a moment I might have veered away from it, when the commotion exploded once more directly in front of me. A large, brownish-black object near the base of a tall beech was heaving upward, flapping in the air, and hitting the ground with a thudding might.

It was an eagle with a five- or six-foot wingspread. His beak was clamped around a protruding root—I couldn't see how, but evidently in such a way that he couldn't free himself.

The great wings spread, shuddered, rose; and cracked down over and over again. The neck writhed and yanked, and I thought the body might tear itself from the head. At the same time the talons ripped and scratched under the root; dirt and bits of molding leaves hurtled in all directions. To no avail. Then, as if done in at that instant, exhausted beyond fear or rage, the eagle collapsed; the crown of his head matted with blood where crows had pecked at him. The eyes—redbrown with an almost black center—were glazed, fixed as if in an unseeing stare, and utterly distressing. The head, though distorted by strain, possessed a fierce kind of dignity.

A sharp wind swirled about the mountainside. It cut low amid the bare trees and lifted away some of the loose eagle feathers. I shook with cold. The crows cawed high in the branches of a near-by tree.

They set the eagle off into another frenzy. His wings and tail lashed the ground and air. The talons scratched under the unyielding root. They groped for it and missed. They clawed the earth while the wings thrashed and dirt and leaves and sand and feathers flew. Then the eagle's long neck twisted itself as one might twist an empty waterhose, the wings folded down on themselves, the fanned-out tail drew together, and the whole body flopped over, bottom side up—again without result. The mandibles remained wedged. Presently the neck unwound itself tortuously, the body turned top side up, and the eagle sank into another spell of near-exhaustion.

The westering sun vanished behind a bank of clouds. The wind whistled steadily. There was a brief snow flurry, and I watched the flakes melting on my cold, tensely clasped hands. A crow cawed again.

Another shudder shook the eagle. He was still alive—not yet dead, anyhow. I touched his head, meaning to brush off the dirt and investigate how bad the wounds under it were.

Suddenly the great bird heaved himself in another tremendous convulsion so sudden and swift that the fear it evoked in me flung me backward. In a blur I saw his head jerk itself loose, and he shot past me.

He half-dropped, half-alighted about twenty yards away. His partly spread-out tail and wings trailed the ground. Tilted in a lopsided stance, he tried with partial success to right himself. He seemed to find it especially hard to hold up his head: but what worried me most was his beak. It remained open. I wondered again how badly his tongue was hurt. Were the jaws dislocated? Cracked? If they were, he might just as well still be trapped in the root, for he would have died sooner and easier than by starving to death.

But after a while I began to think he would pull through. His efforts to right himself became smoother. His wings spread out, fluttered, folded. His head straightened on his curved neck and stayed straight. He managed to go through a series of hopping, awkward movements.

The cold wind drove the snowflakes at me and past me. The wind closed my eyes. When I opened them, the eagle was well on the way to being an eagle again. He paced, stopped, hopped a bit; then spread his wings and fanned the air. Unexpectedly, he sailed to a stump twenty or thirty yards down the ridge.

I wanted to cheer. But my lips were nearly numb, and I could hardly keep my teeth from chattering.

The disheveled eagle huddled on the stump awhile, his back to me —a heap of uncertainty. Then, rather abruptly, he straightened up, half unfolded and flapped his wings, crouched again, and took off. For a moment he sailed precariously down the ridge, barely clearing the stumps and undergrowth. The wind almost grounded him again, but his wings adjusted themselves to its drive, and he rose with it.

Unable to cry out, I waved to the eagle, then watched the patch of bleak sky over the adjacent mountain until he vanished from view. I was conscious of a trembling inside me.

I knelt by the snake-like root and put on my glasses to examine it closely, especially the bloodied spot where the beak had cut in. I couldn't determine how deep the jaws had been in the twisted wood, so I seized the root with both hands and yanked as hard as I could. It broke more easily than I had expected—at the place where the eagle's beak had been.

Returning to the lodge, cold and drained emotionally, I recalled Melville's curious footnote about the albatross. "Through its inexpressible, strange eyes, methought I peeped to secrets . . ."

The next day was bright and sunny again. The false spring continued for another three weeks.

For months after, as I delved into the Yugoslav story, the incident of the eagle recurred to me again and again. I told others about it, and learned that it is not unusual in Yugoslav forests to find skeletons of eagles, their beaks still fast around protruding roots or ground-crawling vines.

Back in the United States, my attention was drawn to a passage in W. H. Hudson's *The Book of a Naturalist* dealing with oddities the author had encountered in Nature. One story told of a heron whose fate differed from my eagle's, but whose predicament was similar. He had "impaled" his beak in a bony fish. Hudson follows the tale with this comment: "Death by accident is common enough in wild life, and a good proportion of such deaths are due to an error of judgment, often so slight as not to seem an error at all."

Gradually, "my eagle" established himself in my mind as the symbol of Tito, of the Yugoslav Revolution, while the roots began to represent the Soviet and the "Western" systems of life.

BOOK ONE
CHAPTER EIGHT: *Operation Bootstrap . . .*
"Coming up out of the dugout,
out of the filth"

NE MORNING during Preseren Week, Boris Kid-
ric asked me if I'd like to go through Litostroj, the
big new machine and die works visible from the
distance on the outskirts of Ljubljana. I said I certainly would.

"I haven't been there myself for months," Boris said. "Shall I pick
you up at two this afternoon? It takes about three hours to see it all.

And if I get hold of Luka, I'll ask him to come along. Litostroj is his baby, really."

"Luka" is the wartime name of Franc Leskosek, a tall, large man in his mid-fifties; a metal worker before the war, a Communist and trade-union leader since the 1920's; the first commander-in-chief of the Slovenian people's uprising (1941–42); now a member of the CPY Politburo and, as Federal Minister of Heavy Industry, a kingpin in the Yugoslav planned-economy setup which the Cominform split, then in its eighth month, intended to throw out of kilter. I had met him a few days before at a reception which was part of the Preseren centenary, but only to shake hands.

In the car on the way to see "his baby," Leskosek said he was observing Preseren Week mainly by attending to business: and it was a business he wouldn't wish on Stalin even! Open-faced, direct, and humorous, expansive in manner, he made no bones about what a damned nuisance it was that Hungary and Czechoslovakia hadn't delivered vital machinery and that Yugoslavia was short of Western *valuta*.

Boris, nearly twenty years younger that Leskosek and his immediate superior and close co-worker within the Five-Year Plan, waved him off, smiling.

"Listening to Luka, you'd think he was Jeremiah in person. The fact is he's the exact opposite—an incorrigible optimist, the visionary who dreamed up Litostroj.

"Before the war, he was foreman in a small machine-shop. The owner went bankrupt in 1930; he blamed it on the economic crash in America. Luka told the workers they would build a great factory there." As the car passed through the heavily guarded gate in the high barbed-wire fence enclosing the small industrial city, Boris pointed: "There's Luka's conception but he insisted it should be called 'Titov [Tito's] Litostroj' [the sign over the gate] because without *tovaris* Tito there might have been no thoroughgoing Yugoslav Revolution in our time.

"Litostroj is only about half completed, but even so it's a crucial factor in our economy right now. Without it, parts of the Five-Year Plan might be in jeopardy; with it and with three or four related plants in Croatia, Serbia, and Bosnia we'll pull through this period, and in the end"—Boris' eyes glinted mischievously—"our Jeremiahs of today will say that the Cominform did us a favor by making us rely on our own resources."

Luka grunted. The car halted in front of the administration building.

Although only about half completed in February 1949, as Boris said, Litostroj was turning out dies and parts of machinery for other factories and major equipment for sawmills, coal and ore mines, and hydroelectric projects. Its thirty-year-old director was a locksmith when the war began. Its chief engineer, not much older, had never built a factory before. They had three thousand men and women and teen-aged boys working under them. This was about half the personnel the First Five-Year Plan called for by the end of 1951.

Litostroj was a combination factory and vocational school. At the time of my visit in 1949, there were three hundred apprentices between thirteen and eighteen years of age whose schedule was divided between practical work in the expanding plant and technological theory in the school. A modernistic structure set apart from the immense work-halls, the school was required, under the Plan, to increase the number of its apprentices to six hundred by the middle of 1951. Many of the apprentices were orphans of fallen Partisans.

Within walking distance of the factory gates were rows of new apartment houses, and more were going up. Boris said this housing project—typical of others at the new plants—was a mistake. The directors had begun to discover that a good many workers didn't like to live in big apartment houses; they preferred individual cottages with small plots for gardens; and as soon as practicable, though not nearly as soon as he'd like, they would get what they wanted. But the cottages, too, would be built near the plant, for much of the workers' cultural life was already organized around it.

I guess I smiled, for Boris asked what was amusing me. I said that many state-financed housing projects in the United States built during Roosevelt's New Deal were groups of huge buildings, each with scores if not hundreds of small, modernly equipped apartments: highly compact communities with their own shopping and service centers. "In other words, under the dictates of its free-enterprise system, individualistic, capitalistic America tends toward a way of life which requires cooperation, compactness, and uniformity—collectivism, almost —while workers in communistic Yugoslavia rebel against collectivist housing, and you, the 'dictators' of this totalitarian setup, are giving them what they want. . . ." I told him of a curious novel, *The Fountainhead,* published in the United States early in the '40's which ranted against the popularity of quasi-collectivized housing. The architect hero, a super-individualist, went so far as to dynamite a housing project; and I said I wondered how the author would deal with this individualistic cottage-and-garden tendency in collectivist Yugoslavia.

At each of the gates and at the approaches to the large work-halls, the school, and the administration building special industrial guards were posted. Heavily armed, they were members of a division of the State Security Organization—tried and tested former Partisans.

"Are they actually necessary?" I asked Boris.

"We think so," he answered. "It's in plants like this and in the mines and hydroelectric projects that we're carrying out the mandate of the Revolution—building socialism—and we can't take any risks."

Outside and in, on walls, wire poles, flatcars, machines, dusty window panes, everywhere, were "Tito" signs: *Tito, Our Country's Foremost Metal Worker. . . . A better future can be built only by hard work. Are you fulfilling your daily commitment?,* etc. I had seen the same reminder in the Spinning and Weaving Mill in Trzic.

At periodic pep meetings, workers committed themselves to achieve at the very least the "norm" set—and raised as production methods improved—by the representatives of the trinity ruling every industrial plant in Yugoslavia in 1949: the *uprava* or administration consisting of director, deputy directors, engineers, and department superintendents; the workers' union, and the Communist Party. In Trzic, I had learned the details of how this interlocked triumvirate worked—by calling a meeting whenever a problem arose, and solving it as best and as quickly as they knew how.

As we walked through the noisy work-halls between rows of whirring machines and beneath cranes bearing large objects from one end to the other, I remarked to Boris that the place would be considered large even in America.

Leskosek didn't hear me. "Luka," Boris shouted, "this *Amerikanec* says no self-respecting American capitalist would look twice at this puny shop of yours."

"You tell him to go back where he came from or we'll give him a bath in this juice," Luka shouted, his eyes on the molten metal pour-

ing into a mold in the floor. His face aglow, he came over to us, and
said: "Wonderful, isn't it? Like seeing the birth of something."

"Like a birth," echoed one of the men. "That's been my thought
many a time, *tovaris* Luka."

The director and the chief engineer who accompanied us introduced
me to several of the men. Some of them were *udarniki*—literally "hard-
hitters" or shock-workers—whose performances were well above the
norm. Several were already working "in 1950," or even "in 1951"—a
year or two ahead of their individual assignment under the Plan. A
friendly observer might have described the expressions on many of
the faces as fervent or dedicated, especially in the glow of the molten
metal; an unfriendly observer would have called these workers fanatics or victims of an obsession. In departments where it wasn't too
noisy to talk men and women gathered around us to listen or to inject
a word or two of their own.

"Joking aside," Leskosek said to me, "how long would it take to
build a plant like this in America, and get it going?"

"What you have here now or the plant you envision at the end of
1951?"

"The whole plant—about twice the size of what you see here now."

The group of workers close around us were all ears. They sh-*sh*-ed
the ones further back. Some of the machines were stopped.

"If there was no rush," I said, "my guess is it wouldn't take more
than eight to ten months."

"*P'r moj dus!*" someone exclaimed. "By my soul!"

"When was Litostroj begun?" I asked.

"In 1946," Leskosek said.

"In other words," said Boris, somberly, "it'll take us six years to
do what you say takes from eight to ten months in the United
States."

"Yes," I said; "but American industrialization is an old story, and
now it's at a climax. The conditions are all different. In the first place,
the building and engineering firms that are given the contracts to erect
and equip a plant have the talent, materials, and machinery at their
fingertips—at the end of their telephone wires, at any rate. Their
orders are filled and delivered to the site on specified days, and if the
contractors have fairly good relations with the unions, the engineers
assemble the factory in no time according to blueprints worked out by
special industrial architects or designers. During the last war, when

the government financed and pushed plant expansion, it probably took less than eight months to raise a unit like this and get it into operation."

"*P'r moj krvav dus*—by my bloody soul!"

At Litostroj, as in other factories that I saw later, the Yugoslavs were doing it the hard way, made harder by the Cominform split. The director and the chief engineer told me that at the moment, in February 1949, forty percent of Litostroj's production was going into Litostroj—into enlarging and equipping itself.

I said, "You're lifting yourself by your bootstraps."

"We have no other way," Boris said.

Several other workers nodded.

"Will you make it?" I asked one of them.

"*O ja!*" he replied.

Boris smiled, nodding emphatically. "Don't worry about that. That is, if there's no war. We're proceeding on the chance there won't be another war."

"We must make it," the worker added.

"There's no alternative," said Leskosek.

Boris and I returned to Ljubljana without Leskosek. He stayed behind at the request of some workers who were having trouble with one of the new machines. "As Minister of Heavy Industry," said Boris, "Luka is our mechanic-in-chief. Whenever he comes near a plant, he stays there half the night exterminating operational bugs. He's a born fixer-upper. The trouble is he can't be everywhere at once. And of course problems like that aren't Luka's job, but he loves to help out, especially when an old-timer he used to work with in some small shop before the war asks him."

We drove in silence part of the way.

"Well, Lojze, what do you think of our Litostroj?" Boris asked.

"Quite a place," I replied. "I'm beginning to think you really will make it—'that is, *if* there is no war.'"

"You stress the *if* a little more than I do," Boris said.

"It really is a big *if*, if you ask me," I said, "and it was your reservation in the first place."

"What are you driving at?" Boris asked. "Are you saying that we're not sufficiently worried about the possibilities of another war?"

"I'm not sure what I'm driving at," I said. "Offhand though, seeing you people work like mad to build socialism with that *if* dangling over you, I just wonder——"

"But if we worried about it, we'd be done for on that count alone," Boris said. "*Tovaris* Tito says our only prospect is to work as hard as we can on the assumption that another war won't break out."

"I'm not worried about your not worrying," I said, "but I wonder if you people in the leadership are doing anything, whether Yugoslavia is doing anything, to help prevent another war."

"There you go again," said Boris. "We're sitting on the story, and all that? . . . What's America doing? What are the American people doing to prevent another war?"

I said that didn't answer my question, and we were quiet for a while.

"When you arrived you said you wouldn't write about New Yugoslavia," Boris smiled. "Have you changed your mind? I just ask."

"I haven't changed my mind," I said. "Of course I'm making notes. It's a habit. At home I write a page or a paragraph if my cat has kittens."

Boris' eyebrows rose.

"Cats are very interesting," I said. "Not that New Yugoslavia isn't. I'm writing notes on Yugoslavia too, as complete notes as I can. I don't know what I'll do with them. They're just a means of figuring things out for myself. I'll probably write a note on this visit to Litostroj. I suppose it's top-secret too, isn't it? Like everything else. Incidentally, if your security organization cares to confiscate my diary, it's a big loose-leaf notebook with limp black covers, on the bedside table in my room. The chances are I'll never use it, anyhow."

We smiled.

"Are you doing anything tonight?" Boris asked.

"Having supper at one of my relatives'," I replied, "and I expect to be the life of the party. I'll tell them about Litostroj. Thanks to your press, or rather to your *konspiracija* system and atmosphere, I'm sure they know nothing about it beyond the fact that it exists, and they'll listen to me with even greater interest, perhaps, than when I talk about American factories."

"That last dig is pertinent," Boris said. "The people ought to be informed—about Litostroj, et cetera. The question is how can our story be told without affecting our security."

I didn't know what to say to that.

"*Tovaris* Tito is of the same mind," said Boris. "But it's not an easy matter. Patience, Lojze, have patience," he smiled as I got out of his car in front of the guest-house.

On my arrival in Ljubljana I met a young man with a fluid, matter-of-fact manner whose name I didn't catch when we were introduced in the hubbub at the railroad station. He was seeing about my bags, instructing someone where to take them. The next day he came to the guest-house to make sure I was comfortable. Was there anything I wanted? I thought he was in charge of the place, and it turned out he was, in a way. After a while it came to me that he was Marijan Brecelj, Vice-Premier of the People's Republic of Slovenia. Everybody assumed I knew, so no one told me he was directly responsible for Slovenia's part of the Yugoslav Five-Year Plan—not for Litostroj and a few half-dozen or so other big plants and projects which were under federal authority but for everything else industrial in the tiny republic. And he didn't mind when I asked him if I could have another pillow for my bed, as I liked to read and scribble before going to sleep. He promptly saw to it that I got another pillow.

After my "rest" in the Upland, I returned to the same guest-house. It was formerly owned by a rich man who died in Dachau, and, before the Cominform split, was used by cultural and commercial missions from Russia and the East-European countries. Now the villa was empty most of the time and Brecelj wanted me to make myself at home.

The housekeeper—a government official—was a small, elderly woman, at once timid and eager, with a hesitant voice, but not un-talkative. Everybody called her *tovarisica* Jozinka. Her only son had fallen in the War of Liberation and her husband had died in Dachau; she was alone in the world. She cried, telling me her story. One day she reminisced about the Czech, Polish, Hungarian, and Russian guests she used to serve before the Cominform break. Some of them had been as nice as anyone could wish. The trouble was she didn't always understand what they said, but when she made a mistake they just laughed. That was the kind of people they were. Just folks. But many of them, most of the Russians, had behaved badly. Until lately she had scarcely dared to breathe a word of this to anyone except *tovaris* Vice-Premier Brecelj. He was a fine man, didn't I think so? He never failed to stick his head into the kitchen to ask how she was, and wasn't there something he could do, like lifting or moving something heavy? If not for his kindness she couldn't have done her job when the house was full and some of the guests were so demanding.

Had I met his wife—Ancka Brecelj? A wonderful young woman, a leading actress of the National Theater of Slovenia, as good in tragedy as in comedy; I must see her——

The last week in February at my request Marijan Brecelj let me accompany him on a three-day trip through Styria, a part of Slovenia I hadn't visited in 1932–33—famous for it vineyards and hopfields, now in process of transformation into a leading industrial center. We spent the night at the Strnisce (Stubblefield) aluminum factory, not yet completed, sprawling in the middle of a valley formerly known for its grain fields.

"The project is so vast," I noted in my diary, "that we got lost in the dark looking for the main gate, although both Brecelj and the chauffeur have been here many times before. . . . Yugoslavia is rich in bauxite and other raw materials that go into aluminum production and Strnisce will be one of the largest aluminum plants in Europe and for a time perhaps the most modern. It's a federal or all-Yugoslav enterprise, but some of the construction work is being done by a branch of the building trust of the People's Republic of Slovenia which is under Brecelj.

"We spent the next forenoon giving the project the once-over. It's about two-thirds finished with a dozen enormous buildings still in the rough, but some machinery is already installed in most of them. Materials are piled up everywhere, approximately three thousand workers swarm about—a scene pretty much like any big construction job in America. Some of the workers, Brecelj told me, are Italians from Trieste and Italy. They want to live in a socialist country and Yugoslavia let them in. Eventually they'll become Yugoslav citizens. They help relieve the manpower shortage.

"I said 'like any big construction job in America'—with one big difference not perceptible to the naked eye: the C.P. The construction manager, Viktor Stopar, is a veteran Communist. He's not forty yet, and this is the first big plant he's putting into operation. He was a metal worker before the war, earning the equivalent of a dollar and a half a day. He's never made aluminum; but when about half of the plant starts working near the end of the First Five-Year Plan, while the rest of it is being completed, he'll also be the director of production. And somehow there's no doubt in anyone's mind that, *if* there's no war, Strnisce will turn out so much aluminum by the end of 1952, so much by '53, and that by '55 the whole factory will be completed and producing —— tons, its ultimate capacity. The figure is confidential.

"When I asked Stopar how it happened he was assigned to this job and how he felt about holding it, he smiled. 'I can answer in three words, *"Partija in Tito"* [the Party and Tito]. The Party assigned me to the job. The Party's ability and strength are my ability and strength, so I don't expect too much trouble in pulling it off. *Tovaris* Tito is a metal worker and he's head of the state; *tovaris* Leskosek is a metal worker and he's Minister of Heavy Industry; so, perhaps, another metal worker ought to be able to run this plant.'

"It was a straightforward answer to a question. Behind it was the Marxian idea that ordinary workers possessed hidden capabilities which the Revolution brought out. Stopar looks 'ordinary.' He's a member of the Central Committee of the CP of Slovenia and a deputy in the Slovenian parliament.

"His chief engineer, who isn't a Communist in the strict sense of Party membership, never built a plant before either, and was never inside an aluminum factory until 1947, when he went through one in Switzerland. He's the No. 1 technical man on the project. His prewar profession was chemical engineering but in Old Yugoslavia he never had a chance to practice it. He roamed about Central Europe, working here awhile. there awhile. Now he's a key man in Operation Bootstrap, and he looks happy—but very tired. He works from fourteen to twenty hours a day. There's a dire shortage of engineers and technicians. All the engineers I meet show fatigue but it doesn't occur to them to take time off for rest. I asked Brecelj about this. He said it was part of the whole *élan*—a word used a great deal in speeches and conversation. These men, each doing the work of five or more, are spurred on by the new setup, by the zip in the new atmosphere, by personal and supra-personal motives, by day-to-day satisfaction in getting the job done in the face of lacks of equipment and materials.

"The Cominform crisis put a crimp on Strnisce before the open split occurred. Some of the machinery was on order in Hungary. It should have been delivered late in 1947 as part of Hungarian war reparations. It wasn't. To be on the safe side, the Yugoslavs ordered the equipment from Switzerland and it has begun to arrive. Some of it was on order in Czechoslovakia, to be delivered early in 1948. It was finished on time, but not delivered. Unbeknown to the Soviet secret police in

Czechoslovakia, the Swiss bought the machinery from the Czechs for half the price, since the Czechs had no use for it, and shipped it to Yugoslavia.

"Brecelj was quite prosaic about Strnisce, as he was about our next stop—Mariborski Otok, the hydroelectric project on the River Drava which will supply the aluminum plant with power.

"When fully completed [in 1954, if everything goes well] Mariborski Otok will be one-ninth the size of the Coulee Dam—but that's big for tiny Slovenia and even for Yugoslavia. It took me two hours to go through the section already in operation.

"Brecelj had to attend to some business nearby, and left me with the director, a young fellow, who was also new at bossing a big job. Talk about zeal. He and his men are priests in this religion of socialist construction and production. Maybe they're what some of the Ljubljana ideologists I sit with at their discussions have in mind when they think aloud about the precursors of the 'New Man.' Like some of the men at Litostroj, these, too, appear ready to die a hundred deaths to prevent anything happening to the project.

"As at Litostroj and Strnisce, special industrial militiamen are on duty at Mariborski Otok—only there are more of them, for the place is closer to the border and more vulnerable. On the hillside above the dam is a pillbox; inside it are a couple of alert machine-gunners. Men with tommy-guns stopped us at the approach to the gate. Brecelj couldn't get me past them until the director came out and identified us. A guard stands at the entranceway to each gallery.

"The dam went into partial operation in the spring of 1948. Brecelj told me of the moment when the water was let into the turbines. The men who had built it could scarcely breathe waiting to see if it would 'work.' When it did, when the revolutions gathered momentum and the powerful, rhythmic hum they had dreamed of began and continued, they shouted with joy, they danced and embraced one another.

"In the city of Maribor [continuing from my diary]—the second largest Slovenian town, about two-thirds the size of Ljubljana, whose rapidly growing population reached 120,000 at the end of 1948, compared to 95,000 in 1940—Brecelj took me to the office of the president of the people's committee. In prewar days the mayor of Maribor was invariably a pompous stuffed shirt. Now at the same desk in the city hall sits a good-humored, businesslike chap in his early thirties, an ex-Partisan, a Communist, a candidate for membership in the Central Committee of the CP of Slovenia, who had every detail of the information Brecelj sought at his fingertips.

"Everywhere in local affairs, key positions are held by young men and women. . . . At the Agricultural School just outside of Maribor I felt as though I were splashing in a pool of enthusiasm. The young dean, who looks twenty-eight but may be in his mid-thirties, introduced me to the assembled student body and faculty. He said he hoped I would like the school. It was a tiny but to them very dear part of Tito's New Yugoslavia. Whereupon the nearly four hundred students burst into hand-clapping and chanting 'People, Party, Tito! People, Party, Tito!' for four or five minutes.

"It was the same kind of *skandiranje* I had heard and seen at the Serbian CP Congress. Tito wasn't here in person, but 'Tito' the symbol was. The mere mention of his name touched off, ritualwise, an outpouring of enthusiasm. But this may be describing it too simply. It was a mingling of ardor, faith, determination, desperation, reaching for a Messiah.

"The students are between sixteen and twenty-five, boys and girls from all over Slovenia. A handful of them come from other parts of Yugoslavia. Scores of them are all that remain of their families. A good many went through the worst of the war and Revolution, and are permanently maimed, or are scrawny and ill-looking. Some may be actually ill—and to swim in that pool of enthusiasm may be the best medicine for them, at least temporarily.

"Brimming with facts and figures about the school and the agricultural problem in Slovenia, the young dean was tremulous with eagerness that I grasp the significance of their work. The school was started in Old Yugoslavia. It never had more than 80 students enrolled at a time. In 1948–49 it had 389. In the eleven years of its existence before the war a total of 38 boys were graduated. In 1948 the graduates numbered 79; the expected figure for June 1949 was 108. About half of these would continue their studies at the universities of Ljubljana, Zagreb, or Belgrade to prepare themselves for agricultural posts in the Second Five-Year Plan beginning in 1952. Most of the others would find places in the new peasant cooperatives; ultimately, in from five to ten years, in scientific farm collectives. And some would teach or do research in laboratories.

"The study program is about 60 per cent in the classrooms and laboratories, about 40 per cent in the fields and greenhouses. The equipment is largely improvised and would be considered inadequate in a similar school in the United States, but the dean, the faculty, and the students are very proud of it.

"Before 'the Tito Revolution' (as one of the teachers, who is probably head of the CP organization in the school, kept referring to it) this was the only agricultural school in Slovenia. Now there are 27 of them in Slovenia alone and about two hundred of them in all of Yugoslavia. From 1950 on, between three and four thousand more or less scientific agriculturists will come out of the 27 schools in Slovenia every year. Impelled both by their own conviction and their technical and ideological training, 'a great majority will work to help bring all of agriculture into the socialist sector of the economy as quickly and smoothly—and as *humanely*—as possible,' said the dean.

"'About 90 per cent of our students,' he continued, 'are all for socialism. Among them are sons and daughters of one-time well-off peasants.'—'Are the other ten per cent against socialism?' I asked.— 'Yes; or rather, yes and no. They feel it's too bad private property is on the way out, but most of them admit it would be untenable for Yugoslavia to continue it. They have no alternative to propose to the building of socialism. . . . No, no; they're not discriminated against in any way. They receive stipends like the other students. Their presence in the school is desirable on two counts: one, the other students sharpen their minds trying to convert them; two, some of the students who tend to be over-zealous learn to practice patience toward those who are slow in seeing the necessity and wisdom of a collectivist society.'

"There's a room called 'the Red Corner' with a small library of 'Marxist-Leninist' literature. The executive committee of the school's Party organization meets here nearly every day. Small seminars are held on the psychological problems the Revolution has created or brought to the surface. What to do with the crust of custom, tradition, and habit still overlaying parts of the peasant population: crack it or let it crumble slowly? How to liberate individuals and communities from their old mental and emotional patterns and lay the basis for a new, conscious socialist patriotism? Is force justified? If it is for whatever reason, is it desirable? Especially if it can be avoided? . . . Persuasion? Yes, yes; but how go about it without running serious risks to the Revolution? How cope with some of the peasants' subtle, often unwitting opposition to change? How help truth and the people's commonsense prevail against lies concocted by *reakcija*?

"But youth [my diary notes continue], while on top, is beginning to discover that older people and even the aged may still have something to contribute.

"Brecelj and the president of the Maribor people's committee, who is even younger than Brecelj, took me with them to a small machine shop in a backyard lean-to, where the boss is a rheumatic, asthmatic, nearly blind seventy-three-year-old German named Ferdinand Kocelli. This is his story:

"He was born in the Sudeten region [then in Austria, later in Czechoslovakia]. He was always tinkering with one kind of gadget or another. As a young mechanic working for others, he invented simple machines. In his late middle years, during the 1930's, he owned a prosperous factory in which he manufactured his own devices. After Hitler seized Czechoslovakia, the Nazis trumped up a charge against him, seized his plant, and gave it to one of his newest employees, a Nazi. A political babe-in-the-woods, past sixty, Kocelli didn't know what had hit him. His wife, a few years younger and a good deal sturdier, had relatives in Maribor and, fearful that the Nazis might kill them, she persuaded him to seek refuge in Yugoslavia.

"World War II caught them there. In 1941 Hitler declared Styria part of the Reich and the Nazis held Maribor with a strong garrison. But the Kocellis were permitted to live in peace in their small comfortable apartment . . . until 1945, when the revolutionary Slovenian Partisans took the city and for a while made life tough for all Germans in sight.

"They knew nothing about Kocelli except that he was a German. He and his wife were evicted from their flat, and their predicament worsened until the pressure of the Cominform crisis reminded the city people's committee of a rumor that the old man was an inventor.

"Two committee members called on him and asked him if he'd work for socialism in New Yugoslavia—he'd be fairly compensated. Old man Kocelli wanted to throw them out, but he lacked the strength. He wouldn't talk with them. They came again and again. At last, he opened up enough to say that he had no use for Communism and even less for Communists, they were as bad as Nazis. They had treated his wife and him harshly for no reason at all and he would have no truck with them. Besides, he was old and ill, his eyesight was almost gone and he didn't think he could design any more machines, anyhow. 'Leave me alone.'

"Brecelj suggested to the president of the people's committee he should contrive to see *Frau* Kocelli alone. And in the end, a few months ago [in November 1948] it was she who persuaded the old inventor to accept the offer conditionally.

"The people's committee set up the shop according to Kocelli's specifications and assigned him a draftsman and three mechanics who knew German. His wife comes to the shop daily as his nurse and also because she understands how his mind works and can tell the draftsman and the mechanics what he wants them to do.

"The people's committee moved the couple back to their old flat, within a few minutes' walk of their work. Twice weekly a doctor examines the old boy and tries to help relieve his asthma, rheumatism, and arteriosclerosis.

"Now Brecelj was calling on him at the shop in the name of the government of the People's Republic of Slovenia to congratulate him on the completion of his first machine designed especially for New Yugoslavia—not a big job but important. It will turn out wire brushes and save the country foreign *valuta*. Brecelj, presenting him with a draft for a million dinars ($20,000), made a little speech in German. The old man was dumfounded. His wife cried, and she made him sit down and held his head to her breast."

In Ljubljana, immediately after I returned from the Upland, I became reacquainted with Bozidar Jakac, one of the leading Slovenian artists, just turned fifty. Twenty years earlier he had lived in Cleveland and the Southwest and painted many scenes of northern Ohio and of Arizona and California. During the war he had been an official Liberation Front artist and photographer of the Slovenian sector of the Yugoslav *borba*. Now he was one of several non-Communist members of the Slovenian Parliament representing the arts in addition to his district.

As we talked, he dwelled on the new Slovenian Academy of Fine Arts, of which he was director. Taking me through it, he said:

"Of course, like all of our institutions, we're terribly underequipped. We lack paper, colors, crayons, pencils, erasers—the most elementary articles. Look, we call these few shelves of art books and journals our library. But it's a beginning. Nearly everything in New Yugoslavia is in its initial stages. . . . The history of the Slovenians' fight for an art school in Ljubljana goes back to 1703. The Austrian rule wouldn't let us have an art school. In Old Yugoslavia, the Belgrade regime promised us one, but that was as far as we got. Now, thanks to Tito, thanks to the Revolution, here's the Academy of Fine Arts which—with the University of Ljubljana, the Slovenian Academy of Arts and Sciences, and the new Academies of Music and of the Drama—helps to form Slovenia's higher-educational system. A great step forward, and apparently there was no other way of making it. No wonder that nearly all of our foremost painters and sculptors participated in the Revolution. Some of them died in battle or as hostages. The Revolution was no picnic. It still isn't. But looking back, I believe events had to happen as they did. . . . The tremendous experience we went through calls for expression. It may need new forms and special emphases. Now we have the chance to work them out organically in the atmosphere of the rest of our unfolding. This doesn't mean that our students won't go abroad to study and to see; they will, when our *valuta* balances allow us to send them; but their taproot will be here. And that's not nationalism; it's ordinary horse sense."

The models in the drawing, painting, and sculpture classes were all aged men and women. I remarked about this.

Jakac explained, "That's because no young person will just sit or stand still nowadays. They feel they have something better to do than to pose for artists. The impulse is to move, to be on the way, to strain."

The students were anywhere between eighteen and thirty-five. One had a leg off. Another didn't answer when I spoke to him, and Jakac said, "He's deaf."

One evening I asked Jakac what wartime experience came back to him most often, most vividly.

"The sunbeam," he said, then grinned at my puzzled expression. "It happened during the big German offensive in the autumn of '43.[1]

"Thirty of us, twenty-one men and nine women, found ourselves

---

[1] Another version of this experience appears in the book *Tovarisija* (Comradeship) by Edvard Kocbek, a Christian Socialist intellectual who during 1942–45 was a member of the wartime executive committee of the Liberation Front of Slovenia.

To simplify the narrative I omit most of the names.

in a wood, pursued and finally encircled by a German battalion aided by a detachment of White Guards. I thought our goose was cooked— overdone, in fact—and I thought it was a pity because it was an exceptionally beautiful autumn. The Germans usually shot the Partisans they captured, even women. We were *'Banditen,'* you know, not soldiers worthy of being regarded as prisoners-of-war under the Geneva Convention. Worse yet, most of the political leaders of the Liberation Front of Slovenia were in our group.

"Our ammunition was just about gone and there was no way of escaping the encirclement. Ironically enough, knowing we couldn't get out, the enemy was in no hurry to round us up. That saved us.

"One of our men who had been in the Partisans since 1941 (the bodyguard of a Liberation Front leader) insisted this looked like the forest where two years before he'd helped build a dugout in a hollow exactly like this one, above which we were holding our position. He didn't remember its exact size but he thought we might all be able to squeeze into it. It was a 'wonderful bunker,' he kept saying as he dashed about seeking it.

"Well, he found it . . . and we all got into it through a hole that he afterward carefully closed behind us by manipulating back over it the lichen-covered rock which fit perfectly, and by which he had recognized it. All around it and on top of it, amid a thick growth of underbrush, were many other rocks of all shapes and sizes. Stepping lightly on the lichen-less parts of the rocks, we left no trace. With all our belongings we literally sank into the ground.

"The subterranean bunker had originally been built for a command post, but it was fairly large, perhaps twenty-five feet long, about as wide, and just six feet high from floor to ceiling. The thirty of us were pretty crowded. But this wasn't a serious matter at first. If the Germans didn't find us with bloodhounds, we thought we'd be out of the dugout in a few hours. We expected them to leave the forest believing we had somehow slipped out of the encirclement.

"The trouble was they suspected we had some high-level *'Banditen'* in our group, and they didn't give up the search so quickly. For three days they tapped over and over again every square foot above us and perhaps a couple of square kilometers around us. They blew up cliffs, thinking we might be behind or under them. In a hollow near ours, they did find a bunker, but no one in it. No one in our group knew it existed. Our 'wonderful' hole-in-the-ground was even deeper and so tightly packed with us and our rucksacks and bundles—for instance, I had all my art and photo supplies with me—that when they tapped above us it produced no hollow sound. And as luck would have it, this German unit had no bloodhounds.

"Down below, our problems mounted and multiplied with the passage of time. The dugout was fairly dry, and half of us could sit down if the other half stood—no easy stunt if you were six feet or over. But the tightness of our quarters was the least of our woes. As I say, it was what saved us.

"The big trouble was the ventilation system. It consisted of two rusty cast-iron pipes sticking out of the ceiling in opposite corners of the bunker, and it didn't provide adequately for thirty pairs of lungs or thirty noses. The pipes, I imagine, were about ten feet long and laid slantwise in the earth above the hole. One was straight; the other, slightly bent. Each emerged under a bush and, like the entrance, was camouflaged perfectly.

"When we moved in, the pipes were stopped up with leaves and dirt. There was the skeleton of a small animal in the bent one, probably a squirrel, that had got in somehow and couldn't get out. In the bunker we found a long stiff wire (part of the equipment of the previous occupants) and we cleaned out the pipes. Peering through the straight one in the daytime, we saw a splotch of light on top.

"The Germans decided to camp in the forest. And for one of their latrines they selected a spot in the bushes very close to the outlet of the bent pipe. By-and-by Nazi urine started to drip down it. This added to the stench of our own excreta which, beginning with the second day, was enough to drive us mad.

"Of the thirty of us, eleven were Communists. One—a veteran of the Spanish Civil War—was a political commissar who died in a battle later. He asked if he might take charge, then taxed all his will power and stamina to conduct himself to set an example for the rest of us. 'Don't talk,' he kept saying in a low, deliberately calm whisper. 'If you want to say something, whisper. Smother your cough; suppress your sneeze. Whether or not we come out of this depends on each of us individually and all of us together.'

"You have no idea how hard it is not to cough out of nervousness when you're in a spot like that. Again and again the commissar said, 'If you can't control your cough, ask a *tovaris* near you to help you cover the sound.'

"With breathing such an effort and the air so fetid, it was difficult not to get hysterical or panicky. Over and over the commissar said, 'If you feel you're losing control of yourself, ask the *tovaris* nearest you to hold your hand or talk to you—in a whisper.'

"By bringing our ears as close to the end of the bent pipe as we could without being dripped on, we heard the Germans' footsteps, voices, and—other sounds. Those of us who knew German understood what they were saying in the latrine—among other interesting topics, that we, '*die gottverdammten Banditen,*' were bound to be somewhere within a radius of a few thousand yards.

"Four days of it! . . . Often the tension was unbearable to the point where I thought we would explode out of the bunker by spontaneous combustion.

"I imagine that, beginning with the third day if not before, because of the stench and the thirst, many of us thought of suicide. We had one or two cartridges left in our rifles or revolvers. One young man, when the thought seized him, made his way through the packed dugout to the straight pipe for a squint at the daylight above. The next time, however, it was night and, seeing no light, he almost went crazy. We had to hold him down. But before anyone could clamp a hand over his mouth, he shrieked out, and we feared the Germans would find us. I don't know what time of night it was; perhaps most of the enemy were asleep. If the guards heard the outcry through the pipe, they probably attributed it to one of the sleeping supermen.

"The crisis began on the third day. The food was gone but that didn't matter—who could eat? The commissar kept a little water in his canteen—'for emergency,' he said, as if the whole episode wasn't an emergency, as if the worst was yet to come. Now and then he annoyed me so I could have screamed at him. Later I told him this, and he smiled and pressed my hand.

"He had a bent for symbolism. He said in some ways this dugout— dark, stenchy, dripping, suffocating—was 'a replica of most of the world.' At that time, no doubt, he excepted the Soviet Union.

"Early on the third day those who smoked each had a puff of the last cigarette. It was lit with the last match. Because the air was so thin, or so thick, I don't know which, it almost went out before it was used.

"One *tovaris* whispered to me, 'This is our Musa Dagh. Only, instead of a clean mountaintop it's a goddamn filthy hole in the ground.

Strictly speaking, it's an inverted Musa Dagh. And we have no idea how many days we'll be in it. Frankly, forty days is too much to look forward to.' In the 1930's many of us had read Franz Werfel's novel and soon after the outbreak of the *borba* in 1941 literary-minded Slovenians referred to Slovenia, some to Yugoslavia, as a Musa Dagh with sixteen million people. . . .

"There was humor—even on the third day. Some of it had to do with our natural functions. Those jokes would sound coarse now; but in the dugout they were a kind of barricade against insanity. . . . Humor helped us both to transcend each other's filth and to love each other in spite and because of it. . . .

"After we burned our last match, most of us kept our eyes closed most of the time—— It was pitch dark and there was nothing to see—not even dim figures. In self-defense, too, our sense of smell gave out. Our bodies were toxic, heavy. We dozed a lot, sometimes standing up. In our sleep, our knees folded; but we didn't go down—we were packed so tight.

"We lost track of time. A man and a woman near me whispered whether this was the third, fourth or fifth day. Someone *sh-sh-sh*'ed them. We determined later it was the fourth day—the fourth 'eternity' some of us called it.

"By then it didn't matter. . . . Truth? I've heard the story of this experience told three or four times by different individuals who were in the dugout. It sounded different each time, and yet all the versions are true, more or less.

"At any rate, the story ends as happily as a Hollywood film. Near mid-afternoon of the fourth day a thin strong streak of light suddenly reached down from the ceiling in the corner with the straight pipe. It quivered gently and illumined a part of the dugout. From where I leaned against a wall, I saw three faces and several others less clearly: a picture I shall never forget. It was an El Greco! Wonder erasing lines of anxiety and despair. Sudden hope mingled with incredulity."

Jakac placed a hand over his eyes for a moment. "When I close my eyes, I see the picture as sharply as I saw it then. The few times I tried to catch it on paper, it evaded me: there's too much in it. I tore up all the sketches. . . .

"One of the three faces belonged to a peasant from the village of Frankolovo, a middle-aged man . . . The spring before [in 1943] a German officer was killed near that village: no one knew by whom, but probably by a Partisan patrol. In retaliation the Germans rounded up one hundred men in Frankolovo and the neighboring hamlets, gathered up all the rope they could find, and hanged ninety-nine on the blossoming boughs in the apple orchards and wherever else was handy. . . . This peasant, the hundredth, fainted of horror. The Germans booted him a few times, decided he was dead, and left him on the ground.

"Regaining consciousness, he saw men dangling from trees all around him. The Germans were gone. He crawled away and hid in a woodshed. The villagers were forbidden to touch the bodies until the next morning. Then the women and children came out of the houses to take down the ninety-nine bodies, and the hundredth man emerged and took charge of digging a great pit in the orchard, near the highway . . . and they buried the victims. Then the peasant put an arm around his wife's waist, walked with her to their home, filled a sack with food, and vanished into the woods.

"He tried to find his sixteen-year-old son who had joined the Partisans near the end of '41, but the boy probably had fallen in battle long before. The early Liberation detachments kept almost no record of their casualties, or the records were lost; besides, most Partisans went by *noms de guerre*. . . . The upshot was that this middle-aged peasant from Frankolovo became a fierce fighter, a hero. The woods were full of heroes who didn't regard themselves or each other as heroes. They were doing a job: fighting the enemy, fighting a revolution, liberating their soil much in the same spirit, on the same principle, that they weeded their fields. It had to be done. . . .

"How this fellow got among us, I don't know. Someone casually told his story a few days before we ducked into the bunker. Now here he was, with that strange spotlight on him, with his soul in his face. . . . Like many of us, he fainted when we left the dugout. The good, fresh air was too much for him. But, unlike the rest of us, he never came to. Heart failure. We buried him in the forest. It was a beautiful autumn day. There were still some wildflowers around, and the women in our detachment gathered them and placed them on his grave.

"But to go back. I'm not sure how I felt when I saw the light, or what we all thought. Two days later, trying to review the episode, one of the four women who was anything but religious confessed that the exclamation '*Jezus, Marija!*' "—common among Slovenian peasants—

"almost burst out of her. It didn't, she said, because her nerves had tightened so they choked her voice. Others told how they exclaimed '*Zivijo* Tito!' (Long live Tito!) inside themselves. Or '*Zivijo* Stalin!' I wonder if some of that wasn't afterthought. . . . I think awe was my chief emotion. I was stunned by the beauty of the light on those gaunt, unshaven faces. Never, never have I loved my fellow-man so much.

"Who saw the ray first? I believe several of us became aware of it instantly. We stirred and jostled those nearest us. In a second all of us were staring at it, except those who were very ill or virtually unconscious. No one uttered a sound.

"Afterward we argued how long the light lasted. I'd say ten seconds, at the most. Before it went, leaving us in darkness darker than before, the commissar cautioned us to remain silent, and for a long while no one moved or made a sound—except a sob.

"Earlier in the day we had heard some dull thundering above-ground, but we were so numbed that none of us—not even the commissar, as he admitted—so much as dreamed the Germans were leaving the forest. Now roused by the light, our senses tingled. In a rush, with the most acute awareness, the instinct of self-preservation re-asserted itself. We listened. There was no sound above. Nor any distant sound reverberating through the earth. The latrine over the dugout wasn't frequented any more.

"The commissar begged us to remain still. Then he and the Partisan who had found the bunker groped their way up the ladder to the exit and between them collected enough strength to push up the lichen-covered boulder. They peered from under it and saw nothing except the forest and the autumn sun, its rays slanting low from the sky behind the trees. To make sure that the enemy was gone, the commissar crawled out . . . then returned and told us to come on out, too. . . ."

Jakac continued: "I mentioned that the commissar fell in a skirmish near the end of 1944. If he'd lived, he'd be one of our top men now: surely a member of the government of the People's Republic of Slovenia, probably of the Slovenian CP's politburo. . . . I think the man who located the bunker also died. . . . I know at least half the people who were in that dugout and who survived the rest of the war. One of them is my wife."

One evening I met Bozidar Jakac in the street, and he took me along to see a friend of his and his wife's from Partisan days—Malci Albinec, a war heroine of whom I had heard. Her name is disguised. When, months later, I thought I might write about her, she begged me not to. Jakac helped me to overcome her objection after I promised not to use her right name. She said her "heroism" (the way she uttered the word makes me put it in quotes) was nothing beside that of many others, most of whom were dead.

"Incidentally, she was in the dugout too," Jakac said.

Her appearance on first sight was almost weird, especially in the dimness of her quarters, into which Jakac steered me from the even dimmer corridor on top of three flights of unlighted stairs. Most of her left cheek was covered by a large star-shaped scar. As I watched her talk to Jakac, however, her face, her whole personality grew more and more appealing. She had had little or no formal schooling, obviously; but her mind was bright, quick, and direct. She wore a shabby house coat. The room she and her husband and children lived in was large and warm, but not very attractive. Unpleasant odors sifted in from the corridor. However, unlike one of my relatives whose family were well-off before the war and who now lived in similar circumstances, Malci was not embarrassed and made no apologies. She asked me to take the one chair and Jakac to sit on the bed. Her husband, a shock-worker in Litostroj, was doing overtime this week.

She was just out of the hospital with her third child and still a bit weak, she said. And she didn't have a thing to offer us. Yes: the new baby was fine. A great big boy, just now asleep in his crib. She uncovered him a little so Jakac and I could see him.

At Jakac's urging to tell me about herself, Malci said what was there to tell? She was an orphan. A poverty-stricken aunt took care of her for a few years—"just so I didn't die before I grew up enough to be able to work," she added with a little laugh. When she was twelve, in 1939, her aunt "gave" her to a well-to-do peasant. She became a shepherdess.

She was going on fourteen in the summer of 1941, when the mountains where she grazed her master's sheep and cows suddenly livened up with people who called themselves Partisans. Their fervor impressed her. She thought they had the right idea and the right way of going about it. Some of them were boys and girls her own age, or a little older. She told her master he would have to watch his herd himself, and she joined the Liberation forces.

By 1942, as I knew from Jakac, Malci was considered one of the bravest Slovenian *partizanke*. In the woods she learned to use various weapons and to read, cook, sew, and clean and bandage wounds. She listened to talk about the Soviet Union, Lenin and Stalin, Tito and Kardelj, and about what life in Slovenia, in Yugoslavia, was going to be like after the war.

"Those were wonderful days," she said. "I remember the first time I heard somebody talk about *nase perspektive* [our perspectives]. It took me a while to grasp what the words meant."

Early in the summer of 1943, near the end of a crucial four-day battle with the White Guards for the control of the medieval castle of Turjak, a bomb burst in front of Malci while she was dragging a seriously wounded Partisan commander from the danger zone. The bomb finished the commander and tore a hole in her left cheek and scattered thirty-one smaller pieces of metal through the rest of her tiny body. Several fragments punctured her chest, two lodged themselves near her heart.

Italy capitulated; Tito's representatives in Bari arranged with the British military hospital there to take a limited number of Yugoslavs; and Malci was sent off on the first of the Allied planes that landed on a hastily improvised airfield in Lower Slovenia. This was two weeks after the battle, and her cheek wound had already begun to heal. It looked like the five-pointed star which by 1943 was well established as the symbol of the Liberation movement.

The British doctors in Bari extracted all the metal from Malci's body, then suggested doing a job of plastic surgery on her face which—they smiled—would make her even prettier than she was before. She said no, and it took her a while to explain why. The Englishmen were nice enough but they always smiled at her as if she were a child who had suffered a mishap. Their words, translated to her, merely deepened this impression. The surgeons showed her some before-and-after photographs of men who had undergone plastic surgery, and she realized it would have been normal for her to want to have a pretty face. But after a while she asked the interpreter to tell the doctors not to be angry with her: she wished to live out the rest of her life with the star-like scar on her cheek, even if it did seem crazy to them.

Also, she wished to return to Slovenia right away. She was told she was only fifteen years old and underweight and not well enough to fight any more. She protested she was old enough to know her own mind, and quite fit . . . and late in September 1943 the British hospital authorities yielded to her insistence, and put her on an American plane flying to Slovenia to pick up more wounded Partisans.

Back in the Slovenian woods, Malci was assigned to work in a secret hospital, and she was on her way there when she met the group with the LF leaders and Bozidar Jakac and his future wife, and wound up in the dugout with them.

The war ended. Malci was seventeen. She married another badly mangled ex-Partisan—"we cripples belong together," she said. Tone, too, was an orphan and a prewar shepherd who, between battles, had developed the ambition to become an industrial worker and a member of the Communist Party. He was both now. Three times a week, after work in Litostroj, he went to a CP evening school.

Malci said she wasn't smart enough to be a "good Communist." She was satisfied that under the leadership of the CP, headed by *tovaris* Tito, the working people of Yugoslavia were assured of a worthwhile future. She wanted to have as many children as possible because in New Yugoslavia they would have a chance to grow up into decent, healthy men and women. She was twenty-one now; maybe someday she would be smart enough to be a Communist too. Some of the things Tone was bringing home from the CP school were very interesting.

The two older children were in the Litostroj nursery—"a wonderful place"—until she regained her strength. Tone dropped in every day to see them on the way home from work.

"If it weren't for our *borba*," she said, "I might still be a shepherdess or a *dekla* [a peasant's maid-of-all-work] with never a chance to marry. The same might be true of Tone. He'd be a *hlapec* [a man-of-all-work] and would sleep in the barn."

As Jakac and I made ready to leave, I asked Malci if she remembered the sunbeam in the dugout.

She looked at me, surprised. Jakac explained.

Turning toward the crib, she said in a low tone, "How could I forget it?"

We stood silent a moment.

Malci turned to me and asked, worriedly, "There won't be another war, will there?"

I said I hoped not. Then Jakac and I walked silently down the unlighted stairway.

Religion is what the individual does with his own solitariness.

History, down to the present day, is a melancholy record of the horrors which can attend religion: human sacrifice, and in particular the slaughter of children, cannibalism, sensual orgies, abject superstition, hatred as between races, the maintenance of degrading customs, hysteria, bigotry, can all be laid at its charge. Religion is the last refuge of human savagery. The uncritical association of religion with goodness is directly negated by plain facts. Religion can be and has been the main instrument for progress. But if we survey the whole race, we must pronounce that generally it has not been so.

—ALFRED NORTH WHITEHEAD

URING the luncheon at his house on January eighteenth I mentioned to Tito and his co-leaders that the New York Archdiocese, headed by the able, influential, and ambitious Francis Cardinal Spellman, had named a large parochial high school near New York City for Archbishop Stepinac, who in 1946 started a sixteen-year sentence in the Lepoglava Prison for his activities against New Yugoslavia. "During 1947 and '48," I said, "perhaps the most persistent and successful propaganda against you in the United States was based on the charge that you're persecuting religion."

" 'Persecuting religion,' " bristled Tito, then took a long draw at his cigarette. He turned to X, at the other end of the table, and suggested he answer me if he wished.

X, surprised, said he wasn't exactly an expert on the question. He took a moment to organize the facts and opinions at the tip of his tongue, and began:

"Non-Marxists and anti-Marxists are familiar with the 'opium of the people' phrase. But that wasn't all Marx said. He said that 'religion is the sigh of the hard-pressed creature; the heart of a heartless world.'

"In our country some of the older people as well as a small number of younger ones are religious. As you know, the two main faiths in Yugoslavia are the Serbian Orthodox and the Roman Catholic. Besides, we have a small Moslem population, a few thousand Jews, and a number of very small sects. Having 'sighed' all their lives, having sought 'the heart' in 'a heartless world,' these people continue to need something that religion or churchgoing gives them. Our new system, just beginning, hasn't yet made it unneeded, hasn't yet replaced it for them, and possibly may never be able to replace it—for them.

"All the propaganda to the contrary, we Communists respect the people. Or rather, in view of our present position, at the risk of being accused of nationalism again, or of self-righteousness, let me state it this way: we Communists in Yugoslavia respect the people. We respect human beings. As Marxians, unlike the priests of many if not most organized religions that I know of, we believe people are essentially good."

"Even if they aren't entirely for socialism?" I asked. "Or think they are against it?"

"Oh yes," said X, "if they're not plotting or working against the socialist program, and most certainly if they're willing to work constructively. And even then they're not given up or rejected. Communist morality rests on work, on a person's social usefulness. In Yugoslavia, that's basic.

"There are Communists, to be sure, who would convert churches and mosques into museums, garages, and tractor stations, but they're a very small group in the CPY. The majority of the CPY want people who need religion to practice it in their different ways as long as they need it. If some of them continue to need it, it's partly due to the in-adequacy of socialism at its present stage.

"It's no secret that many of the clergy are exerting every effort to make the churches centers of political opposition, or that agnostics and atheists of the former ruling class now go to church on Sundays and even on weekdays to 'worship'—for political purposes. But this doesn't worry anybody in authority in New Yugoslavia.

"In so far as organized religion is under attack, it's so only indirectly, in the general sense that we're determined to build socialism and create a new set of values based on reality, on a realizable program, and bring about a new set of relations among people and between people and their environment—relations that will give the country a strong, throbbing heart and an avid mind.

"However, while people are free to worship as they please, bishops and priests are *not* permitted to participate in political schemes origi-nating outside the country. Let me make it clear that this doesn't mean we want to keep the individual priest out of politics because he's a priest. Not at all. He's a citizen—even if some of us don't approve of him, even if some of us look upon him as a member of a parasitic pro-fession that we hope will soon be obsolete. We don't demand he be pro-Communist. If he engages in politics, however, he must engage in them as a citizen of Yugoslavia and not as a subject or an agent of a foreign state. If his loyalty is primarily to a foreign state, as is largely true of most of the Catholic clergy, he's required to be nonpolitical and to confine himself to priestly functions.

"Hundreds of Orthodox and Catholic churchmen are in favor of the new system and are active in the People's Front. Monsignor Ritig of St. Mark's in Zagreb, for instance, is a member of the federal parlia-ment. Communists generally regard him as a fine man, even if he and we don't see eye to eye on many issues. During the war he wanted to join us in the woods, but he was too old and frail to be a Partisan. Other priests whisper out of both sides of their mouths. For reasons of their own or on orders from their masters outside the country they give lip service to New Yugoslavia. We'd rather they didn't, but they're left alone. By and large, the clergy are asked to bear in mind that the old days are over and that our national constitution—a popularly adopted constitution, if there ever was one—provides for the separa-tion of church and state. That's all.

"In Old Yugoslavia laws didn't apply to priests; they were a privi-

leged group. In New Yugoslavia they apply to them no less than to
other individuals and professions. For years in Old Yugoslavia a politician and foreign agent in the mask of a priest"—Anton Korosec—
"was Minister of the Interior. He was always more responsive to orders
from abroad than to our country's interests and sensibilities. One of his
main jobs was to hunt down Communists and have them tortured in
the Glavnjaca [the political police headquarters under King Alexander
and Prince-Regent Paul] and slap long prison sentences on those who
didn't die under torture. In New Yugoslavia a man like that has no
chance. Nor can any other priest, even a bishop, commit crimes at will
and with the certainty that no one can touch him. A priest, a bishop,
even an archbishop, is treated like any other man. If he commits an act
which is a crime under the laws of our new state, he's punished. He's
not sacrosanct. He's a citizen, a member of our society, of our world. If
he breaks the law, he comes before a people's court; and if he's found
guilty, whether he committed the crime 'for the glory of God' or 'in
the interest of the Church' or for some other reason, he's sentenced
and punished.

"About Stepinac. I said that even an archbishop is treated like any
other citizen if he commits a crime. But that's not quite true. For a
time an exception was made in the case of Stepinac for reasons"—he
smiled—"which come under the heading of what you, *gospodine
Adamicu,* call 'public relations.' Stepinac is a war criminal according
to the definition of that term established by the Nuremberg and Tokyo
war-crime trials. Goering, Tojo, and other high-ranking war criminals
were found guilty not because they killed helpless civilians with their
own hands but because they were held responsible for the acts of their
subordinates, bound to obedience by rigid discipline; because they
ordered the slaughters or didn't stop the inhuman acts of their subordinates. In our country hundreds of priests who were under the
authority of Archbishop Stepinac, and bound by vow to carry out his
directives, participated with gun, knife, sledgehammer, and other weapons in the massacres of hundreds of thousands of Serbians and Jews.
That's a *fact* (at the same time, parenthetically, that it's true, too, that
Stepinac arranged for some Jews with a lot of money to escape to
Italy and then to Cuba or the Argentine). Thousands of other priests,
also under Stepinac's jurisdiction, explicitly or implicitly approved of
the massacres of Serbians in Croatia and Bosnia and Herzegovina and
helped to create the atmosphere for the massacres, although they them-

selves took no part in the actual slaughter. As the responsible head of the Catholic Church in Yugoslavia, to whose orders, wishes, and slightest whims all the bishops and priests were always sensitive, Stepinac was responsible for the acts of those killer priests no less than Tojo and Goering were for the acts of their men. He was also partly responsible for the whole massacre program initiated by Ante Pavelic [the Axis-sponsored quisling ruler of Croatia from 1941 to '45. A main function of the Pavelic government was to put an unbridgeable river of blood between the Croatian and Serbian peoples by butchering, as he did, between six and eight hundred thousand Serbians and tens of thousands of Jews]. Stepinac was in the closest collaboration with Pavelic. That's a *fact* too; a matter of absolute proof which would be accepted in any court of law worthy of the name. The whole voluminous record of the Stepinac case is available—alas! most of it only in Serbo-Croatian—to anyone who's sincerely interested in the legality and the justice of it. . . . But it's not a simple case. To understand it truly, one needs to look not merely into the court record but at the whole complicated religious background in the Balkans.

"Proof that Stepinac was a war criminal existed as far back as 1943 and '44, before the term 'war criminal' was defined and used by the Allied world. In '45, when the Communist Party of Yugoslavia came into power, some of the *drugovi* in and out of the Central Committee wanted to put him in the dock at once. But, as I recall, the Politburo urged patience and caution. The argument ran that religion, especially religion which isn't what it professes to be, is dynamite. We had a new state to build; we needed good will outside the country wherever we could find it. You see," X smiled again, "we *did* try to practice 'public relations' vis-à-vis the West.

"It's a matter of public record that *drug* Tito talked with Stepinac at that time. Stepinac promised not to work against New Yugoslavia. I surmise *drug marsal* didn't think we could believe him, but he also felt we should avoid bringing him to court if it was at all possible. It's a matter of public record, too, that the Marshal saw the papal nuncio here, who is the American Bishop Hurley, said to be close to Cardinal Spellman. Hurley was urged to induce the Vatican to take Stepinac out of Yugoslavia. He was informed that, although Stepinac was a war criminal, we didn't want to try him and would be happy to let him go. All we wanted was to be rid of him, to have him demobilized as a politician who in the guise of religion and behind a barrage of foreign propaganda worked against our people's democracy."

"Weren't you a bit naïve?" I interrupted, looking at Tito.

Tito's mouth tightened, then he regarded me for a moment, smiled, and nodded to X to continue.

"Naïve?" said X. "Too bad you didn't come here in 1945 or '46 and see the wreckage Yugoslavia was immediately after the war. If you'd seen the country then, you'd have no trouble understanding why we tried to avoid the international rumpus a trial of Stepinac was bound to provoke. However, Nuncio Hurley was told that unless the Vatican took Stepinac out of Yugoslavia we'd eventually be forced to bring him to trial. In '45 or '46 we had proof that on top of his wartime crimes Stepinac went right on working against the Revolution, which our laws forbade—naturally: no revolution ever tolerated counter-revolution. . . . On orders from the outside, Stepinac was giving moral and material support to the *Krizari*"—the Crusaders, a Croatian guerrilla organization that Western espionage services were starting, to replace the shattered Ustasi outfit and help overthrow the Tito regime.

"Then too, late in 1945," X went on, with a glance at Aleksandar Rankovic, "our security organization was tipped off that the crypts in the ancient church next to the Archbishop's palace in Zagreb contained not only the dust of Stepinac's revered predecessors but also the gold and other valuables that the Pavelic-Stepinac massacre squads had stripped from Serbians and Jews they killed in 1941 and '42. The church was raided; and cached in the crypts were numerous large wooden chests filled with watches, watch-chains, rings, earrings, brooches, bracelets, and tooth fillings extracted from the mouths of massacre victims. There were tens of thousands of articles worth tens of millions of dinars, all carefully itemized in documents found in each chest. Each list was signed by a representative of the Pavelic gang and countersigned by a priest. They were part of the appropriation for the *Krizari* 'war budget.'

"As we see now, the Vatican and the various Foreign Offices *wanted* us to try Stepinac. There's reason for the belief that Stepinac himself— a murky, cunning individual—wanted to be tried and become a 'martyr' and an international *cause célèbre* . . . Naïve? As a Communist, I think we were right to take every possible step to avoid the affair. I feel differently as a Serbian. I have relatives who aren't Communists, and in 1945 and '46 they were turning against the new regime because Stepinac wasn't brought to justice when nearly every Serbian *knew* he was partly responsible for the butchering of hundreds of thousands of Serbians in Croatia. In other words, Stepinac was an internal political problem. . . . At the end, since the Vatican refused to relieve us of him, Stepinac was tried and given sixteen years, though his crimes far exceeded those of many war criminals who were executed in Germany, Japan, and Norway as well as in Yugoslavia. The worst you can say is that we discriminated in his favor.

"And, if I'm abreast of our policy, we're prepared to continue to discriminate in his favor. Bishop Hurley, the Vatican, and your 'able, influential, and ambitious' Cardinal Spellman know that our government is always ready to consider releasing Stepinac from Lepoglava Prison, provided he leaves Yugoslavia and quits his role of a politician and counter-revolutionary."

"Why should they want to relieve you of him? Stepinac in Lepoglava has wide propaganda value."

A few of the men around the table nodded. Tito inserted a new cigarette into his holder.

"We may be stuck with him," said X. "And that's a kind of unpoetic justice. Stepinac is a product of what passed for civilization in Yugoslavia before the war. He's a product of religious history in the Balkans, going back not hundreds of years, but a thousand. In a way, he's a delayed climax of the Rome-Byzantium rivalry. He's part of the 'heart' of 'a heartless world.' Remnants of that world are still with us. Our task is to work ourselves clear of them. . . .

"As for that school near New York named after Stepinac. Someone sent *drug* Tito a picture of it out of a newspaper. The clipping is filed in our Central Committee library. The school is a fine building. But we're appalled that American parents wish to send their children to a school named for a war criminal."

A pause.

One of the other men at the table said, "I'd like to add that much of the thinking in our country on priest war criminals these past several years has been less objectively Marxian than old-fashioned reacting to an ugly phenomenon. Some people hold that it's more reprehensible for a priest to commit a crime than for anyone else. This implies that a priest is a better man than another man because he's a priest, or that he was 'ordained' or 'consecrated' because he was a paragon to begin with. Of course that's nonsense. To me, a criminal is a criminal, a crime is a crime. Someday we may all be more detached about this.

"For moments once in a while I can see our priest criminals as dim figures in an unpleasant procession, far off, that fits into an ancient pattern of conflict in the 'inverted world' Marx saw; and I don't hate them as persons or as priests. They're part of the whole tumultuous process of man trying to find himself in the darkness of the feudal-capitalist-imperialist evolvement. I find no satisfaction in seeing them punished. There's no satisfaction in trying a Stepinac or keeping him in prison—in the same prison where *drug* Tito and *drug* Pijade served time. There's no fun reading summaries of American and British worldwide-Catholic propaganda built around the trumped-up charge that we're 'persecuting religion.' As though we had nothing else to do! We merely leave religion stewing in its own crisis. . . .

"But moments of detachment are a luxury none of us can afford too often as yet. . . . Another aspect of the Stepinac case. It's rumored in the West that he's in Lepoglava for revenge, because *drug* Tito and *drug* Pijade served time there in the 1930's, when a Catholic priest"— Anton Korosec, a Slovenian—"was Minister of the Interior of the royal government. Actually, *drug* Tito and *drug* Pijade had nothing to do with Stepinac being sent to Lepoglava. He is there because Lepoglava is in Croatia. If he were in the penitentiary at Sremska Mitrovica or Maribor, the rumors might be the same, for *drug* Marshal was in both of those prisons too. The fact of the matter is we simply don't know what else to do with Stepinac, since the Vatican refused to take him off our hands. We have to keep him in one prison or another. If we wanted revenge, Stepinac would be in a cell as desolate as the one *drug* Tito had; instead he is in an airy apartment. *Drug* Tito's cell had no Marxist literature except what was smuggled in. Stepinac's apartment in Lepoglava contains a small library and a well-equipped chapel. There are priests of lesser rank in Lepoglava—war criminals, too— who assist him at Mass, as befits an archbishop. Again, discrimination in his favor. But I'm off on a tangent."

"An interesting tangent," I said.

"We have our leftovers from the past," X said. "What can we do with Stepinac, or that other bishop we have in prison at Zenica? [The Bishop of Mostar, Herzegovina. He was released in 1950, before the expiration of his term.] How can we handle our atavisms? . . . Detach-

ment *is* a luxury we can afford only in small doses. New Yugoslavia is
a revolutionary state. Our Party and government leaders and we who
assist them are not hermit philosophers. Life swirls around us and
pounds us with the most compelling motives and demands.

"The war and postwar crimes of some of the clergy," X went on,
"are part of Yugoslavia's present consciousness. Who can reasonably
demand that the CPY urge our people to forget and forgive? How can
any friend of New Yugoslavia reasonably recommend that our Party
ask our citizens not to memorialize the heroic victims of those crimes,
simply because some people elsewhere in the world who know nothing
of what happened in Yugoslavia, and why, are persuaded that that
means we are 'persecuting religion'? . . . For at least a generation
the Yugoslav people will be unable to forget. Their attitude toward
organized religion, the Church, and priests personally, has been pro-
foundly affected. To those who blame the Communists for that attitude, I can only say the obvious: we didn't create it. Stepinac created
it, and some of the priests under him. It exists, and our Party and
government leaders have no magic wand to wave the wrath of the
people away.

"But what happened in Yugoslavia during the war is nothing new.
Long before there were Communists, men like Stepinac behaved in
this fashion. There was the Inquisition. In France during the twelfth
and thirteenth centuries, there was that horrible case of those people
—what were they called? They had some connection with our Bogomili. . . . Yes, the Albigenses. . . ." (See *The Heretics,* a novel by
Humphrey Slater [Harcourt, Brace: 1947]. Part One deals with the
slow murder of thousands of orphaned Albigensian children during
the papacy of Innocent the Third. . . . The Bogomili were a "heret-
ical" sect of anti-Church Christians in what are now Yugoslavia and
Bulgaria.)

Late in January and through February 1949, going about Slovenia,
a country with a long Catholic background, I was impressed by several
scenes and incidents—"some of them palpable and understandable
enough," I wrote in my diary on February 28 as part of a general note
on the subject, "others subtle and endlessly baffling."

In Ljubljana, not a single priest, monk, or nun was to be seen in the
street—or so I thought until one of my brothers said of a man we
passed, "That's a priest," and informed me that the diocesan authority

required all priests to wear secular clothes out-of-doors. There were two explanations for the requirement. One, that it was a gesture of protest against the "godless Tito regime." The other, that when the clergy appeared in religious garb they drew so many angry looks they were uncomfortable, and that, besides, they aggravated the anti-Church attitude of many elderly people and nearly all the youth.

In rural Slovenia I saw thousands of roadside crosses and hundreds of little shrines dedicated to the Virgin Mary, St. George, and St. Florian. True, none of them were new; they had all been put up before the war, and some were in need of repair. But evidently the new regime was in no hurry to make them disappear. Some were decorated with artificial flowers and freshly picked wildflowers.

Passing through Kranjska Gora, a mountain town in the northwestern corner of the Slovenian Upland, I encountered an old priest wearing a soiled turned-about collar. He was over six feet tall and built in proportion, with a large head under a big black hat. His shabby, unbuttoned fur-lined coat made him look even bigger than he was. He needed a shave and carried a rough cane. He stopped in the middle of the main street and, eying me angrily, muttered something in response to my "Good morning," and stalked on. I inquired about him at the office of the local people's committee and was told that his wartime record was *"proti-ljudski—anti-people"* but that no charges had been brought against him. Most of the community regarded him, pityingly and otherwise, as deranged. This attitude was encouraged by the local CP *aktivisti,* who preached that hating a man for his misdeeds during the war was harmful to the community.

Slovenia is thickly dotted with churches. Every town and every sizable village has one. It usually dominates the scene. Hundreds of churches stand on hilltops alone. They are ancient and fortresslike, and some of them are quite beautiful. Long ago they were used for defense against the foraying Turks. During World War II various armed forces but especially the Italian- and German-armed quislingist *Belogardisti,* or White Guards, used them for fortifications, and many were damaged or destroyed.

At the end of my first month in Slovenia—on February 18—I wrote in my diary that "of the dozens of churches I have seen close by so far, two-thirds or more are pockmarked with rifle and machine-gun fire. Some were repaired by voluntary-labor 'brigades' organized by local people's committees in compliance with the wishes of the villagers.

Having repaired their homes and barns and *kozolci* [drying sheds] or built new ones, they couldn't bear to see the old church stand in ruins or disrepair, even though the services had been discontinued either because of the shortage of priests or because people no longer went to church.

"The church as a building remains part of the Slovenian landscape. What will be done with it eventually as the socialist culture unfurls, I don't know. Nor does anyone else, it seems. Apparently no one is giving the matter any thought. The CP leaders may feel the people will handle it themselves in their own different ways, depending on local traditions.

"A few churches stand in disrepair by popular demand as monuments to wartime crimes perpetrated within their walls in the name of religion by priests and their fanatic lay followers. One of these is Sveti-Urh [St. Ulrich] on a hilltop about an hour's walk from the center of Ljubljana.

"This church—from the summer of 1942 to the war's end, when the Liberation Forces finally captured it at the climax of a four-day battle— was a minor Dachau. In it a priest-commanded outfit called the Black Hand, a branch of the priest-recruited White Guard organization, tortured and killed about a thousand 'Communists,' most of whom were not Communists but pro-Partisan civilians or relatives of Partisans. The Black Hand's motto was: 'In the name of the wounds of Christ, this Partisan must die!' [the same motto under which my cousin, now in South America, went about his massacres]. Each member of the organization wore a medallion said to have been specially blessed by somebody high up in the hierarchy in Yugoslavia if not in Rome. They were distributed by priests holding official positions in the diocesan chancellery of Bishop Gregorij Rozman in Ljubljana.

"I visited Sveti-Urh twice, a few days apart, and listened for many hours to a young woman, Stefka Podbevsek, who taught school in the village just below the 'horror hill.' She is writing a book about the place and let me read her script, still in rough draft. She wasn't a Communist before the war; she is an ardent one now.

"Everything inside and around the church is as it was immediately after the battle, except for the bodies of the clerical and non-clerical war criminals who fell in the fight. Of their comrades who survived, some escaped to Austria and made their way to Brazil, the Argentine, and the United States. One is said to be in Cleveland. Several were

captured, tried by a people's court at the end of the war in the presence of two thousand men and women on the slope in front of the
church, and executed.

"During the trial, which lasted several days, a battalion of the New
Yugoslav Army was deployed on the hilltop. Stefka Podbevsek was
there. 'The troops were needed,' she says, 'to protect the prisoners from
the mothers and other relatives of the victims who wanted to tear
them to bits.'

"I went through the ruined parish house and down into the window-
less basement where the prisoners were tortured. On damp warm days
the floor and walls are still 'sticky with human blood' [my guide's
words]. There's a tunnel through which the Black Handers dragged
the battered captives from the basement into the church where priests
offered them the sacraments. . . .

"I asked why the priests acted that way. How could they? No one
can say for sure. Like X, Josip Vidmar brings up the Inquisition and
the Albigenses. Stefka Podbevsek shakes her head: it's beyond her
understanding, and she has no idea how she'll end her book. She
showed me pictures of the priests directly responsible for the horrors.
One priest looks like a dedicated ascetic.

"I walked in the woods around the hilltop where every few nights
for nearly three years several men and women were shot, hanged, or
knifed in the heart by men who, from all accounts, experienced a kind
of spiritual orgasm killing them 'in the name of the wounds of Christ,'
while at the same time they were enriching themselves with the loot
they confiscated from their victims.

"Driven into a tree trunk is a steel ring, now rusting, to which hundreds of martyrs were tied for the final installment of torture if they
had refused the last sacrament of the church. Then they were killed.
[Details like these came out during the trial and are a matter of record.] . . . The forest was illumined with floodlights. All this business
took place between one and four at night. Then the killers passed
through the church and genuflected before the main altar and crossed
themselves with holy water, and went to the parish house to wash up
and have a drink or two and a bite to eat; whereupon they were ready
for sleep. At the trial they told on each other: how they paced in front
of the church nervously before the night's load of victims was brought
in from Ljubljana. Once when the truck broke down and arrived two
hours later than usual, one of the sadists almost went stark mad. By

daybreak, after he had done his night's 'work,' he was calm again, at peace with his God.

"A few steps from the tree with the steel ring is a *tolmun*—bottomless pool. It sucks down everything heavier than water and nothing ever returns to the surface. Into it, by their own statements made during the trial, the Black Handers dumped hundreds of their victims.

"Two high barbed-wire fences about a hundred feet apart, now rusting and in disrepair, encircle the hill. During the war they were charged with electric current which came up from a near-by factory, whose owner was on good terms with the diocesan chancellery and a moving spirit behind the Black Hand. Close around the church and the thick cemetery wall are rows of trenches and blown-up pillboxes.

"Hundreds of graves are scattered haphazardly among the trees within a thousand-yard radius of the church. Some are only two, three feet deep, covered over by a growth of brush and ferns. Workers were opening them up both times I visited Sveti-Urh. They've been at it for months and don't know how much more there is yet to do. I watched them for a long time. There was an official in charge of disinterring the remains and searching the dirt for identifying objects. In grave after grave they found nothing. The bones were gathered, put into unpainted caskets, and borne into a massive tomb, still unfinished, a stone's throw from the church. . . . Two or three times I felt I was about to keel over, and sat down or grabbed hold of a tree.

"The tomb will be a monument. In Ljubljana three sculptors are working on various sections of it. They hope to produce a work of art people will want to come to see.

"People already come to Sveti-Urh from all over Slovenia: relatives and friends mostly of the men and women known to have died there. Others make the pilgrimage because they think their sons, brothers, or husbands who disappeared during the war may have been among the victims. They wander in and out of the church, all about the place, and gaze at the 'gallows trees' in the forest, and touch the steel ring in the tree trunk, and stare into the black *tolmun*. To see them is to glimpse a bit of Slovenia's wartime agony. (But I'm told that Sveti-Urh is nothing compared to the priest-directed horrors in Croatia and Bosnia-Herzegovina.)

"Still others come because they're Communists, intent on paying tribute to the memory of the victims, or interested in seeing how the monument is progressing. Most of them are young. They transcend the horror with Marxist ideology and hard work in the Party-government apparatus or as students in the university and the technical schools. They discuss it without hate.

"I talked with two of them who fought in the final battle in 1945 which resulted in the Partisans breaking into the church and capturing the surviving Black Handers. One of them, a young man named Gaspercek, took me all around the hillside and told me of the battle in great detail. It was the climax of his life. To him that battle was *the* Liberation.

"The church building isn't seriously damaged. Inside, though, the pews and other fixtures and objects are in utter disarray. St. Ulrich, the patron saint who was a bishop, is intact but leans to one side in his niche in the center of the main altar. Nearly everything else is busted up and strewn about. Most of the pictures of the Way of the Cross are on the floor covered with plaster dust. The walls inside are almost more thickly pockmarked with bullets than outside. The window panes are broken and birds and bats fly in and out. The doors are down, and dogs and cats come and go.

" 'Everything,' said Gaspercek, 'will stay as it was when we captured it, except as time and the elements change it. The name Sveti-Urh will remain.' "

In the forenoon on February 26, 1949, I came to the town of Metlika. The main street was crowded with people. I asked what was happening. A trial before the people's court. Who was being tried? A priest. What for? The people exchanged glances and were silent. Could I see the president or secretary of the people's committee? The president and the secretary were called, and they took me aside and said the priest was a homosexual charged with perverting two boys. They telephoned to Ljubljana—to the UDBa or the public prosecutor's office, I imagine— and obtained permission to admit me to the already overfull little courtroom. For two and a half hours I listened to the proceedings.

The accused, in his late thirties, had pleaded guilty a few minutes before. Without much prompting from the examiner he told how he himself had been seduced twenty-odd years ago by the parish priest in his town and then been persuaded to enter the seminary. This, he said, was a common procedure for two or three decades. When he graduated from the seminary, he became the parish priest's *kaplan* (assistant pastor) and steady sweetheart.

The narrative, while marked by the exhibitionist streak found in a good many homosexuals, had a straightforward quality. It involved at least one bishop and one head of the seminary in Ljubljana. Every now and then it evoked shocked exclamations from the spectators. Twice the president of the court, a school teacher in a near-by village, rapped for order.

The poor creature was sentenced to four years in prison—no solution of his abnormality, but justified in the minds of the people because of the two boys. I also sensed a satisfaction that *now they, the people, could do something* about a matter of this kind. Before the Revolution priests were outside the law.

I saw no report about the trial in the newspapers, so I went to Boris Kraigher—who, as already mentioned, was Minister of the Interior of the PR of Slovenia, head of the local security police, and a leading member of the Politburo of the Slovenian CP. I learned that in recent years several such cases had come up. The press refrained from reporting them at the request of the Party and the government for fear the news would spread outside the country and be distorted into propaganda that Tito was hounding the Church—or that homosexuality was ripe in Yugoslavia. "Actually," said Kraigher, "there's less of it here than in Europe generally."

Quoting from my early-March notes, "There *are* priests—a small minority—who were pro-Partisan in wartime and who are now in favor of the new regime. Last week I saw the Reverend F. S. Finzgar of the Ternovo parish in Ljubljana, a popular novelist, close to eighty years old but hale and hearty. He and nearly two hundred other Slovenian priests are members of the People's Front organization. He's not a Communist of course, perhaps not even a pro-Communist, but he's for 'Tito'—although with reservations, I believe.

"Another pro-Tito priest is Father Anton Cernugel of Babna Gora. Long-time Communists speak of him with affection. The theme of a speech he delivered in 1943 after blessing a Partisan brigade going into battle was: 'You are better than we are.' I couldn't work up much of a discussion with him. He's either a very simple man or ashamed of his fellow-priests, or both.

"In the village of Stopice I came upon a Franciscan who is the parish priest. He agrees with the Marxists that constructive work is the firmest basis for a sound morality. He joins every voluntary-labor group he can and although he's anything but robust works harder than anyone else.

"I'm told that in the Slovenian Littoral and in the Croatian parts of Istria [both regions were under Italy between the two wars] about half the priests are anti-fascist from 'way back and so, now, they're pro-Tito with or without reservations. A handful of them form the core of an anti-ultramontanist movement for a national autocephalous Church —divorced from the Vatican."

My sister Polda's few words about the Prior of the Carthusian monastery at Pleterje, in Lower Slovenia, kept recurring to me while I was in the Upland. When I returned to Ljubljana, I asked others about him and everyone, Communists and non-Communists, spoke highly of him. I inquired if I might visit the place and soon after an invitation came from the Prior, the Right Reverend Doctor Josip Edgar Leopold.

The monastery compound takes up the level bottom of a secluded valley in the foothills of the Gorjanci Mountains, an hour's walk from the village of Sent-Jernej (St. Jamesville). It is a small walled-in city, a compact civilization with a way of life all its own. Surrounding the enclosure is an upsweep of fields, vineyards, and orchards; and beyond, of forests.

There is a large building near the main gate, and there are rows and clusters of smaller buildings, some of them built centuries ago to last forever, all strung together in an unrigid symmetry along the high, thick quadrangular wall and amid small orchards and gardens. There are two churches, several chapels, assembly rooms, offices, a kitchen, a library, numerous workshops and storerooms, and about forty very small houses—hermitages—all alike, one for each full-fledged monk.

The aged gray Prior and a husky young monk—the *ekonom,* who manages the monastery's practical affairs and some of its relations with the outside world—showed me through the compound and many of the buildings. The unoccupied hermitage they took me in had a small walled-in garden, a tiny living-room, bedroom, oratory, workshop and storeroom. There was an aperture for the passage of food and other requirements—books, tools, workshop materials, garden seeds. The new tenant would write his needs on a slate, I was told, and the lay brother assigned to him would fulfill them.

The Carthusians are not complete hermits. They talk among themselves and with the lay brothers and occasional visitors—but as little as possible. Once a week they walk in silence outside the compound. At midnight they gather in the main church and pray until two. On Sunday and on feast days they eat in silence side-by-side at long tables in the refectory, a bare room with uniquely simple, lofty lines.

In the large library, where I would have liked to spend a week, a monk with a thin boyish face was in charge. He answered my questions with a quick, precise practicality that was somehow incongruous with his abstracted personality. Except when he spoke, he seemed to be beyond the point of returning to everydayness. Crammed on the ceiling-high shelves and stacked on tables and benches were twelve thousand volumes in two dozen languages, among them hundreds of ancient and rare items as well as a lot of trash, judging by some of the English titles I noticed in passing.

We went through the ruins of the eighteen buildings destroyed during the three-day battle in mid-February 1943, between the Liberation Front—or Partisan—forces on the one side and the White Guards and their fascist-Italian masters on the other.

The afternoon passed so quickly I didn't feel I had learned very much about Pleterje and the Prior, and I eagerly accepted his invitation to stay for supper. While I ate he and the *ekonom* sat opposite me. A lay brother brought me an excellent *kranjska klobasa* (a Slovenian sausage), horseradish, dark bread, red wine, and a bowl of big yellow apples. From an odd-shaped blue bottle the brother filled a small glass before me with Chartreuse, the finely flavored green liqueur the Carthusians make, and the otherwise taciturn Prior kept urging me to take one sip after another.

With less success, I kept urging the Prior to tell me about the battle with which I was already familiar from other sources with other viewpoints. Finally, as though sensing he had failed to satisfy me, he said a *kartuzija* was a place of silence and he'd never been much of a talker anyhow; if I wished, he would give me a copy of a typescript of about a hundred pages containing extracts from his wartime journal. He also gave me a beautifully printed book in Slovenian, *Kartuzijani* (The Carthusians), a history of the Order from its beginnings, with a section on Pleterje.

Silence and seclusion are two main features of the Carthusian way of life whose tradition goes back to the early eleventh century, when a French priest now known as St. Bruno founded the Order. (Pleterje itself was started in 1406.) And so when war engulfed Yugoslavia on Palm Sunday 1941, and when the *borba*—resistance to the enemy, revolution, and civil war—blazed up in the wooded Gorjanci region, the Pleterje monks' clearest and strongest inclination was to pretend it was none of their concern, and to bypass it. This turned out to be impossible. In the second half of 1941 all of Slovenia, all of Yugoslavia, was deep in a "total situation." There was no vantage point from which one could merely look on. In one way or another the tide of events snatched up everyone.

Every now and then the silence of Pleterje Valley was broken by the not so distant *rat-tat-tat* of machine-guns or the crack of a sniper's rifle. Refugees from the occupation's terror and wounded Partisans appeared at the monastery's heavy main gate. "Naturally," said the Prior, "we helped them with what little we had." Soon couriers came with messages from Partisan commanders in near-by hills asking for medicine and bandages. "Naturally, we gave them from what little we had."

The Prior meant "naturally" as a Christian. From other sources, however, I knew that his attitude wasn't shared by all the Pleterje monks. Three among the thirty or so were Germans, and the Prior was said to have had quite a time with them. Most of the others were in a state because the Partisans were said to be Communists: a species of sinners the world over. They were alleged to deny God, to have dealings with Stalin, to have shot monks and nuns in Spain——

But the Partisans didn't behave badly. Well-written notes from their commanders came addressed to "The Right Reverend Doctor Josip Edgar Leopold, Prior of Pleterje," thanking him and the *kartuzija* for the medicines and their kindness. Quite early in the struggle a few commanders and commissars called in person, and the Prior thought they certainly didn't look like the ogres their adversaries painted them in *Slovenec* (The Slovenian), the priest-edited Clerical Party's newspaper published in enemy-occupied Ljubljana, to which the monastery had subscribed before the war and which kept coming irregularly in the mail. The Partisans could have looted Pleterje, but not one of them took even an apple from the orchards or a bunch of grapes from the vineyards outside the compound when they passed through the valley. Their restraint impressed the most bitterly anti-Communist monks. Besides medicines, the Partisans needed other supplies—horseshoes, for example, which the monastery had in abundance in the autumn of

'41—and the commanders and commissars asked for them and gave a receipt. They told the *ekonom* that after the war the monastery could claim payment from the new state which they would found on the principles of social and economic justice. The Partisans had no doubt whatever how the war would end.

One commander told the Prior he was "a Communist of course": he had fought on the Loyalist side in Spain in 1936–37, and was very proud of it. He added that most of the commanders and all of the political commissars were Communists, and that Communism was a great philosophy with the only scientific social-economic-cultural approach to man's problem. If the Prior had never read Marx and Engels and Lenin, he didn't know what he was missing. He pointed out that, from what he had seen of it, the Carthusian way of life was a medieval form of Communism, whereas the Communism he believed in was *modern* Communism, destined to sweep the earth.

This caused the Prior some uneasiness. He couldn't shake off the idea that Marxian Communism was sheer sin. Yet he wondered. He couldn't find it in his heart to condemn these men. Was Marxism really bad? It must be, for Communists didn't believe in God, which was dreadful—it gave him a pang whenever he thought of it. Nor did they genuflect and cross themselves when they entered a chapel or passed the main altar in the church. But they always left their weapons outside the compound, apparently in deference to the *kartuzija*. And their conduct toward him and the other monks was as agreeable as one could wish, and not put on.

The Communists brought him neatly handwritten excerpts from the works of Marx and Engels and their followers which they thought might interest him—such as:

. . . Men make their history themselves, but hitherto they have not done so with a collective will according to an all-embracing plan. Their efforts oppose each other; thus they are ruled by necessity, completed and expressed by chance. When society seizes the means of production, the product will no longer dominate the producer. Conscious organization will replace the anarchy which tyrannizes over social production, and the struggle for individual existence will cease. Only thus can man, in some sense, detach himself definitely from the animal world. He will pass from the conditions of animal existence to the conditions of human existence. It will be the leap of the human race from the reign of necessity into the reign of liberty. . . .
—From Engels' January 25, 1894, letter to Heinz Starkenburg

. . . Communism, as a real appropriation of the human essence by man and for man and thus as man's return to himself in his social, i.e. human, aspect . . . a return that is complete, conscious, and sustained by all the riches of former development . . . is naturalism fully achieved and thus coincides with human- ism. It is the true end of the quarrel between essence and existence, between objectivization and the affirmation of self, between the individual and the species. It resolves the mystery of history, and it knows that it resolves it.
—Marx, in 1844

The Prior didn't look at these excerpts for weeks, wondering if he should; and when he did, they *were* "interesting" in so far as he under- stood them, but he couldn't bring himself to comment upon them to the eager young men to whom Marxism was a religion—a religion rivaling his, and wrong for other reasons besides. It bypassed God; it said that man could take hold of nature, of himself in nature, without His help. A blasphemy, or close to it, *but*——

On July 16, 1942, about seventy thousand of Mussolini's crack troops —aided by about three thousand Italian-equipped Whites,[1] many of them armed priests wearing officers' insignia on their tunics—began an elaborate "offensive" against the Partisans, who then numbered only about five thousand men and about one thousand women, but who had the support of a big majority of the population. The "offen- sive" lasted nearly four months. Using the Whites as guides, the Italians fine-combed the whole of Lower Slovenia. Their objective was to de- stroy the "communist bandits" once and forever. The first week a few battles and several minor skirmishes took place. Then, of a sudden, the Partisans vanished like rain in the ground; or, as "Lawrence of Arabia" described a similar instance, like an odorless, colorless gas. For the next few months the Italian Fascisti and their White fellow-travelers crawled through bushes and up and down hills and mountains search- ing for them; and enraged by the futility of the hunt, topped by the unfriendly attitude of the populace, they sporadically burned hundreds of villages and slaughtered thousands of hostages. Throughout this period Italian commanders were sending elaborate communiqués to

[1] The Italian occupation authorities' official name for the "White Guards" was *Milizia Volontaria Anticomunista*. Almost without exception, the MVA's recruiting officers— and, in many instances, the commanders—were young Slovenian priests, lately out of the seminary. After the Italian capitulation, most of the White Guard units became adjuncts of the German occupation, of the Gestapo specifically.

the High Command in Rome telling of far-flung, savage battles all over this new *provincia* of *Il Duce's* expanded empire, and that in each of them, employing fascist generalship at its best, they killed, wounded, and captured thousands of *banditi*. It may be that the fascist generals half believed these reports or that their intelligence officers succumbed to some of the Whites' exaggerations. Both the Italians and the Whites apparently did believe, though, that their superior numbers and equipment had scared the Partisans out of existence.

To the Prior of Pleterje, who followed the "offensive" as well as he could, it looked for a time late in the autumn of 1942 as if *partizanstvo* had been vanquished.

Suddenly just before Christmas, scorning all the protests of the monks and the lay brothers at the main gate, a White unit, under four officers, marched into the Pleterje compound. One of the officers was a priest, Father Janez Kolesnik from a near-by village, who used to visit the monastery in prewar days. Now, as the Prior subsequently noted in his journal, he was "armed to the teeth." Asked why, he replied that he had his orders. From whom? The Bishop's office in Ljubljana. He hinted that his right to bear arms came from Rome. "Impossible!" said one of the Carthusians. "That would be against the laws of the Church." Father Kolesnik guffawed loudly.

(Kolesnik is a near-anagram of his true name which almost anyone in Lower Slovenia will recognize. I disguise it because just before the war's end he escaped from Yugoslavia and is now in America, still a priest and capable, I am told, of violent action. He means nothing to me, and I have no desire to expose him and turn him into my active enemy.

(In Ljubljana, through much of 1949, I often talked with Ivo Pirkovic, a writer, a Christian Socialist before the war and an emphatic pro-Communist since 1943, a son of a well-known family in the town of Sent-Jernej, which is near both Pleterje and the village of Kolesnik's birth and priesthood. Though crippled by arthritis since the middle 1930's, Pirkovic became a Liberation leader in his home territory, running a minor war from his bed after two of his brothers were killed— one of many Yugoslav stories I came upon that are barely credible to an outsider unless he visits the country. Pirkovic is a close personal friend of Prior Leopold and an authority on the Partisan warfare in the Gorjanci Mountains and on Kolesnik.

("Kolesnik came of a poverty-stricken family," Pirkovic told me, "and was a strange lad even while he was attending school in the city. Once when he was home during vacation he picked up a gun belonging to a hunter who was having a drink in the village inn, and shot the innkeeper's rooster—just like that, for no reason at all except, as it later occurred to me, that he liked to kill. On being ordained he was assigned to his home village as assistant pastor. He was a passionate hunter. He owned three shotguns and a rifle. . . . What led him to become a priest? The *kartuzija* in Pleterje gave him a small stipend, which carried the wish of the monastery that the beneficiary study for the priesthood. But in all probability that wasn't what decided him. His mother, a pious woman, wanted him to be a priest. More decisive still, in Old Yugoslavia, a young fellow going to school in the city soon realized that the priesthood offered him higher security if not income than, say, engineering or almost any other technical profession. But that's another story: the story of the educated young person in Old Yugoslavia. . . .

(". . . During the war Kolesnik fascinated me in a repugnant sort of way," Pirkovic said. "After the Liberation I did a little research job on him. Two peasant women, Kozeljeva from the village of Zapuze and Zagorceva from the village of Orehovica, claimed he killed their sons, Stanko Zagorc and Stanko Kozelj, both of whom I knew. They told his mother, Kolesnikova, who declared she no longer recognized him as her son even if he was a priest. . . . One day immediately after the war my wartime comrade, Rudolf Kocman, roamed the woods near his village of Dolza seeking the grave of his father. A woman gathering mushrooms, whom we both knew well and liked, led him to it—a mass grave containing about sixty other White Guards' victims. She had witnessed the massacre from behind a cliff fifty yards away. At first the White troopers refused to shoot, she said; then Kolesnik pulled out his gun and showed them how. . . . In October 1942, when his soldiers again balked, Kolesnik himself shot dead a prewar friend with whom he used to go hunting. . . . Explain him? Ask me something easy."

(I visited all the people mentioned above. They repeated their stories to me. They couldn't explain Kolesnik.)

The Whites took over an entire wing of the monastery, and, to the Carthusians' abhorrence, made themselves at home. Most of the soldiers

—about a hundred of them—were peasant boys from the vicinity, with scant education, who in normal times would have become more or less normal men. Their village priests had roused them to a pitch of anti-Communist fanaticism and induced them to enter the service of the enemy.

Twice—at the end of December 1942, and of January 1943—an Italian army paymaster came to Pleterje to pay the Whites. One morning an Italian general named Gomara turned up on a tour of inspection and gave the White commander a wad of lire to buy drinks for the boys. He was seen chatting and shaking hands with Kolesnik.

On first coming to Pleterje, some of the boys didn't realize the Carthusians were religionists of a different stripe than Kolesnik and the other priests they knew. They boasted that in such-and-such a village they had killed so many "Communists"—men, women, and children whose brothers, husbands, and fathers were in the woods with the Partisans.

On the walls in the wing of the enclosure they had taken over, the Whites painted slogans like *For God and the Faith—the Partisan Must Croak—This Is the Will of the People.*

No White entered either of the two monastery churches. But every Sunday, wearing priestly vestments over his uniform, Father Kolesnik celebrated Mass at an outdoor altar and preached a violent anti-Communist sermon. The service had all the forms of Roman Catholic ritual, and many of the boys kneeling in the grass prayed with such fervor that several monks believed they must be truly religious, while others suffered as though living through a nightmare. They talked more during those few weeks than they had for years before. The bulge in Kolesnik's vestments where he carried his gun—of Italian make—shocked them more than anything else.

The Prior didn't join in the discussions. Nor do the extracts from his journal tell how he felt about Father Kolesnik's services. Others told me that he sank into "a chasm of silence." He didn't utter a word for weeks.

The other three White officers obviously were ordinary criminals to whom the complex "total situation"—war and civil war, and revolution *versus* counter-revolution—was a chance to loot. They made forays into near-by villages and returned with hauls which they stored in their quarters. In the compound they helped themselves to almost anything they saw. This was true of many of the young soldiers but not of all. Pleterje awed some of them who had been brought up religiously.

The presence of a woman in a Carthusian monastery is unthinkable, but the Whites kept several of them in Pleterje. They wore uniforms. When asked about them, Kolesnik laughed and said the girls were *kurirke*—couriers. At night while the monks tried to sleep or pray in their hermitages, or as they assembled in the main church for the Midnight Office, sounds of wild parties came from the Whites' wing.

Again and again, the monks begged them to depart. The lay commanders laughed at their pleas, but no louder than Father Kolesnik, whose position in the garrison, the Carthusians eventually realized, was analogous (with many differences) to a political commissar's in the Partisans. If they, the monks, had a complaint, the commanders said, they should address it to Bishop Rozman in Ljubljana, or to Archbishop Alojzij Stepinac in Zagreb, and wait for a reply . . . *ha, ha, ha!*

The Whites kept accusing the Carthusians of being pro-Partisan, the Prior particularly; which was true ("How could I not be?" Doctor Leopold said to me)—and of having given the "Communists" medical and other supplies: also true. They said the Prior and his whole white-robed pack, with their piety and stuff, were no better than those goddamn Reds in the woods whose boss and master was not the man called Tito, said to be operating somewhere in Bosnia, but the world's chief atheist and Antichrist, Stalin himself. Tito, if there was such a bastard, was a Russian general or a Comintern operator, whom the world's No. 1 Communist and God's No. 1 enemy had sent to Yugoslavia to destroy religion. Helping the Partisans in the Gorjanci woods was helping Tito, was helping Stalin, was helping atheism, and—following this line of logic—the Carthusians were practically atheists and Communists, and goddamn lucky they were still permitted to toddle around in those silly white robes. Actually, they deserved to be shot and dumped in the field out there for the carrion crows and buzzards to feast on, or to be chased out of the monastery into the woods, where they belonged, with their beloved Communists . . . *ha, ha, ha!* . . . and as they ran, stumbling over their robes, wouldn't they make fine targets? . . .

These and similar details came to me from a man now in the UDBa in Ljubljana. A prewar CP member and a Partisan since 1941, he was assigned by the Slovenian Liberation Front high command to work his way into the monastery for two weeks in January '43 and pretend to be a White and size up the quislingists' strength.

The Prior didn't tell me this, nor is it in the parts of his journal that I read; but, from what I learned in Ljubljana before my visit to Pleterje and after, it appears that the events there late in '42 and early in '43 were no mere Partisan-*versus*-White or revolution-*versus*-counter-revolution conflict. In part they were the most recent—and not the last— act of an old, long-drawn-out struggle between two factions within the Catholic Church in Yugoslavia: between the "truly religious priests" like Dr. Leopold, some of whom were more or less anti-Vatican, and the "political priests," or Clericals, who were fanatical ultramontanes. (The word *ultramontane,* long familiar in Europe but unknown to the general reading public in the United States, means, literally, "those beyond the mountains," usually beyond the Alps, *i.e.,* in Italy. In religious controversy *ultramontanism* is, briefly, the idea and movement which favors the Pope or the Vatican as the source of all jurisdiction.)

In various forms, with various emphases, the struggle was—still is— worldwide. A phase of it began in the nineteenth century. In the Balkans, for a time, it revolved around the Croatian bishop, Josip Strosmajer, who lived from 1815 to 1905. He was a staunch anti-ultramontanist who followed the tradition set by Bishop Grgur Ninjski, a Dalmatian, who centuries before Luther defied Rome. Strosmajer fought the dogma of accession of the Virgin Mother and the concept of papal infallibility, and in the 1890's he was in a heretic's doghouse. From the start of the twentieth century, however, and until the success of the Tito-led Revolution, the political priests were in the ascendancy in Croatia, Slovenia, Dalmatia, and Bosnia-Herzegovina. For fifty years the Archbishop of Zagreb and the bishops in the smaller centers like Ljubljana, Maribor, Sarajevo, Mostar, and Split were political hatchet-men disguised as ecclesiastics.

Prior Leopold was a Croatian, son of an old and prominent family. Friends like Ivo Pirkovic in Ljubljana who knew him longest told me that he grew up in the Strosmajer tradition. In the 1920's, when he was a young priest in Zagreb, he was one of the leaders against the cynical, money- and power-hungry political faction in the Church nominally headed by old Archbishop Bauer, but actually by the young Monsignor Stepinac, who was in charge of the archdiocesan chancellery. At Bauer's death it looked as if Stepinac would succeed him, and the "purely religious" faction prevailed upon Leopold to stand as the anti-Stepinac candidate for Archbishop of Zagreb.

In the ensuing struggle, the political hatchet-man won. On the urging of King Alexander, who was Serbian Orthodox, the Vatican made Stepinac archbishop and thus head of the Catholic organization in Yugoslavia.

Father Leopold then "retired into silence," into the Carthusian Order . . . and eventually became the Prior of Pleterje. . . .

In April 1949 I revisited Pleterje in the company of Josip Vidmar and Ivan Levar, a leading Slovenian actor, both wartime friends of the Prior; and John N. Rogelj, of Cleveland, an insurance man, on his first trip to New Yugoslavia.

I found the Prior aging, white-haired, thin, rather ashen-faced, with a quiet fire in his gray-blue eyes, which rather resembled Tito's when the tumult within him was quiet. Listening closely to his barely audible speech and looking at him, I thought that a religious-minded romantic would describe him as "saintly." Fitting together my impressions of him, I wondered if he belonged in the priesthood, in a monastery. I thought he was a singular, possibly superior man who never functioned to his full capacity and who, on that basis, was in the twentieth century a very unsingular man. . . .

Early in 1943, from the monks' point of view, the state of affairs inside the enclosure went from bad to intolerable. The behavior of the Whites and their *"kurirke"* grew so offensive that even the monks who were most strongly anti-Communist began to mumble that the Partisans' *borba* had a point, and offered prayers for their upsurgence.

Now and then the Carthusians tried to appeal to the Whites' sense of decency, but if any vestige of it existed they couldn't reach it. As the *ekonom* monk told me, they "prayed like crazy day and night," addressing their special appeals to St. Bruno, while the ashen-faced Prior sat in his hermitage or walked through the corridors of the main building, sunk in deep silence . . . thinking no one knew what.

Meanwhile the Partisan units dispersed by the Italian offensive were reorganizing in the Gorjanci Mountains as they were elsewhere in Slovenia.

Early in February 1943, the Prior found "in my hands" a two-page typewritten letter signed "The Liberation Front of the People of Slovenia" and ending with the Partisan motto *Death to Fascism! Liberty to the People!* Recalling the kindness of the Carthusians, the LF stated its deep gratitude to the Prior personally and to the entire monastery, but said that the existence of the criminal White force inside the compound was intolerable.

The letter went on to say that in the opinion of the LF's central committee (its president was Josip Vidmar; its secretary, Boris Kidric) the Whites in Slovenia, like the Ustasi in Croatia and Bosnia-Herzegovina, were criminal bands, appendages to the enemy occupation, which had at least the tacit approval of the Catholic hierarchy in Yugoslavia if not of Rome itself. Unless Prior Leopold promptly found a way to rid Pleterje of the intruders, the LF's armed forces would attend to them in their own way. The mere thought of destroying or damaging any part of the monastery was painful to the members of the LF's central committee, as they knew it would be to the Carthusians, *but——*

Circumstantial evidence tends to support the idea, not unprevalent in postwar Slovenia, that the Prior agreed to the Partisan attack on Pleterje and even helped to plan it so it would succeed with the least damage to the monastery. The Prior wouldn't discuss this with me, nor would anyone in the Liberation Front Museum and Archives in Ljubljana. I pieced together the climactic section of the story from bits of Doctor Leopold's journal and hints from other sources.

Perhaps largely or even only *pro forma* and for the record, but conceivably also because he hadn't yet abandoned all hope of avoiding a military battle, the Prior did his spiritual utmost to make the Whites leave the compound. He urged the monks and the brothers to pray harder than ever before. He communicated with his bed-ridden friend Ivo Pirkovic, a Partisan leader in near-by Sent-Jernej, asking his advice. He sent copies of the LF ultimatum to the White commander in Pleterje, to the Italian commander in the region, to the priests in the Gorjanci territory who he either knew or suspected were behind the Whites, and to Bishop Rozman in Ljubljana, who had recently Italianized his first name from Gregorij to Gregorio. He implored the Bishop, as one priest to another, to do everything in his power to induce the Whites to leave the monastery. His primary concern, he declared in all his communications, was to prevent the destruction of Pleterje. The reply he received from Bishop Rozman's office was to the effect that the Bishop had no authority over the White Guard if any such organization existed.

At the same time he was making these efforts, the Prior followed Ivo Pirkovic's advice and ordered the lay brothers to remove as unobtrusively as possible everything moveable and valuable from the buildings on the side of the compound where the Partisans, six hundred strong, struck at ten o'clock in the evening on February 18, 1943.

For some reason that I was unable to pin down, the attack took the Whites by surprise, although they had a copy of the LF letter announcing it. Possibly they didn't expect it so soon or their intelligence pertaining to Partisan movements was poor. But even taken by surprise, the Whites, inside the compound, had a tremendous advantage over the Reds storming the walls. The initial attack was repulsed. The Whites sent up flares for help.

The Italians deployed several thousand troops, compelling the Partisans to bring all their available forces into action; and for two and a half days the battle zigzagged over an area of about ten square kilometers, while the Partisan units which staged the opening assault on Pleterje held their position in the woods immediately around the little valley. In all, they stormed the walls three times. They failed to capture the compound, but threw the Whites inside it into a semi-panic. Then, late in the afternoon of the third day, Italian tanks and armored cars moved against the Partisans and created an opportunity for the White unit to evacuate the compound at leisure.

Before the White unit left, however, its three lay officers confronted the Prior with drawn revolvers and told him they had just shot two Partisans disguised as Carthusian monks; and, war being war, they would shoot anyone else they saw in Carthusian garb during the evacuation. But, to be fair, they would give the Prior ten minutes to gather all his monks and lay brothers into the main church with him. They must not move for five minutes after they heard three shots fired in rapid succession outside the church door.

Father Kolesnik, "the political commissar," was not present at this meeting. He avoided the Prior generally. Ivo Pirkovic thought he had a guilty conscience: the Prior had approved the Carthusian grant to him a few years before. . . .

The Prior rounded up the monks and lay brothers, and locked himself in the church with them. When, about an hour later, they emerged —five minutes after the three shots—they discovered that the Whites had looted the monastery. There had been no Partisans in Carthusian robes. The threat had been a ruse to get all the monks out of the way, to facilitate the haul. Perhaps, too, Kolesnik had felt squeamish about looting the place in full sight of the Prior and the monks.

The Whites had carted away most of the *kartuzija's* food supply, most of the blankets and linen, all the leather from the shoeshop and the harness-shop, the best tools and materials from the other shops, most of the kitchenware, all the fruit, all the wine and Chartreuse. For one reason or another, possibly because they didn't know their value, they hadn't touched the books in the library or any of the paintings, carvings, and statues in the corridors of the main building.

Nor did the Whites make any effort afterward to recapture the monastery.

A week after the battle, a Partisan detachment approached the Pleterje gates. The commander and the commissar asked to be admitted and inquired how the Prior was, how the other monks were—did they need any help? They inspected the wreckage and said that the future government of Slovenia would make it good. They saluted and marched off with their men.

Thereafter the Partisans too steered clear of Pleterje. But they made it known that the monastery was under their protection: if the Whites moved in again, the Liberation Front would do everything it could to drive them out.

Throughout the rest of the *borba,* refugees from the enemy and quislingist terror who knocked on the Pleterje gates were helped "with what little we had."

In the spring of 1943 the central committee of the Liberation Front of the People of Slovenia, consisting of Communists, Christian Socialists, and non-Party *kulturniki* like Josip Vidmar, established contact with the Prior. In the two meetings they had with him, LF representatives discussed the possibility of the Prior's making a trip to Rome and delivering a letter to the Pope telling him of the unpriestly behavior of many Slovenian priests. But the idea was abandoned—it was certain to prove futile.

"Now the People's Republic of Slovenia," I wrote in my February 26, 1949, diary notes, "has it 'in the Plan' to restore the ruined wing of the monastery as soon as some of the other, more urgent, reconstruction and construction jobs are completed."

During the three-day battle, the actual fighting immediately around Pleterje was sporadic. By order of the Prior, the monks prayed behind the thick walls of the main church where they were safest. The Prior himself spent hour after hour leaning upon a window sill on the top floor of the central building, looking out at the scene.

The parts of his journals I read contain no hint of his thoughts as he watched the grenade-tossing Partisans storm the walls. I asked him what went on in his mind and heart; his reply was a faint smile. Probably no one will ever know.

"Was he thinking of Stepinac?" I wondered in my diary. By then he knew that Stepinac was collaborating with the quisling government in Croatia, as Rozman did with the quisling government in Slovenia. "Did he imagine that the White Guards' incursion into Pleterje— possibly even the looting—was ordered by someone high up in the hierarchy? That Kolesnik acted as an agent of the political-power faction within the Church, of Stepinac or Rozman personally, bent on destroying the little there was left of the 'purely-religious' faction? In other words, did the Prior see the battle as a continuation of the old struggle between him and Stepinac?"

I didn't feel free to ask him these questions, but I did ask him what he thought of the wartime behavior of some of the priests in Slovenia and elsewhere in Yugoslavia. And how did he explain the "Sveti-Urh horror"? Did he know that Bishop Rozman, convicted *in absentia* as a war criminal by the Tito regime, was now in Cleveland, Ohio, USA? And that the New York archdiocese, headed by Cardinal Spellman, had named a parochial high school for Stepinac? . . . For a moment after each question, the gray old man studied the transparent skin of his clasped hands resting in the lap of his robe. Then he looked up, smiled, and waited for my next question.

I summarized the conversation at Tito's on the subject of religion, and the Prior looked keenly interested. I waited for his comment. He only motioned me to take another sip of Chartreuse.

Was he familiar, I inquired, with the American nineteenth-century essayist Ralph Waldo Emerson? The Prior shook his head. I said I wasn't sure of the exact wording but Emerson had written that among the low religion was low. The Prior studied his hands again, then he looked up; not at me but at the white wall behind me. He didn't answer.

I have never listened to such eloquent silence.

BOOK ONE
CHAPTER TEN: *Wading in a scoop*
. . . and the eagle's ordeal
to free himself

THE MORNING OF MARCH 1, 1949, winter returned to Slovenia with a vengeance. Driven by a cold alpine wind, the snow fell for two days and a night. It brought on much discomfort, even suffering, and optimistic talk about the prospect now of a good harvest also in northwestern Yugoslavia.

For three weeks I had been going to parties, visiting relatives, and getting accustomed to a pack of small fry calling me "Uncle Lojze";

receiving visitors whose relatives were in prison; making short trips, stopping to read inscriptions on roadside mass graves; sitting in on meetings of people's committees and peasant cooperatives; asking questions, listening to people, watching their faces. The storm suspended this activity, all social life in the city. The streets presented a problem in navigation even after the snow ceased falling; then, too, few households had enough coal or wood to heat the living-room for company. For many, the best way to keep warm after working hours in shop or office was to join the neighborhood snow-removing "brigade" and shovel as vigorously and as long as their calorie intake allowed.

For a week I pretended to have a head cold and stayed in bed eighteen to twenty hours a day. I wanted a chance to go over the nearly three hundred pages I had written in my loose-leaf diary since leaving New York, to fit in copies of my recent letters to friends in the United States, and to fill about two hundred pages more with notes on Franc Leskosek and Boris Kidric and Litostroj; on my trip to Styria; on Bozidar Jakac and the sunbeam in the dugout, on Malci Albinec and her outlook; on Sveti-Urh and Pleterje——

Scribbling these notes, I sharply realized what had been occurring to me every once in a while before: that I was wading in a scoop.

"To write or not to write another book on Yugoslavia?" reads my March 5 entry. "Some people in Ljubljana expect me to 'complete the trilogy,' as Jakac put it a while ago. Lately others have remarked about it. But there's no use explaining. Will Rogers was right: we're all equally ignorant, only on different subjects. People here have no inkling of American publishing. If I told them that *My Native Land* almost wasn't published in 1943 because it went against the news pattern of that period [giving Mikhailovic's Cetniki, who collaborated with the enemy, credit for the military operations of Tito's Partisans], I'd have to deliver a lecture why the publishers' hesitation was justified, and then I couldn't be sure that I hadn't laid the groundwork for more misconceptions about the United States than I had dispelled.

"Even 'the best-informed' people in Yugoslavia know only of [J. Parnell] Thomas and the Un-American Activities Committee. And most of what they 'know' isn't quite so. They lack all knowledge, not to mention understanding, of other groups and individuals now astride American life and fanning the 'cold war' hysteria, from the very politically minded Catholic hierarchy to the stupidly impolitic Communist

Party, from the lunatic and hoodlum Right to the crackpot and un-scrupulous Left—factors whose intense activity in the present interna-tional nightmare would cause most American publishers to shun a script on Yugoslavia that didn't mop up the floor with Tito—even though there suddenly appears to be a change of attitude toward him by the State Department and in the last few numbers of the New York *Times* I've seen.

"On the other hand, how can I *not* write about New Yugoslavia and Tito? If I dodge this one, I may as well quit. . . . Reading my notes on X's outburst about truth and America, I disagree with him on at least one point. There *are* people in the United States and elsewhere in the 'West,' I suppose, who want to know about the Cominform split and what's happened in Yugoslavia, and why.

"But what do I really know? All I have in these scribblings so far, and in the impressions not yet down on paper, is a nagging sense of the importance of this moment in Yugoslavia and a scent of the atmos-phere surrounding and permeating the story. . . . I've never felt so strongly about any material and, at the same time, so wobbly about my chances of grasping it fully and my ability to turn it into something worthwhile.

"It's clear now that I won't get a Soviet visa; also that if by a miracle I do, no Russian leader will discuss the Cominform split with me, ex-cept possibly to say that Tito is a no-good so-and-so; and that it would be inadvisable for me to go to Czechoslovakia, Poland, or Hungary. So even if I learn every detail of the Yugoslav side of the split, what will I have? A limited, 'biased' story. Can I say so and expect the reader to accept the limitation and consider the partial picture and make up his own mind?

"Again, what about my Yugoslav origin. Both the Communists and the Rightist crackpots, as well as people in between, will dismiss any-thing favorable I write on Tito and Yugoslavia with 'What can you expect? He's a Yugoslav.' I'll have to make it clear that, while my inter-est in the country isn't separated from my background, I'm looking at the picture as 'objectively' as I can because I want to know what Tito means to New Yugoslavia and what 'Titoism' represents in the world.

"Of this I'm almost sure (and I hereby gulp a chunk of crow): that Yugoslavia has no future in the Soviet orbit, or in any other orbit. I don't know all that has gone through Tito's mind since I saw him [six weeks ago], but if he's still thinking of the possibility of a patchup, he's off the track not only because the Kremlinites are out to make away with him and destroy the quality he and his co-leaders have given the country, but also, in fact chiefly, because independence is the core of the Yugoslav character. Yugoslavia's future is in becoming, if she can, what the United States was to the world's progressive impulse at the end of the eighteenth century, what France became in the nineteenth, the Soviet Union in the 1920's, and Spain in the '30s. Yugoslavia may produce historic results even by making only a stab at it.

"So where am I? In a quandary. . . . I've decided to go to Italy for two, three weeks, to see Florence; then return to Yugoslavia or not, depending on how things look by-and-by, on whether Tito & Co. get off 'my' scoop, on whether New Yugoslavia ceases to be a 'top secret' even to herself . . . I may go to France for a while, or to Israel; I don't know. I may return home sooner than I expected. Perhaps in time to see the lilacs bloom. . . .

"Yesterday I went to the Ministry of the Interior and obtained an exit visa, and to Putnik [the state travel agency] where they made a reservation for me on the Simplon Express leaving Ljubljana on Sunday the twelfth. . . . Last night the *Slovenski porocevalec* [Slovenian Reporter, one of the two Ljubljana dailies] called me: Was it true I was leaving? Was I coming back? Yes, I said—with an uncomfortable feeling that I might not be, and that eventually they might think I had lied. . . ."

Near the end of February 1949, the Trieste radio reported that Tito was on Brioni, an island off the tip of Istria, formerly (under Italy) owned by a British-controlled international syndicate which had made it a hunting reservation and minor Monte Carlo. The American broadcasting station in Frankfort, Germany, and the BBC repeated the report. The Budapest radio blew it up into a red-hot Cominform sensation:

". . . The fascist Tito is on Brioni to confer with Wall Street agents and Anglo-American warmongers, plotting with them the next move in his betrayal of socialism and the international working class. But this vile traitor's days are numbered! His island fortress is not impregnable. Not even James Forrestal and the rest of Wall Street can save him from the wrath of the Yugoslav people, for their love of the Soviet Union and the peoples' democracies remains steadfast. They will rise against the jackal. Brioni is the foul beast's last refuge on Yugoslav soil. In the bay facing his villa, in which he hides and cringes like the criminal he is, his seagoing yacht—a gift from Wall Street—is under steam, loaded with loot, ready at a moment's notice to take him to the United States or the Argentine."

This sort of "news" kept ripping the air waves for days. In Ljubljana people discussed it with a mingling of amusement, outrage, and anxiety. "Have they gone completely mad?"

Trieste picked up the Brioni story again, paraphrasing the Budapest version of it for background, and declaring that the "day before yesterday [Thursday, March 2, 1949] a motorboat full of men was seen leaving Fiume, Brioni-bound." Almost immediately the Budapest radio identified the passengers as more "Wall Street agents and Anglo-American warmongers visiting their vicious tool, Tito."

On Monday, March 6, one of the motorboat passengers burst into my room in Ljubljana—Vlado Dedijer, in high boots and mackinaw, looking like Paul Bunyan's twin brother.

"Leaving us, *ha!*" he exploded as though we had last talked seven minutes ago instead of seven weeks, and he was angry because I had neglected to tell him of my projected departure. "Going to Italy, *ha!* What's the big idea? And why are you in bed in an unheated room, worrying poor Jozinka out there, not letting her make a fire in your stove, refusing to see a doctor or anybody else? You don't look sick. Why aren't you out shovelling snow? What's the matter with you, anyhow?"

I was glad to see him, but by then *zafrkavanje* (a native form of jesting) had become part of my own tactic in personal relations, and I said: "The answer to the last question is that I'm sick and tired of this country—specifically of some of the people who are supposed to be running its affairs. I was brought up too well to mention names."

Big-eyed, uncertain how serious I was, Vlado unbuttoned his mackinaw, sat down and looked at me, and I at him. We grinned . . . then talked for hours.

This was the Brioni story. When the Cominform radios stepped up their attacks on "the Tito clique," early in February, Tito was so outraged he became ill again. Dr. Djoni Popovic prevailed on him to return to the island, so he could take long walks and work off his anger and think calmly. Last week Kardelj, Djilas, Rankovic and a few others went there, by way of Rijeka (Fiume), for their early-in-the-month conference with Tito; and he, Vlado, went along. *"We* were the boat-load of 'Wall Street agents, warmongers, et cetera,' " he said. "No other launch came to Brioni last week. But of course all this is off-the-record."

I groaned.

"All right," cried Vlado, "what do you expect us to do—deny that Tito is conferring with Wall Street agents and warmongers? To issue such a statement would be like denying that he kicks Tigar every morning before breakfast. . . . By the way, Tito asked about you: how you were, if you had a rest, if you obtained a Soviet visa, and what your plans were. Then someone said you had left or were about to leave for Italy. So I came to Ljubljana to check up on you. Are you really leaving? . . . When?"

"Sunday."

"When are you coming back?"

"Who said I'm coming back?"

Vlado hesitated for a moment.

"Boris Kidric told me," he said, "that you're writing a diary. Do you intend to publish it?" . . . Vlado's own two-volume *Dnevnik* (Diary), covering the Yugoslav Revolution from 1941 to '43, was (and is) the most widely read work in Yugoslavia.

"Not a diary. That's your field."

"I thought you meant it," Vlado said, "when you told us you didn't want to write another book on Yugoslavia." He jumped up and stalked about the room. "If you aren't leaving for Italy before Sunday, you still have nearly a week here. Why don't you run down to Brioni for a few days and talk with *Stari?*"

"What—and be identified as another visitor from Wall Street, or engage in another off-the-record conversation?"

"If I could," said Vlado, ignoring my remark, "I'd go back to Brioni with you and tell *Stari* in your presence what's bothering you, but I must be in Belgrade tomorrow. . . . Look, the auto that brought me from Rijeka is outside; let me arrange to have it take you down. I'll telephone *Stari* you're coming."

"And further upset his health?"

"His health is excellent; this was only a momentary upset. He'll be glad to see you."

I wanted to go to Brioni and talk with Tito again, and see some of the seven thousand deer and thirty thousand pheasants and other wild life in the sanctuary there. But after a moment's thought, to impress

Vlado with my strength of character and for other, more valid, reasons, I decided: No.

Vlado shook his head, amused. "The correspondents in Belgrade would give their eyeteeth to talk with Tito for a few minutes on Brioni or anywhere, and you—you refuse to spend several days with him—oh boy! Wait till I tell him."

We talked until Vlado's train time. How long would I be in Italy? Where could he reach me?

As we parted at the station, Vlado said, "Florence . . . I've never been to Florence. I wish I could go with you. Send me a postcard, will you?"

Ten days later I sent him one with a picture of Michelangelo's *David*.

In Florence, then in Rapallo, Genoa and Milan, I went through a batch of printed matter every day. Nearly every Italian newspaper contained several stories about the "civil war" and the "terror" raging in Yugoslavia and about Tito's "secret conferences" on Brioni, his imminent liquidation by Stalin's gunmen, and his love affairs: spiced and heated hogwash, all of it.

The *Daily American,* published in Rome; the Paris edition of the New York *Herald Tribune,* the international edition of the New York *Times* and the air edition of the London *Times,* each had from two to eight items daily on Tito's "defiance" of Stalin and the consequent turmoil in Yugoslavia. Most of them were Cominform stuff seasoned for American and West European tastes, partly or wholly untrue, some of it idiotic from any angle.

Belgrade denied nothing, released nothing that clarified Yugoslavia's new position in the world.

At the end of my first week in Florence I wrote to the editors of the *Daily American* in Rome and the *Herald Tribune* in Paris that I had just spent two months in Yugoslavia and the country was calm and extremely busy lifting itself up by its bootstraps. I had seen no "terror," as the word was meant in the "West," and the "civil war" was pure fiction—the "anti-Tito guerrillas" didn't exist.

The letters were published and I received nice thank-you notes from the editors. One of them said he had felt right along that the stories he had been featuring on page one "smelled."

Through the letter in the Rome paper I met a number of Florentines of diverse political affiliations and leanings and they gave me letters of introduction to friends in Genoa and Milan.

Condensed excerpts from my March 14–26, 1949, diary notes and letters written in Florence:

"To come to Italy from Yugoslavia is a leap from one world to another. In Yugoslavia you can't get everything you need or want, no matter how much money you have. In Italy, for money you can buy almost anything imaginable, up to the very best. In Yugoslavia those who work hardest are favored and rewarded; in Italy idleness if combined with money is the most respected occupation.

"It costs me about five thousand lire [$8] a day to live in a second-rate hotel. The average city family is said to exist on less than fifty thousand lire [$80] a month.

"Of course I can't be sure from such brief and limited observation, but as I took a look at the Italian Communists and Socialists (most of them personally very nice in the vivid, extroverted Italian way) and listen to them, my impression mounts that, numerous as it is, the Left in Italy is a pretty faint and timorous not to say empty business—as of this moment at any rate. I may see it so because of my two months in Yugoslavia. . . . If the Italian Left has any revolutionary spunk, it's too subtle for my perception. There's none of the diehard quality suggested by the hero of [the Italian film] *The Open City*.

"Italian conservatives, 'former fascists,' people addicted to the *status quo,* have oblique praise for the CP of Italy. They seem to be grateful for it. K. [an English-speaking correspondent in Florence for newspapers in other cities with whom I spent a good deal of time], an 'antifascist before and during the war, now privately a leftist intellectual,' took me to the house of his uncle, a highly cultured, widely traveled man in his sixties, with a creased, sophisticated face, who is a Demo-Christian, although 'privately an agnostic,' and who says: 'If there were no Communist Party in Italy, we would have to invent one.'

"There are, I'm told, many such people. Clever, cunning, 'educated' but essentially ignorant, confused, egocentric: lawyers, doctors, journalists, absentee farm-land owners. They may know how to play on the American fear of Communism, but their ideas about the United States, derived in part from Hollywood movies, are downright fantastic. . . . Newsstands are loaded with American printed matter both in Italian and English. When it comes to knowing America, however,

Italians are even worse than Yugoslavs, few of whom ever see *Life,
Time,* or *Reader's Digest;* but no worse than Americans (myself included) who, reading no end of articles about Europe, know next to
nothing about Europe. One way not to inform people is to litter them
with fragmentary information.

"Italian politics have curious twists we in America know nothing
about (just as Italians, like Yugoslavs, know nothing about the sub-
tleties in American life). Many well-to-do Florentines and other Tus-
cans, I'm told, are dues-paying CP members because it's in their tradition to be against the party in power in Rome. To be a 'Communist'
often is simply to be anti-Rome, nothing more.

"You only need a glimpse of Mayor Fabiani [of Florence], a member of the Central Committee of the CP of Italy, to know he's no
menace to things-as-they-are. He calls himself a *moderato.* The working-class CP leaders in and around Milan and Turin are said to be
'different, many with Titoist tendencies.' But even if they are, I don't
believe they can get anywhere revolutionwise in the foreseeable future
—not because of the Marshall Plan but because of the Machiavellian
kinks inside Italian politics, including inside the Kremlin-controlled
CPI. Also because Catholicism, now openly political, is a tremendous
force in Italy. And, last but not least, because no people ever heave up
in a revolution if they can avoid or postpone it.

"Currently in some of the Demo-Christian and outright fascist papers, the name of the head of the CPI is spelled Togliatt*off,* signifying
he's a Russian agent, not an Italian leader. K. tells me that a discreet
effort by 'really intelligent conservatives' is afoot to stop this subver-
siveness. The CPI membership has been slipping too fast, and if the
anti-Togliatti, anti-Communist sentiment increases, it will be 'bad for
Italy,' bad for those on top in Italy. The American people might begin
to suspect that Kremlin-controlled Communism is really counter-
revolutionary in effect if not in intent: little more than a bogey the
Vatican and the lay interests are scarifying them with. To all appearances, the Kremlin is quite willing to let it be that. Perhaps the Kremlin figures if Italy and the rest of Europe mulct the United States,
American capitalism will suffer. But where does that leave the average
Italian city family [living on $80 a month]? And the honest Italian
leftist? And Italy? Does Togliatti give a damn?

"K. says the Kremlin probably figures that Western Europe, Italy
included, is too shattered by wars and impelled in too many directions

by her class structure and regional jealousies, is too complex and too
decadent to be worth bothering about now; that she needs to be shattered further by World War III or fragmentized culturally by the impact of American bounty. This may be Kremlin ratiocination, or
merely an echo of a bull session in which K. participated. Whatever
its source, it parallels Josip Vidmar's belief that Western Europe is too
played out biologically, too debased by imperialistic exploitation of
'backward' peoples, too deep in the inner chaos of its past to be able to
contribute substantially to a social revolution and the creation of a
sound new order. It may be that Vidmar tentatively excepts Italy.
Some of her conditions do tend to deteriorate character, but that was
also true of Old Yugoslavia, possibly even more so. Has Italy a few
tens of thousands of do-or-die individuals like those who made up
Tito's underground in the late 1930's, or like the hero of *The Open
City*? K. shrugs his shoulders: he doesn't know: it's hard for him to
believe there are any do-or-die individuals in the world. He doesn't
think *The Open City* character was true to life. But my guess is that
in Italy corruption doesn't go deep. K.'s opportunism, for instance, is
quite aboveboard. In many respects Italy is sound even according to
the severe Yugoslav-Communist (specifically Vidmar) standards. She's
biologically vigorous. Ingrained in many of her wonderfully skilled
people is a tradition for good work that amounts to a passion. Nothing
like this skill and passion existed in Old Yugoslavia. Interestingly
enough, Italians who emigrated to New Yugoslavia and are now helping build socialism there are more at home than many Yugoslavs.
Many Italian qualities were undermined by the wars and by fascism,
and now, says K., the Marshall Plan is more effective in promoting
Coca-Cola and *Reader's Digest* than self-reliance and pride in work-
manship, while the Communist propagandists, extolling the Soviet
Union's big-industry system, also belittle individual craft skills of which
a man can be proud. Does Togliatti care? Or the Kremlin? Apparently
not. But, just on a quick glance around, I'd say that a good many
Italians are still going about their business of producing quality
goods. . . .

"The streets in midtown Florence are full of priests whose faces and
movements, unlike those of priests in Yugoslavia, are very impressive.
They evidently know what they're about and what they have. They
want to hold on to it. Many, I'm told, come from the 'best' (richest,
oldest) families. Premier De Gasperi is their man before he's an

American puppet. They're the big and little wheels in a well-functioning political machine. If a citizen wants a problem in a government office straightened out quickly, he goes to a priest, not to a notary or lawyer in his town, and he pays a fee in the form of a donation to a Church institution. The churches contain a large share of the world's greatest art. The purposeful, power-minded priests are its custodians and thereby custodians of the finest symbols of European tradition. No would-be revolutionary movement will get anywhere soon if it doesn't succeed first of all in drawing at least some of that tradition to itself as the Slovenian CP leaders, for instance, have drawn the Enlightenment to themselves through France Preseren; and if it doesn't encourage with the greatest respect and patriotic concern the Italian tradition of good work—again, in some such way as Yugoslav Communists are using the old craft skills to build socialism, making the skills and the character growth that goes with them a vital part of the new Yugoslav culture.

"The anti-Atlantic Pact 'riots' I'm witnessing obviously are not a serious matter either to the giggling, laughing young 'Communist' demonstrators or to the militia which rushes to the scene in screaming, careening American-made armored cars. Nobody gets hurt. The demonstration lasts half an hour, then *finis*—'mere theater,' says K. with a faint smile. Three days later the latest international edition of the New York *Times* carries a story about it, usually on the front page: and I'm sure that to American tax-payers who see these stories the Marshall Plan outlays for Italy and the Atlantic Pact are justified anew.

"This doesn't mean that serious leftists don't participate in the riots; many do—for very real *Italian* reasons. It means that the CPI leadership probably has scant interest in those reasons.

"What Tito said to me [on January 18, 1949] is interesting—that the billions of dollars which the USA is spending to 'contain Communism' is a waste and confusion: that if Italy and France hadn't received American 'aid,' they might have had Communist-led revolutions and, like Yugoslavia, they might now be at odds with the Kremlin if the Russians had tried to butt into their internal affairs and to use them as pawns in the power game against America: and that *that* might have reduced the danger of World War III. But I think this is beside the point. In a sense, American aid to Europe is really European aid to the American system.

"The fact of the matter is that Italy—and not just her most cunning, cynical layer—prefers to play America for a sucker rather than go through a revolution, while America—the dominant section of America—doesn't consider herself a sucker. To maintain her economic system at its present pitch, America must throw off her financial and production surpluses someplace, fast. And her improvised statesmanship combines the disposal of those surpluses with a 'contain Communism' policy, which is less anti-Communism than a cover-up for expansionism.

"In other words: the competitive spirit of American capitalism, impelled by internal and external forces to abandon isolation, is pitting itself against Russian expansionism, whose impulses—for different reasons, using different slogans—are similar.

"On the face of it, this effort promises to pay off big.[1] Italy, for example, is rapidly becoming an American colony. She's a pawn in Washington's power game against Moscow (also against London). Italy must be held for herself; but, like Greece, even more so for the sake of the Mediterranean, the route to the Middle East with its vast oil deposits, which Russia would rush in to control and exploit if America didn't.

"But Russia, alias the USSR, under the 'Marxist-Leninist' anti-imperialist slogans, isn't doing badly either. Her anti-imperialistic imperialism is almost as successful as America's. If she manages to inhibit or suppress 'Titoism' in China, her success may surpass America's.

"In still other words: the 'cold war' is as useful to the Kremlin as it is to the baffled, fear-driven powers-that-be in America. It justified the seizure of Czechoslovakia. It helps Stalin to keep Gottwald, Beirut, Rakosi, and Dimitrov in line. It's indispensable to the leadership of the Bolshevik Party in dealing with the discontent said to permeate the Soviet peoples. The fear of American imperialism, however un- or anti-imperialistic it may seem to Americans, is apt to make Mao Tsetung think twice before he goes the Tito way.

"In America the 'cold war' justifies the activities of the Un-American

[1] In the fall of 1949, Dr. Sumner H. Slichter, the Lamont Professor of Economics at Harvard, declared before an audience of American bankers that the "cold war" was "a good thing for [American] capitalism. . . . In the absence of the 'cold war,' the demand for goods by the government would be many billions of dollars less than it is now and the expenditures of both industry and government on technological research would be hundreds of millions less than they are now. So we may thank the Russians for helping make capitalism in the United States work."

Activities Committee. It makes it easy to brand Henry Wallace and his uneasy adherents subversives at the same time that the President of the United States, as a candidate for re-election, 'steals' most of their domestic thunder and wins the election with it. . . . The 'cold war' is a terrific invention. Barney Baruch and Winston Churchill invented it, but in ten or twenty years the Russians may claim the credit—*if*——

"One anti-imperialistic imperialism needs the other to justify itself, to feel itself pushed into reaching out. And everything would be ducky if the two 'giants' now on the loose, uninhibited by considerations of a third, weren't expanding at the expense of the smaller countries and of such ex-powers as Italy, France, Japan, Germany, etc.—of hundreds of millions of people—and if this two-way drive weren't heading for World War III and *Amen!*

"This—quickly, roughly—is one aspect of the world at the midpoint of the twentieth century.

"Another is that in Italy (as in other countries, doubtless) the most definite long-range political factor is the sentiment against another war. It has little or no connection with the sporadic Kremlin-dictated outbursts of anti-war propaganda by the Communists or the 'peace' declarations by the Pope. It's simply the longing for peace that exists even among the most blatantly opportunistic pro-Americans and seemingly the most fanatic pro-Soviet Communists. By and large, this longing is the equivalent of Vidmar's and Saurès' 'anti-gigantism.'[2] If

[2] On page one of the February 20, 1950, *Figaro*, a conservative Paris newspaper, the well-known French novelist and polemic François Mauriac published an article maintaining that the United States and the Soviet Union were similarly if not equally menacing to Europe. "It is not what separates [these two powers] that should frighten us but what they have in common. Their ideological oppositions are perhaps less to be feared by us than their agreement regarding the scale of human values. [They] are dragging humanity in the same direction of dehumanization. . . . [In both of these countries] man is treated as a means and no longer as an end—this is the indispensable condition of the two cultures that face each other."

Mauriac's article was a comment on and an elaboration of an essay which had appeared in *Figaro* a few days earlier, written by André Siegfried, a French professor of political science widely known in the United States. Siegfried's article pointed out that American education was dominated by technical subjects while "the humanities are practically abandoned." In this respect "the American appears the true successor of the German," he commented.

Reporting on these articles, Harold Callender, a Paris correspondent of the New York *Times* (February 21, 1950) commented as follows:

"These philosophical voices are raised in criticism of the American way of life—which they consider very alien to, and even menacing for, Europe—just at the moment

there's another war, Italy won't be worth much to America. (Ditto, France, perhaps, etc.) And in all probability the Cominform states won't be worth two cents to Russia.

"In short, 'successful' as the two anti-imperialistic imperialisms are at present, with one helping the other, the process is utter madness, as a great many people know—but they don't know how to change it, where to turn. There's no honest leadership. K. says that in Italy many people are quite fatalistic: another war is coming, and there's nothing they as individuals or Italy as one country can do about it, so they 'riot' on the Left and yell for American aid on the Right, or burn candles at the altars of their favorite saints."

The papers I read in Italy during the last half of March 1949 reported the hysterically hostile behavior of obscurely identified "Catholic" and "war veteran" groups in New York toward the Cultural and Scientific Conference for World Peace called by the National Council of the Arts, Sciences, and Professions; sponsored by a great many American progressives, liberals, and leftists, including Communists; and held under the co-chairmanship of the distinguished Harvard astronomer Harlow Shapley and the famous sculptor Jo Davidson. The hysteria reached a climax when the three Yugoslav delegates who had been given American visitors' visas were confronted at La Guardia Airfield by a contingent of women shrieking, "You shot down our planes, you have Archbishop Stepinac in prison—go back, you filthy Communists! . . ." Josip Vidmar, president of the Slovenian Praesidium, who was supposed to have headed the delegation, couldn't get an American visa in time for the conference.

---

when other voices are raised against the North Atlantic Treaty and in favor of neutrality for Western Europe. They happen to coincide also with more active opposition to that treaty by the Communists. The United States seems to be catching it on all sides in France these days.

"There is probably no political intention behind the critical jabs of Messrs. Mauriac and Siegfried, both of whom detest Communism and the Soviet Union. M. Mauriac is a Catholic polemic, while M. Siegfried is a Protestant. Yet it is a striking fact that the aspersions on the United States have long been left almost entirely to the Communists, until the last few weeks, when the bourgeois intellectuals have come forth again with their old theme that the United States is more like Russia than like Europe. . . ."

Henry Wallace said in Chicago on February 24, 1950: ". . . The United States and Russia stand out today as the two big brutes in the world. Each in its own eyes rests on high moral principles, but each in the eyes of other nations is guided by force, and by force alone."

These indications of the American mood tended to sharpen my occasional doubt that a large American publishing house would be willing to bring out a book I might write on "Tito's Yugoslavia." But it also strengthened my conviction that if the Yugoslav leaders managed to extricate themselves sufficiently from the early effects of the Cominform crisis to release the story for me to use as I wished, I would write it even if I had to borrow money to publish it privately.

Stirred as I was by many things in and near Florence, my unwritten book kept pushing on my mind even when I was roaming through the Pitti Palace and the Uffizi Gallery, the Medicean Chapel, the Duomo, staring at the Giotto Belfry, Ghiberti's Door of Paradise, Michelangelo's Bacchus, riding in a bus to Vinci (Leonardo's native village), or sitting in the old amphitheatre in Fiesole, listening to wild political harangues by priests in S. Maria Novella, the edifice across the street from my hotel, watching the Communist "riots."

I expected a letter or telegram from Vlado Dedijer; none came.

Then, late in March, from a Belgrade dispatch appearing in several papers, I drew the impression that the Yugoslav leaders might be edging to a point where they could be argued into cooperating with me. The dispatch said that Tito, still on Brioni, was working on his "most important speech to date concerning the Cominform rift" to be delivered at the opening session of the Third Congress of the People's Front of Yugoslavia on April 9. He was "expected to reveal what really brought on the crisis."

From Milan I telephoned to Vlado Dedijer (it took two days to get the call through to Belgrade) and learned that the dispatch was accurate. Hadn't I received his letter written in mid-March informing me of a "disposition" to accede to my "demands" and urging me to return to Belgrade in time to attend the People's Front Congress? I hadn't. (It was one of the half-dozen or more letters that went lost.) . . . Yes, he got my postcard with the picture of *David* from Florence. . . . No, he hadn't seen the speech yet; *Stari* was still working on it; but he, Vlado, was certain I wouldn't want to miss it. . . . So was I.

Between Zagreb and Belgrade, after I returned to Yugoslavia, I traveled in the same compartment with Lieutenant General Danilo Lekic, a Montenegrin in his early thirties. My old friend, Dr. Stampar, had introduced me to him at the station. Now, on the train, as the young general and I talked, I learned that he—a university student before the war—had been close to Tito during 1942-44. I asked him what he could tell me about him. Not much. I pressed him with specific questions, and he said:

"Yes, *drug* Tito is a Croatian and I'm a Montenegrin, but that's unimportant. Tito is Tito. You understand? . . . I mean his biography doesn't interest me the way it interests you. . . . I understand you met *drug* President Nazor. . . . Too bad you didn't ask *him* about Tito——"

(In 1943, when he was nearly seventy, Vladimir Nazor, the dean of Croatian writers—novelist, poet, essayist—agreed to a Partisan task force slipping into enemy-held Zagreb and smuggling him out of his apartment, past the quislingist guards to Tito's rough, perennially moving headquarters in the Bosnian mountains. He became a chief non- but distinctively pro-Communist spokesman for the Liberation cause. Now in his mid-seventies and growing frail, he was a leading member of the Yugoslav Academy and president of the Praesidium of the People's Republic of Croatia.)

"After Nazor came to Supreme Headquarters in '43," Lekic related, "he saw Tito every day for three or four months. Then one evening the two of them were in Tito's hut alone. An oil lamp burned on the table between them. They were talking about something or other; Nazor himself didn't remember about what when he told me the story. But he remembered that at one point in their conversation they fell silent. Tito looked at him and said, '*Drug* Nazor, I know who you are; do you know who I am?'—'Of course I know,' Nazor said, 'you're Tito, you're the Supreme Commander.'—Tito shook his head. 'I mean, do you know who I am apart from Tito and the Supreme Commander; what my real name is, where I came from, and so on?'—Nazor was taken aback. Although he was a writer, he had never asked anyone, had never even wondered *who* Tito was. To be sure, the whole *konspiracijska* atmosphere surrounding most of our leading personalities and Supreme Headquarters discouraged questioning; but that wasn't the full explanation of Nazor's disinterest in Tito's identity. 'Well, who are you?' asked Nazor.—'My name is Josip Broz,' Tito said. 'I was born in Kumrovec. I'm a metal worker.'—But to Nazor too, as he himself told me, this information didn't matter. He was impressed by the *way* Tito told him these few facts. It confirmed his feeling that Tito was Tito. That was enough. He wrote several poems about him. . . ."

(About ten weeks after Lieutenant General Lekic told me this story, Nazor died of old age and war-time privations. Two hundred thousand people passed his bier and walked in the funeral procession, Tito among them.)

For eight to twelve hours a day, for three days (April 9–11, 1949) the Communist and non-Communist leadership of the Yugoslav Revolution, of Yugoslavia as a federated state and of the six component republics, was jammed into a drafty pavilion in the middle of a park. Tito, the president of the national executive committee of the People's Front—with the ribbon of the Hero of Yugoslavia on his marshal's tunic—sat or stood in the middle of the vast stage throughout each session: a picture of health, the acme of glamor. In form and enthusiasm the congress resembled the Serbian CP meeting I had attended in January.

Tito delivered his address in two installments. During the first half, the whispered remarks of the foreign correspondents from the "West" and their native-Yugoslav interpreters, with whom I sat in the press box, gave me the impression that most of them were interested primarily in the shot to be fired by someone who might have slipped in through the security arrangements. These were no more obvious and stringent than those of the Serbian CP Congress had been. . . . I kept thinking of the carrion crows in the Slovenian forest waiting for the eagle to die. . . . During the rest of the sessions I sat with Krleza and other delegates elsewhere in the hall.

At the close of the address, the twelve hundred delegates gave Tito a twenty-minute *skandiranje*.

Vlado Dedijer, his face glowing, asked for my reaction to the speech. I said I was disappointed. He stared at me blankly, then grimaced and said, "I'll tell *Stari*," and left me.

Vlado next appeared on the platform with a sheaf of cables and telegrams from Yugoslav embassies and legations. He read quotations from news stories in the American, West European, Trieste, and Cominform press and from radio broadcasts reporting the "savage battles raging in the Yugoslav mountains between Tito's forces and the pro-Cominform guerrillas." Each "communiqué" provoked a gale of laughter, in which Tito joined.

On the second day of the congress Tito's aide, the young colonel whom I remembered from January, came over and said *drug marsal* would like to see me backstage during the next intermission.

Tito's manner wavered between cordiality and reserve. He said he hoped I'd had a pleasant and interesting sojourn in Italy. I said it was a pleasure to see him looking so fit. He said he felt quite well now, thank you—and asked why I thought his speech was no good. I said Vlado's title should be changed to director of *mis*information. I was disappointed with the speech not because it was no good but because it didn't go beyond accusing the Soviet leadership of "revisionism," which, as I had told him once before, few people outside the Communist movement would understand.

Tito responded that was as far as he could go at this time. Why? No answer. . . . Why couldn't Stalin, admittedly a big man, revise "Marxism-Leninism" to "Stalinism"? He could, said Tito; he *did;* but he couldn't make him like it. "Why raise the question of revisionism at all?" I asked. Tyro or not when it came to Marxism and "Marxism-Leninism," I felt that raising questions about Stalin's adherence to "M-L-ism" was, if not irrelevant, certainly a bit late. Wasn't Stalin a "revisionist" long before the Cominform outburst? Tito nodded. Then why stick the label on him *now?* Why not stress, instead, the concrete, specific details the fuss was all about? The facts and circumstances? The Stalin-Churchill "fifty-fifty" deal, for example? . . . But the Cominform had labeled the Yugoslav leadership "revisionist" first, said Tito, and he felt obliged to show the accusation was absurd; that it tried to disguise what the Kremlin itself felt guilty of. I remarked that that would interest the Freudians; as for most of the rest of the world, who cared?

The conversation lasted about twenty minutes in the middle of a large room full of federal and republican CP and People's Front leaders, all engaged in lively discussions and chit-chat, and was no great success. Tito doubtless felt this wasn't the time or the place to be assaulted by my questions and comments, and I agreed with him. It didn't occur to me then, as it did later, that he was trying to dodge them for a number of reasons, among them that the CPY, not to mention the People's Front, was made up of people with various shades and tempos of thinking. But he had asked me why I was critical of his speech, and I wanted to be sure to correct Vlado's hasty—and doubtless intended-to-be-humorous—interpretation of my remark.

Tito inquired if I was comfortable in Krleza's, and how long I planned to stay in Belgrade. He said that these days, after the sessions, he was seeing many of the delegates from the various republics, but he hoped I would visit him after the congress. He asked for my impressions of Italy, and listened very attentively to my remarks on "Togliat*off*" and the current position of the CPI within the Machiavellian ramifications of Italian politics bent on postponing needed reforms, mulcting America, and generally making the most of the "cold war" insanity.

Before the first bell rang for the session to resume, I renewed my questioning and extracted from Tito a tentatively worded and slowly uttered observation that the Cominform crisis now spinning around Yugoslavia might not be an isolated affair but, rather, one of the lesser results of a far-flung counter-revolutionary effect the Russian leadership was having—perhaps wanted to have—on the world. He hoped he was wrong. But Soviet actions in the past had played havoc with progressive developments in other countries, and were playing the very devil with them now. In Eastern Europe at the moment, the Kremlin's method and purpose were conquest—in some respects much worse than Western-capitalist imperialism—and I might be right about Italy. The picture in France was similar. All this was likely to depress progressive impulses everywhere. "Why didn't you say so in your speech?" He replied he had, which was true—only in such opaque Marxian phraseology it evaded me. Why not say it plainly so the world would understand? The world was waiting to hear his side. Tito shook his head: there was much I didn't know. He was going to say something more when his secretary reminded him for the third time that the second bell had rung minutes ago.

I stayed in Belgrade for a week after the congress.

From Vlado—who brought me a copy of the note he had sent to Florence—I learned that the top leaders' "disposition" to withdraw their off-the-record injunction on my material for the book had gone through several ups and downs in the past month. At the moment, Vlado hinted, they still didn't know whether they wanted to help me write the kind of book they imagined I had in mind, at the same time that they hoped I'd write a book anyhow. Did Tito feel that way too? Vlado, who wasn't his buoyant self, nodded dully and looked at the floor. He said their attitude was no reflection on me: the *drugovi* simply were in stew. He knew what the trouble was but he couldn't tell me.

I learned what the trouble was months later. . . . Shortly after the Cominform radios had increased the violence of their attacks on the "Tito clique," a Kremlin representative mentioned to Ales Bebler in London that the Soviet leaders might consider a patchup if the Yugoslavs took the first step. What the "first step" should be, he didn't specify. He repeated it would have to come from the Yugoslavs. Why? *Because.* But *why?* Because the USSR was a great power with tremendous responsibilities in the world and she couldn't permit herself to be humiliated: or words to that effect. The Yugoslav leaders considered the suggestion. Early in April they informed the Soviet representative that they had no wish to humiliate the USSR; but, since they were not responsible for the cleavage and had done everything possible to avoid widening it, they—as Communists and as responsible leaders of the CPY and the Yugoslav peoples—found it morally and politically impossible to make any "first step." If they made it, it wouldn't be a step but a crawl, unsuitable to a people accustomed to an upright posture and to looking up and ahead. They were eager to close the split, however, and they would await any recommendation for a mutually dignified solution befitting two socialist states. (By the end of 1950 Yugoslav leaders ceased considering the USSR a socialist state. See Milovan Djilas' essay *Contemporary Themes,* in which he branded the Soviet system under Stalin "state capitalism.")

"Vlado gave me a *précis* of what you have in mind," said Tito at our next meeting. "We'd like to cooperate, but"—hesitating—"there are considerations. You want 'the whole story'? What is 'the whole story'? How can anyone aspire—how can anyone imagine he can tell it? Forgive me: I'm not suggesting you're presumptuous; rather, that the idea, if I understand it correctly, isn't easily achievable.

"Every once in a while I rant because our novelists and journalists aren't recording our recent and current history, but then I realize I'm unjust. Most of them [like X, like Vlado Dedijer] have jobs in the Party or the government, or in both. They're everywhere; and so, as writers, perhaps nowhere. Also, there may be something to the excuse that they're still too close to our complex and massive experience to see it: that to gain perspective takes time.

"This may not apply to you," he smiled. "But you will be handicapped too. So far, our researchers, most of them inexperienced, have gathered only fragments of the material necessary to grasp the glory and horror of our *borba*. We're just beginning to dig into the enemy archives we captured."

I said I wasn't unaware of these—and my own—limitations. I had no definite idea of the kind of book I would write *if* I wrote one; but in all likelihood I wouldn't draw heavily on the enemy archives or the rest of the material the researchers had or hadn't gathered. I didn't aspire to do a definitive work. I'd probably write a narrative of my second return to Yugoslavia as a personal experience in understanding.

"What do you mean by 'understanding'?"

"Nothing fixed or final for myself or for anyone else," I said. "To me understanding is a relation, a process, between a mind and a subject which comes to a point or climax. If it doesn't, it doesn't. If it does, something clicks. Things begin to make sense. If I achieve that here, it won't be complete; and if I write a book, it won't wholly satisfy anyone, least of all me—or you."

"Meaning—what?" asked Tito.

"Nothing specific, nothing you need worry about. All writing, all communication, is a matter of selection." I tried to tell him about Alfred North Whitehead and Alfred Korzybski, but my Serbo-Croatian and his English were too sparse to meet on that ground. I made a poor job of remembering the gist of Whitehead's chapter on understanding in his *Modes of Thought,* and an even worse one of formulating Korzybski's idea that words were not the objects they represented, that they did not cover everything about anything, that nothing was "so and so"—it was "so and so, et cetera," and the et cetera carried the greater measure of the meaning.

Tito said that et cetera allowed too great an opening for obscurity, fence-straddling and misunderstanding. Such finicky unpreciseness might be all right for writers, for philosophers. In politics, it would be dangerous. One had to be definite, explicit.

I mentioned that Korzybski had once written me a letter that a chief trouble in the world was the use of such words as "democracy" and "communism" which meant all sorts of things to all sorts of people, none of whom gave a damn what they meant to the other fellow. Most people weren't even sure what they themselves were saying when they used them. "To you, Marshal Tito," I said, " 'communism' means something different than it does to Stalin, Rakosi, and Togliatti, to say nothing of what it means to Churchill, Truman, Baruch, and the Pope; and the same is true of democracy."

Tito walked about the room, Tigar at his heels.

He sat down again opposite me and said, *"Gospodine Adamicu,* at the risk of seeming evasive, we at the head of the Party and the government in Yugoslavia come nowhere near knowing 'the whole story.' Take the Cominform crisis. We don't know everything about it. Or about other matters. Our position isn't exactly pleasant. Every now and then one of us wants to lash back at the Cominform radio lies— but what good would it do? We love the Soviet Union; where would we be without the Russian Revolution? So how can we throw back at them all the filth they're hurling at us? How can we proclaim our repugnance for their behavior toward us the past several years when we're afraid it will only help them to hurt the cause of the international working class? Eventually their insanity or cupidity, or whatever it is, may *force* us to fight back; and to fight back may yet prove the healthiest of tactics; but now, for a while longer, we must wait and see."

"For how much longer?" I asked.

"It depends on them," said Tito. "To return to the subject under discussion a moment ago, I think I see what you mean by 'understanding.' If I understand you, you're not far from that 'click'—at least if Vlado didn't exaggerate too much. He said you already have 'a ton of notes,' some of which will be news even to us who you think know everything. Nobody knows 'the whole story,' not even in your 'et cetera' fashion. Certainly it doesn't revolve around us, the leaders. Stay in Yugoslavia a little longer, as long as you like. Go anywhere, look around; and if it's important to your sense of independence, pay your own way.

"My biography? Like anybody else's, my life means little except as it's written in the lives of the masses of the people. There's entirely too much focus on me. I wish I knew what to do about it. Your own slant, if I see it correctly, is too much on me. Again: go look at the people, at the country, at the projects already completed, and those underway. If you see me there, well and good; the rest of me isn't worth delving into, isn't worth writing about in a serious book. You shake your head, but I feel I am right.

"A year or two ago an American publication called me 'a self-made man.' If I understand that expression as it is used in America, I am nothing of the sort. I didn't 'make' myself. I *was 'made'* by the international working-class movement; more specifically, by the Communist Party of Yugoslavia. I was 'made' by the sense of a need for a revolution here, for a fundamental change; the sense that wasn't mine alone, or the Party's, but that sprang out of the people's instinct for self-preservation in the face of conditions in Old Yugoslavia and in Europe and the world generally.

"According to your *précis,* you want to know why the Kremlin has failed to destroy the Yugoslav leadership—specifically, me. Go look at the people; the answer is there, not in me or Kardelj or Rankovic or Djilas. If you want to know what we think, we're on record. Vlado tells me you read our languages with fair ease. You know about his *Dnevnik.* Other wartime diaries have been published. There are volumes of speeches and articles by Kardelj, Pijade, Djilas, and me. Read them if you like. Not that every word is conclusively true or the height of political wisdom, or that I wouldn't change a single word I said and wrote in the last ten years, although I should say that I think we made no serious mistakes. It's possible too," he smiled, "that much of this printed matter *is* long-winded and obscure. By and large, however, inadequate as this material may be, it's honest. As far as we know, no one in the West has studied it in order to help formulate a concept of New Yugoslavia. Use it as you see fit, if you wish; use it as it falls in with your first-hand observations.

"But I hope you'll not insist that we cooperate with you in the way and to the extent you outlined. We'll be happy to see you whenever you come to Belgrade and talk with you and hear your impressions. But please remember it's one thing to talk about this *kriza* privately in a small group of like-minded or sympathetic people; it's another to talk for publication, especially when aspects of the situation change from day to day and are dim, if not utterly baffling, in the first place. However, don't think we're completely at sea. We're Marxists and I believe we have a fairly firm grasp of the objective facts in the world situation, both as they bump into us and in a larger view. That is to say, we know where we are and what we're doing. Around the objective facts, however, which are the stuff of history, there's a swirl of imponderables—of nip-and-tuck shifts in juxtapositions—which, if put in black on white, gain undue importance.

"Besides, as I think I said or meant to say to you the other day, there's one very delicate matter which I wish you'd respect—and this is very much off the record. Without having anything specific to go on, some

of us continue to hope—against hope, if you like—that this nightmare
will pass somehow."

I shook my head.

On an impulse, the day after my talk with Tito, I copied from my
Florence notes the paragraphs on how I felt Yugoslavia's new position
might be turned into a significant stroke in the world picture, and gave
them to Vlado, saying this was what interested me most. If he felt it
made sense, he was free to show it to anyone he liked.

Later I learned, from people who didn't see my notes, that essentially
the same thought—of Yugoslavia trying to become an anchorhold for
people now adrift in the world chaos—had been popping up uncertainly, speculatively, throughout the CPY since about October 1948,
four months after the Cominform outbreak. Only in most of these
Yugoslav Communist conjecturings the probable need of a change to
a new and clear position was weighted with grief and anxiety, whereas
I saw the need—potentially—as the best thing that could befall Yugoslavia or the world since 1945: a development comparable to that on
March 27, 1941, when at a moment of utter depression in the so-called
free world, Yugoslavia suddenly heaved up against the Axis' Tripartite
Pact.

Most of the week in Belgrade (April 12–18, 1949) I had no firm idea
how matters stood with "my book." Every evening I resolved to clear
out, return to the United States, and devote the rest of my days to a
sensible pursuit like growing petunias. But the next morning I felt that
Tito and the men around him, their "beaks" still stuck in the old protruding root, would loose themselves and I wondered how I could best
fill in my time meanwhile.

A friend in New York had sent me a batch of John Gunther's magazine and syndicated newspaper articles on his recent (late 1948) findings *Behind the Curtain* (published as a book in 1949). One of several
pieces on Yugoslavia contained a résumé of most of the rumors about
Tito's true identity and way of life that the Josef Goebbels machine, the
pro-Mihailovic royal Yugoslav government-in-exile in London, and the
Vatican had begun to manufacture back in 1942, and that industrious
information attachés of the British and American embassies and the
English-speaking legmen of New York and London correspondents in
Belgrade had been revamping for postwar usage since V-E Day.

According to John Gunther, no one knew where the Yugoslav "dictator" lived in Belgrade. A village somewhere in the wilds near Zagreb had been picked as his "official" birthplace. Gunther didn't name the village or say who chose it.

Every morning at breakfast Miroslav Krleza and I talked of people and places in and out of Yugoslavia, among them of Tito, whom he had known since the 1920's. One morning I read one of Gunther's articles to him; and after he asked me if I knew Gunther and what his motives were for writing such a piece; and after I said that the blame for this flummery was partly due to official Belgrade's reluctance to supply foreign journalists with authentic biographical material, Krleza repeated: that Josip Broz—now Tito—*was* born in Kumrovec, a village fifty-odd kilometers from Zagreb; and that this fact was easily ascertainable.

It occurred to me then that if I stayed on in Yugoslavia to get "the whole story" I might first go to Kumrovec—and to the devil with the idea that details about Tito's life were unimportant.

My April 17 notes cover—inadequately—the previous evening I spent with Milovan Djilas and his mother. "*Majka* [Mother] Djilas," I wrote, "is a thin, restrained, mild-seeming woman. Her husband, her only daughter, and two of her sons were killed in the war. She mourns them but sees their deaths as the price for *sloboda*—a word which when uttered by a Montenegrin woman has a different meaning than 'liberty.' . . . 'He could have been killed too,' she said, glancing at Milovan Djilas. 'He wasn't; he's here.' (Is this the so-called Slavic or peasant fatalism? It sounded the opposite: active, affirmative, almost frightening.) 'My husband was under the weight of years when he was killed, but my daughter and my sons were young.' She paused, then quoted two lines from Njegos [Peter Petrovic-Njegos, the Montenegrin ruler and poet in the middle of the nineteenth century] which I didn't immediately understand. Djilas wrote them down for me:

> *Mlado zito savijaj klasove*
> *Prije roka dosla ti je zetva.*

[Freely translated: Young grain, you
must be reaped ahead of harvest-time.]

"In Montenegro almost everybody knows some Njegos by heart. After the war *Majka* Djilas wanted to stay on the stony little Djilas farm and till it herself and join the peasant cooperative when it was formed. But finally, as she told me, she gave in to Milovan and his wife Mitra and came to Belgrade to keep house for them. Now, alone in the house most of the day, she scanned the papers and listened to the radio, and much of what she read and heard was 'not good.' Especially evil were these broadcasts from Moscow, Budapest, and Prague about the 'Tito clique.' They made her old blood boil.

"The telephone rang in another room and Milovan Djilas went to answer it. I asked *Majka* Djilas how she sized up the Cominform split.

"'I'll tell you what I tell my son,' she answered quietly. 'I say to Milovan it would be better for him, for *drug* Tito, for all of them, for New Yugoslavia, to die rather than to give in to the Russian rulers.'

"Before the war, Djido (one just naturally begins to call him Djido) wrote poetry; Vlado told me that whenever he has a little time to himself he works on a novel he started years ago; and he still looks and talks more like a thinker and poet than a warrior and political leader. Now he is head of 'agit-prop'—the agitation and propaganda department—in the Central Committee of the CPY, as well as a member of the CPY Politburo. During the war he was a colonel general in the army. I asked him if he knew how John Gunther sized him up—a rough, fierce Montenegrin; a one-time favorite of Stalin; intensely anti-American and anti-British.

"'Yes,' he replied. 'I don't read English, but Vlado told me about it.' He shrugged and frowned as if to say there was nothing he could do about it.

"He drove me home in his Buick convertible. We talked of automobiles: he loved to drive, he said, almost as much as to fish. He hoped to visit America before long; to see Detroit, Pontiac, Toledo, Pittsburgh, Niagara Falls, the Grand Canyon. He was astounded that I had never been to Niagara Falls and the Grand Canyon. I explained that I have an unnatural resistance to viewing over-ballyhooed natural wonders, and Djido, driving, turned to me and smiled as though I suddenly struck him as a strange duck.

"It was a mild spring night, and we sat in the car in front of Rumunska 5 for perhaps an hour. He was very disappointed with me also because I had never read Jack London's *The Call of the Wild*. A great story, he said, written with a superb dramatic sweep. He had read it at least ten times in Serbian and Russian translations.

"I said my literary enthusiasm right now was *Moby Dick*. Djilas hadn't heard of it. I told him about it briefly, stressing that it went deeper into the innards of America and of the white world generally than any other book I knew. He wondered if it was available in French, German or Russian. I didn't know. . . .

"Djilas referred to the book I was thinking of writing. Vlado had told him I was discouraged about it. Was there anything he could do to help? I said I wasn't sure. If I decided to write anything, it would only be after I experienced the feeling that I had touched the heart of the story. Hadn't I experienced it yet? 'No,' I said. 'Frankly, I'm confused. I have moments when I almost feel that you, Tito, Kardelj, and the others in the leadership *kolektif* are the heart: that without Tito (not to mention the rest of you again) there would have been no upheaval in Yugoslavia. Then I have moments—tonight, for instance— when I feel that people like your mother, like the boys and girls I saw working on the new highways near Zagreb, are the heart.'

" 'You might be on the right track both times,' Djilas said slowly. Perhaps the answer to my dilemma was to lay the tracks side by side, and also not to overlook the CPY, for without the Party there might have been no story; and without Tito, the Party and the story would have been different: how different was anyone's guess. But, first of all, I shouldn't neglect the super-fact that a revolutionary potential had existed in the Balkans for decades if not centuries.

"The question, What is truth? reared up again. I was unable to follow his Marxian emphasis on 'objective facts,' and I can't attempt to summarize what he said. To me, I said, a 'fact isn't truth until it connects with a mind and excites it and changes it; and then truth is a relative business.' Djilas said nothing to this. Possibly he couldn't follow me any more than I could follow him. Possibly he thought I verged on mysticism. And I on my part feel more and more that 'Communism' belongs in quotes; that, as it works in Yugoslavia, and in Russia too, no doubt, it's a *mystique*—in some respects not unlike Christianity, capitalism, or any other big idea and would-be practice barging around the earth.

"I said that in a bookshop in Florence a couple of weeks ago I had picked up a paper-bound collection of short stories called *Open the Door* by the English writer Osbert Sitwell. 'One story, "Pompey and

Some Peaches," intrigued me especially. It's really two stories in one; or, rather, a story in two distinct and yet connected, sections in which the author lets the same "objective facts" about the same man, an artist, sift through the make-up of two different people who are the narrators. One narrator is a rural doctor. He sees the artist, who liked to paint peaches, reflected in the mirror of the aggrieved frustration and sentimentality of his widow, who liked to *eat* peaches; and he presents the painter as an egocentric who victimized the poor woman, who after his death quite naturally and properly cashed in on his paintings, although he, the doctor, can't see their artistic worth any more than she can. The other narrator is an art critic. He doesn't give a damn about the widow or the high prices which the pictures she inherited bring. He sees the late artist in the light of his work, his passion for beauty which found expression particularly in painting peaches; and he presents him as a rare and wonderful man who followed his inner directives that had nothing to do with "success." To me, the critic's version is the truth, is the man. It tells how the artist put on canvas everything a peach is and radiates, all its beauty—especially after it's a bit over-ripe and no longer fit to be eaten. But there are other readers, doubtless, who see him the doctor's way. As I say, the two versions of the story use identical facts about the same man in the same period of his life. In other words, facts in themselves are not truth, are not anything you can hang on to. They can be arranged and emphasized to produce a downright lie or another version of "truth." They are the necessary building material; but you need something else. What else? Maybe an open mind. Sympathy for the subject. Or a set of values, a set of instincts, that face the "good" and the "bad" in the subject dispassionately. We could talk about this all night. But, roughly, I think that what I'm trying to say is that this applies when the subject is a man like the artist in Osbert Sitwell's story, or Josip Broz Tito or Milovan Djilas, or whoever; or when the subject is a revolution or a country like New Yugoslavia.

"'Tito is disturbed because Yugoslav writers aren't writing masterpieces about the Yugoslav *borba*. I'm disturbed, as you know, because you leaders are perched on top of a great story. If I had anything to say in New Yugoslavia, I'd try to give out the facts as I saw them, good or bad, favorable and unfavorable; and take a chance on truth emerging somewhere by-and-by. I'd try to liberate the Yugoslav authors from whatever obstructs them from writing meaningfully about the Yugoslav experience, about this phenomenon called "Tito," especially from whatever keeps them from writing books and pieces that would be translatable into other languages; and I'd invite all kinds of people from America and elsewhere to come to Yugoslavia, and let them see for themselves, let the facts touch their minds.'

"I wish I could recapture Djilas' remarks. He seemed to agree about the relativity of truth, but he didn't say so outright. Like Tito, Djilas has immediate political responsibilities. He must hold on to absolutes, or he cracks. Open approaches to truth must wait awhile. But this may be doing Djilas an injustice. Almost nothing in New Yugoslavia is as it strikes one at first sight. Almost no one really thinks or believes what he says, and it's not that everyone is lying; rather, that everyone is caught up in a furious process, and everything is tentative, being fused and re-fused into something else, changing from placidly flowing water to power bent on breaking into a roar. A curious thing, a revolution. Even the 'facts' about it are only relatively factual, depending on your vantage point, on the level to which your perception can penetrate.

"As I got out of the car, saying I didn't want to keep him up any longer and I was tired myself, Djilas detained me for another couple of minutes. 'I hope you won't be impatient with us,' he said. 'We're in a complicated frame of mind.' He paused. 'As you know, *Stari* and some of the other *drugovi* continue to hope that a change of attitude in Moscow isn't excluded. Those of us who don't share that hope respect Tito's inner problem. Somehow, perhaps because he's the top man, this so-called Cominform crisis hit him worse than anyone else. But you'll see, gradually we'll unravel ourselves. Give us time—a few weeks, a month or two, I can't say exactly. *Drug* Vlado told me you're leaving Belgrade in a few days. Come back for the May Day Parade, won't you?'

"I said I might.

" 'Where are you going from here, if I may ask?'

"I said I was thinking of going to Kumrovec——"

During the next three and a half months, while I had many long interviews (some taken down by stenographers) and many informal meetings with Tito, Kardelj, Pijade, Rankovic, Djilas, Kidric and others, I sensed every once in a while that vestiges of the old hope-against-hope sentiment clung on. In Tito and Kardelj they lasted until the end of June.

The eagle didn't succeed in wrenching his beak entirely clear of the protruding root until early in the summer of 1949. Then, with tortured wings, injured tongue, and crow-pecked head, he was free—in a plight, but free.

Between mid-January and the end of August 1949, I traveled eleven thousand miles in my native land. I crawled through a half-dozen primitively operated coal and copper mines, and about a dozen unfinished hydroelectric projects. I visited scores of factories, large and small, recently set in operation or nearing completion; peasant cooperatives, schools, and army camps. I spoke with, or looked into the faces of, thousands of people in various stages of well-being and poverty, of enthusiasm and weariness, in every region of the country—Communists, non-Communists, and anti-Communists, political prisoners, and ex-prisoners.

By midsummer I was satisfied that I had as much of the Yugoslav story as I could understand and manage.

CHAPTER ONE: THE STORY: *1892–1951*

The beginnings of a "beginner" . . .
or, The boy is the father of the man

*Truth is such a fly-away, such a sly-boots, so
untransportable and unbarrelable a commodity,
that it is as bad to catch as light.*
—RALPH WALDO EMERSON

*No human being is constituted to know the
truth, the whole truth, and nothing but the truth;
and even the best of men must be content with
fragments, with partial glimpses, never the full
fruition.* —WILLIAM OSLER

*The exceptional man is one who possesses qual-
ities which make him most capable of serving
the great social needs of his time, needs which
arise as a result of general or particular causes.
Carlyle, in his well-known book on heroes and
hero-worship, calls great men* beginners. *This is
a very apt description. A great man is precisely
a beginner because he sees* further *than others
and desires things more strongly than others. . . .*
—S. V. PLEKHANOV

*Veracity does not consist in saying but in the in-
tention of communicating truth.*—S. T. COLERIDGE

THE northwestern corner of Croatia bordering on Slovenia is
called Zagorje. The name means literally "the land beyond
the mountain (or mountains)." In mountainous Yugoslavia
there are several Zagorjes. This one is "beyond" the mountains that
rise abruptly outside of Zagreb, the Croatian capital and the second
largest Yugoslav city.

From an airplane about to land at the Zagreb airdrome on a clear spring day, Zagorje looks like a great green lake which a playful wind has whipped up into little waves, earth-waves—*brezulki,* or knolls—which crowd upon one another in a rhythmic turbulence on the verge of subsiding. The region is almost treeless, densely populated, and intensely cultivated (anything but "wild," as reported by writers who never saw it). Driving through it, one discovers that the occasional clumps of trees are oaks, aspens, acacias, beeches, linden, and fruit trees.

On the slopes and in the narrow valleys and swales there are tiny fields, some fenced in, others framed by hedges, ditches, and footpaths —except those around the settlements where the new-style peasant *zadruge,* or cooperatives, have begun to forgo walls and fences along with small-scale farming. There are tiny meadows, tiny vineyards. To a visitor from America accustomed to large dimensions, nearly everything is small. In the spring, especially after a rain, areas of the rolling countryside resemble billowy patch-quilts freshly washed and laid out in the sun to dry.

Towns, villages, and hamlets lie tucked and hidden in the valleys and ravines. Steepled churches with walled-in graveyards perch on nearby knolls. The ruins of feudal castles stand on the highest hilltops —relics from the second half of the seventeenth century when Zagorje was the scene and the heart of the *Seljacka buna* (peasant revolt) under the command of Matija Gubec, a serf leader whose makeup had touches of Joan of Arc, John Brown, and Garibaldi.

In the 1670's Matija Gubec organized ten thousand rebels and led them against the feudal lords and the city aristocracy allied with the Church. The serf legions threatened even Zagreb for a time, but in the end they were crushed by the superior forces of the established order. The well-armed mercenaries of the landed and urban aristocrats and the Church slew six thousand peasants up and down Zagorje. They captured Matija Gubec, brought him to St. Mark's Square in Zagreb and—by order of the Bishop, a precursor of Stepinac in more ways than one—crowned him "peasant king" with a red-hot iron "crown" as he sat chained to an iron "throne" under which a great fire blazed . . . and thus made him a hero, a national saint, in Croatian and generally in South Slavic history and folklore.

The 1946 Chevrolet which the Croatian Writers' Union put at my disposal took an hour to cover the fifty kilometers from my hotel in the center of Zagreb to the squeaky garden gate of the stone cottage in the center of Kumrovec where a somewhat weather-beaten sign reads: DRUG TITO'S BIRTHPLACE. The gravel highway—built when Croatia was a province of the Austro-Hungarian realm, long before Tito's birth —is narrow and dusty in dry weather but fairly smooth most of the way.

The night before, in the course of a five-hour bull session at the Writers' Union Club in Zagreb, the orthodox Marxists agreed with Tito on the role of leaders in history. But I stuck to my thesis—really Carlyle's—that outstanding men, while they are products of their periods, are also catalysts in historic processes and as such are interesting, and their biographies, down to the most ordinary details, are history.

Afterward, walking me to the hotel, Secretary Petar Segedin of the Writers' Union asked me if he could come to Kumrovec with me. He had never been there.

We arrived in the village a little after eight in the morning. Most of the Kumrovcani were at work in the fields or in school. We inspected the exterior of the house where Tito was born, and the life-size bronze statue by Antun Augustincic, a leading Croatian sculptor, done from memory as Tito looked at a critical moment in 1943. I knocked on the door—no answer. Segedin recalled that in 1945 or '46 the local people's committee had declared the house a national shrine.

We strolled through the village. Like scores of the small peasant communities we had just passed through or seen from the highway, it was almost primitive. Manure water ran in slow trickles down the main road and lay in puddles. The new wirepoles showed that electricity had just been brought in; it was connected with only a few of the twenty-odd dwellings. On a near-by slope stood an unfinished building. Segedin thought it was a hotel.

Homes and barns damaged during the war were largely repaired. A peasant was mending his roof. Here and there a face appeared in a window. A child with a running nose and scabby face, in a soiled linen shirt, stood barefoot in a half-open doorway, sucking his thumb.

As we walked back to Tito's birthplace—the neatest house and yard in the village—a peasant past middle age with a slow, dragging step, and smelling of fresh soil and well-fermented manure, appeared. He wished us good day, introduced himself as Sandor Krajcer, said he was the custodian of *Drug* Tito's Birthplace, let us into the house, and opened the Visitors' Book for us to sign.

The man peered at our names and announced he'd heard of both of us. He'd lately read an article by Petar Segedin and only last night he'd heard over the radio I was in Zagreb. A cousin of his lived in Pittsburgh. An aunt of Joza's lived in Pittsburgh, too; did I know her?

I said I didn't, and inquired who "Joza" was.

"Tito," the custodian said. "We call him Joza here in Kumrovec, those of us who grew up with him. Marshal Tito is his name for the world to go by. When he was a small boy, he was Jozek [Joey]; when he grew older, he became Joza [Joe]; after he left the village to learn the metal trade, he was promoted to Josip [Joseph] Broz."

On first impression, peasant Krajcer's loquacity didn't quite jibe with his awkward personality. His Zagorje dialect was vividly expressive: a mixture of about two-thirds Croatian and one-third Slovenian as spoken by the people across the river Sutla which flows by Kumrovec and forms a length of the border between Croatia and Slovenia.

"As you know," the custodian went on in the manner of ciceroni the world over, "this is where Joza—Marshal Josip Broz Tito—was born. In this very room, on this very bed. That's the cradle his mother rocked him in. The bed and the cradle are genuine. So, I believe, is that spindle; his mother brought it with her from Slovenia. She was a Slovenian girl. Strictly speaking, Joza is half-Slovenian and half-Croatian, but we in Kumrovec regard him as a full-fledged Croatian. Try and stop us. ... The stove is original too, but it looks better now than it did a couple of years ago. We fixed it up. We fixed up lots of things. The hinges on the front door, for instance, are new. ... Now, there's a dispute about this bootjack. Some say it was here in Joza's boyhood, others say it wasn't. To me, it looks worn and lopsided enough to have belonged to his father, who I definitely know had a pair of high boots he couldn't take off without a bootjack. ... The table and the benches are replacements. Guesswork.

"After the people's committee decided to take the house over and declare it a monument, there was some awful squawking in Kumrovec, I can tell you. Joza has three aunts living right here in the village. They and the aunt in Pittsburgh are on his father's side. Across the river in Slovenia, just outside the village of Podsreda is Aunt Ana, on his mother's side. Quite a character, Aunt Ana—just like Joza. I read in the papers you met Joza, I mean Marshal Tito, didn't you? . . . You should see him and old Ana together. They're a pair, let me tell you. They talk and move their hands exactly alike. She tells him off, even if he is Marshal of Yugoslavia. You'd think they were mad at one another, but Aunt Ana loves him even if he doesn't listen to her, and he's crazy about her, I guess. She doesn't think much of Communism, but he doesn't care, not where she's concerned. She helped him a lot when he first got started in the Revolution. . . . But, as I was saying, Joza has four aunts all told. All in their seventies and eighties. All strong characters, and women besides; and if you know anything about *old* women, well, you know what I mean.

"The four of them got into a row about the kitchen. Should the walls and ceilings be left sooty or should we scrape them and whitewash them? Then there was the question: should the sauerkraut vat be left by the door in the vestibule where it always stood? What was genuine, what wasn't? . . . Well, at least half of this kitchenware isn't genuine. That is to say, it wasn't here when he was a boy. Those new wooden spoons, for example. When Joza was a boy, the Broz family ate with wooden spoons like the rest of us Kumrovcani—if we had anything to eat. Some of the people here still eat with wooden spoons, and food is only a little more plentiful than it used to be.

"But the people's committee pulled the best one," chuckled Krajcer. His eyes lit up and his narrative sprang into the present tense. "All of a sudden after Liberation, lots of people hereabouts discover they're Communists even though they're not Party members. In fact, like a burst of morning, it dawns on them they've been Communists all their lives, ever since they were no bigger than a fist in their mothers' wombs. And others take the hint and feel that's the thing to become, since a lad from Kumrovec made such a success of it. So they're elected to the people's committee, and they decide to put pictures of Marx, Engels, Lenin, and Stalin on the wall over there by the stove. There's a hot argument how big the pictures should be, and finally a delegation goes to Zagreb and buys them. And what happens?" Custodian Krajcer chuckled again. ". . . Joza comes home for the first time since the end of the war; only now he's Marshal of Yugoslavia, and with him come other leaders from Belgrade and Zagreb, and his dog Tigar. The kids go crazy over Tigar: they can't make up their minds who's more wonderful, Joza in his uniform or Tigar with his clipped ears and tail.

"Joza steps into the house and looks around and is very serious. I stand right where you're standing now, *gospodine* Adamic. I'm the custodian, which is a fancy word for watchman. The people's committee pays me seven hundred dinars a month [about $15 at the official exchange rate], which isn't exactly a fortune; and I'm not supposed to take tips—that's not the thing to do in New Yugoslavia—but I do if somebody makes me. . . . No, I'm not a Communist. I don't know enough to be one. And I didn't want this job, but the people's committee appointed me custodian because my house is across the street and I can see visitors who come by auto unannounced like you two did. . . .

"So, as I say, I stand right there and I watch Joza, and I say to myself, 'Here he is—Marshal Tito, Prime Minister of Yugoslavia, who was born right here in our village.' He looks at the pictures of Marx, Engels, Lenin, and Stalin on the wall, and he can't believe his eyes. He scowls, then he laughs a little, and he looks at me, but he realizes I'm not to blame because I'm only the custodian. So he turns to the president of the people's committee and says he doesn't think these pictures belong here because they weren't in the house when he was a boy. He never heard of Marx, Engels, Lenin, or Stalin until after he left Kumrovec."

Segedin and I laughed.

"Joza takes a few steps around the room and seems to be thinking, as if he's trying to remember something, and he turns his face sideways to me—like this—and he says, 'Sandor, when I was a boy, there was a picture of the Holy Trinity over there,' and he points at the spot where the people's committee put Marx and Engels and Lenin and Stalin. 'It was really a music box,' he says. 'It had a key, and I used to wind it, and the picture played a little tune. I was winding it all the time.' And he asks me if I remember the music box. I say no, I can't say that I do. He says I was the closest neighbor then as I am now, and I used to come to the house often; I must've seen him wind the music box and hear it play. But I don't remember—can I help it if I don't? So Joza says that's all right, but I should look around. I should ask his aunts and others; and if I find the picture which is really a music box in somebody else's house, I should believe they came by it honestly. I should buy it and let him know how much I paid for it and he'd send me the money, and I should put the Holy Trinity where the people's committee put Marx and Engels and Lenin and Stalin, because that's what belongs there."

A question now and then kept Krajcer going.

"On Sundays visitors arrive in busloads. During the week from none to twenty come a day—on the twelve o'clock bus which picks them up at three. . . . *Drug* Bakaric [Premier Vladimir Bakaric of Croatia] was here about a year ago with some visitors from Belgrade. He's interested in the house. He arranged the loan from the Croatian Republic's budget to the people's committee of Kumrovec to build the hotel, so in the years ahead visitors can stay overnight if they wish, or spend their vacations here. It's a very healthy place. Lots of people in Kumrovec live to be ninety, even a hundred. Who knows why? I'd say some people live to a ripe old age just because they don't die when they're younger. A granduncle of Joza's lived to be nearly a hundred. He died a couple of years ago. He ran the flour mill in Zelenjak, not far from here. He learned to read when he was past seventy, then he wrote poetry and things that some say aren't bad at all.

"The hotel? It's up on the knoll over there; you saw it. The work on it is at a standstill right now because everybody's busy with spring, in the fields. Also, the people's committee, which is building it, can't get pipes, locks, door-knobs, and other metal fixtures for love or money; and I guess it'll take awhile before the hotel can put up guests."

A battered jalopy of Czech make sputtered to a halt in back of our Chevrolet and a young man stepped out and joined us. He was Josip Druzinec, a trained CP *aktivist* and secretary of the regional people's committee in Klanjec; a nice, intelligent fellow.

"The new hotel isn't finished," he said, "but if you want to stay overnight or for a few days, we can put you up. We'll have lunch at the hotel between one and two, as soon as it's ready. Too bad you didn't let us know you were coming."

Krajcer suggested we move into the room across the vestibule where there were some benches and a table and bronze busts of Matija Gubec and Josip Broz Tito. He said the village people's committee met here once a month.

Other men and women came in, most of them in their late fifties or older, all of whom knew Jozek, or Joza, or *drug* Tito, as they variously called him, since his childhood. I talked with them for hours. Segedin volunteered to take notes.

In the afternoon, after lunch at the hotel, the young *aktivist,* Segedin, and I drove across the river to Slovenia, as close to the village of Podsreda as the car would take us, and walked the rest of the way—

to a hut pressed up against the base of a mountain, where we stayed past nightfall.

It was the home of Tito's seventy-eight-year-old Aunt Ana—Ana Kolar (her husband, also in his late seventies, was away somewhere) —whose features and expressions, manner of speech, gestures, and energy were startlingly like Tito's. She hadn't seen Joza for two and a half years, she said; and when I told her I'd been with him the week before, she made me tell her everything I could about him. Questions tumbled out of her. There had been a rumor he was ill: was he all right now? How did he look? Was he in danger? . . . well guarded? . . . careful? What was wrong with the Russians anyhow? Those liars!

She'd read I was in Yugoslavia, that Joza had received me when I arrived—when was it? In January; yes, it was in the winter: how time passed. But she never dreamed I'd come to see her. Did Joza tell me to come? He didn't? She was disappointed. "Just like him! Just like a man! I guess he's forgotten his Aunt Ana. I'll have to die to make him think of me. I may never see him again."[1]

After a while, the old woman bustled me from her sooty, low-ceilinged little kitchen to her small bedroom . . . and we talked alone

[1] In 1949 Tito said he planned to visit his native village in 1950, and he might also go to Podsreda. But, apparently, he couldn't make it. Late in December 1950, I received a letter from Aunt Ana. She apologized for not previously acknowledging the postcard showing a group of New York skyscrapers I had sent her in the fall of 1949, soon after my return to the United States. How was I? She was getting old. There was no escaping the ravages of years. . . . Hadn't I said I would write a book about her nephew Joza? Was I still writing it? Would there be pictures in it? When was I coming back to Yugoslavia? . . . As for her nephew, she had a favor to ask of me. During 1950 she had written him three times, and he hadn't answered. *Zakaj?* Did I think he was angry at her? Had I repeated to him what she had told me? Was it that? Or were his adjutants and secretaries ("those young devils around him") keeping her letters from him, figuring they were from some old crank who imagined herself Marshal Tito's aunt? Oh, sure, their job was to spare Marshal Tito's time and energy so he could run the country; but after all, she *was* his aunt; or had she been dreaming all her life? . . . "So won't you please write Joza and tell him about my letters? That I've written him three times? Say I'm nearly eighty and worried about his safety. Especially now that Stalin is so mad at him. Say I pray for them both—for Stalin, to be sensible and not start a war; for Joza, to have the wisdom and strength to take care of himself and of Yugoslavia. . . . Please write Joza and tell him to come to Kumrovec and Podsreda soon. I want to see him once more before I die. . . ."

Aunt Ana died on July 16, 1951, at the age of 79. The announcement, signed by her relatives, included the name of Josip Broz Tito, nephew.

for an hour of more. On the walls were three pictures of Tito, one of the Virgin Mary, and a crucifix. She had no photographs of herself, nor of her sister Mica (Tito's mother), nor of Tito as a boy or a young man. I said I would send a photographer from Zagreb to take a few shots of her.

At parting Aunt Ana asked me to tell Joza, if I saw him again, that she was angry at him but she prayed for him.

"And when you get back to America, send me a postcard, won't you? One with those tall buildings on it. Are they really so high? . . . A hundred stories! I don't believe it. . . ."

All rumors to the contrary, Josip Broz *was* born in Kumrovec on May 25, 1892. He was the seventh of fifteen children born to Franjo Broz and his wife Mica—the peasant form of the name *Marija* (Mary).

Of the fifteen Broz children, seven died within a year after birth. Fifty percent was the approximate infant mortality rate in Kumrovec, in Croatia, in much of the rest of Eastern Europe in those days . . . and long after. Of the eight who grew up, seven were still living in 1949.

None of Tito's four brothers and two sisters is exceptional in any apparent way. The oldest brother is an aging railroad man in Hungary, where he went in search of work in his youth. The second oldest brother died a peasant in his middle years in Kumrovec in the 1930's.

Two of this brother's sons joined the Partisans in 1942 without knowing that the man called Tito was their uncle. They were captured by the quislingist Ustasi forces in 1943 and executed because their name was Broz.

Tito's sisters are peasant housewives. Three brothers are workers, one takes care of his house in Zagreb.

Tito's relatives have not benefited materially from his rise to power. Nepotism was a curse in Old Yugoslavia, it is discouraged—on the whole—by the ranking leaders of New Yugoslavia.

Tito's native village was in many respects little better off in 1949 than it had been in 1939. The outlook for its inhabitants as for other Yugoslavs hinged on the strength of the Tito regime, on whether it would be able to withstand the opposition from the "East" and the designs of the "West," and on socialist construction and production which was just getting underway in 1949.

The name Broz appears in old and modern Dalmatian records. In inland Croatia, in Zagorje itself, it appears from 1552 on.

When I laid before Tito for corroboration the facts, legends, and suppositions about his background that I had gathered, I found him uninterested in the genealogy of his family. His reaction to my persistent questioning was polite boredom. The one clear-cut response on the subject was that his first forebear in inland Croatia had probably come from the region where Dalmatia runs into Herzegovina: his father undoubtedly was of the "Dinaric type"—so called after the Dinaric Mountains. He also confirmed that living to a ripe old age was not unusual in his family—for those who evaded death in infancy. He knew about his nearly-one-hundred-year-old granduncle in Zelenjak, the miller named Blazicko, who learned to read at seventy and took to writing poetry and a philosophic diary. He'd seen some of his verse and notes: they were "rather good and interesting in a—shall I say?—primitive way."

Many of the older Kumrovcani, as well as Aunt Ana in Podsreda, had vivid memories of Tito's father, perhaps because his looks, manner, ways, and outlook were different from theirs.

Like everyone else in the little village (about the same size in the 1880's as in 1949), Franjo Broz' parents were poor. They kept their family going on their few acres with the hardest and (in modern eyes) stupidest kind of toil. Franjo was strong and a good worker when he felt like working but, unlike the more or less typical Kumrovcan who remained in the village, he had no passion for the drudgery of grubbing. He let his parents and sisters do the major share of the farm work.

By all accounts, Franjo Broz was tall and dark, lean as a flail, and handsome. He had a prominent beak nose which—in his youth and early manhood—added to the shrewd challenge of his eyes. He was uneducated but he could read and sign his name. He was a great talker, a braggart, an individualist. He was ambitious and didn't care who knew it. Had he emigrated to America, he might have made out all right. Why he stayed in the village, no one remembering him could say. Everybody agreed that young fellows with only a touch of Franjo's nature forsook over-populated, backward, hard-pressed Zagorje in their teens or early twenties. In the 1880's America was a mere rumor in Croatia; but, as in previous and subsequent decades, enterprising men and girls—every third male, every fourth female—went to seek a livelihood elsewhere in Austria-Hungary, or in Germany or Italy, rather than knuckle under to the mediocre pattern of village existence.

Franjo Broz stayed in Kumrovec but he never quite knuckled under to the pattern of its life. He may have stayed because he was an only son and as such heir to his father's meager farm . . . or because in his early twenties luck faintly caressed him as a trader in horses, cattle, and grain, and then he clutched on to the idea of success . . . or because he was not as self-confident and venturesome as he liked to appear . . . or because the Slovenian girl in the village of Podsreda, across the river, hesitated to marry him, as if she sensed that for all his fast talk and bold posturing he wasn't quite the fellow he made himself out to be.

The girl was one of several children of a poor peasant family named Javorsek—a common Slovenian (*not* Czech) surname. Until her mid-teens they called her Micka, then Mica. At eighteen, when Franjo Broz won her, she was tall and well-built, with regular features, red cheeks, light-blue eyes, and a mass of tawny hair. Her carriage and movements held a quiet pride. Her older sister Ancka (the Aunt Ana I visited), who was short and round but equally good-looking, opposed the marriage. She never understood why Mica accepted Franjo, and bemoaned the union for nearly sixty years—until her nephew Joza turned out to be Tito.

Franjo brought his bride to Kumrovec in 1883. He built a new house —destined to become *Drug* Tito's Birthplace—and for about six years they were a good match. A child was born every year or so, and died as likely as not; but, as already mentioned, this was normal in Zagorje. Franjo owned nine acres of land and Mica did most of the work, for now ambition prodded him more than ever and he roamed the countryside buying and selling horses and cattle and hay and grain. The life that went with trading appealed to him. It took him to fairs and brought him in contact with other go-getters—quick-witted, articulate men. It meant sitting around a jug of wine in an inn while going through the ritual of transacting a piece of business. He liked animals, horses especially, and harness and wagons.

Occasionally Franjo Broz owned a team of horses, which set him above the other peasants who at best had only oxen, and many of whom plowed with their only cow pulling the wooden plow. Off and on, he hired himself and his team out to lumber merchants and, hauling logs from woods situated in various parts of Croatia to the urban centers, he earned what passed for big money. Hauling took him away for weeks at a time. Once—a year or two after Tito was born—he returned without team and without money. He had sold the horses, he explained, and been robbed. It may have been true. It *was* true that more and more he liked to sit in inns and talk and drink.

From 1895 to 1910 Franjo Broz tried to get on his feet, and for each failure he built an elaborate excuse. His wife begged him to give up trading and drinking. He resented it bitterly. The criticism of his two oldest children, one of whom once told him to his face that their poverty was all his fault, sent him into a rage. From about 1910 on, his decline continued with brief intervals of seeming regeneration.

The Broz house was among the newest in Kumrovec and one of the neatest inside and out. Flowers grew in the garden amid cabbages and onions and in pots on the window sills from early spring until mid-autumn. Mica was a *dobra gospodarica,* a good housekeeper: the pride of her youth remained with her. But from, say, 1895 on, when Franjo sold four of his nine acres in order to make another stab at horse- and grain-trading, the children and she often had next to nothing to eat. It was a period of drought and poor harvests; times were hard generally. People began to hear of America. In 1900 one young man emigrated and sent for a younger sister of Franjo's and married her in Pittsburgh, and for a while it looked as if Franjo too, although late in his thirties by then, might "go across the big pond." But his brother-in-law didn't send him a "ticket." This depressed him still more. He could never get enough money together for the trip. By then his personal disintegration was too far advanced.

Mica's family across the river couldn't help her very much. The circumstances of Franjo's three sisters who were married and settled in Kumrovec were almost as bad as her own, except that their sister in Pittsburgh occasionally sent them a few dollars. Besides, they appeared to dislike Mica, presumably because she was "from across the river" and "different." So she asked a girl named Tereza, a neighbor's daughter, to look after her youngest children—Jozek especially, for he was always up to something—while she and the two oldest boys slipped out of Kumrovec before daybreak and went to a neighboring village to work for a "rich" peasant. Evenings they returned with half a bag of corn flour, a fistful of beans, a slice of hog-fat, and a few coins.

According to Tereza—whom in 1949 I found a gnarled, talkative little woman in her early sixties and in the thirtieth year of her marriage to a peasant named Vilce Stefan—Mica and the boys went out several times a year. A week's labor provided the family with food for the next two weeks. At times the Brozes had no cow and Mica bought a liter or two of milk for the youngest from neighbors with the money she and her sons earned—never more than the equivalent of forty or fifty cents a day for twelve to fourteen hours of work. Off and on, when the crisis was downright tough, she took a couple of the children to her mother's in Podsreda, where they had two cows. She nearly always took Jozek.

Occasionally during this dire period Franjo pulled himself together. Swearing off drink, he worked hard at whatever job he found in the vicinity and brought home every penny of his wages or a sack of grain or a slab of bacon.

Mica bore her last child in 1902; it died at birth, as did the two immediately preceding it. By then her proud body had shrunk and bent; yet a curious beauty lingered on her face through the rest of her life, which ended in 1918 when Joza, then twenty-five (and already a convinced but uncrystallized revolutionary) was an Austrian prisoner-of-war in Russia.

A few months before she died Mica Broz turned up unexpectedly at her sister Ancka's. It was either in September or October 1917. Thirty-one and a half years later Aunt Ana told me:

"It took a well person under an hour to come from Kumrovec to Podsreda. It took Mica the whole forenoon, she said when she got her breath back. She had to sit down by the roadside every few steps, and rest. She was all worn out and barely made the steep parts. She didn't want my husband to know how poor she was, but I said never mind him, never mind anybody, and I made her stay with us for a few days. I thought she was just hungry, starved; so I killed a chicken and fed her broth, and she picked up a little. She wasn't sick, she was just done in. I walked back with her across the river. I was forty-six then, Mica was forty-four. But I remember when I parted from her in Kumrovec I thought she looked sixty. She was skin and bones, but beautiful still. It was the last time I saw her alive. . . . One day her youngest came running to me all out of breath, crying she was dead.

"While she was with me, I made her stay in bed—that was something new: she'd never stayed in bed before except for a day or two after each childbirth. Fifteen of them! . . . I loved Mica more than anyone in the world, even more than my mother. There was never anyone finer and more beautiful. And she had such a miserable life!

"She lay here on this bed for two days and talked to me as she never talked to anybody before. She felt she was going to die. She didn't know where Franjo was; he hadn't been home for a couple of days; but she begged me not to think ill of him."

Aunt Ana sighed deeply. Then: "I can't tell you everything, I just can't. But Mica did say three or four times that Franjo was a good man: it was unjust to think he was a ne'er-do-well and a failure. He drank, but he wasn't a drunkard. He never bullied her, never hit her. That's what she said, that's what she wanted me to believe. There was no use arguing with her. I thought it was right she stood up for him. He was her husband, and maybe she knew him better than I did. She said he drank because something gnawed inside him and he couldn't find his way through *zmesnjava* [the jumble and maze]. That was how she sized him up, and Joza too.

"This is something I often tried to figure out. Mica's children were as down on their father as I was—all except Joza. If I remember rightly, when he was going on twelve and insisting I call him Joza, not Jozek, he stuck up for his father against the whole bunch of us. I used to think he disliked me because I said mean things about Franjo and the way he shirked his responsibility to my sister and the children." Aunt Ana threw up her hands and was silent for a long moment, looking at the crucifix on the wall. Then:

"Where was I? . . . Yes. About Jozek; I mean, about Joza, when he was twelve or so. He defended his father even against me, and he was right. Does anybody ever know anybody *really?* So, then, what right has anybody to judge anybody? Human nature. . . . When I was in Belgrade in '46, I got to know Joza pretty well. He gives you a piece of his mind, but he doesn't nurse a grudge. I don't believe he ever really disliked me. When he was a boy, he didn't approve of what I said about his father, but he didn't hold it against me. He told me what he told his two older brothers: to shut up because I didn't know what I was talking about. And of course he wouldn't stand for his aunts in Kumrovec blaming my sister for Franjo's drinking either. *There* he had his hands full; me, he only saw once or twice a year. . . . His father was the way he was, Joza said, because he was the way he was.

"I remember I asked Mica if Jozek (*she* always called him Jozek)

picked this up from her. She said no, she thought *she* got it from
Jozek. You figure it out. . . . Yes, I did ask Marshal Tito about it. He
wouldn't say. He's touchy about this; you better not write about it
either. It's nobody's business. If you must mention Franjo, just say he
was a good man: and you know, I think he was. Who's to say who's
bad? When I was young, I was seldom in doubt; now the older I get,
the less sure I am about anything. When Joza came back from Russia
in 1920, he was full of revolution and Lenin and Communism, and I
used to think he was crazy. I thought so right along, especially from
1934 on up to the war, when he used to come here to hide from the
political detectives who were hunting for him.

"Now look at him! I must have been wrong. So I don't trust my
judgment any more. Who's bad, who's good? Who's crazy, who's sane?
Maybe communism isn't all bad, all insane. What do you think? . . ."

"What did your sister Mica say to you that time in 1917?" I asked.

"You want to know everything, don't you? Well, I won't tell you.
You won't say what you think of communism, or you say, 'That's a
big subject.' So why should I tell you what you ask me? Besides," with
a quiver of her lips, "I like to hug my memory of Mica all to myself.
She was my beloved sister; a finer woman never lived. . . . Why I
think so? Just like Jozek! Every time I opened my mouth, he said,
'*Zasto, tetka Ana?* [Why, Aunt Ana?]'" She imitated a boyish voice.
"Or he'd say in Slovenian, '*Zakaj, tetka Ana?*'

"But"—hesitating—"I guess I will tell you why Mica came, just the
same. It was to talk about Jozek mostly. As I say, she still called him
Jozek, even though he was twenty-five then—in 1917. He was always
her favorite: you know how mothers are. Some of them like the worst
or the sickliest child. I've seen it myself.

"Mica wasn't educated either, like me. Just another peasant girl,
only different. . . . How different? I'll tell you. When Joza had me
for a visit in Belgrade for two weeks in '46, he made me go to the
theater, to the opera, to the *kino,* for the first time in my life, and I
was seventy-five. One of Joza's generals took me; a young Montenegrin: the handsomest devil you ever laid eyes on. . . . So there I sat
in a box at the opera, with everybody glancing at me when the lights
were up, wondering who I was. They say I look like Joza, like Marshal
Tito; and I do—naturally—because he took after his mother and she
and I resembled each other. . . . So I was at the opera with his Montenegrin general, and I listened to the singing and the applause, and I

kept thinking of Mica. I tell you, if she'd had the chance—and *this* I'm sure of—she would've been as good as those girls, all done up, singing on the stage, or better maybe.

"When Mica was about seventeen, before she married Franjo Broz and went to Kumrovec, it was a joy to be in the same world with her. She had a fine strong voice. It came right out of her so the air shook, and if you were near her and she sang full and loud, it tickled the insides of your ears: you know what I mean? . . . That's what her voice was like. She knew so many songs; Croatian songs too, because here, on the Croatian border, most Slovenians know Croatian as well as Slovenian, and the same is true of Kumrovec the other way around. Also, hundreds of years ago, during the peasant revolts, Matija Gubec was stirring up the peasants in Slovenian Styria almost as much as in Zagorje. In fact they say Gubec was half-Slovenian, just as Joza is, although Croatian lore says Gubec is a Croatian. Not that it matters. . . . Our Mica knew five, six songs about him. And could she tell stories! About Matija Gubec and King Matjaz"—the legendary Slovenian hero sleeping with his army inside a great hollow mountain and destined to emerge at the dawn of Slovenian liberation.

"Mica sang all the time. She liked to, I guess, and she knew people liked to hear her. And when she went to Kumrovec she kept right on singing. When the children came she sang to them and told them stories—in Croatian, because it was the custom that when you married in Croatia you became a Croatian, and the other way around, you became a Slovenian if you married in Slovenia.

"Mica sang till she was about twenty-eight or thirty, but less and less as her life with Franjo and the children became harder, and there was no bread in the house sometimes—which I didn't know for sure till lately when a woman in Kumrovec told me how Mica hired herself and the older boys out so she could feed her family. . . . Yes, Tereza Stefan. She knows *plenty*. . . . My, my! Who would ever have thought all this would be important and you'd come all the way from America to ask me? . . .

"It was late in the autumn in 1917, and Mica lay in this very room, worn out, talking of dying. All she knew about Joza was that he was wounded in Galicia and captured by the Russians. She felt she would never see him again, and she asked me to keep an eye on him if he came back, because she was afraid for him because the world didn't suit him as it was and he wanted to change it, and she knew the world would try to beat him down. She was smart, Mica was—only not in that request. How could *I*, an ignorant woman stuck in this gully, help Joza when I didn't even know where he was or what he was up to most of the time, or if I'd ever see him again?

"Joza was a grown-up man then; twenty-five, as I said; he'd been around—to Zagreb and Trieste and Ljubljana, to Bohemia, to Vienna, to Germany and Switzerland; I don't know where all. He was a metal worker and"—she whispered—"a socialist, with a head full of schemes that were beyond me. He was mixed up in all kinds of doings I didn't understand and didn't like either, because he was against religion, although I've known priests who were ordinary *barabe* [scoundrels]. But I was taught a priest was one thing: human—and religion was another: divine. Joza's talk, when he came to see me before the war in 1912 and '13, was heathenish and dangerous too. And I guess it sounded that way to his mother also, because she and I were brought up together. I mean she felt he was in danger. I don't think Mica disagreed with him, except maybe when it came to religion. She thought he was a good boy. Not that she was a socialist or communist any more than I am. She just had a mother's feeling for him.

"No, *no*, I'm not making this up. What do you take me for? Why should I lie? I tell you, she lay on this very bed and said, 'I have a feeling about Jozek.' How should I know 'exactly' what she meant? The chances are she didn't mean anything 'exactly.' Mothers have a feeling about their children, or about one child, and it turns out right or it turns out wrong. If it turns out wrong, nobody mentions it; if it turns out right, somebody remembers it. Mica's happened to turn out right, so I remember it. Maybe Jozek was her favorite because when he was still very little he always begged her to sing just one more song or tell one more story, or because he always wanted to wind that music box on the wall. Oh, you know about the Holy Trinity! I think Franjo bought it at a fair in Klanjec a year or two after they were married and brought it home for Mica. That was when it still looked as if he might turn out all right. No, I don't know what happened to that music box; I only wish I did.

"Did Tereza Stefan or anybody else in Kumrovec tell you that all the children took after Mica except one boy who grew up to be the image of his father? But Jozek resembled her most. That may have had something to do with her loving him so, too; what do you think? I don't know, either; nobody can know for sure. She may have felt that when he grew up he'd somehow make good the hardship she went through—if the world didn't beat him down. But she was afraid it might beat him down. That's just a guess. What did Tereza tell you?"

"When Jozek was six, I was eleven," Tereza Stefan had told me in the presence of Petar Segedin and about a dozen of her fellow Kumrovcani. "It was in 1898, a bad year for Aunt Mica—I called her Aunt Mica although she wasn't my aunt: no relation at all. For many weeks in a row, for three or four days each week, she asked me to watch the children while she and the oldest two went out to earn enough so they could eat.

"Jozek, as we called him then, wouldn't be still for a minute. Always hungry. There was no end to his questions. He always wanted me to sing and tell him stories. I had no voice but I sang the few songs I knew for him over and over, and I told him stories, although everytime I finished a song or a story he'd tell me I couldn't sing and I couldn't tell a story like his mother. But when Joza, when Marshal Tito, came to Kumrovec in '45, looking so fine in his uniform, with his dog and all those *drugovi* from Belgrade and Zagreb, and saw me in the crowd, he recognized me and he reached for my hand and pulled me to him and laughed and said he remembered how I used to sing for him and tell him stories. It was the most wonderful thing that ever happened to me.

"What else do I remember? Well, when Aunt Mica baked, she made three, four loaves at a time, as many as she had flour for, that week. Then she locked up the loaves and hid the key. She had a houseful of kids and they were always hungry, always reaching for anything they saw: you know how children are. She figured out exactly how big a piece each child could have how many times a day so the bread would go around and last until she baked again. Sometimes that meant till she got hold of the next batch of corn flour. But Jozek, not to mention the others, pestered her, '*Majka,* why can't I have the next piece now? If you give it to me now, you won't have to give it to me later.' When he and the others carried on like that, her face tightened and she told them they'd have to wait till the time came for her to give them their share. 'But if you give it to me now,' Jozek said, 'you won't have to remember.' This became a bitter long-drawn-out joke between them, only it was no joke. Jozek was always testing her to see how far he could go. Children can be cruel.

"And he was smart, that boy. He knew she was proud, especially in front of her sisters-in-law. So if one of them dropped in while he was home, he'd say offhand-like, '*Majka,* please give me a piece of bread, I'm hungry'; and although she trembled inside, she'd open the cupboard and cut him a piece as if that were what she did whenever he asked for bread. When the aunt left, though, she'd scold him and she'd weep. This happened seven or eight times that I know of. It must have happened fifty, a hundred times. What was going on in her mind, I don't know.

"My mother was often angry with me because I was at the Brozes' more than I was at home even when Aunt Mica didn't need me to mind her kids. She was so nice to be with, I liked to look at her. The Brozes were as poor as we were but Aunt Mica's house was brighter. No, that wasn't what drew me to her. I don't know what it was. Maybe it was her singing; and, later, my sorrow because she sang less and less, and then stopped singing altogether. I was nearly thirty when she died; I cried for days, worse than when my mother died.

"Aunt Mica and Jozek were close. There was a bond between them. She worried about him more than she did about the others. She always told me to watch out for him especially, when she left me in charge. Sure, he was thin and pale, but that was only because he didn't have enough to eat. There was nothing else wrong with him. He was healthy as a sparrow and quick as a flea. You couldn't spring anything on him and catch him off-guard. Pepek"—her husband's cousin, Pepek Stefan, a peasant who had come into the room a while before—"can tell you about that. I mention it because once I said to Aunt Mica—it must've been 1903 or 1904—that I thought she didn't have to worry about Jozek. 'He knows how to take care of himself,' I said. The next morning I heard her sing—she hadn't sung for a long time—and I came over, and she gave me a piece of embroidery she'd brought in her hope chest from Podsreda.

"What else? . . . Well, I used to help Aunt Mica outdoors, just as she and her two oldest helped us when something had to be done. One day when I was fourteen and Jozek was nine, he came to the cornfield with a hoe and started to work the soil. He could barely lift the hoe, it was a foot longer than he. So I told him to run along, he was in the way. No, he said he had to work. I said again he should run along and wait until he grew up—I meant it kindly, the way you speak to a child—but he wouldn't look at me and smile back. He said, 'I must work,

'Tereza,' and he sounded angry, as though I should've known better than to have him tell me. I said, 'Why must you work?' He said, 'Mother says if I'm to eat I must work.' "

Pepek Stefan—a slouching peasant with a long blank face (blank till he spoke) and a short gray mustache and a rawboned, almost fleshless frame in dirty, patched-up work clothes—had come in with a slow, side-lunging stride while Tereza and I were talking. Custodian Krajcer had sent someone to call him from the field, and interrupted Tereza to say, "Pepek can tell you more than anybody else." When I took his hand it felt like a hunk of earth. Like the others, he had a gift for simple narration with a touch of humor, usually at his expense. The story of Pepek's and Joza's boyhood reminded me of Huckleberry Finn and Tom Sawyer.

"Joza will be fifty-seven next month," he said, "I was fifty-eight in the autumn. He's a year and a half younger; when we were kids together, though, from the age of nine on to about fifteen, making mischief, he was the leader and I, you might say, was his *oproda* [shield-carrier: aide, bodyguard]. When he was around ten, he led a gang of four to six boys; when we got older, he had a dozen or fifteen. Our gang always won. We were always getting into jams but Joza got us out of them. No, I'm not saying this because he's Marshal of Yugoslavia now. People in this room will swear I'm telling you the truth. Deep down in him, Joza was the same at twelve as he is today. The boy's the father of the man, they say.

"I remember when he was thirteen and our gang fought battles with other gangs, he ordered flanking movements, not only frontal attacks. We ambushed and surprised the enemy. We sneaked up on his position. Real *taktika*." Pepek tapped his forehead.

"I don't remember how I came to be his sidekick. Maybe because he saw I wasn't so bright but not so dumb either. Reliable. I was the only one he let in on his schemes, and even if I wasn't the smartest partner in the world I stuck with him through thick and thin. I guess that's why he liked me. Oh, we didn't do anything so bad." Pepek grinned. "We prowled in the woods and along the river bank and we swam, the two of us or with the gang. We fished with a worm on a filed, hooked nail at the end of a string. Adventures like that.

"I don't know if you saw it or not, but on the summit of that steep hill outside the village, a ways as you come from Zagreb, there's an old,

old castle. It's been a ruin for hundreds of years and it's overgrown with moss and vines and crawling with lizards. One story is that Matija Gubec's serf army laid it waste, another is that it was ravaged farther back than that. The scholars in Zagreb may know; they know everything; but I like to be ignorant, so I can imagine as I please how it came to be a ruin. Take a look at it on your way back to Zagreb: it'll be on your right, the hill beyond the first hill after you leave Kumrovec. Well, Joza and I explored that ruin many a time. He thought it was wonderful. I did too. We played there often, just the two of us sometimes. He was a knight and I was his *oproda*. Or he was Matija Gubec and I was Ivan Pasanec [another seventeenth-century peasant rebel leader]. From stories he heard about the *buna,* he knew that Matija Gubec's men covered their hats with periwinkle sprigs and tree leaves to disguise themselves; and when we fought our wars with gangs from near-by villages, Joza ordered us to put on greenery before we crawled up on the enemy through the bushes. *Taktika.*

"We fought three, four battles a year, usually with the Slovenian kids from across the river. Joza had a bit of a grudge against the Slovenians, and I'll tell you why—but if you see him I'd sooner you didn't mention it. When his mother first took him over to his grandma's in Podsreda, he was going on five and he didn't have his first pair of britches yet, or his first pair of shoes—on the Croatian side of the river we only wore shoes in winter, most of us seldom before we were seven and starting to school. So when his mother took him to Podsreda that first time, I guess it was the summer of 1896, all he had on was a long homespun linen shirt with a string around the waist, according to Kumrovec custom. The Slovenian boys, who got their britches a year or so earlier than we did, thought he was very funny, and taunted him. He was humiliated, and for a while he had it in for the Slovenian kids, even though he liked to stay with his Slovenian grandparents in Podsreda. He fought many battles to uphold his pride, or because he heard the Styrian-Slovenians looked down on us Croatians. If he preached to me once, he preached to me ten times that I mustn't let anybody make fun of me because I was poor or a Zagorac or a Croatian.

"Of course we did things, Joza and I and the gang, that weren't exactly proper. We climbed people's trees and ate the cherries before they were ripe. Your father, Sandor," turning to the custodian of Tito's Birthplace, "once caught us up one of his trees—or, to be exact, he caught *me*. Joza had dropped down and run off, and I got the beating and a kick. Joza hid in a bush and watched. Afterward did he give me a talking-to! You'd think *he* was the one who got the beating. He said I mustn't ever let anybody catch me again. It wasn't so much that a beating hurt, it was the humiliation. We went through a ceremony: he made me solemnly swear that the next time I found myself in a tight spot I'd risk breaking a leg or my neck—anything—rather than let myself be caught and kicked.

"He said I mustn't be afraid, ever. What was there to be afraid of? At night we went to the cemetery. He made me go with him to prove that there were no ghosts. I shook all over, but Joza said the dead were dead: they couldn't harm us. We hadn't harmed them; so why should they bother us? That's how he spoke. He asked the questions and he answered them. One evening, I remember, he and I were passing by a wood when a noise made me jump. Joza laughed—it was only an owl.

"Another time when he was about thirteen, the late Antun Jurak"—a Kumrovcan of a couple of generations back—"caught *him* up a pear tree. I was on the ground and saw old Jurak—may God rest his soul—and I yelled and ran, but there wasn't enough time for Joza to climb down." Pepek chuckled. "There was Jurak under the tree with a club, cursing so the air turned blue. He kept yelling at Joza to get down and take what was coming to him. Joza had to think fast. What could he do? The moment Jurak wasn't looking he dropped, *plunk!* straight down on Jurak's head and knocked him over, picked himself up and ran. Of course he was a hundred times quicker than Jurak, and he even grabbed a few of the pears I'd left on the ground. Joza wasn't hurt except for a little scratch on his hand. He licked it, and that was all. He was so proud he didn't even bawl me out for not seeing old Jurak sooner, and warning him. All he said was 'You see. That's the way to handle your enemies.'

"Once we picked up a pup on the road. Later, when the owner charged us with stealing him, Joza claimed the pup was a stray—he picked *us* up. We almost got in serious trouble over the critter because he was a hunting dog somebody in Klanjec was raising specially to sell to a well-known sportsman in Zagreb. The pup disappeared soon after we found him—just before his owner traced him to us. We never found out what had happened to him: if someone stole him from us or if he ran off trying to find his way home. Anyhow, Joza convinced the owner we were innocent. He didn't get around to telling me about this right away, but it was Lent, and we had to go to confession. I was in the confession box; Joza was right behind me, as usual, listening. He didn't mind if I listened to his sins either—we were pals. Afterward he'd talk things over with me: that it was all right I'd confessed this sin, but why hadn't I kept mum about that one, because now the priest knew that he had been in on it too, and he had to confess it also, and it wasn't a sin to begin with. Who knew what was right and wrong, anyhow? This time, though, after I confessed everything I could think of without bragging what a rascal I was, the priest asked me was there anything else—had I stolen anything? I thought of the pup and began to mention it, when I heard Joza whisper, 'You *budak* [dunderhead], you, what are you telling him that for? The dog followed us and we aren't to blame if he disappeared.' When his turn came, he convinced the priest we weren't thieves."

I asked Pepek Stefan if he thought his friend Joza Broz had been religious.

Pepek pondered; everybody in the room was silent.

"Was he religious?" he said. "You know how boys are. His mother made him go to church as long as he was in Kumrovec. It's a little dim in my head now, but I think he once told me he liked to go to church. He liked the singing, the ceremony, and the smell of incense. That's what I liked too; and, although the resemblance between him and me now isn't so strong you can notice it on first glance"—laughter—"when we were boys, Joza and I were alike in many ways."

Pepek cast a mock furtive look at his fellow-villagers. Tereza cleared her throat; several others fidgeted in their seats, aware that Pepek was coming to an episode they had often discussed in late years, and wondering whether he should tell it.

"The priest I confessed to about the pup," Pepek said, "was a good priest. Then, around 1903, a new one came. He was a big man so morose everybody was afraid of him. People said maybe the bishop sent him to Kumrovec as punishment. Nobody liked him. The other priest had trained a couple of altar boys, but they quit to go somewhere and learn a trade. My father, who was the sexton, asked me if Joza and I would like to be altar boys. I was twelve then, Joza eleven. Joza said sure, why not? The new priest began to instruct us. We discovered he smelled like a still. Once he fell into a stupor in the chair right in front of us, but we didn't tell anybody. Joza said we shouldn't; it wasn't anybody's business.

"We became altar boys. I felt funny in that get-up—the bottom of the red gown was always getting under my feet and I tripped over it all the time, or I spilled candle wax on the surplice. Once I almost set myself afire. I just wasn't any good at it. I couldn't say those Latin responses at Mass like I should; all I could do was mumble them as loud as I dared. Joza, though, took to it like a duck to water. He didn't know the meaning of the Latin responses either, but he snapped them back at the priest one-two-three.

"He was a strange one, that priest. He drank more and more and looked meaner by the day. God or the Devil only knew what was eating him. The chances are he wasn't bad, but he had no business being a priest. Maybe he had become a priest, as so many others did, to please his mother or because some girl jilted him in his student days. At Sunday Mass and at funerals, processions for rain, and other big ceremonies, Joza and I served together. On weekdays, we alternated. Only a few people were in church and the priest hurried through Mass so he could rush to the parish house and take his first swig.

"One morning when it was Joza's turn, the priest was in a bad way. For some reason my father, the sexton, wasn't in the sacristy to divest him of his robes, so Joza had to do it. As I said, the priest was a big man, Joza was smaller than I, and he couldn't reach all the way up his back to unbutton him. The priest was in a hurry as usual, and he flew into a fit of rage and he kicked Joza and hit and cursed him. He used pretty bad words——"

On June 9, 1949, in Belgrade, in the course of a seven-hour interview, I asked Tito about the several incidents that stood out in Sandor Krajcer's, Aunt Ana's, Tereza's, Pepek's, and others' narratives. He was annoyed at my interest in "all these trivia," but he confirmed most of them and elaborated on some. I waited for him to comment on his experiences as an acolyte. He said nothing, so I asked him what he did after the priest cuffed and kicked and cursed him.

"What could I do?" he said. "He was a mountain of a man; I was twelve and small for my age. Before that incident I don't suppose I either liked or disliked him. He was the priest; I was an altar boy; this was the church, his place of business; and he and Pepek and Pepek's father, the sexton, and I had our work to do. The priest was the boss. I think that was about how I looked at it. What did I know? Of course, when he kicked me, I stopped being an altar boy, inside and out. I didn't know, still don't know, what was the matter with him; but when I saw him drunk, I understood quite clearly that he was no better than any other man. It was an important discovery, although at the time I didn't fully realize that it was. Naturally, telling about boyhood incidents like this, one is apt to inject afterthoughts; and I'm not certain, but I think those kicks and curses began the process in me leading to active disbelief in organized religion. Although I continued to go to Mass on Sundays because Mother wanted me to, I think I was through with the Church from then on."

I gave Aunt Ana the highlights of the story Tereza and Pepek Stefan and other Kumrovcani had told me of Tito's beginnings, then I asked her to give me, in concrete terms, her own remembrances of Tito as a boy.

"Some of the stories Tereza and Pepek told you I know too," she said. "They're true, but each of us tells them differently. Naturally." Her speech was slower, quieter than at first. "What else can I tell you? Sometimes when Jozek came to stay with me in Podsreda, up to about the age of fourteen, I thought he was a *falot* [a rascal] and he *was,* but that isn't the whole picture. . . . In what ways was he a *falot?* He was never bad in any way you could put your finger on really, only in the little ways Pepek told you about, which wasn't bad: just mischief. In Podsreda he behaved better than in Kumrovec. He had few friends here—no close friend like Pepek—and he never got into serious trouble. He liked it with us partly because we always had plenty of milk and *zganci* [corn or buckwheat meal]. But he never forgot how the Podsreda boys had humiliated him when he first came, and he kept more to himself than in Kumrovec. In many ways he was a very *good* boy," Aunt Ana emphasized. "He pastured our cows and treated them kindly. He loved a bull calf we raised one year. He named him Pepek. What a funny pair they were! They scampered around. One warm Sunday afternoon I found Jozek fast asleep under a tree, using the calf for a pillow. The calf was asleep too. It made me smile.

"When there was other work to do, he did it right away and well. He got that from his mother. He'd do anything you asked him: bring in wood and water, gather up the two or three eggs a day, and so on. The worry was you often couldn't find him. You called and called—

no answer. But sometimes you just knew he was nearby and he heard you. When he turned up and you asked where he'd been, he'd say 'in the woods' or 'somewhere' or 'all over.' He never told you definitely. He never lied either, he just kept you guessing. He liked to gather berries, and to look for mushrooms after a rain. He could tell good mushrooms from poisonous ones better than I could. Smart as a whip.

"After he started school and learned to read, he had a passion for printed matter. He pored over every book and every scrap of paper he found. He loved pictures. He always had something in his pants pockets: a picture, a nail, a pebble: stuff like that. Almost any time of the day you'd see him carrying something under his arm: a stick, a tool—something. When you asked him what he was clutching in his fist, he wouldn't tell you, or he'd say 'Nothing.' That's what I mean by *falot*. He worried me and I loved him like my own and I knew how much he meant to Mica, and I guess I had a feeling he was too smart for his own good. You know how we are, we *kmecki ljudje* [peasant people]. We're cautious. We think it's wise to look even a little dumber than we are. Jozek looked too bright. So I was afraid. His hands and forearms and feet were always full of scratches and cuts. He climbed trees and crawled over rocks and brambles, as boys will. But I couldn't help thinking he'd have a mean fall and break a leg or arm and be unable to come home, or be bitten by a rattlesnake.

"I never could figure him out. He was little and thin, but his face was so alive, his eyes were so big, and his step and gestures so quick, he made you dizzy watching him. The way he turned his head made you almost sure he was up to something that might land him in grief. He was forever going someplace, and if you asked him where, he'd twirl around on his bare heel, eye you, make a face, and twirl away again.

"Once when he was about eight, I called him. No answer. His grandma called him. I went to look for him, and there he was—right behind the barn. 'Why didn't you answer?' No answer. A couple of weeks before that Grandpa had bought him a *pipec* [a cheap pocket-knife] and I saw he was cutting a switch. I asked him what he was doing. I repeated my question. 'Can't you see, *tetka* Ana?' he said at last.—'But what do you need another switch for?' I said. 'You have one to drive the cows to pasture with.'—'This switch isn't for cows.'—

'What's it for, then? For me to give you a lacing with when we call you and you don't answer?'—Jozek glared up at me. 'Don't be silly, *tetka* Ana,' he said. 'No one ever beats *me*. You just try!' He was so serious it took my breath away.—'Very well, Jozek,' I said, for of course I didn't mean it. 'What's the switch for?'—'For horses,' he told me finally. I knew he loved horses more than any other animals except calves and dogs (and years later it occurred to me that maybe he loved his father because Franjo had once had a team and was trying to trade in horses). 'But we have no horses,' I said. Again no answer. I said I didn't see how he could use his new switch if it was only for horses. 'Don't you worry, *tetka* Ana, we'll have horses.' We were so poor I don't think my father even dreamed of ever owning a team, and Franjo had already had his reverses by then. So, as I watched Jozek cutting the switch with his new *pipec,* I said that people like us didn't aspire to own horses; they cost too much money. Jozek squinted up at me again and said, '*Tetka* Ana, stop worrying. I'm going to get horses without money.'

"That's what he said," chuckled Aunt Ana, "and look—he's got them! When I was in Belgrade in 1946, he drove me outside the city where the new army—his army—keeps its horses, and I said, 'Joza, now you have your horses and you got them without money.' I reminded him of our talk about the switch forty-five years before. He laughed and said, 'Is that what I said? But the horses are yours too, *tetka* Ana. They're *ours;* they belong to the people. The new army is *our* army; I just command it for the time being. The whole country now belongs to the people.'

"In Belgrade, seeing Joza, I thought a lot about my sister Mica and about Franjo Broz. Back in the 'eighties, as a young blade coming over to woo Mica, and later, Franjo was, I thought, a vain, cocksure man.

"Mica was proud too, but differently—if I can explain it. She was proud of being alive, of me, of our whole family, and our village. I remember when I was young I noticed that peasant backs started to bend early, already when we were in our teens or twenties; and long before they began to dim, peasant eyes started to bore into the earth. But not Mica's. When she was a girl and later for a while in Kumrovec, she stood straight as a pine and held her head up as though she wanted everybody to know how good it was to stand and walk straight and look up and ahead. I think Joza is that way, only much more so: he's a man—and now he has this high position.

They tell me the whole world knows about him. My sister Mica's boy——

"Watching him in Belgrade, I could see Joza—Marshal of Yugoslavia —was trying to carry pride for the whole country, for all of us lowly ones. But Joza is his father's son too, and I suppose that bearing of his is pride in himself also. But it's different than Franjo's was. Franjo's pride was empty; Joza has something to be proud of."

My longest interview with Tito—the one already referred to: on June 9, 1949—began in the afternoon in a large room in Beli Dvor. The exchange was taken down in shorthand—the first three hours of it. Then Tica Stanojevic, Tito's stenographer, announced his hand was turning numb.

We laughed; we were just getting started. Tito let Tica go; it was seven o'clock, and he invited me to supper at his house at Rumunska 15. We had meat balls, potatoes, peas, dark bread (no butter), and coffee. We talked alone, with the supper dishes on the table between us, and Tigar yawning on the floor, until eleven o'clock: too tired for anything but simple directness.

"You know, *gospodine Adamicu,*" said Tito, striding about the large room in Beli Dvor as he got over being annoyed at me and my questions, "this sort of probing into my 'beginnings' is rather strange" —he smiled—"because it's not ill-intentioned. In recent months I was uncooperative with two or three foreign writers who wanted to write my biography: for good reasons, I believe. First, I was sure they wanted to write my 'life' because of the lunatic idea which seems to have traveled around the globe that I, personally, am the center of the Cominform storm. Second, I knew they would twist anything I told them. Third, I continue to feel that apart from its political aspect my life is my own business. . . . You disagree. Very well. It appears you're not easily discouraged." He looked at the heap of cards in front of me, one for each fact or supposition about him I had picked up in Kumrovec, Podsreda, and elsewhere. "It may be that nothing you have here is untrue. The truth, however, is another matter, I'd say. . . .

"I see my parents and Kumrovec quite simply. My father was a good man. You think he might have done well in America. He *might* have if we don't inquire into what 'done well' means. Or he might have died in a mine cave-in, or in some other untimely way, as many of our people did who emigrated in those days.[2] In Zagorje, years before he died [in 1925], my father drowned in the vast morass of poverty and frustration, of pointlessness and uselessness. I knew him. I remember his struggle, when I was a boy, to make something of himself. He wanted to, he *tried* to do right by his family. When I grew up and Marxism began to illumine life for me, we had some discussions, my father and I, and I was convinced of what I'd vaguely felt as a boy: that he wasn't so much a personal failure as a social phenomenon. Typical of millions of men in this section of the world in the last hundred years or so. Ambition, enterprise, initiative: what good did they do him? Wherever he turned, he bumped into semifeudalism—the best crop and pasture lands and forests and cattle and horses were owned by the Church and the remnants of the aristocracy.

"Aunt Ana is a chatterbox. Not that I'm not fond of the old girl; I love her dearly; I always did, at the same time I often wanted to wring her neck. She really talked to you too freely about matters that aren't anybody's concern. The same goes for Tereza and Pepek Stefan; I'll give them a piece of my mind when I see them. . . .

"I have little to add to Tereza's and Aunt Ana's blabbings about my mother. My remembrances of her are a blend of delight and pain, gratitude and sorrow; sorrow, that she died while I was a prisoner-of-war in Russia and that I didn't see her again, and for other reasons. She was a lovely woman, intelligent but tragically limited by the lack of education and opportunity. She was obliged to recognize early that for such as she and hers life was an unremitting struggle for bread and dignity. She drowned in the same morass as my father.

"That's their story." Tito was silent awhile, thinking, hesitating. Then: "To elaborate a little on the details you obtained about my mother. She had a set of values which were—are—inherent in our people. In my twenties and thirties, looking back, I marveled at how she managed to hold on to them in the awful struggle she waged to bring us up. I recall how she used to talk to us children, telling us to

[2] According to a story published in an early-summer 1949 issue of *Time* magazine, a friend once pointed out to the late United States Senator Robert F. Wagner, born in Germany, that his life testified to how wonderful America had been to immigrants: how it had been and still was possible to rise from the slums to success. "That is the most god-awful bunk," said Senator Wagner. "I came through, yes. That was luck, luck, luck. Think of the others!"

be honest, truthful, and considerate of anyone who was considerate of others." Tito rose, walked to a window and looked out, and returned to the table where his stenographer and I waited for him to continue. "I don't mean to present myself as a paragon of virtue, but I think that many of her beliefs and admonishments remained with me as I grew up.

"The lot of most of our peasants and working people was dismal not only in Croatia but, as I saw later, throughout Yugoslav lands. Zagorje, in fact, was much better off than Bosnia, Herzegovina, Montenegro, and Macedonia, than parts of Galicia, Bukovina, and Slovakia.

"In the United States, I read somewhere, the idea exists that Europe's poorest emigrated there. Most of the emigrants doubtless were poor, but they weren't the poorest. The poorest in Zagorje didn't leave for America. They couldn't. Around the year 1900 you needed a minimum of two hundred *forinti* for the trip.

"In my village, when I was in my mid-teens and later, that is, from five to ten years before the First World War, nearly everybody between fifteen and thirty wanted to go to America; I did myself when I was about eighteen, as I told you. The question was where and how to get passage money. For most of us it was next to impossible to save that much from wages, or to raise it in any other way. You had to have something to sell and find somebody to buy it.

"In my time, between sixty and eighty percent of the youth growing up in Kumrovec—a fairly typical community in Eastern Europe— were surplus. There wasn't anything for them to do in the village. After they completed the four years of schooling, they had to leave. There just wasn't enough food to go around. If they stayed beyond the fifteenth year, public opinion—the entire culture of the village, of Zagorje—pushed them out. Their parents were caught too tightly in the bog of poverty to even dream of sending them to Zagreb to continue their schooling. Education was mainly for the children of the city gentry and of the few well-to-do peasants. For such as my brothers and me almost the only road open was to leave the village, become apprentices, and learn a trade. And *that* road was steep and stupid: so stupid that some of us wanted to do something about it. And when we came upon Marxism, especially from 1917 on, with the Great October Revolution before us, we had the answer.

"In spite of everything I'm saying, however, the culture of Kumrovec wasn t wholly mean or low. In fact, those are scarcely the words for it. True, most of us children were half-hungry much of the time, but, as Pepek Stefan told you, we had wonderful times too. Those who stayed beyond their teens, however, were caught in one of two tendencies: to stagnate, to become emotionally dull, mentally blank, and personally shapeless; or to pit themselves against impossible odds and suffer defeat upon defeat. Some of the villagers were caught in both tendencies, now more in one, then more in the other. In between, in spite of everything, there was the stubborn attachment to life. An unspoken hope. A persistent faith in *pravica"*—justice. "There was the vital tradition of peasant revolts, of Matija Gubec—a great potential for the future. Few Kumrovcani read even if they weren't illiterate. Who had the money to buy printed matter? But there was a lot of spirited talk, of singing, and of storytelling. Day-to-day circumstances held the people in a vise and pressed many of them dry before their middle years. Before that happened, however, many a Kumrovcan, as I say, fought hard to retain his self-respect. This struggle sharpened the villagers' intelligence and their morality. You probably noticed those qualities talking with Tereza and Pepek, Sandor Krajcer, Aunt Ana, and the others.

"Even some of the poorest peasants had one good suit or dress for church, for going to fairs, baptisms, and funerals. When I was twelve or thirteen, and the burning issue was which trade I should learn, there was a lot of talk in Kumrovec about the importance of having good clothes. How this talk originated, I don't remember exactly. I suppose somebody like my father started it every once in a while to show he was not so supine as some people might think, and then somebody would repeat it, and pretty soon the talk about having good clothes in order to hold up your head was all over the village.

"Just then—when I was about thirteen—our family was passing through an ordeal about that very problem. So I wanted to become a tailor and see to it that everybody had decent clothes to wear. The tailor in the village was ready to take me on as his apprentice, but the village teacher pointed out that tailoring was a sedentary occupation and I was an active boy. He told my father to encourage me to choose carpentry, masonry, or the metal trade."

In 1893, when Mica and Franjo Broz' son Jozek was one year old, Thomas H. Huxley wrote in *Evolution and Ethics* that character "is the sum of tendencies to act in a certain way."

In the spring of 1905, a Kumrovcan who left the village ten years before and now was a waiter in the best restaurant in Sisak—a town near Zagreb—came "home" to visit his relatives. Well-dressed, glib, polished, he called on Mica Broz, who had done him a kindness in his boyhood; and he made quite an impression on Joza Broz, aged thirteen. A waiter's job wasn't bad, he said. The pay was low, but if you knew how to please and flatter the customers, you received tips. You ate better than most folk. You came in contact with the best people and heard interesting talk while you served. Unlike workers in other trades you weren't in continual danger of having your fingers or hand crushed, or having something fall on your head. It was, in short, refined work; and, alert and quick as he was, Joza might make a successful waiter. In the fall there would be a vacancy for an apprentice where he worked, and he was sure he could induce the proprietor to accept him.

For three months Joza Broz hired himself out to a peasant to earn enough for a pair of shoes, and his mother made him two homespun-linen shirts and went in debt to the village tailor to provide him with a suit.

In Sisak, Joza quickly learned the tricks of a bus boy, but he soon decided that working in a restaurant wasn't for him. It required altogether too much scraping and bowing. His fellow Kumrovcan, the waiter who had impressed him so much a few months before, now appeared a poor worm, servile during business hours and nasty-mouthed about the customers afterwards.

Joza struck up an acquaintance with two boys slightly older than himself who were apprentices in a machine-shop down the street. They declared they'd rather starve than wait on tables. That was work for a sissy, whereas it took a *man* to be a machinist, a locksmith, or a mechanic on a train. Their boss wasn't half bad, and he might take Joza on.

Joza saved every penny he received in tips to buy himself a pair of overalls. Then he presented himself to the machine-shop owner—a master mechanic named Karas, a Croatianized Czech, a big, hearty, middle-aged man who was in love with his trade. Looking down from his height at the small fourteen-year-old boy, Karas roared and shook with laughter as Joza related his reasons for not liking to work in the restaurant. Karas said his resourcefulness and independence appealed to him: they were two qualities essential for a good mechanic. And, accepting him, the master mechanic entered his name in the records as *Josip* Broz. He said "Josip" was more dignified than "Joza" and gave him a lecture on the dignity and importance of being a mechanic—in this vein:

"Why, my boy, without us mechanics the modern world wouldn't begin to be what it is. If all of us quit today, tomorrow the human race would be at a loss to know how to proceed. The whole scheme would come to a standstill."

The term of apprenticeship was four years.

There were seven apprentices, all teen-agers. They slept in a loft over the shop. A small room next to it was occupied by a young mechanic who looked after them outside of working hours. Their workday was twelve hours; it often stretched to fourteen, fifteen. The boys were exploited but weren't beaten or otherwise mistreated. They received no wages but they each had an opportunity to pick up a tip now and then for fixing a lock or a bicycle or doing some other minor job around town. Usually they spent the money for tobacco, rolling their own with whatever paper was available—newsprint mostly.

The young mechanic in charge of the apprentices was a Croatian-speaking German named Karl Schmidt and a good fellow. He encouraged the boys to practice cooperation and comradeship among themselves, and spoke to them about how indispensable workers were in the world, of the evil of organized religion, of their duty on the completion of their apprenticeship to join a union and the Social Democratic movement, and thus help bring about a better future for mankind. Disagreeing with Karas, Schmidt said over and over that the future depended not only on metal workers but on a class-conscious proletariat generally. Though the literature in his room was mostly German, Josip Broz liked to leaf through it. In 1907 Schmidt began to take a special interest in him. He taught him German and elucidated some of Marx' and Engels' more complicated ideas.

These ideas made sense to Josip and he mentioned them to his mother when he went home once a year. At the same time (1908–10) he became enormously interested in *The Adventures of Sherlock Holmes,* which came out in Zagreb, in Croatian translation, at two-week intervals in booklet form. Karas' apprentices pooled their money to subscribe to the series and took turns reading the installments.

The trouble was that they worked in the shop from dawn till dark and there was no light in the loft, so now and then one of them would read on the sly during working hours. When Karas caught him, he twisted his ear, yelled, and confiscated the booklet.

By 1910 Josip had become an expert mechanic. His regular job was to run a drilling machine. It stood in a corner of the shop where Karas couldn't easily see him, and Josip read with one eye and watched the metal under the drill and for the boss' possible approach with the other. One day, however, Sherlock Holmes and Doctor Watson were taken up by so absorbing a case that for a minute Josip's attention was more on the printed page than on the whirring machine. Suddenly, *zing!* the drill broke . . . and the next instant Karas loomed up before him, a mountain of wrath. A huge paw connected massively and sharply with Josip's face, and he reeled and fell under the blow.

It was the first serious unpleasantness between master and apprentice. Relating it in June 1949, Tito said in an aside that he hadn't thought of it for years, and he smiled, musing.

"What did you do then?" I asked.

"I picked myself up," said Tito. "Karas was yelling and all the mechanics and apprentices were looking on. Their faces were tense or blank, and the thought went through my head: They're waiting to see what I will do. I was a little groggy from the blow, and very humiliated and angry. Karas was thrice my size. I could reach up and try to hit him back. But, quite apart from my physical disadvantage, I couldn't bring myself to try. He was a master mechanic; I'd had great respect for him. I don't know how long I stood there, perhaps no longer than a quarter of a minute, while he roared about the damage I had done. I reached for the Sherlock Holmes booklet, which I hadn't finished, but Karas grabbed it first. I went upstairs, put on my jacket . . . and left Sisak.

"I was eighteen. In two more months Karas would have given me a certificate and I would have been a mechanic qualified to seek employment anywhere and join the metal workers' union. Karas had always liked me. A week before he'd asked me if I would stay on when I finished my apprenticeship, and I'd said I might. Now this had to happen—in front of all the boys and Schmidt and everybody!"

Josip Broz had a few coins and took the train to Zagreb, where the station platform teemed with people bound for America. A steamship-ticket agent mistook him for an emigrant and wanted to know why he wasn't wearing his identification tag.

Joza—he suddenly felt more like "Joza" than "Josip"—walked the fifty kilometers to Kumrovec. His arrival surprised his mother and father. They argued whether Karas had the right to strike him. Franjo Broz ordered him to return to Sisak and ask Karas to take him back. Mica Broz said nothing. Then, alone with Joza, she asked him what he wanted to do. He said he wanted to go to America.

Karas, meantime, had reported his apprentice's unauthorized departure and three days after Joza arrived in Kumrovec a gendarme came and took him back to Sisak, and locked him up after he refused to return to Karas' shop.

"Then," Tito told me, "something very nice happened. Karas came to the jail and laughed and put his arms around me and said we'd both been wrong and we should forget the whole unpleasantness. He stuck out his big hand and, naturally, I took it and we shook. We were both very happy. . . . Karas wanted me to be released immediately, but it required hours to fill out all the forms. So he went to the restaurant where I used to work, and ordered the waiter from Kumrovec to send me the best lunch on the menu that day."

"Is that what you're waiting for Stalin to do now?" I asked.

Tito made a face, then he smiled and said, "No comment."

Completing his apprenticeship, Josip Broz remained with Karas for a few months as a paid mechanic. He kept thinking of going to America, but Schmidt discouraged him: "Our duty is here, to help bring about a change so people won't have to emigrate and live in strange lands." Josip saw the point, but for a year or more he was torn between it and America.

In October 1910, he went to Zagreb and joined the union. This automatically made him a member of the Social Democratic Movement. He found a job in a machine-shop in the big city and planned to save every penny he could for passage money to New York; and when he had the money, to decide whether he wanted to emigrate or not.

Circumstances decided for him. Late in 1910 an acute economic crisis gripped all of Central Europe. Just before Christmas, Josip lost his job. He had a few *forinti* left after paying his board and union fee and contributing to a Social Democratic publication fund. His shoes were holey, and he was on his way to have them soled, when his father showed up at his lodgings and asked him for a small loan.

For the next three and a half years (1911–13) Josip Broz was one of a large straggly crew of metal workers following rumors of employment possibilities in Austria-Hungary, Germany, and Switzerland, going hungry between jobs, and talking and thinking socialism and revolution. From Zagreb he went to Ljubljana . . . to Trieste . . . to Kamnik, a town in the Slovenian Upland with a small absentee-owned metal works . . . to Chenkova, in Bohemia . . . back to Zagreb (*via* Podsreda and Kumrovec) . . . to Ljubljana again . . . to Vienna . . . to Munich . . . to Berne . . . to Mannheim in the Ruhr . . . back to Zagreb (*via* Kumrovec) again . . . to Vienna——

These were his formative years as a revolutionary. He experienced or observed every phase of the class struggle Marx and Engels had distilled into their heady ideology. In 1911, for example, when he lost his job in Kamnik because the factory there suddenly closed, a labor agent appeared and offered the dismissed workers "much better jobs" in Chenkova, Bohemia. About twenty of them signed up and the agent paid their fares and supplied them with provisions for the two-day railroad journey. Reaching Chenkova, they discovered that the workers—two hundred of them, of several nationalities but mostly Czechs—were waging a bitter strike, and that the man who had hired them was an agent of the owners of the Kamnik and Chenkova plants.

"Naturally, we refused to be strikebreakers," Tito said. "The strikers took us into their homes and to meetings and made heroes of us. They won the strike. A condition of the settlement was that the plant employ us too."

Josip learned Czech, and his German improved so that by-and-by he was able to read Goethe and Heine and political articles. To his pleasure and chagrin, he found that the workers in Bohemia, Austria, and Germany were further advanced in their outlook and firmer in their proletarian character than the workers in Croatia, Trieste, and Slovenia. He attended every meeting he could and participated in six or seven strikes besides the one in Chenkova.

At nineteen he read a pamphlet which so stirred his interest in the French Revolution that for several years afterwards he spent hours reading up on it in libraries all over Central Europe.

In Kamnik in 1911, he was drawn into the local *Sokol* (Falcon) gymnastic movement.

The Sokol idea, which originated in Bohemia, was then taking root in Slovenia. Its physical-culture program concealed a subtle nationalist revolutionary purpose which—directed by Thomas Masaryk—was already undermining the Hapsburg Empire. Through group and individual exercises, the Sokol movement encouraged the Slavic peoples of Eastern Europe to self-esteem, to concern for and pride in their health, posture, dress, and athletic prowess. It also urged them to think well of their fellow-nationals and fellow-men generally.

This fitted Josip Broz' makeup like a glove. Later he joined the Sokol in Bohemia and the *Turnverein* in Austria, and excelled on the horizontal bar and the parallel bars, and at wrestling and fencing.

When he was twenty-one, in the spring of 1913, His Imperial and Royal Majesty Franz Josef called metal-worker Josip Broz into the Imperial and Royal Austro-Hungarian Army. Broz requested assignment to a Croatian regiment and in June 1914—just before the fateful Sarajevo assassination—wound up in the Twenty-Seventh Guards, whose entire personnel from the colonel to the latest recruit were Croatians. Soon he was promoted to sergeant, partly because he won the regimental fencing championship.

He made a good soldier, but he disliked soldiering on two counts: *one,* under the Austro-Hungarian system, it was utterly stupid—a matter of endless, exhausting drills whose chief aim was to dull and finally kill a man's spirit; *two,* as a socialist he considered old Franz Josef's army an instrument of oppression and imperialism. Two men who served under him as privates told me he was one of the best liked sergeants in the regiment. He was also one of the youngest noncommissioned officers. He couldn't very well preach socialism and revolution to his platoon, but the men were aware that he was trying to make the best of a bad predicament for all of them and to reduce the stupefying effect of the drills as much as possible. His fencing impressed them. Once during war games one of the two men overheard Sergeant Broz mutter *"Budala!* Blockheads!"—meaning the officers who ran the show. Another time he had his platoon execute an "attack" in direct variance with orthodox military rules which turned out so successful that it caused talk throughout the regiment.

I asked him about this "attack," but Tito only vaguely recalled it.

He said he had worried about himself while he was in the Austro-Hungarian army because he apparently had a talent for military matters.

In the autumn of 1914 the Twenty-Seventh found itself on the Austro-Russian front in Galicia, and young Sergeant Broz and two other men—one also a socialist, the other a pan-Slavist—began to scheme how to desert to the Russians with the entire platoon. They had just worked out a stratagem when the entire regiment was "captured" by a troop of fierce-looking Circassian horsemen. Telling me of this, Tito laughed and was almost certain that "captured" belonged in quotation marks: that the pro-Russian or pan-Slavist officers, conceivably including the colonel and the battalion commanders, had arranged for the outfit, over a thousand men, to be taken.

If they had, the scenario called for a "battle" in which Sergeant Broz happened to be one of a half-dozen men who were seriously wounded. While he and the rest of his platoon stood with upraised arms in the attitude of surrender, a Circassian mounted on an enormous, snorting piebald steed dashed by and plunged his lance several inches deep into Broz' right armpit—"perhaps for the devil of it," said Tito, "or because he was unaware that the surrender and the 'battle' had been arranged, *if* they were arranged."

Josip Broz and a soldier named Bohacek, a Croatian of Czech descent, also seriously wounded, spent their first two months of captivity in an improvised hospital in a monastery at Sviyazhesk, near the larger city of Kazan, in central Russia. Very unlike Broz, whom he never understood yet grew to like and respect, Bohacek was destined to play a minor role in Broz' revolutionary career in the late 1920's, when a court set up to safeguard King Alexander's dictatorship sentenced him to six years in prison and he was sent to the Lepoglava Penitentiary, near Zagreb, where Bohacek was the warden.

During his first two months in the monastery hospital Broz learned enough Russian to make himself understood and to read slowly. Transferred to Alatir, in the Simbirsk *gubernia* (later the Ulianovsk province within the Russian Soviet Socialist Republic), where there was a better hospital, he mastered the language rapidly under the inspiration and tutoring of two girls who were students at the *gymnasium* across the street. Twice weekly after school, they visited the prisoners-of-war ward to do little favors for the patients. One girl, very pretty, was the daughter of the ward doctor; the other, her friend, was the only child of a mechanic exiled to Siberia, years before, for anti-czarist activity. They both read a lot, and became interested in Broz because he asked for books and the meaning of words and phrases. They brought him a Russian-German dictionary and loaned him the literature they had at home and could borrow: Tolstoi, Gogol, Dostoievski, Chekhov, Kuprin, Turgenev. By the time he was ready to be discharged, early in 1916, he had read eighty to a hundred books, and discussed many of them with the girls.

Under the Geneva Convention, a POW who was a sergeant was not required to work. Broz volunteered. From Alatir he was sent to Ardatov, in the same *gubernia,* and was assigned as a mechanic to a flour mill in the near-by village of Kalasiyevo. The mill was owned by three well-to-do peasants whom Socialist Broz found objectionable chiefly because they were "typical kulaks." They treated him well enough but systematically overworked their other help and took one-fourth or more of the muzhiks' grain in payment for milling the rest. The economy of the village revolved around them—"a typical condition midway between feudalism and capitalism."

Broz worked only when repairs were needed. Most of the time he read the books and journals he borrowed from the Kalasiyevo school-teachers, with whom he had quickly made friends. Or he roamed the countryside and talked with people, or he visited Ardatov, where he chanced upon an anti-czarist movement. Its members had never heard of Croatia and they listened raptly to his tales of Matija Gubec and the peasant uprising, of conditions in his native Zagorje, of the class struggle in Zagreb, Ljubljana, Trieste, Kamnik; in Austria, Bohemia, Bavaria, Switzerland, and the Ruhr. They thought he was a man of the world. He liked them and their cause.

One of the anti-czarists was a government official whose job was to arrange the disposition of POW's. Broz told him he disliked working at the kulaks' mill; besides, he wouldn't mind seeing some other regions of Russia—the Urals, say. Could he be transferred? *"Honosho!* Why not?"

In the autumn of 1916, he was sent to a camp for Austrian POW's working on a railroad project near the city of Kungur, in the Urals; and was made camp administrator. He kept the records and handled the prisoners' mail and the International Red Cross packages.

Immediately following the outbreak of the February Revolution—which overthrew the Czar, brought the inept Kerensky to power, and all but took Russia out of the war—Broz suddenly found himself in jail in Kungur on the charge of being connected with the local revolutionary organization. "Of course I denied it," Tito told me thirty-two years later. Then he gave me a flashback:

"Soon after I reached Kungur in October 1916, a couple of local worker-leaders approached me. They'd had word about me from Ardatov, and it seemed something was brewing. What were my views? I said I was all for the overthrow of czarism and would induce as many of my fellow-POW's as I could to join the uprising if one occurred in Kungur. I put myself under their orders. . . . No; I don't believe they were Communists or Bolsheviki. Looking back now, I'd say they were revolutionary, as I was, in a general, instinctive, proletarian and specifically anti-feudal, anti-czarist way. My contacts with them were too few for me to be sure, but I think I was ahead of them ideologically.

"For a few weeks, several of these revolutionaries were in jail with me. They'd been betrayed by a member of the inner group. Then they were taken from this jail and sent who-knows-where. Whether the informer had given the police my name too, I don't know; in any case, the local bureaucrats felt that as a prisoner-of-war I couldn't be exiled to Siberia. They kept me in Kungur—the worst prison I've ever been in. It may be that I wasn't a victim of the informer at all but was arrested because as administrator of the POW camp I had accused the office of the chief of the Czar's police in Kungur of stealing our International Red Cross packages.

"When I was finally released in mid-May 1917, and returned to the camp, the information I heard on the developments in Petrograd and on the Eastern Front filled me with boundless enthusiasm. I decided to escape and make my way to Petrograd, the center of the Revolution. Rail and river transportation was disorganized. I walked perhaps a thousand versts. The country was in a fluid state. I heard the word 'Bolsheviki' and Lenin's name—Lenin's much more than Kerensky's, as though the people felt that Kerensky was a transient figure. The Russian people were in suspense, waiting, smelling freedom. I saw them close up in one of their finest moments. Wonderful people! . . . Several times I was picked up by police who didn't know for certain any more what was lawful and what was unlawful. I spoke Russian as well as, if not better than, most Russians, and I easily extricated myself from various tight spots. But there was a great deal I didn't know, and more I didn't understand. I was twenty-five.

"I arrived in Petrograd in July 1917, just in time for the street battles resulting from the Bolshevik-led demonstrations. I mingled with a group of workers and soldiers who hinted a decisive something-or-other was about to occur in Finland, so I went to Finland with them. I was arrested on suspicion of being a 'dangerous Bolshevik,' but I convinced the police that I was only an Austrian POW adrift in the revolutionary storm. They released me and I returned to Petrograd and witnessed spasms of the process that culminated in the Great October Revolution.

"Shortly before that tremendous culmination, however, I was nabbed again. My Russian was so fluent that no one believed I was an Austrian prisoner-of-war. And the next thing I knew I was in a slow, sulky Siberia-bound train carrying a couple of hundred other prisoners whom Kerensky's bungling police investigators considered 'dangerous Bolsheviki.' The train carried almost as many guards as prisoners—rather characterless fellows.

"Fifty, sixty miles from Omsk I jumped off the exile train and reached Omsk the next day on an ordinary passenger train. I had no money, no ticket, but the conductor didn't care. He smiled at me as though he knew a secret that reduced such trifles as money and tickets to utter insignificance. It was the day after Lenin seized power. . . . At the Maryanovka railroad station in Omsk, armed men wearing caps and armbands I hadn't seen before questioned all the passengers. They were the revolutionary Red Guards. They asked me who I was, where I came from, and what brought me to Omsk. I told them, and one of the Reds took me to a courtyard full of Austro-Hungarian and German prisoners-of-war who were joining the local International Red Guard unit. . . .

"Stories have been published about my extensive participation in the Russian Civil War. Alas! they are not true. I served in the International Red Guard from the late fall of 1917 until the early summer of 1918. Although we petitioned repeatedly for a chance to fight the White Guards, our unit wasn't sent to the front. Our petitions were returned with the message that the Revolution needed us in Omsk. This turned out to be true, not only because we were helping to guard the key installations and because some of us were skilled mechanics, but because the front came to Omsk.

"As a Red Guard doing sentinel duty and repairing locomotives and cars at the Maryanovka station, I had no way of knowing what was going on in the world, in Russia, in Omsk, or even at the railyard where on some days I spent twenty-four hours at a stretch putting some old engine in shape. . . . It was early in the summer of 1918. Rumors abounded. One was that America was beating the Germans and the war might end any day. Another was that Austria-Hungary's days were numbered, and that after the war there would be three new countries: Poland, Czechoslovakia, and a South-Slavic state that might be called Yugoslavia. . . .

"Suddenly several trainloads of Czechs passed through Omsk. . . ."

These Czechs were former Austrian soldiers who in 1914 and '15— because they were nationalists or socialists, Sokols or "soldier Shweiks" —had deserted to the Russians individually, in small groups, and in battalions and regiments. Once they were prisoners-of-war, their leaders had begun to organize them into a Czech army for the new state that Thomas Masaryk, backed by President Woodrow Wilson and many Czech-Americans and some Slovak-Americans, had announced in Pittsburgh, USA, in 1916.

"When the first trainload of Czechs went through Omsk," Tito recalled in June 1949, "a Czech member of the International Red Guard, a mechanic named Lupsek who worked with me in the Maryanovka railyard but whom I didn't especially like because he had a rather cold manner, suddenly warmed up and stuck out his chest. 'Ah, our Czech army!' he cried. And it *was* a splendid-looking army. Well-armed. Disciplined. Smart uniforms. The troops stopped in Omsk for several hours. Their noontime meal was cooked in field kitchens which they set up in the railyard close to where Lupsek and I were working on a boxcar.

"Lupsek explained that his fellow-countrymen were going to Vladivostok, where they would embark on ships provided by the Allies. Wasn't that wonderful? Yes, I replied; but, as I say, I didn't care for the fellow. And it occurred to me: why hadn't we prisoners-of-war from Croatia and Slovenia thought of organizing an army like this? At the same time, watching Lupsek and the trainload of Czechs, I couldn't help feeling that something was amiss.

"Czech troop trains kept coming through. I was impressed. . . . One day Lupsek didn't show up. I inquired about him, and it turned out

that all other Czechs in the unit were AWOL also. But no one in
authority in our unit was disturbed by this; everybody assumed they
had gone with the Czech army. I considered them deserters from our
Red unit. But being only a mechanic without rank, I wondered if I
should say something to my unit's commanding officer, who was a
Russian, or to a higher-up in the Red Guard organization . . . when,
lo and behold! the trainloads of Czechs that had recently passed
through Omsk returned.

"They seized both the Tatarka and Maryanovka stations, and occupied the city. We Reds were greatly outnumbered and underequipped. Many of the Slavs in the International Red Guard unit
couldn't believe that 'our Czech brothers' would engage in counter-
revolution; and, frankly I myself found it difficult to fire at them in the
street battles which lasted only about an hour.

"By nightfall there was no sign of the Red force. Our international
unit was shattered physically and morally. With several other survivors
—who were sincere revolutionists but, as I later saw, naïvely idealistic
—I tried to get into the pro-Soviet underground which I thought
would or should be formed to function while the Czech occupation of
Omsk lasted. But I was rebuffed with the rest of them. Some of the
men found this almost harder to take than our defeat by the Czechs,
and they scattered over the steppe.

"I was bewildered. . . . Why did the Czechs behave this way?
Socialism had been widespread in Bohemia, and I estimated that one-
fourth of these Czechs must be socialists. So how could they do this?
Was it counter-revolution, plain and simple, hooked to the White
counter-revolution led by former czarist officers like Kolchak, Denikin,
and Wrangel, which in turn was tied to French and British imperialist
interests? Or did the Czechs decide to take Omsk because it was a
strategic transportation center and they felt they must control it until
all of their troops reached Vladivostok safely? . . . As for the Red
leaders in Omsk, their attitude toward us really hurt; but, thinking it
over, I couldn't blame them. After all, we were foreigners. None of us
was a Bolshevik or communist in any concrete sense that meant anything to them. And some of the men in the international unit, Czechs
and others, had turned out to be traitors. . . .

"Oh yes, Lupsek." Tito hesitated, glancing at the stack of research
cards on the table in front of me, studying me. "For a purely personal
reason, I stayed undercover in Omsk for a few days after the Czechs

took over, and one morning I ran into Lupsek in a Czech officer's uniform. We didn't stop to talk, but a glint in his eyes told me that Omsk was unhealthy for me. So I went into the steppe too. . . ."

The "purely personal reason" was Pelagia Belousek, an Omsk girl, with whom he had fallen in love.

For a week Broz roamed the steppe. He was twenty-six—and in a quandary. He loved the Russians. Their vast raw land, their deep-reaching literature took his breath away. In spite of the spreading White counter-revolution, supported by the capitalist powers, the Russian Revolution was off to a start. He was a communist in outlook, and he felt that his brief service in the International Red Guard entitled him to consider himself a Communist with a capital C, in the sense of being a member of the International Revolutionary Working-Class Movement. And he thought he might stay in the Soviet Union, especially now that he was in love.

At the same time, Broz had the opposite—and stronger—urge to return home. He had last written to his parents (through the International Red Cross) from Kungur. He was unaware that his mother had recently died. He often thought of her . . . of Kumrovec and Podsreda, of Aunt Ana . . . of Sisak, of Schmidt and Karas . . . of Zagreb and the metal workers' union there . . . of Trieste, Ljubljana, and Kamnik . . . of the persistent rumor that a South Slavic state might be formed. There was a Yugoslav Committee in London which allegedly had won the support of Lloyd George and of Woodrow Wilson. Broz had heard the names of a few members of the committee, but he didn't know whom they represented and what they stood for. Some were said to favor a republic, others a monarchy. Would the people have a voice in deciding? Did the people at home know what was happening in Russia?

To Broz—roaming the flat, almost treeless plains between fifty and eighty kilometers from Omsk—the prospects in the Slavic Balkans were alluring. He had asked Pelagia if she would go back with him. She wanted him to remain in Omsk.

The region of the steppe that Broz chanced into was dominated by semi-nomadic Kirghiz Moslems living in tents in the summer and in sodhouses from midautumn to early spring. One day, walking along a tributary of the Irtysh River, he came to a big flour mill. It was owned by Hadji Issai, who needed a mechanic as much as Broz needed a job.

In addition to the mill, Issai owned many square versts of the best pasture land and about three thousand horses. He spoke Russian and was delighted with Broz' Kirghese, scant as it was. Tall, handsome, and on the sunny side of middle age, Issai had a score of wives, about a hundred children (he didn't know exactly how many), and jurisdiction over all the Khirgiz for fifty versts around. His expansive, almost arrogant bearing and gestures implied he was the center of the universe. In business dealings he drove a hard bargain. Somewhere inside him, however, as Broz gradually perceived, the man had a core of intelligence, humor, and even honor of a kind.

Broz told him that he was an Austrian POW, a former Red Guard, a political refugee from Omsk, and a convinced communist. Issai revealed he had no use for communism. Nor for czarism. As for Kerensky, the less said the better. The same went for Kolchak, head of the White Guard, who declared himself dictator of Siberia soon after the Czechs occupied Omsk, and made his headquarters in the city. Issai had no use for anybody but Issai, for anything but Mohammedanism; and even though he was a hadji who had made his pilgrimage to Mecca, he didn't believe in Mohammedanism as a religion, either. It was so much horse manure, but also the warp and woof of the Kirghiz way of life. Or, more accurately, it was the shovel with which a fellow like himself scooped up the gravel (the masses of people) and put it where it belonged, namely, on the road to wealth, power, beautiful horses and women, and so forth. What else he valued, if anything, Issai never let on to his curious mechanic—unless it was creating pleasurable relations with men he took a liking to.

He liked Broz right off. Besides being a good mechanic, Broz knew horses, and horses liked him. He carried himself proudly "like a good Kirghiz," almost as well as Issai himself. He looked well in Kirghiz costume. In two months he spoke fluent if imperfect Kirghese. Issai urged him to become a Kirghiz. Why not? He could have any four or five of his two dozen good-looking daughters, then in their middle teens, that he wished. Broz told him about Croatia and about his girl in Omsk. Very well, said Issai; if that was how he felt, he'd respect his wishes, for every man who was a man had the right to his own folly; and Issai had Broz' letters delivered to Pelagia Belousek by the messenger who periodically took the business mail to the city.

Meantime, in Omsk, Lupsek had reported Broz was a "fanatic

Bolshevik." He knew about Pelagia, and in the next few months her home was searched repeatedly, first by the Czechs, then by Kolchak's White Guard troops and secret police. Somehow, shortly before Kolchak took over Omsk, Lupsek traced Broz to Issai's mill, and Czech soldiers came to arrest him. But Issai hid Broz and, bursting with indignation, lied that all his employees were Kirghiz who didn't care one way or another about the so-called Revolution. And when Kolchak's soldiers came he lied again.

News of the end of the war reached Broz about a month after it occurred. The Siberian railway wasn't running, partly owing to the deep snows but mostly to the disorganization brought on by the civil war. Broz couldn't move.

One week in the spring of 1919, about a month before the Reds captured Omsk from the Whites, a group of Kirghiz hadjis gathered at Issai's to celebrate a Moslem holiday.

"Issai invited me to join the feast," Tito told me thirty years later, "and presented me to his guests as one who, alas! was a 'Christian dog' but a respectworthy biped, nevertheless. He said I'd been all over the world, even to Istanbul where the Padishah himself had received me and engaged in a political and theological discussion with me. So he was sure, Issai said, that they, his honored guests, wouldn't object to my sitting with them. They might even be interested in my experiences.

"Issai had given me no warning that his peculiar sense of humor was on tap that day, and of course I couldn't very well make a liar out of him. . . . The hadjis were very impressed. Issai kept encouraging me to overcome my shyness and to give the distinguished hadjis at least a glimpse of my sojourn in Istanbul and of my audience with the Padishah.

"I told as good a cock-and-bull story as I could invent on such short notice. The fact that none of the hadjis had been to Istanbul helped my imagination to soar. . . . A discussion followed. We sideswiped a number of subjects. Issai knew I was thinking how to get even with him, but he smiled, oh, so benignly, as he remarked how unfortunate it was that the Kirghiz couldn't claim me as one of their own: for I had, he insisted, the making of a man who knew how to progress on the smoothly graveled highroad to success.

"One hadji held forth that the Kirghiz were the most cultured people in the world: they washed after each meal and after sunset, whereas adherents of other religions, the Christians especially, were cultureless and 'dirty.' I said everywhere I'd traveled in Moslem lands, in Istanbul too, and even in the Padishah's palace, I'd seen plenty of dirty Moslems. Behind their veils, I said, Moslem women were unclean and smelly.

"The hadjis were speechless; their host pretended to be. I went on to say that, in most instances, people the world over were dirty for the same reasons—poverty and the lack of education. And they were poor and uneducated because organized religion helped the upper classes to keep them underprivileged. I said, too, that as much as I liked Hadji Issai, I didn't care to travel on his 'smoothly graveled highway.'

"Years before, in a Vienna library, I had read a pile of books on religion—in one of them, that Mohammed had started as a herdsman. So when the hadjis regained their speech and united in an uproar that the Christian prophet, Jesus, was a hobo criminal who was hanged, whereas Mohammed was the greatest man who ever lived, I was ready for them. My extended views on Mohammed turned the uproar into a typhoon of indignation, and all that kept the hadjis from thrashing me was that Issai apologized to them, ordered me from the tent, and promised them that he'd deal with me after they left.

"That evening Issai came to the mill, shaking with laughter, and said the hadjis were fanatics, idiots. He thanked me for the shock treatment I'd administered to them. They needed it."

Through most of 1919 the Civil War blazed along great stretches of the trans-Siberian railroad, and it continued to be impossible to get out of Siberia except eastward with the approval of the Kolchak counter-revolutionary dictatorship in Omsk. After the thaw began—in April—the steppe swarmed with White refugees heading for Omsk and points east. Among them were czarist noblemen and industrial tycoons from Petrograd and Moscow journeying with their families and retinues on horseback. Some stopped at Issai's for rest, provisions, and fresh horses. Issai relieved them of their gold, while Broz eyed the pursued, weary, saddle-sore "best people" of czarist Russia and listened with a straight face to their stories of the terrifying Red hordes moving up behind them.

In Omsk, unsanitary conditions owing to overcrowding brought about one epidemic after another. Disguised as a bearded Kirghiz, Broz made his way to the city twice to see Pelagia. She refused to leave because of her family. On both occasions he tried to get into the Omsk underground, but the Red leaders held his membership in the international unit during 1917–18 against him. Both times he was arrested by Kolchak's secret police, and he barely extricated himself.

In the autumn, the steppe around Issai's domain became the scene of skirmishes between the Reds and the Whites. In November, the Reds took Omsk, forcing the remnants of Kolchak's forces to withdraw to Irkutsk. But it wasn't until January 1920 that westward passenger rail service was restored, and then it was very sporadic and limited.

When Broz parted from Issai, he had several hundred rubles in gold. In Omsk, a high-ranking Red officer who had been a Red Guard in 1917 and had helped to recapture the city now recognized him, and he was suddenly acceptable to the Soviet regime. Pelagia Belousek and her brother, a Red, reminded him of his earlier enthusiasm for the prospects the Soviet Union offered young people, and tried to persuade him to stay. But Broz prevailed on Pelagia to come to Yugoslavia with him. (This version of Tito's sojourn in Russia, often referred to as a period in his life about which nothing is known, is based on the story he told me. It was taken down by his stenographer, whose notes in the original Serbo-Croatian are in my possession.)

The Soviet authorities made him commander of a contingent of POW's from former Austrian lands now within Yugoslavia. Some of these POW's were Reds, others anti-Reds; most of them only wanted to get home. Broz organized them into Croatian, Serbian, Slovenian, Bosnian, and Dalmatian detachments. When they reached Stettin, Germany, the anti-Reds rebelled, saying that his principle of organization-by-nationalities smacked of Sovietism; and in the ensuing squabble the contingent voted to break up and for each man to find his way home as best he could.

Josip Broz and his Russian bride crossed the Austrian border into Yugoslavia at Maribor, Slovenia. They were arrested and detained for a week's questioning. Whether or not the Yugoslav police had advance information about him, Broz' and his bride's striking Siberian clothes were enough to make them suspect. Their names went on the suspicion list to stay.

Released, they took a train from Maribor to Sent-Peter, the station nearest Kumrovec. It was even nearer to Podsreda, so they went to Aunt Ana's first, although Josip was eager beyond words to see his mother and have her meet Pelagia.

"I'd given up all hope of ever setting eyes on him again," Aunt Ana told me in April 1949. "Now here he was—with a Russian bride. Just like Joza! She was tall and beautiful. When she took off her fur hat, I almost gasped—she looked so much like Mica when Mica was a girl.

"It broke my heart to have to tell Joza that his mother was dead, that she'd died two years before. He turned pale. He sat down. His wife couldn't understand me; she was upset and kept asking what was the matter. Joza pulled himself together and told her in Russian, then asked me to tell him all I knew. So I told him how his mother had come to me that morning in the fall of 1917, and what she had said about his being in danger because he was against the world, and so on. He listened and didn't say anything. I said I didn't know how I could help him, but I wanted to, and if he was ever in danger he could always come and hide in my house. Pelagia wanted him to translate, but he didn't—not then, while they were here, anyhow. When they were leaving, he put his arms around me without saying anything and he pressed me to him. I'll never forget it. . . .

"He hired a carriage to go to Kumrovec. It must have been very depressing there. Franjo was home, and Joza's second oldest brother. His other brothers and his sisters had left the village by then."

It was spring; the year was 1920.

Josip Broz went to Zagreb, renewed his membership in the metal workers' union, and joined the one-year-old Communist Party of Yugoslavia. The party had been formed early in 1919 as a branch of the Third Communist International (Comintern) which had come into existence under Lenin's leadership in Moscow the same year. Broz found a relatively well-paid job in a machine-shop, and Pelagia and he rented a modest two-room flat.

For a time Broz was a sensation in Zagreb's working-class circles. His five years in Russia had made him an authority on the country toward which nearly all Left thinking in ten-month-old Yugoslavia was orienting itself. Here was a man who had "seen The Future with his own eyes" and could tell about it. Men gathered around him to listen. They asked him and his Russian wife to their homes.

"If I were you, *drug* Broz," a man remarked one day, "I'd have stayed in the Soviet Union. There, under Lenin, the Revolution has a chance to create a paradise on earth."

"I think that would have been a mistake," Broz said. "We need a revolution too." A man I met in Zagreb remembered hearing this conversation. Tito didn't recall it.

Thus began the career of Josip Broz, Yugoslav revolutionary. He was twenty-eight—thin, wiry, agile, attractive, quick-witted, dedicated.

Thus, too, began the hallucination among the Yugoslav workers and intellectuals which—linked to the existence of the Soviet Union, and feeding on the complex crisis engulfing Europe and the world generally—culminated in the Yugoslav Revolution on the Soviet model.

BOOK TWO
CHAPTER TWO: *The way through the underground
toward something bigger than himself*

ALKING with people in different parts of Yugoslavia, especially from May through August 1949, I quoted (from memory) whenever I had the chance the American Seabees' motto:
"The Difficult we do at once, the Impossible takes a while longer,"
because it illustrates a likeable American conceit and because I enjoyed
watching the Yugoslav Communists' faces simultaneously light up and

darken as though here at last, in a boast, they found a common ground with capitalistic America. Since then I have discovered that the Seabee motto is a rephrasing of George Santayana's sentence "The Difficult is that which can be done immediately; the Impossible that which takes a little longer." I find, too, that La Fontaine wrote: "Man is so made that when anything fires his soul impossibilities vanish" ... and Emerson wrote: "Every man is an impossibility until he is born."

In 1949 I came upon scores of middle-aged and elderly people in New Yugoslavia—apart from Tito's relatives and other Kumrovcani—who knew Josip Broz during his genesis as a revolutionary in the 1920's. Of the seven I talked with, three said without leading questions from me that they remembered him as a *fanatik,* and two others agreed that the word was not inaccurate. I use the Yugoslav form because in Yugoslavia, at least as applied to Josip Broz and to the movement and the Revolution he led, *fanatizam* has a different popular meaning than "fanaticism" as the Americans and the English use it in the middle of the twentieth century—though, perhaps, *fanatizam* is no more a concentrate of what it takes to achieve the Impossible than what the Seabees had.

A Croatian writer, touching on the subject in an essay published while I was in Yugoslavia, recalled the words of the heretic Dominican monk, Giordano Bruno, to his judges: "You who are pronouncing my death sentence tremble worse than I who listen to it." The essayist then defined *fanatizam* as "that which fills and activates those who are fighting for a better future. It is a fusion of all sound passions into a single high aspiration which is not blind but, on the contrary, is a matter of wide, calm consciousness and clear, pointed thought that dominate a man's whole being, and of the sense that his own will is in consonance with the urgencies in human affairs."

Not that fanaticism of this kind, as already suggested, has been complete anathema in England and America. In the United States: William Lloyd Garrison, the Abolitionist, started his *Liberator* in Boston in 1831 with these words on the masthead: "I am in earnest—I will not equivocate; I will not excuse; I will not retreat a single inch; and I will be heard." Eugene Debs, one of the few respectworthy American Socialist leaders, was an out-and-out fanatic. In an undated clipping of Sydney J. Harris' "Strictly Personal" column in the Chicago *Daily News,* sent to me by someone in 1948 or '49, I read that "the world has always needed fanatics ... It was fanaticism that gave St. Joan her glory and John Brown his immortality. . . . [Fanatics] are the only people who are willing to work for something greater than themselves."

This just about covers Josip Broz from 1920 on, as well as a growing number of his countrymen.

For six months after his return from Russia in 1920, Josip Broz worked from ten to twelve hours a day as a machinist in a shop in Zagreb. During most of the rest of his waking hours he agitated for the trade unions and for Communism, which to most of his listeners meant "the same system they have in the Soviet Union." (To many American and English ears in 1950 or '51, the word "agitator" also has a disquieting sound; in Tito's Yugoslavia I found it to be a title of distinction.) Having been in Russia during the Revolution, and having the ability to talk about it in simple, direct, heart-lifting words, Broz —without consciously meaning to—laid the first blocks for the construction of his prestige.

He had no doubt that in Russia he had seen the future. "We need to follow the Russian example," he said. "If we want a better future for our country, we have no alternative. Socialism is the answer. We, the workers, must study, must prepare ourselves to take over." His emphasis was always on the workers. *They* were the harbingers of the future.

Broz was a pleasant companion, a good fellow with a lively sense of humor. In company, conversing on his favorite subject, he would sip wine or *rakija* (brandy) if a glass of it was set before him. He liked good food, neat clothes—on others, too. He was ready to give away almost anything he had. On payday his father often came for a "little loan" and he always gave it to him, even if he had to borrow the money. One winter evening, walking home from a meeting with an older man (whom I met in Zagreb, where he was still a worker, in April 1949), Broz took off his coat and hat and gave them to a shivering, desolate man they came upon in the street. His companion remarked that he need not have done that. Broz didn't answer; he resumed the conversation.

His manner of speech and bearing indicated that he thought well of himself, and demanded respect. In turn, he respected and liked others. He cared keenly about the personal welfare of his friends and acquaintances. If someone he knew was in a scrape, he took steps to

get him out of it. He felt that nearly everybody was in straits of one
kind or another, and that collective action was necessary to navigate.
His use of the adjectives "important" and "significant" was reserved
for *"nasa partija*—our Party," the CPY; for *"nas sindikat*—our union";
for "the international working class" (he used this phrase often); for
Marxism, for socialism, a classless society without exploitation—"an
association," he quoted Marx, "in which the free development of each
is the condition for the free development of all," and from which the
government would eventually wither away.

Now, however, the class struggle was the central reality of the times.
The workers must wage the *borba* and win it, the workers of all lands.
They must stick together. The goal was to come to power. Everything
hinged on that. Victory could be achieved only through a strong fighting, conspiratorial Communist Party modeled after the Bolshevik party
in Russia. Their first job was to strengthen the Party, make it bold,
give it direction. Naturally, the bourgeoisie—on the defensive, trembling
before the spectre defined in *The Communist Manifesto*—employed
terror to prevent the Communist Movement from spreading; but
the workers must not be immobilized by fear. Rather be caught for a
lion than a lamb. *Djavo* (devil) take the provocateurs, informers, and
stool pigeons!

"Here, read this." Broz was forever handing out leaflets. "When you
finish it, pass it on to someone else." He saw issues simply. He was
like a bow tensed to loose an arrow at a mark. But he was not impatient with anyone who was slow to grasp his meaning. He would have
made a good teacher.

Except when he observed ostentatious waste, luxury, or posturings
on the part of the rich, he didn't hate, nor even dislike, them personally. He didn't envy those who were well-fed and well-dressed. And
he didn't point out the difference between them and the majority of
the people. It was obvious enough.

Having just returned from Russia, Broz wasn't substantially active in
the elections for the Constituent Assembly, which laid the groundwork for the new state. But he helped to organize the metal workers'
strike in Zagreb in the second half of 1920. The strike, which drew in
other workers, was partially a protest against the *Obznana,* the regime's
anti-Communist terror, that was sideswiping the trade unions. At the
end of it, Broz found himself out of a job and on the blacklist. He had
no connection with the assassination of Milorad Draskovic, the terror-

istic Minister of the Interior and the inventor of *Obznana,* which occurred in the town of Dalnice, Croatia, in August 1921. But he did not disapprove of it. It was an act of war.

Broz was a Party *aktivist*—agitator, union organizer, strike leader, professional revolutionary. He had a keen instinct regarding people. Every now and then he distrusted someone in the Party or the metal workers' union, sometimes without any concrete reason; and sooner or later that person turned out to be a stool pigeon. Broz was not discouraged. All in all, numerous as they were, creatures like that were a minor flaw, an inevitable weakness, in a sound movement geared to the onrushing future. Look at the Soviet Union—nothing, not all the forces ranged against it, could stop it.

Broz possessed the attribute of Joseph Conrad's central character in *Nostromo*—"an energy of feeling, a personal quality of conviction." He spotted quixotry or romanticism at a glance. Sometimes his facts and arguments came like hail. He laughed heartily and a great deal, but no one could say he was light-minded. He liked humor in others; he noticed that it helped to take them over the bumps. Yugoslav humor was not frivolous; often it was *zafrkavanje* (baiting), often tinged with bitterness; many of the jokes contained insights into social affairs. They were akin to Jewish humor, originating from the fix the people were in.

"But seriously, *drugovi,*" Broz would say after a release of laughter, "what will count in the long pull ahead is the Party—the Party, the Party." It was, he maintained, more than the aggregate of the qualities of all its leaders and members. It was Everything: the *mystique,* the vehicle of Progress. The vehicle must be kept greased and moving. He zealously carried out each order given to him, whether or not he knew by whom it was conceived, and why.

Early in 1921, Broz went to a small village near Bjelovar (7,800 pop.) in Croatia. He organized the workers in the several shops and small factories, and created a CP cell. In four and a half years he led three strikes and was arrested and jailed seven times. His son Zarko—who lost an arm twenty years later defending Moscow as a Soviet soldier—was born in Bjelovar in 1923.

In 1925, his assignment in Bjelovar accomplished, Broz was recalled to Zagreb, and a few months later he found himself in the little boat-building town of Kraljevica (Kingsville) in the Croatian Littoral, just south of Susak and Fiume.

The story in Kraljevica is as follows. In 1925 the Belgrade terror relaxed somewhat, and employers scanned the blacklists less carefully. One day a pale, thin man appeared at the boatyard employment office and said he wanted work by the sea partly for his health's sake. He was hired. He rented a little shack and his Russian wife, who by now spoke Croatian, and their two-year-old son joined him.

Twenty-four years later I visited Kraljevica and listened to two old-timers reminisce—one retired, the other still on the job, now in the enlarged and booming boat-building plant named for Tito. They took me to a building on which a metal plaque reads: "On this spot stood a hut in which *drug* Josip Broz Tito lived as a boatyard worker in 1925 and 1926." They showed me the page in the employees' register of the absentee-owned company with the signature "Josip Broz" and the information "—Kumrovec—married—machinist," also in his handwriting. On one side of this entry, written by another hand, was his employee number "445"; on the other, "6.50"—his hourly wage rate in dinars: about fifteen cents.

Among other jobs he did in Kraljevica, Broz helped build a new speedboat for Milan Stojadinovic, a young minister in King Alexander's latest government, a Belgrade speculator, and a principal agent of foreign agents in Yugoslavia. A few years later Stojadinovic became head of the Belgrade Bourse, or stock exchange. In 1935 Prince-Regent Paul made him prime minister. In that capacity, complying with official Britain's (the Cliveden set's) wish at the time that Yugoslavia enter the Axis parlor under the coattails of Britain's appeasement policy, Stojadinovic neatly switched the country from the Paris-London sphere into the Hitler-Mussolini orbit.

Within a week of his arrival in Kraljevica, Broz made friends with several men in the shop. He mentioned that the company employing them was half-foreign-owned. He didn't need to say it paid poor wages, skipped paydays, and laid men off without notice, frequently without paying them. Nor did he have to tell them that individually they lacked the financial means to engage attorneys to present their claims against the company in court. The only way to cope with this outfit, said Broz, was to organize. The company's main office was in Susak. Its bank account was located across the bridge in Fiume, which was under Italy. It was a tricky setup in which a dismissed worker, trying to get a few hundred dinars back-pay, was out of luck.

Although Broz' proposal to organize wasn't exactly new, it scared the workers who still had jobs. Living from hand to mouth, they feared that if they formed a union, the company would discharge all of them and replace them with Italian workers. Then the company helped Broz achieve his purpose. It once more skipped a payday, and Broz said to his fellow-workers, "What have I been telling you?" In two months he had the core of a union. Early in 1926 a strike broke out in the hitherto moribund Kraljevica. In two weeks the men won higher wages which were to be paid on set dates twice a month without fail.

Broz didn't have time to form a CP cell in the boatyard. Before the strike ended, gendarmes escorted him out of town.

His next assignment was the French-owned factory in Smederevska Palanca, Serbia, which made and repaired railroad cars. His experience there was similar to that in Kraljevica, except that before he was run out he had organized a CP branch. In fact, the Serbian workers elected him, a Croatian, their envoy to the central committees of both the CPY and the countrywide metal trade-union council, then being formed. This occurred at a period when the politicians, the press, and the priests were blowing up "the Serbo-Croatian problem" into the biggest issue in the land.

Terror was rampant again; in recent months two or three CPY and trade-union organizers had been found dead. One day the foreman informed Broz that the manager of the plant, a Frenchman, had ordered him to discharge Broz at once. The next day the local gendarmerie ordered him to leave town—or else! Broz queried the Party; it instructed him to return to Croatia. Soon after this, to his surprise, he was elected secretary of the Metal Trades Union Council in Zagreb.

By now (early 1927) King Alexander's secret police—whose character was a fusion of Byzantine cunning and cruelty, sexual abnormality, corruption, stupidity, and anti-Communism rationalized into patriotism—had scant doubt that Broz wasn't just a trade-union organizer but a Red operator. The trouble was that the Law for the Protection of the State required tangible evidence of his ties with the Comintern or of concrete activity directed at destroying the state. And "the state" meant the existing order: the monarchy, the "best" families, the Church, the foreign agents and industrial managers: their will and whims and their power and their "take." But the police were not troubled; they were receiving plenty of help from within the Communist movement riven by the Stalin-Trotsky feud in the Soviet Union. So-called "Trotskyists" and "anti-Trotskyists" were informing on each other and on other Reds who, like Broz, were against both. Meanwhile the secret agents were making hay—arresting hundreds of "suspected" and "dangerous" Communists.

Broz was arrested as "dangerous" soon after he was expelled from Serbia and elected secretary of the Zagreb Metal Trades Union Council. The police had no concrete evidence and held him incommunicado —*pod istragom,* under investigation—for weeks. Questioned, he said it was no secret he was a class-conscious worker and a trade-union organizer. To be sure, he favored strong unions. As for the security agents' other questions, it was *their* job to find out the answers, wasn't it? He spoke with a proud look, a cocky grin. The royal gumshoers eyed him, then one another. Was he a Stalinist or a Trotskyist? He asked *them* to tell *him* what they meant by the terms. They were stumped.

Actually, Broz himself knew little about the schism rocking the All-Soviet Communist (Bolshevik) Party. He had been too busy building the Yugoslav working-class movement so it could bear up in the class struggle at home, and help fill out the international revolutionary picture. He hadn't had the time or the inclination to listen to a lot of theoretical dissecting of the goings-on in Russia by obviously uninformed CP and fellow-traveling intellectuals. Not that he wasn't interested in the Moscow split or in its world repercussions; but first things came first. Besides, how could he, how could the tiny CPY, influence the great Party in the USSR? No one but the Soviet leaders themselves could iron out their differences. All the CPY could do was perform to the best of its ability in Yugoslavia and hope the Soviet Union endured and continued to be an inspiration to the working people elsewhere. Broz had been too busy even to ascertain whether commonsense had led the majority of his fellow-workers in the Leftist unions to arrive at this attitude. He simply assumed they had arrived at it when they elected him secretary of the Metal Trades Union Council. . . .

But now (in 1927), as I said, the royal security-police agents had Broz in the lockup, and they followed the procedure which had been so successful in the past couple of years. They showed him to the other political prisoners in the Zagreb jails on the chance that one or more of them might turn against him and give them a case that would hold up in court. But although several of them knew that Broz was a CP member, no one turned against him.

One day the agents took Broz to the town of Bakar, near Susak-Fiume. In the jail there, they confronted him with seven leaders of the Kraljevica union he had aroused to militancy the year before. Like himself, they were in chains. "Is Broz a Communist? Is he a Party organizer?" the agents demanded. "What did he preach in Kraljevica?" Each of the seven men answered that they recalled him only as a fellow-worker favoring a union. Later he learned from them that when they were arrested and taken out of Kraljevica in chains, the townspeople—workers, fishermen, storekeepers and their families—lined the streets and waved to them, grim-faced and silent.

After a week in Bakar, the agents loaded the eight prisoners in a truck and took them to Ogulin, the nearest large town inland from the Croatian coast. Broz insisted on knowing why they were being moved around like this. The agents didn't say. They shoved him into a cell by himself in the centuries-old jail whose damp walls exuded an intolerable stench. The straw mattress on the floor crawled with lice and other vermin. Rats scurried about and now and again stopped to contemplate him with beady eyes.

Broz pounded on the cell door and demanded to be let out. Why was he in prison in the first place? And the seven men from Kraljevica, what had they done with them? Where were they? The guards had instructions from the political-police agents to ignore him. So, exhausted from banging on the cell door, Broz went on a hunger strike, and for five days refused to eat—"the stuff they stuck in through the opening was awful, anyhow," Tito told me twenty-two years later.

The presiding judge of the Ogulin County Court, Stjepan Bakaric, was a decent, liberal man who worried remotely about bad social conditions and extreme political trends, less remotely about individuals who were in prison for their opinions and activities, and acutely about his fifteen-year-old son Vladimir (now Premier of Croatia; I met him when I was in Zagreb). Like so many other students at the time, Vladimir—attending the *gymnasium*—was beginning to glance Left.

One day Judge Bakaric received in his mail from an anonymous source in Zagreb a copy of a mimeographed underground sheet with a marked item about Josip Broz, secretary of the Zagreb Metal Trades Union Council, whose "disappearance is causing concern and unrest among the working people. *Secretary Broz is believed to be in prison in Ogulin.*" The last sentence was underlined in pencil.

On the same day, or the next, a prison guard informed a member of Judge Bakaric's staff that a political prisoner named Broz was on a hunger strike. The guard took the liberty of suggesting that the judge look into the case, for should the prisoner die there might be repercussions.

The judge hurried to the jail and ordered the turnkey to bring Prisoner Broz before him. But the turnkey had strict orders from the security police not to let Broz out of his cell under any circumstances. This incensed Judge Bakaric and he demanded the turnkey take him to Broz' cell. "Old man Bakaric was all right," Tito told me. "He was evidently shocked by the filth and stench. He asked me why I was on a hunger strike. I asked him, 'Would *you* stay here without protesting?' He wanted to know if I was a Communist. I suggested he ask the agents: they were being paid for doing an intensive research on me. This amused the judge. He and I had quite a chat. Taking it for granted that I was a Communist, he said that if he were the leader of our movement he would forbid his lieutenants and followers to hunger-strike: that might do in India, here it was stupid; I was endangering my health and life. I countered that there were far more stupid ventures in the world, and he knew it. He argued that if he were the boss of the Communist movement, he'd want strong, healthy aides; what good would I be to the cause if I starved myself to death? In a struggle, I said, one was apt to die any moment. We batted our ideas back and forth. Judge Bakaric begged me to be sensible. Well, I asked him, would *he* think me 'sensible' if I ate the slop they gave me, and sat calmly in this stinking hoosegow until somebody took a notion to let me out? Why the devil was I in here anyhow? If they had no definite charges against me, I demanded to be released. And the seven men from Kraljevica—where were they? The judge summoned the prison official and found out they had been released. . . . So, presently, the judge and I made a deal. I promised to eat if he saw that I received decent food, and if he promised to take steps either to have me released or indicted. He promised, and he kept his word. Moreover, he had his cook bring me excellent meals from his own kitchen during the two weeks it took him to get me out of that damned hole. Meantime, as I learned by chance years later, the security-police agents were snooping around Kraljevica and Smederevska Palanca for evidence against me, but none of the Serbian workers there would oblige them."

The ensuing sixteen months (1927–28) were decisive in molding Josip Broz into a Communist and revolutionary leader. Even more of a *fanatik* than he was before, he developed a scrutinizing attitude toward everything he encountered, including the CPY, which he realized was a failure, in danger of its life. During the eight years of its existence the Party had had no real leadership. It had muffed its chances during the 1919–21 revolutionary spell. ("In a revolutionary situation strikes are not sufficient for the victory of the working class," said Tito in his long report to the Fifth Congress of the CPY in June 1948, referring to the "weakness and immaturity" of the Yugoslav CP leaders in the 1920's. "A revolutionary situation demands revolutionary means . . . armed struggle . . . since it must be expected that the bourgeoisie will act quickly and energetically to beat the working class by taking the necessary measures.") Since then—in spite of all the work that men like him had done or tried to do in factories, shops, and mines—the movement had been declining alarmingly under the blows that Belgrade, with all its stupidity, knew how to aim at the underground, which didn't know how to parry them and strike back.

The successive secretaries-general of the CPY lived abroad. *Who* were they? *Who* were the other members of the Central Committee? *Who* elected or appointed them? *Were* they in touch with the Comintern? And had they anything to say in it? *What* could they say, since they probably had no clear idea of what was happening in Yugoslavia? They couldn't know that the tension over the "Serbo-Croatian problem" was rising to a dizzy climax: that employers, taking advantage of the police terror, were beating down wage scales and, thereby, the class morale of thousands of workers: that a small yet substantial part of the Left was embroiled in the Stalin-Trotsky feud which, Broz could see, involved far-reaching questions but which, if continued, would benefit no one but the mob dominating Yugoslavia.

As secretary of the Zagreb Metal Trades Union Council, sensing his popularity with the workers, Broz felt more deeply identified with the *trudbenici,* the toilers, in industries and crafts than with the absentee CPY leadership. No doubt, the workers, the skilled workers especially, were the *avantgarda* of progressive forces. Practical, determined, self-disciplined, they did not engage in endless verbal bouts which only fragmentized the Left. But, compared to the rest of the population, they were a mere handful. What about the peasants who comprised the great majority? Their leader, Stjepan Radic, seemed to be fingering the edges of the problem and had at least ninety percent of the Croatian peasants with him. He was gaining support among the peasants in Serbia and Slovenia and as far down as Sandjak and Macedonia. . . .

Early in 1928 Josip Broz suddenly felt the need of spending a few days in Kumrovec. He walked across the river to Podsreda to see Aunt Ana. She was in her late fifties then. He remarked that the way people in the villages lived was no way to live. He had seen one of Tereza Stefan's children standing in a puddle of manure water; what chance did a kid like that have?

Ana (as she told me in 1949) turned on him sharply. "See here, Joza. You're young yet, you've been places, you're smart, you know things. Kumrovec and Podsreda have been the way they are for hundreds of years. What can *you* do about them? And how do you know they want to change? Maybe we peasants are so dumb we want to stay the way we are, each of us in his own puddle of manure water. Why should you care? Is it any of your business? Forget us. Go your own way. You've got a good head; use it to make something of yourself. You have a son; Pelagia will give you more children—do something for them. Start a machine-shop. Anything. You'll succeed. . . ."

Josip Broz returned to Zagreb angry, but not at Aunt Ana, or at Stjepan Radic about whom everyone in Zagorje was talking, or at Radic's Croatian Peasant Party. He was angry at the CPY because the CPY was missing the bus. (Said Tito in his report to the Fifth Congress twenty years later: "Because of the erroneous stand of the CPY leadership [in the 1920's] as regards the national and peasant questions, the working class remained isolated from the strong peasant movement not only in Croatia . . . but in other regions as well. The CPY leaders had then a completely negative Social Democratic attitude toward this peasant movement which [besides being peasant] also represented the struggle of the Croatian and other peoples for national equality. They even ridiculed this movement, which might have been a powerful ally of the working class. . . .")

The failure of the CPY in the 1920's was an extension and a deepening of the Yugoslav movement's failure in the preceding decade. Way down, it was nobody's fault; it was organic with the confusion of a transitional moment. In a superficial political sense, the responsibility lay with all the Yugoslav Communists. In 1921, when their leaders began to be hounded and imprisoned as enemies of the new state, they numbered about sixty thousand, but a preponderance of them were not communists in any meaning of the word that would survive a ten-minute argument. They were ex-members of dead or dying socialist parties, held down by the ballast of the past.

Early in 1928, again to Broz' surprise, the "sound elements"—those opposed to the three or four kinds of "fractionalists of the Right and the Left"—elected him secretary of the underground CP organization in Zagreb. If his life had been in constant peril during the violent strikes in 1927–28, it was even more so now. Trusted workers stood guard in their homes so he could catch a few hours' sleep—but he never slept in the same house more than three times in a row. He had no home life.

One pitch-dark evening the political-police were tipped off by a "fractionalist" informer, and raided the apartment over a butcher-shop where he expected to spend the night. He leaped blindly from a second-story window—on the chance that the open drayload of fresh meat he had seen directly beneath it hours before was still there. It was. He dropped on several newly skinned porkers which shifted under his weight and lessened the impact. He got away without a scratch.

Apart from his narrow escapes, however, this chapter in the Broz biography was no scenario for a Douglas Fairbanks film. But the thirty-six-year-old Kumrovcan was a hero to a large section of Zagreb workers.

In May 1949 I met several men who knew him well during 1927–28. Now in their fifties and sixties, some of them were foremen in the sprawling new "Rade Koncar" machine factory in Zagreb, one of the triumphs of "Tito's Five-Year Plan." Back in '28, two of them were Broz' frequent companions and bodyguards. They posted watchers wherever he held meetings with his *aktivisti,* or whenever he went to gulp a meal that some worker's wife had cooked for him, or to get a wink of sleep. One of these two companions, gray-haired Branislav Resinic, told me of Broz' arrest in '27 that led to the Ogulin episode, which Tito subsequently confirmed. Here is a spliced summary of the narratives I drew from them:

"Every now and then *drug* Broz matter-of-factly instructed one or more of us in the Zagreb CP organization to do thus and so if he was killed or if he 'disappeared' that day or next week. He risked his neck oftener than the rest of us, routine-fashion as part of the task at hand—

never foolhardily, though. We took all the precautions we could with the means at our disposal. An actor on the Zagreb theater staff, who was one of our many sympathizers among the intelligentsia, taught us how to change Broz' looks with makeup every once in a while, so that police agents and even informers who knew him well couldn't recognize him. In May 1928 he 'disappeared' like so many *drugovi* before him whom we never saw again. But he turned up and said he'd been in jail for three weeks. . . . In June 1928 four agents nabbed him again, but he escaped and went to a fellow-worker's house to have the shackles filed off his wrists. . . .

"But that was nothing," said Resinic, "arrests, beatings, gunfire were commonplace for anyone who fought in the class war. . . . Broz was in agony because the CPY was torn by *frakcijanastvo,* because Communists like us, the CP membership in general, had no idea where our leaders were *if* we had leaders; because the Party was falling to pieces. Allegedly between 1920 and '28 the membership had declined from sixty thousand to three thousand. (I say 'allegedly' because nobody knew for sure.) . . . It was this sort of thing that made *drug* Broz pace up and down the room and talk with tears in his eyes and rage in his voice. . . ."

Another man said: "How early and how clearly *drug* Broz saw our peasants' revolutionary potential is hard to say. But I guess he saw it as early as 1926. He was a peasant, you know; or a former peasant— almost all of us workers were peasant boys who had gone to the city to learn a trade."

Resinic: "I was with him a lot in '28. He was in a sweat over the peasant and nationality questions. *Djavo,* why didn't we tackle them? Why did we leave it all to Radic and the Croatian Peasant Party? Not that Broz wasted any time on being anti-Radic. Radic had been to Russia, had met Lenin; but he was not a Marxist. He was playing by ear; he didn't know the revolutionary music required in the twentieth century. We *did* know, said Broz; so why didn't we and Radic get together? Or why didn't we move in on the peasant movement he was running in all directions? . . . But in the early '20's our Party leadership had been against Radic; now Radic was sore at us, at Communists generally; and in '28 *drug* Broz and the rest of us didn't know how to correct the CPY's early mistakes. Or whether we had the right to. We weren't top CP leaders—just sergeants and corporals fighting a succession of skirmishes in the class conflict. As I say, we didn't even know if we had a leadership, not to mention if we had a party; and if we had one, what it thought about the hullabaloo Stjepan Radic was raising. Sometimes, when this subject came up, *drug* Broz' face would tighten and he'd shut up and brood for hours, even for days, without speaking a word."

On June 20, 1928, one of King Alexander's trigger-men in Parliament, a *mangup* (pervert, scoundrel) named Punisa Racic, who "represented" a district on the Albanian border, emptied his gun at the opposition benches. He killed or mortally wounded four Croatian deputies, among them Stjepan Radic.

"In God's name," cried Deputy Sava Kosanovic, a progressive-minded Serbian Independent Democrat, "what are you doing to the State!"

Answered Vojvoda Lune, a notorious Cetnik and pan-Serbian extremist: "This is how we cleanse our honor! In blood!"

The assassin walked out of the Parliament Building unmolested. He reported to the Reverend Anton Korosec, the same Slovenian Catholic priest at whose order scores of railroad strikers were killed in 1920, but who now was Minister of the Interior and who doubtless knew that the royal clique, if not the king personally, had instructed Punisa Racic to shoot Stjepan Radic. The killer was not arrested until several hours later.

Stimulated by the "Balkan experts," the civilized world's reaction to the news from Belgrade was "Those Balkanites! What do you expect!"—while the Yugoslav people were outraged or stunned. Stjepan Radic lay dying in a Belgrade hospital. The streets of Zagreb filled with townspeople and peasants from near-by villages. Even before the city CP organization accepted Josip Broz' proposal to call the workers off their jobs, mechanics and barbers, tailors and coffee-house waiters, carpenters and hotel porters quit—spontaneously—many of them the moment they heard the news.

Broz saw an opportunity for a revolutionary uprising against Belgrade. He scattered a leaflet addressed "To the Workers and Peasants" and ordered the *aktivisti* to distribute the few guns and grenades they had managed to collect. But, as Tito later admitted, his estimate of the situation was "erroneous . . . naïve." Broz may have been led into error by his overeagerness to bring the working class and the peasant movements together in a common action, though in back of his mind he knew it was doomed to fail. Others thought of action too, but only he acted. Coming on top of years of confusion, however, the incident revealed that there weren't enough un-stunned individuals to de-stun quickly a substantial number of others, whereas King Alexander's vast police apparatus had been alerted in advance.

Informers ("fractionalists" who were really diverse blackguards) aided secret agents and uniformed gendarmes the country over, but especially in Zagreb, to pack the jails with Leftists, Peasant Party leaders, and ultra-nationalists opposed to the regime. Simultaneously, King Alexander deepened the popular confusion by calling on the mortally wounded Stjepan Radic at the hospital, expressing his royal sympathy and his royal outrage over the shooting, and then starting the rumor that Radic had asked him to declare a dictatorship in order to save the country. At the same time, the entire regime-controlled press ran "Shame! Shame!" editorials, appealing to the people of Yugoslavia, who were calm, to becalm themselves, lest the world think even less of them than it already did.

Broz' information was that Radic couldn't survive the wound; and he thought his death might set off demonstrations, which the CP organization could point up. But Radic lived for nearly seven weeks after the shooting, until August 8, 1928; and when he finally died, a great sob went up in the villages . . . and that was all. The people were leaderless.

A week before, the political-police inspectors in Zagreb and other Croatian cities were informed that Radic couldn't live much longer and that, to be on the safe side, they had better pick up any dangerous agitators their dragnets had missed in June and July. In Zagreb, Josip Broz' name headed the "dangerous" list. As secretary of the city CP organization he was responsible for the distribution of the leaflet in July calling for a popular uprising. He had evaded arrest by frequently changing his looks, posture, and gait. Now, from about August first on, half the Zagreb political-police force was assigned to get him and enough evidence to send him to prison for at least a two-year stretch. They were not to kill him unless they had to in self-defense: he was popular with labor, and killing him at this juncture might, just might, spur the workers to a general strike.

This time the agents succeeded in buying a low-life character who hung out on the fringes of Broz' inner circle and knew his guise that week. On August third (five days before Radic's death) the informer bellied up to Broz in the street and whispered that some *drugovi* at 50 Vinogradska Street were in a jam and desperate to see him.

Broz had a temporary headquarters and hideout at that address. The *aktivisti* on his staff were all dependable, as were the middle-aged couple occupying the rest of the flat. He had been up all night; so, too tired to heed his suspicion of this fellow, he hurried to 50 Vinogradska —and straight into a police trap. Five agents pounced on him, put him in irons, and drove him to the *Glavnjaca,* the royal political-police headquarters—there was one in each large city in Yugoslavia.

An examiner eyed Broz and told him to take that look off his face. Broz failed to comply and the examiner struck him in the face.

"I suppose you think you're quite a fellow," Broz said, contemptuously. "Hitting a man in irons and held by two gendarmes."

He refused to sign a paper which he wasn't permitted to read, and the examiner grabbed a stool and swung it at his head. Broz ducked and the stool crashed on his chest. He spat blood for three weeks. It availed him nothing to demand a doctor. For two months he was in an *iztraga* (investigation) cell of the political-police headquarters.

In other cells up and down the corridor, prisoners—regaining consciousness after they were brought from the torture chambers— groaned day and night. Broz knew some of them. He himself was not beaten again, possibly because his fearlessness inhibited the examiners, or perhaps because he admitted that, yes, he *was* Josip Broz; and, yes, he *was* secretary of the CP organization and the Metal Trades Union Council in Zagreb: and they could make the most of it. Yes, he *was* responsible for the distribution of the "uprising" leaflet. Yes, he *had been* carrying a revolver when he walked into the police trap. Yes, he *had* rented the room at 50 Vinogradska. But trying to protect the couple who had rented it to him and the *drugovi* who were sleeping there when it was raided and others who were arrested subsequently and connected with his case, he accused the police of planting the bombs, revolvers, and ammunition they found in a wicker-basket under the bed.

Two Zagreb newspapers gave the "bomb case" a great deal of space before and during the trial. It involved sixteen persons who had been caught in the police net during the raid on 50 Vinogradska. Most of them pleaded not guilty.

Broz was the center of the case. He was one of the first Yugoslavs who had the effrontery—in the eyes of the police, the press, the Church, and some of the public—to boast of being a Communist.

On August 15, 1928, the *Novosti* (News) published a biographical sketch of Broz, giving 1892 as his birthdate and Kumrovec as his birthplace. It mentioned that Pelagia Broz, *née* Belousek, whom "he claims to have married in Russia," was also arrested. Later his wife, who took care of their son Zarko and who had not participated in his activities, was freed.

The trial opened on November 7, 1928; it lasted three days. Most of the first day was occupied with the hearings of the other prisoners, who were either released or sent up for short terms.

The moment the gendarmes installed Josip Broz in the dock, his personality stood out in the packed courtroom. The editor of the *Novosti* rushed an artist to make a drawing of him, and on November 8 the paper reported that "Broz is unquestionably the most interesting figure in the case. His face has something of those visages that suggest steel. His eyes have a cool, energetic, calm look. When a question is addressed to him, the spectators turn very still to hear his answer." The spectators were mostly university students.

An altercation developed between the presiding judge—named Bacic, who occasionally handled "subversive" cases—and Broz:

The Judge: Guilty?

Broz: Of course I'm "guilty"—according to the interpretation of my thinking and behavior as they are presented in the indictment. In truth, however, I am *not* guilty.

The Judge (wearily amused): Tell us, then; in what respects, precisely, do you consider yourself guilty?

Broz (scorning the word "guilty"): I admit that I'm a member of the Communist Party of Yugoslavia, which the regime has declared illegal. And I admit I've urged the proletariat to resist injustice and to study the scientific theses of Karl Marx which we Communists maintain spell out a better future for all mankind. I do *not,* however, recognize this court. I am responsible only to the Communist Party of Yugoslavia.

The Judge: You are familiar with the Law for the Protection of the State?

Broz: I've already indicated that I've heard of it. I've never read it. It's a transient business; it doesn't interest me.

The Judge: That law forbids Communistic propaganda—you know that, don't you?

Broz: Yes; but I repeat, it's a transient law.

The Judge: It's the law in force now. It was initiated by the people to protect them against you Communists, who they believe threaten their way of life. Anyone who is caught breaking that law goes to Lepoglava [prison]. The people are protecting themselves against your destructive actions.

Broz: The so-called law is in force now, yes. However, it wasn't the people who initiated it. I'm not afraid of it. It will be an evil day when the Communist Party permits a "law" like this to frighten it.

The Judge: Obstinate fellows like you are only throwing your lives away to no good purpose.

Broz: That's how you see it. It's my life, and I'm ready to "throw it away."[1]

Followed a long delving by the prosecution into the evidence to determine the other prisoners' connections with the room in which the agents found the basketful of bombs, revolvers, and cartridges.

Broz: I'm not concerned about the length of the prison term ahead of me. If I'd had anything to do with those bombs, I'd readily admit it.

The Judge: Now, about this leaflet calling for an uprising of peasants and workers—you wrote it yourself?

Broz: I won't say who wrote it.

The Judge: During the pre-trial examination you confessed you were ready to shoot all and sundry if you got the chance.

Broz: I confessed nothing of the sort. I said I carried a revolver in self-defense.

The Prosecutor: Against whom?

Broz: I go about a great deal, and experience has given me hints that my life is in danger.

The Prosecutor: And you would fire?

Broz: Of course—if necessary to protect myself.

The Judge: Tell us something about your life.

Broz: Gladly. . . .

The accused told of his career as a metal worker in half a dozen

---

[1] This and the ensuing exchanges between the judge and the accused are not literal translations. The subjective qualities of the Serbo-Croatian language are so different from those of the English language that a literal translation of words spoken in a tense moment like this would be false. Taking the liberties of a novelist, almost (believing that novelists often approach truth more closely than most historians), I try to give the altercation in self-interpretative equivalents.

countries before the war. He mentioned that in 1914 he found himself driven by the rivalry between capitalistic forces into the "slaughter-house" on the Eastern Front, where fortunately he was captured by the Russians. Then he decided to re-tell his story, beginning with his parents, his childhood and boyhood, the poverty in Kumrovec.

The prosecutor and the judge perceived that the latter's expression of interest in the accused's life had been a mistake. Broz' narrative evidently was leading to an explanation of why he was a Communist: which was not legitimate defense—it was Communist propaganda prohibited by law. If they permitted him to go on, they themselves might be guilty of an infraction of the statute to protect the state. So the judge stopped him.

Broz reminded the judge he had asked the question, hadn't he? Well, he, the accused, was answering it. He insisted that he be allowed to continue. The judge said his court was not a platform from which Communists could spout propaganda for their party, and he told Broz to sit down.

Broz remained on his feet. "When you asked me to tell about my life," he said after a moment, "what did you expect me to do—'spout propaganda' for your Radical Party?" (Like the Radical Party of France, the Serbian Radical Party in Old Yugoslavia was ultra-conservative, a political arm of the Pan-Serbian cause.)

It was a tense moment. The spectators wriggled in the squeaky seats. Some put their heads together and whispered.

In response to a gesture from the judge, a courtroom guard told Broz to obey His Honor and sit down. Broz ignored the guard. Addressing himself to the spectators, he began to declaim on "bourgeois justice," when the gendarmes seized him. Before they removed him from the court he cried out: "Long live the Communist Party of Yugoslavia! Long live the Third International!"

Most of this was reported in considerable detail in the *Novosti* and less thoroughly in another Zagreb daily, and in the ensuing week the Leftist-student and working-class groups buzzed with excitement about Broz. The "bomb case" became the Broz trial.

Some non-Leftists wondered why the man had so proudly affirmed he was a Communist. Had he denied he was a practicing Red, he would have received two years at the most; now the judge could not avoid giving him a stiffer sentence. Was Broz crazy? Were all Communists more or less crazy? . . .

In Broz' own opinion then and later, he behaved in court as an agitator should behave. He exploited the opportunity to advance his cause. As for admitting, or not denying, "guilt" to all the charges except the responsibility for the bombs (for which, in a way, he was also responsible), what else could he have done? And if he was going to plead "guilty," why not plead "guilty" with pride? The trial might then stir a handful of spectators who would tell others. In that way his having walked into that damned police trap could turn into an asset to the Party, which was at an all-time low in membership, morale, and influence—even labor unions were drifting away from it.

Broz had long been critical of those who broke under torture when they were taken to the *Glavnjaca,* and betrayed other members or Party secrets. A Communist must be strong enough inside to withstand anything the sadists could inflict on him. He also had expressed himself about Party members who tried to crawl out of imprisonment by denying that they were Communists, or by bribing the examiners, or by permitting their attorneys to pull strings in bourgeois circles to sway the prosecutors and judges. So now he acted as he had preached.

On November 14, 1928, Broz was brought back to court. The judge sentenced him to five years. He again demanded the right to resume telling the story he had been invited to tell, and was again denied. As they hustled him out, he cried once more to the spectators: "Long live the Communist Party of Yugoslavia! Long live the Third International!"

This scene, too, was reported in the *Novosti.*

The Belgrade newspapers didn't print a word about the case, but the *Novosti* was read in Belgrade; and it is estimated that several thousand Leftist students and workers there were impressed by Josip Broz, of whom they had never heard before. To a lesser extent, this was true in Ljubljana, Sarajevo, Split, Kragujevac, perhaps even in Skoplje, and in the small towns and villages. The news of Joza Broz' encounter with the law didn't penetrate to Kumrovec and Podsreda, slightly over fifty kilometers from Zagreb, until almost the end of 1928.

Broz' courtroom manner impressed a number of student spectators at the trial, so much so that they never forgot him. Some of them were not Leftists; they were only seeking answers, or had come to court out of curiosity. One young man (who died a Partisan in a battle in Bosnia in 1942, perhaps without knowing that Tito was Josip Broz) sent his brother in Belgrade clippings from the *Novosti* in November 1928, and wrote on the margin of one of them: "The first free man I've ever seen."

Few workers had attended the trial, but the newspaper writeups sparked thousands of them in Zagreb. They told one another to save the papers. They penciled lines under Broz' answers to the judge. The Metal Trades Union Council elected a secretary *pro tem,* retaining Broz as the official secretary.

Before Broz' arrest, there were still at large in Zagreb a few hundred members of the all-but-nonexistent CPY—mostly metal workers, men like Branislav Resinic and the others whom I quoted—who felt that the worst was yet to come. It came on January 6, 1929. King Alexander proclaimed a dictatorship and made General Pero Zivkovic, Commander of the Royal Guards, his Premier and assistant dictator in direct charge of the drive to extirpate Communism. Immediately the "White Terror" cut loose. But before this happened some of the Communists realized that if the Party was to survive it would have to rid itself of "fractionalism" and reorganize into a closely knit do-or-die conspiracy which, as a first step, would bring into full view the festering revolutionary situation as a precondition to revolution and socialism in Yugoslavia.

These men called themselves "anti-fractionalists" and Leninists. Most of them were not deeply familiar either with old Marxian literature or with more recent Russian writings. Like Broz, they didn't know that toward the end of his life Lenin had publicly expressed his doubts about the Bolshevik leadership of the World Revolution. Lenin was a magic name. They had read leaflets containing excerpts from his works. They heeded his insistence that revolution was no picnic, that it must not be undertaken lightly, never without regard for the broad masses of people who must be readied for it.[2] . . . These men

[2] Two paragraphs from Lenin's work *The Infant Disease of "Leftism" in Communism:*
"One must ask not only if the vanguard of the revolutionary class has been convinced, but if the historically active forces of *all* classes, absolutely all classes of the given society without exception, are so apportioned that the decisive battle is altogether ripe—1) so that all enemy class forces have entangled themselves sufficiently, have quarreled enough among themselves, have weakened themselves sufficiently with a struggle to which their forces were not equal; 2) so that all irresolute, uncertain, unsteady middle elements—that is, the petty bourgeoisie—have been sufficiently exposed to the people, have been shamed to a satisfactory degree as regards its bankruptcy in deed; 3) so that mass disposition for support of the most determined and boundlessly

dominated the Zagreb CP organization of which Broz was the secretary. Similar but much smaller "anti-fractionalist" or "Leninist" groups existed within the CPY in Belgrade, in Slovenia, and elsewhere. But the Zagreb leaders had no liaison with them, and did not presume to take the national leadership. When Broz was arrested, the "anti-fractionalist" idea floundered.

The arrest hit the Zagreb group between the eyes. In fact, while Broz was hermetically sealed in the *Glavnjaca* for two months, the city CP organization almost caved in. The *Novosti* story of his conduct in court, however, revived the Leninist element.

Resinic told me: "I remember hearing two or three *drugovi* remark, 'That's the way to act!' or similar words. Broz had set us an example. Without even meeting to discuss the matter, we decided that the Party must rid itself of all fear of the White Terror."

At the secret Fourth Congress of the CPY in 1929, the "anti-fractionalists" failed to sweep the Party clean of the "fractionalists"—neurotics, agents, adventurers—but they succeeded in electing Djura Djakovic, one of their group, the organizational secretary within the Central Committee. A few months later, however, the political-police agents of King Alexander's dictatorship, just then hitting its stride, captured and killed him in so barbarous a fashion that it is beyond recording.

It may be that Djakovic was captured with the aid of informers who were members of the Central Committee. The "fractionalists" certainly gained full control of the national CP organization immediately after his death. They claimed to be in the good graces of the Comin-

---

courageous revolutionary actions against the bourgeoisie has begun to awaken and grow strongly in the proletariat. It is then that the revolution has ripened, it is then that victory is ours—if we have accurately estimated all the above-mentioned and outlined conditions and if we have accurately chosen the right moment, our victory is certain.

"The ideological conquest of the vanguard of the proletariat has already taken place. That is the main thing. Without that not even the first step toward victory can be taken. But from that point it is still rather far to victory. Victory cannot be won with the vanguard alone. Throwing the vanguard alone into a decisive struggle, while the whole class, while the wide masses have not yet taken a stand either of direct support of the vanguard or, in an extreme case, of well-disposed neutrality toward it and utter incapability of helping its opponent—would be not only foolish, it would be a crime. And propaganda alone, agitation alone, is not enough to get the whole class, the wide masses of toilers and those exploited by the capitalists to take such a stand. For this, the masses must have their own political experience. That is the basic law of all big revolutions."

tern. At the same time, some of them unquestionably were cooperating with the Alexander-Zivkovic White Terror and were also in touch with French and British Intelligence agents in Yugoslavia, as well as with the Jesuit organization in Central Europe. During 1929–31 about ten thousand Leftists and other oppositionists passed through the various *glavnjace.* Over one hundred of the most dedicated and aggressive members of the CPY were tortured to death in the Belgrade *Glavnjaca* alone, while the Lepoglava, Mitrovica, Maribor, Zenica, Nis, Pozarevac and Skoplje penitentiaries were filled with approximately twelve hundred "politicals," nearly one thousand of whom were Communists sentenced to from one to fifteen years.

By 1931 the CPY was almost completely ineffectual—"almost" because the CP in Zagreb *did* hold together by the skin of its teeth. Broz, remaining its secretary, ran it from Lepoglava, where the warden was his wartime buddy Bohacek, who didn't understand him now any more than he had in 1916–18 but, somehow, had an even higher regard for him.

Warden Bohacek put Political Prisoner Broz in charge of the prison power plant and made him a trustee. This enabled Broz to meet with his Zagreb CP lieutenants in the town of Lepoglava . . . and helped to make G. B. Shaw's maxim "The most anxious man in prison is the warden" fit Bohacek like a glove.

In Nathaniel Hawthorne's *The Scarlet Letter,* a prison is "a black flower of civilized society." Whether the society in which the Lepoglava Penitentiary flourished was civilized is another question. The prison, however, wasn't the worst in the Balkans and Central Europe; and twisting the Hawthorne characterization a bit further, one can say that in a half-dozen prisons in Old Yugoslavia red flowers came to bud.

The Communist prisoners converted the several bastilles into "Universities of the Revolution" and their sentences into graduate and postgraduate courses in socialist, anti-imperialist thinking and underground techniques. Except for that, Josip Broz might never have crystallized into Tito and there might not have been a Yugoslav revolution capable of the audacity of standing on its own feet. Indeed, had he not been forcibly enrolled in Lepoglava, Broz' chances of survival might have been very slim; and in view of Djura Djakovic's fate, it may be said that he was enrolled in the nick of time.

By the end of 1929—the first year of the undisguised Belgrade *dik-tatura*—several hundred Communists were in state prisons serving sentences of varying lengths. Of these, as it turned out, the most note-worthy was Mosa Pijade.

Mosa Pijade was born in 1889 in Belgrade, Serbia. His father—a de-scendant of Sephardic Jews who fled to the Balkans from the Spanish Inquisition—was for a time a mildly successful merchant. Mosa, who grew five feet tall and then stopped growing, received the best formal schooling available in Serbia. After graduating from the *gymnasium* he went through the Belgrade Academy of Arts, then studied painting in Munich.

"Mosa" is the Serbian form of "Moses"; how "Pijade" was spelled in Spain, Mosa never heard. His father wasn't specially conscious of being a Jew (there was almost no anti-Semitism in Serbia) and Mosa grew up a Serbian. Being a Serbian, however, was never the central theme of his life. For a time he considered himself an artist and an aesthete.

In his early twenties, Mosa was influenced by socialist thought, which was "Marxism, but"—— The *but* covered various Balkan nuances and emphases, or the lack of them. Socialism had a long tradition in Ser-bia. Now—between 1908 and '14, the half-dozen years before World War I—a strong Social Democratic movement was gathering ad-herents under the leadership of Dimitrije Tucovic, who was well known in European Socialist circles.

At a Second International Congress in Copenhagen in 1910, Tuco-vic described the Serbian Social Democratic Party's anti-war efforts in Serbia: how his co-leaders and he were fighting Czarist Russia's in-fluence in Belgrade: and how the comrades in Austria-Hungary, con-demning the old Balkanite "war-swindlers," "dynastic intrigues," and "corruption," were aiding them in this fight. "Although they might well have left it to us to square accounts with our potentates," he de-clared, "we are grateful for their help! In the future, however, we would appreciate another kind of assistance from our comrades in Austria-Hungary even more—*energetic opposition*," he stressed, *"to the colonial policy of enslavement pursued by the rulers of Austria-Hungary."* He pointed out that the Socialist parties in Central Europe weren't doing a thing to thwart the Berlin-Vienna-Budapest imperial-ist designs on the Balkans. The Serbian people were letting their rulers get away with murder because they were afraid of the Germanic *Drang nach Osten.* He called on the Socialist parties in the big countries to engage in a "principled and energetic struggle [against] the policy of conquest pursued by powers" whose intrigues were turning the Balkans into a witches' brew; and "to establish contact with the parties of the small, oppressed peoples . . . to facilitate their fight against chauvinism and militarism." Tucovic's speech got a big hand —and that was all. The parties in Germany and Austria-Hungary made no honest effort in their own lands to stop the trends toward war. In 1914, when Austria invaded Serbia (following the Sarajevo assassination in which official Vienna was almost as deeply involved as Serbian nationalist fanatics), the Tucovic ideals of international cooperation among Socialists were drowned in blood. He was himself— early in the First World War an Austrian bullet pierced his Serbian officer's tunic and his heart.

The Socialist tradition in Serbia goes back to the early 1870's—to Svetozar Markovic, a neophyte with a mind of his own. He was the first Serbian to analyze his country's social-economic predicament in the light shed by Marx and Engels. He was educated in Belgrade, St. Petersburg, and Switzerland; he died at twenty-nine in 1875—a Marxian when Marxism was still in flux and creative social thinkers added to it and utilized it in developing their own schemes for their countries. It was just about the time that Marx said cantankerously, "If those people," referring to some self-styled revolutionaries, "are Marxists, *I* am no Marxist."

A Serbian who knew Serbia, Markovic didn't blame Serbian capitalism for the peasants' shocking poverty—there was no Serbian capitalism to speak of. He blamed it on the feudal-minded officialdom installed in the rural sections by the Belgrade regime to misgovern them. This corrupt bureaucracy, Markovic wrote, must be replaced by *narodni odbori,* people's committees, which would become the pulsebeat of self-government, the instrument for economic and cultural progress, a source of liberty.

The *odbori* were not Markovic's original idea. Centuries before, under Turkish rule, Serbians had had local undercover committees to uphold their national-religious identity and to assist individuals and communities economically. Markovic theorized that a primitive society could skip over the capitalist phase into a cooperative order by adapting the traditional economic, social, and cultural forms. He envisioned the state becoming a vast *zadruga,* a cooperative of cooperatives.

Markovic may have been influenced by the works of Alexander Herzen which were published in exile in Western Europe during the middle third of the nineteenth century. An honest man with a core of his own who often suspected that revolutionaries were "not the doctors of humanity but part of the disease," Herzen believed that Russia could hurdle the capitalism which had corrupted the "West." He averred that the Russian peasant was a potential revolutionary and socialist, capable of expanding the old-time democratic functions of his institution, the *mir,* or commune, until it operated on a state-wide basis.

Thirty years later, however, when Svetozar Markovic's successor, Dimitrije Tucovic, came to the fore, Serbia had the beginnings of capitalism and a working class; so, within the frame of the Second International, socialist agitation used the more or less orthodox Marxist technique, playing up the proletariat, trade unions, and the class struggle. Socialism made sense to any number of people in Belgrade and other large towns. The agitators scarcely addressed themselves to the peasants. Yet in 1912 some twenty thousand peasants voted for the Social Democratic candidates. One reason for this was that the long memories of the people in the primitive villages began to link the socialist theories of 1910 and thereabouts with Markovic's ideas of 1869–75, which had reached them through two of his energetic disciples, Mita Cenic and Vaso Pelagic.

With all this unexpected support, the Social Democratic leaders and agitators in Belgrade might then have veered peasantward; but immediately after the 1912 election the Balkan Wars came, followed by Sarajevo, followed by the First World War. Like Tucovic, many other Socialist leaders fell in battle as national patriots and anti-imperialists. Threads of the Serbian socialist tradition, however, from Svetozar Markovic on, were invested in the intellectual makeup of a few young men who survived the ravages of all three wars.

Mosa Pijade was one of these. He read everything by Svetozar Markovic. He discovered Alexander Herzen.

About this time, his father's business failure, from which he never recovered, compelled Mosa to resort to writing for a living. His vivid newspaper pieces, which had a socialist, radical, libertarian tone, made a hit; and soon he was better known as a writer than an artist. During 1911–13 he was secretary of a journalists' association.

In 1919, after the creation of Yugoslavia, Pijade and the pseudo-liberal owners of the paper which employed him were at loggerheads; and with a small group of young journalists he started a weekly called *Slobodna Rec* [Free Expression]. The name described it. The paper offered itself as a compass to a bewildered new country in a world in upheaval. Way over to the Left, it met all issues head-on. It stressed that liberty was "an absolute public good . . . the property of all mankind."

Pijade joined the CPY in January 1920 and, as Yugoslavia went from bad to worse, the content of his writing deepened. He argued less and became more analytical in terms of class forces. He defended the Russian Revolution, the Soviet Union. He exposed the corruption of the Belgrade press. He was a partisan of the homeless, of war invalids in need of hospitalization, of artists without studios, of authors whose books were not published because their ideas clashed with the publishers' interests and obsolete ideas. At first he assailed the Law for the Protection of the State. Then he decided: "I can't be sentimental about terror. It's not my purpose to rail against it. That might be proper for believers in bourgeois 'democracy.' Well, I don't believe in bourgeois 'democracy.'" He announced he had joined the ranks of those Europeans who "are making history" by following "the line of pride and heroism"—a typically Serbian phrase. He iterated the remark a Serbian people's leader had made two decades earlier to a group of peasants, "You have no history, your history is yet to begin."

In 1925 Pijade was arrested as a menace to the state, given a twenty-year sentence, and lodged in the Mitrovica Penitentiary, near Belgrade. The stiff sentence was meant more to warn Stjepan Radic—who, with his growing popularity in Serbia and elsewhere, was publishing vitriolic editorials against the Belgrade hegemony and in favor of a republic—to watch his step than to punish Mosa Pijade.

Pijade appealed his case and his sentence was reduced to twelve years. But later it was upped to fourteen because one day, in the course of a demonstration by Communist prisoners for better conditions, he joined in the singing of "The Internationale"; and he did not get out until 1939, shortly before the outbreak of World War II.

Prior to Pijade's incarceration, Communist prisoners had no organized life. They were ensnarled in "fractionalism," which led nowhere except to personal disintegration. Pijade and a few others started reading and discussion groups. In 1927, through collective demands which were dramatized periodically by hunger strikes, and with the aid of such friendly liberal deputies in parliament as Sava Kosanovic, the Communist prisoners succeeded in being put together in a block of cells. They also won the privilege of meeting in a large room for an hour or two daily. Sympathetic guards slipped out their requests for printed matter and smuggled in whatever literature their relatives and friends procured for them. They had no systematic contact with the declining CPY underground organization outside of prison. The Party "leadership," living abroad and engaging in fractional disputes, had no interest in them—except, in many instances, to keep them in jail.

By 1926 the Pijade study group in Mitrovica had done so well that reports of it, smuggled into other prisons, brought about demands for the same conditions elsewhere; and when Josip Broz reached Lepoglava, he found a Marxian study group there.

Broz had known of Pijade since 1921. Pijade first learned of Broz late in '28 through the *Novosti* clippings describing his trial, smuggled in to him. He showed the articles to the other Communist prisoners. One of them said, *"Hvala bogu*—thank God, here at last is a man who acts like a man."

In the spring of 1929 Mosa Pijade completed on contraband paper the first draft of the first translation into Serbian—or any Balkan language—of Karl Marx' *Das Kapital*. He made the translation from a paper-bound three-volume German edition, also smuggled in. The long job of translating sustained his mind. In addition, he painted portraits of his fellow-prisoners. But at forty he still had a full decade to serve out his sentence, with no chance of a commutation. So, having long been interested in China, he decided to study Chinese and his friends outside procured the books he needed. In 1929, however, he didn't get very far with his Chinese studies.

The White Terror—intensified by order of the King-Dictator, supervised by Premier Zivkovic, executed by Minister of the Interior Korosec, approved by the French and British Legations (through their agents), at least tolerated by the American minister, and ignored by all the correspondents of the "free press" in the "West"—filled the state prisons with "politicals."

The prisoners were herded into Mitrovica by Belgrade gendarmes or political-police agents. Some of these agents were former Czarist or White Guard officers who had fled to Yugoslavia from the Bolshevik

Revolution.[3] To show their disdain for the prison guards who "pampered the politicals," the gendarmes and agents slapped, kicked, and pushed the inmates around every time they brought in a new batch. Mosa Pijade had his hands full inducting the newcomers into the Communist organization in the prison, keeping out "fractionalists," re-forming study groups, and starching the men's morale for a new hunger strike he had in mind. It was to be of such dimension and duration that it would communicate itself outside the prison and, he hoped, end the brutality in Mitrovica, register a protest against the entire terror program, and build character in the Communist prisoners.

Reports of the strike, which friendly guards smuggled out, had repercussions in several parts of Yugoslavia. Some of the newly enlarged "politicals'" study groups in other "colleges" struck too. The cumulative effect, although the general press printed not a word about the hunger strikes, added to the restlessness within the trade unions and among the intelligentsia. Hundreds of thousands of non-Communists openly expressed interest in the "politicals" or even sympathized with them. And extreme brutality in state prisons ceased—though it continued in the *glavnjace*.

In the ensuing decade, some of the "politicals" serving long terms, particularly the obvious or suspected leaders, were transferred every so often from one penitentiary to another. Thus, early in 1930 Mosa Pijade and several other Mitrovica "politicals" were sent to Lepoglava.

By then the pattern of the Mitrovica study groups was established in Lepoglava. The emphases were on Marxist theory and on drawing deductions from the men's class-war experiences and observations so far. Pijade knew many of the prisoners. Most of them were very young.

When thirty-eight-year-old Josip Broz and forty-one-year-old Mosa Pijade met, the metal worker was more impressed by the intellectual than the other way about. Eager for contact with a man whom he judged to be a learned revolutionary, Broz induced his friend, Warden Bohacek, to make Pijade his assistant in the power plant. Pijade had even less understanding of machinery than Broz had of Chinese,

[3] In the 1920's King Alexander admitted about 20,000 "White" Russian refugees. He put thousands of them on the payroll of the Belgrade government.

In 1946–49 scores of these refugees from the Bolshevik Revolution found their way into the espionage service of the Soviet Embassy in Belgrade. When the Tito regime arrested them in '49, Moscow sent threatening notes to Belgrade, demanding the release of these "Soviet citizens." The Yugoslav foreign office then asked the Soviet government to permit them to return to the bosom of their motherland. But Moscow did not bite.

which Pijade now resumed studying in the comparative quiet of Lepoglava. By-and-by, Broz inducted him into the mysteries and arts of oiling, greasing, and wiping the dynamo. The chief mechanic and his assistant had a good deal of time to talk and become friends. Pijade painted Broz' portrait, which was lost in the course of the artist-prisoner's subsequent peregrinations in the prison circuit.

In May–June 1949 I saw a lot of Mosa Pijade—at Tito's; in his office in the Praesidium of the Federal People's Republic of Yugoslavia, of which he was the first vice-president; and while traveling with him and Edvard Kardelj and Ales Bebler through Serbia, Montenegro, Dalmatia, and Bosnia-Herzegovina. Looking back across two decades, Pijade recalled that during their first year together Broz impressed him mainly as the man who in 1928 had conducted himself so valiantly in the Zagreb courtroom, and as a good mechanic with an uncanny instinct for machinery. A slight change in the hum of the dynamo which Pijade's ears never detected made Broz jump up to attend to it. He was no great conversationalist. Oh, his questions and his responses to what Pijade said—about Svetozar Markovic, for instance, and his *narodni odbori* and *zadruge* ideas and about Dimitrije Tucovic—were intelligent enough, even acute; but Pijade had known dozens of such worker Communists in Mitrovica.

In their second year together, the highly intellectual, witty Pijade tumbled to the realization that his boss-mechanic had a very good head. His theoretical knowledge wasn't wide and deep, but it widened and deepened steadily with voluminous reading. The Lepoglava study group received numerous books and journals, most of them in German and Serbo-Croatian; Broz read them all. His remarks at the bull sessions were to the point and simply stated. Unlike many other inmates, he never slumped into behaving like a prisoner for even a moment. He was thin and pale, quick and alert, with a bright, straightforward look.

Broz hated prison life; and being a trustee free to go to town, he could have escaped. He didn't, partly because he was a disciplined member of the CP group in the prison which disapproved of "breaks." Then, too, according to various estimates, the Belgrade *diktatura* employed between thirty and fifty thousand plainclothesmen and gendarmes to concern themselves solely or mainly with the "disloyal opposition"; and an escapee would have had no chance to evade them and flee the country. It was wiser to stay in jail and study.

Broz' other consideration was the warden. Although he didn't respect Bohacek, he didn't want to get him in trouble or to destroy his decent qualities. He induced Bohacek to make life more tolerable for all the prisoners in Lepoglava.

Broz' natural interest in people drew him to thieves, murderers, and other criminals in the prison. Most of them, he believed, were products or victims of social conditions. Among these convicts was a lifer who escaped late in 1930. Captured the next year, he mentioned he had discussed his plans for the "break" with Broz. Actually, he had invited Broz to join him. Broz had refused, but it had not occurred to him to inform on the man.

Thus Broz lost Bohacek's goodwill anyhow, and he was transferred to the penitentiary in Maribor, Slovenia . . . Pijade lost track of him for the next eight years, until he (Pijade) served out his term in the spring of 1939.

The Maribor prison was known as "Alexander's toughest pen." There was no brutality but everything was so rigidly managed that if only half-alive a prisoner felt hemmed in on all sides. This rigidity was a reflection of the character of the warden, a morose old bureaucrat, a carry-over from Austria, to whom a prison was a prison, and that was that. (One day in mid-May 1949, when I was in Tito's office, he told me about the letter he had recently received from the son of the old man who was the warden in Maribor for thirty-five years: under Austria, in Old Yugoslavia, and finally under the Nazis. "When our forces took Maribor in '45," Tito said, "he was unceremoniously kicked out. . . . Now, years later, his son writes me that his father is past seventy and a burden to him, and won't I please intercede so that he will receive the pension which he believes is due him. They realize, both the father and the son, that I was a prisoner in Maribor for three and a half years, but I shouldn't hold that against the old man. It was not his fault that I was sentenced. He had only been the warden, a loyal official carrying out his duties under whatever government was in power. Perhaps I recalled—I'm paraphrasing the letter—that the prison had been well administered. . . . I turned this over in my mind and saw that the old man and his son had a point. I sent the letter to the Ministry of the Interior, with the notation that I personally had no objection to the warden being put on the pension list.")

In Maribor, the CP "politicals" lived in a hall which doubled for a work-room, where they were required to sew so many flour bags daily. Broz, who had been elected program secretary soon after he arrived, organized the work so that it took only two or three hours, instead of the seven to ten it had consumed before. The rest of the time was spent in reading, study, discussion. If a "political" showed signs of depression, Broz peppered him with arguments that he must study and prepare to become an *aktivist:* that, in the first place, studying and thinking of the future were the only ways to save his sanity and fortify his spirit. In this preaching he was aided by Rodoljub Colakovic, another protegé of Pijade from Mitrovica. (Colakovic is now Minister of Culture in the federal government.)

"Broz *did* want respect," Colakovic said (in 1949, when we met), confirming the information Pijade gave me. "But he also felt a great need to respect those around him. If he had to associate with somebody who was mentally or physically shabby, he tried in some way to bolster and spruce him up.

"We received quantities of printed matter, almost anything we wanted, through the good offices of the man in charge of the prison supply-room who was a criminal of some kind but who sympathized with us and had contact with all manner of people outside. He was never caught helping us, nor was our Marxist literature discovered. *Das Kapital* came to us bound in the covers of *The Arabian Nights.*" . . . (In the one prison in New Yugoslavia which I visited, I found a sizeable library of Marxist-Leninist books which a good many of the prisoners read avidly, I was told. Some of them became Communists. Those who were hungry for anti-Red literature had to have it smuggled in—Winston Churchill's memoirs bound as *Das Kapital,* for instance.)

"Marx and Engels headed the reading list," Colakovic said. "We didn't receive any current Soviet literature because scarcely any came into the country through underground channels. Years later we discovered why. Most of the CPY 'leaders' living in Vienna were agents of the Belgrade regime, yoked to agents of foreign-capital interests in the Balkans, at the same time that they were in the Comintern apparatus: for the whole Central Committee was appointed by the Comintern. . . .

"In '32 we began to receive the London *Economist,* which Broz and I found worthwhile reading. Whenever it came, he made me sit down with him and in time, with the aid of a dictionary, we learned enough

English to follow the American Depression and other capitalist dol-
drums. . . . Several of us read everything on religion that came our
way. For a while, after reading a booklet about the Quakers, Broz was
fascinated by them. Next, it was a book on Pavlov's conditioned re-
flexes that roused his interest."

Colakovic served out his twelve-year term in 1933, and soon after
went to Moscow. He spent the next three years in the Foreign Section
of the Marx-Engels-Lenin Institute. Edvard Kardelj and Ivan Gosnjak
were two other Yugoslavs who attended the same school.

Broz was released from the Maribor "college" in 1934. He was forty-
two years old.

His release order directed Broz to report forthwith to the mayor of
Zagorsko-selo, then the seat of the township of which Kumrovec was a
part; to proceed by the shortest route to his native village; and to stay
within its confines until further orders, except for a weekly trip to
Zagorsko-selo to show the mayor he was still around.

Mayor Josip Jurak—a peasant, a master mason, and a shrewd character (I met him in Kumrovec)—received a copy of the release order.
Thirty years before he and Joza Broz had fought on opposite sides in
the "wars" for the control of the castle ruin midway between their villages. Now, when Joza—scrawny, and wearing a cheap, ill-fitting suit
from the prison supply-room—entered his office, Jurak shut the door,
bade him sit down, cleared his throat, and said: "I've been thinking
about you, Joza, ever since that day in '28 they sent you up. I can't
make you out, but I know you're a driven man. Law or no law, you
won't stay in this township. . . . I wouldn't be mayor if they didn't
think I was for the regime, so let's not talk about that. Somebody has
to hold this job; I took it, and I aim to make things as smooth and easy
as possible. You're smarter than I am, Joza, so you'll realize I can't be
helpful unless people cooperate. Now, then——"

They agreed that Broz should stay in Kumrovec for a while, visit
Aunt Ana in Podsreda, apply for permission to go to Zagreb on personal
business—and "disappear." That would clear Jurak of responsibility.

Broz stayed for ten days. He was uncomfortable in Kumrovec, particularly in his native house and his brother Karlo, who now owned the
place, and his wife, whom he hardly knew, were uneasy with him
there. He had the village tailor make him a suit in a hurry. Evenings,

he dropped in on his old friend Tereza and her husband Vilce Stefan, and on Pepek Stefan and his wife.

"Sometimes he came two, three times a day," Tereza told me. "I guess he didn't know what to do with himself. He asked a lot of questions: how much cash Vilce and I saw a year, how much a spool of thread cost, or a half-kilo of salt. . . . One evening I lit the lamp and put a common-bowl of boiled cabbage on the table. Vilce wasn't in; the children were over at the neighbor's across the way to see the new calf, and I was opening the door to call them when Joza stepped in. He wrinkled his nose, looked at the cabbage, and tasted it. 'What do you call this?' he asked. 'Cabbage soup,' I said. 'Soup!' he said. I knew you could hardly call it soup; there was hardly any fat in it: fat was scarce, and salt too; I'd only put in a pinch. 'The children's supper?' he asked. I nodded. 'Tereza,' he said, 'aren't you ashamed to feed them slop like this?' He made me so angry I could've shaken him or told him to mind his own business, and I guess I did give him a look. I *was* ashamed; but what could I do? Hardly anybody in the village had any money. The crop was poor; most of us were out of potatoes. Joza knew all that, but still he asked. Did I have bread for the children? I wouldn't tell him. So there he stood, looking at the cabbage for I don't know how long; and I felt awful. The light from the lamp was low, almost dark, but I saw his face. He touched my shoulder, then walked out. . . . When the children came in, I couldn't tell the oldest, who asked me, why I was crying.

"Another time Joza spent the evening with us and he and Vilce got into an argument. 'If I were half as bright as you are, Joza,' Vilce said, 'I'd make the best of life *for myself.*' Joza said that was the wrong attitude. 'Why?' asked Vilce. Joza didn't answer. So I said, 'If you keep on, Joza, you'll lose your head someday.' 'Maybe I will,' he said, 'but until then I'll try to use it.' Vilce said, 'Joza, you're crazy!' Joza didn't mind. Sometimes he sat in my house for an hour without saying a word, and just looked at the children."

"When he came to Podsreda," Aunt Ana told me, "he wore the new suit. He was so thin and pale his cheekbones stuck out too much. I asked him if he was well. He said not to worry about him. I said I was his only aunt on his mother's side and I had a right to worry about him if I wanted to. . . . While he was in prison, he wrote me once a year, but he didn't want me to come to see him, and I was glad. I didn't want to see my sister Mica's son in jail! It was politics; he didn't kill anybody or break the Commandments; just the same I woke up nights thinking about him. I didn't read about his trial, but I heard how he talked back to the judge. I wondered what Mica would have thought— God bless her soul.

"It was in '29 or '30 when Pelagia, his wife, came to see me, to say good-by: she was going back to Russia. I didn't blame her. She wrote Joza he should come there too when he got out. She told him that in Yugoslavia he was throwing his life away. She was sure they would kill him if he kept on. So now, when he came, I told him I agreed with Pelagia. I begged him to think of himself for a change. He said he *was* thinking of himself. If he didn't follow what he believed in, he couldn't live with himself. It took me a while to figure that out."

When Broz dived back into the underground in 1934, he found the Zagreb CP a going concern in charge of young men who had gone through the torture chambers and had served prison terms. They had close contact with the key trade unions and with the vital student movements—specifically with such youths as Vladimir Bakaric—which were boldly resisting two opposing fascist pressures in the University of Zagreb. One pressure was exerted by the Belgrade regime, the other by the ultra-nationalist, fascist Ustasi underground outfit led by Ante Pavelic from Italy and linked to Archbishop Stepinac's office and to the conservative city elements of the Croatian Peasant Party. The Croatian Peasant Party was now headed by Vladko Macek, who was nowhere near the leader Stjepan Radic had been.

By the summer of 1934, the Zagreb group of young CP leaders (Broz knew one or two of them from Lepoglava, a few others by name) had sized up the Yugoslav situation. They believed a Red revolution was overdue. The CPY now had hundreds of new leaders; more were coming out of prison every month. These men had been tested. They knew each other. They could spot a "fractionalist" at a glance. They took no chances with possible informers in their midst. . . . But it was later than most people supposed. Hitler was in power in Germany. The inevitable and imminent Second World War might be the opportunity for the CPY. The thing to do was to prepare for it. . . . A first task was to look into the Party's top leadership. Who were the men in the Central Committee? Gorkic? Schmidt? Copic? Why were they in Vienna? It was high time somebody investigated. . . .

After prison, Broz had expected to resume his post as secretary of the Zagreb CP or go back to itinerant agitation. He was sure his wife and son were being taken care of in the Soviet Union; he was free of personal ambition and ready for whatever the Party wanted him to do. Then he discovered that the Zagreb group had been waiting for his release from prison, to make him their leader. They remembered his stand in court in 1928. And Mosa Pijade had spoken well of him in the presence of a man released from Lepoglava the year before.

One of the Croatian CP leaders was Rade Koncar, a handsome young locksmith from Split, Dalmatia, who had worked in Belgrade a while. He had a record of dauntlessness under torture and a prison term behind him. He knew several Serbian Communists and spoke with quiet enthusiasm about the CP leadership emerging in Belgrade. Broz liked and trusted him instinctively. (Rade Koncar was in his native Split when Mussolini's fascist army seized the town in 1941. He was betrayed, captured, and tortured; confined in one of the buildings within the fabulous Diocletian Palace, and finally hacked to death.)

Two action-ideas came out of the conversations between Broz and the young men: *one,* that the Croatian Communists create a regional Party committee for Croatia; and, *two,* that he, Broz, go forthwith to Vienna and get the lowdown on the Central Committee of the CPY.

Broz noticed that most of the young CP leaders dressed almost elegantly and were always immaculately groomed. They explained to Broz that a good appearance was in the long run the best and the cheapest disguise. It exploited the gendarmes' and plainclothesmen's single-track minds, which were so steeped in bourgeois lore that Communists were dirty, uncouth, and "wild," that it never occurred to them that a clean-cut fellow in a well-tailored English-tweed suit with shined shoes, a natty bowtie, a corner of a white handkerchief peeping from his breast pocket, a flower in his lapel, and a fine felt hat set at a jaunty angle on his head could be a Red.

Broz thought this was very funny. He liked it otherwise too; it fit in with his Zagorje-born flair for clothes which had been repressed during his prison years. For his trip to Vienna he was outfitted with typical tourist luggage, a costly if small wardrobe, expense money (out of local CP funds), and a false passport—expertly forged by the *tehnika* department of the Zagreb CP.

Seeing him off at the station, his natty young friends suggested that he stop in Ljubljana and take a look at the Slovenian *tovarisi.* If he managed to get in touch with the "sound elements" there, he was to use his own judgment whether to inform them about the movement in Croatia and why he was going to Vienna.

In Ljubljana, Broz found the beginnings of the same development that filled him with such satisfaction in Zagreb. He was impressed by and attracted to several young men—Edvard Kardelj, Boris Kidric, and three or four others (who died in the *borba* during 1941–45). They all remembered his name from 1928; he knew two who had recently been released from the Maribor prison. Kardelj, as I mentioned earlier, had been tortured in the Ljubljana and Belgrade *glavnjace* and had spent two highly profitable years in a Serbian penitentiary, studying the subtler points of "Marxism-Leninism."

At the end of their first session with Broz, the Slovenian *tovarisi* suggested that he represent them, too, on his mission to Vienna, and stop in Ljubljana again on his way back. He said he would.

IN THE AFTERNOON of June 16, 1949, I sat with Tito in a box at the Belgrade Sports Stadium for three or four hours while the local physical-culture organizations—thirty thousand young people or more—went through their annual calisthenic and gymnastic routines. As we talked between numbers against the blare of bands and loudspeakers, Tito didn't conceal his disappointment at my patent inability to answer comprehensively his questions about sports in the United States in which he appeared greatly interested. "I was under the impression," he said, "that Americans spent most of their time at ball games and boxing matches and listening to on-the-spot descriptions of them on the radio and reading the sports sections of the newspapers." Well, I was an exception, I replied. I had a friend in Hollywood, Abe Roth, who was a boxing referee and a friend of Jack Dempsey's and that was the extent of my contact with sports. I hadn't been to a ball game or a prizefight in ten years or more. I didn't have the time. . . .

Before the afternoon was over, however, Tito's estimate of me as an American may have risen a notch, thanks to a young lieutenant general sitting among a group behind us who leaned over to ask me if I could tell him something about the *"cuveni americki general Josip* [famous American general, Joseph] Stilwell, in whom many of us here are very interested." Despite the din, Tito heard the question and the answer. I summarized as much as I remembered of Stilwell's diary notes and letters about his experiences in China and Burma that I had read a year or so before in *The Ladies' Home Journal*. In an aside, I mentioned that during World War II he had adopted as his motto a labor union's slogan: *"Illegitimati non carborundum*—Don't let the bastards grind you down." Tito smiled long, and I had the impression that for a while he paid little heed to the activity in the stadium.

In the last half of 1934 Tito could not help realizing that he was becoming a leading *illegitimatus* (to the royal Belgrade regime) and that he was in danger of being ground down or rubbed out. However, the "bastards" (from his angle) he had to be most wary of were the Moscow-appointed leaders of the Yugoslav branch of the International Communist Movement he believed was his country's hope.

From 1929 to '37, the secretary-general of the Central Committee of the Communist Party of Yugoslavia—the CC, CPY, for short—was Milan Gorkic, whose red hair and mustache were the reddest part of him. His real name was Josip Czizinski. He was born of Polish-Czech parentage in Bosnia during the Austro-Hungarian occupation of that former Turkish province which brought to the Balkans a good many Poles and Czechs in Austrian uniforms and as civil-service administrators. No other solid facts about Czizinski's early life were available in

Yugoslavia in 1949. At least I couldn't find anyone interested in them or in helping me to dig them up.

But I did gather that Josip Czizinski was a metal worker with no liking for his trade and a bent for "revolutionary" multiloquence who came into the inchoate Yugoslav Communist movement when he was twenty-three or -four, in 1921 or '22. He joined *SKOJ—Savez Komunisticke Omladine Jugoslavije,* the Union of Communist Youth of Yugoslavia. I was told that there was no record of his ever having been accepted by the CPY as a full-fledged member. Just when, how and why he left Yugoslavia, or when he assumed the name Milan Gorkic, nobody with whom I talked in 1949 could say. For a time in 1926 he worked in the Vienna office of the International Communist Youth organization which was part of the Third International (Comintern) network, and which sent him to Moscow for a course given to Comintern operators. The probability is he was an anti-Communist agent even then.

From the mid-1920's on through the 1930's, Moscow's population included numerous Communists from other countries: Duclos and Thorez of France, Togliatti of Italy, Pauker of Rumania, Beirut of Poland, and many, many others whom Fate neglected to mark for historical roles, or at least for newspaper headlines after 1945. Some came and went, others were more or less permanent *émigrés* who regarded the USSR as their "Socialist fatherland." Some worked at jobs in the Comintern offices. Others sought to become "part of Soviet life." The simplest way to achieve that was to get into state bureaucracy. For one thing, it was easier to squeeze yourself into a niche in Moscow than to plot revolution and dodge the police in your native land. For another, as a "good, disciplined Communist" you recognized the paramountcy of the Soviet CP and slumped, comfortably or otherwise, into an acceptance of the emerging Stalinist gospel that the Soviet Union was the most progressive and enlightened land in the world (whereas Lenin had held, realistically, that Russia was a backward country), and that the world's future depended solely on the USSR's success in "building Socialism in a single country."

Some of these foreign "Communists" were, or became, anti-Soviet spies and anti-Communist agents. They were a relatively unimportant detail in a vast sick state of affairs.

In November 1922, less than two years before his death, the already dying Lenin spoke at the Fourth Congress of the Third International.

He warned against Soviet Russia's insistence that the Communists in other countries learn only from her experience and follow her example to the letter. "I have the impression that we [Russian Communists who dominate Comintern meetings] have made a big mistake," Lenin said, ". . . that we ourselves have blocked the road to future [revolutionary] success." (The speech, entitled "Five Years of the Russian Revolution and the Prospects of the World Revolution," was in part a criticism of a resolution on the organizational structure of the Communist parties and on their methods and the content of their work which was adopted at the Third Congress of the Comintern in 1921. See Vol. X of Lenin's *Selected Works,* originally published by the Marx-Engels-Lenin Institute in Moscow; issued in English in the United States by International Publishers, New York.)

Stalin and his Comintern apparatus ignored Lenin's warning, however. From about 1928 on, the insistence that the USSR was all that mattered, at least for the time being, was the core of Comintern policy.

For about five years (1928–33) the big-wheel in the Comintern's central office was Ossip Pyatnisky. He was its treasurer and paymaster and also Stalin's deputy and chief of the division which picked the cadres and briefed the Comintern's special agents. He was closely linked with the GPU (then the initials for the Soviet security police), one of whose centers was in the same building, on Mochovaya Street in Moscow, as the main offices of the Comintern. He stretched Stalin's ideas into the "line" for the parties in other countries to follow—a *Russian* "line," based on the *Russian* experience, calculated to benefit *Russia*. In 1931–32, for instance, the "line" laid down for the German CP unquestionably paved the way for Hitler's ascent to power in 1933.

Large sections of the world's Communist movement reacted very unfavorably, subversively; so down the drain went Pyatnisky as a sop to the international working class . . . and in 1935 Georgi Dimitrov, the Bulgarian hero of the Reichstag Fire Trial in 1933 and the originator of the People's Front "line," became secretary-general of the Comintern. He was the boss in some matters, but not in the important ones, such as picking the cadres to run the CPs in other countries and briefing the super-secret special agents. His connection with the GPU was tenuous. In all weighty organizational and policy matters, the actual boss of the Comintern was Dimitrov's "deputy," Dmitry Manuilsky, who during 1945–50 became a familiar figure as a Soviet delegate to United Nations meetings. He had been a Ukrainian revo-

lutionary since 1905 and a key member of the Central Committee of
the All-Soviet (Bolshevik) CP and of the praesidium of the Comintern
since 1924. He was a Stalin-man, hand-in-hand with the GPU.

In the middle 1930's Togliatti of Italy and Duclos of France were
among Dimitrov's leading "assistants" or "deputies." Doing what? In
1949 I couldn't get a concrete answer to this question from the Yugoslav Communists who had been in Moscow in the 1930's. My impression
was that Togliatti and Duclos helped Dimitrov go through the motions
of being secretary-general. They yessed Manuilsky's "proposals" (read:
Stalin's directives) in unison with Dimitrov. Stalin seldom appeared at
the Comintern executive committee meetings. Few Yugoslav Communists ever got close enough to talk to him at these meetings. Molotov
was also a member of the Comintern's Central Committee, but he
seldom had anything to say, either. He let Manuilsky do most of the
talking.

To go back to Milan Gorkic. In 1928, when he was in his early
thirties, he married a woman whose name (according to one of my
sources) "was something like Broenstein." She was the director of the
children's playgrounds in Moscow and one of the better known women
members of the Bolshevik party organization in the Soviet capital.
Gorkic's marriage to her may have helped elevate him to the post of
secretary-general of the CPY in 1929. The more or less official gossip
at the time was that Pyatnisky had chosen him for the job and had
convinced Manuilsky, Molotov, and the rest of the Comintern's inner
group to appoint him by arguing that the Communist movement in
Yugoslavia was a "mess" and needed a new leader who had had no
share in making it that way and might be able to tidy it up.

The Central Committees of most of the CP's outside the Soviet
Union were appointed or "approved" by the Comintern insiders. This
was to enable Stalin to use the whole movement as a tool of Soviet
foreign policy, whose ultimate aim may or may not have been to realize
world conquest disguised as messianism, but certainly was to achieve
the Industrial Revolution in Russia at whatever cost no matter to
whom.

Some CC members and even secretaries-general of the various CPs
were almost continually in Moscow, and had no first-hand idea what
went on "at home." They hung around, drawing stipends from the
Comintern treasury; or worked in the Comintern offices, in the superb

library and reading-rooms of the Marx-Engels-Lenin Institute, or in other Soviet institutions. Others, provided with false identification papers, resided in the least inhospitable countries adjacent to their own, where they kept in touch with Russian GPU "resident" and transient agents. Their assignment was to keep the revolutionary home fires burning by remote control. When the flames showed signs of flaring, they were supposed to subdue them by one means or another and produce a counter-revolutionary effect. The idea was to kindle the fires just enough to keep the Western foreign offices in a mild sweat, so they would think twice before making things hot for the USSR.

Secretary-General Milan Gorkic and most of his wrecking crew, who were members of the CC, CPY, lived in Moscow until 1930. Then some of them moved to Paris and others to Vienna, which was not drastically inhospitable to foreign revolutionaries even after Dollfuss' rise to power. One reason Gorkic may have moved was that his marriage had gone on the rocks. A more likely reason was that the CP in Yugoslavia was getting a bit too headstrong again. In 1933, the entire Politburo of the CC, CPY established itself in Vienna.

For six and a half years Milan Gorkic was the Moscow-appointed "leader" of the Yugoslav Party. During 1933-35 he and the rest of the Politburo of the CC, CPY under him sat in Viennese coffee-houses and split hairs over Moscow's latest "directives." On the backs of menus they penciled rough drafts of their "reports" about the developing "revolutionary situation" in Yugoslavia. The "reports" were compiled, signed "For the Central Committee, CPY: *Gorkic*," and picked up every once in a while by the Comintern's shadowy underground couriers. While there is no proof that the entire CC consisted of agents, it is very close to a fact, as already mentioned, that even the least disloyal of these "leaders" had next to no connection with the Communist movement in Yugoslavia—almost none with the non-"fractionalist" groups, like the one in Zagreb which sent Josip Broz to Vienna late in July 1934. In reality, Gorkic's ties with Yugoslavia were mostly with the deadly enemies of the Party Moscow had selected him to head.

Years later it was established beyond a shadow of a doubt that while Milan Gorkic was a cog in the Comintern machine he was also an informer for the anti-Communist forces in Europe—the royal regime in Belgrade, the Pilsudski government in Warsaw, the British-French interests in Eastern Europe, and the Jesuits. His connections with the latter and with the Pilsudski regime were through the CC of the Polish Communist Party which for a time consisted exclusively of anti-Red agents. How much money the secretary-general of the CC, CPY received for this work is unknown. Possibly he was a member of King Alexander's secret political police even before he left Yugoslavia in the middle 1920's. The first meeting between him and his future wife, the Moscow children's playground director, may have been a rendezvous of two spies. Possibly he engaged in this business not only for the money he received but to satisfy the twists and turns of his nature.

Two items concerning Gorkic are certain: that in Vienna he lived in comfortable middle-class style, and that in the middle 1930's he informed on scores of key people in the Yugoslav and Polish Communist undergrounds who were then liquidated by the Belgrade and Warsaw political police. In addition, during 1930–36 he sent, on various pretexts, many devoted Communists to the Soviet Union where they were interned or liquidated on his say-so as "Trotskyites" or "imperialist agents." In other words, he was a GPU man as well.

In his report to the Fifth CPY Congress in June 1948, after the Cominform outburst had made it necessary for him to tell a little of the inside story of the CPY, Tito stated categorically that during 1934–37 Gorkic, while holding the position of secretary-general of the CC, CPY, to which Moscow had appointed him, was "very closely connected" with Slobodan Jovanovic and Dragisa Vasic, two founders of the "Serbian Cultural Club" in Belgrade. This "club," ostensibly a "patriotic" and "idealistic" pan-Serbian organization, was really an agency for British and French financial interests in Yugoslavia and for the Paris-London diplomatic-military policy in the Balkans. Colonel (later General) Draza Mihailovic belonged to it. During World War II, Jovanovic, a historian who evolved questionable theses with great literary skill, rose to premiership of the royal Yugoslav government-in-exile in London; Vasic, a close prewar friend of Mihailovic, long an agent of British and French agents in Belgrade, became one of Mihailovic's props in Serbia.

In the summer of 1934—and long after—Josip Broz had no reason to suspect Milan Gorkic or any of the other CC, CPY members in Vienna of treason to the cause they were supposed to be serving.

Right now, late in July and early in August 1934, Josip Broz was on a mission. These fellows he had been sent to find were lazy, loose, objectionable; but they *were* part of the Comintern sub-hierarchy. His job was to inform them about the shape of things in Yugoslavia as the Communists living in Yugoslavia saw them, specifically as the CP in Zagreb, then going through a rebirth, saw them. Subconsciously, however (as he realized later), the half-dozen shifty-eyed characters, including Gorkic, whom he found himself among in a Vienna coffee-house appalled him.

Most of them had not been in Yugoslavia for years. They eyed him with expressions mingling degrees of stupefied surprise, resentment at his breaking in on them, cunning disbelief, and curiosity. As he saw himself reflected in the stares of two of them at any rate, he might just have emerged from Darkest Africa dressed in the best Central European style for a summer tourist. And his words, the eyes fixed on him seemed to say, verged on impertinence.

Broz spoke quietly, simply, to the point. One of his first assertions was that no real Communist in Yugoslavia whom he knew or had heard of, in or out of prison, had any active faith in the CC, CPY—in *them*.

Gorkic twisted his red mustache. It did not become him; it only set off his pallor. Now he interrupted Broz with a spate of vile language.

Broz dammed it with the calm statement that the *drugovi* in Zagreb who had sent him intended no disrespect for the CC, CPY or the Comintern as organizations. On the contrary, they loved the Soviet Union, they revered the memory of Lenin, and were ready to follow Stalin's leadership and the Bolshevik Party to the ends of the earth. Living under Alexander's monarcho-fascism, however, the *drugovi* in Zagreb, as well as elsewhere in Yugoslavia, felt that their leaders ought to live under it too, right in Yugoslavia with them—or at least take turns at living there, so they would know what monarcho-fascism was like. Then maybe the Party could cope with it.

Gorkic realized he was confronted by no flyweight and after a while he assumed a calm, reasonable enough attitude, one befitting a leader. Explaining his outburst as a tactic to test Broz, he agreed that, from their vantage point, the Zagreb comrades might be right. From the international point of view, however—which was important too, no?— there were more *howevers* than they, with their limited Yugoslav outlook, could imagine. The whole situation called for very careful pondering.

Broz stayed in Vienna a week and saw the CC members or Gorkic alone every day. The questions Gorkic asked him indicated that his information about conditions in Yugoslavia came from sources on a different wave length than the Zagreb underground CP leadership. Still, Broz' feelings did not spiral to a pinpoint of suspicion. He told the CC members what he knew. At the same time his instinct about people, which sharpened with the years, nudged him. . . . But, then, why should he be uneasy? Under Moscow dispensation, these men were his leaders.

The day Broz left Vienna, Secretary-General Gorkic informed him in a friendly tone that his visit might mark the beginning of a positive development within the CPY. He had given the CC a lot to think about; the consensus was that he, Broz, was a valuable man. The night before, they had held a plenum meeting and had elected him to the CC. The election was subject to approval by the Praesidium of the Third International, but in all probability it wouldn't run into any obstacle in that corner of the Red Olympus, at any rate. If any difficulty did arise, he, Gorkic, would take care of it.[1]

Surprised and pleased, Josip Broz told Secretary-General Gorkic he would like to visit the Soviet Union soon. His wife and son were there. And if he was to be a useful CC member, he ought to spend some time in Moscow. Gorkic agreed: he would fix that too: just leave everything to him. It was too bad that neither he, Gorkic, nor any of the other CC members stationed in Vienna could go to Yugoslavia at the moment; they were all tied up with pressing matters that would take weeks, months to complete. But Broz could rest assured that he, the secretary-general, and some of the other CC-men would visit Yugoslavia as soon as possible to look over the whole picture—just when, he couldn't say. They couldn't flit about at will; Moscow would have to pass on the trip "in principle"—a phrase Gorkic used over and over.

Meantime, Gorkic went on, it was the wish of the CC that Broz should serve as its liaison with the Party in the homeland. Broz was to tell the members in Zagreb that their CC was with them in so far as their ideas didn't cross—unwittingly, of course—the Comintern policy.

---

[1] There were Communists in Yugoslavia in 1949 who believed that Josip Broz was a member of the CC, CPY before he made his first trip to Vienna in 1934 to find Gorkic. This belief was based on the fact that the Zagreb CP organization and the CP group in Slovenia had authorized him to represent them. I am not prepared to argue this point. I think it makes little difference. Tito himself appeared indifferent about the exact date when he became a member of the CC, CPY. He said that from about 1935 on he had had a "consultative body" on whose counsel he largely relied.

Broz should tell them to curb their youthful impatience and impulsiveness. They needed to bear in mind that, as secretary-general of the CC, CPY, he was the historically responsible head of the Party and ever eager to keep in touch with its membership. It was entirely possible that the whole movement in Yugoslavia needed overhauling—but *why*, specifically?—and *how*, concretely? These questions needed to be thought over and discussed on the highest levels. Perhaps by Stalin himself.

Broz reminded Gorkic that that was exactly what he had been talking about all week. He stressed again the Zagreb proposal that the various branches of the CPY should hold underground regional conferences in the near future, to be followed by a national conference which would decide on the ways and means of building a party from the ground up. Easier said than done. After all, they were operating under a terroristic dictatorship. Still, it was an excellent suggestion even if a bit dewy-eyed. It would be considered. But he would have to have each and every detail about these conferences in advance—the dates, places, routes to and from the rendezvous, means of travel, passwords; who would attend them, and why; and agendas. This would call for exhaustive checking in order to reduce the risk of betrayal to a minimum. Broz understood that, *ne?* Broz did and, at the same time, he had a curiously tight feeling in his chest.

Always, *always,* Gorkic emphasized, the comrades "at home" must remember that while Yugoslavia and the CPY were one thing, the Comintern and the Soviet Union knew best what was desirable, and when, from the point of view of world politics. To achieve all-around effectiveness, everything had to be coordinated. Each step of any significance had to be cleared, at least "in principle," with Moscow.

Broz couldn't help thinking that the secretary-general was extremely adept at dodging the immediate problems in Yugoslavia. He kept wrapping them in anticipated difficulties and tying them with the strings of long-range world considerations. Yet his mission, Broz felt, was a success. He could report to the *drugovi* at home that there *was* a CC, CPY: he had seen it, he had talked with it.

When Gorkic, seeing him off at the station in Vienna, asked Broz for the alias under which he was traveling, a shapeless uneasiness made him give another. Two hours later he decided to stop at a small mountain resort that night and take another train the next day.

And the next day—amid the salutes of conductors, customs inspectors, and police officers impressed by his prosperous appearance and his casual manner—Broz arrived safely back in Yugoslavia with the expertly forged Austrian passport which the CP organization in Zagreb had provided.

In the late summer and early autumn of 1934 Josip Broz went to Vienna three times at few weeks' intervals. He traveled under a different identity and wore different clothes each time, keeping his identity a secret from Gorkic. He said good-by to the CC, CPY in Vienna, then changed the schedule of his arrival at the Yugoslav border —just in case one of them might tip off the Yugoslav authorities or the *Orjuna,* the fascist outfit organized on the Nazi pattern by special interests in Belgrade as an auxiliary to the gendarmerie and the political police. He thus evaded the fate of Djuro Djakovic.

During this period his role as the envoy between the reviving CP inside Yugoslavia and the CC in Vienna grew. To the young leaders in Zagreb—all of them a bit naïve but patriotically desperate: the collective eagle diving toward the protruding root of "Soviet Communism"—Broz was the key man in the organization they thought the CPY ought to become: an indigenous, democratic party coordinated with the international working-class movement. They cautioned him not to risk his life, and put at his disposal every means of disguise and security they and he could think of and that they could afford.

In Zagreb, Josip Broz renewed his acquaintance with Miroslav Krleza, who had been a CP member since the 1920's and was a friend of Mosa Pijade. At forty (two years younger than Broz) Krleza was Yugoslavia's most distinguished living writer in the high European tradition of Romain Rolland, Stefan Zweig, Thomas Mann, H. G. Wells—except that Krleza was a Communist. He had a score of books to his name and was almost equally famous as a playwright, novelist, poet, essayist, and political and cultural polemist. He was a scholar of aesthetics, human values, and phases of South Slavic history no one else probed. His naturally well-endowed, deeply cultivated, and helplessly honest and radical mind ranged over other fields of knowledge and theory as well. It was no secret that he was a Leftist. The police and the regime were almost certain he was a CP member but did nothing about it except search his rooms now and then, and invite him to the political-police headquarters to answer questions. An explanation for their restraint was that Krleza enjoyed great prestige among the intelligentsia in Yugoslavia, especially in Croatia, and that he was well-known in Czechoslovakia and France where his arrest or disappearance would have caused a furore. It was wisest to let him alone. There were about a dozen other Yugoslav intellectuals, writers and artists, in the same position. One of them was Marko Ristic, scion of a Belgrade family which is as important in Serbian history as are, say, the Adamses or the Roosevelts in American history. Another was Koco Popovic, scion of a banking family in Belgrade. Most of the other notable dissidents died in the war during 1942–45. In the 1930's both Popovic and Ristic were surrealist writers. In 1949 Popovic was chief of staff of Tito's new army and Ristic was Tito's ambassador in Paris.

Speaking a half-dozen languages and able to read three or four more, Krleza was a brilliant conversationalist. His talk—in the 1930's, no less than in 1949, when he and I conversed for hours on end—was a subtle interplay of carefully gleaned and coordinated information, much reflection which roamed the labyrinths of the side issues of every subject he dug into, and humor bouncing from gentle irony to sardonic derision. He was also a man of deep silences as well as a good listener. Listening to Josip Broz' views in the summer and fall of 1934, and to the occasional autobiographical passages of the man's odyssey from Kumrovec, Krleza was impressed by the quality of his mind and feelings. It was simplicity itself articulated with a matter-or-fact directness that automatically placed significance where it belonged. To a trained, conscious intellectual like Krleza, this characteristic—plus Broz' mixture of instinctual alertness, physical courage, and controlled *fanatizam* —was very interesting.

On his part, in the second half of 1934, Josip Broz found Miroslav Krleza the fulfillment of a need he probably didn't realize he had. To be in touch with Krleza's intellectual expanse and roving inquisitiveness was a happy sequel to his two-year contact with Mosa Pijade in the Lepoglava prison.

Between his first and second trips to Vienna, Josip Broz visited Belgrade. The Zagreb CP organization had a number of reliable contacts there who accepted him after he and they exchanged passwords. He discovered first-hand that the pleasant rumor he had heard was true: the new CP development in Serbia *had* even greater vitality and scope than the CP in Croatia had. It took in or influenced a majority of industrial workers, many university professors and students, some government officials, lawyers, doctors, journalists, and Left-tending sons and daughters of bankers and speculators, and of present and former ministers in King Alexander's regime. This Leftwardness was less theoretical Marxism-Leninism than it was ordinary patriotism appalled by the corruption of the existing order in semi-colonial Yugoslavia. It sought a movement that would overthrow the *status quo.*

On this visit to Belgrade in September or October 1934, Broz met a number of young men whom he sized up favorably and who three or four years later became his co-leaders and assistants. Most of them fell in the war during 1941–45 fighting in Serbia, Bosnia, and Montenegro or died under torture in Gestapo prisons. In '34 many of them were still only members of the underground *SKOJ*—Union of Communist Youth of Yugoslavia. A few were in the secret local CP organization whose leadership, as in Zagreb, consisted largely of men recently released from prison who were known to no one outside the inner circle. Its small membership roster was a super-secret document, unavailable even to some of the top local leaders—to say nothing of the CC, CPY in Vienna. Broz was impressed. In turn, he impressed the new Belgrade leaders. They told him about Milovan Djilas, a young Montenegrin poet, a student at the University of Belgrade, who was a grandson of an anti-Turkish *haiduk;* and about Aleksandar Rankovic, a young tailor who hailed from a hamlet near Kraljevo. Both had recently been captured, tortured in the *Glavnjaca,* and sentenced—Djilas to three years, Rankovic to six. It was not until years later that Broz met them.

Whenever Broz made a trip to Vienna he stopped for a day or two in Ljubljana, where the Slovenian branch of the CPY was reviving around two young men—Edvard Kardelj, twenty-three, a janitor's son; and Boris Kidric, the same age, whose father was an internationally known Slavicist, Professor France Kidric of the University of Ljubljana. Kardelj had been graduated from teachers' college in 1929 but he hadn't been given a teaching job because the authorities suspected he was a Red. Kidric had studied chemistry at the university but he didn't want to work in that field; at seventeen, six years before, he had announced to his parents that he would devote himself to revolution.

Kardelj and Kidric had studied Marxist-Leninist literature since their middle teens—since 1926 or '27, when another young man, Vlado Kozak—the youngest son of a Ljubljana innkeeper—had introduced them to it. Each had several encounters with the police behind him. They were as unlike as they could be, each was remarkable in his own way. They worked well together, without rivalry. They were in contact with all social levels in Slovenia, including the peasants. They were out of touch with the CC, CPY in Vienna, but kept in contact with several Slovenian Communists in Austria, Czechoslovakia, and France. Their co-workers in Ljubljana were as devoted to the Party organization and its cause as they were.

"What else about them impressed you?" I asked Tito in the long June 9, 1949, interview. Lighting a cigarette, he did not reply immediately. I tried again, broadening my question: "What criteria did you go by in sizing up people within the movement?"

"Oh, I just noticed how they went about their business," Tito said. "Were they good revolutionaries? Or bureaucrats by habit? (For there was a tendency to bureaucratism, officiousness, and cliquishness even in the underground.) If a man was a glib phrasemonger, I was wary of him—a good many people are revolutionary in words only. On the other hand, as I saw even then, some of the best-intentioned revolutionaries were thrown off the track by side issues and incidental roadblocks. I liked people who didn't fret and fuss about details but kept their minds on the task at hand, and scaled obstacles as they appeared. *Drug* Kidric was like that. No prevision of hindrances prevented him from getting started. . . . *Drug* Kardelj was so quiet you scarcely noticed him at first; but decisions were made, goals were achieved, then you realized that it was he who had formulated the decision, persuaded others to accept it, and put the task in motion. No setback dismayed him. He was free of pretense and bluff. He steered clear of fractionalism. His mind dwelled on essentials. He studied. After my first meeting with him I had no doubt he was honest and a true revolutionary. I felt the same about *drug* Kidric. Good organizers, both of them. . . . Neither was ambitious for himself, only for the Party—to do what they could to make it a force."

. . . On June 1, '49, in answer to my questions, Kardelj said:

"First of all, I feel it would be a mistake to look at the Revolution in Yugoslavia by spotlighting the leaders. Not that I want to underestimate our share, least of all Tito's, in the process. But our biographies are unimportant. I have never been interested in knowing the personal details of Tito's life. I know *him* and I feel I know the scene and the period out of which he and the rest of us grew. We simply fell into various roles in the drama of forces in which our lives, our country, and the world were involved. The essences of Tito's Yugoslavia were clearly in the air in Old Yugoslavia—injected, in part, by the efforts of the CPY, inadequate as they may have been. . . . My own role, since you insist that I describe it, took shape very naturally. But, I warn you, it isn't a particularly interesting story.

"My parents were of the working class, life-long Socialists both of them. When I was nine, I carried a banner in the May Day parade; that was in 1918, when Slovenia, as you know, was still under Austria —but Austria-Hungary was on its last legs, even I knew that, at the age of nine. At ten I was reading Socialist and other progressive litera- ture and followed world events. You may be interested to know that in 1924, when I was fifteen, Senator Robert La Follette's candidacy for President of the United States absorbed me. The Sacco-Vanzetti and Tom Mooney cases were discussed in our home.

"My two brothers, my sister and I, all four of us, were teen-agers attending school, when my mother went to work in the tobacco factory in Ljubljana. My father's wages as a janitor in a public building and the little we youngsters earned at odd jobs after school weren't enough to keep us in food and clothes. After my sister finished commercial school and got a job, she turned over her salary to the family fund. I saw how meager our life was. So did my brothers. One of them never became a Communist; he died a Socialist fighting in the War of Liberation, in 1943.

"In 1924 a Communist named Kocmur (whom the Ustasi hanged in Zagreb in 1942) tried to enroll me in the Communist Youth. But I was under the influence of my Socialist family and I held out until 1926. Then one day Vlado Kozak talked to me. He had a wonderful man- ner with people, and he convinced me that I ought to join the Com- munists. It was the only movement that made any sense. It meant busi- ness. Yes, Vlado Kozak persuaded Boris Kidric to join the Movement, too. Vlado had a small library of Marxist and Leninist books and brochures, and during 1925–28 I read all of them, besides others which I obtained elsewhere. Attending teachers' college, I enticed several of my fellow-students into the underground Communist Youth organiza- tion. Many of them fell in the War of Liberation fourteen, fifteen years later.

"Why did we become Communists? One reason was economic. Most of us were very poor." (Young people of well-to-do families were spiritually affected by the poverty they saw about them. Professor France Kidric—who died in April 1950—told me during a casual conversation early in 1949 that his son Boris probably wound up in the Communist movement because at the age of ten or eleven he couldn't bear the poverty of the other boys. "He asked me and his mother questions which we couldn't answer," said Dr. Kidric; "so he went elsewhere and brought home the answers.")

"The other reason," Kardelj said, "of almost equal importance, was the national question. Even as boys of thirteen or so, we resented the pan-Serbian crowd in power in Belgrade. Through the centralized rule they had established with terror they dominated and exploited Croatia, Slovenia, and Macedonia, and they weren't good to the Serbian people, either.

"Some students came under the influence of the Clericals and emerged as a clero-fascist group which favored separatism—Slovenia and Croatia breaking away from Serbia. In other words, breaking up Yugoslavia. The rest of us were in, or on the fringes of, the Communist movement which, in spite of all its flaws of leadership and organization, showed that the economic and national questions were one and that it could be solved only through a revolution whereby the people took over control of their country. I recall that in 1923 or '24, in our mid-teens, some of us had a great deal of sympathy for Stjepan Radic, who was a peasant leader but who, we thought, was fighting for national equality within the Yugoslav state. Then in 1925, when Radic made a temporary agreement with the Belgrade hegemonists, disappointment pushed youngsters like Boris Kidric and me closer to Communism. And when Vlado Kozak approached us, we were ready for him. He had been a Marxian for two or three years.

"A struggle was going on in the CPY. We young Communists were dissatisfied with the old leaders who had come into the movement in 1920. They were mostly Social Democrats and not leaders, really. To them, Party work was a petty job which paid a small salary. . . . The brutal monarcho-fascist dictatorship begun by King Alexander in January 1929 was hard on the CPY, but it caused the old 'leaders,' all the deadwood, the irrelevant elements, to slough off. The movement was left small and puny; although, actually, by 1931 or '32, as it turned out, it was stronger than ever.

"I remember in 1930, when I was nineteen, there was no Party organization. In Ljubljana the CP appeared to be shattered by the terror. In reality, quite a few of us went on working alone or in small teams of three or four or in slightly larger groups: persons who knew and trusted one another. But for a year or two these groups had no connection. Vlado Kozak, if I remember rightly, worked by himself—almost free-lance, you might say—converting young people to Marxism. Boris Kidric and I each belonged to a different group and didn't know that the other was active. What did we do? Oh, little things like distributing mimeographed leaflets and lettering slogans on walls. One night a friend (who twelve years later fell as a Partisan) and I waited hours for a chance to stencil the hammer-and-sickle on a wall of the central police station in Ljubljana.

"At first glance, activity of this sort may look silly. But it had a point. We were testing ourselves, testing one another. As I see it now, in the early 1930's the CP was entering the prelude to its heroic phase. At the same time, some of the older trade-union leaders and Social Democrats who hadn't joined in the early 1920's now came into the CPY. Franc Leskosek, for one. He joined the Party in 1926 and stuck with it through the terror. Except when we were in prison, Kidric and I kept in constant touch with Leskosek. He'd had a lot of experience. His advice was always sound, often invaluable in a death-or-life sense.

"It was no fun going through the *glavnjaca,* being pounded and having pins stuck under your fingernails, and worse. But those who endured it discovered they had something inside themselves that counted for a good deal. They were usually sentenced to a term in prison and that was as good as going through a course in human collectivity.

"When I was sentenced, they sent me to the Pozarevac prison, in northeastern Serbia. There were about forty of us 'politicals': Serbians, Montenegrins, Slovenians, Croatians, Macedonians. Our personal stories were essentially alike. We had a Party organization in prison and a small library of Marxist literature hidden under the floor boards. We took turns reading and keeping watch. Our activity went on from daybreak to nightfall. It was an intensive, rich life. You felt yourself growing. Discipline, comradeship, the sharing of responsibility—a collective life; and, personally, I discovered freedom—in jail. When we were released, we knew something, and not only in our heads—we'd had actual experience. We were free, just as we had been in prison, because we had learned how to live together and strive together for ends we collectively believed in, even if some of us would have to die to achieve them.

"Early in 1934, when the CP revival was on, we in Ljubljana established contact with the Zagreb, Belgrade, and other CP underground organizations, and we found some of our former fellow-prisoners among the new leaders. This gave us a feeling of confidence, for we knew them—we knew we could trust them utterly. It also gave us a feeling of being part of a national movement—the only movement in Yugoslavia that, small as it was in 1934 or '35, embraced the whole country. All the other parties and the religions in Old Yugoslavia were regional.

"Then one summer day a well-dressed man who gave the passwords we had agreed on with our Zagreb contacts appeared in Ljubljana. He had credentials from Zagreb and said he was Josip Broz on his way to Vienna to have a look at the CC, CPY. Some of us recalled his name from the court case in 1928. We knew he'd been in prison. I hadn't met Mosa Pijade but I knew he'd been a leader in organizing CP units in prison; and I recalled that someone had quoted a favorable comment Pijade had made about Broz. Boris and I exchanged looks which told each other we trusted him.

"What was my first impression of him in detail? In *detail?*" Kardelj smiled as if to say that when he'd agreed to talk with me he hadn't expected to be cross-examined. "I don't remember very well. So much has happened since 1934. Certainly I had no idea that our party would unfold under Broz' leadership. But I do recall, though not too clearly, that a few of us discussed Tito, or rather Broz, after he departed at the end of the first visit in the summer of 1934. We agreed that he was very direct of speech and manner. He was in his early forties, about twenty years older than we were, and looked it; but he wasn't a bit like the old-time Party 'leaders' who were bureaucrats. Broz didn't talk about himself but you felt he was experienced. He knew theory too; yet when you asked him something, he didn't answer with a quotation from Marx or Engels or Lenin. He spoke in practical commonsense terms. This is what we the Party and we the country are confronted by, he said; this is what he thought has to be done—did any of us think differently? If none of us did, he urged us to think. I remember this because Tito conducts conferences the same way now.

"Back in the summer of '34 we were getting ready to hold a conference of Slovenian Communists, and he gave us good advice. He didn't talk down to us because we were young. He asked us when we were planning to meet and said he would try to be back from Vienna in time to attend it as an observer if there was no objection. There was none; on the contrary we urged him to try to make it. Ten days later he was back and sat in as an observer. Having been to Vienna, however, and having seen the CC, CPY, of which he was a new member; and being the man he was, he became the center of the meeting. He was in favor of each nationality or region in Yugoslavia having a CP of its own which all together would make up the CPY. Thus we would lay the foundation for a new federated state. The discussion that ensued showed that a good many of us had been thinking along the same lines, especially those of us who had been in prison.

"Incidentally, the conference was held in the Bishop's Manor in Medvode [a town near Ljubljana] which was the summer residence of the Bishop of Ljubljana. Bishop Rozman wasn't there just then. His half-brother, who disliked him very much, was in charge and the gardener—one of our boys, a Communist—induced him to put the manor at our disposal. *Tovaris* Broz was highly amused. We couldn't have had a safer place for our meeting. Twenty-odd *tovarisi* came from all over Slovenia, and Bishop Rozman's relative couldn't do enough for us. He cursed the bishop, said that nothing was too good for us, and saw to it that the meals, wines and liqueurs served to us were first-rate. I forget who slept in the bishop's bed.

"Most of the *tovarisi* who attended that conference died in the War of Liberation. They were the nucleus around whom the underground Communist Party of Slovenia grew into a power. By 1940 it was a factor keenly felt in the political and cultural life of the country. In fact, by '39 or '40, the CP in Slovenia was, for all practical purposes, an above-ground if somewhat irregular organization. The populace was with us. Even the police were on our side. They received orders from Belgrade to arrest us, and they raided our rooms and hauled us off to prison; but none of this was serious. They treated us well. I remember that late in 1939 Pepca, who wasn't my wife then, and I were in a roundup of 'dangerous' Communists. She was taken to the women's section of the prison. The guards in both sections were only too glad to carry our notes back and forth. Ales Bebler was in prison at the same time. His guard wanted to do something for him. Bebler couldn't think of anything. Finally he remembered that he had learned how to play the guitar, in Spain, so he asked for a guitar. Now, guitars weren't exactly plentiful in Slovenia, as you can imagine; but this guard found one for him. The investigating officers were on our side, too, as were most of the judges. Old Yugoslavia was already dead in '39 or '40."

To return to the summer and early autumn of 1934. A half-dozen regional conferences were held in Yugoslavia. Their main purpose was to give the CPY a sound democratic base, to prepare outlines for the agenda of the national conference to be held in the winter.

Josip Broz was the only CC member in the country, the only CC member whom the new regional leaders trusted. He was the center of all this clandestine activity. It had been approved "in principle" by the CC, CPY in Vienna. But plans for the meetings which Broz submitted to it were invariably changed at the last minute to foil the political police who might have got wind of them, he feared.

The police were aware of the regional conferences and of the countrywide CP resurgence; and beginning in mid-August 1934—in compliance with King Alexander's personal orders—hundreds of Communist-supporters were rounded up and "processed" through the *glavnjace* torture chambers in the principal cities. Very few prisoners broke under the tortures; none who knew the plans for the regional conferences or that Josip Broz was ascending to the Party's national leadership.

The political police probably half-believed the people in Kumrovec that Broz had gone to Russia to join his wife and son. Gorkic may have withheld his information about Broz from his pan-Serbian superiors in Belgrade because he felt this upstart might become valuable to him later on. Perhaps he speculated on drawing Broz into his own game eventually; or, if Broz was the *fanatik* he seemed to be, to let him mature and then, by destroying him, pull a *coup* that would lay the whole CPY low again for another few years. He may have plotted such an act in connection with the national CPY conference to be held in December which he and two or three other Vienna-residing CC members planned to attend.

On October 9, 1934, King Alexander was assassinated in France . . . and the secret-police agents in the larger Yugoslav centers went berserk. They arrested thousands of oppositionists of all persuasions. Corpses were found in alleyways, in beds. Prisoners were pounded to death in the Belgrade *glavnjaca* and dumped into the Danube. Others were thrown out of upper-story windows and declared suicides.

Shortly before the assassination, the political police learned that Josip Broz was in Yugoslavia; and now, in mid-October, they did their best to capture him. He eluded them by hiding out in a shed in the woods near Aunt Ana's in Podsreda.

At the end of October, two of his Zagreb *drugovi* brought him a new wardrobe, hair dye and other makeup, a Czechoslovak passport, money, and the recommendation of the Croatian CP leaders that he make his way to the Soviet Union at once. They related that the Zagreb underground had been in touch with the CP organizations in Belgrade, Ljubljana, and Sarajevo which concurred with their estimate of the situation. The next year or two would be extremely difficult in Yugoslavia. Terror might be even worse than it had been in 1929–31. It was advisable for the leadership material which was not safe in prisons (as were Pijade, Djilas, Rankovic, Boris Ziherl, and scores of others) to leave the country. As many as possible were to go to Moscow and take advantage of their opportunity in the Soviet capital to ready themselves for the coming upheavals. Broz was to seek a post in the Comintern headquarters; one that would enable him to keep an eye on the interests of the CPY.

No one person or small group formulated this program. It was a conviction rising out of the Party and the circumstances in the country.

Broz decided to leave the country as he had the previous two times— by train, by way of Ljubljana and Jesenice, a town in the Slovenian Upland, near the Austrian border. Before proceeding to Moscow, he meant to stop awhile in Vienna; and, having a Czech passport, he bought a ticket to Prague.

In Ljubljana, after King Alexander's assassination, the CP leadership had gone *v globoko ilegalnost,* "into deep underground," to dodge the secret-police squads roving the city. Broz managed to find Kardelj, who told him that Kidric was hiding in Zagreb where he was not known to the police and their informers, and that Kidric and he and a half-dozen other Slovenian leaders were about to go abroad for a while in compliance with Party decision. Kardelj hoped to be in Moscow before long. He was waiting for his false passport to be completed. Broz told him how to reach him in Vienna.

The police network in Ljubljana tightened so much that Kardelj decided not to wait for the passport. He made his way to the densely wooded mountains along the Austrian border . . . and, walking a good part of the way, came to Vienna. There, as a member of the CC, CPY, Broz had the Comintern apparatus provide him with papers and money for the rest of his journey to Moscow, where he became first a student, then a lecturer at the Marx-Engels-Lenin Institute.

Kidric reached Vienna a few weeks later. He was arrested and jailed by the clero-fascist regime. His father, who had friends in Vienna, got him out . . . and eventually Boris went to Prague, then to Paris.

Before Broz arrived in Moscow he had two experiences worth relating. The passports and visas with which the Zagreb CP organization had provided him for his two earlier excursions to Vienna had been so expertly forged that he assumed his Czech passport and his visas for this trip were also perfect. After leaving Ljubljana, however, he took a close look at them and discovered they were very crude—no doubt because the impact of the new terror had thrown the whole underground setup in Zagreb out of kilter. What to do? Broz correctly anticipated that, owing to the tense atmosphere evoked by the regicide, the passengers' papers would be scrutinized more thoroughly than ever.

Traveling in the first-class compartment with him was a lovely young Austrian lady with an adorable baby. Whenever Broz looked at the baby, the baby gurgled and cooed and stretched out his arms to him. The woman tried to hold him still and Broz, worrying about his passport, smiled absently at the baby's wrigglings. The mother told him the baby would soon fall asleep; she hoped his momentary activity was not disturbing the gentleman. On the contrary, said Broz in fluent Viennese German, he was delighted: he loved children: he had a boy of his own. The woman and he conversed sporadically. How old was the baby? Six months. His name? Karl.

The train slowed down . . . came to a stop. At the border station a team of uniformed gendarmes, special inspectors, and the *Orjunasi* fascists came aboard.

To get her passport from her bag, which was on the luggage rack, the woman placed the baby on the seat. Little Karl squirmed; and Broz, afraid he would tumble to the floor, took him on his lap. When she found her passport, the lady wished to relieve the gentleman of her offspring, but *der Kleine* wanted to stay where he was. Both she and Broz laughed. Then, without warning, the baby sprang a leak. Broz' first concern was for his finely creased gray trousers, but he delayed reacting until the inspectors entered and their chief asked for the passports . . . whereupon he rose pathetically abashed, as though the mishap which he was trying in vain to conceal had just occurred. He handed the baby over to the mother who, beside herself with embarrassment, apologized to the gentleman, who went through a flustered effort to make light of the matter and at the same time retain his dignity. He spoke German to the lady, Czech to the Yugo-slav inspectors. They were all smiles, thinking the couple were hus-band and wife; then, seeing they were chance co-occupants of the same *coupé,* they found the scene even funnier. Now the gentleman was apologizing to them in Czech because he couldn't find his passport straightaway. The chief inspector, stamping the lady's passport, hand-ing it back to her and looking at the baby, told him to take his time. When the gentleman, excusing himself again in Czech, finally pro-duced his document, the inspector perfunctorily stamped it and re-turned it. He saluted and bowed, and the whole crew representing the law and order of the doddering Yugoslav monarchy withdrew, grin-ning at each other and chuckling, leaving the Austrian lady and the Czech gentleman with the baby, their embarrassment, and the prob-lem of a pair of wet pants. . . .

Broz remained in Vienna for six weeks. He rented a small room with a separate entrance on the fourth floor of a lower-middle-class tenement from a Jewish widow who occupied the rest of the flat with her three daughters. He never got to know his landlady well but felt she was an honest, sensible person. She appeared to be a typical Viennese Leftist intellectual. She probably knew or suspected he was a revolutionary but didn't pry into his business or—in the face of his reluctance—insist he fill out the police-registry form. This was four months' after the Dollfuss assassination, Austria was under a rigid clero-fascist regime, and Viennese hospitality to underground foreign-ers was waning. Broz realized it and came and went as inconspicuously as possible.

The daughters, seventeen, nineteen, and twenty-two, worked in stores and offices and turned their pay over to their mother, who kept house for them. Afternoons she spent a few hours in a near-by coffee-house reading the journals and conversing with friends. Walking by, Broz saw her at the same table, beside the same window.

Secretary-General Gorkic of the CPY wasn't in Vienna. Broz couldn't learn his whereabouts and he wasn't in close touch with the rest of the CC, CPY. On his last visit to Vienna Broz had met an Austrian Comintern agent who now provided Kardelj and him and a few other Yugoslavs with the papers they needed for a smooth journey to the USSR by way of Czechoslovakia and Poland.

In the afternoon of the day he was to leave on a late-evening train for Czechoslovakia, Broz sat in his room, arranging his material on Yugoslavia which he felt might interest someone in the Comintern headquarters in Moscow . . . when there was a sudden outcry, followed by a hubbub, in the corridor. Broz jammed the papers into a suitcase, put the suitcase under the bed, donned his hat and overcoat, and stepped into the hall.

One of his landlady's daughters had just attempted suicide. A neighbor had smelled gas, and, finding the door to the flat unlocked, entered and discovered the girl lying on the kitchen floor. Her outcry brought other tenants into the corridor. Someone called the police and a doctor. Before they came, Broz, who had learned how to treat such emergencies in the Austrian army, gave the girl artificial respiration and brought her to.

On the way downstairs, he met three policemen and the doctor coming up. He found his landlady at her customary table in the coffee-house and told her what had happened—not to worry, the girl was all right now—and begged her to be so good as to pack his belongings and bring them to him at the railroad station between nine and ten that evening. The woman nodded and hurried home.

She and her oldest daughter were at the station promptly at nine with his two bags. They thanked him warmly: his quick action had helped save the girl, who had lost her job, they explained, for stealing from her employer so she could buy herself some sweets and trinkets and go to the movies.

In mid-December 1934, an underground national CPY conference was held in Yugoslavia. The extreme terror kept away many of the new leaders who lived in the country, whereas the more or less pro-Gorkic delegates had no trouble traveling to and from it. Gorkic himself showed up at the meeting.

In hundreds of magazine and newspaper articles in my files and in about a dozen books on my shelves, published during 1944-51, Tito is described as "Moscow-trained," a "Comintern operator," and a "Stalin agent." According to all the testimony I could gather in Yugoslavia in 1949, none of these descriptions applied. When I tossed them at Tito, he merely smiled and shrugged. Later on, one of the officials in Tito's office who happened to overhear me said, "If *druze marsal* is 'Moscow-trained' and was a 'Comintern operator' and a 'Stalin stooge,' it may be equally fitting to say, *gospodine Adamicu,* that you're 'American-' or 'New York-trained,' or 'trained' wherever else you have lived in the United States, and a 'State Department agent' and a 'Truman stooge.' "

On his arrival in Moscow around December 20, 1934, Broz found his wife Pelagia ill. Their son Zarko was twelve years old and a joy to him. The little family moved into a room at the Hotel Lux, which had been assigned to the Comintern some years before to provide foreign Communists with living quarters and to give itself additional office space. The Brozes lived there until Josip left Russia in the summer of 1936. Though Pelagia's health improved while he was in Moscow, he didn't want her and the boy to return to Yugoslavia with him. He knew life there would be hard for some time to come. On the other hand, he was deaf to her plea that he give up the idea of a revolution in Yugoslavia and stay in Russia with her and Zarko.

In 1932 the Ossip Pyatnisky "line," as already mentioned, had been discarded. Now, late in 1934 and early in '35, the Comintern was in a between-and-betwixt state, with the Georgi Dimitrov "Popular Front line" ascending. Broz met Dimitrov briefly before the Bulgarian hero of the Leipzig Trial became the Comintern's official secretary-general. Later in 1935 and during the first half of '36 they had frequent brief talks. Their ideas jibed at many points. But the various replies I received to my questions about Dimitrov convinced me that there had been no deep friendship between him and Broz during the middle and late 1930's, and that considerable hostility had been directed toward Broz by the other Bulgarians in the Comintern offices.

Broz' written and verbal reports on the revolutionary possibilities in Yugoslavia impressed a few people at the Comintern headquarters. None of them carried any weight. But the "Yugoslav desk" was vacant, and Broz had no trouble being assigned to it. It was what he most desired. Now he could size up the CPY's position within the Comintern.

During the nineteen months he was in Moscow, Broz did not attend any Soviet or Comintern school, political or military. He was not "trained" by anybody for anything. No one of any importance within the Comintern, least of all Dimitrov or Manuilsky, took a special interest in him. Broz didn't "push" himself; on the contrary, he avoided all links with the bureaucracy entrenched in the Comintern head-quarters. He sought no favors from anybody. And, according to the information I gathered from him and those who knew him well in those days, he was not "training" himself for the top spot in the CPY. His central thought, as always, was the cause, the cause . . . the Party, the Party, the Party which needed new leadership; not merely a string of new names on the CC, but a *kolektif* that meant business. Hell was about to break loose and the CPY needed leaders who could withstand it. . . . So much misinformation has been published and broadcast on this point that I want to repeat that this was not merely Broz' own conviction. It was a conviction he shared with Kardelj, whom he saw frequently, and with thousands of Croatian, Serbian, Slovenian, Montenegrin, and Macedonian Communists. It was a party idea. Broz was not an agent of the Comintern; he was an agent *to* the Comintern of the grass-roots elements in the CPY. These elements sent Broz to the Mecca of all true Communists, to learn what he could from the Soviet setup, but primarily to find out what the CPY's membership in the Comintern meant and how it could best perform at home and strengthen itself and the International Communist Move-ment—for, the strength of one, as the city and regional CP leaders in Yugoslavia saw it, was the strength of the other.

Not given to hasty dislikes, Broz found that he detested Gorkic and most of "the Gorkic members" of the CC, CPY, some of whom lived in Moscow almost regularly during 1935–36, while others showed up every few months. He began to distrust Gorkic consciously, as did Kardelj and several other Yugoslav Communists temporarily living in the Soviet capital. But Broz wouldn't intrigue against him within the Comintern or within the "Yugoslav colony" in Moscow. That would lead to the formation of a new clique. Broz felt that no matter what specific corruption he was up to, Gorkic was not the problem. The problem was the whole setup of which "leaders" like Gorkic were a symptom. Intrigue couldn't change it; intelligence, integrity, sacrifice, work could: that is, if the Soviet Union was basically a sound revolutionary state. And of course it was. You believed that utterly. . . . *But!*

This sharp *but!* was never clearly uttered by Broz or Kardelj in Moscow during 1935–36. Nor by Rodoljub Colakovic, Broz' friend from their Maribor prison days, whom he frequently met. For had they begun to discuss it and attempted to think it through, even on the basis of the little they then knew, there was no telling where they would end, what diffusion of energy and confusion of mind would engulf them. The most they ventured to say to each other, or think to themselves, was that So-and-so, high up in the Comintern hierarchy, was not a real revolutionary: he lacked fire: he had a vested interest in his position—which was true, more or less, of all the others. But this, they felt, was superficial criticism. The Comintern's basic defect —its increasing use as a tool of Soviet foreign policy without keen regard for the revolutionary stirrings and needs of other countries— was a matter for all the member parties to correct. The job of the Yugoslav Communists was to find a way to make the other parties' leaders see this without upsetting the revolutionary applecart.

The thing to do now, for those in Moscow, was to study, study, study . . . to count on returning to Yugoslavia as soon as possible . . . to keep free and honest within themselves . . . to get ready, on the basis of Marxist-Leninist principles, for the Big Showdown . . . to create a party in Yugoslavia that would be an example to Communists elsewhere . . . to bear in mind such "self-evident" truths as Lenin wrote in *State and Revolution:* "The essence of revolution is not that a new class shall govern by means of the old governmental machinery but that it shall smash up this machinery and govern by means of a new machine. This is a fundamental idea of Marxism." And as Marx said: "The existence of the State [meaning *any* kind of State] is inseparable from the existence of slavery."

"I found it extremely satisfying to be in Moscow," Kardelj told me in June 1949. "There were wonderful libraries full of books I had long been wanting to read, and many more I had never heard of. There were reviews and newspapers from all over the world. I read and studied to my heart's and mind's content. In this aspect, I was never happier in my life. All the publicity in the Western press to the contrary notwithstanding, the Russian or the Comintern higher-ups left us Yugoslavs completely alone—too much alone, I felt at the time. No one pressured us into doing anything. Nor, as far as I know, did they pressure any of the other foreign groups. A couple of American Communists, for instance, were supposed to be studying at the Institute but they spent nearly all their time strumming an instrument called the ukulele, which I learned originated in Hawaii.

"We few Yugoslav Communists at the Marx-Engels-Lenin Institute had our own organization. We formed it on our own initiative, under a chairman we elected, in order to coordinate our study hours, lecture- and theater-going, etc., merely to make the most of our opportunities in the Soviet capital. We each received a small stipend as students occasionally do at schools almost anywhere. When I became a lecturer on the Balkan problem at the Marx-Engels-Lenin Institute (my class consisted mostly of Yugoslavs), I received a small salary as an instructor does elsewhere.

"I was in Moscow until January 1937, a few months longer than *tovaris* Broz. In those twenty-five months I seldom slept more than five hours a day. I studied day and night, literally; and the more I studied, the more I wanted to see Marxism-Leninism applied to Yugo- slavia. Often, after four hours of sleep, I woke up thinking that all of us must go home as soon as we had even one chance in a hundred of not walking into death. *Tovaris* Broz thought the same. But we were obliged to leave the timing to the *tovarisi* in Zagreb, Belgrade, and Ljubljana. *They* had sent us to study in Moscow.

"What was Broz like? Full of life, often humorous and gay; *cisto navaden in domac v razgovoru*—completely simple (ordinary) and homey (informal) in conversation. I always found it pleasant and rewarding to be with him. I couldn't keep up with world events as closely as he did; he usually had something to tell me, or show me. He knew Dimitrov, of course, and Togliatti of Italy, Pick of Germany; but only as acquaintances. No, not Stalin—not yet. He met him during the war, in 1944. Toward the end of 1935 it dawned on me that Broz had great powers of analysis and an uncanny talent for probing to the core of a problem and stating it simply. At times he made us younger men self-conscious and unhappy, although of course he didn't mean to. The self-criticism which he unwittingly induced in some of us made us realize that we were too pedantic, too apt to be impressed by our learning. He knew all the phrases and clichés which were part of the furnishings of the Comintern mind, but he seldom used them. Their overusage was one of the blights of the international working- class movement and all its branches.

"No, it still didn't occur to me that some day *tovaris* Broz would be secretary-general of the CPY. We were collective-minded and didn't think in terms of who was going to supplant whom and become the top man. However, he *was* the only CC member I trusted, which was true of the great majority of other Yugoslav Communists at home and abroad. I suppose, without knowing it, we were growing and coalescing into the *kolektif* we felt was needed, and Broz just naturally, quite apart from his being one of the oldest men among us in Moscow, became the candidate for the leadership of the Party, long before either he or any of us realized it."

Much of what Rodoljub Colakovic told me of Broz' sojourn in Moscow was a repetition of Kardelj's replies to my questions on the subject. "No, no; *drug* Broz didn't attend school in Moscow. He went to a lecture occasionally, as almost anybody did. He read stacks of Marxist-Leninist and general Soviet and European-revolutionary literature. The French Revolution, which he'd begun to delve into in Maribor, continued to interest him, especially the Commune period, I believe. The Soviet form of government absorbed him. He studied the whole system thoroughly. Engineering and industrial accomplishments like the Dnyperstroi Dam and Magnitogorsk, the steel city, excited him no end. '*There* is the answer,' he would say. '*Industrializacija!*'

"No, I didn't see Broz as our inevitable leader. Not until 1937. That question never came up in Moscow. Looking back, now that you ask me, I'd say we all assumed that whoever became our future secretary-general would depend on the membership of the CPY.

"Still looking back, trying to remember, I'm struck by Broz' foresight. He had *no* doubt that a revolution in Yugoslavia would come. It was linked to inexorable forces. It would occur in the context of the European process. In that process the existence of the Soviet Union was a prime factor. But 'of course' the revolution in Yugoslavia would also come for specific Yugoslav reasons. Our people had to get hold of their country. It was their last chance. If they muffed it, the great imperialisms, then shaping up for a showdown, would trample them down. . . . He *knew* it. Talking with him, you had a sense of trailing on a historic directive.

"But behind all this, call it historic instinct, or whatever you like, I was always conscious of a deep humility, an epic ordinariness. I liked to drop in on him. He would greet me with a smile and a funny remark, then clear a chair of books and papers for me to sit down on. 'Rocko,' he would say, 'the more I dig into the entire *problematika,* the more I realize how little we know'—meaning us Yugoslav Communists. Or, 'Rocko, I'm just beginning to see daylight.'"

Every other day or so, during most of his stay in Moscow, Broz spent several hours in the Comintern library reading the world press, Communist and non-Communist, whose contents spelled out ever more sharply the imminence of a bloody climax in world affairs. He was at his desk from six to ten hours daily studying and compiling the reports from Yugoslavia. Some of these reports, dealing with routine matters, came through the CC, CPY in Vienna; some—from the "deep underground" sources inside the country and from Boris Kidric and others who lived in Central and Western Europe—came through a special channel Broz had arranged with his Comintern *kontakt* in Vienna.

As already suggested, Broz was on smooth but not intimate terms with Dimitrov. Broz began to sense that, great figure that he was in the World Communist Movement, Dimitrov was not entirely at ease in Moscow, especially after he was made secretary-general of the Comintern. Broz saw Manuilsky three or four times; he spoke with him once. Twice he was in the same room with Stalin during Comintern conferences attended by fifty or sixty people, but he did not speak to him.

Somehow, Broz' prestige grew. Shortly after the Seventh Congress of the Comintern, at which Dimitrov was elevated to the post of secretary-general, a delegation of seven men unexpectedly arrived from Yugoslavia. They proposed that Broz be made the CPY's official delegate to the Comintern, which would mean, in effect, that he would become a candidate for membership in the Comintern's Central Committee. This move, apparently, came spontaneously—naïvely—out of the churning of ideas and impulses in the depths of the Zagreb, Belgrade, Ljubljana, and Sarajevo undergrounds. It kicked up a crisis in the CC, CPY, all of whose members were in Moscow at the time. Secretary-General Gorkic called an emergency meeting and permitted the seven delegates from Yugoslavia to attend. Broz did not enter the debate. Gorkic and another CC member (Copic) at first opposed the motion of his candidacy, then joined the majority in endorsing it. This was a maneuver. When the proposal came up before the Central Committee of the Comintern, Gorkic & Co. protested that making Broz—the newest member of the CC, CPY—a delegate to the Comintern would only further "fractionize" the Yugoslav Party. Result: Gorkic, who was both a GPU and an anti-Communist agent, was accepted for possible membership in the Comintern's inner circle, not Broz.

Broz—maintaining that Gorkic, devious as he was, was not the prob-

lem: the problem was something deeper—didn't fight this undemo-
cratic Comintern action. The seven delegates from the Yugoslav underground were furious and Broz had quite a time calming them and
impressing them with the need for patience.

Until this candidacy incident, Gorkic had no notion how strong the
Yugoslav Communist underground had become under the stimulus
of its expanding consciousness of the forces converging on it, not to
mention the impact of the Belgrade terror which he was aiding and
abetting. After each regional CP conference in the second half of 1934,
and also after the CPY's national conference at the end of that year,
so many of the young hotheads had been arrested, liquidated, sent up
with long prison terms, or impelled to flee abroad, that the secretary-
general had thought he had the situation well in hand. Now, suddenly,
he wasn't so sure—from three angles: that of the Belgrade regime
which he served first of all; that of his own strategic position in the
Comintern apparatus which he had to keep if he was to be worth his
salt to Belgrade and to the Pilsudski-Jesuit agents in the Central Committee of the Polish Party; and that of the inner group in the Comintern which was virtually a branch of the GPU, and which, he knew,
did not want a real revolutionary dénouement anywhere in Europe,
certainly not in the Balkans—if for no other reason than that it might
frighten the capitalist imperialists and hasten a new war.

Gorkic knew the underground in Yugoslavia didn't trust him and he
didn't particularly care. It obviously trusted Broz.

In the summer of 1936 the Spanish Civil War became the metacenter
of the international crisis pitching headlong toward World War II.

The legal, democratically constituted government of the Spanish
republic, which was mildly Leftist and potentially revolutionary, supported by a strong Popular Front movement, was attacked by the
armed forces of Francisco Franco, a fascist general in Morocco. He
had the open backing of Hitler, Mussolini, and the Pope, and their re-
spective international networks, which stretched to the United States;
and indirectly also of the ruling classes of Britain and France. When
President Franklin Roosevelt, in the midst of his second campaign
for the Presidency, gingerly picked up the idea of circumventing the
arms-embargo law and of shipping badly needed war supplies to the
legally established Spanish government, the Catholic hierarchy told

him—with the lips of Jim Farley, in the presence of a friend of mine, who told me—to drop it if he wanted enough Catholic votes to be re-elected. Roosevelt dropped it.

In Moscow, Secretary-General Dimitrov of the Comintern, the initiator of the Popular Front "line," with his great prestige around the world, was all for aiding the Spanish government. Maxim Litvinov, then Soviet commissar of foreign affairs, also urged resistance to the aggressors assembled behind Franco. So did a few members of the Kremlin's inner circle, while others remained in doubt and still others demurred. For six months or longer, a group within the Kremlin had been uneasy about the upsurge of the Popular Front movement in Spain, because it increased tension and instability in Europe and accelerated the approach of a new war, which the Kremlin was not ready for.

Simultaneously, over much of the globe, Leftists, progressives, and liberals, perceiving the world significance of the Spanish crisis, wanted to jump in to help stop the Hitler-Mussolini-Vatican-sponsored counter-revolution. The Kremlin couldn't openly oppose this widespread impulse, so it gave Dimitrov the nod . . . and Communists and non-Communist liberals by the hundreds, then by the thousands, began to slip into Spain to stake their lives against fascism.

At the same time, the Kremlin slipped into Spain hundreds of special agents whose assignment was to fight "Trotskyism" and other "deviationisms"—actually to create discord where it didn't exist among the Loyalist forces, so they would mince themselves up politically or psychologically if Franco didn't finish them militarily. The Stalinist logic was that if the Madrid regime won, the Spanish Popular Front revolution might continue, its international dynamics would disquiet the ruling classes in Britain, France, the Americas, everywhere, possibly to the point of leaning toward Hitler . . . and conceivably wind up in a concerted West European-Japanese attack on the Soviet Union. A Franco victory would neatly take care of all that: stop the Spanish revolution in its tracks, silence its repercussions over the earth, postpone a large-scale war. This might favor fascism or counter-revolution in some countries for the time being. In the long run, however, it would favor the Soviet Union, which was to say a Soviet-led world revolution (Soviet expansion or conquest). Therefore——

Besides, while it had obvious virtues, the Popular Front formula was too broad, too vague. It was neither fish nor fowl; it was apt to get out of hand. The Comintern-controlled CP "leaders" in the various countries might not be able to guide it in the interest of the Soviet Union. The New Deal was a kind of Popular Front; Roosevelt had invented his version of it independently of Dimitrov; and although the American CP, coached by "resident" Soviet agents, was infiltrating into the Roosevelt administration and into labor unions and supporting Roosevelt, it was a very minor factor in American life. No fool, Roosevelt was expediently using the CPUSA to postpone the demise of capitalism, to expand labor organizations, to begin a Social Democratic period, to advance general welfare through the capitalist system. . . .

After Dimitrov got the nod from Stalin *via* Molotov and Manuilsky he proceeded to give his own nods to Josip Broz and others to go ahead and help the democratic regime in Spain. Thus, it came about that in August 1936, Broz, disguised as a well-dressed Austrian tourist planning a few weeks' stay at a Dalmatian coast resort, crossed the border into Yugoslavia.

One of his first "contacts" was Franc Leskosek, the rangy, big-boned Slovenian metal-worker whose long-time reputation as a Social Democratic trade-union leader screened his membership in the CPY from the royal political police. He was forty-four in 1936, Broz' own age, and probably as open-faced, hearty and humorous, and direct of manner as I found him in 1949, when, as already mentioned, he was a member of the CPY Politburo and the federal Minister of Heavy Industry. Near the beginning of my four-hour talk with him on May 31 he said:

"My first impression of Broz? . . . Well, he showed up all of a sudden. I wasn't home. My wife came for me. She said a well-dressed man wished to see me on important Party business. We rushed home and I asked her if she thought he was genuine. 'How should I know?' she exclaimed. What was his name? He hadn't told her. He had said he had a letter from Levc. Levc? Both my wife and I had forgotten that in the Ljubljana underground during 1933–34 Kardelj was called Levc. ("Bevc" and "Kristof" and "Birc" at other times and places.)

"Shaking hands with the stranger, I was worried: he was so well-groomed. He smiled agreeably, and I tried to appear glad to see him. The letter of introduction from Kardelj, who had remained in Moscow, introduced the bearer as 'Rudi,' which I recalled was Josip Broz' alias when he stopped in Ljubljana in 1934 on his way to and from Vienna.

I didn't meet him then, but I remembered Kardelj and Kidric telling me that 'Rudi' was the Josip Broz of the 1928 court case in Zagreb, and quite a man. . . .

"So here he was, in my house. As we talked, I kept thinking, and later I remarked to my wife, and she agreed, that he had a very plain way, outspoken and to the point, like a *sloser*" (locksmith, mechanic), Leskosek smiled. "His hands were manicured, but I could tell by the shape of the fingers on his right hand that he was a metal-worker. And he had a good face, wide across the cheekbones, with darkish-green eyes which looked straight at you and could be nice and friendly and coolly thoughtful at one and the same time. . . . Well, he wanted me to take charge of recruiting Slovenians for the war in Spain. I said I would, sure. A week later he was back and gave me a big sum of money——"

"Ah, Moscow gold!" I interrupted Leskosek.

"That 'Moscow gold,'" Leskosek said cheerfully, "was from the underground treasury of the CPY—every bit of it. It was collected by our *aktivisti* all over Yugoslavia from working people and from well-to-do sympathizers in Belgrade, Zagreb and Ljubljana. Of course, members of the CC, CPY, headed by Gorkic, living abroad, received their salaries and operational funds from the Comintern treasury—you can call it Moscow gold—but those fellows had nothing to do with us in Yugoslavia; we didn't elect them: they were a hundred-percent Moscow outfit. *Tovarisi* like Broz, Kardelj, Colakovic, and others lived on their small salaries in Moscow which were paid to them on their jobs. If you ask Tito, he'll tell you that when the Comintern sent him to Yugoslavia in '36 to organize the recruiting of fighters for Spain, he was given just enough for his travel expenses to Zagreb." (On June 9, 1949, I did ask Tito, and he confirmed Leskosek's information.)

"The CPY," said Leskosek, "I mean the *real* Party in Yugoslavia, never received one kopek from Moscow aside from what I mentioned was paid to *tovarisi* like Broz and Kardelj, and my guess is the total of that didn't amount to the total CPY contributions to the Comintern, assuming that Gorkic turned them over to the Comintern treasury as he was supposed to. Nor did we get any sort of coin from any other source outside of Yugoslavia. In fact, I remember that in the middle and late 1930's, the CPY—the underground organization in Yugoslavia, primarily in the cities—gave money to our *tovarisi* in Austria, Czechoslovakia, and France who couldn't earn a living, or weren't supposed to have jobs because their duty was to study and keep us informed of what went on in the world at large. Several times our CP organization in Slovenia helped out financially CP groups in Italy and Austria. Anyhow, the money that Broz gave me to get my Slovenian recruits on their way to Spain was pure Yugoslav currency.

"How many did I send? I don't remember exactly, offhand; but quite a few. I'd say close to a hundred. Lots of them fell in Spain or died later in French internment camps and hospitals. But we Slovenians didn't have nearly as many volunteers proportionately as the Croatians, Serbians, and Montenegrins who worked under Broz' over-all direction."

Broz knew intimately several of the new CP leaders in Zagreb who took over recruiting-for-Spain in Croatia. He also knew underground leaders elsewhere who attended to the chore in Serbia, Montenegro, Bosnia-Herzegovina, Dalmatia, Macedonia. His headquarters, with Rodoljub Colakovic as one of the executive officers, was in Paris, the penultimate station on the underground railway. In Yugoslavia, Milovan Djilas, just twenty-five, recently out of prison, was an active recruiter; but he didn't meet Broz until 1937.

Within a few months the secret Aid-for-Spain organization they created sent—by various routes—close to a thousand members of the CPY and Communist Youth organizations, and other Leftists and progressives to the hard-pressed Loyalist army. Those who could traveled at their own expense and with genuine passports; the CPY took care of the others. The total expenditure ran to several hundred thousand dinars.

"Moscow gold, no doubt," I said to Djilas during my three-hour session with him in his office in the CC, CPY Building in Belgrade on June 3, 1949. He was unaware I had made the same remark to Leskosek four days before.

"No," he smiled slowly, looking at me as if to ascertain whether I was joking or not. "During the Spanish war we had all the money we needed. That struggle made a profound dent on a diversity of people. From personal observation, I can say that Belgrade reacted intensely. As I recall, considerable sums came from the clergy, members of banking and business families. But the bulk of it came from the workers. In Belgrade, Kragujevac and other places some of them gave one-third or half of their wages throughout most of the Spanish Civil War."

The war in Spain was a specially dramatic event to the Yugoslavs, for by then millions of them had perceived that the Belgrade regime, headed by Prince Paul, Milan Stojadinovic and Anton Korosec, was selling the country to Hitler.

In the summer and early autumn of '36 Yugoslavia was overrun by German tourists many of whom were top Nazi agents—an advance guard for another stab at *Drang nach Osten.*

It was a state of affairs to rouse any halfway decent person. Yet no force in Yugoslavia was organized to act against it—except the illegal CPY, which began to receive such mass support that (as I quoted Kardelj earlier in this chapter) it gradually ceased being underground. Everybody knew it was the Communists who were responsible for the "Defend Spain!" leaflets strewn on sidewalks and stairways every morning and found in one's coat pockets after having been in a coffee-house. The CPY's rallying cry, even before Broz came from Moscow, was: "Spain is the military anti-fascist front for the Yugoslavs no less than for the Spaniards." By then the Communists had strong youth organizations in all big cities, many small towns, and even some rural areas. They consisted of workers, students, peasants: sons and daughters of working-class and business families.

One of the chief leaders of the Communist Youth movement was a Belgrade University student, Ivo-Lola Ribar, whose *fanatizam* and precise organizing ability spread his influence throughout Yugoslavia. He was a close friend of Milovan Djilas and Vlado Dedijer. His father was Dr. Ivan Ribar, a liberal Serbian politician from Croatia, then (in the middle 1930's) living in retirement in Belgrade and best known for having been president of the unfortunate Constituent Assembly in 1921, soon after which the CPY was decreed illegal and driven underground. The Ribar home, located in one of the most respectable residential sections of the capital city, became a principal meeting-place for the Communist Youth leaders in Belgrade. Ivo-Lola Ribar led into the movement scores of sons and daughters of ministerial, banking, and industrial families, whose heads were the core of corruption in Yugoslav life. It was the intimate insight into that corruption and their idealistic (moral-patriotic) revulsion to it that impelled many of these young people into the CP movement. In the summer and early autumn of 1936 they, who lacked nothing materially in their home life, joined the half-starved university students and young factory workers and unemployed engineers and helped collect money "for Spain." They only had to whisper the phrase and total strangers took out their billfolds and gave.

Thinking aloud during one of my talks with him in 1949, Djilas was certain the contributors generally knew that the money went through Communist channels, and that it could easily be misused. They weren't even certain the collectors were bona fide representatives of the Aid-for-Spain cause. They donated anyhow. Their sense of identification with Loyalist Spain compelled them to. They felt they must back the anti-fascist front. "I believe," said Djilas, "that even then, in the middle 1930's, partly because of the struggle in Spain but mainly under the stimulus of the Belgrade regime's treasonable policies, the Yugoslav people's national instinct, their instinct for sheer survival, was beginning to work. It was the same instinct that rallied them against the Axis and its quislings and collaborators in 1941 when *drug* Tito issued his call for a national uprising."

As a matter of practical necessity, without meaning to set up a group whose authority would rival Gorkic's CC, CPY, all of whose members continued to live abroad in 1937 (mostly in Paris), Broz gathered as his assistants for running the underground railway to Spain a number of men who, as it turned out, became the nucleus of a new CC, CPY. These included Djilas, Ribar, Rade Koncar, Miha Marinko and Leskosek who operated in Yugoslavia; and Kardelj (who had left Moscow soon after Broz had), and Colakovic and Kidric to help him in Paris. When Aleksandar Rankovic was released from prison early in 1937, he became part of the inner group.

In Paris, from the late summer of 1936 to the mid-spring of 1937, Broz worked with Secretary-General Gorkic and the rest of the CC, CPY, in so far as they helped him run the underground railway through a half-dozen countries and over the western Mediterranean. But for the key spots he used his own assistants—in Yugoslavia and France. He was in touch with the Loyalist Spanish Legation in Paris. He worked with the Comintern agents who handled the recruits of all nationalities on their last lap to the front, although the motives of some of them had no kinship with his. The French authorities knew of this traffic, but hardly interfered with it.

This was also the policy at first of the royal regime in Belgrade which made no strenuous effort to stop the exodus of young men eager to reach the Spanish front. Although the propaganda conducted by the CP was dangerous, the riddance of some of the most energetic CP *aktivisti* compensated for it.

As Broz shuttled back and forth on his own underground railway between Yugoslavia and France, supervising the traffic, he never used the forged passports Gorkic's shadowy staff of forgers prepared. He used the documents prepared by the Aid-for-Spain organization in Yugoslavia which also supplied him with money for himself and his staff. Nor did he ever travel by the route he had told Gorkic he would take. He changed his facial makeup and wore different clothes for each trip. Every now and then he spent a few days at Aunt Ana's, to rest and think. On these occasions he scarcely spoke to her.

In Paris, his distrust of Gorkic and two or three other members of the CC, CPY heightened after he heard a few of their cynical remarks which coincided disturbingly with the gossip in Paris and elsewhere that the Comintern's Aid-for-Spain movement was a trick to liquidate the cream of the CP's outside the Soviet Union, of which the massacres and other disasters that befell foreign fighters on the various fronts in Spain were part and parcel.

Broz wanted to go to Spain to fight and also to see if the "fractionalism" weakening the Loyalists' military operations could be overcome. He had no proof and consciously rejected the gossip that the GPU was behind it. There was no denying that the Soviet government had sent fighter planes and other supplies to the Loyalist forces in considerable quantities.

The young CP leaders who remained in Yugoslavia eagerly subscribed to Broz' leadership; but when he mentioned his desire to fight in Spain, they objected. They insisted that he continue to run the underground railway, and that he must take as few chances with his life as possible. They had decided that he was to be their future leader, though no one told him so outright. Only the details of displacing the Gorkic group remained to be arranged with the Comintern. How that would be accomplished, they didn't know; all they knew was that the CPY needed Broz at the top.

Some of the young CP leaders in Yugoslavia couldn't dismiss the rumors about Spain. But most of them blamed the Trotskyites and the Spanish "anarcho-syndicalists" rather than the GPU for the apparently needless losses which international units suffered. They advised Broz to instruct the Yugoslav fighters to avoid "fractionalism," stick to the purpose which had taken them to Spain—to fight fascism and learn all they could about the civil-war type of fighting. Whatever the provocation, they must stay clear of conflicts within the Loyalist ranks. They should bear in mind, too, that the Spanish war, if they survived it, was just a beginning. The climax of the struggle against fascism was to come, for them, in Yugoslavia.

This sequence of thought—which wasn't the effusion of any single mind in Yugoslavia but the consensus of many, including Broz'—was communicated to the Yugoslavs in Spain by Broz personally on his one trip there.

Meeting Tito in 1949, I found it difficult to believe that he didn't realize that the Party leaders in Yugoslavia had chosen him to be their future chief; that he had actually been their chief in many respects since 1934.

After his first visit to Madrid, Broz might have returned to Spain in spite of his group's objection, had it not been for Gorkic, who late in 1936 or early in '37 suddenly told him that he saw no reason why he, Broz, shouldn't go fight for the Loyalists. Gorkic suggested that now that the underground railway was established someone else could run it. Who? Oh, one of the other members of the CC, CPY. This caused Broz to stick to his job.

Meanwhile, hundreds of thousands if not millions of non-Communist Yugoslavs, aware that by now between two and three thousand Yugoslavs had gone to Spain, and that many had died fighting fascism there, reached still deeper into their pockets to aid the Loyalist cause— even after it began to appear hopeless. At this point the Belgrade regime, possibly prodded by the British Legation or the German "tourists" swarming over Yugoslavia, tumbled to the probability that all this pro-Spanish sympathy might be dangerous and decided to stop the traffic of recruits and medical supplies.

In the summer of 1936 a vast CP-sponsored mass meeting held on a plateau near Cetinje, the capital of Montenegro, was attacked by a large force of gendarmes and secret-police agents, while a plane of the royal Yugoslav Army from the nearby Mostar airdrome strafed it. Seven Montenegrins were killed and twenty-five were wounded. Later similar incidents occurred elsewhere in Yugoslavia. Student riots in Belgrade and Zagreb were quelled with tear-gas bombs and gunfire.

One dark night early in 1937 several unlighted Yugoslav naval craft carrying a few hundred well-armed secret-political agents from Belgrade and Zagreb surrounded a darkened tramp steamer off the southern coast of Dalmatia, just as she weighed anchor after having taken aboard six hundred recruits for the International Brigade from Dalmatia, Bosnia, Herzegovina, and Montenegro. Of dubious registry, the ship had been chartered by Broz' representatives to deliver the men in Barcelona. In all likelihood the Gorkic crowd had learned of it and notified the royal secret police in Belgrade, perhaps through the royal Yugoslav Legation in Paris. At any rate, all six hundred, most of them members of the CPY or the Communist Youth organization, were arrested, taken ashore, and put through the terror wringer in the various *glavnjace*. It was Belgrade's biggest haul of Leftists. It rocked the whole CP underground. In Paris, Broz first learned of it from one of the "Gorkic men," who mentioned it as a rumor. Broz couldn't help but suspect that Gorkic had betrayed them. He guardedly expressed his suspicion to Kardelj, Kidric and Cokalovic who were in Paris at the time, and to Vladimir Popovic, a huge twenty-three-year-old Montenegrin, a recent Zagreb University student who was on leave from the Spanish front (in 1950 he came to Washington as ambassador). What to do? The probability was that if his suspicion of Gorkic & Co. was justified no one could ever prove that they had betrayed the ship.

Broz and his *drugovi* in Paris need not have brooded. Months before, Gorkic's Russian wife or ex-wife in Moscow had implicated him, and the GPU had probably had him under surveillance in Paris ever since. The incident in the Adriatic probably did not interest them especially. (If it had, they might have intervened.) When in the spring of 1937 Gorkic and several other members of the CC, CPY went to Moscow to attend a periodic Comintern meeting, they were seized by the GPU for political crimes against the Soviet Union . . . and that was that.

Broz had no inkling of this finale until a few weeks later. Nor, subsequently, did anyone in the leadership ever learn what the charges against them were and what the GPU, or whoever, had done with them. Gorkic & Co. were never heard of again.

After the 1936–37 winter deadlock, the Spanish Loyalist military operations began to go from bad to worse. In Paris, following the events through the press, Broz—now forty-five—was anything but happy. In the midsummer of 1937 his principal job was to hospitalize in France the many wounded Yugoslavs, Ales Bebler among them, who managed to come from Spain. But the Spanish catastrophe, important as it was, was abruptly displaced from the center of Broz' consciousness by word from Secretary-General Dimitrov of the Third International that he wished "Valter" (as he was known in the USSR) to come to Moscow immediately.

Enroute (with a false passport), Josip Broz wondered about the summons. But nothing his imagination had conjured up prepared him for the shock Dimitrov had in store for him.

The Comintern's secretary-general told Broz that he was now the sole member of the CC, CPY—the others had just vanished behind the GPU curtain; that he (Broz) wasn't under suspicion and had nothing to worry about; that the Comintern's inner group had sized up the CPY and decided to abolish it. When Broz regained his voice, he ventured to inform Dimitrov that, with all due respect to him personally and to the Comintern, the decision was a mistake and he hoped it could be rescinded. The CPY rank-and-file was *not* corrupt. On the contrary, it was brimful of integrity and heroism. There were hundreds if not thousands of young leaders and potential leaders in it. True, some of the best Yugoslav Communists had died in Spain while others lay in hospitals in France, seriously wounded and none too well cared for; but hundreds of Yugoslav survivors of the Spanish war were now experienced in a way that might be invaluable in the perilous years ahead. He looked Dimitrov squarely in the face. The CPY should *not* be disbanded, he repeated. It contained a hard core of members, most of whom had never seen Gorkic, and a multitude of followers. What would they do if the CPY were abolished by a Comintern decree? Why should *they* be penalized? With another world war imminent, Yugoslavia needed a CP. So did the Comintern. So did the Soviet Union. He begged Dimitrov to induce the Comintern leadership to reconsider its decision. He suggested that it authorize him to return to Yugoslavia and recommend to the city and regional CP organizations that they call a national conference and elect a new Central Committee.

For several days, which he spent with Pelagia and their son Zarko (now in his mid-teens and a student at a Moscow school), Broz didn't know where he stood politically. Dimitrov had eyed him strangely. All at once he realized that Dimitrov had never been quite friendly to him and he remembered the snide remarks other Bulgarians had made about the CPY in Moscow during 1935-36.

Pelagia had a job. She again appealed to him to give up the idea of a revolution in Yugoslavia, and to settle in the Soviet Union: he was risking his life—for what? He saw her point, but he did not like it, nor the way she put it. Instinct told him he was right: the young CP leaders in Yugoslavia vibrated with the Marxian vision of a better life for the working people: he must return home and do what he could to help the CPY organize its own Central Committee.

But first he must get the Comintern's consent. The state of the world being what it was, there could be no effective CPY unaffiliated with the Comintern.

To Broz' relief, Dimitrov called him for another interview and told him with a wry smile that he could go ahead. He added that the Comintern's decision to abolish the CP's in Poland and Korea, whose CC members had almost all been liquidated at the same time as the Gorkic group, remained in force. The Comintern was reversing itself only in the case of the CPY, to give Broz an opportunity to see what he could do.

Broz thanked Dimitrov for the Comintern's reversal of its decision to liquidate the CPY, adding: "I feel certain that our rank-and-file can wash the face of our Party which the Gorkic crowd fouled." Dimitrov grimaced and remarked, "Don't boast too soon."[2]

---

[2] I believe this incident not because Tito told it to me but because the atmosphere and circumstances in which details of this kind popped out of him confirmed it for me. I also accept other details in this narrative which I got from Tito and others for the same reason. Frequently I learned from Djilas, Pijade, Kidric, Josip Vidmar, etc., that Tito had casually told them the same thing years before. Besides, there was no reason, within the context of our relationship, why Tito should lie to me. Finally, I felt that certain information he and the others gave me was true because it fit the rest of the Yugoslav or the Balkan picture as I began to see it in May or June 1949.

I checked and double-checked most of the information which I thought was of some historical importance—not because I considered my source a liar (for I developed the impression that no one was consciously lying to me) but because I hoped to evoke additional data. In the instances where, say, Tito's and Pijade's or Djilas' statements diverged, as on the question of Dimitrov vis-à-vis Yugoslavia, I weighed the difference and presumed to decide who was closer to the truth. Sometimes I couldn't decide, and there was no way to get to the bottom of the point, at least not in 1949, when most of the archives of the Yugoslav Revolution were still in a rather chaotic state, or in charge of people who didn't know how to turn around within the mess; and so there were things I was told which you won't find in this book, or you will find them contradicting other statements.

Dimitrov? In Yugoslavia in 1949 I received conflicting opinions
about him. Tentatively, however, I am satisfied that in the 1930's and
at least until 1947 or '48 he was, for all practical purposes, a "Greater
Bulgaria" Communist, a Stalinist in favor of the Dardanelles going to
Russia and of a Balkan "federation" dominated by Sofia, or rather
by Moscow-via-Sofia. Tito told me that he never felt Dimitrov had
any deep affection for him. Yet, back in 1936, in connection with the
war in Spain, which was the CPY's first plunge into international
revolutionary politics, Dimitrov had agreed that Broz might return
to Yugoslavia and develop an internal CP leadership while the Gorkic
group stayed in Moscow or Paris.

It is a fact, too, that the Central Committee of the CP of Bulgaria,
headed by Dimitrov, was consistently opposed to the Tito-led Revolution in Yugoslavia in 1941–45. On the other hand, beginning late in
1945, Dimitrov either honestly favored Tito's concept of a Balkan
federation or gave a very good imitation of it. During 1946–47 he let
several leading Yugoslav Communists, including Kardelj, know that in
1937 it was he who had induced the other Comintern leaders to rescind
their decision to abolish the CPY and authorize Josip Broz to return
to Yugoslavia.

Perhaps every leader of a mass movement has a streak of naïveté—
of innocence, even—in his makeup. If he didn't, he would sink into
cynicism and inaction or into depravity. He is a special type of realist
who half-deliberately and half-unconsciously wears blinders. If he
saw the whole scene, with all its obstacles and hazards, he would never
begin.

Returning to Paris, Josip Broz told Kardelj, Kidric, Vladimir Popovic, Ales Bebler, Rodoljub Colakovic, and perhaps a half-dozen others
what had transpired in Moscow. They organized a committee to aid
the Yugoslav survivors of the Spanish Civil War straggling over the
Pyrenees into France to return home as soon as possible. By then,
along with many non-Communist analysts elsewhere, the "Broz group"
had sized up Spain as a prelude to a new world war. The Party must
be established on a sound basis under a democratically chosen leadership and Josip Broz was the obvious candidate for secretary-general
of the new Central Committee.

To compress a two-volume story into a paragraph: In 1937, under
fantastically secret circumstances, a conference of regional and city CP

leaders was successfully held in Smarna Gora, near Ljubljana. The
meeting was—"had to be"—held in the deepest underground and
fewer than a hundred delegates were there, but these were widely
representative. From several of them with whom I discussed this
conference twelve years later, I gathered that Broz' election as secretary-general had become so inevitable it simply occurred. The delegates
were cautioned to keep the new secretary-general's identity a secret.

Broz needed an intra-party name. Several thousand persons in Yugoslavia and the USSR knew or knew of him as "Valter." Several hundred had heard of him as "Rudi." "Rudi" was also Rodoljub Colakovic's underground name. Broz adopted a new name—Tito.

The most widely publicized explanation of how he came by it is that
it was given him by his fellow-members of the CPY, first in jest because, as the only CC member in the country and one of the oldest
Yugoslav Communists widely accepted as a leader, he often said when
assigning them to various tasks, *"Ti to, i ti to.*—You do this, and you do
this." In 1949 I asked Tito if the story was true. He laughed and shook
his head. "No one called me Tito before 1937. Then I needed a new
intra-party identification and 'Tito' popped into my head. I think I
heard it once or twice at home in Zagorje. It isn't a common name as
Josip is, or Juraj [George], but it's used. No, I don't believe it has any
relation to the name 'Titus' or anything Roman. It's a Zagorje name or
nickname. That's all; any other story is poppycock."

Tito established his headquarters in Zagreb. There had been such
a turnover in the political-police and gendarmerie personnel since 1928,
when he was sent to prison, that he wasn't recognized. He decided to
live openly in the guise of a well-to-do engineer named Babic and
bought a small villa with a grape arbor on the outskirts of Zagreb. He
drove an automobile. These possessions, plus his good clothes (everything paid for with Party money) and his naturally gallant yet simple
manner, gave him such an air of respectable wellbeing that no one
dreamed he could be a Red, least of all the top Red in the country.
His *legitimacije* were expertly forged, and whenever he traveled to
Belgrade, Ljubljana, Cetinje, Sarajevo, or Split, the police inspectors
on trains, who barely glanced at his papers, saluted and bowed. When
he was summoned to Moscow—to answer objections raised by the
Comintern—or traveled elsewhere abroad, his documents made him
out to be a Czech engineer named Tomanek. As "Tomanek," his facial

makeup, the color of his hair, and his gait were altered to prevent anyone recognizing him as "Babic." In Moscow he continued to be known as "Valter" and signed his reports to the Comintern with that name.

He always framed his reports as diplomatically as possible in order not to upset or offend some Comintern bureaucrat in Dimitrov's or Manuilsky's office.

Between 1937 and '41, the year when Yugoslavia was attacked and conquered by the Axis, Tito was frequently tied up in knots. One such dark mood may have occurred when Pelagia died, in 1939, just before his last prewar visit to Moscow. An earlier instance occurred in 1937, a few weeks before he was chosen secretary-general of the CPY.

Suddenly, a few days after his arrival in Zagreb from Paris, an inner necessity took Broz to his native village in Zagorje. He got off the bus a couple of stops before Kumrovec and walked the rest of the way in the dark. He didn't visit his aunts, his late father's sisters, or Pepek or Tereza Stefan, for fear word of his being back in Yugoslavia might spread. He sat long on the ground by a fence on a knoll overlooking the hamlet. He saw the dimly lit windows, heard the usual noises of the early-evening chores being done around the barns. A light breeze brought to his olfactory centers the mingled smells of cabbage "soup," cow manure and urine, and the good rain-drenched earth.

I heard of this strange visit from two sources early in 1949. When during my longest interview with Tito (on June 9) I asked him without preface what had gone through his mind as he sat by the fence that evening, he started, then thought a moment and begged me to excuse him—he didn't wish to talk about it.

Even so, I know that that night he made his way by a roundabout route to Aunt Ana's hut outside the village of Podsreda, across the River Sutla in Slovenia; and that he woke her and her husband, had a bite to eat, and told them he was back in Yugoslavia to stay—that hereafter he might come to see them off and on but they mustn't tell anyone. To Ana, as they talked in the low-ceilinged little kitchen, he mentioned that he had recently been in Moscow, found Zarko doing well in school, and told Pelagia to get a Soviet divorce if she wished. He put his hand over Ana's mouth when she started to upbraid him for being a fool and throwing his life away. He asked her to be patient: he had to do what he had to do; and in the course of doing it he might occasionally need to come to her for refuge—"they" wouldn't look for him here. An hour or so later, he pressed her to him in the dark, and left. Aunt Ana didn't recall the exact day of this visit but she remembered it was early in the fall of 1937. It was about midnight and drizzling when he left her in front of the hut.

The next evening, in Zagreb, during a rain storm, Miroslav Krleza sat in his unlighted study, watching the rain beat on the window panes and thinking, when his doorbell rang. He was vaguely annoyed and made his way through the apartment to the entrance, turning on the light in the anteroom. He admitted a man in a dripping topcoat and hat. It took him a second or two to realize that the voice which said, "Good evening, *druze,*" belonged to his old friend Josip Broz. They hadn't seen each other in a long time. Krleza had often wondered and worried about Broz. He assured him that he was alone; that, as usual, Bela, his actress wife, was at the theater, and wouldn't be back until midnight. Broz said he would like to sit with him for a while. No, he didn't want anything to eat or drink—no, not even coffee, only a glass of water. He just wanted to talk. They talked most of the night. When Bela came home, she was too weary to find out who was with Miroslav —he often had late-evening visitors—and she went to bed at the other end of the apartment.

Broz told Krleza he had been to Kumrovec the night before. He hadn't seen any of the villagers, although he wanted to. Looking at the cluster of houses from nearby, he had been assailed as never before by a sharp sense of the backwardness of the *selo,* the village, using the word generically. "We *must* do something," he said. He rose and stepped to the window against which the wind-driven rain beat. Then he sat on the divan again and told of his recent visit to Moscow.

In 1949 I often found Miroslav Krleza deeply, unshakeably taciturn and then again all at once, at two or three in the morning, he might begin to talk so interestingly or entertainingly that I would sit with him until daybreak. I imagine he was much the same in 1937. At any rate, he let Broz spill out his mind about Gorkic, the Comintern, Dimitrov, the Spanish Civil War, his observations in Paris, and what he'd read in the English press about the upheavals in China. He switched to Austria-Hungary: the botch it had been. This led him logically to the new South Slavic state squirming under the hegemony of Belgrade which until recently was dominated by Paris and London, and now in '37 by Berlin; to the terror in the *glavnjace;* to the dry-rot characterizing the Social Democratic movement, what was left of it. As he finished each subject, he returned either to the potentiality of the CPY or to the achievements of the Soviet Union.

"Magnitogorsk! You should see it. Tremendous. But Yugoslavia is rich too. We only need to create a chance for our people to industrialize. Every beginning, though, is difficult." Broz uttered this last remark in a low, held-in voice. In another connection, he said:

"Someone should explain why it was that before, during, and immediately after the war [World War I], which contributed to bringing on the October Revolution and the downfall of the Austro-Hungarian and Turkish empires, no one in our South Slavic lands ventured to analyze the European and world situation and indicate where the whole sweep of contemporary history put us. . . . We Communists can't boast of any high perspicacity, either. We have followed the Russian line too closely. Don't misunderstand me. I think the revolutionary beginnings that Lenin set underway in 1917 were a great stride. But the question is: should we imitate the Russian way? I had glimpses of the Russian Revolution, both in 1917–20 and lately. A revolution isn't like writing a book, painting a picture, or cooking a meal. It's a very complex enterprise. I suppose that, to a large extent, we'll have to follow the Russian example: we have similar problems here. But where are we going to draw the line? . . . Last night, walking from Kumrovec to my Aunt Ana's across the river and through the woods, I thought, 'The agony of it! The agony of our people! The darkness in which we are groping—the primitiveness of Kumrovec! The smells of Zagorje.' I recalled what I had read in an early issue of *Borba* back in the early 1920's: that the terror regime under [Prince-Regent, later King] Alexander was bound to collapse and that then the people would find themselves in utter chaos. I don't know who wrote it. I think it appeared in the spring of 1922 or '23." (The prediction Broz recalled was probably from an unsigned article that Krleza found in 1947 on p. 2 of the March 23, 1922, *Borba,* as he was about to jot down a description of that evening in '37. My version of the episode is partly drawn from Krleza's unpublished manuscript which he regarded as notes requiring further thought and work.)

"Now suddenly, since last night, it seems to me we *are* on the verge of that chaos. Will this insanity called the Serbo-Croatian problem be the chief phase of it? How will we emerge? . . . Again, with all that is wrong there, I turn to the Soviet Union: to Lenin and Stalin, to the

flames leaping from the ore ovens of Magnitogorsk. Twenty-seven
million tons of steel! In Russia! Think of it. I know you're critical of
the Soviet theories of art. But bear in mind Magnitogorsk and Dnyperstroi—*Industrializacija!* If that isn't the answer for us, what is?
I think, in fact I *know,* the beginning of the answer for us is in steel
and copper and coal owned by the people; in harnessing our rivers, in
electrification.

"However, if you go to Kumrovec, if you visit my Aunt Ana and
talk to her—or listen to her, rather—the whole idea strikes you as
fantastic. So how are we to take our first steps toward electrification,
industrialization, and a people's economy? Yet there must be a way. The
Russian way. We'll need a strong people's regime, a plan, the determination to carry it through. We'll have to be careful not to frighten ourselves into a stupor by the immensity of the *problematika* facing us. First
things first. We'll need cool heads, firm hands. . . . Again, I turn to the
Russian Revolution. Our Revolution will take after it. Lenin was a
great man. I saw Stalin a few times, never talked with him, but I felt
he was a strong man. His five-year plan worked. On the other hand,
the way he handled the peasant problem was dreadful. Perhaps he
couldn't help it. I don't like these purges, either. People simply disappear. Not that I'm shedding any tears over Gorkic; but was his case
looked into? . . . In some respects, our Revolution will have to be
different. . . . Say something; what do you think, *druze* Krleza?"

Krleza was deeply engaged by his visitor. Josip Broz was a striking
individual.

After a few moments of silence, during which Broz lit a new cigarette, Krleza responded. He was a writer, he said; not a political leader.
Theories on art and artistic practices *were* important to him, but he
didn't disagree with Broz; on the contrary, he was very sure kilowatts
and ingots were part of the maze of preconditions to a decent life for
the South Slavic and other Balkan peoples. It was just that his thoughts
coursed along different channels—cultural, historic, artistic, human.
One thing he had observed at home and while traveling abroad:
European literature and especially the drama were on the downgrade.
This applied to so-called "Left" writing, to certain "Left" operettas he'd
seen. Also to painting. "Leftism" had become a fad. Synthetic. Lifeless.
Perhaps its most prominent characteristic was dialectical snobbism.
He wanted none of it. It was worse than having no Left at all.

Krleza paused, then asked (with an inimitable chuckle) how could one be against dialectical snobbism without becoming snobbish one-self? How would Broz deal with *that* in the CPY?

A long pause. . . . Broz said he thought he understood Krleza's point. At the moment he was unprepared to discuss it. It might be that much of this "dialectical snobbism" was whistling in the dark or trying to cover up gaps in the knowledge of Marxian-Leninist theory.

Krleza said there was no disputing that the Belgrade regime and the whole *carsija*—ruling group (literally: the marketplace)—were center-less individuals, pompous shadows converging into a new nocturne. However, he (Krleza) knew a few members of other governments—French, Italian, etc.—who were no better than the Belgrade hegemo-nists, terrorists, and grafters. They were just a trifle more refined and played more expertly for bigger stakes. War and chaos *were* imminent. To watch contemporary Europe; to travel in Italy or France, to spend a week in Rome or Naples or Paris and observe the faces of people, trying to imagine what went on inside them; or to walk about here in Zagreb and to study the faces was enough to dismay anybody, espe-cially if one considered the inadequacies of the Left. There *were* some wonderful *drugovi* in Yugoslavia and elsewhere; but could they pull together and give tone and quality to a movement—political at heart, yes, or, rather, political and economic in its immediate drives; but something more, much more, if it were to cope with the chaos ahead. . . . Ingots and kilowatts *were* among the first steps; but what else?

Broz said that Marxism-Leninism was inclusive; it took in nearly all facets of the human makeup and its requirements. He spoke again of Magnitogorsk, of the great number of Soviet planes he'd seen over Moscow. Yet Krleza was right, he assented; the Left in Europe was full of serious defects. It permitted fascism to supplant the democratic government in Spain. It lacked morality. It was too much a matter of words, of quotations, of sloganeering. Too many Leftists dropped by the wayside soon after they set forth. . . . However, he (Broz) wished to defend the Left in Yugoslavia. He had great faith in these young Communists who had been in prison or in Spain. As for the USSR, lots of the unfavorable criticism about her was true. Yet she provided the world with two beacon lights: Lenin's revolutionary principles and Stalin's five-year plans. These lights had their dark sides, but it was a mistake to over-emphasize them. The lights turned, and there was the great glow of the classical directives of historic materialism.

Krleza didn't disagree. Stimulated by his visitor, he spoke of his recent delvings into South Slavic history. In the libraries in Rome and elsewhere in Italy, he had been startled by such facts, for instance, as that Michelangelo's teacher was a Slav from Dalmatia; that Slavic artisans and sculptors from Dalmatia built palaces in Italy—almost entire cities—which were still the pride of Italian culture. Why hadn't these artists and craftsmen worked at home? Why had Nikola Tesla gone to America? The answer was the whole history of the Balkans. During the last two or three thousand years there were rare pauses between wars, invasions, conquests, massacres, and other forms of havoc and dislocation which ripped the seams of normal life; and men emigrated where they could work in relative peace. But here was a wonderfully redeeming phenomenon, as Krleza saw it. Whenever the Macedonians, Serbians, Croatians, Bosnians, Dalmatians, or Slovenians had a decade of peace, or a semblance of it, they made the most of it. They produced artists, mathematicians, astronomers, physicists, and other scientists of high talent, and saints galore. And in spite of everything, they survived.

Krleza had been mulling over this when Broz rang his doorbell. . . . *Survival*. Why? . . .

In any case, these peoples now called Yugoslavia had passed through an endless series of nocturnes and given off flashes of genius between the nocturnes. Krleza's theme was that a way must be found, at whatever cost except the human essence, to put an end to havoc—wars, invasions, massacres—so that people could go about their business.

Broz listened attentively. He hoped to have many more opportunities to listen to Krleza, he said. These matters *were* important. But, as he had remarked a few hours ago, first things came first. Nocturne? That was an artistic word. A new war was in the offing. Call it a nocturne or imperialism, it was bound to engulf Yugoslavia. . . . And take Kumrovec: what could it do if a war came? Nothing except put up with it. That was intolerable. The *selo*—the villages generally—must be prepared to join the proletarians' rising against fascism, join the Communist-led working-class and intelligentsia in the cities and towns. Or did Yugoslavia's future, and the world's, depend on Magnitogorsk and Dnyperstroi entirely? He hoped not——

Krleza insisted on making coffee. They drank it in silence. Shortly before dawn Broz put on his wet topcoat and hat, and slipped out of Krleza's apartment. . . . Two years later Krleza learned that the new

CPY secretary-general, whose intra-party name was Tito, was Josip Broz, the man from Kumrovec.

Meanwhile, all of Yugoslavia was in a ferment. In the summer of 1938 tens of thousand of young Yugoslavs, most of them under direct or indirect CPY leadership, were ready to fight Hitler in Czechoslovakia. The CPY informed the Czechoslovak Legation in Belgrade about this. Hundreds of young people besieged the Legation daily, begging for visas. Thousands were in Prague when Eduard Benes knuckled under to the Munich pact. Most of them had come without passports and visas.

As Kardelj related, by 1939 or '40 the populace—even gendarmes, police investigators, prison guards, judges—were on the side of the Communists: not only in Ljubljana but in Zagreb, Belgrade, Sarajevo, Split, Skoplje, Kragujevac. *And the village was stirring——*

One evening in February 1949 I met a peasant Communist. I asked him why and when he had become a Party member.

"It all began with a couple of students from Ljubljana, Boris Kidric and Boris Ziherl. Both were Borises. I'm not sure which one came by my place first. I remember I was working in the field and Boris handed me a leaflet. That was in 1932 or '33. Then the other Boris came by and handed me another. I read everything they gave me. I didn't dream it had anything to do with revolution and communism. It just made sense. I could prove it from my own experience. Hard as my wife and I worked, things-as-they-were didn't add up for us. The first thing I knew I was arrested. My wife wept: that was the worst of it. The political agents beat me. Where did I get the literature? On the foot-bridge which spanned the creek, I said. Maybe they knew I was lying. They beat me some more. Maybe they liked to. I stuck by my story, and ended in the Maribor penitentiary. Two years. . . . Yes, *tovaris* Broz was there; but I didn't get to know him especially well. There were too many of us. He was just one of us 'politicals.' In prison I joined a study group and discovered how important printed matter can be. I came out a convinced Communist. My fellow-villagers looked at me askance. I was an ex-convict. But I didn't care. Soon they were willing to listen to me. I procured every item of Marxian literature I could. Some of the other peasants asked their sons attending school in the city to get them books and brochures. They passed them around. In '36 a few of us formed a reading club and made contact with the workers at a near-by sawmill. They had a Communist cell and loaned us their books. Sunday afternoons some of them came to our village and we talked. By '39 or '40 nearly everybody in the vicinity was either Communist or pro-Communist in varying degrees. I was admitted to the Party in '37; three years later over a dozen peasants signed up. A few got off on the wrong foot. They thought that as Communists they had to prove there was no God, which only disturbed the priest and some of the older women. We straightened that out; we concentrated on economics and politics.

"The most effective propaganda was information about the Soviet Union. Even well-to-do peasants not only revered Lenin for his anti-imperialism, they wanted to hear all about Stalin, particularly about his ideas on the nationality question. Naturally, the *aktivisti* preached about the USSR and Lenin and Stalin. They were politicians; their main directive was to prepare the peasants so they would join in the impending upheaval."

In short, the eagle diving from on high to clamp his beak around the exposed root was not so much Tito as the Party—was not so much the Party as large sections of the population.

Meantime, as already mentioned, Tito, alias Babic, alias Tomanek, alias Valter, had to make a number of trips to Moscow to mollify the Comintern.

Early in 1939 he was summoned there. When he didn't return to Yugoslavia two weeks after he had said he would, some of his principal lieutenants—Kardelj, Djilas, Rankovic, Kidric—began to suspect the worst: that he had disappeared behind the GPU curtain. But, while he was in Moscow, a sixth sense had told Tito that he might be in danger. It was just before the Stalin-Hitler pact; he had been asked some odd questions—whether he considered himself a disciplined Communist, for instance. He said he did and was one.

He had two sets of identification papers with him, a wad of CPY money, and a couple of valuable diamond rings which had been part of his paraphernalia—a sort of backlog—when he ran the underground railroad to Spain. Instead of returning to Yugoslavia by way of Poland, Czechoslovakia, and Austria under the *nom de guerre* Tomanek, he became Spiridom Mekas, a Turkish citizen of Greek descent, and took the shortest route to Istanbul. If his Turkish and Greek speech was a bit lame, it was because he had spent most of his life in Canada and the United States. In Istanbul he had no trouble convincing everyone concerned that he had a great deal of money in Paris. Mr. Mekas reserved a first-class cabin on the New York-bound motorship *Conte di Savoia,* made a sizable deposit, and told the Italian Line agent he would pay the rest of the fare in Paris. He traveled first-class on the Orient Express *via* Sofia and Belgrade. The train stopped briefly in Zagreb, Mr. Mekas took a stroll on the *peron* to smoke a cigarette, then scooted —or, rather, turned into Engineer Babic—who took a cab to his suburban villa with the grape arbor.

A week later the mysterious disappearance of Spiridom Mekas was news in the European press. The *Conte di Savoia* had waited six hours at Gibraltar for him to turn up. The Italian Line agent in Constantinople swore he knew Mr. Mekas, a man of wealth, personally; he couldn't get over his disappearance. Foul play, perhaps. Police in two or three countries were investigating. The luggage contained only some clothing and toilet articles.

While this story, along with the report of the Hitler-Stalin pact, was agitating Europe's newspaper readers, Tito, Kardelj, and several other members of the Politburo of the CC, CPY held a conference in Aunt Ana's hut near Podsreda. By then old Ana was used to having them show up almost any time of day or night.

She began to like Herta, a girl from Maribor, who was Joza's new wife. He had met her in Zagreb when she delivered an underground message to him. By 1940 Ana had decided that Herta wasn't just Joza's wife but a member of his staff. Herta and Ana talked. A war was coming; Hitler would take Styria and much of the rest of Yugoslavia, leaving some of it to Mussolini; then there would be hell to pay.

One day Joza said to her, "When war comes, Aunt Ana, hide in the woods." He said they would resist the conqueror and even pull off a revolution, and Ana shot back,

"How—with your bare hands?"

Joza replied, "Not quite; we'll have arms. But if necessary, with our bare hands."

"You're crazy," said Ana.

"Then we're crazy. But when war comes you go to the woods or lie low."

The Stalin-Hitler pact was a blow to the CPY leaders. But they rationalized it. It was a tactic. Nazi Germany and the USSR were bound to clash. And Yugoslavia and all the Balkans would be drawn into the war. Meanwhile, the thing to do was to be disciplined Communists.

The late 1939 issues of *Proleter* were full of tortuous verbiage on the subject.

In the autumn of 1937 the CP cells in the various prisons in Yugoslavia were informed that the CPY had a new Central Committee and secretary-general.

In '38 Mosa Pijade, serving the thirteenth year of his prison term, needed an operation and was sent under guard to a Belgrade hospital. Afterward he discovered that at least half the hospital staff (apart from the Catholic nuns) was Communist. The doctor in charge of his ward was a Party member, the head of the cell in the hospital, in fact. Mosa Pijade wrote a letter to the CC, CPY, reporting on the "politicals'" activities in his prison, and asked the doctor to have it delivered. A few days later he received a reply. It was signed "For the CC, CPY: *Tito,* Secretary-General." It began: "My dear *drug* Mosa" and thanked him for the report. There was a postscript expressing hope for his speedy recovery and looking forward to seeing him the following year when he was due for release. The postscript was signed "T." So—Tito knew the length of his prison term, Pijade noted. Interesting.

When Pijade was released late in 1939 and feeling rather lost in the Belgrade underground, which by now appeared to be practically aboveground, he eagerly accepted a young CP member's invitation to a party at his home. The young fellow was Ivo-Lola Ribar. Pijade knew his father, Dr. Ivan Ribar.

There were about eighteen people in the large living-room—young folk, mostly, in their twenties and early thirties: all Communist or pro-Communists, it seemed. They hailed Pijade as their *drug* who had been absent too long. Pijade pressed old Dr. Ribar's hand and noticed his enigmatic smile. He was introduced around. He knew only two or three of the young men. They were his one-time fellow-convicts. One was Aleksandar Rankovic, the other was Milovan Djilas. There was a huge youth, Vlado Dedijer, nicknamed "Gangster" because he had lived in the United States. His job in the Party was to procure printing presses and ink and paper. There was a girl named Olga Nincic, the daughter of Momcilo Nincic, the erstwhile foreign minister.

Over in a corner was a debonair, well-dressed man who looked dimly familiar. Ivo-Lola Ribar had introduced him as Engineer Babic, and Babic had greeted Pijade familiarly as Mosa. After a while Babic advanced, all smiles, and drew Pijade aside.

"Don't you remember me, Mosa?" he asked.

"No," Pijade said; "but ever since I came into the room I've been trying to place you."

"I'm Josip Broz"—in a low voice, with a finger over his lips.

"Da, da!" whispered Pijade.

"And I'm Tito"—in a voice lower still.

"Oh!" whispered Pijade. *"Kolosalno!"*

The next day Tito and Pijade had a long talk.

In June 1949 Boris Ziherl, whom I saw off and on in Belgrade and Ljubljana, told me that at a CPY conference held in June 1940—after a long discussion of the existing situation and impending events, mainly the end of the Stalin-Hitler pact and the Soviet Union's entrance into the war against the Axis—Tito rose and said:

"Well, *drugovi,* this about exhausts the agenda. This is our last 'illegal' Party conference. The next Party conference will be held openly—after our victorious Revolution."

BOOK TWO

CHAPTER FOUR: *The climax: "Death to Fascism! Liberty to the people!"*

LATE in June 1949 I went to Paris for two weeks, mainly to find out if it was true that printing costs in France were considerably lower than in the United States. The anti-Red hysteria in American newspapers and news-magazines was so apparent that I continued to feel that any substantial publishing house in the United States would hesitate to accept a book having the views I had

on Yugoslavia and Tito and the rest of the world, and that I might
have to publish and distribute it myself—if I wrote it.

Returning to Yugoslavia in mid-July to finish gathering the material
I might need, I flew from Ljubljana to Belgrade and thence to Skoplje,
the capital of Macedonia, where an almost pre-Homeric primitiveness
was reaching for almost non-existent bootstraps in its determination to
lift itself to modern industrialism. Everywhere the name "Tito" was
the symbol of the difficult present promising a better future. It was not
merely popular here, it was a passion.

With Dimce Koco, a young teacher at the University of Skoplje, I
trudged up steep mountainsides to crumbling monasteries that had
lately been declared national monuments. The Communist regime was
reinforcing the ancient walls to preserve the pre-Renaissance frescoes
inside. I had seen photographs of them at Krleza's. Now, half-listening
to the learned talk bubbling out of Koco, I looked long at the originals.
Some of them were almost Picasso-like modernism—except that this
medieval art, dating back to the ninth, tenth, and eleventh centuries,
had an emotional quality—a tense, yet matter-of-fact expressiveness
that the modernistic painting I knew in America and had glanced
hurriedly at in Paris lacked. It had a fervent significance; and it occurred to me that the CPY was at once closely related and incidental to
them culturally. In 1946 or early in '47 I had come on F. C. S. Northrop's mind-opening book *The Meeting of East and West,* and I kept
thinking of "The Madonna of Guadalupe" around which he had
organized the meaning of much of the culture of Mexico; also of José
Orozco's frescoes at Dartmouth College and Grant Wood's "Daughters
of the Revolution." According to Northrop, art in the United States
was "an afterthought." In his chapter on American culture, he dealt
with the all-pervasive influence on "Western" culture of John Locke,
the eighteenth-century English philosopher who postulated that a
man's soul is "a blank tablet." Now, I thought, I understood those three
faces in "Daughters."

On August first I returned to Skoplje, to hear Tito speak the next
day. A crowd estimated at 300,000—nearly half the population of Yugoslav Macedonia—jammed the great plaza in front of the Government
House, the side streets, and the banks of the River Vardar to listen to
him over the amplifiers. He warned the Soviet Union and her Cominform satellites—Bulgaria, Albania, Rumania, Hungary—to think twice
before they attacked Yugoslavia. The Yugoslav peoples, he said, would

fight them to preserve their independence, just as they had fought the Axis; and if necessary, would die fighting. It was harvest time, and I was told the CP *aktivisti* had had a job inducing enough people to stay home to take care of the crops whose harvesting couldn't be postponed. Everybody wanted to come and hear Tito.

It was hot as blazes. I was on the platform, a few feet behind Tito. At my side were Dr. Bozidar Lavric and another surgeon to tend to Tito if someone took a shot at him. But apparently he gave no thought to the possibility of being assassinated. He spoke impromptu, fluently, fervently, without notes, wiping the sweat off his face every two or three minutes. He summarized the history of the South Slavic nations to show that while they desired peace above all else they had no alternative but to fight *anyone* who menaced their hard-won opportunity to build states of their own around their native cultures—states grouped in a federation with a central government dedicated to finding ways and means to implement mutually their social and economic well-being. It was a good speech, one of the best I ever heard, full of meaning which I felt should electrify the world but I knew wouldn't—partly because Grant Wood and F. C. S. Northrop were right.

Later that day I had what I thought would be my last talk with Tito before I left Yugoslavia to return to the United States. I told him I didn't know whether I would write a book or not: the material was overwhelming. I would have to pit it against the mass of superficial writing about Yugoslavia in the "West," against the whole "anti-Communist" *un*sanity (and against things I couldn't begin to discuss with him because he wasn't familiar with Northrop's book and Grant Wood's picture). I knew at once too much and not enough. I was sorry I had put everybody to so much trouble helping me get information. I shouldn't have returned to Yugoslavia from Italy in April. Tito grimaced eloquently. Then he smiled, turned serious and said he thought he understood my problem. The previous night, in the train coming from Belgrade, he hadn't been able to sleep. He had outlined his speech in his mind, going over what had happened in these regions through the centuries, and why. It awed him, he said. He wouldn't blame me if I abandoned the book; as he remembered, the idea had been tentative anyhow. . . . Then he seemed to want to talk of commonplace matters. How was I? Did the heat bother me? What did I think of Macedonia, of the crowd today? Milovan Djilas, who was with Tito, remarked he had just heard a Macedonian *drug* say that about eight hundred people had fainted from the heat during the speech, an old man had died, and six women had given birth. I said that either "awesome" or "elemental" might be the appropriate adjective for the occasion. Looking at the mass of people—Slavs, Albanians, Turks, most of them in picturesque homespun costumes—I had seen it move during the speech like the waves of a sea, like the wind-stirred wheat I had once stopped to watch while driving across the Kansas prairie. Whether this was good or not, I said, I didn't know; I didn't know, either, how good it was for a man, any man, to have 300,000 people come to hear him speak. Tito grimaced again, then smiled and nodded. I said that the night before I had walked about Skoplje (normally a city of sixty thousand) and had gotten the impression that a couple of hundred thousand men and women were sleeping on the sidewalks, along the walls, on stones, in the dust, in the grass, all over; some of them upright in sitting position because there was no room to lie down. I had also been impressed by the multitude's orderliness and self-discipline, and how natural and altogether decent it had seemed for thousands of them to urinate and defecate in the River Vardar, thus avoiding what might have been a serious sanitation problem. Someone in the room anxiously inquired if I was going to write about that. I asked why not. A delegation of Albanians came in at that moment to talk with Tito, and I never heard his answer.

I stayed in Macedonia for about two weeks after Tito had left. Dimce Koco and Pero Korobar, a young official in the Macedonian information bureau, took me to the ancient city of Ohrid, by the lake of the same name (with Greece and Albania visible in the distance), one of the places where the Communist regime was uncovering frescoes. They were under layers of whitewash and mortar in the Orthodox cathedral that had been a Moslem mosque for half a millennium. From Ohrid we went to the immense half-completed Mavravo hydroelectric project. It was in charge of an engineer who before the war had never had a chance to tackle anything bigger than a road- or bridge-repair job. From there we drove up a new mountain road to Lazaro Pole, a very successful farm cooperative maintaining fifteen thousand sheep, where the air was so cool and good and the people were so direct and fervently friendly, yet restrained, that I wished I could stay there for a few weeks or months.

We stopped briefly in Titov Veles, Bitolj, Resen—communities marked by a mixture of primitiveness and crude beginnings of modern progress. We crawled over the ruins of the castle of Royal-Prince Marko, the tragic hero of the Saga of Kossovo.

On the Skoplje-Ljubljana plane—on August 18—the discomfort of having so much of the Yugoslav Story in my consciousness amounted almost to physical pain. I couldn't possibly contain more and hope eventually to digest and fit it into the context of the world problem and turn it into publishable form. I had heard and seen and read so much that was "darkly wise and rudely great"—a phrase from a poem by Alexander Pope that kept occurring to me. Somewhere over Croatia, where I could see the ribbon-like Belgrade-Zagreb turnpike, I decided to leave Yugoslavia immediately without saying good-by to anyone except my mother.

Directly from the Ljubljana airport (a pasture from which cows were barred) I drove to my native village, stayed less than an hour and told Mother that I was leaving—I didn't know just when: possibly to-night, perhaps tomorrow night, depending on when I got a reservation on the Simplon Orient Express. She shouldn't worry about me; I had to return to the United States to see if I could find a publisher for my book.

In Ljubljana again, I opened some of my mail which had piled up while I was in Macedonia, and found a letter from a group of American liberals or progressives who were traveling in Europe to see whether there was going to be peace or war. Professor Kirtley Mather of Harvard and Professor Henry Pratt Fairchild of New York University were in the group. The letter expressed the hope that I would still be in Yugoslavia when they arrived and would serve as their interpreter if they could arrange to have an interview with Tito.

They turned up in Ljubljana on August 24. They had an appointment with Tito on Brioni Island that evening. A snag in transportation delayed us and we didn't get there until late. Tito had waited until eleven o'clock and then decided to see us the next day.

He spent five hours answering my fellow-Americans' questions. He understood most of them as they were asked but replied in Serbo-Croatian, which I translated. During lunch a telephone message came from Ljubljana that I was expected by six. I didn't understand why; the Simplon Orient on which I had a reservation didn't leave until ten. Tito's adjutant couldn't explain it. I had had enough of the interview anyhow, and was glad to leave Brioni. A car brought me to Ljubljana about six-fifteen and, dusty and tired, I found myself in a big room full of people laughing at my surprise. It was a farewell party someone had thought up that forenoon in revenge for my attempt to leave the country without saying good-by. I was allowed to wash up before we sat down to dinner. The meal over, Prime Minister Miha Marinko of the People's Republic of Slovenia made a brief talk, funny and serious, typically Slovenian. President Josip Vidmar spoke next, at his witty best. I glanced at my watch; it was past nine and I said I had to catch my train. Everybody laughed again. My baggage, they explained, was in a car below, all set to drive me to Sezana, the last station in Yugoslavia, where the train stood until 4 A.M. before crossing into the Free Territory of Trieste. I had nothing to worry about; I would be in Genoa, Italy, the next afternoon.

The party lasted until 2 A.M. Nearly everybody present had been at one or another of the discussions I had taken part in early in 1949. At that time they had been, if not anti-American, at least very skeptical of America's role in world affairs. Four other men made speeches. Not a word was said about what weighed on me most: my unwritten book. I suppose no one thought of it. Two speakers thanked me for the light I had thrown on America for them, and I squirmed, afraid I might have misled them. I felt especially shaky in view of the fact that even such well-meaning and intelligent Americans as the group I had accompanied to Brioni had shown scant ability to understand Yugoslavia and Tito. They were interested in peace, as I was; and peace *was* a precondition to the future, but there were preconditions to peace. The problem was something else than peace-or-war. . . .

Returning from Brioni, I had wondered if anyone (except a poet or artist or philosopher: a Byron, a Goethe, a Beethoven, a Northrop) could apprehend a culture other than his own—even with the best will —during a period of transition when the culture was both in flux and in conflict inside itself: like America's, like Yugoslavia's. There was great confusion in the world, a rudderlessness, a desperate reaching for straws of certainties. The straws themselves were negatives but so emphatically proclaimed they seemed the opposite. Yesterday I had received a letter from a friend teaching at an Ohio college.

   . . . *The disheartening element* [he wrote] *in the intellectual world hereabouts in this year of 1949 is the increasing tendency to take the word* liberal *to mean "anti-Communist," and in a very unprecise way. . . . This is an impression I can't shake off. And I fear it's a condition which isn't restricted to this college, or this section of Ohio which I know rather well, but that it is a general*

American condition. . . . I suppose it was natural enough for people of a certain disposition, with some reputation, and a stake in academic life to wish to continue to call themselves liberal and to change the meaning of the word rather than to give it up as a label for themselves. And they are the inevitable result of force applied to mush. . . . But am I any better than they are? Am I not one of them? I have no use for the pro-Sovieteers who have vanished under the impact of hysteria; but what do I believe in? Where is America? What are we doing in the world? I don't know. So I keep silent and merely teach sociology and as innocuously as possible. . . .

Not having succeeded in getting away in time to catch the train in Ljubljana, I realized that I would have to speak too. About midnight I found myself on my feet and, although I intended to say only a few words, I rambled on until two o'clock, when Miha Marinko's secretary came up behind me and whispered that I'd better be on my way if I wished to be in Sezana by four. I don't know if I would have remembered what I said; but after I had been talking five minutes or so, someone took down my remarks in shorthand and a month later sent them to me, neatly transcribed:

". . . When I first arrived in Yugoslavia in January 1949—it seems like only a moment but also like ages ago—an officer in Tito's new army stationed in Belgrade, a veteran of your revolutionary-Liberation *borba,* a Slovenian (most of you know him), said that he himself couldn't tell me about the war, about your Revolution, but that someday, perhaps, a Tolstoy would appear among you and dash off a Yugoslav *War and Peace.* Seven months later I want to say that it will take more than a Tolstoy to write your story. First of all, perhaps, there's need of a five- to ten-volume documentary history. I say 'perhaps' because, unlike some of you who call yourself Communists, I'm not sure the world, which includes you, has much of a future. I think the deepening shadows around the globe are converging into a dimout which may last for centuries and which will preclude any intelligent interest in your Revolution.

"I hope I'm wrong but I feel it is necessary to express my pessimism because all of you seem so gay and confident—not just because at long last you're going to be rid of me but because some of you are suddenly hopeful of America and you have said that your hopes are partly based on my remarks last winter. What really helps you to see America in a better light, I believe, is that Washington has granted you a small loan and the State Department will let you buy an American steel mill. I think that is an illusion. How could a steel mill be an illusion? I won't answer my own question. I can't without running into some of your most insistently held beliefs; and I don't want to do that—it would lead to a superficial argument, which I might have found enlightening seven months ago, but wouldn't now, I'll tell you why later, if I don't forget. . . .

"I suppose nothing I told you last winter was untrue. America *is* a great place from many angles whether you're in the right mood; or if you're hostile to her; even from the communist angle—we have bigger and better communistic institutions than you have: the post office, the public school, library, and water systems, to name the most obvious. But I didn't, I couldn't, begin to tell you the whole truth about America; and I can't tell it to you tonight. I don't know it, nor does anybody else. All I'm fairly sure of is that America is a 'giant' and, like the Russian 'giant,' dangerous to herself and the world right now, because she is a 'giant'—wound up with a wonderful technology which operates under a system and on a scale too big for anyone to understand thoroughly and lead wisely. I'm not a student of Marx, and it can be argued that I have no business saying what I'm going to say; but I think that Marxism doesn't cover America, at least not all the way. Marx in the British Museum in the 1870's couldn't possibly imagine America in the middle of the twentieth century.

"As of 1949, from the little I know of the situation, I'd say that a war between America and Russia may not be inevitable but it is more than likely. Whose 'fault' it will be is not even an academic question. A practical question to ask here tonight may be: Where will you be then? And I'd like to ask again the question I asked seven months ago: What is your outlook? I still haven't received an answer. I think you have one (as Nehru has, perhaps) which reaches even beyond the next war if it comes, even if it destroys you; but you're not stating it so the world can hear and at least pause to wonder what you mean . . . The next war? What can we do to prevent it? Can the Cominform schism be used to help prevent it? How? . . . If World War III begins, America is apt to 'win' it. But what will America do with the 'victory'? This question is up your alley as well as mine. I don't know the answer.

"But let's drop all that; let's say I'm wrong; let's say there won't be a new world war and the world does have a future, that a Yugoslav Tolstoy-plus is possible: and that you should prepare a five- to ten-

volume documentary history for him to use as a basis for his novel.
Most of you are writers, poets, and editors, and perhaps you're able to
guess what I'm trying to say. I spent the last few months tracking
down your story, and I have tracked it down but I haven't whipped it
into a neat form. I made you talk, I made you tell me about your
borba. I badgered Belgrade into giving me information. I took about
thirty hours of Tito's time as if he had nothing better to do than talk
to me. I've been all over Yugoslavia and I've talked to hundreds of
people. Some may have fibbed; the rest told me what happened as best
they could, I'm sure. But I still don't know if I can write an honest
book. And, if I can, whether I should. Who will believe me? Should I
write a superficial, believable book? Should I simply tell what I believed on top of my mind to be true seven, six, five months ago?
Should I tell the story of Tito's life and let it speak for itself? But,
then, who—what—is Tito apart from the rest of the story? . . .

"I think your *borba*—the period from 1941 to '45—is the climax of
your story. I can't swear that your wartime statistics are accurate, but
I've met very few people who haven't lost at least one relative in the
war. Two of you in this room, as I remember, told me that you are the
sole survivors of your families which before the war numbered seven
and nine, respectively. So I don't doubt that Yugoslavia lost about
1,706,000 people in the war, and that about two million others were
wounded or otherwise injured; that, in other words, your total casualties were over twenty-three percent of your total population. But what
of it? Who—in America, for instance—will believe me? Or care? And
why should they? Do any of you care about the plight of our Navajo
Indians in the Southwest? Or even know about it? Even superficially,
the way I thought I was beginning to know or 'understand' New Yugoslavia six months ago on the basis of first impressions which were
factual enough but not deeply true? The riddle is how to tell you so
you will care, see it as an all-human problem, and not just blame it on
an abstract bugaboo like 'Wall Street.'

". . . I pause every once in a while, and you may be thinking I'm
tired, which I am; but that isn't my main trouble. Things occur to me
which I want to say; then I change my mind, first because my Slovenian vocabulary is too limited, then because it would take days of
conversation to extract them from the lump in my mind.

"To get back to something relatively simple—to the American who
has no more incentive driving him to curiosity about Yugoslavia than

the average Yugoslav has to learn about the Navajos. How can I make the Yugoslav Story mean something to him? By making him feel that it is to his interest to know more about your country? For me to say that Yugoslavia's 3,700,000 casualties are the same as if America had had somewhere between thirty and forty million casualties in three and a half years isn't a fact likely to stir him in itself.

"I was in Lika, Krajina, Bosnia, around Kocevje, where I saw the ruins of entire villages and towns. I found whole counties virtually depopulated. I was told that four thousand villages and towns, or about 57,000 buildings, were totally or partially destroyed; that you lost sixty percent of your livestock and about half of your fruit trees, and so on. Will it mean anything if I tell Americans that that is relatively equivalent to several states of the Union being almost completely wiped out? I doubt it. I doubt if any American can conceive of such a thing as even a remote possibility, at least not until he learns that the Russians have a lot of atomic bombs too; and possibly not even then.

"I was in Kragujevac [Serbia] where the Germans had rounded up about fourteen thousand men and boys, and mowed them down with machine guns. This story was published in America in '43. I told it, myself, as a bare fact, as a piece of information. Who cared? Maybe some Americans were shocked; but if so, mostly in terms of what beasts the Germans, then our common enemies, were—or of how fortunate it was that America was not the Balkans where Germans could move in and do a thing like that. . . . Should I tell the story again? Why? How? Who'll give a damn? Yet Kragujevac is an important reason why New Yugoslavia is the way she is—unwilling to serve as a football for the 'giants' to kick around.

"Should I exploit your quarrel with Stalin? If I do, won't I be dishonest by omission if I don't also emphasize that your bringing down those two planes in 1946 was part of the same psychology? That you don't want to be pushed around by anybody? That you've had a revolution for that reason. . . . If I tell that, where am I? Who'll read my book? For the two planes and the five airmen who died in one of them are mixed in the amalgam of America's present hysteria. I will be accused of having said that America is as bad as Russia. . . . What should I do to be published and at the same time retain at least an illusion that I'm saying something true?

"I was in Bihac, Bosnia. In and around that town, as some of you know, the Ustasi, led by Catholic priests armed with guns and high purpose and righteousness, massacred about twelve thousand Orthodox Serbians. After spending a day there I'm convinced that it happened. But will America believe it? I heard the Bihac facts four or five years ago in America; I don't recall having experienced a deep reaction to them. Now, when I was in Bihac, they almost numbed me. . . .

"In the village of Ripac [near Bihac], which had about one hundred and fifty Serbian families in 1941, one male adult now survives. He was away when the Ustasi massacre squad, which included a Catholic priest, slaughtered the others. I met him and I saw that Ripac has almost no middle-aged men. . . . Who will believe it? People in America are like people in Yugoslavia, whether they are Communist or anti-Communist: they believe what they can bear to believe, what they want to believe. . . .

"In Bihac there's a pile of stones. The story—and I believe it—is this: The Ustasi dynamited the Orthodox church in '41. They razed it to the ground. Then the Catholics in Bihac used the stones from the ruins of the Orthodox church to add an annex to the Catholic church across the street; and from the Catholic angle those people weren't bad. This is a new chapter of the old story of the struggle between Rome and what used to be called Byzantium, between the 'West' and the 'East.' As I see it, it is only incidentally a struggle between the Serbians and the Croatians who speak the same language. But how can I explain away the fact that hundreds of thousands of these people *were* slaughtered? Or why should I? . . . Toward the war's end the British bombers destroyed Bihac, the Catholic church with its new annex included. The few surviving Serbians gathered the stones from the wreckage of the new annex to the Catholic church and piled them across the street where the Orthodox church used to be. And, from the Orthodox angle, they did right. They thought—still think— those stones are Orthodox stones. If I write about this, some Americans may exclaim, 'That's the Balkans for you! Let's keep out of it.' At the same time, after reading some statement by Cardinal Spellman, they will condemn Tito for keeping Archbishop Stepinac, who *you* believe is responsible for the massacres, in prison. I looked into the Stepinac case; and *I* believe Stepinac could have stopped the priests from working with the Ustasi squads which massacred Orthodox Serbians along with Catholic Croatians who didn't believe in the massacring of Serbians or anybody else, and blew up Orthodox churches. Stepinac worked hand-in-hand with the enemy occupation and the quisling apparatus: no doubt about it. I didn't want to go to Lepoglava Penitentiary to see him; but I imagine he still thinks he did the 'right' thing. . . . Tito asked me if I thought he should let Stepinac out of prison. I said no, not on moral grounds; however, Stepinac is the personification of a world-wide issue, and world politics is another thing. It has no morals; in spite of all the verbiage of foreign ministers and ambassadors, it has no interest in morals, in humanity at large. I don't know what Tito should do, or can do. . . .

"I was at Jasenovac where a gang of Ustasi headed by two men, one of them a priest, did away with about seventy thousand Serbians, Jews, Communists, and Catholics who opposed the massacres. It's a story beyond belief, yet I was forced by the evidence to accept it as factual. . . .

"I walked through a wood in Bosnia. Something cracked under my foot. I looked; it was a human skull, Partisan or Cetnik, or conceivably neither. A member of the people's committee, nearby, offered to take me to a forest where the bones of about fifteen thousand people (his figure) who fell in battle or were massacred are still lying among the trees and in the chaparral. I didn't go. I took his word for it, along with his explanation that the community lacked the manpower to collect and bury the skeletons. . . .

"In Bosnia, too, I talked with a middle-aged couple. In 1941 or '42 he was married to another woman and had four or five children, and she was married to another man who was the father of her three or four children. Their story is that the Cetniki compelled the community to dig an immense pit, then shot everybody—but missed these two, who found themselves alive under a pile of bodies. They crawled out of the common grave of their families and the rest of their fellow-villagers; and after the war—two of the few survivors in that region—they married. They are a very nice couple.

"In a town called Loznica, in southwestern Serbia, people told me that during the war the place changed hands so often they couldn't always remember whether they were under the Cetniki, the Partisans, or foreign occupation. . . . If I'm not mistaken, the town of Nova Varos, in Serbia, changed hands thirty-five times. All or most of you here know what that means: it occurred in Slovenia too—but I don't think what happened in Slovenia compares with what happened in Bosnia. . . . How can I convey this information to the average American so he'll understand why Yugoslavia is such a difficult country to come to terms with—why she's so 'fanatical' on the subject of the big-power game and religious fanaticism? Why, for the time being at least, she stands alone. . . .

"A couple of months ago, one of you here told me the story of Jazo, a young peasant in Bela Krajina, a happy-go-lucky fellow who before the war liked to drink a little wine on Sunday and play the mouth organ. His father had died, and sometimes when Jazo had had a glass too much he went to the cemetery and sat on the old man's grave and played the tunes his father had sung. He was a little eccentric but harmless, and everyone in the village liked him. He was handy at many chores and full of fun. So far, so good. . . . Then the War of Liberation, the Revolution, started in Slovenia, and Jazo became a Partisan. He could cook, and he became the cook in his brigade. The Germans captured him and turned him over to the native White Guards, who killed him in the name of Christ—literally chopped him up in little pieces with the cleavers from his kitchen, in the presence of a priest who now lives in America. . . . *But——*

"In Lika a young man named Ivo, a good Catholic, became a Ustasa and the leader of a massacre squad. The rest of his family, also good Catholics, were anti-Ustasi who sided with the Serbians, hiding and protecting them from the massacre squads. Ivo's father, Jovo, was particularly anti-Ustasi. When Ivo's massacre unit, accompanied by one of Archbishop Stepinac's priests, came to his native village to kill the Orthodox Serbians and blow up their church, old Jovo went forward to meet his son and forbade him to carry out his assignment. Ivo told his father to shut up or he'd shoot him along with every other pro-Serbian Croatian. Jovo hurried home and told his wife and two daughters that Ivo and his squad were rounding up the Serbians, and that he must find a way to stop him. He seized a pitchfork and said he would kill his son if he couldn't stop him otherwise. At that moment Ivo appeared in the doorway. Jovo ordered him to disarm. Ivo laughed. His mother and sisters cursed him for the criminal he was. He shot them dead and reloaded his gun. The gun jammed and Jovo lunged at his son with the pitchfork. Ivo ducked and fell, then lay still; Jovo didn't have time to see whether Ivo was dead or unconscious, because at that moment several Ustasi came looking for their leader. Jovo slipped out the back door and staggered to the woods. He found a number of his fellow-villagers there, Croatians and Serbians. He sat with them in the bushes and helplessly watched the Orthodox church go up with a blast while more than half the houses burned. The next day the survivors drifted toward Bosnia. The others shunned Jovo because he was Ivo's father. He left the group and ended up in Dalmatia, where he eventually became a minor Partisan hero. What happened to Ivo is unknown. Jovo is in the village again, one arm gone that he lost in battle. His face holds a curious expression and there's an undertone in his voice. . . . Should I tell all this and assert that Ivo, or rather what was behind him, is one reason why New Yugoslavia stands against the big powers which try to use religion to foul her Revolution? And that behind your bravado and humor and weariness flows a great idea, a deep feeling that humanity needs to get together? . . .

"In [a Croatian city] I was told about the daughter of a middle-aged professor whom the narrator had previously pointed out to me in the street. Her name was Zorica. She was an only child and lovely. The professor and his wife were a well-to-do genteel couple. They couldn't do enough for Zorica. She had a governess, and as she grew up a personal maid drew her bath, combed her hair, and kept her wardrobe in order. In 1939 Zorica came across some Marxian literature. She wanted more of the same. In '41 she rebelled against her parents, the bondage of their love and their gentility, and joined the Communist Youth organization. A year later, somewhere in the south of Croatia, she was well-known as a heroine *partizanka* and also as the filthiest person in her detachment. She wouldn't wash or comb her hair or clean her clothes. She wanted only to fight. In '43 she fell in battle. . . .

"My head and notebooks are crammed with stories like this. You know some of them; having gone through the *borba* as a chore you couldn't avoid if you wished to have a chance for anything else, they may seem ordinary to you and, therefore, not specially interesting. Or else, as writers, you know how graphic they are but you leave them alone because you don't know, as I don't, the effect they'll have. You write and talk 'Marxist-Leninist' jargon, instead, which scarcely anyone in America wants to bother to understand. Not that I know what I'm going to do with the material I've collected, either. Much I haven't even read thoroughly or at all; there hasn't been time. Maybe I won't do anything with it. I do know I must leave Yugoslavia or I'll burst. . . . I have read many of the speeches of your top leaders, many of their state papers and the now-famous correspondence of 1948 between the Soviet and Yugoslav CP leaders. Some of the information may be useful, but official stuff is official stuff, here as anywhere else—none of it conveyed nearly as much to me about you as the stories I've related—or as the story of Gromovnik.

". . . Who is Gromovnik? Some of you, apparently, don't know. Vlado Dedijer has a paragraph or two about him in the first volume of his *Dnevnik;* aside from that, I don't know of anything about him in print. He's a brigadier general in Tito's army and a National Hero of Yugoslavia. I talked with him in the Officers' Club in Belgrade one day in June, and literally pulled his story out of him. . . . His name is Brigadier General Ilja Gromovnik-Heris, but once it was plain Ilja Heris. I'd say he's in his late forties; born in 1901 or 1902, of peasant parents in a hamlet near Karlovac [Croatia]. There were two hectares of tillable land and ten or eleven children. Ilja was the youngest. Nearly all of them went *'s trebuhom za kruhom*—with stomach after bread.' Some left home to work in the mines in Belgium, France, Germany. Early in the 1920's Ilja emigrated to Canada. He first heard of Socialism there, and of the Soviet Union. He took part in strikes. Reading was difficult for him, so he skipped Marx and Engels and Lenin (and I suspect that to this day he's read only excerpts from their works), but what he heard of their ideas appealed to him and he became a Communist. He joined the Party in Canada; just when, I don't remember—it's not important. . . . In America a fellow like Ilja is called a working stiff or a bindle stiff—colloquialisms for itinerant worker. His story is a bindle stiff's odyssey. He worked in mines and at other jobs in Canada, then in the United States, then Mexico, and Argentina. Why and how he drifted as far south as Argentina, I don't know. Ilja became a 'powder monkey'—an expert at dynamiting rocks, stumps, and mountainsides. Came 1936, and Ilja went to Spain and learned military sabotage and demolition, and after the Loyalist defeat he was interned in France for a while. He escaped and, in '40 or '41, made his way to Yugoslavia where he hadn't been for nearly twenty years.

"When Tito issued his call for an uprising, Ilja 'didn't even have a pocketknife,' as he told me, but he pitched right in. The Party had told him to. I asked him what he meant by 'the Party.' He looked at me as though my question was a little silly. He is a slight, short fellow but strong and agile. He jumped on a German superman and choked him and took his weapons and ammunition, then killed more of the enemy until he accumulated a small arsenal. He formed a Partisan detachment and for about a year operated independently of Tito's high command. The detachment never consisted of more than a hundred men. Its job was demolition and sabotage. It worked on its own initiative even after it made contact with Tito's headquarters and became part of the new Yugoslav army: for when a man or an outfit was doing well, Tito let him or it alone. . . . The demolitionists' task was simple. They captured explosives from the enemy and blew up as many installations, trains, trucks, railroad tracks, tunnels, bridges, hangars, etc., as they could, incidentally killing as many Germans, Italians, and quislingists as were within the range of their destruction. Ilja was wounded twice, slightly. He lost relatively few men. In about four years he personally dynamited 167 trains. (The figures given here are from the notes jotted down in June 1949. In Ljubljana my remarks, made from memory, were less exact.) His detachment destroyed 1,203 trains, 204 bridges, 122 enemy trucks and automobiles, eighteen tanks, five tunnels, thirty airplanes, eleven factories, between thirty and forty thousand sections of railroad track, and about twenty ammunition dumps and supply depots. Hundreds of wrecked locomotives and railroad cars which Ilja and his boys sent up are still rusting along the Zagreb-Belgrade and other lines. Altogether his outfit executed 2,011 sorties, or an average of more than one a day. Ilja kept track. How many of the enemy his detachment killed is guesswork. Ilja's estimate is 'tens of thousands.' He knows that at least four German generals died in the trains he and his men blew up. Men? Some of them, he told me, were boys in their teens.

"One day Gromovnik himself blew up Ante Pavelic's airplane which Mussolini had presented to the quisling; but 'Pavelic wasn't in it,' Ilja said regretfully.

"In spite of misgivings based on his observations in Spain, Ilja was pro-Soviet. He tried especially hard to stop trains carrying German troops to the Soviet front. He and his men worked mostly in Croatia but they also went to Istria and Hungary to blow up anything that was necessary to advance the program Tito had summarized in the phrase 'Death to Fascism! Liberty to the People!' which they first heard sometime late in 1941 or early in '42. Ilja liked the slogan. It covered everything he had in mind. He still thinks it's great. . . .

"After the war Ilja Gromovnik-Heris received the decoration of the National Hero of Yugoslavia, was promoted to general, and put in command of the sabotage and demolition division of the New Yugoslav Army. He also received the highest Czechoslovak, Polish, and Bulgarian decorations. In '46 Moscow awarded Gromovnik the Lenin Order of the Red Flag.

"Gromovnik-Heris didn't tell me all this. I got some of it from other sources. I asked him what he thought of Stalin and the Soviet Union now, and of the Cominform, Radios Moscow, Budapest, Prague, etc. 'What do I think?' General Gromovnik-Heris asked. In his general's uniform, he still has the look of both a Croatian peasant and an American bindle stiff. 'All of a sudden Stalin says the Yugoslav *borba* is no good. What we did, we didn't do. We are "megalomaniacs." I never heard the word before. What do I think? I don't think; I *know* that Stalin and the Cominform are wrong. But it's not up to me to argue with them; I have my hands full. *Drug* Tito made me a general, so now I go to school four to six hours a day and try to become educated and learn how to act like a general. I think it's nonsense because all that I really am is a powder monkey; but I'm supposed to be a disciplined Party member; and it serves me right. I'm supposed to study Marx. I was a Marxist before I ever heard of Marx. But I'm in the army and orders are orders; and all I can say is that these studies are harder than anything I went through in the war. My job is demolition—training task forces which, if necessary, will do better than my outfit did during 1941–45. They *will* do better. Tito needs us. Our country must be independent and respected. We've got to keep it independent or die trying.'

"To me, Ilja's story speaks volumes. It's his version of Tito's speech in Skoplje early in August. I think Gromovnik is a terrific little fellow. He knows Tito the way most of you here know him: Tito is Tito, and that's enough. In my estimation, the two of them are quite a combination. They personify the climax of the Yugoslav Story so far. A high climax. . . . The postwar period has been anti-climactic, here and everywhere, I believe. Some of you may disagree; very well. Perhaps we can say that Yugoslavia is now striving for the next climax. But it's not easy to move from an anti-climax to a new climax.

"At this juncture my mind splits in two streams of uneasiness.— Tito and Gromovnik? They have to prepare for the next war as well as they can. *But*—— The next war, if it comes, is going to be demolition on a super-Gromovnik scale. I know Tito won't start it. Can he, can this New Yugoslavia, do something to prevent it?

"Tito? . . . Some of you here may know him better than I do, the essence of him; but I know details of his life that add up to make him a very extraordinary man. . . . I don't like uniforms, but I'm willing to go along with the argument that it was politically expedient for him to wear one in Macedonia, since he spoke as Marshal of Yugoslavia and also since the Macedonians like uniforms. That's politics, and Tito has a political position in Yugoslavia and in the world. I like him. I liked him especially late one evening last June. We had been talking all afternoon and evening. When we started, he was Marshal Tito, and I was the writer interviewing him. Toward the end, six or seven hours later, he was too tired to be the diplomat or statesman. I was tired too. We had worn each other out. We sat at a table with the supper dishes between us. He was full of painful memories of the *borba*—of the climax, as I call it—and of reasons why the spirit of New Yugoslavia, born in the Revolution, must not be destroyed. He spoke of the Fifth Offensive: how he felt realizing in advance that thousands of his *drugovi,* hundreds of whom he knew personally, would die. That was one big and bloody reason in itself why the Cominform and the 'West,' separately or together, must not be permitted to destroy or befoul New Yugoslavia.

"Tito recalled his visit to an improvised hospital in Foca, Bosnia, in the winter of 1942, after a battle in which hundreds of men and girls had been seriously wounded. The hands and feet of some of them were frozen. To save about 160 lives, the few doctors worked day and night amputating limbs. They had no anaesthetics. 'Imagine that!' Tito said. 'But as their hands and arms, feet and legs were sawn off, the patients didn't scream with pain. Instead, they cried, "Long live Stalin! Long live the Soviet Union! Long live Tito!"' As Tito told me this, there was a curious beauty in his face. Pain.

"'That was in 1942,' Tito said, 'when the Germans were advancing deep into the Soviet Union, when the fall of Moscow seemed imminent. Our people knew that; yet they had faith in the invincibility of the USSR, in Stalin. They didn't know that Mosa Pijade and I had been trying to get medicines and anaesthetics from the Russians. Soviet planes could have dropped them to us, but they didn't. . . . Now the Cominform, the Kremlin, Stalin says that our sacrifices were as nothing. . . .'

"Tito spoke to me like this in reply to my question asking him what he remembered most vividly of the *borba* days. Then he asked me what impressed me most vividly in New Yugoslavia in 1949. I told him it was the great effort the people were making to lift themselves by their own bootstraps, and he nodded. I said: 'I don't think I'll ever forget the squeaking of wooden wheelbarrows on your construction jobs.' Tito nodded and again there was that curious beauty in his face.

"Yesterday I drove to Brioni with a group of American liberals and progressives, nice men, intelligent and full of good will. I liked two of them especially; they were seeking answers. But, oh! the mass of misconceptions behind their questions about Yugoslavia. I tried to tell myself that they weren't misconceptions, just part of the cloud of half-truths and nonsense enveloping the world; that you people here were no better when it came to America; and that I was no better on a variety of subjects. But, by the time we got to Brioni, I had lost patience with them. . . .

"The next morning Tito sent someone to ask me to come to see him ahead of the group. He wanted advice about what to tell them. I didn't know myself. I told him that the members of the group were fine men, what we in America called liberals or progressives; I knew most of them personally or by reputation; they would ask him a lot of questions; he should answer them, just be himself. And he was, but he was his official self, the statesman—the Marshal of Yugoslavia, although he wore civilian clothes. He answered all their questions, the friendly ones, the nasty ones; some of them at great length and informatively; and at the end I felt the group was satisfied. But he wasn't the Tito I knew, nor were his answers vibrantly true. He wasn't able to be his human self. What he told them was not untrue, but it was far from the truth that I think I know.

"What was the matter? It may have been the latent hostility in some of the questions which weren't consciously hostile but simply an echo of a mixture of American anti-Red and Cominform anti-Tito propaganda. It may also have been Tito's pride—a defensive tactic against that latent hostility or against America as he knows her through her official actions, which I believe and which I tried to tell him—and you—aren't a fair reflection of the America I know and care about. . . . Back in June, when both of us were too tired to be anything but ourselves, we had talked of the squeaking wheelbarrows in Yugoslavia and of America's great technology. On a few previous occasions I had tried to impress on some of your top leaders in Belgrade that America's technology was good but that her tremendous industrial or production advantages weren't good as a factor in world politics, weren't good either for her or for a country like Yugoslavia, by which I meant also China— in fact, between two-thirds and three-fourths of the world. I had pointed out that America's production capacity was so vast that if, for instance, you here in Yugoslavia were a hundred years behind America when you started your Five-Year Plan, you would be—roughly speaking, technologically speaking—two hundred years behind her after even the most successful completion of your Plan, for in the intervening five years America was apt, if not almost certain, to leap ahead productionwise beyond your wildest imaginings. . . . Tito had said nothing to this. Nor had any of the others among your top leaders on whom I had inflicted this unpleasant thought. I inflict it on you now, as I make ready to run. If you get that little steel mill (little in American terms), what will it really mean? I don't mean to be unpleasant, to take revenge on you for this hospitality, to intensify your worries. I'm worried myself, not so much about you in the anti-climax here, which is part of a bigger anti-climax, as I am about America—what she, the biggest 'giant' in the world, will do with her immense power, with her wonderful technology. If I am worried about you Yugoslav Communists ——"

Here I interrupted myself to tell about the self-trapped eagle with his beak around the protruding root I had come upon in the Slovenian Upland during the false spring of 1949. I had already mentioned the incident to a few of those present, adding that I regarded it as a symbol. It helped me to grasp their situation: it cast no aspersion upon them or their ideology. America, with her tremendous drives, her great production, had a hallucination too, now shot through with endless fear. To a few of them, months before, I had tried to convey the symbolism of Captain Ahab in *Moby Dick*. . . .

"If I'm worried about you Yugoslav Communists, it's not because I question whether you're wise or entitled to call yourselves Communists, or whether your Party is more truly communistic than the Soviet Party. That scarcely interests me. I'm worried because I feel that 'Marxism-Leninism' and your fight with Stalin doesn't even begin to touch the problem we are caught in. As far as I can see, your fight with Stalin merely points up that problem, and our American diplomats—as it seems to me—are merely being clever in trying to find out if they can use the Cominform split in the 'cold war' game or in the hot war which is likely to come.

"The past few months—particularly since I've been in Macedonia and seen the primitive super-human effort that is being exerted on the Mavravo hydroelectric project, two currents of uneasiness have throbbed in my mind. I think our great American technology, as I've said, is good in itself; and I think your social Revolution in itself—and Tito standing up to Stalin—is good. Two kinds of good. But each regards the other as evil, or at least with suspicion. How can we change that? Is it idiotic, is it utopian, to ask the question? *Can* we stop, or at least curb, our hallucinations? Can one good and the other good pull together? If not, we *are* in a world-wide anti-climax and your climax, your *borba,* may be canceled out, may already be in the process of cancellation, not because of Stalin but because he too—more than anyone else, perhaps—is caught in this predicament of inequality, of *increasing* inequality, which was brought about by the Industrial Revolution whose chief base, I insist as unmegalomaniacally as I can, is in America, which can sell you a steel mill, then tell you on a whim that you can't have it. . . . To find a way out of your anti-climax to a new climax, you (along with most of the rest of the world) need America. America doesn't know it yet but she needs you, she needs the world to be on her side: or, rather, she needs to become part of the world on a basis of mutuality—not of being able to give or not give. She doesn't know it, but she needs terribly this phenomenon called Titoism, *not* because it is anti-Stalin but because it is human and, despite some surface appearances which foreign journalists have played up, you are seeking freedom and cultural respect along with material betterment —because you are bent on creating a society which will be primarily social, not industrial and financial, or military or bureaucratic, because you and America together may be able to find the way out of this Anti-Climax.

"I don't know you as well as I should after being among you these past seven months. But even if, or because, you call yourselves Communists—a word than which there's none more obnoxious in the current American language—I know that you're striving toward something called progress. I know a little about America, after living there for thirty-odd years. She changes quickly; now you see one aspect of her, then you don't. I have been away eight months; but judging from the press I have read and the radio broadcasts I have listened to, I think she's as dangerous right now as she was in 1948—to herself first of all, to the essence of America. That essence is good. Lincoln, whom I have been quoting or paraphrasing to some of you, is part of that essence. I'm not a thorough student of Lincoln; but some of his biographers show him as a practical politician, almost a shyster, at the same time that he was able to deal with large human questions. I recall, inexactly perhaps, something he said concerning our Declaration of

Independence—that it offered liberty and an equal chance not only to all Americans but a hope or promise of liberty and equality to men everywhere, now and forever. Lincoln said that, by virtue of the Declaration of Independence (whose soundness scarcely any American questions), America carries within her makeup, her ethos, her soul, a promise 'that in due time the weight shall be lifted from the shoulders of all men and that all shall have an equal chance.'

"Of course this is easier said than done. . . . But now I'm reminded I must leave in order to catch my train. I've talked too much anyhow. I little realized how quickly time passed. I guess it passes most quickly when we are in a hurry trying to cover too much ground. But it was you who rigged up this occasion, so blame yourselves—in part, anyhow. *Zdravo!* Perhaps: *Do svidenja!* So long."

An anti-climax is inherent—and later appears to have been evolving —during the climax. The 1945–51 anti-climax in the world was uncoiling during World War II if we take that conflict as a climax. And if the Tito-led Revolution was a climax in South Slavic history, the anti-climax was apparent in Yugoslavia in 1949. Shakespeare's perfidious Antonio—in *The Tempest,* Act II, Scene I—said it well:

> *We all were sea-swallowed, though some cast again,*
> *And by that destiny to perform an act*
> *Whereof what's past is prologue, what to come*
> *In yours and my discharge.*

The South Slavic climax began to spin to a head when Tito rose to the leadership of the CPY in 1937.

In his Political Report to the Fifth Congress of the CPY late in June 1948 Tito said: "Long before the war—in 1938, long before Yugoslavia was attacked—the Party sent directives to the Communists [in various parts of Yugoslavia] to learn how to handle arms and to become acquainted with the war. In Belgrade, the pre-military training of students formed in battalions began, although the regime in power was not in favor of this. Further, in compliance with Party directives [sent out as early as '38] . . . women and girls attended courses for nurses in cities and towns and some villages."

Many Yugoslav women decided to join the men in the impending struggle, or were drawn into it by or with them. About one hundred thousand of them went into the fighting units; between three and four millions helped in the rear. Nearly twenty-five thousand fell in battle or died of wounds or disease. Forty thousand were wounded. Two thousand became officers. In 1949 I was told that 1,171 women veterans were entitled to wear the 1941 Partisan Badge, which indicates the number of survivors among the unknown total who joined the *borba* in 1941. Approximately 282,000 women were massacred in towns, villages, and concentration camps, many of them with their children.

In Slovenia and elsewhere I was shown caves in the woods, remote mountain cabins and city cellars where Communists had cached weapons and ammunition as early as the autumn of 1938.

In 1939 the CC, CPY appointed a special military-revolutionary committee to prepare people for action against the consequences of the Belgrade regime's sellout to the Axis. The CPY leaders had reason to believe that most of the members of the successive governments, as well as many or most of the generals of the Yugoslav Army, were Fifth Columnists in the service of the Axis. In an attempt to cope with this top-level treason parading in the resplendent uniform of patriotism, the CP military committee assigned a young Montenegrin veteran of the Spanish Civil War, Mitar Bakic (now a general in Tito's new army), to work among the royal officers' cadre. Vladimir Popovic and Milovan Djilas were also members of the CPY military committee, headed by Tito—to mention only those I met.

During 1938–40, under directives from Tito, Yugoslav Communists moved about the country, acquainting themselves with the terrain, spotting likely strategic positions, building bunkers, caching arms. In 1949 I crawled in and out of a number of dugouts in Ljubljana from which, beginning in the spring of 1941, Edvard Kardelj, Boris Kidric, and Boris' wife Zdenka, whose underground name was Marjeta, conducted revolutionary operations during 1941–43. One of these bunkers is about ten feet under the backyard flowerbed and beehives of an old postal clerk and his wife. Their name is Jezak. Their address is Dalmatinova Street 19. What took place there is material for a cloak-and-dagger novel.

In reference to the Stalin-Hitler Pact and the Soviet-Finnish War, most Yugoslav Communists, as disciplined members of the Kremlin-dominated International, outwardly followed the "line" which the Comintern had stretched around the world. At the same time, without having the faintest anti-Soviet feeling, they worked like beavers preparing for war against the Axis. Many "Western" writers have insisted that prior to the German invasion of Russia on June 22, 1941, the CPY was inactive *versus* the Axis. Hamilton Fish Armstrong, for instance, in *Tito and Goliath* (p. 15) says that Milovan Djilas' claim, published in May 1948, that the Yugoslav people under CPY leadership were responsible for the overthrow of Prince-Regent Paul's regime on March 27, 1941, and Yugoslavia's refusal to adhere to the Tripartite Pact, "is of course pure fantasy." Mr. Armstrong could have learned the truth: that Djilas' claim was accurate, had he shaken off the English-speaking leg-men of the American and British correspondents living in the Hotel Majestic and been able to communicate with the Yugoslavs in their own language. It is possible to maintain that without General Dusan Simovic, then chief of the Royal Air Force, Prince Paul's pro-Axis government would not have been overthrown on March 27, 1941; but the Simovic *coup* could not have taken place without the pro-CPY officers around him, and *they* would not have revolted had it not been for the CPY-led crowds which filled the streets of Belgrade, of Kraljevo, Cacak, Valjevo, and many other Serbian towns, as well as of other Yugoslav centers, for two or three days before the fateful date, muttering *"Bolje grob nego rob*—Better death than slavery," which was no momentary political slogan but a centuries-old folk-saying.

"The importance of March 27, 1941, was not in the actions of the small group of dissident Yugoslav officers led by General Simovic," wrote a British group in 1947, "[but in] the mass demonstrations of the people against the Axis, against the internal quislings, and for the independence of their country. The demonstrations were of historic importance. They gave new life and hope to the people of occupied Europe. They delayed Hitler's attack on the Soviet Union—but they made inevitable the Axis invasion of Yugoslavia."[1]

Mr. Armstrong also questions the veracity of Tito's outline of the period immediately before and after the conquest of Yugoslavia and the flight of her new "government" under the boy-king, Peter II, and

---

[1] See p. 1 of the pamphlet "Yugoslavia Faces the Future," a report by James Klugman, a member of the British military organization responsible for liaison with Yugoslavia from September 1942 to April 1945 and executive assistant to the chief of the UNRRA Yugoslav Mission from April 1945 to July 1946; Betty Wallace, author of *World Labour Comes of Age* and *The Trial of Dr. Aloysius Stepinac, Archbishop of Zagreb;* Doreen Warriner, head of the UNRRA Yugoslav Mission's Food Division; and K. Zilliacus, M.P. My only disagreement with the above statement is that it was General Simovic who was led by the "dissident officers," not the other way about.

Prime Minister Simovic to the Middle East and thence to London. The "Balkan experts" generally have made much of the fact that when the Stukas bombed Belgrade, Tito, "the Moscow-trained Kremlin stooge," was in Zagreb. They didn't seem to know that several other leading Yugoslav Communists were in Zagreb as well. Before me is a copy of the March-April-May 1941 issue of *Proleter,* whose extensive contents indicate that off and on in the first half of the spring of 1941 most of the CC, CPY members were in Zagreb, meeting with Tito, analyzing Yugoslavia's new position, and plotting a general uprising.

This issue of *Proleter* reached Moscow in mid-June 1941 and upset the Kremlin. The Kremlin, apparently, continued to hope for peace with Hitler and did not believe the warning of the British Foreign Office and the American State Department that Hitler had already set a date for invading the USSR, which Yugoslavia's March 27, 1941, action and its consequences postponed five weeks.[2]

The *Proleter* gives the gist of discussions and decisions of a secret CPY plenum meeting held in enemy-occupied Zagreb early in May 1941. Several score of regional CP representatives from Croatia, Slovenia, Montenegro, and Bosnia-Herzegovina convened for two days with the CC, CPY, under Tito's chairmanship. Dalmatia and Macedonia were not represented because their delegates couldn't get through the heavy enemy concentrations between their regions and Croatia. The chief decision reached was that, since the Simovic "government" had gone into exile, the leadership of the Yugoslav peoples devolved on the CPY. Tito was appointed commander-in-chief of any resistance to the enemy the CPY could evoke. It was this that upset the Kremlin when it learned of it about a week before Hitler broke his pact with Stalin—and there was hell to pay in the Comintern. Why hadn't

---

[2] See the article "Light on Nazi Foreign Policy," by DeWitt C. Poole in the October 1946 *Foreign Affairs,* edited by Hamilton Fish Armstrong. An old State Department man and one of the Americans who examined high-ranking Nazi war criminals before they were tried, Mr. Poole wrote:

"Germans we talked with stressed that events in Yugoslavia contributed decisively to the German defeat. The order to prepare an offensive against Russia, which Hitler communicated to the General Staff on Dec. 18 [1940], envisaged May 15 as the date for the opening attack. The *coup d'état* in Yugoslavia, and the consequent need to conquer that country, delayed the beginning of the German campaign eastward until June 22. Karl Ritter, who for some time represented the Foreign Office with the General Staff, told us with sober mien that the delay cost the Germans the winter battle before Moscow, and it was there the war was lost."

Manuilsky and Dimitrov prevented such foolishness? . . . The explanation follows:

On April 6, 1941, when the Nazi planes bombed Belgrade, a bomb fell on the building where the CC, CPY radio transmitter-receiver connecting it with Moscow was hidden. Had it not been for that stroke of good luck, the Comintern (read: Manuilsky—read: Stalin) would certainly have forbidden the early-May 1941 plenum meeting in Zagreb and reminded the CC, CPY that they were supposed to be "disciplined Communists" and as such must abandon their plans for an uprising against Hitler; and Tito might have had a problem on his hands. As it happened, unable to communicate with Moscow, the CC, CPY didn't learn of the Kremlin's mid-June 1941 displeasure until months later, and meantime had gone about its business of preparing an insurrection against the Axis, assuring the CP membership and the Yugoslav people generally that Russia would soon be in the war, and at the same time creating the first basic difference between the Russian and the Yugoslav revolutions. *Lenin's revolutionary cry had been: "Peace! Land to the peasants!" Tito's was: "War! To the woods, peasants, or whoever you are: for the enemy is going to burn the roof off your house and kill you and yours!"*

As I mentioned before, Yugoslav Communists had been convinced long before March 27, 1941, that the Soviet Union would eventually enter the war against the Axis in spite of Stalin's pact with Hitler. Immediately after that date, assuming the possibility that some of the generals of the Royal Yugoslav Army might not be out-and-out Fifth Columnists, the Communists organized Popular Front delegations which called on the commanders of the local garrisons to offer their services. Ales Bebler was a member of the delegation which called on the commanding general in Ljubljana. He and the rest of the group were almost arrested and thrown into jail for their patriotism. In Zagreb, Vladimir Bakaric and other delegates who had sought an interview with the corps commander, an old pan-Serbian, were severely reprimanded as warmongers.

Hoping that some parts of the Royal Yugoslav Army would make a stand in the Bosnian mountains, several Slovenian and Croatian Communists, Boris Kidric among them, headed south. But all they found along the way were treason and confusion. Axis troops advanced at will. It wasn't until mid-April 1941, however, when the Chief-of-Staff of the Royal Yugoslav Army surrendered to the Nazis while thousands of Yugoslav soldiers wept with shame and a sense of unspeakable frustration, that the CPY leadership fully realized that nearly all the generals of the Royal Yugoslav Army, most of them pan-Serbians, were German agents.

On April 27, 1941, the CP leadership of Slovenia, notably Edvard Kardelj and Boris Kidric, called a meeting of all political Party leaders who had opposed the Belgrade hegemony. They also invited prominent individuals like Josip Vidmar—and like Joze Rus, a judge, a passionate "Sokol" patriot—who were not affiliated with any party but were known to be anti-Belgrade-hegemony, and who perceived as clearly as the Communists that the very existence of the Slovenian nation and of Yugoslavia was at stake. Then and there they formed the Slovenian Liberation Front, a political organization whose duty was to organize resistance against the Italians, Germans, and Hungarians occupying the country. Similar popular-front meetings were held at approximately the same time in other Yugoslav centers. And the CP military committee ordered some of its *aktivisti,* especially the veterans of the Spanish Civil War, into the woods and mountains, to collect as many of the weapons abandoned by the disintegrated Royal Yugoslav Army as possible, to size up the quality of non-Communist individuals and groups hiding in the forests, and to begin forming the nuclei of future detachments.

According to Vlado Dedijer's *Dnevnik,* Tito—*Stari,* the Old Man— appeared in Belgrade early in May 1941. By then, he had organized the apparatus which was to become the leadership of a people's Partisan resistance movement. As Commander-in-Chief, he had given the *aktivisti* in the mountains and woods a spell of time to reconnoiter and rally adherents. He figured they and he had five or six weeks. They were obliged to wait for a politically opportune moment to issue the call for the uprising. That moment, he expected, would come when Hitler's attack brought the Soviet Union into the conflict. He reasoned this way less because he was a Communist and a pro-Sovieteer than because he knew that large numbers of Yugoslavs were pro-Russian and pro-Soviet, and because he was aware they could count on no other power for the political backlog a small country needed when it engaged in revolution. America had not entered the war yet, and Roosevelt's lavish promises to the royal Yugoslav government just before and immediately after March 27, 1941, had proven empty; while Britain, sustaining her inner patriotic structure mainly on Churchill's eloquence, was a chief exploiter of Yugoslavia's natural resources and corrupter of her government and culture, and was unpopular with the masses of Yugoslavs.

In mid-May 1941, Tito's military intelligence reports deepened his conviction that Hitler soon would attack the Soviet Union, and German troop movements that month and during the first half of June supported it. Tito had no direct contact with Moscow; he conveyed his conclusions to the Kremlin indirectly, but the Kremlin apparently ignored them. Stalin continued to act as Hitler's loyal "neutral" ally, shipping him supplies according to agreement; and it appears that the June 22, 1941, attack caught him completely by surprise.

For five weeks in the late spring of 1941 Tito awaited the inevitable. He lived almost openly in the house of a Serbian Communist friend in the Dedinje residential section of Belgrade, changed his quarters a few times, and passed two or three hours daily in coffee-houses listening to the drift of German and Serbian-quislingist purposes and plans. His elegant attire and refined manner fooled both the Germans and their Serbian stooges, headed by General Milan Nedic, a pan-Serbian who had been sold on a German victory two or three years before World War II began. Tito had several sets of identification papers.

Among his closest lieutenants during this period were Vlado Dedijer and Lola-Ivo Ribar, Milovan Djilas, and his wife, Mita Mitrovic; Olga Nincic and her husband Avdo Humo, a Moslem from Sarajevo studying in Belgrade, and Vladimir Ribnikar, an editor of *Politika*—to mention only those, most of them Serbians, whom I met in 1949. They mimeographed the aforementioned issue of *Proleter* and had couriers deliver copies to leading Communists throughout Yugoslavia. They mimeographed or printed several propaganda leaflets, served as Tito's couriers, and organizers of various conspiratorial actions within the city, and collectors of medical supplies. Dedijer was busy with plans to resume publishing *Borba,* which had been an illegal paper in Belgrade since the late 1930's.

During this time Tito became well acquainted with a number of other young Serbians and Montenegrins in the Belgrade underground whose qualities impressed him and destined them to play major roles in the impending upheaval. Again, to mention only those I met in 1949: they were Aleksandar Rankovic, tailor and ex-political prisoner, who, like Djilas, became a member of Tito's inner group; Petar Stambolic, who took over Partisan operations in eastern Serbia; Blagoje Neskovic, who did a comprehensive job of organizing the city of Belgrade against the occupation-quislingist authority; and Svetozar Vukmanovic, whom Tito nicknamed Tempo because at the 1941 plenum session he persistently argued that there was no time to lose, the CPY had better step up its tempo. All of them were unusually strong men, less physically than in purpose and the spirit to sacrifice themselves.

In May and June 1941 Tito and his closest collaborators estimated that the strongest resistance against the Axis would develop in Serbia.

Tito heard of an officer named Colonel Draza Mihailovic, who was said to have evaded capture by the Germans and to be hiding with a small band in Ravna Gora, a mountain range in western Serbia. He was said to be a British agent to whom the Cetnik organizations in different sections of Serbia and Bosnia were eager to subordinate themselves. There was little doubt that many leaders of these Cetnik outfits had been members of the royal Yugoslav secret political police and now still functioned in the same capacity under Quisling Nedic and the Gestapo, while the others simply sought over-all leadership along the pan-Serbian "line." Tito sent Rodoljub Colakovic and two other *drugovi* to the heart of Serbia to ferret out information about Mihailovic and his forces if any. They reported negatively: Mihailovic had no forces: he was a semi-dissolute type of army officer: a number of would-be "Cetnik commanders" of questionable repute wished to give an impression of strength by claiming that they were under orders from Mihailovic's eyrie headquarters somewhere on Ravna Gora— which tended to fit the pattern of Serbian folklore romanticism.

When I talked with Tito, he couldn't recall the main tenor of his thought in that period; but I surmised from him and others that he had brooded a great deal. He was outraged by the deliberate or careless negligence of Governor Ivan Subasic of Croatia, the right-hand man of Dr. Vlado Macek, head of the Croatian Peasant Party, who, when he had joined the fleeing Yugoslav government, had left about two hundred Communists in Croatian prisons to be slaughtered by Ante Pavelic's Axis-sponsored Ustasi regime. Tito continually studied a roughly drawn map of Yugoslavia which showed the areas occupied by the Germans, Italians, Hungarians, Bulgarians, and Italian-backed Albanians. The situation was further complicated by the quisling governments headed by criminals and traitor generals established in Zagreb, Belgrade, and Ljubljana which were supported by the Church.

Efforts were under way to install quislings in Dalmatia and Montenegro; and sections of Slovenia had been declared an integral part of
the Third Reich, while other Slovenian districts, with the city of
Ljubljana, and Dalmatia were attached to the Italian Empire. Word
reached Tito that Hitler had ordered Styria and Upper Slovenia to be
cleared of Slovenians and settled by Nazi Germans, and that his *Gau-
leiters* had begun to carry out the order. Reports of the early Ustasi
massacres of Orthodox Serbians in Lika and other parts of Croatia
strained Tito's credulity. They were horrible beyond belief. But here
were the photographs the Germans circulated in Belgrade and throughout Serbia with the story that the Croatians were liquidating the Serbians. Tito knew the Ustasi were a specially organized gang of a few
thousands criminals and perverts of Croatian birth who were willing
to serve the purposes of Rome and Berlin. Another report he received
was that the Germans had ordered their quislings to exterminate the
Jews in Yugoslavia, and that the extermination had begun. . . . Could
the CPY ever hope to start a movement that would transcend or coun-
teract all this horror and confusion? What if he were wrong and the
Soviet Union didn't enter the war? The CPY-led resistance, as he now
envisioned it, would scarcely have more than a toe to stand on. He
couldn't shake off the feeling that Moscow didn't like him, that it had
no real interest in Yugoslavia. If the Soviet Union did go to war, could
the Yugoslav resistance movement under his command expect any
help from the USSR? . . .

The approximately two hundred *aktivisti* in the woods—about half
of them "Spaniards," or veterans of the Spanish Civil War—had orders
not to start big-scale military operations until Tito issued his call for
an uprising to the Yugoslav people. Meanwhile, operations should be
restricted to demolition and not be engaged in foolhardily. Local commanders, in charge of resistance nuclei in the woods and villages,
should take care not to spill patriot blood in vain. They must calculate
their chances realistically, exactly; and, whenever possible, clear their
plans with Supreme Headquarters. These general instructions were
not followed by all local leaders. Some interpreted them differently
than others.

The CP cells in the factories had "military committees" whose
general orders were to start anti-Axis sabotage the moment they heard
the Soviet Union was at war. Aside from hampering the Axis, the
purpose of their operations was to electrify the people who, according

to information Tito received, were in a resistance mood but needed a kick-off signal as well as a severance from the notion that the old Cetnik organization—with its fine tradition in the period of the Turkish conquest, lately fouled by its bond with the Belgrade hegemony— would take a serious action against the foe. The following is one of several stories I authenticated which represents hundreds of instances of anti-Axis action by CP military groups in factories, shops, and mines during the last week of June 1941.

A man named Caco was head of the military committee of the rather strong CP cell in the railway repair-shop at Sisak, Croatia. At seven o'clock in the morning of June 23, 1941, when he appeared at his usual place of work, he noticed that his fellow-workers' "Good morning" had an extra hearty ring, and that some of them kept looking at him afterward.

"What's up?" he asked.

"Don't you know? Didn't you listen to the radio this morning?"

"No."

"Hitler attacked the Soviet Union."

Caco took a deep breath. "In that case, *we,*" meaning the Yugoslav Communists, "are now actually at war with the Axis. You all know what to do. Each of us slips out of the shop as circumstances permit, and attends to the assigned task."

By the end of the day, one locomotive, a bridge, and several sections of the railroad track near Sisak had been blown up.

Sorties between Axis patrols and Yugoslav resistance groups, some of which called themselves Cetniki but many of which had no label, occurred as early as mid-May 1941, mostly in Bosnia. These Cetniki had no connection with Draza Mihailovic. He was unaware of their existence. The CPY had nothing to do with them, either. They had sprung up spontaneously. Many of them disintegrated after their first defeat; others, reached by CP *aktivisti* in time, were convinced that this free-lance fighting wouldn't get them anywhere. Some of them elected the CP *aktivisti* to become their commanders.

During the two weeks immediately following the Nazi invasion of Russia a few premature local uprisings occurred in southern Yugoslavia and ended in defeat, in pointless loss of life. They occurred despite Tito's caution to commanders that they calculate the prospects of every operation very closely and make every blow count.

One of the first military operations carried out on Tito's direct order occurred in Belgrade late in July 1941. The Gestapo had captured Rankovic while a small task force under his command was preparing to blow up a Nazi radio station. He was beaten half to death, first in the old royal *glavnjaca,* then in the Gestapo headquarters. He realized the Germans had nothing but contempt for the old crew of sadists in the *glavnjaca.* After giving him their first going-over, the Gestapo officers treated him moderately—by their standards. Apparently, they didn't want him killed for the time being. One of the *Gestapovci* seemed to suspect that he, Rankovic, was an adjutant of the "Communist Commander-in-Chief" and thought he could make him reveal the commander's identity and whereabouts. The Gestapo knew the name "Tito." Rankovic acted as though he'd never heard it. They beat him again, then dragged him through the streets. He was bleeding, his clothes were torn, his eyes were so swollen from the blows he could barely see. They took him to a hospital, dumped him on a bed, strapped him down, posted guards nearby, and instructed the doctor to see to his injuries and give him food.

Somewhere along the way he had been dragged two of his best friends—Lola-Ivo Ribar and Lazo Kolisevski—had seen him. They hastened to inform Tito, who forthwith ordered one of his several secret task forces in Belgrade to attack the hospital and rescue "Marko" —which had lately become Rankovic's *nom de guerre*—at all cost.

In the hospital Marko had lost consciousness; regaining it, he remembered seeing Lazo in the street and (as Marko told it later) he was sure the Party would find a way to pull him out of the Gestapo's clutches. He decided to simulate unconsciousness. Efforts to bring him to, to administer internal medication, to pour tea into his mouth were useless.

Suddenly, there was shooting and a brief hullabaloo in the corridor outside the ward. From a corner of one swollen eye Marko saw several men grapple with the Gestapos guarding him. Two men cut the straps, asked, "You're Marko, aren't you?" and stood him on his feet. Marko recognized some of the Partisans. They were part of a thirty-eight-man task force which had captured and held the hospital for the few minutes necessary to effect the rescue. Rankovic was badly battered; but he was hardy, just thirty, a veteran of torture chambers, and in a few days he was well enough to resume his duties.

Tito sent him to central and southeastern Serbia. Some correspondence between them, carried through enemy-held territory by dare-devil CP couriers, followed. Tito's letters dealt with the organization of the National Liberation Partisan Detachments, the qualifications of the commanders, the need for limiting themselves to demolition and sabotage and other small actions for the time being, and the prospects of finding a common ground with the Cetniki groups whose commanders were sincere resistance men and not Axis agents. In mid-August 1941 Tito closed a letter to Marko with the words "Death to Fascism!" In his next letter he added "Liberty to the People!" It didn't occur to him that the two sentences made a perfect slogan for the over-all program of the CPY-led Liberation Movement. It did to Marko, who quoted the two phrases to Rodoljub Colakovic or someone else in the "agit-prop" division of CC, CPY, which that autumn began to use them as a slogan on all its printed and mimeographed matter. Soon "Death to Fascism! Liberty to the People!" was the way to close letters and speeches and became the customary exchange between Partisans meeting in the woods or where non-Partisans couldn't overhear them. One would say, "Death to Fascism!" and the other replied, "Liberty to the People!"

There was a CC, CPY man in the Comintern office in Moscow—Veljko Vlahovic, who had lost a leg in the Spanish war—but, with the CP radio transmitter-receiver in Belgrade out of commission, Tito couldn't communicate with him. He had little to convey to the Comintern anyway. The Soviet Union was at war and Stalin had broadcast an appeal that the European peoples resist the Hitlerite hordes. Having built Stalin up as a great leader in the Yugoslav mind the previous four years, Tito found it difficult to restrain the CP-led Partisan units in various sections of Yugoslavia from hasty action. But the Stalin broadcast worried him: how was a solid resistance movement possible anywhere without a clear revolutionary motive behind it? . . .

Edvard Kardelj was in Belgrade for several days around April 6, 1941, when the Stukas pulverized about one-fourth of the city. Vlado Dedijer, as he tells in his diary, had had the devil of a time keeping him out of the way of falling bombs. Then Kardelj went to Zagreb, to Ljubljana, back to Zagreb, back to Ljubljana; and now, in the mid-summer of 1941, as he had promised Tito, he turned up in Belgrade again. Slovenia, he reported, was ready for a major uprising. Boris Kidric was the chief political commissar there; Zdenka Kidric, his wife, was in command of the Ljubljana underground, which was practically the municipal government—most of the police being at her beck and call, while *Il Duce's* security officers were going crazy trying to locate the bunker (under the flowerbed and beehives at Dalmatinova 19) from which she issued her orders. Franc Leskosek was Commander-in-Chief in the field. Ales Bebler was his Chief of Staff. . . . The CC, CPY estimate made in May 1941, that Serbia would be the center of resistance ferment, was re-examined and found to be correct.

Nazi intelligence had come to the same conclusion. German garrisons were reinforced. The Gestapo strung up "Communist suspects" on lampposts in Belgrade and other cities, and machine-gunned hostages by the hundreds. As elsewhere in Yugoslavia, these atrocities numbed a few with fear and fired others with the spirit of resistance.

On August 10, 1941, the underground Supreme Headquarters of the National Liberation Partisan Detachments, as it was originally called, issued its first military-political bulletin. It was intended primarily for the top- and second-level CP leaders, detachment commanders, political commissars, and leading non-CP members of the Popular (or Liberation) Front organizations in various sections of Yugoslavia.

In it Tito referred to the proclamation he had made after Hitler invaded the Soviet Union, and continued:

All you groaning under the invader's boot who love freedom and independence, who refuse to endure fascist slavery, know that the hour of liberation is near. Therefore, contribute your share to the struggle for liberty under the leadership of the CPY. The struggle of the Soviet Union is your struggle; the USSR is fighting your enemies. . . . Do not allow yourselves to be misled by the diverse domestic reactionaries who serve the fascist bandits. Your place is in the ranks of the working class. . . . Your future and the future of your children depends on this struggle. If you love freedom and independence, if you do not want to be foreign slaves . . . join the righteous struggle of the great peace-loving homeland of socialism, the Soviet Union. Unite against the oppressors, the fascist invaders who enslaved you and are plundering your country.

To proletarians [class-conscious industrial workers] in all parts of Yugoslavia: Take your positions in the front ranks . . . around your vanguard, the CPY. Each stand at his post. Do your proletarian duty resolutely and with discipline. Ready yourselves quickly for the final and decisive fight. Do not allow the precious blood of the heroic Soviet peoples to be shed without participating in the struggle. Your slogans must be: Not one [Yugoslav] worker shall go to Germany to swell the bandits' power with his labor! Not one rifle, shell, not a

single grain of corn, shall fall into fascist hands by our default! . . .
Mobilize your forces to prevent our country being made a base for supplying
the fascist hordes which, like mad dogs, are attacking the Soviet Union . . .
our hope and the beacon light of the toilers of the world.

   To the Communists of Yugoslavia: The grim hour we foresaw . . . has ar-
rived. We knew the fascist criminals were preparing to attack the Soviet Union
and [thereby?] all working mankind. The bloodthirsty fascist rulers, who keep
both their own peoples and those of the invaded countries in slavery, declared
a war of extermination on us. . . . We accept the struggle. We expected it, we
are ready for it. "In this struggle there will be no mercy for any Communists,"
the fascist slaughterers have declared. We reply: "In this struggle there will be
no mercy for the criminal fascist leaders and their faithful henchmen. In this
struggle there will be no mercy for the fascist financial oligarchy and its satraps!"

Tito also addressed the Partisan Detachments which were being organized in the woods:

   . . . First, [your] main task . . . is to liberate the people of Yugoslavia from
the invaders and to fight the invaders' domestic agents who are helping to
oppress and terrorize the populace. Second, [bear in mind that] German fascism,
with its marauding allies now plundering our country, is the greatest enemy of
our liberty and independence; [and that], accordingly, it is the sacred duty of
all patriots to fight unremittingly until this fascist gang is annihilated. Third,
[let us be clear in our minds that as] National Liberation Detachments you are
not the formations of any single political party or group—not even the CPY,
although Communists are in your front ranks. You are the fighting detachments
of the peoples of Yugoslavia which all patriots . . . should join regardless of
political convictions. . . .

He then listed in detail the tasks the detachments should perform:

   . . . destroy all installations of service to the enemy: telegraph and telephone
lines, railways, bridges, factories, shops, munition stores . . . prevent the invader
from taking grain, livestock and other supplies . . . take such supplies from the
enemy by force and distribute them among the people, retaining only what your
detachment needs to maintain itself . . . defend our settlements from fascist
terror . . . safeguard women . . . protect people's property from the plunder-
ing invaders . . . kill enemy officers, Gestapo-men, Black Shirts, etc., and their
domestic agents . . . rouse the spirit of resistance so the people will face the
danger our country is in——

This, roughly, in the midsummer of 1941, was the counter-strategy
for meeting the Axis scheme, as the CC, CPY had learned it, to turn
Yugoslavia, with her sixteen million population, into a needed cross-

roads between Germany on the one hand and Italy, Bulgaria, Turkey, Rumania, and Hungary on the other; to exploit her undeveloped resources; to use the rich plains of Vojvodina to feed German armies in southeastern Europe; to export Yugoslav manpower to German factories; to ship Yugoslav girls to Nazi brothels on the Eastern front; to spur production in the small industries in Slovenia, Croatia and elsewhere to increase the fascist powers' war potential.

Tito had half-known since 1938 or '39 that the Germans had worked out an elaborate blueprint like this. Even so, when in mid-July 1941 he first saw copies of the German documents, he tightened into a cold rage. They were undoubtedly authentic. They had come from a dozen or more of his most trusted people who spoke fluent German, posed as Nazis, and held positions in the occupation forces, even in the Gestapo. . . .

Nor could Tito question his *aktivisti's* reports that many of the "resistance leaders" issuing "mobilization proclamations" were provocateurs. In the *Bulletin,* he urged skepticism about them. He also warned against narrow-mindedness and pointless arguments about this or that man's religion and political affiliations. At the same time, he ordered local commanders and commissars to be on their toes for spies and informers in their ranks. If any were discovered, and after a thorough investigation there was no doubt of their guilt, they were to be shot.

During a meeting which Tito held with Rankovic, Djilas, Lola-Ivo Ribar, Blagoje Neskovic, and other CP-men in Belgrade one day in the second half of July 1941, he referred to reports he had been receiving from Partisan commanders who implied that their outfits were entitled to "live off the country"—to take by force whatever they needed wherever it was available. "We've got to quash that idea," Tito said. "If such behavior isn't checked forthwith, there will be no stopping it. Steps to check this 'requisitioning,' really looting, limited as it is, must be taken at once, or you have my resignation now. I am *not* going to be the Supreme Commander of a plundering army. . . . First of all, I don't like stealing. Secondly, if our detachments 'requisition' food and other supplies from the countryside, our movement will repel, *not* attract the wholesome majority of our people, many of whom may not see eye-to-eye with Communists politically but who are good men and women, nonetheless. On the contrary, even if only a few of our detachments loot, we will attract riff-raff, the kind of scum I hear some of the Cetnik outfits are attracting. The people generally will be against us (and I won't blame them); our operations will disintegrate before we get started. . . . The movement that I want to head, if I am to head it, will have to bring to a point all goodness, all sense of outrage against evil, and the desire for a new society that I feel exist in the present chaos of our people. . . ."

The small council was silent for a minute or so after he finished. Then there was a general, whole-hearted assent. Tito wrote briefly on the subject in the first *Bulletin:* honesty must be the byword of every detachment: every member must be fully cognizant that he or she belonged to a people's liberation army: no act of dishonesty must be overlooked: no act of plunder, however trivial and "justified," should go unpunished. The commanders and commissars must ascertain that supplies taken from the enemy had been shipped in from Germany or Italy. If they were found to be confiscated by the enemy from the countryside, they must be returned. Supplies which the detachments could procure from the villages must be purchased with the peasants' consent. . . .

The second issue of the *Bulletin,* dated August 19, 1941, contains a list of Partisan demolition and sabotage activities during the first half of that summer, and severe if oblique criticisms of Partisan groups whose impetuosity had caused them to initiate battles prematurely.

In September 1941, relying on intelligence reports stating that considerable sections of Serbia were temporarily under Partisan control, and even more on his instinct, Tito decided—with the approval of the rest of Supreme Headquarters—to leave Belgrade and start major operations on his own.

To leave Belgrade, however, was no easy matter. The city was a concentration point of German power and was surrounded by troops. The least suspicion of irregularity in one's documents was enough for one to fall into the Gestapo's hands and never be heard of again.

In the previous few weeks, Marko, alias Leka, alias Alexsandar Rankovic, who wasn't in Belgrade at this time, had created the nucleus of a security organization, eventually to be known under the initials OZNA, whose chief function was to protect Tito. It consisted of trusted, resourceful Communists. Tito was all set to make his own way through the Nazi lines when they reminded him that his life was not exclusively his own but also belonged to the Party. They found an Orthodox priest named Milutinovic from Ivanica who was going home, and Tito crossed the Nazi barriers around Belgrade in his disarming company.

Meantime, considerable elements of the liberty-addicted population of central and southeastern Serbia were in a state of subdued frenzy, bewildered by the ups and downs of the sporadic guerrilla operations, and looking for leadership. Some CP commanders insisted on holding their fire in order not to shed blood in vain. They waited for Supreme Headquarters to work out an over-all strategy, while Cetnik "leaders" —most of them enemy or quislingist agents—called for action which, when it occurred, only served Nazi purposes and those of headline writers in London and New York. Aside from the numerous, well-disciplined Partisan detachments deep in the woods, several of which Tito inspected, and the small Partisan task forces whose members masqueraded as humdrum civilians in towns and villages, the people had few arms—none to match the Nazis' modern weapons. Word had spread that, for the time being, they must wait and endure the occupation.

There were Partisan headquarters in several small towns in Serbia —out in the open during liberation, underground when the Nazis reconquered them.

"Tito . . . Tito?" The name had a clear ring. By August 1941 only a few people had seen the man and knew who he was. Now legend had it that he was a Communist, the leading Communist in Yugoslavia. This upset some people but nonetheless added resonance to his name, for Russia—"Mother Russia" herself—was said to be Communist. This connection with Russia, both in spite of and because it involved Communism, had special appeal in Serbia and Montenegro, which were traditionally attached to Russia on illusory pan-Slavic grounds and even more because they were small states dependent on the friendship of a big power.

In midsummer of 1941 some would-be Cetnik leaders spread the rumor that Tito was a Russian. But few people in Serbia and fewer still in Montenegro—as elsewhere in Yugoslavia—paid much attention to it or believed it. It was hard to know what to believe. Suppose he was a Russian——

The daily realities engulfing them were enough. Conquest. Humiliation. Horror. Nazi soldiers made passes at women. Men whom you knew hung from lampposts and the boughs of trees. Your turn might be next. A German truck or armored car was blown up on the outskirts of town; the Cetniki spread word that the Partisans had planted the mine; and the Gestapo retaliated. They rounded up five, ten, twenty hostages (never any Cetniki), shot them against a wall or in a field and left their bodies for days, posting an order that they must not be moved—not even close relatives were permitted to come near them. . . . People in Serbia proper learned that in Croatia the Axis-sponsored Ustasi were slaughtering Serbians wholesale. Then there was a rumor (true) that in revenge Cetnik groups in Bosnia and Herzegovina, claiming to have the support of London, were slaughtering Croatians. . . .

"Tito?" Whoever he was, Communist or not, he issued leaflets which denounced the Ustasi massacres as sheer criminality—they had to be stopped, but they couldn't be stopped by slaughtering Croatians. The leaflets quoted Hitler's man Himmler who wanted to put "a river of blood" between the Serbian and Croatian peoples, thereby making a reconstitution of Yugoslavia impossible. And the peoples of all South Slavic regions were called upon to join together in a righteous struggle to stop fratricide, to save their country at any cost. If they couldn't save their homes or their lives, they might—they could—save their country: Serbia, Croatia, Slovenia, Yugoslavia: a spot under the sun where homes and normal human living eventually would become possible again.

Tito established his first operational headquarters in Krupanj, a small town in Serbia. The few Partisan detachments he inspected filled him with "an indescribable love for these men," many of whom were Belgrade and Kragujevac metal-workers, Bor and Trepca miners, and peasants. He knew some of them personally. Most of them didn't know who he was; a rumor was started within the detachments that he was their Supreme Commander Tito!

There were, as yet, few women in the fighting ranks.

Several of the commanders—among them Sreten Zujovic, popularly known as Crni (the Dark One, because of his swarthy complexion), a Serbian, formerly a teacher; Koca Popovic, of the Belgrade banking family; Danilo Lekic, a quiet young Montenegrin; Petar Stambolic, a dull-faced Serbian giant; most of them Spanish veterans—captured Tito's affection. Also, there were the endlessly resourceful Marko, and young Vlado Dedijer with his childlike devotion.

Nor were all the Cetnik "commanders" he met Nazi agents, Tito conjectured. There was the priest, Vlado Zecevic whom Colakovic introduced him to one day—evidently a sincere resistance man: and Zecevic said there were others who felt as he did. The people as a whole impressed Tito. They were confused, yes; but they were turning their eyes Leftward, looking for a possible exit from their predicament, from the shame of conquest, and were ready to risk their lives for a new start.

The reports on German troop movements convinced Tito that the Nazi High Command in Belgrade had ordered an offensive against the liberated and semi-liberated territories of Serbia. It might begin in October or November, or even earlier—late in September. A few days after reaching Krupanj, Tito called his first war council in the field. It was held in the near-by Strlac mine. *Drugovi* from Serbia, Bosnia-Herzegovina, and Montenegro had been summoned on short notice. Kardelj, who had slipped out of Belgrade, represented Slovenia, but like the others—Rankovic the Serbian, Djilas the Montenegrin, Tito the Croatian—he was regarded as an over-all Yugoslav leader. Years before among Yugoslav Communists, one's national origin had ceased to matter. . . . The council decided that the Partisans should try to collaborate with Draza Mihailovic and with any local Cetnik commanders if it could be established that they were neither directly nor indirectly in the service of the invaders. Tito's staff, which included Rankovic and Djilas and would include anyone else he wished to add to it, was renamed the High Command for Guerrilla Detachments; and departmental headquarters were authorized for Croatia, Slovenia, Bosnia-Herzegovina, and Montenegro, with instructions to maintain as close a liaison with the High Command as possible. To begin with, western Serbia was to be cleared of Germans and made the principal base for future military operations.

The Cetniki? In spite of its unprincipled conduct in King Alexander's days and later, the organization—if it could be called an organization—was a factor in Serbian political lore. Mihailovic? He constituted a question mark. No one actually knew him. His name was wrapped in an aura of romanticism. One thing appeared certain: up to the end of August he hadn't authorized a single act of sabotage against the occupation forces. Tito decided to see him personally and went to Ravna Gora.

The two men, each accompanied by a small staff, met in the village of Struganik, in the house of a Cetnik "leader." Mihailovic was sober and at first didn't impress Tito too badly. Making no secret of being a Communist, Tito proposed that they join forces and give the Germans something to worry about. But Mihailovic and his staff—notably Dragisa Vasic who subsequently was proven to have been a principal contact between the prewar Belgrade regime and "Western" interests in Yugoslavia—argued that this wasn't the time to attack the Germans. Draza was vague about whether the Cetnik outfits in western Serbia were under his command or not. He said he hated Croatians: they were slaughtering Serbians and must be punished. Tito declared Draza was wrong to blame the Ustasi atrocities on the Croatian people. The massacres had been ordered by Himmler and apparently approved by the Catholic hierarchy. Tito maintained that the overwhelming majority of Croatians were as outraged by the massacres as the Serbians. Draza shook his head, repeating he didn't like Croatians; they didn't deserve any sort of independent or autonomous state; if they remained in Yugoslavia, they were only fit to be vassals of Serbia. Tito was appalled. Draza tried to speak Russian; which led Tito to think that Draza believed the rumor that he was Russian was true. All Tito could get Mihailovic to agree to was that he wouldn't interfere with his guerrilla operations and his attempts, then underway, to unite with some of the Cetnik groups.

Some of these attempts made by Tito's lieutenants were temporarily successful. But most of the battles which the Tito forces and small Cetnik detachments fought together in mid-September in western Serbia were not.

Meantime, Tito had moved his Headquarters to the town of Uzice, in southwestern Serbia. It had a small rifle and cartridge factory and the townspeople generally were pro-resistance. A large proportion of them were clearly pro-Partisan. A delegation from the latter turned over to Tito's staff pouches of Yugoslav currency abandoned by an old general of the Royal Yugoslav Army who had surrendered to the Germans in April. The amount handed over was in the neighborhood of fifty million dinars, or about a million dollars at prewar exchange rates —enough to resume production in the rifle factory. Tito induced the local bank to reopen, and the huge sum was deposited to the credit of the High Command. The townspeople began to assume that Uzice was the capital of the Liberated Territory; a few spoke of it as the capital of a new Soviet republic. When Tito heard of this, he ordered his staff to discourage such prattle.

The Nazi offensive began early in October and quickly spread over Serbia. Its main force was directed against Uzice. Many Cetniki, some under their own commanders, joined Tito and fought at the side of Partisan detachments. The exact number is unknown. A fair guess is that twelve hundred Cetniki, who claimed to be under the over-all authority of Draza, participated in battles in the area between the towns of Kraljevo and Valjevo.

Encouraged by this, Tito sent a courier to Draza with a letter urging that he induce other Cetnik groups to join them, and Draza replied he would. In November, allegedly in compliance with orders from Ravna Gora, numerous Cetnik commanders drafted "in the name of the King" the male inhabitants of many villages and towns. At the same time, other Cetniki spread the word that the guerrillas didn't have a chance—if you were smart, you would lie low or hide and save your life and home.

The guerrillas won several battles, captured or recaptured a number of key communities, and seized considerable matériel and other supplies, with which they then equipped the men and women waiting to enter the struggle. The rifle factory in Uzice operated day and night, turning out 420 rifles and 80,000 rounds of ammunition every twenty-four hours. Tito thought the outlook wasn't bad. Captured Germans confessed that they wished they had never laid eyes on Serbia.

Accompanied by two of his most successful guerrilla commanders, Sreten Zujovic and Mitar Bakic, Tito made another trip to Ravna Gora. Mihailovic was sober and amenable, and in no time they concluded a pact of collaboration on the basis of a draft Tito had brought with him. In the next room during the negotiations was a British officer, Captain Bill Hudson, a young man but an old Balkans hand. Tito asked that he be called in. Draza said no; a member of his staff added that there would be no point in having a foreign witness to a purely internal transaction. The agreement covered divisions of armaments and monies in Tito's possession. Tito saw to it that these provisions were carried out immediately to the letter.

Four days later, during a battle against a large body of German troops intent on capturing Uzice, a sizable Cetnik force—*undubitably on orders from Ravna Gora*—attacked Tito's forces from the rear. The battle lasted over a week. One day the rifle factory, next door to Tito's headquarters, blew up—an act of sabotage executed by a few Cetniki.

I visited Uzice and traversed the scene of the battle where at the

end of November 1941, with a cold spell coming on, Tito's forces suffered a serious defeat. . . . The gist of the tale, as I heard it, is that
Mihailovic, with approval from London, helped the Germans—*a practice pursued throughout the rest of the war*—and that Tito was obliged
to pull the ragged remnants of his army into the adjacent plateau
region of Sandjak. I followed the route of this retreat, which took place
during a blizzard. I slept in the house in the Zlatibor forest in Sandjak
where Tito, after a few hours' sleep, held a war council. What now?
Other members of the High Command and the detachment commanders wanted to re-form here and return to western Serbia. Tito,
on the other hand, was for moving on to Montenegro and Bosnia. His
instinct, quickened by recent experience, told him that their chances
in those endless high Montenegrin and Bosnian mountains were better
than in Serbia. At long last everybody agreed.

Tito developed his plan as he talked. Only "plan" is too exact a word.
It was instinct in a critical moment leaping into focus as a fairly concrete outline of procedure, subject to change as circumstances demanded. At work in his mind were these considerations: The high
mountain ranges which run into one another in Sandjak, Montenegro,
Herzegovina, and Bosnia, would provide an immediate hideout. It
would be very cold right now, true; but they would have to cope with
that somehow. Later, when it came to battle, the terrain would be in
their favor, especially against the Germans and Italians with their
cumbersome equipment. More important, *there* they could get the
movement underway better than in western Serbia, where collaborationist *cetnistvo* was well advanced and where the Germans had heavy
troop concentrations protecting the Belgrade-Salonika railroad. Small
demolition outfits could take care of the railroad, he said, and Petar
Stambolic could develop—as he did—tactical detachments in eastern
Serbia. Tito's decision to move the High Command and most of what
was left of his army to Montenegro and Bosnia was also based on reports from those regions he had read in the last five months. The ones
from Mosa Pijade influenced him particularly. They tied in with his
political instinct.

Along with hundreds of other former political prisoners, the royal
security police had arrested Mosa Pijade in 1939 and sent him to a concentration camp in southern Yugoslavia. He had escaped in 1940 and,
after hiding here and there, had made his way to Montenegro. When
Yugoslavia folded up under the Axis assault, Tito had sent him a

message to stay there. By then he was already quite at home. He was just past fifty, graying; and the young Montenegrin *drugovi* had begun to call him *cika* (uncle) or *Cika* Janko (Uncle Johnny).

It was in December 1941 when the defeated column—fewer than three thousand men and three hundred women, perhaps one-fifth of them CP members since prewar days—moved on through the forests in the bitter cold.

There were almost no enemy troops in Sandjak. The advance guard of the column encountered detachments many of whose members vaguely regarded themselves as Cetniki. On inquiry, however, it turned out that "Cetniki" was just a word. Not only did these detachments have no connection with the Cetniki in Serbia; the name "Draza" was virtually unknown to them; *and their commanders were Communists* whom one or another member of the High Command detachment knew personally from prison days or the Spanish war. Tito learned that the woods and remote settlements in Bosnia were full of "Cetniki" of this breed. The CP commanders had no objection—wisely, thought Tito—to their calling themselves "Cetniki" if they wished. The matter of designation would clarify itself eventually. Tito recalled that he had heard of these CP-led "Cetniki" before. The discovery of them now was a slightly confusing but good sign. Here was resistance manpower and he felt encouraged. His decision to head into southwestern Yugoslavia had been right.

One afternoon, the battered column, dragging its feet westward, passed through a narrow valley which was windless and warm. It was near a place called Zlatar. Tito ordered a "Halt!" The past few nights he had slept huddled in a German officer's greatcoat, usually under a tree, with one or two of his bodyguards shivering nearby. Often the temperature was near-zero. And waking suddenly, he'd lie there brooding until at dawn, without breakfast, he ordered "Forward!" Then, trudging silently with them, he'd listen to the talk among members of the High Command detachment and commanders, and reflect that nearly everybody in the column was inadequately clad and hungry, that many of the men and women had no arms or even cartridges for their rifles and revolvers; and that yet—in a subtle way, humanly, spiritually—hard to define in words—they were the finest outfit any man ever commanded.

There was something magical about this narrow valley. The winter sun poured all its faint warmth into it. The talk in the High Command detachment didn't interest Tito—he'd heard most of it before. He was tired but didn't want to sit down and yield to weariness. One of his bodyguards offered him a slice of meat. Though he was hungry, Tito declined it, knowing that most of the men in the column wouldn't have anything to eat either. He ordered the bodyguard to leave him and he walked the length of the sunlit valley, among his sprawled-out army. Most of the men were dead to the world; others were consciously enjoying the rest, the sunshine, and pure mountain air. They helped pick lice off one another, rewrapped their bleeding feet, doused themselves in the cold creek, or were mending their garments.

Tito knew several hundred of them by name—workers, peasants, intellectuals, mostly Serbians. He stopped here and there, asking, "How are you, *druze?*" Most of them replied, nobly, "Very well, *druze* Tito." One man, however, who sat in a group delousing themselves, gave him a sidelong glance and replied:

"How am I? Look at me. You can see for yourself. This is how I am: none too good. *Druze komandante,* now that you have asked me a question, may I ask you one?"

"Naturally," Tito said.

"Tell me, *druze* Tito, tell all of us, what is this war about? You're our leader; we'll follow you because we feel you're honest and the country has been betrayed. As far as I can make out, there isn't a mother's son or daughter of us in this column who won't go wherever you take us, except if he or she drops dead on the way. But it would help us to know not where we're going—that's your business as commandant, *druze*—but what we're doing, what we're up to. There are Cetniki and "Cetniki," for instance. Some of them are here with us, disgusted with Draza. Others are in the Sandjak woods; good men too— you can tell that just by looking at them. Then there are those who attacked us at Uzice. There's Draza. He and his crowd are the King's men, as were some of those who fought on our side last month. Is the King going to return? Are we going to permit him to return? I don't mean just him personally; he's a slip of a boy in London—what does he know except what those around him put in his head? I mean: after this war is over, will we have to return to the same conditions that brought on the disaster we are in now? Or are we going to try for something else?"

Tito didn't answer immediately. The man's queries were right and he mustn't give him a snap rejoinder. Other men around the questioner looked at him too—they all wanted to hear his response. Tito asked them to excuse him for a while; he wanted to think; he would be back.

He sat alone on a stump.

Presently he returned and noticed that the group around the man had at least trebled, and he said:

"*Druze,* you're right. The King must not come back without the permission of the people. A change *is* needed. As Supreme Commander, I hereby create the First Proletarian Brigade. Its personnel and commander will be selected later—you will be in it. It will be a shock unit. The men will wear red stars on their caps. CP members serving in the brigade will be entitled to put the hammer-and-sickle symbol in the star. This will be done as soon as we get some red cloth and cut out the five-pointed red stars. . . . A social revolution *is* needed."

"Death to Fascism!" one man said.

"Liberty to the People!" another responded.

The Yugoslav Revolution started then and there—if it hadn't before. That was also the beginning of the New Yugoslav Army.

Tito's radio contact with Moscow had been re-established.

Two weeks after the rest period in the sunlit, warm valley he formally created the First Proletarian Brigade and made Koca Popovic, the banker's son, its commander. Then, after most of the men in it had sewn five-pointed red stars on their caps, Tito received a message from the Comintern office in Moscow. The Kremlin was deeply displeased. It was furious. It wanted no "proletarian brigades" and no red stars in Yugoslavia or, presumably, anywhere else in Europe. They signified social revolution, and this was not the time for social revolution—only for resistance, for aid to beat Hitler. Proletarian brigades and red stars would disturb Britain and America (Pearl Harbor had recently brought the United States into the war), and Britain and America must not be disturbed. It might endanger Big Three unity. "The Yugoslavs have stuck a knife in our back," someone in the Kremlin had remarked, and the remark reverberated in the Comintern.

Tito was expected either to disband or rename the First Proletarian Brigade and to order his guerrillas to rip the red stars off their caps. Well, he couldn't do either even if he wanted to, and he didn't want to. It would have wrecked the whole movement. The movement was growing *because* of the red star. Other units wanted to wear it. There was a growing demand for red cloth. Some of the "Cetnik" outfits under Liberation commanders which he found in Bosnia stuck the red stars on their caps beside the old Cetnik emblems. . . . And he was supposed to abolish the red star! Did the Kremlin think it had a monopoly on it? Actually, the five-pointed red star—*danica*—had been a South Slavic symbol of hope for centuries.

Tito had never received a more depressing and enraging message in his life. But, typically, he remained calm. For two or three days he scarcely said a word. Late one evening he sat listening to a London broadcast with a group in the High Command's hut in a Bosnian forest. Mihailovic was the big news. His heroic resistance was extolled as an inspiration to the whole Allied world. A big-name American classified Draza with General MacArthur on Bataan and with Marshal Timoshenko. . . . Next came the Radio Moscow broadcast. It, too, extolled the widespread Mihailovic resistance in Serbia.

Tito rose. "If they don't want to help us, they could do us the favor of not mocking us. They know the facts." He stepped out of the hut into the cold air.

London and Washington weren't upset by Tito's proletarian brigade and the red star they wore on their caps. London and Washington probably knew nothing about them until much later, when Tito had two more proletarian brigades well organized. The British and American press and radio continued to glorify the Mihailovic "resistance" against the Axis, while Mihailovic lay drunk in his Ravna Gora eyrie half the time, using unquotable language about Communists or Ustasi one minute and about Germans or the British the next, while some Cetnik commanders openly went over to the Germans and Italians against the Left-tending people in the towns and villages.

There was a report that someone in the Kremlin had remarked, "The fools!"—meaning Washington and London, because they had failed to sit up and growl at the proletarian brigade and the red star in the Bosnian woods.

The anti-climax was germinating in the climax.

This isn't a book about Mihailovic. I went through most of the published material on his case and talked with Rankovic's men who as early as 1943 had infiltrated Draza's staff. In 1946, when Tito was in power in Belgrade, these OZNA-men—who by then secretly controlled Draza's headquarters—one night induced him, with the unwitting aid of the anti-Titoist British mission on Ravna Gora which fell for the stratagem—to go with them in a car to central Serbia where an anti-Communist army supposedly awaited his command. The army was a figment of the OZNA-men's imagination: a plot to take him alive to Belgrade as a prisoner charged with treason. . . . "Treason" is a debatable word. But I want to say that if Benedict Arnold was guilty of treason, so was Draza Mihailovic. Those who differ with me are referred to Winston Churchill's statement (to my mind, an understatement) in the House of Commons on May 25, 1944: "The reason why we have ceased to supply Mihailovic . . . is a simple one. He has not been fighting the enemy, and moreover, some of his subordinates have made accommodations with the enemy, from which have arisen armed conflicts with the forces of Marshal Tito, accompanied by many charges and countercharges and the loss of patriot lives to the German adversaries." It might be recalled, too, that on July 8, 1944, King Peter of the Yugoslav government-in-exile dismissed Mihailovic from his post as minister of war.

From the early autumn of 1941 to May 1945 the strange warfare under Tito's command whirled and zigzagged, expanded, contracted, and expanded again and again over much of Yugoslavia. Most of his forces were surrounded almost continually by Germans, Italians, Hungarians, or Bulgarians; or by quislingist Croatians, Slovenians and Serbians who ended up by being—if they didn't begin as—criminals dressed in Axis uniforms; or by Cetniki who were not exactly quislingist, who one day claimed to be operating independently and the next day swore by the beard of General Draza or the youthful King in London.

In the eyes of orthodox military experts, Tito's forces were doomed at every tick of the clock, but the double- and triple-encirclement tactic suited him perfectly. Four or five times he barely escaped with his life; but these tactics worked like magic not because they were sound but because most of the enemy commanders, trained in the best military schools, couldn't figure them out.

One day in 1943 a Soviet military mission appeared at Tito's hut in Bosnia. It was headed by a general. Could he see the maps, please— the Yugoslav resistance positions and the whereabouts of the enemy? Tito showed them to him. The Soviet general blanched.

"You're completely surrounded!" he exclaimed, loosening the collar of his tunic. "How will we get out of this trap?"

"We won't," Tito laughed; "we don't want to. Everything is much as it should be. I'm told the Nazi general in command in the sector here, for instance, is newly arrived. My guess is he doesn't know yet what's happening to his neat disposition of troops. By nightfall he'll know that *something* has happened but not just what. The poor fellow won't sleep all night, he'll be so puzzled or so enraged at his officers."

The Soviet general's expression showed he thought he had dropped into the middle of military insanity.

It was horrible warfare. Tito didn't like it, but he insisted that it be kept going ceaselessly in order to kill as many of the enemy as possible and not permit him to re-form and catch his breath, to force him to bring in green units under too-well-trained officers; and, more important, to keep his own forces busy and growing by leaps and bounds in Bosnia and elsewhere. Lying idle in the woods or remote villages wasn't good for morale; besides, the boys and girls hadn't joined up to have a picnic or go on a safari. They wanted to kill the enemy and capture his weapons and stores to equip the waiting recruits. Tito had learned from experience that even the best-intentioned detachment, consisting of the most moral, patriotic individuals imaginable, ready to fight and die but a week ago, tended to degenerate if it lay around. Sometimes his losses were enormous, which almost drove him mad; but action, action, action was all important, regardless of immediate consequences. There was no substitute for it. If a hundred Partisans died, two hundred surged up from somewhere to take their place. Young men and girls pressing into Tito's ranks who didn't know how to read knew by heart Bosnian poems like those by Jure Jaksic written in the 1870's, and intoned them during and between battles:

"Fall, brothers! Drown in blood! Leave the village, let the roof blaze. If need be [lest they be reared as janizaries] *cast your children into the flames! Shake off slavery, let us free ourselves of shame! . . ."*

In Slovenia, a country in many ways far more different from Bosnia than Connecticut is from Mississippi, a new poet, Matij Bor, began to write battle hymns whose spirit was akin to Jure Jaksic, although he wasn't familiar with the latter's verses.

"We go forward without you, tovarisi, *our blood having caught the fire from yours as it went cold, and that fire now lights our way."*

This spirit motivated the *borba.*

Tito's brigades often were badly beaten. The enemy thought they were finished. The remnants dispersed and the Liberated Territory shrank. A short time later there was the recently vanished brigade, stronger than ever; to the enemy it seemed to have sprung out of the ground; and the Liberated Territory expanded once again.

In four years 305,000 Yugoslavs died in battle or of wounds for which there was no immediate or subsequently adequate medical care. I don't know how Tito's statisticians arrived at that figure, how detachment commanders could possibly have kept track of their turnover. But, going about the country, listening to survivors, I couldn't avoid the impression that a multitude of Liberation-Revolution fighters had been killed in action. Tens of thousands of Partisans froze to death. It was a grim business. There were days in 1942, in '43, when Tito thought he couldn't run it any longer. Yet in many places it was safer to fight as a Partisan than to stay at home. Some of the veterans told me they had never felt as free as when they fought and were in mortal danger.

Partisan life had other compensations. It had flashes of humor; with death all around there was more laughter than weeping.

One afternoon after a three-day battle in Bosnia in which about three thousand people died, the enemy commander sent an envoy with a white flag to the Partisan side—which could hardly be called a "side," for the Liberation forces were not a line but gusts of storm which swiped the enemy here, then there. Even command posts were not fixed, nothing you could pitch a grenade at or land a bomb on.

Nonetheless, the envoy did locate a Yugoslav who seemed to be a commander. He saluted, *"Heil Hitler!"*—presented the compliments of the German general, and conveyed his message. It was a suggestion for a cease-fire in order that both sides might gather their dead and wounded. If the Yugoslavs sent one or more emissaries of some rank, the Nazi general would personally meet them at a designated clearing in the forest and guarantee their safe return with his honor.

The First Proletarian Brigade had spearheaded the Yugoslav side of the battle—only "spearheaded" was not the word the German general would have used to describe its share in the melée. The commander of the First Proletarian, dapper Koca Popovic, now bore the title of general. Tito heard of the message and asked Milovan Djilas, also a general, serving as secretary of the High Command, to find Popovic and meet the German after making sure it wasn't a trick.

They found him a youngish Prussian with a monocle, spick and span (which Djilas wasn't), straight as a ramrod, affecting a sophisticated air. He spoke French almost as well as Popovic and received the Yugoslavs in the grand manner which was part of the Prussian military tradition, full of formality and worship of honor. Wouldn't they dispense with this vast bodyguard of theirs and come to his headquarters? Popovic didn't see why not—— He and Djilas discovered themselves in a newly built house, smelling of fresh lumber and furnished luxuriously—this in Bosnia, mind you. The Nazi general had had the furniture, rugs, paintings, and knick-knacks shipped from France, where he had served *der Fuehrer* before coming to the Balkans.

On meeting them, General Kurt von Weygeist (or some such name) had given Djilas and Popovic the *"Heil Hitler!"* salute. He said he knew of both of them and considered it an honor to receive them. They returned his salute with the Communist clenched fist and all three smiled at the incongruity of the formalities.

At headquarters, there were food, drinks, and heel-clicking dog-robbers who dashed in and out of the room. Djilas and Popovic were invited to sit down.

"Oh, before I forget—congratulations, General Popovic," said the Nazi.

"What for?" Popovic inquired, twirling his mustache.

The Nazi laughed ever so lightly. "Have you been so busy, General Popovic, that you forgot today is your birthday?"

"So it is," Popovic said after a moment. *"Merci,* General von Weygeist. . . . You appear to know a good deal about us."

The Nazi laughed again. "It is my duty to keep track of the birthdays of enemy generals. To your health!" He lifted his glass. *"Heil Hitler!"*

Djilas and Popovic were silent.

An adjutant, as slick-looking as the general, appeared; but his rank, perhaps, didn't entitle him to sit at the same table with generals. His superior uttered a curt order and he whirled out of the room.

"Now, where were we?" said the German general. "No matter. . . . As for my knowing a good deal about you, General Popovic, I mean about your setup and your style of warfare, I must confess I don't, really. All I know with any degree of certainty is that you gentlemen —*pardon,* you comrades, as you call yourselves—are causing us a devil of a lot of trouble. I'm told that over two thousand of my men are lying out there"—he waved an arm elegantly—"dead or dying; and that many of them were punctured with bullets fired from German weapons which you captured from one of my predecessors. I consider that the height of something or other. Shall I say, audacity? Perfidy? Or irony, perhaps? . . . But, of course, you're not really as clever as you think. This isn't intended to disparage your Supreme Commander, Tito, or either you, General Djilas, or you, General Popovic, personally; I'm referring to your style of war, as it appears to me. Of course, *Heil Hitler!* we are a modern army. We have heavy artillery, tanks, mortars, and all manner of other paraphernalia. But in these goddamned mountains, if you will forgive me, we can't use our equipment to full advantage. This terrain is a fitting habitat only for goats. Your rabble army—*pardon,* your guerrillas in their *opanke* [handmade sandals]—can easily crawl and dash about these crags and crevices. My men with their fine, heavy boots, cannot. We fire our heavy artillery pieces and our mortars; we send for our planes, and they come over and spew out streams of fire and seeming destruction —to what end? Oh, we do inflict some casualties on you, no doubt, as you know better than I—but at too great an expense. Our tanks can't get up there, so they park down in the gorge; and what happens? Your goddamned monkeys—and, *pardon,* here I won't apologize for that slurring reference—your monkeys leap out of the nearest bush onto the tank, open the turret if it is closed; in goes a 'Molotov cocktail' and a grenade or two and up goes the tank. At least, it is put out of commission for the time being. This is bad enough; the really outrageous part of it is that if a Molotov cocktail is used, not only the gasoline inside the bottle but the bottle itself is ours. As for this goddamned terrain, if it must be anywhere, it ought to be on the moon, which, as far as I know, isn't yet on *der Fuehrer's* list." The general smiled.

"I'm sorry if this terrain is not to your liking," said Popovic, with mock sympathy, "but please bear in mind that we didn't invite you."

The German's eyes flashed, then dimmed, under pulled-down brows.

"You're here, however," Popovic went on, "and we will be glad to help you out of your trouble."

"Meaning—what?" snapped the German.

"I propose the following," said Popovic with earnest mien, "that you give us your heavy artillery, your tanks and planes, your mortars, and as much of the rest of your modern paraphernalia as hampers you and you can bear to part with; and we, in return, will give you our *opanke.*"

"Never! Never!" the Nazi cried, his sense of humor failing him for an instant. He regained it and laughed. *"Grossartig! Grossartig!"* he exclaimed. "I shall write my wife about this."

Then they settled down to the business of trying to make a truce in order to gather their dead and wounded.

Sidelights often tell more than history, though dates, places, names, battles, statistics, communiqués, and other official statements—usually false—are considered important. The military history of the Yugoslav *borba*—which, to repeat, was at once resistance to and liberation from the enemy and his quislings, and a social revolution frowned upon by the Grand Coalition no less than by the Axis, and a gradually mounting climax imbued with an anti-climax—is divided into seven major Axis offensives and one Liberation offensive.

The first five enemy offensives resulted in the "complete annihilation" of the Liberation Forces—so the enemy commanders thought or wished to think, and reported to their higher-ups in Berlin and Rome. But the Liberation Forces always reappeared, each time stronger than before. The last two offensives involved troops in vast numbers but were launched with limited objectives. And they were too late.

The Sixth began in October 1943, seven weeks after Italy's capitulation, whereby in spite of "Anglo-American" efforts to forestall him,

Tito came into possession of great stores of arms and other supplies. Joseph Goebbels earlier had scribbled in his diary:

September 21, 1943: . . . *The Italian question has created difficulties for us in the Balkans. The Slovenians are now in open rebellion and have gone almost entirely over into the camp of the Partisans. At the moment we lack the police powers to knock out this somewhat dangerous movement.*

The "police powers" which Hitler finally collected to mount the Sixth Offensive and "knock out" Tito from the Yugoslav areas formerly held by the Italians consisted of sixteen German divisions plus the probable equivalent of seven divisions of quislingists, Cetnik, Bulgarian, and Hungarian troops, plus a horde of "Vlasovci," anti-Kremlin Russian deserters whom the Axis allowed to roam through eastern Europe, raping and looting. The campaign to expel the "Communist *banditen*" simultaneously succeeded and failed. The Germans did take over some of the erstwhile "Ljubljana Province" of Mussolini's empire and some of Dalmatia, and come within sight of Montenegro. But Tito's Liberated Territory in the interior had expanded; a new surge of recruits exceeded his losses; and his troops—renamed the National Liberation Army—were better equipped than before; while forty thousand Germans had been killed and other "anti-Communist" forces had also suffered heavy casualties.

The Seventh (and final) Offensive began in April 1944. Fifteen German and five Bulgarian divisions were thrown into it, and approximately another five consisting of Cetnik, Ustasi, Slovenian White Guard, and other units. This time about fifty thousand Germans were killed. Shortly before and during the offensive Tito received minor Allied aid, mostly American supplies shipped from Italy *via* the Partisan-held island of Vis, off the Dalmatian coast, by the efforts of a small group of American officers who had got fed up doing nothing in Cairo. Their superiors' interest in the operation was casual and faint.

Historically speaking, the peak of the Seventh came at dawn on May 25, 1944—Tito's fifty-second birthday—in the form of a sudden and massive parachute attack on his secret headquarters in a cave near the little town of Drvar, Bosnia. General Rommel, "the fox of the African desert," was personally in charge of the operation. The objective was to capture Tito. Rommel almost succeeded. . . . In 1949, both before and after I visited Drvar in company with Kardelj, Pijade, and Bebler, I talked with dozens of Yugoslavs who were positive that a "certain foreign mission" had had a hand in arranging the parachute attack with the Germans. I was allowed to assume they meant the British mission, most of whose members had left Drvar a few days before. I asked Tito about it; he lowered his eyes and didn't answer.

In my June 7, 1949, interview with Kardelj, I asked him.

"We have no official opinion about the incident," he replied carefully. "But some *tovarisi* are unable to shake off the memory of particular circumstances that convinced them that the Anglo-Americans wanted the Germans to liquidate us. They point out that for a week or so the sky above Drvar was full of Allied aircraft, but then for two days immediately before the attack no Allied planes appeared, nor did the Germans have to cope with a single British or American fighter on May 25. . . . Chance?" Kardelj's shoulders lifted in a slow shrug.

In the summer of 1944 the National Liberation Army launched a country-wide offensive and kept it until the war's end in Europe, allegedly engaging thirty enemy divisions. Virtually the only aid it received from the Red Army was during the liberation of Belgrade in the last half of October 1944. By then Tito had a well-organized, well-equipped army of 300,000, and about half a million more who wanted to fight but couldn't for lack of arms and other supplies.

By then the Yugoslav Revolution had become a factor recognized more or less over the world. Schemes were afoot to quash it. The schemers had agents and some Church and other support in Yugoslavia. But most of their plans revolved—until 1947—around the tens of thousands of diverse Yugoslav collaborationists relabeled royalists or democrats, who had fled into Austria and Italy just before V-E day, where the "Anglo-American" occupation authorities, both knowingly and ignorantly, received them with open arms. The "Anglo-Americans" financed their overt return to Yugoslavia to overthrow Stalin's No. 1 stooge, Tito; and the "Anglo" part of the combination *knew* that that would suit Stalin. In Austria, the "Anglo-Americans"— without the least knowledge of the British and American peoples— permitted the organization of a royalist army which, came the day, would return to Serbia, Croatia, and Slovenia and restore the good old *status quo*.

By then Tito was a world figure: the Commander who, lacking a production and supply system, ignoring logistics, relying on the truism of the Yugoslav proverb that big rivers owed their volume and strength to little brooks, had done more with less than any other. He was head of the Provisional Government of New Yugoslavia recognized by the major powers.

The history of this Provisional Government, integrated and synchronizing with military developments, is briefly this: There had been CP-initiated Popular Front meetings in the spring of 1941. Then, on November 20, 1942, on the initiative of Tito's Supreme Headquarters and with much popular support, a country-wide organization, AVNOJ, the Anti-Fascist Council of National Liberation of Yugoslavia, had met in Bihac, Bosnia, the momentary capital of the Liberated Territory. The delegates, representing nearly all regions and nationalities, and including priests, created an Executive Committee which would free the High Command of political and administrative responsibilities unlinked with military operations, and inspire the formation of regional political bodies by general elections wherever possible. Accordingly, in September 1943, elections were held in the liberated territories of Slovenia, which had a broad Liberation Front. Eighty percent of the total Slovenian electorate voted; whereupon the first Slovenian Parliament—572 deputies—convened and created the nucleus of a new regional government with a clear-cut anti-royalist and Left program. Similar political developments occurred elsewhere. In Serbia and Macedonia, where strong occupation garrisons precluded elections, Provisional Anti-Fascist Councils were created.

On November 29, 1943, the AVNOJ met again, this time in the ancient Bosnian city of Jajce, where 240 delegates from all sections constituted themselves the supreme legislative body, virtually the national parliament. It elected a Praesidium of fifty-six members headed by Dr. Ivan Ribar, a non-Communist, the father of Communist Youth leader Lola-Ivo Ribar. And it created a National Liberation Committee under Tito who, on the motion of Josip Vidmar, non-Communist head of the Liberation Front in Slovenia, was proclaimed Marshal of Yugoslavia. The National Liberation Committee consisted of seventeen members: six Serbians, five Croatians, four Slovenians, one Montenegrin, and one Bosnian Moslem. It was the government of the

Liberated Territories. The AVNOJ made several sweeping decisions. For instance:

> *In order to carry out the principles of sovereignty of the nations of Yugoslavia, and in order that Yugoslavia may be the true home of all its peoples, and no longer an arena for the machinations of reactionary influences, Yugoslavia is being built on the federal principle which will ensure full equality for the nations of Serbia, Croatia, Slovenia, Macedonia, Montenegro, and Bosnia-Herzegovina.*

The Big Three thought this was going a bit too far, too fast. It set a bad example. If other European countries followed it, the Big Three would have an explosive situation on their hands. At Yalta, therefore, early in 1945, Roosevelt, Stalin, and Churchill worked out the so-called Tito-Subasic formula, under which Tito was required to affiliate the NLC with the royal Yugoslav government-in-exile. Tito almost choked on that one, and his apparatus had to work overtime to quiet the outraged multitudes in the Liberated Territories and assure them the King wouldn't return, that the Soviet Union favored the arrangement only because it wanted Big Three unity, and that Ivan Subasic and other leaders-in-exile who came into the Provisional Government under the premiership of Tito were as provisional as any other members. A general election would be held as soon after the whole country was liberated as possible, and the people would adopt a new constitution and vote into and out of power anyone they wished.

By then the Popular Front that included the CPY, which at least thought it knew what it wanted, had become a holding company of Yugoslav patriotism, an effective political organization taking in all the elements untainted by collaboration or out-and-out pan-Serbian royalism. The widespread and solid basis of this coalition, of which the royal government-in-exile and its friends in London and Washington had no more understanding than the Man in the Moon has of Swiss-cheese manufacture, was the tens of thousands of people's committees which had sprouted into existence during the war under the ideological guidance of Mosa Pijade, Edvard Kardelj, and a few other leading Communists as well as several non-Communists with a precise sense of statehood.

As I suggested earlier, these people's committees had a long tradition in South Slavic history. The majority were elected as democratically as any group could be elected during a revolution, in the Balkans or elsewhere. Its members held office for one year, then were eligible for re-election or could be replaced. The majority were headed by local Communist *aktivisti* because Communism was hitched to the Soviet Union, which was bearing the brunt of Axis might, and because they were the ablest individuals around or could go through the motions of knowing what needed to be done. Not a few people's committees were headed by pro-Communists, non-Communists, anti-Communists, or anyone regarded as competent to run the affairs of the community. Real or sustained administrative competence, however, irrespective of politics, was a rarity, especially in the chaos which ruled in Yugoslavia during and immediately after the war. There was much awkwardness and muddling; here and there local leaders, both Communists and non-Communists, tried to screen their inexperience by bluster and the insistence that this was how things were done in the Soviet Union—— Long live Stalin!

Wherever it was possible, people's committees were formed in the autumn of 1941; many of them in cities, towns, and villages occupied by the enemy. By '44 they had become a general institution in the liberated territories. They displaced the prewar administrations and, most emphatically, the gendarmerie which, in most cases, ousted itself by siding with the quislingist or occupation authorities. The old gendarmerie was replaced by a people's militia.

In many instances, the new committees were democracy at its best. Through them the populace began to participate in the administration of local affairs and register its wishes in larger issues. Many committees held mass meetings three and four times a week. They worked up a terrific popular abhorrence of illiteracy and fatalism, and a driving enthusiasm for education and programmatic action. During 1941–45 one of their chief functions was to help supply food for the fighting forces in the near-by woods. Going about it, many of the committee people, particularly women, even the very old, were as daring as the fighters. Enemy snipers could pick them off far more easily than they could the armed Partisans. How many of these folk fell is unknown.

The democratic procedure of the few people's committee meetings I attended in Slovenia early in 1949 impressed me, but later in Slovenia and elsewhere I met leaders of people's committees, both Communists and non-Communists, who depressed me. On the whole, however, they were a vast improvement over prewar royal bureaucracy. In all cases, they were as democratic as the people wished or could make them, or were full of potential democracy whose actualization depended on the people, on conditions in the country, on the wisdom of the analyses and recommendations reaching the villages and towns from the top- and second-level leaders in Belgrade and the other five republican capitals.

During the war, too, a powerful security organization, the OZNA, had developed under the organizing genius of Aleksandar Rankovic. It had been essential to the fighting phase of the Revolution. After the war, the OZNA's main duty was to help the leadership implement the Revolution, create a new state, and build socialism. It consisted of tried and trusted Communists loyal to the CC, CPY, and remained a component of the New Yugoslav Army.

The OZNA was not subservient to the Soviet security police. Indeed, its development as part of the Yugoslav Revolution precluded its subservience to anything outside of Yugoslavia. After the war, OZNA-men promptly reported every effort of the Soviet secret-police agents—who came to Yugoslavia as members of Soviet cultural and commercial missions—to lure them into the Soviet espionage service which was being set up in the rest of eastern Europe.

In 1948 the initials OZNA were changed to UDBa. In 1949 I became quite well acquainted with Rankovic and two of his aides in the Ministry of the Interior, of which the UDBa is the principal division, and with the ministers of the interior of three of the six republics of the Yugoslav federation, and numerous operatives. I have never encountered a more intense devotion to a cause. My impression was that every member of the organization was ready to die not so much for Tito personally, whom they revered, or for Marko, whom they loved, as for "Tito," the symbol of "everything."

"Tito" had become a name to several tens of thousands of Leftists by 1938 or '39. Most of them had never seen him; but, somehow, they felt that here at long last was an honest and energetic leader. In the second half of 1941, in the midst of uprisings which at first glance seemed to have failed, the name "Tito" began to assume legendary proportions. For security reasons, his whereabouts and true identity were kept secret. "Agit-prop" didn't publicize him. Inevitably, as the war whirled on, however, thousands of people caught glimpses of him —and knew or thought that he was the Supreme Commander. He looked the part. Enemy propaganda directed specifically against him helped build him up in the popular imagination as a legend and a heroic leader. If the Axis hated him, he must be good. Occupation authorities also offered a reward for Mihailovic, but Cetniki were heard to say that that was a joke. No one said that the announcement of a reward for Tito was a joke. People talked. They put two and two together and got five.

In the chapter about the Pleterje monastery, early in this book, I mentioned the Gorjanci range of mountains in Slovenia. In 1942, peasants in some of those remote villages, which I visited in 1949, claimed they had seen Tito riding through the forest, sometimes alone, sometimes at the head of an army. One tale led to another. People prayed for him. . . . Popular imagination seized upon the name of a new figure and set it among the other names of messianic characters in Slovenian folklore.

The growth of the legend elsewhere in Yugoslavia is explained similarly. It worried Tito. The CC, CPY discussed it, the "agit-prop" was instructed to put a stop to it. It couldn't. The legend ran rife. Partisan detachments began to make up songs about Tito. Commanders were ordered to order them to cease singing about him. They said that would be a mistake, for they had discovered that the name "Tito" was like a tonic. So the CC, CPY and Tito personally gave up. During 1942–45 a whole cycle of "Tito" songs sprang up, and a number of first-rate poets who had joined the Partisan ranks composed epics about Tito the man and the leader. When the "agit-prop" hesitated about permitting the publication of the first of these compositions, the poets protested: weren't they fighting for liberty, including the freedom of expression?

Throughout much of the war, to a majority of Yugoslavs, Tito was a strange combination of symbol and leader. Millions were concerned about him. Was he well? In danger? Learning that he had been wounded in the Fifth Offensive (it was a slight wound), many wept. The wound brought him still closer to the people. It was said (correctly) that he carried the tommy-gun of an enemy soldier he had killed. He used it when he had to. He was one of the soldiers of the people.

On May 25, 1944, when the town of Drvar was half demolished by Stukas—perhaps as a diversion from the parachute attack—the first question everybody asked was: had Tito escaped? When they learned that he had, the sight of their homes in ruins wasn't quite so crushing.

A few days later Tito arrived on the island of Vis, to establish a temporary headquarters. Several hundred people on the quay were dumbstruck when someone said this was Tito. Then, after a minute's complete silence, some of the crowd broke into wild cheering, others wept for joy, embraced one another, and fell on their knees in thanksgiving.

(I shan't try to explain this phenomenon; for I would get entangled in a complex leader-people ecology if I did. I merely say, parenthetically, that its 1949 form struck me as good and bad, climax and anticlimax intermingling; and I thought as I did when Franklin Roosevelt died: that no public figure should become so important, and no people so dependent on the life of one man. *But——*)

There is no doubt that Tito had turned out to be a military genius. I was satisfied that he hadn't been "trained in Moscow." I asked him how he explained his military ability. He shrugged, puffed at his cigarette, and patted Tigar. I asked him again at a subsequent meeting. He frowned and said that within the whole CP *kolektif,* as it had developed from 1937 on, he just naturally did what the Party or he personally thought should be done. I asked Miroslav Krleza; he repeated what he had said in a public address a few months before: "If it weren't for Tito, we wouldn't be here"—which was no answer to my question.

That Tito was the mainspring in a very taut situation not of his making, is also part of the picture. I asked his closest associates how they accounted for him. I asked Kardelj. At first he said he didn't know how to reply, then he thought aloud:

"Tito just knew how to work with others whose minds worked differently than his, and who used different methods. His whole makeup was—is—geared for collective work. Somehow, he 'nullified' the weak side of those about him and brought out their good features. He had an almost infallible instinct about people. He often blew up over nothing but remained cool and calm at the critical moment. Even when he groused, he was endlessly patient—with people and with adversities."

Djilas' answer was similar; instead of "instinct" he used a Serbo-Croatian word whose nearest English equivalent is "intuition." He stressed Tito's faith in people, in the human race.

Pijade's views, I thought, were more precise.

"*Drug* Tito is a Marxist-Leninist," he said. "His principles and ideas are open to discussion but they are always before him. I think I got to know him during the war. He had an incredibly acute sense of our Yugoslav actualities in the world arena. He never thought we'd have it easy; Yugoslavia was a small country with a primitive economy; we'd have to work hard to get through. With battles raging, this or that man dying whom he had just assigned to a task, Tito's mind was forever busy with the probabilities and possibilities facing us, with the imponderables we might meet. His orders, his conversation, his casual remarks, his jokes, showed that he never lost sight of revolutionary perspectives. . . . His military genius? I can't explain it. Maybe his own explanation [which I had quoted to Pijade], that the need drew forth the ability, is all there is to it. All I know is that his decisions were invariably right, though militarily they looked wrong often enough. As the war raged on, for instance, there were hundreds of thousands of refugees, old people and women with children, following or preceding our columns, getting in the way. Tito maintained that they were our people—we had to help them, feed them, if we could. For a while some of the commanders growled about this; then it became the general attitude, and in the long run it acted in our favor. It showed that we *were* a people's army. Our casualties were enormous, but we grew and grew, nonetheless, because the people were on our side. Another thing, Tito gave orders that the wounded were not to be abandoned, and sometimes more men were killed rescuing the wounded than were rescued, but this too paid off in the long run. Our fighters knew they wouldn't be left to die and you can see how that affected their psychology and that of the people supporting them. . . . Some would say the motive was purely political. I say that Tito's general orders were based on his sense of right. They turned out to be good politics because they coincided with the people's sense of right. . . .

"But speaking of Tito's military talent: Military actions which Tito ordered often were important as military actions, both in scope and result, sometimes even when we seemed to have lost. To Tito, however—to the High Command, to the CC, CPY, to the commanders in the field—they were also, continually and emphatically, the means to our political ends. These ends, besides the immediate aim to hurt the enemy, were: social revolution and the assumption of power by the

CPY, the Party with the greatest prestige in the Popular Front: to overcome the effects of the Ustasi and Cetnik massacres and unite the country, to draw people into the *borba* or into supporting it.

"Perhaps the most immediately evident result of the Liberation *borba* was the unification of the Yugoslav peoples in the face of the big powers' disbelief (to put it mildly) that we could unite. The CC, CPY, and Tito personally, spent endless time and energy to frustrate the Axis and its dupes in the anti-Axis world who were bent on blasting a gorge between our peoples to prevent the restoration of Yugoslavia. The Hitlerite scheme of finishing off Yugoslavia once and for all collapsed, I believe, by the middle of 1942, although details of it continued to interest certain circles in London, Washington, and Rome even after '45.... By '42 we had numerous Liberation detachments and brigades and hundreds of people's committees in which Serbians, Croatians, Catholics, Orthodox Christians, Jews, and Moslems served side-by-side, not because the CC, CPY wished them to but because they—the people—wanted to. Old Yugoslavia had been despised; here, in this many-sided Tito-led *borba* was the perspective of a new—a people's—state, and the mixed detachments and people's committees experienced a special satisfaction in the fact that they were mixed, as though they sensed that their very existence erased the whole Himmler-Rome-Pavelic-Mihailovic-etc. insanity or criminality, and that a decent new society was possible. . . . I can't tell you why I think so, but without Tito, or rather without the CPY headed by him, the passion to re-create Yugoslavia against such odds, if it had appeared at all, might have foundered. . . . During and immediately after the war, although we had, *ugh!* various and many unpleasantnesses with Moscow, we were unwilling to believe that the Soviet Union didn't want the Yugoslavia we envisioned. But this is a chapter of our story that as yet [early in June 1949] some of us don't know whether we want to go into."

Throughout the war and until 1948 the CC, CPY and the Party membership and the Yugoslav peoples at large were strongly pro-Soviet. The Soviet Union's defeat by Hitler would have been calamitous to the Communists' cause in Yugoslavia. In an article entitled "Join the Partisans!" published in September 1946, Kardelj proclaimed that it was the duty of the Yugoslav peoples to put up as stiff a fight as possible in order to reduce the concentration of enemy troops on the

Eastern Front. "We will be unworthy of freedom if we wait for others to win it for us."

In the summer of 1942 a vast armada of German planes bombarded Partisan positions in Bosnia. Tito had no aircraft, no anti-aircraft guns; but watching the attack, although (as we shall see) he had recently had an unpleasant exchange with Moscow, he remarked, "Well, if they're here, they're not on the Eastern Front." This remark became a byword popularly used thereafter especially when enemy attacks were extra severe. Late in '43 the Liberation Movement was immensely proud that it was holding twenty-odd Axis divisions in Yugoslavia which otherwise would be fighting the Russians. News of German retreats on the Eastern Front, of the Soviet victory at Stalingrad, of the retaking of Kiev, were causes for celebration. Somewhere in his immense *Dnevnik* Vlado Dedijer mentions that one day Milovan Djilas, having just heard a radio report of a Soviet victory, gave vent to his joy by stepping out of his hut in a Bosnian forest, firing his pistol in the air and shouting the news to Partisans, nearby, who hadn't heard it yet.

At the same time, several CC members and other leading Communists, Tito and Pijade among them, often were highly uneasy—with good reason—about their uncritical attachment to the USSR, about their Party's and their country's emotional-political dependence upon her existence. As ardently as they believed (amid fleeting doubts) that the Soviet Union was the Socialist homeland, that the Kremlin was the citadel of the International Working Class, that Moscow was the Athens of Marxist thought, they felt that their attitude was too exclusive, too single-tracked. Tito talked with American and British newspapermen who were superficial writers but seemed decent fellows personally, trying to find out if the "West" might be willing to accept the Yugoslav Revolution. Re-reading a letter I received from him early in 1944, in which he thanked the South Slavic Americans for their efforts to interpret the struggle he was leading to other Americans and the American government, I see now that that was the gist of it. But most of the time the official and journalistic "West" literally went out of its way to indicate its disapproval. When "Anglo-Americans" began sending aid to the Partisan forces, airplanes dropped quantities of shoes which were all left-footed, and food where there was an abundance of it, not where people were starving. This occurred too often to be accidental. More than a year after the Foreign Office and the State

Department had absolute proof that Cetniki collaborated with the Axis, London and New York radios were still glorifying Mihailovic. And both the British and American armies maintained missions at Mihailovic's headquarters after Churchill had publicly declared that Cetnik commanders were "accommodating" themselves to the enemy.

Major Jones, a middle-aged Canadian, a devout Christian, was parachuted into Slovenia in 1943 and worked heart and soul for the Liberation Forces. He radioed endless messages to Cairo asking his superiors for crucially needed supplies. His pleas went unheeded, and eventually he was pulled out of Yugoslavia on allegations that he was a crackpot.

In the summer of 1943 Brigadier Fitzroy Maclean, a personal friend of Prime Minister Churchill, head of the Allied missions to Tito, informed him that he must not take any of the arms of the Italian army which was about to capitulate. Tito took them anyhow. Maclean suggested that British troops land in Dalmatia. Tito warned him that that might lead to complications. A group of American officers, under Major Louis Huot, started delivering supplies to Tito's forces across the Adriatic. Maclean hotfooted it after Huot and, catching up with him in Bari, Italy, lectured him with cold fury. Huot was recalled to the United States.

Eisenhower's forces in southern Italy favored the Cetniki above the Partisans. On an impulse in '44, I cabled General Eisenhower requesting that someone on his staff take an interest in the pro-Tito Yugoslavs in Italian prisons and help them get back to Yugoslavia to fight our common enemy. Back came the reply, signed "Eisenhower," that So-and-So was in charge of the matter. I knew that So-and-So had been a leader of the old fascist *Orjuna* organization in prewar Yugoslavia, and now was pro-Cetnik. General "Ike," of course, knew nothing about this. I suspected that he hadn't seen my cable, that someone at his headquarters had replied to me in his name. I was sure he was too busy with other problems for me to go on badgering him about So-and-So.

Incidents or conditions like this were commonplace all the way down the line. American officers just naturally took the recommendations of British officers in the Mediterranean area or of Italian bishops before anyone else's.

Early in 1945 the British had a secret "Slovenian government" set up in Ljubljana, consisting of their agents. This outfit was to grab control of the country when British troops passed through the "Ljubljana Gap," as Churchill called it, on their way to Hungary. At the same time, on orders from London, tens of thousands of Cetniki had made their way toward the "Gap." Tito was obliged to order a forced march of an army corps from southern Yugoslavia—less to help the Slovenian Liberation forces capture Trieste, which Yugoslavs felt belonged to Yugoslavia, than to fill the "Gap" with sufficient armed power to deter any venture to detach Slovenia from the rest of Yugoslavia.

Some members of the CC, CPY were one-hundred-percent pro-Soviet, which in certain respects meant being one-hundred-percent anti-"Anglo-American." In the long pull, the CPY pro-Sovieteers who had reservations about the USSR, who in fact often were appalled by the Kremlin (at a time when Hollywood on Washington's urging produced films showing Russia as a promise of paradise), were obliged to go along with the one-hundred-percenters not all of whom were Communists. Among them, for example, were such non-Communists as Dr. Stanoje Simic, of a well-known Serbian family, who because of his prewar experience in diplomatic formalities became Tito's first ambassador to Washington. . . .

On June 19–20, 1949, traveling from southwestern Serbia through Sandjak to old Montenegro, I rode now in Kardelj's car, then in Pijade's. We discussed the *borba,* the Cominform, and related subjects. I asked questions. In America, I said to Kardelj, he had been presented as violently anti-American, as having declared that the movement of which he was a part and the United States were separated by "an unbridgeable chasm": was that true? He said no.

We stopped here and there to get a glimpse of the primitive beginnings of a new mine and shake hands with the shock-workers, who I imagined were Communists assigned to set the example and work tempo for other miners to whom the occupation was a new experience. We crawled over mountainsides to see if anything was left of some cabin where the CC, CPY or the High Command had met on such-and-such a date seven years before. I sat in on the conferences Kardelj and Pijade held with local *aktivisti,* many of whom were rather awkward and all of whom were passionately sincere. As veterans of the war, they were indignantly anti-Soviet because the Cominform resolution had condemned the CPY leadership and declared the Yugoslav *borba* wasn't worth recognizing. But they were anti-Soviet for other reasons too, which weren't mentioned, or were only hinted at.

We stopped in a small town at an extremely high altitude. To make conversation, I asked a man who a while later I discovered was president of the people's committee, if they didn't have a lot of snow in the winter.

"Oh, it gets two, three meters high," he said. "We're cut off completely for four or five months."

"What do you do during that time?"

"The same as we do the rest of the year: work: liquidate illiteracy. We have a peasant cooperative, a couple of new industries, a school for the young and a school for adults who can't read or write. Pretty soon our adult school will be closed for lack of pupils. 'Building socialism' covers all our activities. Let me tell you something. Up here we can go on building socialism not only without the Cominform and the Soviet Union but also without Yugoslavia, in fact even without the People's Republic of Montenegro. Furthermore, we don't care to quibble with anybody whether we or they are true Marxist-Leninists. The Cominform propaganda calls us megalomaniacs—we hardly know how to pronounce the word. But if it means what it's supposed to mean, it doesn't apply to us. We feel as we do for our own good reasons, though we don't claim we're one-hundred-percent right. *Who* is? We try to face reality. The Soviet Union is the way she is, Stalin is the way he is; let them be. If they want to call us names, we'll be patient for a while. But there's a limit to everything. In our own dumb way we believe we have discovered what will work up here and we're sticking to it."

For the next thirty or forty kilometers I rode with Pijade and Blazo —Montenegro's Prime Minister, Blazo Jovanovic, in his early forties, who had been associated with Pijade during the *borba*. They enjoyed my repeating the words of the man in the town we had just left. I added that I thought the Cominform crisis might be a blessing for Yugoslavia. Blazo looked at Cika Janko, as he called Pijade, who pondered a bit; then, nodding, looked back at Blazo, and said, "We were mere copyists of the Soviet system; now maybe we can become creative."

"Spoken like an artist," I said.

As we approached the town of Zabljak, at the foot of beautiful Mount Durmitor, Pijade asked the chauffeur to stop. We were on a spacious plateau. We got out and Cika Janko called to Kardelj in the next car that he and the rest of our party should go on—we would soon follow.

"This is off-the-record for the time being," Cika said. "But it won't be six months or a year from now. In fact, it's silly to say it's off-the-record now. Half of Montenegro and a good many *drugovi* elsewhere can tell you the story. Blazo knows it.

"I believe you mentioned that *drug* Tito told you he was in Foca, over in Bosnia, early in 1942. Foca was our supreme headquarters then, but we weren't supreme in any respect except in spirit. And, frankly, *my* spirit had its ups and downs. It was a hard winter; we'd been pushed around and beaten. At first glance, no one would think we had a chance. We had hundreds of wound and frostbite cases in our hospital in Foca, and thousands of *tifusari* [people with typhus] roamed about or were dying in the villages.

"At the beginning of February 1942 we informed Moscow, through our representative there, that we desperately needed anaesthetics, antityphoid serum, bandages, et cetera; weapons, munitions, boots, cloth for uniforms, and so on. For a time it looked as if Moscow would send it. I was assigned to handle our end of the delivery. It was a high moment in a dismal minute. Moscow had apparently forgiven us for putting red stars on our caps and for calling a few of our decimated units proletarian brigades.

"This plateau beneath Durmitor was picked as the spot where the Soviet plane or planes would drop us supplies. Tito had several exchanges with 'Grandpa,' as he referred to Moscow in conversations with me. He requested that 'Grandpa' be good enough to send also some binoculars and special weapons. He mentioned that if we had weapons for them we could mobilize one hundred thousand men and women in Bosnia, Herzegovina, and Montenegro alone—the masses were on our side and wanted to fight and liberate the country. I have the whole correspondence: a package of papers about so thick. When you return to Belgrade, remind me to show it to you—and even then you won't believe what's in it. I hadn't re-read them myself until recently, thinking it was just so much slop down the ditch. And what I'm telling you now may not be exact in every detail but it's true in rough outline. Blazo, correct me if I mix up dates or the like.

"In one of his messages to 'Grandpa' Tito asked Moscow to parachute to us—along with the medicines, et cetera—a few members of the Soviet armed forces. He assured 'Grandpa' they would be completely safe in our Liberated Territory, and very welcome. They could observe our resistance movement first-hand and report to him. 'Grandpa's' recent messages had bristled with misconceptions about us, which worried Tito and the rest of us. Tito admitted to 'Grandpa' that right now we were up against it, but he also said that the potentialities of the fight we had started against the fascist invaders were great and that a few Soviet men dropped amongst us would have a wonderful effect. (I'm paraphrasing from memory.)

"One of 'Grandpa's' first messages asked us to issue a manifesto to other peoples in Europe, particularly the French and the Czechoslovaks, to rise against the occupation. Tito agreed. 'Grandpa' then specified that we should call on Europeans to cease manufacturing munitions for the Germans and to disorganize the transportation systems. Tito was all for this. We proceeded to draft the manifesto and Tito reminded 'Grandpa' that our need for medicines, et cetera, was desperate: could we please have them right away? It was a matter of life and death for many of our people. Moscow replied that sending us supplies involved technical problems. This went on for a couple of weeks while in Foca our doctors had to go on amputating arms and legs without anaesthetics.

"Finally, the date for the arrival of the Soviet plane or planes was set—February 23. I'll never forget it. First of all, it was the anniversary of the Soviet Army which our Liberation Forces celebrated; secondly, the day before I had had to hoof it to Zabljak through snow deeper than I am high in order to make sure that a beacon would be lighted when we heard the aircraft approach. The Russians had the exact latitude-and-longitude location of our 'airfield,' but they asked us to light a beacon. Reasonable enough.

"You see that village over to the left? That's Junca Do. It looks close but it's seven kilometers from Zabljak, and I know. I walked the distance I can't count how many times through spots where snowdrifts were six feet deep. . . . The people of Junca Do had four stacks of hay a little this end of the village. They gave us permission to burn one haystack. They were on our side and asked no questions. We were Tito's people, that was enough.

"About sixty Partisans, none too well clad for near-zero weather, were distributed over the plateau. The wind sang around Durmitor and whipped up snowdrifts. . . . The man who first heard the planes was to fire his gun; then the others were to listen hard; when they heard the roar too, they were to fire; whereupon the crew at the haystacks, fifteen men under my command, would clear the snow off the haystack and set it blazing. That would be the signal, and down would come the supplies and, we hoped, several Soviet army men.

"We were on the alert the whole night of the twenty-third, straining our freezing ears. No planes came. I thought it was due to some misunderstanding of dates between us.

"There was a telegraph line between Foca and Zabljak, but the blizzard had knocked it out. Our men couldn't repair it immediately. So Tito and I communicated by couriers. They tracked through blizzards—through winds that pushed the breath back into their lungs. We sent two together so one could pull the other out if he sank in a drift.

"I also thought the delay might be due to bad weather. If it was bad here, it might be worse in the Caucasus. But we kept vigil in the cold every night. . . . Our 'operation,' incidentally, was top-secret. We had closed all approaches to the valley except for couriers. Deep snow closed most approaches to the plateau, anyhow; and, as I said, everybody was on our side in any case. The villagers watched with intense interest, but swallowed their curiosity. I suspect everybody knew what we were about.

"No planes. But I had no doubt that at least one would come. To make things easier; or, rather, so as not to freeze to death, we erected a makeshift hut near the haystacks. Except for its smokestack and the top of the roof, it wasn't visible above the snow. I felt like the head of a polar expedition. We reduced the number of spotting crews and posted all of them near habitations so the men could go inside and warm up after standing watch in the snow.

"No planes! Not even one! We kept vigil every night until March 29! Thirty-seven nights!

"During the first half of March I received three messages from Tito which indicated he was still exchanging radiograms with 'Grandpa.' He asked me not to worry about having to wait; then he wrote me to be patient a while longer. . . . One message [dated March 11, 1942] was longer than the other two. *Drug* Tito revealed that he and 'Grandpa' were having an argument alongside of which, I thought, the delivery of the medical supplies was of secondary importance. Believe it or not, 'Grandpa' objected all over again to our struggle as being too communistic, we had no business having proletarian brigades, and why didn't we have a Popular Front, and—most objectionable of all—we had no consideration for the Soviet-British-American Coalition. We had heard those objections before, as you know; and when I left for Zabljak, I thought they were over with. Now here was the whole to-do again, burning hot. Tito wrote me that he had told 'Grandpa' he was mistaken: we *did* have a Popular Front, our movement had a broad national base and appeal; we *did* see the value of the Soviet-British-American Coalition, and we wouldn't do anything to disturb it. Our movement didn't bring on the quislingist regime nor the Cetniki; they had existed before our uprisings. As for the proletarian brigades, they were exceedingly popular and by their heroism were setting an example of fighting for freedom and independence.

"This latest exchange began a day or so after I left for Zabljak to make sure about lighting a beacon when the Russian planes came over with the supplies. It began when 'Grandpa' wanted us to redraft our manifesto, which, it seemed, had too many revolutionary phrases like 'Long live Stalin!' and 'Long live the USSR!' Tito and the rest of the High Command in Foca wondered about this, but it was decided to follow 'Grandpa's' suggestions as long as they didn't threaten to stop our struggle dead in its tracks, and as long as the wording of the manifesto had a kinship to truth. . . . Message followed message; more suggestions, more criticisms of our newest draft. From our angle, each criticism was more fantastic that the one preceding it; and what ultimately became clear was that 'Grandpa' didn't like our *borba*. He had diplomatic relations with the King of Yugoslavia and his government-in-exile in London; and if Mihailovic fought us it was our own fault; 'Grandpa' came within a split hair of saying that it served us right.

"The correspondence is too voluminous and repetitious to read in its entirety. It continued into the summer of '42, until about the time the 'West' began to recognize our existence and call us Stalin's stooges. I'll show you the key messages, if you like—off-the-record for the time being, as I say, because the CC, CPY hasn't yet decided to permit their publication.

"At any rate, we didn't issue the resistance manifesto which 'Grandpa' had originally requested, because now he didn't want us to. He'd changed his mind. Our kind of resistance was all wrong. I don't know what you'll make of the exchanges; but it isn't impossible to conclude from some of them that 'Grandpa' wanted us to cease fighting and relinquish Yugoslavia to the Axis, the quislingists, and Cetniki, and let the massacres continue.

"In the meantime, here we were on this plateau in the winter and snow. We strained our ears night after night. And then, shortly before dawn of March 29, a great hullabaloo went up outside our hut. One of our boys at the far end of the plateau had fired his rifle. He had heard the distant roar of a plane. We heard it, too; it came nearer and nearer. The men nearly went crazy with joy. The plane! At last! Maybe several planes. The Russians! Everybody shot off their rifles. Some fired all their cartridges from sheer joy and excitement. After more than a month of nocturnal vigil, here at last were our allies. The 'beacon' crew was so happy that before I knew it they had set all four haystacks ablaze. I protested that we had permission from the villagers to fire only one, which would have been enough; but the men explained they wanted to make sure the pilots would spot us. The hiss and crackle of the burning hay muffled the roar of the plane. We couldn't hear it so well, then not at all. Our eyes were turned skyward for the lights of the plane, but there was nothing to see—only strands of flaming hay the wind was picking up. A few of us scrambled over the snow, out into the dark plateau, and there we heard the roar of the plane again, except that it was no roar—it was receding, then after a moment or two we couldn't hear it at all. . . . Later we learned that it was a British plane returning to Malta. . . . On the twenty-ninth Tito sent me a message to call off our 'night duty' and explain to the men as best I could. 'Grandpa' had just radioed that the delivery of supplies to us was too full of 'technical problems.' "

In the spring of 1950, eight months after Pijade, Blazo Jovanovic, and I stopped on the plateau near Mount Durmitor, Pijade wrote a series of articles based on the 1942 correspondence between Tito and "Grandpa" and Tito and Pijade. They appeared serially in *Borba* in the form of a reply to the Cominform's anti-CPY propaganda which had reached a crescendo on February 23, 1950—the anniversary of the Soviet Army and of the beginning of Pijade's Operation Haystack. The gist of the Radio Bucharest and Radio Budapest outpourings was the, by then, old story: that Tito had not led a resistance-liberation-revolutionary *borba:* that his "clique" had falsified history: that Yugoslavia, like the rest of eastern Europe, had been liberated with "the moral and material assistance of the Soviet Army." Apparently, this was too much for Pijade and he prevailed on the CC, CPY to let him tell the truth. (Pijade's articles were translated into English and published in London late in 1950—apparently for distribution by the Yugoslav Embassy there—under the tortuous title used in *Borba:* "About the Legend That the Yugoslav Uprising Owed Its Existence to Soviet Assistance.")

Follow a few excerpts from the correspondence:

Moscow to Tito, March 5, 1942: A study of all the information you give conveys the impression that the adherents of Great Britain and the Yugoslav government [in London are justified] *in suspecting the Partisan movement of acquiring a communist character, and aiming at the sovietization of Yugoslavia. . . . How is one to explain the fact that supporters of Great Britain are succeeding in forming armed units against the Partisan detachments? Are there really no other Yugoslav patriots . . . apart from the Communists and Communist sympathizers—with whom you could join in common struggle against the invaders?* [Tito had told Moscow again and again about the diverse composition of the Popular Front and the fighting units in Yugoslavia]. . . .

Tito to Pijade, March 11, 1942: . . . A day or two ago I received a letter a mile long from ["Grandpa"]. *. . . To all appearances, London has been meddling in all this, and I am now making a point of sending* [to Moscow] *daily reports, to keep them off the wrong track concerning our developments.*

Tito to Pijade, March 26, 1942 [after coming to the conclusion that it was useless to argue with "Grandpa"]: *. . . From* [all this] *one can see that the Yugoslav government-in-exile and not our policy is the bar to our obtaining assistance.* [But] *hold on a little longer there; we must see what comes of these talks between the Soviet and Yugoslav governments.*

Tito to Moscow, March 19, 1942: *. . . Tell us if we can expect* [any supplies from you], *and when.*

Moscow to Tito, March 29, 1942: . . . technical difficulties are enormous. You should, alas, not count on our mastering them in the near future. . . .

The same day, after receiving Tito's telegram that Soviet aid was not forthcoming, Pijade assembled his Partisans and "did what I could," he wrote in 1950, "to avoid having them too disappointed and to instill faith in the strength of the Soviet Union which in the end would nevertheless assist us. But the elder men, who clearly saw what a difficult position we were in then in Montenegro [and who knew that the Cetniki were simultaneously getting aid both from the Italians and the British], wept when they had to disperse from that site where for thirty-seven nights we had waited in vain."

Tito to Moscow, May 13, 1942: *At two places astride the village of Stavalj and at Stitovica near Bjelo Polje, British aircraft have dropped thirty-seven machine-guns, four field guns, a large quantity of ammunition, medical material and gold, to Cetniki fighting us. The supplies did not reach the Cetniki but the Moslems* [under a quisling Hitler had imported from Arabia], *who handed it to the occupation forces.*

Tito to Moscow, May 24, 1942: . . . *The people curse the Yugoslav government in London which, through Draza Mihailovic, is aiding the invader. On all sides people and fighting men are asking why the Soviet Union does not send us aid, even if it is only automatic weapons and ammunition. Our Partisans are fighting with unprecedented heroism. . . . Is it really impossible to do anything in London against the present traitorous policy of the Yugoslav government there?*

Tito to Moscow, May 30, 1942: *On May 28 a regiment of the Pusteria Division attacked our Partisan units near Meliak in Sandjak. The Italians were beaten off with heavy losses and thrown back to the town of Plevlje. In these engagements about sixty Italians and twenty-five Cetniki were killed. The Italian Command is doing all it can, here and in Montenegro too, to transfer authority to the Cetniki. To this end it is carrying through a conscription of the peasantry for the Cetnik ranks. The Cetniki now always attack in the vanguard of the Italians, and are much more dangerous than these, since they know every track and attack us from all sides.*

Fierce fighting is in progress in Montenegro with the Stanisic-Mihailovic Cetniki and with the Italians. The Cetniki attack in advance of the Italians, they are well equipped with automatic weapons, while the Italians follow behind with artillery and also bombers from the air. Fighting is going on now near Kolasin and Grahov. We have abandoned Zabljak. In Montenegro we have had heavy losses. We have evacuated about six hundred wounded to Piva. Thanks to the Cetnik treachery, the Italians now are losing very little in Montenegro —their camps are protected by Cetniki.

The B.B.C. has frequent broadcasts in the Yugoslav languages talking about the common fight of Partisans and Cetniki against the invaders. That is a horrible lie. All Cetniki in Yugoslavia, particularly those of Mihailovic, fight on the side of the invaders, against our national liberation units. In bestial murder and terrorization they exceed the invaders. The Cetnik detachments are set up by the invaders, who arm them and hand over authority to them. They are the faithful watchdogs of the invaders. We are deeply convinced that the Yugoslav Government in London is also involved in this, and knows it all. Please do all you can to expose this terrible treachery and acquaint the world with it. In a few days we propose to issue a proclamation against the Cetniki and the Yugoslav Government in London. We have kept silent so far, but it is now necessary to unmask this scurrilous traitor game. Please communicate your opinion.

In Herzegovina a real uprising of the people against the invaders is in progress. Our Partisan army is causing the Italians huge losses, but the Italians are making extreme efforts, with the Montenegrin Cetniki, to crush the uprising. The Cetniki of Draza Mihailovic, together with Italian troops, are trying to penetrate Herzegovina from Montenegro, to drown the uprising in blood. We are carrying on the fight under great difficulties. We have very little ammunition, no medicaments, and have to defend the areas where our hospitals are situated.

London's propaganda is deceiving people with its false communiqués. The enemies of the national liberation struggle in Yugoslavia are being aided from London. But despite all that, the morale of our units and of the people is high. The people are confident of the victory of the Soviet Union and of our own victory.

In the summer of 1942 my attention was called to the dispatches in *The Daily Worker* about "Partisan-Liberation" operations in Yugoslavia. I had known its editor, Louis Budenz, since the early 1930's, years before he had joined the Communist Party. I got in touch with him, and he showed me the long cables coming to his paper from Moscow which quoted Tito's reports without ever giving his name. Communiqués issued by the Yugoslav Government in London, covering the same battles, often giving the same dates, place names, and number of casualties, but attributing the victories to "the Cetnik guerrilla forces of General Draza Mihailovic," were appearing in the New York *Times* and other big newspapers. It was about then that I began to tumble to an approximation of what was going on in Yugoslavia. As I recall, I first heard the name "Tito" from a Slovenian politician living in exile in New York, Dr. Ivan Cok, who had a genuine interest in the future of Trieste but who in '44 admitted to me that he was a British agent, although at the same time he hated the British. He tried to induce me to be sensible too, and get some London gold. In '49 he died in New York a confused, broken man.

Thereafter I followed the Yugoslav situation closely, asking as many questions as I could of anybody who might help me to understand it. I saw everybody from Sumner Welles and Adolph Berle in the State Department to Communists in New York and Pittsburgh, at least one of whom, as I later discovered, was a Soviet agent; from O.S.S. officers, who apparently were considering me for a job in their cloak-and-dagger organization, to a secretary of the British Embassy in Washington who was assigned to watch developments of an idea for European reconstruction I had advanced in *Two-Way Passage* that Eleanor and Franklin Roosevelt had seemed to be interested in, and which apparently had caused Churchill some slight concern; from diverse Yugoslav exiles in New York to Fiorello LaGuardia, who was keenly interested in the future of Yugoslavia.

By September 1942 LaGuardia and I became close friends, and we arrived at the bright conclusion that nearly everybody in authority in the United States and elsewhere was downright stupid when it came to Yugoslavia. LaGuardia, whom I used to see twice a week, told me, "Keep your nose clean!" meaning I shouldn't join the O.S.S. or get involved with any group of probable agents. I was a writer, and my job was to pursue the truth and try to tell it. In '43 he expected to quit the mayoralty of New York, become a general directly responsible to F.D.R.; go to Africa, then to Italy; and he would take me along. We felt Yugoslavia might sharpen to a pinpoint of danger either before or after the war. It seemed to us that the Kremlin was split between Tito and Mihailovic. I had no doubt that Tito, whoever he was, was doing the fighting; I imagined Yugoslavia as a vast Valley Forge; and, in August 1942, I was taken aback by Moscow's elevation of the Royal Yugoslav Legation in the USSR to the rank of Embassy.

In 1949 Pijade showed me Tito's August 11, 1942, telegram to Moscow; in 1950 he published it:

The raising of the representation of the Yugoslav Government in Moscow to the rank of Embassy has made a most unfavorable impression on all patriots of Yugoslavia, particularly those in the ranks of our Army, all the more so since this has come at a moment when the traitor government of Yugoslavia is openly collaborating with the invaders, decorating every executioner with hands stained with the blood of the people, against whom we are waging a life-and-death struggle, just as we are against the invaders. Yesterday the Yugoslav Government demonstratively and openly decorated Pop Perisic Djujic and many other Cetnik executioners.

By this, our national liberation struggle has been made much more difficult. All wavering persons and open enemies of our fight quote this not as recognition by the Soviet Government of our national struggle, but as recognition of the policy of the Yugoslav Government in London. Can nothing be done to ensure that the Soviet Government is better informed concerning the traitor role of the Yugoslav Government, and also of the superhuman sufferings and difficulties of our folk who are fighting the invaders, the Cetniki, the Ustasi and the rest of them? Do you really not believe our daily reports? We are asked on all sides what it means, and how are we to explain it to our people? There is already a lack of spirit showing in our ranks. This may have terrible consequences for our struggle.

We underline: The Yugoslav Government is openly collaborating with the Italians, and under cover with the Germans. It is traitorous to our people and to the Soviet Union. We are quite sure too that the [British] Intelligence Service supports this policy. . . .

Tito to Moscow, September 9, 1942: *Why doesn't Radio Moscow speak of the Cetnik atrocities? Who doesn't it give publicity to our struggle? That is what our people are asking; and justifiably they demand at least moral support. . . .*

At this time, negotiations were underway between the Yugoslav Government-in-exile in London and the Soviet Government for the Soviet Army to send a mission to the headquarters of Draza Mihailovic, who by then had been made a general and minister of war by the King. Tito, Pijade, *et al.,* knew nothing of this until the autumn of 1944, when

Pijade, in Moscow, got hold of a batch of top-secret documents in the Yugoslav Embassy there, some of which he published in 1950. Tito had repeatedly requested that Moscow send a mission to Yugoslavia which would make a complete investigation. He received no response. He then appealed to the British and American governments to send missions consisting of clear-cut anti-fascists who would tell the truth.

Britain had agents with Mihailovic throughout most of the first two years. Among them, for a time, was an engineer and official of the ultra-profitable British-operated Trepca Mines in Serbia. I heard about him from the Anglophobe British agent, Dr. Ivan Cok, who fascinated me but whom I trusted only in matters relating to Trieste. One of Cok's duties apparently was to draw me into the British network of agents —or so it appeared—and either for that reason or because he was a split personality, he divulged the information I relayed to Fiorello La-Guardia, whom I came to regard as objectively patriotic an American as any I knew. "The Little Flower" jumped out of his chair and walked up and down his City Hall office.

"Keep your nose clean, Louis! You and I are both agents. You know whose? The American people's and the decent people's everywhere. Maybe it's up to us Hunkies and Wops to save America. Even if the odds are against us."

The secretary of the British Embassy I mentioned, invited me to lunch at his home in Washington. His manner was hospitality and Western civilization personified. How would I like to receive an official invitation from the Ministry of Information in London to visit the British Isles, see with my own eyes that the English were done with imperialism, and perhaps have an audience with the King? I'd love to, I said; but right now I couldn't; maybe later.

"By the way," I said then, "how is Colonel Bailey [the Trepca Mines engineer] making out at Draza Mihailovic's headquarters?"

"How do *you* know about him?" exclaimed my host.

I smiled, trying to assume a know-it-all look; whereupon the British Embassy secretary (who, incidentally, had asked a mutual acquaintance in the Office of War Information to introduce us) told me a number of details, estimates, and surmises about conditions and events inside Yugoslavia which LaGuardia and I afterward found helpful in visualizing the picture.

Be that as it may, Britain was the first to respond to Tito's request to send a mission to the Liberated Territory. If I am not mistaken, one of the first Englishmen to get to Tito was F. W. Deakin, an Oxford don, Winston Churchill's friend and literary collaborator. He reached Montenegro in May 1943. A while later, as Churchill subsequently mentioned in one of his speeches in Parliament, Deakin was slightly wounded by the same bomb fragment that grazed Tito's hand. Apparently, Deakin was impressed by Tito and his movement, and reported so to Churchill.

Then, by midsummer of 1943, a slew of British Intelligence operatives descended on Tito's Liberated Territories. Fitzroy Maclean—also a friend of Churchill's, a patriot of the old school, and singularly intelligent, who knew a smattering of Serbo-Croatian—was their commander as well as the commander of the American Major Ferish, a Texas geologist. Ferish was the first member of the United States Armed Forces to make his way through the red tape in Cairo to a plane from which he parachuted into Tito's territory. While Tito repeatedly requested that "Grandpa" send in a mission too, he let Ferish and the British roam wherever they chose with or without guides and do whatever they wished with or without the protection of the bodyguards he offered them. Maclean's mission embarked upon a thorough research job which took months, and might have taken longer, had it not been for the intrusion of Louis Huot, the American major I mentioned before, and two or three of his fellow-officers, including Sterling Hayden, a young Marine who was a Hollywood actor in civilian life. From Maclean's elaborate reports, Huot had concluded that Tito and the Partisans were doing a terrific job against the enemy and should be helped even if they were Communists. Stalin was a Communist too, and the United States was sending him billions of dollars' worth of lend-lease aid. Huot couldn't understand Maclean's hesitancy to recommend large-scale Allied aid to Tito, so he simply made his own way to Tito's headquarters—then at Jajce, Bosnia—traveling part of the way through enemy-held territory. He spent an evening there; was impressed by Tito; and while a group of Partisans tracked down Ferish, whom Huot wished to see, he asked the Partisan Commander in Chief what supplies he needed most. He promised to begin delivering the stuff right away without knowing where or how he would get it and how the brass in Bari would look upon his contact with Tito.

Major Ferish, when the Partisans found him and brought him to Jajce, was almost speechless with enthusiasm about the Partisans and the people behind them. Huot asked him why he hadn't reported this;

Ferish replied that he had. The trouble was that his reports had gone through British channels, and were merged with their findings. The two Americans thereupon resolved that Ferish should make his way to Washington and try to see President Roosevelt and give him a first-hand account of the situation. Ferish did see F.D.R. just before the President left for the Teheran Conference late in 1943. And, in an attempt to put Stalin, who was supposed to be a Red too, in a good mood, one of F.D.R.'s first acts—according to Harry L. Hopkins—was to hand Stalin a copy of Ferish's report; however, for reasons unknown to Roosevelt and his staff the gesture didn't go over—the Generalissimo didn't react as he was expected to.

Huot wrote a book *Guns for Tito* early in 1944; but even though he cast his story in semi-fictional form, his superiors in the O.S.S. held up its publication until 1945. He couldn't describe the dressing-down Brigadier Maclean had given him in Bari for ignoring the fact that as part of the Allied setup in the Middle East he was under his command. Huot told me the nub of it—a fascinating encounter between two will-ful men, wherein Maclean was technically correct. I don't doubt, how-ever, that the gun-running between Bari and Tito's base on the island of Vis which Huot and his new Yugoslav Partisan friends organized in October 1943 spurred Maclean into producing a pro-Tito report, which led to some Cairo-approved British aid to Tito and to the sensa-tional reference in Churchill's February 22, 1944, speech in the House of Commons to "Marshal Tito and his gallant bands."

Later Fitzroy Maclean wrote a very readable adventure book, *Escape to Adventure,* more than half of it devoted to his mission to Tito. Per-versely I found it interesting chiefly for its omissions.

There was a diversity of British missions to Tito's Liberated Terri-tories. I mentioned the Canadian, Major Jones, whose pro-Partisan feelings surpassed those of many Partisans'. There was a close relative of Anthony Eden, with a *nom de guerre* and a small staff, who, wrapped in top-secrecy, suddenly descended on the Liberated Territory in Slovenia, tarried a while, and disappeared, presumably in the direc-tion of Hungary.

The foreigner who sized up Tito's movement best, combining hu-man intelligence and sympathy (as opposed to military intelligence), was Colonel Basil Davidson, who before the war was on the staff of the London *Times*. In the middle of 1943 he was on his way to Hun-gary when circumstances led him to parachute into Yugoslavia. He spent several months with Tito and his staff, less in the role of a British Intelligence officer than as a writer. In 1947 his *Partisan Picture* was published in England—in my view, the best non-Yugoslav first-hand account of embattled Yugoslavia. Late in '47 and early in '48 about a dozen publishers in New York and Boston were eager to bring out an American edition; but the "anti-Communist" and particularly the anti-Tito hysteria deterred even the publisher who ranked the book with T. E. Lawrence's famous work on guerrilla warfare in Arabia.

The Soviet Union was the last of the Big Three to send a mission to Tito. I have already referred to "Grandpa's" early unfavorable reactions to Tito's mode of warfare. The mission's personnel included a few pleasantly disposed men and officers; by and large, however, their behavior puzzled the Yugoslavs. It dampened their pro-Soviet ardor and deepened the concern of some of the top CPY leaders about the years immediately ahead. The postwar period was bound to be beset with great difficulties. However, the CPY had survived the corrupt Comintern period of which Gorkic was for them the most obvious symbol; and in 1944–45 the inner group felt that, in spite of all their peoples' technological and administrative backwardness, the Yugoslav Revolution would be worked out somehow. After all, there was Marx, who said so and so; there was Lenin, who said thus and thus; and there was the Soviet Union which, in spite of her failings you could cite by the dozen, *was* a progressive factor in the world. There, too, was all this revolutionary ferment in Asia and elsewhere, bent on putting an end to colonialism and semi-colonialism; and there was Roosevelt's idea for a United Nations which might turn out to be better than the League of Nations. Surely, the European Communist parties would see the point of the Yugoslav Revolution, and help the Soviet leadership to perceive it also.

Pijade, Blazo, and I came to Zabljak in the eerie Montenegrin twilight which begins early even on a late-June day. It had the effect of dimmed indirect lighting. High up on a cliff of Mount Durmitor was a splotch of westering sun. In the glow of the day's end, the mountain breathed a coolness that felt good around my hatless, dusty head, full of Pijade's tale of Operation Haystack. We were at an altitude somewhat lower than the previous town's, but still very high.

Near the first of the Zabljak houses, about a hundred girls, middle-aged and old women met us. "Welcome, Cika Janko! . . . *Zivijo,*

Cika!" . . . "How's *drug* Tito?" Our car slowed to a crawl and the
girls and women all but buried Pijade in flowers. Flowers had been
tossed into our cars as we passed through communities in Sandjak. But
this delightful reception was for Cika alone. It was his day—his first
visit to Zabljak since the war. His face was a study in wry pleasure and
embarrassment. He hadn't expected anything like it, or he wouldn't
have paused on the plateau five or six kilometers back and kept the
women waiting. The car stopped; Pijade knew some of the *drugarice*.
They were delighted that he remembered them. They said they didn't
wish to detain us; the *drugovi* were waiting—we must go on.

In front of a new, still incomplete mountain-resort hotel, a group of
forty or fifty Montenegrins (by then I'd stopped counting people)
hailed Cika as a long-absent much-beloved brother. Many of them were
local CP leaders, *aktivisti* or party whips from around Durmitor. They
were regional *kolektif,* once figures in the armed upheaval, now functioning in another form. Some were very tall, and it was comical to see
them stoop to embrace diminutive Cika. Blazo started to introduce me
around, then gave up. There were too many; I wouldn't remember
names, so—he just made a graceful gesture, saying, "Our *drugovi.*" I
shook a lot of hands. Some were left hands because their owners had
no right arms. Others had no left arms or hands, or lacked a leg, or
their hands were fingerless stumps. There were striking, scarred faces;
but by then all this had become commonplace. The president of the
people's committee in the town we had stopped in early in the afternoon had had part of his face shot off, but I hadn't thought about it
until just before we continued the journey.

Some of the men had come quite a distance. In a way, this assem-
blage was a hastily called reunion of the veterans still living who in the
winter of '42 had engaged in the thirty-seven-day-long Operation Haystack. Ten or fifteen here belonged to that episode. Ten or twelve
others of that group who had survived the war had been unable to
come. The rest—about thirty out of more than sixty—had died in the
borba from the spring of '42 on.

Everybody here knew the story. They also knew that Cika had told
it to me. Blazo may have mentioned it to explain the lateness of our
arrival. Some of them knew I didn't regard myself as a Communist,
yet they all seemed to accept me. A few recalled my visit to Montenegro in 1932.

Pijade and Kardelj were the guests of honor but their real names weren't used. Pijade was called Cika; Kardelj was "Bevc."

Travel weariness had left me. I felt deeply stimulated. I had been placed near the middle of the long table and was crowded on either side but I didn't mind. There was an abundance of food and drink but I couldn't eat or drink anything except water, which had a cold tang. Hardly anyone was interested in food. Somebody behind me whispered that I had a room upstairs, but I never got to it. The crowd stayed up all night. There was so much ground to cover. Time didn't matter. Shortly after daybreak we visitors washed up a bit, and—with Blazo and two or three other Montenegrin CP leaders—departed from Zabljak. An old woman by the roadside cried out, "Greetings to Tito!"

The night passed like a combination of eternity and an instant. Studying our hosts, I imagined that most of them were average in ability, perhaps under-average in precise capabilities required in a would-be industrial society. They all were Communists, or so they would have called themselves had I asked them their politics. Again and again, I glanced at some scarred, curiously expressive face, thinking: "this man *believes* in something." The room was crammed with passionate conviction which might be askew on one level but was fundamentally sound. It was immaterial what this or that man might call it if I asked him. Intermittently, one or another of the men nearest me in the middle of the table asked me a question, or I asked them one. For the most part, I sat, looked, and listened. No one talked loudly, yet those at one end of the long table seemed to hear every word said at the other end. In a low voice I asked the man next to me a question; he couldn't answer it; somebody way down the table, twelve feet away, answered it. I wasn't surprised. I had noticed elsewhere that former Partisans possessed an extraordinarily sharp aural faculty—almost a sixth sense.

Most of the talk, from beyond the fourth or fifth man on either side of me, I didn't hear; and most of the fragments of the conversation near me that I did hear were a repetition, in effect, of what I had recently heard in Slovenia, in Istria, in Croatia, at Uzice and at Zlativor two or three days before. There was wisecracking about the latest Cominform radio slanders. Questions were addressed to Kardelj and Pijade, some to Ales Bebler, a few to me—about the Soviet and the rest of the Cominform's behavior. How was *drug* Tito? When would he visit Montenegro again? . . . Someone asked me if America would start another war. Was American capitalism crazy enough and so true to the Marxian analysis that it had to have another war? I couldn't answer quickly. The others stopped talking and gave me a chance to organize my thoughts. I wasn't sure anyone was satisfied with what I said; perhaps I was least of all. . . . What about the United Nations? Did it amount to anything? Bebler tried to answer that one. . . . The questions directed at Kardelj implied respect; those at Pijade, respect and love.

There was great freedom in the Montenegrins' manner and speech, but also marked restraint. A thought recurred to me: here, too, as elsewhere in Yugoslavia, a New Birth of Freedom impended, *but*——

This was Montenegro, new Montenegro, or at least a good representation of it. Several of the men, besides Blazo, were members of the Central Committee of the CP of Montenegro. The *partizanstvo* I had observed elsewhere was more intense here. Tito was referred to infrequently; but "Tito" was here, the Montenegrin conception of "Tito," which wasn't exclusively Montenegrin. Essentially the same condition or quality existed in other regions of the country. It was an awkward, strained condition in which people were bent on attaining liberty by means of what the "West" called dictatorship.

In the past few months I had had a fleeting sense of a symbiosis, of a union of parodoxical circumstances in New Yugoslavia. Take this: our tour was in charge of the UDBa because Kardelj and Pijade were with us. A dozen former Partisans, under the command of a colonel of the security organization, had been detailed to guard us—with their lives, if necessary. A carful of them drove ahead of us, another carful behind. At each place we came to we were met by the local UDBa officer-in-charge. UDBa-men were posted outside right now, I was sure, to protect the carefree-seeming gathering inside, where nearly all the talk, to which I tried to listen carefully, revolved around liberty and truth and justice. Paradoxical? Yes. But a police state? Fiddlesticks! The room was charged with its antithesis—with piercing honesty. But I also had the feeling of suspense: that this was a between-and-betwixt moment in Montenegro, in Yugoslavia——

Three weeks before, the old Slovenian poet Oton Zupancic had died in Ljubljana. I had become well acquainted with him in 1932–33. During the war he was too frail, too ill, to go into the woods with most of the other leading Slovenian poets, writers, and artists; pro-Partisan doctors kept him in a hospital—he suffered from asthma. But now and then he wrote a poem which was smuggled out of Ljubljana to Mount Rog, the Slovenian "Musa Dagh," and the press department of the Slovenian People's Liberation Front published it under a pseudonym and many Partisans, knowing it was his, learned it by heart.

A unique and, at the same time, ordinary man, Oton Zupancic sometimes didn't write a line for years. He said he didn't have anything to say. For about fifteen years before the war he supported his family by holding the job of director of the theater in Ljubljana, and by translating Shakespeare and John Galsworthy. Then he would write a poem that summed up the whole period. This is true of his wartime poems written mostly in the hospital. One of them said: "The future devolves on faith. He who dies for it rises into life as he slumps into death. . . ."

Early in June 1949, as I say, while I was in Belgrade, Oton Zupancic had died in Ljubljana, and with a trainload of people, including Edvard Kardelj and Boris Kidric, I went to the funeral. The poet's death, long expected, evoked a great outpouring of emotion. For two days and two nights over one hundred thousand men, women, and children passed by his bier. An equal number walked in the funeral procession or stood along the way, many weeping, tossing flowers at the old horse-drawn hearse. University students, young men and women —former Partisans—preceded it, each carrying one of Oton's twenty-odd books of poetry or one of the half-dozen Shakespeare plays or one of the three or four Galsworthy novels he had translated. Three teen-agers carried copies of his three books of children's verse dealing with a mischievous sparrow called Ciciban.

At the cemetery, before the casket was lowered into the grave dug next to the graves of other literary figures of tiny Slovenia, representatives of writers' organizations, academies, and the federal Ministry of Culture delivered short orations in all Yugoslav languages. Some were very moving. Thousands of people lined up and filed past the grave, and each threw in a handful of earth as he or she went by. The burial was a junction of sorrow and festivity. It seemed to be the acme, not the end, of the poet's life.

After the funeral I returned to Belgrade in the special train that had brought the representatives of the federal government and the literary unions of the several Yugoslav nationalities to the funeral.

Everybody was a Partisan and an unwritten novel. Through the long, dragging night I sat in the corner of the uncomfortable car with six or seven men discussing poets: Goethe, Pushkin, France Preseren, Oton Zupancic . . . and Njegos, the eighteenth-century Montenegrin poet-ruler. His epic, *The Mountain Wreath,* became the center of the discussion for a while. Gradually the emphasis shifted from Njegos' form and style to his content. It had to do with man's need to struggle for freedom, to demand and accord respect, to aim at the creation of a free society that would exist for and around him, individually and collectively. Truth and justice, Njegos had held, could exist only in a free society; and humanity would never achieve freedom in states built on power, on covetousness or the interest of a particular group, religious faith, or dynasty. Man, Njegos maintained, needed to find himself, become conscious, extricate himself from his predicament of bondage, and erect a political structure that allowed liberty for the complete, responsible individual.

The discussion avoided practical politics. The two or three men leading it stuck to Njegos—his ideals and concepts, his lofty implication that he, a Montenegrin poet and ruler, had been proud of being a Montenegrin only in so far as he believed that Montenegrins would never cease reaching for self-realization and would never fear risking death to attain a re-direction toward a new society. The philosophy underlying the poetry of Njegos affirmed that everything else in life was secondary. As a ruler, he had been unhappy about his own government. At her best, Montenegro had exemplified the struggle for liberty, or rather the unified strength that the members of even a very small nation experiences in its fight for liberty. . . . The point of the conversation in the Belgrade-bound train was that this was as far as the best of rulers and of poets had advanced: that all men's problems were interlaced and could only be approached internationally, through the liberation and fulfillment of the whole man everywhere.

In Zabljak, now, trying to apprehend the essence of these forty or fifty Montenegrins, Njegos occupied my mind. I kept wishing somebody would mention him but nobody did. One man showed Bebler a copy of a collection of poems by Oton Zupancic in Serbian translation. Bebler passed it to me, and I started to frame a remark which might lead to a conversation about Njegos. Then someone arose and offered a toast to "Tito's Five-Year Plan."

These men were Communists, I reminded myself. . . . Apart from this toast, however, which contained a reference to Marxism-Leninism, nobody made much of it as a philosophy, or of Communism as a social-economic system. As the hours simultaneously dragged and galloped on, and as I watched the faces and caught fragments of the conversation, I felt and thought that, while these men *were* Communists since they called themselves so, they were nothing essentially if they were not the spiritual offspring of Njegos, or of the culture that had produced Njegos. And they were an eddy in the flow of human affairs that had occurred under the leadership of a man called Tito.

Everybody in the room except me had been a *borac,* a fighter in the Tito-led Revolution. In common with the *borci* I had met elsewhere in Yugoslavia they had *partizanstvo,* meaning all the Partisans collectively; a do-or-die purpose; heroism—and more. The word had to be felt. It was synonymous with "Tito" and linked with the CPY. Its history was younger, but its background was a thousand years older if one put the history of the *Party* in a recent chapter by itself, which some of the Yugoslav Communists were trying to do in their, to me, foolish attempts to answer the Cominform.

Partizanstvo was an aggregate of qualities—of spirit—that Njegos and France Preseren and Walt Whitman and many other poets had sung about. The heroism that went with it was matter-of-fact, humdrum. *Partizanstvo* was the mélange of meanings and practices that had crystallized in different sections of Yugoslavia toward the end of 1942 or early in '43, after Tito and some of his co-leaders half-consciously concluded that, while the fiction of their tie-up with "Grandpa" was important, their immediate future rested solely or largely on themselves, on whether the people accepted their leadership, at the same time that many Partisans half-consciously came to the same conclusion that their future depended on the outcome of the *borba* which would continue after the war and branch out variously, and that therefore it devolved on them and the people behind them to achieve the outcome they wanted. This decision, or this cohesion, pressed upon the Yugoslav revolutionary leaders and masses, was at the core of *partizanstvo,* eagerly internationalist in abstract outlook, but sceptical of the world as a whole for the time being, and therefore reaching into Yugoslav cultural and individual resources.

"Heroism" was an ancient word. It had a certain vitality of meaning in the Balkans; just what it meant, was a matter for debate. Early in

the twentieth century some of the city intelligentsia had developed
an aversion to it, because regions like Serbia and Montenegro were
studded with professional "heroes." They sat in coffee-houses sounding
off about their deeds while their women grubbed in the fields. . . .
Now, in 1941–43, the word came up again, and it sounded clean.

Between battles in the woods in Lower Slovenia and elsewhere, I
was told, there had been exchanges of musings about heroes and heroism. What made a hero? What feat did a man have to perform? Was
a hero one who stood up for his rights? Hardly. Anyone who was
half a man did that. And yet, when you came down to it, it did take
something to stand up for your rights, although standing up for
them was the natural, the elemental, in fact the elementary thing to
do; it was what made you human, *ne?*

One day somewhere in Slovenia a man (I couldn't find out who)
said all that was balderdash. As far as he was concerned, there had been
only one hero in all recorded history: Socrates. He advanced quite an
argument, or so the story went; but no one living in 1949 whom I met
had heard it. Those who were familiar with Plato's Socrates in the
early '40's didn't think the old Greek was pertinent to this situation.
He might not have been a hero in a *borba* like this. . . . Christ? The
story in the New Testament made him a martyr; it was his assignment
to become a martyr. . . .

Well, then, was it heroism if you stood up for the rights of the other
fellow? It took courage to do that sometimes, even more courage
than if you stood up for your own rights. On the other hand, if you
came right down to it, what was the difference between standing
up for the other fellow or for yourself? He was simply an extension
of you, *ne?* And if you looked at it that way, what had you? A principle. Very well; so you fought for a principle; but what else were
you to do? And if standing up for the other fellow wasn't heroism
exactly, what was?

For a while, here and there, some argued that "heroism" involved
justice, liberty, truth: right and wrong: good and evil. The hero was
one who consistently stood (fought and died, or lived) for *pravica*—
justice, a much-used word in all Yugoslav languages. What was justice?
Having a thing your way? No; that was bourgeois "rights," said
the commissars; that was selfish (childish, barbaric)—in the long run,
impossible. Justice was having your due, yes; and the other fellow
having his due, yes and that involved many things: your right to speak

freely, to have food to eat and clothes to wear and a roof over your head, and so on. Marx and Engels and Lenin had mapped it all out long ago, the commissars said.

Another thought—distantly connected with heroism—was occasionally explored by the more intellectual Yugoslav Partisans, both Communists and non-Communists, and resulted in observations and views which also favored, or came close to Marxism-Leninism. Social justice, yes. This *borba* was being waged to attain it. But what did the few Partisans not in the leadership *kolektif*, who were trying to think things through, mean specifically? They meant the dominant or central justice, a new system which in Yugoslavia, with her primitive economy, in this era of big powers and of desperate imperialist finance, would have to be collectivist, socialist, communist. Like it or not, there was no other way. That would be an approach to *the* justice from which your various rights would radiate and upon which they would depend. That was commonsense; why call it heroism?

To Partisans who had no intellectual pretensions, justice was social justice, synonymous with liberty—the liberty to express yourself, to say anything you liked within the self-imposed limits of decency, responsibility, and commonsense, to go about your business as one man among many within a *kolektif*, without anyone stopping you, without the other man's or woman's affairs, ambitions, interests, passions infringing on yours. . . . Complicated, if you stopped to think about it. . . . Liberty? Among other things it meant that you could say to the other fellow who tried to hog the show, "Just a moment, comrade, what do you think you're doing?"—and if that didn't work, to nudge him a bit in the tramway, the marketplace, the cinema, on the new project, anywhere; spiritually; at home and globally—politely the first time; then, if he failed to behave like a fellow human being, or like a brotherly state, to bring him or it before a tribunal if you felt it was important. *That* was justice. *That* was liberty. *That* was honesty. *That* was morality; you had to have morality. *That* was utopia—except, if you were a Communist or pro-Communist, you didn't use the word. It wasn't scientific.

The Marx-Engels-Lenin scheme *was* scientific. Even if he had scant respect for Slavs, Marx foresaw such struggles as the Yugoslav *borba*. Even if imperfectly, the system *was* working out in the Soviet Union. Marx visualized a whole era of struggle ending in victory for the people against privileged minorities. "Here read this. It'll help you to understand it all." It was a leaflet or brochure which the regional CP "agit-props" issued, usually in only five hundred or a thousand copies for lack of paper. "When you've finished it, please pass it on and ask the next person to pass it on, too, will you?" . . . Non-Communist Yugoslavs, those who could read, were susceptible to Left reading matter in the '40's, as they had been before to reading matter of many varieties; and this latest material had behind it the prestige of the CPY, the one Party whose leadership had stayed with the people under enemy occupation and which had been so right before the war and immediately after it started. Also, behind these barely legible propaganda items was the prestige of the Soviet Union whose army was said to be engaging over three hundred of Hitler's divisions, first drawing them into the interior of Russia (whether deliberately or not, it scarcely mattered to the embattled Yugoslavs), then pushing them out, chewing them up, demoralizing them, making a stand at Stalingrad, whereas Britain and America—what were they doing? The Partisans had little information about the "Anglo-Americans"; only one thing was certain as far as they were concerned—somebody in Cairo was doing his best to help the enemy-armed Cetniki. True, the USSR wasn't sending any aid, either; but the polit-commissars explained that it was no cinch to fight three hundred Nazi divisions. As it turned out, the patriot-revolutionary Yugoslavs helped the USSR instead; and they died by the tens of thousands doing so. . . . To fight Hitler, to die fighting Hitler, that in itself was a kind of grim utopia.

It was only after months of living with the Yugoslav Partisans [in 1943, wrote the British intelligence colenel, Basil Davidson, in *Partisan Picture* five years later] that I began to be able to assess the motives which underlay their association.

Theirs was far more than a purely political cause. *They saw the future as their own interpretation of Utopia, and this Utopia not a chromium-plated paradise . . . but simply an affair of honest government and self-respect*. It would be enough to remove the fascists and what they stood for, and men would live in peace. Meanwhile there could be no compromise: total war meant everything that a man might know of or possess, and nothing and no one could be spared. Desperation was their mainspring; their beliefs and imperatives arose from the circumstances themselves. [My italics.—L.A.]

The fascists infested the land like filth, and the killing of them had achieved the status of a moral imperative. To gain this new world, this civilization that should arise from 2,500 years of urgent speculation, they proposed in their sublime self-confidence nothing more complicated than the overthrow of tyranny and the establishment of democracy. . . . They were a peasant people concerned with simple and immediate propositions of obvious good and evil.

Heroism? The word, I learned, had popped up again and again in wartime; which caused me to inquire further about it. Heroism? Oh, to the devil with it! It was a romantic concept, strong in Balkan lore. That was true; but it didn't cover *partizanstvo,* others said; in fact, it was almost untrue. . . .

I prodded Josip Vidmar with my questions until he wearied of me. One day he handed me the proofs of a book, *Tovarisija* (Comradeship), the wartime diary of Edvard Kocbek, the leading Christian Socialist intellectual, who had joined the central committee of the Liberation Front in 1941 and who in '49, while a vice-chairman of the Praesidium of the People's Republic of Slovenia, remained a non-Communist.

I found the diary exceedingly interesting (later I met the author: a small man in his mid-forties with a vivid personality and a sharp intellect). A few excerpts, freely translated, condensed:

May 21, 1942: . . . *Here amid the beech-trees are more than five hundred men. Their orderliness amazes me. . . . It is only now that I clearly feel that* [this popular armed uprising] *means a definite break in the history of our little nation. The weapons slung over the Partisans' shoulders are not only the tools necessary for the big cleanup job* [of expelling the invaders] *but the symbol of something new in us Slovenians. They mean the end of our being pushed around; the end of our pessimism, our pettiness and lamentations; the end of our moral non-liberty. . . . Partizanstvo seems to be a sudden focusing in plain view of the hitherto hidden abilities and potentialities of our people. In the eyes of some of these Partisans is a gleam of recent rebirth. . . . One of the young chaps looked familiar. He smiled at me broadly. Then I remembered him. A few years ago he was a withdrawn student in one of my classes* [in Gymnasium]. *Now look at him——*

May 28, 1942: . . . *I met a priest from a near-by town and started to talk with him. "Oh, so you're that Kocbek!" Our conversation was primitive. I was a Christian who held that Christianity needed the dross rinsed out of it; he regarded himself as a Christian too—naturally. The chasm between us. The harder I tried to reach him, the further apart we were—not because he was a simple man but because he utterly misunderstood our realities. It struck me anew that our priests are retarded, immature individuals. Most of them are incapable of grasping what this period is about. . . .*

July 2, 1942: *Rain. I wrote to a* [Clerical] *friend in Ljubljana: ". . . Try to understand us. . . . First of all, the invader must go from our soil; but our struggle, believe me, has a deeper significance. It is part of a new era in Europe; we mean to bring about social changes. . . . This heroism, with all its attendant chaos, is the first release of energies which will take man great distances from his present state, and will frighten him for a while. . . . Our cause is laden with difficulties and fate. The big trials of the human spirit are still to come. Organized religion, as it is today, has sunk so low it cannot help us. Its tieup with fascism is obvious. . . . This poor, ugly fascism with its superficial might. The worst in man given political form. Its chief tool is force—brutality. Its main drive is hate. . . . I find that we here in the forests don't hate. . . . Not that I am optimistic. The new period will need you.* Christian, do you understand me? . . ."

July 13, 1942: *. . . Kardelj spoke. He makes no secret of being a Communist, of his idea that the Party has the only feasible program. At first you resent him, then you perceive that here is a deeply conscious, enlightened man. . . . He and Kidric move at will between our positions in Lower Slovenia and Ljubljana, disguised as railroadmen. It seems that all the men operating the trains are on our side. The Italian guards on the trains are a joke. . . .*

Late July 1942 entries: *. . . Talked with Josip Vidmar. We lay in the grass. Beside him was Zupancic's translation of* The Tempest. *He said something about Goethe, but his highest admiration is reserved for Shakespeare. It is not clear to him what I mean by God, but he said the word for Shakespeare is divine. . . . I sat awhile with Jarc* [a writer]. *We didn't talk. Suddenly he said, "What's happening to me? I feel fear and wonder merging in me." . . . Vidmar and I are worlds apart religiously; he has no idea what I'm talking about when I speak of God; yet I feel he and I are very close. He is not formally a Com-*

munist, but he goes along with the whole Kardelj-Kidric thesis without any serious emendations. . . . Outside the guard was playing his mouth organ. Vidmar paced up down our cabin [on Mount Rog], *then he said: "You know what? The greatest thing one can aim for is a sense of wholeness, of being part of an endeavor that ties in with one's makeup. Culture." . . . A long talk with Vidmar. Then we lay silent in the dark. After a while Vidmar rose: "You know, you're an interesting fellow." . . .*

Late August 1942: *. . . The whole Lower Slovenia is blazing. . . . A big Italian offensive. . . . Nearly all priests are against us; some are actively with the enemy! . . . We're on the run, hiding. . . . No food for days . . . Caught a glimpse of Kidric. His manner leaves no room for doubt that the CP knows what we are about. . . . Vidmar and I stick together. Today he spoke of his travels: Catalonia, Barcelona: France, Paris. . . . Last night we sat around a low-burning fire. Wonderful. And all those men in the woods around us, some sleeping. We are retreating, hiding, but staying on our own soil, not defeated. Vidmar has enormous faith: the enemy can't beat us: our cause is bound to win. . . .* Partizanstvo! *Almost daily I discover new elements in it. It is an antifascist struggle, of course . . . Slovenia's self-defense, of course . . . Slovenia's reaching out for sovereignty within a setup of interdependent nations, and the more nations, the more internationalism, the better. . . . In addition* partizanstvo *has been a complex personal experience. I feel new. Had this war not come, or had I not joined the Front, I'd be going through the old mechanistic routine of so-called duties: teaching, lecturing, writing polemical essays, and of so-called intimate relationships, which I now see were shot through with falsity, pretenses. Back in our "normal" life, all of us used to mill around one another, around our families, friends, acquaintances, and co-workers in the* [Christian Socialist] *party. Here I am divested of all need of pretense and ungenuineness. Here we all have the same direction. We are reduced to bare humanity. There is danger, immediate uncertainty; we don't know what tomorrow will bring, but we know, we just know, this humanity will live. Faith? Yes. But it is realism also. All of us are wide awake as we never were before and ready for anything—no, not unafraid, but confident that even if I, this man, die, there will be a future: a new epoch. Everything we begin, we feel we must complete. . . . Everybody is hungry; our empty bellies are distended;*

*but this is not the crux of our days. Is it that we know this is history?
that through this struggle man is taking a step ahead? ... Most of the
Partisans are so silent. Many don't utter a word for long spells. They
fight; the battle is over; they fall asleep; they awaken to fight again.
... There is a copy of* War and Peace *around. I heard a young man
read a passage from the epilogue to a few others: how man freely de-
cides to do this and that, and how the result then fits into a statistically
defined decision which is called history: how the free will within every
individual realizes itself in large human movements and events: how,
therefore, the exercise, scope, and effect of one man's free will in the
construction of history, swells or shrinks as it comes into play with the
free will of others.... We barely escape, we hide; we are out of breath
from exertion—the first question anyone asks is: Where is Kardelj?
Or: Is Kidric safe? Or: Have you seen Vidmar? And not only about
them, the men whom others regard as leaders, are inquiries made, but
about the rank and file, men whom we know by name and men whom
we know only by sight. This is collectivity——*

Heroism? I found otherwise very articulate people who couldn't
say just what that quality consisted of but who had scant doubt that
the Yugoslav Resistance-Liberation-Revolutionary *Borba* was heroic.
As I have told, I heard men and women yell themselves hoarse calling
Tito a hero, and he allowed it. When I started to delve into him
personally, however, he protested with unquestionable sincerity that
he didn't consider himself heroic or extraordinary. To him, the people
were heroic; and if I wrote anything about New Yugoslavia, I should
write about them. In short, the hero tossed the title back at the people
who tried to tack it on him. ...

Now, in such gatherings as this group in Zabljak, I imperfectly
recalled the nub of passages in Basil Davidson's *Partisan Picture*—
here quoted as he, an emphatic non-Communist, wrote them:

*My own first impression was one of contrast, a contrast between the
utter discrepancy of means available and the end to be achieved. The
only source of supply was the enemy; for it was not until '44 that British supplies began to arrive. This meant that the real issue was a moral
one. The top-hamper of Western Civilization had to go by the board;
only courage and self-sacrifice could be recognized as virtues. Standards
were stepped up until conditions of service in the Partisan Army bore*

no kind of relationship with those of regular armies fighting on the front.

Men could be asked to march barefoot in the snow, or even over the stones of summer, without regular food or drink or the bare necessities of equipment, if necessary for weeks and months; and they were thought contemptible if they complained. And they would do it because for them the war had refined itself into a simple personal equation in which self-respect and survival balanced their pains and wretchedness. Moral comfort had become more to them than feather beds. Nothing like this had ever been heard of in the history of the Balkans. Small wonder that they saw a new world opening before them.

This discipline of courage and self-sacrifice, for which in the first place the Communists were responsible, gradually raised the Partisan Movement to a quite special level of moral probity. Man in the mass is not naturally honest; place him in the middle of a fratricidal war, in which all normal values are swept away in a torrent of bloodshed and violence, and he is liable to be extremely dishonest. . . . The quislingists and many of the Cetniki were to show us to what depths the human organism could sink.

The Partisan leaders knew they could not hope to build a movement with enough moral strength to outlast the fearful handicaps they labored under unless they could inculcate in it a character of moral self-respect. . . . To this end of moral discipline they introduced a system whereby each unit, from company upwards to corps, elected a commissar . . . whose duty first and always was to ensure that his unit remained in every sense of the word a popular unit; that is, of the people and for the people.

Here at the foot of Mount Durmitor, it occurred to me that the hallucinatory aspect of the Tito-led CPY and the *borba* wasn't important, except in so far as it helped to bring about the Revolution and sustain it. This was important: that the Yugoslav climax had had a great content of human values—liberty, the do-or-die spirit, and love, and these values were still here. They were right in this room.

More highlights, more sidelights. The latter especially are for me the inside of the 1941–45 climax of the Yugoslav Story. A few need to be known to perceive the dimensions of its outer bulk. These sidelights are personal tragedies elevated into triumphs, seemingly small events, some seemingly large, and chance remarks about *partizanstvo,* Tito and "Tito," as this personal symbol cropped up in the popular mentality during the war. They are chosen almost at random from an overabundance of entries in my notebooks and from the rest of the several hundred pounds of material I toted out of Yugoslavia. Some are condensed from several pages to a few lines. Others are expanded to a paragraph or more, with the aid of an imperfect memory, from a half-dozen hastily scratched words on slips of paper which I stuffed into my pockets and never managed or bothered to sort. To sort them now would give an impression of sequential causality which wasn't a marked characteristic of the Yugoslav Revolution. In a way, Tito's insistence to me early in our June 9, 1949, interview and on other occasions, probably was right: the people, meaning a lot of diverse individuals pushed into collective action by diverse impulses and circumstances, which the CPY intelligentsia chalked up as "Marxism-Leninism," had more to do with the Revolution than the CPY leadership, more than the CPY rank-and-file, although, clearly, the people couldn't have acted without the CPY.

On June 21, 1949, on the way from Zabljak to Titograd—which used to be called Podgorica and which was being rebuilt into the new capital of the People's Republic of Montenegro—we stopped for an hour in a small town famous for its part in the *borba.* We were met by about a thousand people, most of them not very heroic-looking but full of enthusiasm. I can't decipher the name of the place in my notes which I wrote later bouncing over a road not especially made for automobile travel. I could find it by looking at a map of Montenegro, but I won't because the following could have happened almost anywhere in that smallest republic of the People's Federated Republic of Yugoslavia.

In the spring of '48 a small group of Montenegrin Communists, educated in Moscow to be Soviet agents and who took no part in the *borba,* had tried in vain to stage a revolt against the pro-Tito leadership of the CP and the government of Montenegro, coincidentally with the Cominform resolution. One or two of them might still be lurking around. In the nearby mountains a diehard Cetnik "leader" was said to be still at large. He wasn't worth capturing but he might, just might, try to pull a fast one if he learned that Edvard Kardelj and Mosa

Pijade were coming at a certain hour on a certain date. Therefore, the local UDBa man had arranged for the townspeople to be notified of our arrival only about an hour before—time enough for them to don their best costumes and gather up armfuls of field flowers if they wished. In his over-enthusiasm, however, a local *aktivist* had dashed to near-by villages and spread the word that a couple of men from Belgrade—could be Tito himself—were due any minute and it would be splendid if the countryside turned out in a big way. Meantime, we were held up for an hour by a couple of tire punctures and, as we reached the place, country folk were there in full force. Even Bebler and I, in the same open car, were half buried in flowers simply because we were accompanying Pijade and Kardelj.

Premier Blazo, who knew half of Montenegro personally, noticed that the crowd was about double the town's population. Smiling, both amused and embarrassed, as he introduced the visitors, he said something about "this more or less spontaneously assembled multitude," and the multitude, the visitors, and Blazo too burst into laughter. Pijade, who spoke first, commenced: *"Drugovi* and *drugarice* of 'this more or less spontaneously assembled multitude!'"* That released another gale of laughter. The tone of the rest of the occasion was in keeping, except for a dip or two into sorrow. One night in 1943 was referred to, a night when about thirty Partisans and pro-Partisans in the community were seized by Italian- and British-armed Cetniki. The marker of their mass grave was nearby. . . .

Most of the government of the People's Republic of Montenegro still had its offices in the old capital, Cetinje. I had been there in 1932–33. Now the little city was almost as I remembered it, except that the old professional "heroes" in their gold-braided costumes weren't strutting around. During the war some had become the equivalent of Cetniki and after Italian capitulation had fled to Italy, whose Queen Elena (soon to lose her throne) was a daughter of the late King Nikita of Montenegro. Now all Montenegrins, men and women, worked—in itself a revolution.

Blazo conducted us around. On a wall of the National Library were some enlarged World War II photographs. I was startled by the face and bearing of a young man in one of them, and asked Blazo who he was. Blazo said he was Cedo Cupic; his picture and all the others on the wall were found in the archives of the Fascist Italian occupation

forces which had made Cetinje their center from 1941 to '43, trying
vainly to establish a quisling regime, whereby Mussolini could attach
Montenegro to his empire. . . . As for Cedo, Niksic had been his
home town; he had been a student of philosophy and a Communist.
He was twenty-three years old when this picture was taken. In 1942,
the Fascist Italian secret police, tipped off by the Cetniki who supposedly acted in compliance with an order from the royal Yugoslav
government-in-exile, had captured him.

"This memorandum in Italian," said Blazo, "we found attached
to the picture, and we framed them together, as you see. The memorandum says the photograph was taken a half minute before Cedo
was shot. He knew they were going to shoot him. He had refused
to say *Viva Duce!* and to divulge the identities and whereabouts of
his *drugovi*. I knew Cedo. A handsome fellow, don't you think?
Nearly six and a half feet tall. In this picture, he has a four or five
days' growth of beard, and his cap and clothing look a bit worn, but
even so, I believe, even if one doesn't read the memorandum which
tells the story, if one merely studies his face, his smile, the fearless
gleam in his eyes, and that gesture"—with both his hands shackled—
"one can't but conclude that he was a young man of spirit. . . . You
don't read Italian? The memorandum states matter-of-factly that after
Cedo Cupic was sentenced to be shot he was given a chance to save
his life. All he had to do was reveal the names of other CP *banditi*
in Cetinje and Niksic and elsewhere. His fate was sealed when he
wouldn't say *Viva Duce!*"

Mounted on the same wall was the less striking picture of the
twenty-year-old Montenegrin *partizanka,* Vukosava Ivanovic. She had
been a student too. In 1941 a Fascist Italian army tribunal sentenced
her to death.

"Are you really so self-deluded that you believe you have conquered
Montenegro?" she asked, according to the record. "We have a song
which says we should sing it when scum like you come around and
start shooting us."

An enraged or panicky officer personally fired his revolver into her
forehead.

"The Cominform wants to erase Cedo and Vukosava from our history," Blazo commented, "but we can't go back on them. The other
pictures on the wall tell the same story."

On June 23, 1949, our party spent most of the afternoon crawling over the mountain near Drvar, Bosnia, and into and out of the cave that had been the objective of the German parachute attack on May 25, 1944. I followed the steep trail of Tito's escape. One of the two Partisans who had accompanied him told me that once or twice he had almost fainted from exertion. He had ordered his bodyguard to pick up Kardelj (whose feet are crippled) and carry him to safety. Then he had met Rankovic; and, tears in their eyes, they had embraced. "Where are the foreign missions?" Tito asked Marko. He replied that his men had led the Russian mission out of danger. The Russians had a powerful walky-talky and the last he saw of them they were trying to communicate with Bari, Italy, to get a plane to pick them up. Marko had suggested a possible landing place, and he said that if a plane did arrive Tito should go to Italy with the Russians. . . .

In the evening a party similar to the one in Zabljak was given in a bleak new building in Drvar. These *aktivisti* were Bosnians but their talk was not unlike that of the Montenegrins from around Mount Durmitor. Kardelj and Pijade answered scores of questions. One of the men asked me what I thought of the Cominform crisis. I said I had tried to visit the USSR but hadn't obtained a visa. I didn't know the Soviet Union and the Kremlin rulers first-hand. I simply accepted the impressions of them given me by Tito, Kardelj, Kidric, Pijade, Djilas, and other top-level Yugoslavs who had been to Moscow, though I didn't entirely agree with them. Politically, the Yugoslav CP leadership, with a state, with the very complex Five-Year Plan on its hands, couldn't do anything but resent the Cominform's behavior. Analytically, philosophically, as a writer, I wasn't sure I could blame the Kremlin, which dominated the Cominform, for being the Kremlin. I couldn't blame Stalin for being Stalin. Evidently, the Soviet setup was sick; and if it was, what was the best way to treat a sick society? On the basis of the little I knew, I was anti-Stalinist in approximately the same sense that I was anti-malaria. I wasn't a politician; but as a writer friendly to Yugoslavia I felt it was futile to argue with Stalin or the Cominform.

Kardelj took me up, arguing that the CPY leadership was obliged to disagree with the Cominform, if for no other reason than to keep the record straight, and so on. I didn't object to that, I said; it probably was necessary: all heads of states and parties replied to political attacks as a matter of course. The Yugoslav leaders couldn't dismiss the probability or possibility of another world war, or a localized war against Yugoslavia. War or no war, however, I thought it was extremely important that, in working out her new policies vis-à-vis the rest of the world, New Yugoslavia kept alive the spirit of her Revolution. *That* was top priority. Yugoslavia was obliged to prepare for war as best she could; Tito's new army, what I had seen of it, was a terrific outfit even though it lacked modern equipment; and it might be quite a card to hold in the poker game ahead. My chief interest in the country, however, rested on my sense of the moral, all-human values that I encountered and sensed everywhere, in reading the leaders' speeches (including some of those which they now probably wished they had never delivered), in listening to and looking at the people, in crawling over that mountainside beyond Drvar. Yugoslavia was a small country; but, come what may, ultimately she would make her mark in history as a moral power.

On the wall before me was a photograph of a Croatian *partizanka* (her name in my notes is illegible) just disarmed, held by two Nazi paratroopers. The photograph had been developed from a film found in a German camera which a Drvar boy had picked up in a ditch months after the parachute attack. There was no record of the exchange between the girl and her captors; none was needed; her nobly contemptuous expression was enough. In all likelihood the Germans had killed her soon after one of them snapped the picture. Her body was found a few days after the attack.

Before the war, Drvar's population was fifteen hundred; about eight hundred perished in the *borba*—about two hundred on May 25, 1944.

In June 1949 a hamlet near Drvar (whose name I neglected to write down) had four adult males. Its prewar inhabitants numbered sixty-two; there had been seventeen families. Nine were wiped out.

The county of which Drvar is the center had a population of seventeen thousand in 1940. Over four thousand died in the *borba*.

In Belgrade I met Piva Karamatijevic, a leading Serbian artist. A friend of his talked him into giving me an outline of his family's wartime history. Piva was born and raised in Nova Varos, deep in the heart of the Slavic Balkans, on the southwestern border of Serbia and Sandjak. His father, Prota Jevstatije Karamatijevic, was an Orthodox priest, a conservative Serbian patriot until 1937 or '38, practically a pan-Serbian and a devout Christian. He had a large family. Nine sons and daughters grew to adulthood and were educated. Several became Communists in the last half of the 1930's and gradually the whole family turned Left.

Late in 1941, when some of the remnants of Tito's army, defeated at Uzice and elsewhere, passed through Nova Varos, old Prota—sixty-six years old—joined the column. He discovered Piva, another son, and two of his daughters were in it too. The daughters cursed the Cetniki and Draza Mihailovic for their betrayal. A day later Prota's wife, Efinica, about sixty, caught up with him—she wasn't going to be left behind. She was killed a few months later during a battle as she tried to save a member of her family from the Germans who had captured him. Prota wept; but, as far as it is known, that was the only time. After another battle, he found the bodies of two of his daughters. He pinned notes of identification and money to their clothes, requesting whoever found the corpses to please bury them. Tito's army was moving, retreating; and the ground was frozen—Prota couldn't dig their graves himself.

Later still, old Prota came upon the bodies of his third daughter, two brothers, and four nephews. When time and other circumstances permitted, he buried them. Prota didn't distinguish himself as a fighter in the *borba* whose purpose was to kill as many of the enemy as possible. He was never wounded. Tito and the other leaders knew him; they saw that he was an exceptional man, important to the morale of the guerrillas. He moved from brigade to brigade but spent most of his time with the First Proletarians, commanded by young Koca Popovic. He knew Koca's father, the Belgrade banker.

Whenever he came to a village or town with a priestless church, he held services and christened children. In one town the sexton, who was more or less pro-Cetnik, wouldn't believe the old man was a priest: how could a priest be with a Communist army? Prota started to hold services without the sexton's assistance. He chanted the lengthy ritual from memory. Mid-service, the sexton fell on his knees before him, kissed his cloak, and begged forgiveness. Prota said there was nothing to forgive. The world was full of misunderstanding; the job was to quiet it down, remove the disturbers. Meanwhile, how could any reasonable person blame anybody for anything? At moments, however, he condemned the Ustasi, the Cetniki and Draza, the government-in-exile and the king. . . .

Now, in 1949, Prota Jevstatije Karamatijevic was home in Nova Varos—a tired old man, alone, a shabby figure of immeasurable dignity. He seemed to represent a cause in suspense. I met him briefly as I passed through his town during the tour with Kardelj and Pijade.

One evening in Ljubljana, a partisan by the name of Jan reminisced: "Mount Rog is a beautiful place. If there had to be a Musa Dagh, there couldn't be a more beautiful one in Slovenia. One trouble, there was no water. In the wintertime, of course, we melted snow. Our whole Slovenian High Command was there. Water was brought up by men in barrels on their backs. We had a regular civilization: printing press, offices, radio, and so on. . . . Of course, the water was strictly rationed. Boris Kidric, who was our chief political commissar and secretary of the Liberation Front, and Josip Vidmar, who was president of LF and was translating Molière's *Misanthrope* in his spare time, were obliged to curtail their discussions of aesthetics because of the water shortage—their throats became dry too fast. . . . There's a rock under a tree on top of Rog where Kidric and Vidmar used to sit arguing. Their arguments would make a book. . . . No, I don't think Vidmar finished the translation on Rog; too many interruptions. . . . But I began to tell you about the lack of water. The only way many of the Partisans got a little moisture was to lick dew off the leaves at night and early in the morning. That was *partizanstvo* too: not eating for days, except maybe a berry now and then, or an acorn: and licking the dew off leaves for a 'drink.'

"There was a joke going around that you weren't a true Partisan unless you had a weapon and ammunition, wrote poetry, and were alive with lice. That was just about true; between seventy and eighty percent of Slovenian Partisans wrote poetry: we were lousy at least part of the time: each of us had a gun of some kind. Down south, where a lot of *borci* were illiterate, they composed songs orally. But all this doesn't begin to cover *partizanstvo.*"

Jan told me the history of Silas. "He was a Spanish Civil War hero who became a hero of our own war too. In '43 he was one of our most valorous men; if he were alive now, he'd be at least a lieutenant general. He did an outstanding piece of work—just what, isn't pertinent to the story. As a result of his success, he was idolized and the adulation went to his head. He'd had some Liberation Front money entrusted to him to carry out his mission. He hadn't used it all; so now he spent some of what was left to buy drinks for his admirers. He was arrested and investigated. He pleaded guilty; more than that, he said he'd had a couple of men shot for less, so he deserved no less—he *had* to be shot. He had set a bad example.

"Our field commander in chief in Slovenia at the time was a remarkable young man, ever so gentle and sympathetic: Stane Rozman—Silas' closest friend. They'd been in Spain together. But Stane was in another section of Slovenia just then, and Silas insisted Stane mustn't be informed of the jam he was in. Stane might try to intervene. Get it over with quickly, right now, before he heard of it. Silas smoked a cigarette, embraced all the *tovarisi,* the firing squad too, and said he was ready—'Fire!'

"When Stane learned of the execution, he was plunged into agony. He cried, sporadically, for weeks afterwards. At the end he agreed that Silas had to be shot. . . . Silas was my friend too. Now, years later, a wrench goes through me whenever I think of him. . . . A while later a cannon, which the British had dropped to us, exploded as we were experimenting with it. Stane was killed in the accident, which some of us thought wasn't an accident. But before that Stane and I talked about Silas. We'd have given anything to have had him alive.

"Again, I'm not sure you can understand a fragment like that unless you know our whole story. Nor is our whole story understandable without a few fragments like the case of Silas.

"Often some of our people went hungry for days, then we'd come to an abandoned village. The families had left in a hurry to get out of the crossfire. They had no firearms to join the fight. We knew they would come back if we won. Meantime, there were the loaves of bread on the tables and in the cupboards. Our starved Partisans didn't touch a crumb. That was *partizanstvo.* . . . No, it wasn't orders, nor politics, so much as it was morality. Of course we knew that if the people found out we had taken their food, they'd say that we were no better than the White Guards: a plague on both your houses. Then where would we be, without the support of the people? But it wasn't that thought alone, nor even principally, that kept us from taking the bread. Nor the fear of being shot for it. It was justice. We were fighting for it; we couldn't postpone it until after the war; we had to begin having it right now.

"*Partizanstvo*. On the practical, immediate level, it was essential not only because our country was enslaved, not only because there was treason, but also because the Russians—when a few men of their military mission came to Slovenia—had no idea and didn't want to learn, or couldn't learn, that our plight was so bad that we had to fight as we did. Some members of the Soviet mission were remote, critical of us. We loved that Canadian, Major Jones. He loved us. We couldn't warm up to the Russians. They wouldn't let us. I heard one of the Russians talk about King Peter in London as though there was no question he would return. They knew nothing about us, and in '44 a few of us commanders, who had no precise idea what Tito and the CC, CPY were thinking about the postwar period, came to realize that we couldn't depend on anybody except ourselves. That was hard; but what could we do? This picture seemed to change in '46 and early '47; some of the Russians who came to us were quite friendly; we thought there was an international movement aiming for justice among nations and individuals; but it turned out to be an illusion. Later we saw that they had tried to subvert and subjugate us."

Sometime in May 1949, walking with me in Ljubljana, Vlado Kozak, whom I have mentioned before and who had been with the Partisans throughout the war, said:

"No, no; *partizanstvo* wasn't a morbid movement. On the contrary, it was almost gay. Free! Some of us had never felt so free. We knew we might die any day. We were ready. That released qualities within us—fortitude, commonsense, intelligence, intellectual prowess, abilities and talents of all kinds—we never knew we had. People began to express themselves. You never heard such talk before in Slovenia or anywhere else. The joy of it! The world being what it is, the only way to achieve complete liberty may be your readiness to die this moment for something you believe in. And it may be, the world being what it is, that the liberty thus achieved is the only way to release the faculties and talents in men which are necessary to tackle the problems of man."

In July 1942 Tito's forces in Bosnia and Herzegovina were badly beaten. The field commanders thought they ought to pull their handfuls of troops back into Serbia. Tito said no. He decided to head for Krajina, in Bosnia but close to Croatia. He established his Supreme

Headquarters in Bihac; and, as I mentioned, the first AVNOJ meeting was held there.

"Some of the worst Ustasi massacres had occurred in Krajina," General Danilo Lekic told me seven years later, "and most of us didn't relish the idea of going there. But *drug* Tito was right. Politically, it was all-important that we went to Krajina. . . . It seems to be a characteristic of *drug* Tito that in a moment of crisis he chooses the worst alternative which turns out to be the best. I don't know how he does it, but he does it."

In the summer of 1942 Tito also moved some of his forces toward Dalmatia. He sent several of his experienced commanders there who had survived their detachments. Their assignment was to organize the people who would fight and bring as many of the Dalmatian islands as possible under Partisan-Liberation control. The results? The Partisans organized a "navy," mostly of fishing boats, with which they captured enemy freighters loaded with supplies. . . . What else? In the spring of 1944, the Nazis decided to get tough in the town of Puciste, on the island of Brac. They knew the place was infested with Partisans, but where were the swine-dogs? Where were their leaders? The townspeople were lined up—men, women, children—and questioned. Everybody knew the answers. In fact, half the inhabitants who stood in that line while Gestapo officers barked at them, belonged to the Partisan organization in one way or another. Everyone denied having knowledge of such an outfit. The Germans were positive the people were lying. They executed every tenth one of them.

The most unusual fact about Zezelj is that he survived the war. He was from Lika, a Serbian and wounded nine times. In 1949 I met him at Tito's, a huge, blond, quiet-seeming man in his early or middle thirties. He wore civvies. I hadn't heard of him before. Later, meeting him again, I learned that he was a lieutenant general, one of a handful of living National Heroes of Yugoslavia, and commander of the three divisions garrisoned in the barracks around Dedinje Hill. They liked to be regarded as Tito's bodyguard. Actually, these divisions were shock troops—or crack outfits—of the New Yugoslav Army. Every morning, when I lived at Rumunska 15, I was awakened by their singing.

At first Zezelj disturbed me, he so obviously worshiped Tito. I thought that that wasn't good for either of them. Then I saw that for him the relationship was natural, perhaps inevitable. To General Zezelj, as to several other young men close to Tito, Tito was not merely their Commander in Chief but the man who in 1941–45 represented the opposite of the profound disorganization of life they had experienced. In the midst of the overwhelming chaos of war and revolution, Tito had stood for order, organization, re-integration, culture, the soul, a better future. Now, in '49, with the Cominform crisis upon them, they saw Tito—even more acutely—as the embodiment of everything they had fought for and were ready to fight for again. In utter faith, they trembled with eagerness to do something for him this very minute— if nothing else, to strike a match and light his cigarette.

On May 25, 1949, at a house party in Belgrade celebrating Tito's fifty-seventh birthday, I met another National Hero of Yugoslavia, Lieutenant General Miloje Milojevic, commandant of the Belgrade garrison as a whole.

His story: A Serbian peasant boy. A non-commissioned officer in the old Royal Yugoslav Army. Anti-Communist for a time. Then, somehow, he realized how rotten the royal officer cadre was. The collapse of the Yugoslav Army in the first half of April 1941 didn't surprise him; it appalled him. When his own regiment was ordered to surrender, he and a few others hid in the woods. They crept south and formed a resistance unit. They met up with Tito's column.

During the next three years Miloje distinguished himself as a one-man tank-destroyer. His body was riddled by bullets and pieces of shrapnel. Twenty-odd pieces of metal were never removed. When I met him part of his face, with one eye, was missing.

Vlado Kozak talking to me in Ljubljana in May 1949: ". . . The *borba* was fun. We had schools in the woods. Theaters. We even went in for fine printing. Did you see that edition of France Preseren we got out in three colors? I don't know where we found all the ink, rag paper, and type.

"Our forest theaters, outdoors and indoors, were popular. One skit I remember was about a Partisan commander whose brigade had captured a castle. He made his command post there. The scene showed a wonderful bedroom with a canopied bed. But the poor guy was so used to sleeping on the ground he couldn't sleep in it. To catch a couple of winks he had to sprawl his creaky bones on the floor beside the bed. I don't know who wrote the play; maybe it was a collective job—and not by professional playwrights, although several of them were in the Partisans. One version of the play ended with the *tovaris* commander stalking out of the castle and going back to the woods to sleep."

Veterans of the Spanish war were all-important in the early uprising battles, and later.

"We 'Spaniards' had a good deal to unlearn," General Danilo Lekic said to me in 1949. "But our situation in Yugoslavia was different from that in Spain. There we had a state behind us and international understanding and sympathy. In Yugoslavia, five or six years later, we had little to begin with, no backlog, no real base; only the Party, Tito, and the people. I say 'only'—as it happened, it turned out to be enough. Of course, certain incongruities had puzzled some of us in Spain; but comparatively and by itself, Yugoslavia in 1941 and '42 was a picture of chaos. There were about a dozen different armies in the country. As far as we could tell, our movement had no understanding, no sympathy anywhere. Draza was the big resistance leader, the hope of the civilized world, while the Cetniki, armed by the enemy, fought us. Even Radio Moscow spoke well of Draza's 'victories.' The Soviet Union had friendly diplomatic relations with the royal Yugoslav 'government' in London which made Draza its minister of war. We cheered every mention of the USSR and of Stalin's name. We were sure the Soviet attitude toward us would change. Meantime, however, we were alone —and lonely, let me tell you. We had started from scratch. A commander had to pull off an operation with almost no equipment. Then he discovered it could be done. There were the people. They relied on him; he could rely on them; he couldn't fail. There was Tito. His being in supreme command made everything possible. The Party and he showed the direction—it meant bloodshed: but it also made sense. It was the only way."

Early in 1950 an American "news-magazine" reported that to official Washington, thanks to his split with Stalin, "Tito [still] is a son-of-a-bitch but [now he is] our son-of-a-bitch." Ten months later Hamilton Fish Armstrong's book *Tito and Goliath*—which helped "anti-communistic" President Truman induce the "anti-communistic" Congress of the United States to appropriate funds for Yugoslavia—suggested that

Tito was a low-grade David whose sole qualification for the limited analogy was his standing up to Stalin's "most serious mistake." In the spring of 1951, while Tito was reported to be seriously ill, another book came out, entitled *A Balkan Caesar*. It stressed Tito's "feud with Stalin," America's need to play along with him, and the grave danger of playing along with him. "Caesar" is a many-faceted word, as Shakespeare, Shaw, and others who tossed it around in their minds knew. As for David, there is Michelangelo's *David* and the story about David after he became king. The story of Tito isn't finished yet at this writing. It won't be finished long after he dies.

To me, after reviewing intimate glimpses of a career with some blank spaces, and studying hundreds of pictures and several busts and life-size statues of him, the noblest period of Tito's life was 1942–43. Should he live to be a hundred, I doubt if he can do any better.

Late in May 1949 I sat somewhere with Antun Augustincic, a leading Yugoslav sculptor, a member of the Yugoslav Academy, who had lived for months near Tito's Headquarters in Jajce, Bosnia, and elsewhere; and then I made careful notes of his remarks.

I began by saying that I liked details of his statue of Tito as Marshal of Yugoslavia which I had seen in Kumrovec but I didn't like it as a whole—it made him a bit Napoleonic. Augustincic didn't mind my criticism; defending the statue, he said:

"At Jajce my room was in a house across the street from the guarded enclosure where the High Command had its top-secret maps-and-plans cabin. Behind the fence, in front of the cabin, there was a strip of bare ground, sometimes covered by snow. The cabin was on the mountain crest near the present entrance to the ancient Bogomili catacombs, where those heretics used to hide eight, nine hundred years ago. Tito and his immediate staff were supposed to duck into it when enemy aircraft approached. A few times I took refuge in the catacombs myself —be sure to see them if you get anywhere near Jajce. You have to see them to believe they exist. [The original entrance to the catacombs is —or was—behind a waterfall at the foot of the mountain.]

"Every day after lunch, in sunshine, rain, or snow, Tito strode back and forth across that strip of ground, his hands clasped behind him, mulling over (I suppose) his imaginary chessboard, calculating how and where to move the various brigades. He didn't know I was watching him from behind the curtain of my window. He walked anywhere from one to two hours, back and forth, forth and back, like a caged lion. Outside the fence, the guards stood at their post. They didn't look at him for fear of distracting him. No one addressed him, unless a very urgent dispatch had arrived. Just then Tito was in hot water with Moscow, as he told me, for exchanging prisoners with the Germans. 'Why don't they leave us alone? After all, we're in a better position to know what is good for us than Moscow is. I'm willing to give ten or more German POWs for one of our men in Nazi captivity. But the Kremlin, or whoever is making a fuss about this matter, can't see it that way.' I understood that messages from Moscow were to be shown to him at any time of day or night.

"Napoleonic? I know what you mean. What you tell me about the way his Aunt Ana analyzes Tito's so-called pride may be apt; whether old Ana hit the nail exactly on the head, I don't know, but her explanation fits in with my own observations. In '43, I noticed that it seemed more and more important to him that his clothes were clean and pressed, that he carried himself erect even when he was dead weary. In that very difficult period—when, as I see it now more clearly than I did then, he couldn't tell where he stood with Moscow, and the 'West' was generally unfriendly—he filed his finger-nails daily. He wore a ring or two. I think that subconsciously he developed the need for a bit of bravado, of personifying the pride of his ragged, half-starved army and the working people generally.

"Every few days he invited me to lunch. It was the only time he could give me to make sketches of him. The food was never abundant or fancy, just ample, but it was much better than the food eaten by the army. Once Tito explained that he couldn't think unless he ate. A slight miscalculation he'd made once before he blamed on his not having had anything to eat the day before. Men had died because of it. I suppose there were Party orders, as a matter of practical policy, that, even if others had next-to-nothing to eat, Tito must have food. Perhaps, he agreed intellectually; at the same time he couldn't stomach the inequality. Two or three times when I lunched with him, he wouldn't eat—couldn't touch the stuff because he knew that many of the *borci* in various parts of Yugoslavia were hungry. And, then, sometimes he ate heartily. This sounds strange, if not crazy, as I tell it; and it may be worse than inexact. Who really knows anything about anybody? I'm sure of this: there was a conflict inside him—beyond my ability, then and now, to define in words. I can only guess about it. He knew thousands of his commanders and rank-and-file fighters personally.

When he received word that one of them had died or was seriously wounded, he groaned or turned pale. If the man was wounded, he called for periodic reports of the progress of his recovery. . . . He was restless. Clearly, he carried a burden. . . .

"Once a Partisan who had never seen Tito begged me to let him come to my room for a look at the Supreme Commander. He came hours ahead of time. When Tito stepped out of the maps-and-plans cabin, this Partisan behind the curtain in my room snapped to attention and up shot his fist in the Communist salute. Tito still hasn't heard about this. Nor that I watched him nearly every day. The Party had asked me to do a bust of him; I felt I had to study him, to get to know him; so I spied on him. I was aware that people worshiped him and that he didn't like it—that it weighed on him. Did he wish to free himself and them from hero-worship? Or, if he did, was this the time? Looking back, I realize that that wasn't the time. He wasn't just a solitary individual. He was the center of a closely knit *kolektif,* head of the CPY, commander of this far-flung struggle. He had to consider the entire picture, the country; and the responsibility was permanently imbedded in his soul. Our whole national experience was superimposed on his individuality. . . . I'm sure he doesn't remember all that went through his mind as he paced on top of the catacombs. How could he? He had so many urgent questions to consider: they had to be 'solved' that afternoon: he had to issue orders, had to know what to say when the High Command met at four o'clock. . . .

"Many Partisans called him *Stari*. He was the father of their rebirth in battle. Again, words are not my medium; but I've read a bit now and then. I know a little about birds: how the mother bird pushes her fledglings out of the nest, her little hawks or eaglets, so they must fly. She squawks, they squawk. An old, old story—in human existence too. Where is the climax? In the squawk? Whose? The mama bird's or the fledglings'? In their first flight? Where does paternal or maternal responsibility cease? Where does 'Napoleonism' begin? Who's to be held accountable for it, 'Napoleon' or those who follow him? Or are these speculations simply or largely irrelevant? I think, to me as an artist, they are. I restrict myself to noting when the fledgling becomes a bird, when the child becomes a man, when the slave throws off the yoke; but I don't deny anyone the right to speculate what sort of bird this is we have now, what kind of man the former child has grown into, or how free the erstwhile slave is without his yoke—or whether his freedom has turned out to be a new yoke. Queries of this kind are not my field; not because I don't want it to be—it just isn't. Who can see the exact turning point in a predicament, a life, a career? I can't. I merely make an assumption. My task is to note phenomena, scenes, factors I see and can fashion from my medium. . . .

"If you insist, I will say that I believe there was a climax in our history somewhere during that period. Just what it was, is open to speculation, as is the question of whether Tito, with his qualities and his dramatic personality, was 'responsible' for becoming *heroj* Tito or whether the hard-pressed, embattled people made him their hero out of their need. I haven't got the head for dealing with complexities of that sort. . . . Of this, however, I am quite sure: that it all came about naturally, inevitably. A period ended, another began; and here was this man who paced back and forth inside that enclosure over the Bogomili catacombs. He had had his lunch; he was under pressures from all sides; so much was at stake; he had to think, he had to think. But nothing was solved (nothing ever is). New problems loom. . . . That was the moment I tried to catch him in in my sculpture.

"This delineation of him that you and others call 'Napoleonic'— well, I think it is the result of my seeing the genesis of something. You like the face in my statue. I tried to register his pain regarding the rest of the world's, especially Moscow's, attitude toward our Revolution, his prevision of the internal problems ahead, and the posture of balance he felt he and the country needed to ride out the storms to come. 'Napoleonic' has a derogatory connotation. I saw nothing bad of this nature in him. He was a natural leader then as he is now.

"At Jajce he was proclaimed Marshal of Yugoslavia. A new state took shape around him and the Tito I sculptured is pulled out of that high moment. 'Napoleonic'? I say again, it isn't—unless this is how Napoleon looked at the moment of his first triumph while he was mortally unsure, as Tito may have been because of the tension between Moscow and him, of which people like me now know more than we knew then."

Later it occurred to me that Tito's "pride," his "Napoleonism," his uniform and glamor, are an unsolved personality problem, an unsuccessful attempt to transcend symbolically the backwardness of the country. They are correlated to the appearance of the new state which involved practical politics with its concomitant chicanery and bravado, the wielding of more and more authority, coping with the Big-Power game, the question of a Balkan federation, and other problems beyond enumeration.

Tito knew, long before 1943, that the only kind of Balkan federation that would do New Yugoslavia or any of the other small states any good was one that wouldn't become a Big-Power pawn: and only a federation that emerged from a Balkanwide popular *borba* like Yugoslavia's would be that kind. With this idea in mind, he sent his friend Svetozar Vukmanovic-Tempo, who had distinguished himself as a commander, to Albania, Greece, and Macedonia to evoke Yugoslav-like struggles there. This was in 1943. Tempo (who was Minister of Mines in the federal government in 1949) took many hours from his pressing duties to tell me about his mission. It is material for a Red cloak-and-dagger saga. It was told to me, as other stories were, on the condition that I wouldn't use it if I wrote a book, at least not unless I checked with the narrator before I published it. Since then, however, Tempo has himself indirectly disclosed the gist of it—alas! in a Marxian-polemicist book, entitled *How and Why the People's Liberation Struggle in Greece Met With Defeat*. It appeared in a limited edition in London, 1950.

Briefly, Tempo—who in 1943 didn't know for sure one-third of the material he used in his brochure—returned from Albania and Greece with a discouraging report. The CP leaders in Albania and Greece appeared to be, or were, out-and-out Moscow stooges who had been ordered to lay low. Some of them, he feared, were also British agents; a pack of sneaks *à la* Gorkic. This (almost glaringly clear in the well-documented brochure) gave the inner group of the CC, CPY something to think about. It made it necessary for the emerging new Yugoslav state, small and battered as it was, to try to become a power. . . . Power? In 1651, Thomas Hobbes, in *The Leviathan,* called the power of a man "his present means to obtain some future apparent good." Tito doubtless had "good" in mind without the qualifying adjective "apparent."

The anti-climax began in the midst of the climax. Chicanery, usually called statesmanship, became almost as essential as fighting in order to try to realize desired ends.

In itself, *partizanstvo* was a terrible, wonderful, powerful phenomenon. . . . People chronically ill with ulcers, colitis, and tuberculosis a good part of their prewar lives suddenly became well after plunging into the struggle and experiencing the freedom that, as Vlado Kozak put it, came with their readiness to die. . . . Virtually the whole movement turned not only puritan but celibate. . . . Perhaps owing to the tension of the *borba,* many women fighters didn't menstruate for months, even for years at a spell. Their hips widened strangely, and their stomachs swelled. Some began to look upon themselves as unattractive. Between battles, they confided in one another, wondering if they would ever bear children. Many wept, together and alone. . . .

But young men and women fell in love too; they met in the woods and fell in love and, after the *borba,* if they lived, were married. (Vera and Ales Bebler were one such pair.)

In 1941-42 *tikanje*—calling one another *ti,* or "thou"—was the custom among Partisans. With the prospect of a new army, a new state, this changed. *Vikanje*—calling one another *vi,* or "you"—began. Troopers were required to call their officers "you," not "thou." Here and there they nearly rebelled. The commissars told them that that was the rule in the Soviet army—as though that made it right. To the pro-Sovieteers among the commissars, of course it did. They gained the upper-hand in the Yugoslav Revolution. Tito himself, for the life of him, saw no alternative to crashing into the Soviet orbit in order to win even half a prospect, even a modicum of respect, for the Yugoslav Revolution. In many ways the Soviet system was right; it had to be the model for New Yugoslavia—if only temporarily—if only to rid the country of the "Western" financial interests. Anti-imperialism was the main drive behind the *borba.* It was a prerequisite to the peacetime revolutionary process—soon to come within view, the Partisans hoped.

In 1941-42 commanders and ordinary fighters ate the same food or no food. Then the officers became a privileged caste and had their own messes. Again the men almost rebelled. The commissars explained that their officers couldn't think without a fairly adequate amount of calories. Besides, that was how it was in the Soviet army, in all armies. It seemed that was how it had to be.

On June 25-26, 1949, the Kardelj-Pijade party, which Ales Bebler and I accompanied, toured Bosnia. Until this tour I had known Bebler mainly as a very nice fellow; the Paris-educated son of a relatively well-known, middle-class, prosperous Slovenian family; a diplomat, a linguist, and an Assistant Foreign Minister, whose English and limp dated back to the Spanish Civil War; and the Chief of Staff of the Slovenian Partisan forces in 1941–42. A few weeks before in Ljubljana I had been walking with Dr. Bozidar Lavric (who had operated on my sister Polda) when he suddenly stopped on a street corner and pointed to a wall and said:

"Right here, one day in 1942, I saw several people staring at a poster offering a reward of 100,000 lire for Ales Bebler's head. The poster had just been put up; the glue was still wet. I was about to go on to the hospital, upset and worried, when whom did I see in the little crowd but Bebler, nonchalant as you please. He saw me, smiled, winked, and walked in the other direction."

Now, in the hot, dark little room in Sarajevo to which we had been assigned after the day's traveling from Dubrovnik through Herzegovina, weary and unable to sleep, I said, "Ales, would you mind my asking you a personal question? Why did you become a Communist?"

"I don't mind at all," Bebler replied. "But if you want details, it's apt to be a longish tale. My father was a professor of chemistry in the secondary school in Idria [a town near Trieste whose principal industry was and is a quick-silver mine]. When I was a boy we were still under Austria, but I remember even before starting school, at the age of five or six, I had heard of the Serbians and Montenegrins who spoke a language similar to ours and who had countries—states—of their own. They had armies and artillery and fought wars to keep their independence. After I began school, in 1912, the Balkan Wars started and we youngsters avidly followed the stories of Montenegrin and Serbian heroism.

"There was a 'Yugoslav question' in Idria which came up in our family every once in a while. During World War I, in about 1916–17, that question rotated around the possibility of the Hapsburg Empire consisting not only of Austria and Hungary but of Yugoslavia also, or of a region with some such name, comprising Slovenia, Croatia, Dalmatia, and Bosnia-Herzegovina. I recall myself as a child drawing lines on maps that made the Dual Monarchy a *Triple* Monarchy. There was a rumor that Crown Prince Franz Ferdinand, who was assassinated in Sarajevo in 1914, favored this trialist solution.

"The First World War confused us a bit, adults and children alike: for Austria fought Italy and we Slovenians in Idria were anti-Italian by tradition based on the experience of Italian pressure in this border

area. . . . I was ten when after America's entrance in the war it became clear that the Central Powers would lose and Austria-Hungary
would cease to exist. The first suggestion I heard of what should follow
the old monarchy was its transformation into a triple instead of a dual
State, the third section of it to be called Yugoslavia. But events moved
fast and this suggestion appealed only for a short while. We heard of
President Woodrow Wilson's Fourteen Points. The principle of the
self-determination of peoples appealed to us immensely. My mother
was enthusiastic about it and about Wilson and the United States. She
had found a photo of the President and she had it framed and hung
it on the wall. We also learned that Wilson, Lloyd George, and
Clemenceau were in favor of a new South Slavic State. When Austria
did collapse in the fall of 1918, we—the overwhelming majority of the
3,500 population of Idria, a purely Slovene town—as a matter of
course considered ourselves part of Yugoslavia. The Slovenian political
parties: Clericals, Liberals, and Social-Democrats, formed a National
Council and appointed my father (who had just returned from the
Army), Chief of Defense. We had an 'army' of fifteen or twenty
soldiers who patrolled the streets. They were former Austrian soldiers
and had removed the Austrian insignia from their caps and tunics
and wore red-white-and-blue cockades. We boys participated in street
manifestations and argued trying to guess what the new Yugoslav flag
would look like. . . . But all this lasted only about a week.

"One afternoon an Italian army automobile appeared in Idria. Two
officers who stepped out of it said they represented the Allied Powers
and wished to see my father. The Italian army was on the other side
of the river Soca (Isonzo). The officers wanted to go a bit beyond
Idria to look for some Italian cannons the Austrians had captured and
abandoned. My father called a meeting of the National Council which
allowed the Italian automobile to proceed. . . . The next morning
Idria was occupied by a couple of Italian battalions. Soon the Italian
commander ordered the National Council dissolved and I don't recall
what happened to my father's army. It no longer patrolled the streets.
. . . A bunch of us boys who had read of Serbian and Montenegrin
heroism plotted to form a guerrilla band, retire to the hills, and roll
boulders down on the enemy. But our parents dissuaded us; we were
told that the Italian Occupation was only temporary and the Peace
Conference in Paris would decide in our favor. America—the great

President Wilson, champion of small nations—would take our side. The principle of the self-determination of nations would go into effect. That's how naïve everybody was.

"For months everything was normal and quiet in Idria—on the surface. Underneath, a struggle had begun between the town and the Italian Occupation authority as to whether the schools and other institutions would be Slovenian or Italian. My father was at the center of it. . . . One night he learned he was liable to be arrested and the next morning our house was surrounded by Italian soldiers. We were permitted to go and come if our explanation were satisfactory. A week or so went by. Then one evening my father dressed himself as a peasant, embraced us, and said good-by. I realized he was fleeing to Yugoslavia.

"Several weeks passed and no word from father. Had he been captured crossing the border—killed? Mother could not stand the uncertainty and somehow the idea came up that I should cross the border the same way father had and inquire about him. I joined a group of other town folk preparing to flee to Yugoslavia. We gathered in a farmhouse not far from the new border. We slept a few hours in the barn and at three or four in the morning were conducted by the farmer across the border. Just before we crossed into Yugoslavia an Italian patrol fired at us. It was the first time I felt bullets whiz by my head. I was eleven. . . . On the other side of the line I had expected to find a heroic Yugoslav army backed by President Wilson, awaiting us, and we would tell our story and learn that the people of the Slovenian Littoral at last would have a chance to determine their own future.

"Alas, there was no heroic Yugoslav army. . . . We made our way to Ljubljana. Nobody of any standing there was very interested in the future status of Trieste with its great port and in Idria with its quicksilver mine, or in the rest of the Littoral. I couldn't understand this. I found father through relatives. He was puzzled too. Years later I blamed it on the power politics of the Allies who in 1916 signed the London Pact promising Idria and many other Slovenian and Croatian towns and districts to Italy as a reward for its joining them in the war. And I blamed the Yugoslav bourgeoisie who were unable to defend efficiently our national rights.

"In the spring of 1919 Mother and the rest of our family slipped out of Idria. In 1920 my father—Dr. Boltezar Bebler—found a job as chemist with a firm in Celje, in Styria (a city not far from Kumrovec), and we settled there. For the next couple of years, while attending secondary school in Celje, I continued to cling to the Wilsonian principle of the self-determination of nations. Young as I was, even after Wilson ceased to be President and even after he died, I was positive it would be realized. . . . I was about fifteen when I finally woke up to the facts of political life. There was the centralist pan-Serbian regime in Belgrade, backed by Paris and London. There was a new fascist-like organization called *Orjuna,* small but very obstreperous. . . .

"Father was very unhappy. The firm he worked for—a zinc melting plant—had been Austro-Hungarian state property and under the Versailles Treaties had become Yugoslav state property. But the state suddenly sold two-thirds of it to two private banks, the more important of which was the 'Serbian Commercial Bank.' The representative of this bank, a fellow called Lazarevic, came from Belgrade and started behaving as if he were head of the firm. He created a 'company' to sell the products of the plant; then got the firm to sign a contract with this 'company' obliging it to cede all its products to the 'company' for production costs. In one word all the profits went to the two private banks, the state was robbed. Father was beside himself. He blurted out that the whole affair was a swindle. He wouldn't serve as a front for it. Lazarevic threatened to frame him and send him to jail if he didn't play the game. Father replied that his life was an open book and he wanted no part of this deal. That was in 1923 or early '24. Father had put away some savings and he said we would have to live on that—very sparingly—until he found other work. From this time on Lazarevic and his scheme were for me the symbols of what went on in Belgrade and throughout Yugoslavia.

"Meantime, in the *Gymnasium* which I now attended we students were split into three camps—the fascistic *Orjunasi,* who agitated for a strong centralist regime in Belgrade; a small progressive group who were opposed to the *Orjuna* but had no program; and the Christian-Socialists. I joined the progressives and was elected chairman of the committee for cultural activities. We heard that the *Orjuna* was financed from abroad: it had a lot of money for printed matter, and its members wore silver and gold emblems. We progressives had no money, no printed matter, no emblems. We were called Communists; but it had never occurred to me that I was one and I didn't know anyone who was one or who knew what a Communist was. My father, a very political-minded man, was very vague on the subject when I asked him.

"On June 1, 1924, an incident occurred in Trbovlje (a coal town in Slovenia), which became a decisive factor in orienting many Slovenians Leftward—possibly a majority of Slovenian youth. The *Orjuna* invaded Trbovlje and staged a demonstration. The miners counter-demonstrated. The *Orjunasi* kidnapped a mine union leader named Fakin and killed him.

"I set this incident beside the one involving my father and the Serbian Commercial Bank's crooked deals. A few days before the Trbovlje incident someone had given me a booklet that described the Soviet Union as a federation of workers' states in which the nationality question had been solved—each state had its own language, press, schools, and other cultural institutions: exactly what Yugoslavia needed. I forget the title of the booklet but I remember the very emphatic statement on its last page: that the workers, the proletarians, were the soundest element in every country. I had no doubt about this even before I heard my father say one evening that, from all he could learn the Trbovlje miners had acted as they should and the *Orjunasi* had committed a great wrong. They had killed Fakin in cold blood—on somebody's orders, no doubt. From accounts he trusted, he believed that Fakin had been a nice man, a good Slovenian, who had fought for workers' rights. The Trbovlje mine was partly owned by foreign capital.

"I requested that our progressive group in school call a meeting and take a stand against the *Orjuna*. A meeting was called but the majority of those who attended it couldn't make up their minds. They succumbed to the menacing atmosphere that pervaded the school and the city at large. I resigned. After that everybody began to regard me as a Red.

"Father was a competent chemist and got a job with a small pharmaceutical business in Ljubljana. He did quite well for a while. I was in the seventh or eighth class of the *Gymnasium* at this time. Father gave me all the money I needed for books, and in 1925 when I was eighteen, he let me go to Paris. He had no influence on my political thinking from then on. He remained a bourgeois democrat until he died. What exactly he thought of me I don't know except that I felt he sympathized with my ideas.

"In France, unlike Yugoslavia which was a French semi-colony, the

CP was a legal party. There was freedom I could scarcely believe was real. There was an enormous Marxian and CPF literature. I learned French very quickly and tried to read everything. I sat in the library every evening until closing time. In the daytime I studied law, thinking that that would prepare me for politics. Every four or five months I returned to Yugoslavia. In 1928 I met Edvard Kardelj. We were members of a secret Marxist study group. I remember Kardelj very well from those days. Someone in our group spoke about Josip Broz: how boldly he had behaved in court in Zagreb. That year I was enrolled in the secret Communist Youth organization in Slovenia. I had seen Franc Leskosek in Celje, where he was a Social Democratic candidate running for this or that office, but now I heard a rumor that he was a Communist. In '29 I was admitted to the underground CP in Slovenia.

"In Paris, as I read the vast Left literature, entire new vistas opened to me. There was the upheaval in China. I read piles of books on the Soviet Union. Of course the reactionary press was full of unfavorable reports about Russia—the exact opposite of what I saw in the Left press—but I believed the latter. The USSR under Stalin, Lenin's successor, was a new form of statehood, a new economic system, readying itself to meet the coming attack.

"I was in my early twenties and idealistic. Each time I returned to Slovenia, the Communist approach appealed to me more. The section of Slovenia which was in Yugoslavia we young Communists considered a subject province of Belgrade and, worse, over half a million Slovenians were under Mussolini's rule in Italy, and about a hundred thousand of our people were in Carinthia which the Paris Peace Conference had left in Austria by means of an artificially framed 'plebiscite.' No one except the Communists were interested in the plight of the Slovenians under Mussolini. I met several young men who had escaped from Idria. Among them were my former schoolmates. They were all Communists or they had come to Yugoslavia to join the movement in Slovenia. Slovenia, too, was under a dictatorship then; people were arrested and beaten and killed; but our small secret CP, like the CP in Italy had the cause of the Slovenians under Mussolini at heart. . . .

"Each time I returned to Paris I was more certain than ever that Marxism encompassed the main phases of our Slovenian and general human problem. It could be solved only internationally by people

who cared. I met young Croatians, Montenegrins, and Bosnians studying abroad, some of them from well-to-do families, who felt as I did.
Like myself, they were giving less and less time to the Sorbonne cur-
riculum and more and more time to reading and discussing Marxist-
Leninist books and pamphlets. I met young Serbians from Serbia who
felt as we of the minority nationalities felt. They held that pan-Ser-
bianism, working as it did through the Belgrade hegemony, wasn't any
good for the majority of Serbian people, either. . . . They, too, became Communists. Many fought in the Spanish Civil War, as I did;
for the same reason. Some—many—died in our *borba*. . . . Why did
we become Communists? . . ."

The next day as we continued on our journey, I traveled part of the
way with three Bosnians who tried to explain the *borba* to me in terms
of places, march routes, dates, enemy offensives, and casualty figures
which made my head reel. Then, after we had passed through a village that looked no poorer than any other we had passed through, the
Bosnian on my right (one arm off, one eye out) called to the driver to
stop.

"Very little has been written about our struggle that can be called
history," he said. "Each of us has his own ideas about what's important. . . . *I* think one of the most important incidents occurred right
here toward the end of 1941, when Tito's army was heading this way
from Serbia.

"We had a minor detachment up here in the woods. It was bitterly
cold. All four winters of the strife were severe. At that particular time,
the snow was frozen hard and it was possible to move around. A
couple of hundred Ustasi arrived by train from somewhere at the station a few kilometers away. They were a crew of looters, not a massacre team. They killed only when the notion seized them. They had no
set program. Apparently, this village was on their list to be looted. It
must have got there by mistake, for this was never a rich village, not
by the wildest stretch of imagination. Anyhow, about twenty Ustasi
descended on it like locusts. I think they killed one or two people for
fun. Criminals. The Ustasi 'movement' was not a movement at all, but
a gang organized and turned loose for political purposes by the Axis.
You know that.

"At any rate, one villager came running to us in the woods. We
were freezing to death. Our commander was a Communist. We called

ourselves a Partisan detachment. We went down and reached the village right after the Ustasi had withdrawn with their haul, which wasn't much—some sacks of grain, wool, a few clocks, and some smoked meat. There were about twenty of us. We went after them, gave them battle, lost two men, felled eight or ten Ustasi, and took the loot back. It was strapped to horses and donkeys which also belonged to the village. The remaining Ustasi fled and rejoined their fellows-in-crime who were busy looting elsewhere, I suppose, or were loading the stuff they'd grabbed onto the train. That's unimportant—about them. What's important is that, by order of our Communist commander, we returned the loot to the village—no small thing, believe me, considering our shortages. The women were still weeping. The villagers, when they saw us tramping in, leading their horses and donkeys, couldn't believe their eyes and ears.

"Our commander told them we had attacked and defeated the Ustasi, and here was their property. In a few days the story spread over half of Bosnia—spread and grew—that a Partisan detachment gave the Ustasi a terrific beating and brought back the goods the criminals had stolen. The Partisans could have kept the loot, but they returned it. There was honesty for you. Justice. . . . Then came the Tito column. Were they Partisans too? the people asked. Yes, they were, the Partisans replied, and the people joined them in droves. . . .

"No; that's where you're wrong—our attack on the Ustasi and our returning the loot wasn't mere politics. It was orders, yes; but more than orders. Our commander explained to us that if we kept the loot we'd be no better than the Ustasi. It would be as if we had looted the village ourselves, and that would be like robbing your brother, your family. It was as simple as that."

Nearly all the priests of the several Churches were anti-Partisan. But, as already suggested, in Slovenia early in 1949 I met Catholic priests who had been pro-Partisan. I also met a number of ex-priests who had been unfrocked because they had joined the Partisans.

I have mentioned the ruined castle Turjak, not far from where I was born; and that I had visited it several times. It fascinated me. Over and over again I listened to accounts of the great battle waged there in 1943.

Nearby was the hamlet where Primoz Trubar was born. He was one of the earliest Slovenian authors, famous largely for his pro-Reformation stand when Reformation, which was soon overwhelmed by Counter-Reformation, reached Slovenia. The Austrian-German family which owned Turjak were also pro-Reformation, and Trubar hid in the castle when the inquisitionists were hot on his trail. One of his close friends was a Reformationist priest named Dalmatinov, who also hid in Turjak. Dalmatinov conducted Protestant services in the castle's little chapel.

Hundreds of years later I stood in that chapel. It has a large hole in the three-foot-thick wall. I was told that a Partisan field gun had made the hole, and that then, following a long siege, the Partisans had climbed up the steep mountainside and up a ladder and through the hole into the chapel; whereupon they had fought the priest-led White Guards occupying the castle from room to room.

Once Bozidar Jakac, the artist, went to Turjak with me. Some of his close friends had fallen there in 1943, and he recalled them. He thought the castle should be repaired. First of all, he said, the chapel ought to be repaired because on one of its walls was some art work he considered worth preserving. I had no objection to preserving the art, but I thought the castle should be left as it was. I liked castles in ruins.

I especially liked that great hole in the chapel wall. But its symbolic significance didn't consciously occur to me, and then only as the glimmer of an idea, until after I had re-read a poorly written account of the Turjak battle I had clipped from a Ljubljana newspaper sometime before.

Then, in the course of the Kardelj-Pijade tour, I found myself in Jajce, Bosnia. Both Kardelj and Pijade had been in the Bogomili catacombs during the war. Now they had to hold a meeting with the local *aktivisti* which Ales Bebler and I weren't obliged to attend. We hunted up a member of the Jajce people's committee who had the key to the entrance to the catacombs. Waiting for him to fetch it, we took a look at Tito's maps-and-plans shack; and I recalled sculptor Augustincic's word-picture of Tito walking inside the enclosure after lunch each day.

I think that in all of New Yugoslavia in 1949, except for the ancient Macedonian and Serbian frescoes, I saw nothing more beautiful than the Bogomili catacombs inside that mountain on the outskirts of Jajce. Our guide had a flashlight; Bebler and I followed him down, down; and we went from hall to hall. The lines and proportions in these subterranean chambers bordered on perfection. Here and there were tombs and symbols that meant nothing to me except that they were beautiful.

Neither Bebler nor I knew very much about Bogomili history, and I have been unable to find anything readable on the subject in Yugoslavia or elsewhere. Bogomili history is still to be written. Suffice it to say that the Bogomili were a movement which for two, three hundred years was against both "Western" and "Eastern" theocratic systems with their power-hungry popes, cardinals, and metropolitans. The priestless (almost leaderless) movement spread widely through the Balkans and left thousands of monuments in its wake before its persecutors crushed it. (Miroslav Krleza had told me that the Yugoslav Academy, of which he was vice-president, had recently organized a project to preserve these monuments—a gigantic task.)

In the cool, dim catacombs I had a sense of freedom, of values, of a span of experience. But it wasn't until some time after my return to America, after I began to write this book, that I connected the hole in the Turjak chapel wall with the Jajce catacombs, which had practically been Tito's headquarters—certainly his bombshelter—for a while late in 1943.

While I was in Yugoslavia, I thought of the Yugoslav Revolution partly in terms of the fact that it had been led by the CPY—by Tito, as secretary-general of the Communist Party of Yugoslavia—but chiefly in terms of a popular anti-imperialist move, of a bid by the Yugoslav peoples to pull themselves together, to focus their culture, their values, into social meaning. In America, as I went over my notes while the world quaked, and wondered what my book's thought texture would be if I wrote it, if I finished it, it suddenly dawned on me one day that in all probability the Communist-led Yugoslav Revolution was, in part at least, a delayed re-attempt at Reformation; and that that was why the old Churches had fought it so fiercely.

I have quoted from Edvard Kocbek's diary which I read in proof early in 1949, and I mentioned parenthetically that I met Kocbek, a non-Communist member of the Slovenian Praesidium. I saw him three times; once in his Ljubljana apartment for a couple of hours. He seemed in a state of suspense, beset by a need for mystical groping for consistency or a central *motif*. We talked about his book: its publication was delayed because of the paper shortage. I said I hoped to get a copy before I returned to America. Kocbek promised to send me one. As I was leaving his apartment, he handed me a bulky envelope which, he explained, contained copies of some of the letters he had written to the Bishop of Ljubljana during the war, and to a number of his priest friends from prewar days who were anti-Liberation, anti-communist, and pro-occupation during the *borba.* Josip Vidmar had mentioned this correspondence to me, and had suggested to Kocbek that he give me copies of it. I didn't open the envelope until about a year later.

I had been back in the United States for several months when I received a beautifully bound, autographed copy of Edvard Kocbek's book. I laid it aside; I had read it in proof, anyhow.

Then, late in the spring of 1950 I realized how violent were the political tremors around the world. There was Korea. . . . Should I finish my book? Who would care to grasp the Yugoslav Story? . . . I was tired; I needed time out; and I laid off work for the next few months. But I was interested in seismographic data; and there were days when I picked up almost anything and read it—it was almost sure to contain something about the continuing earthquake. On the floor, tables, and shelves of my room were those heaps of material for my book. One day I leafed through Kocbek's diary and came on an entry I must have missed when I read the proofs:

August 7, 1942: . . . *Last night Boris Kidric and I engaged in a long conversation about Thomas Münzer, the Thuringian cleric, who tied up the need of a religious Reformation in Germany with the uprisings of the German peasants in the sixteenth century. Engels tells about him in his* The German Peasants' War, *but Kidric knows details about Münzer Engels didn't mention. I decided to draw Kidric out, and he almost inundated me with the historic circumstances that made Münzer's Reformation significant, not in the way the contents of Luther's pamphlets were, but in the lives of the German people; with the reasons why Luther turned upon Münzer, namely, because Münzer's movement was a people's movement, as Engels points out, whereas Luther aimed to achieve his Reformation within the existing feudal system. Kidric reeled off Münzer's democratic ideas; Münzer's views that the mainsprings of the peasant upheavals were economic and also a manifestation of God's will; Münzer's sermons to the peasants, quoting the Bible in support of rebellion; Münzer's thesis that religion was so much nothing if it was purely contemplative, that it had to be active, revolutionary, taking in all the peoples of the world, for Christ had sacrificed Himself for all men, and that there was no truth except the truth that resided in all humanity and could be grasped by humanity as a whole living in one society. "Of course that's why they killed Münzer," said Kidric. . . . Isn't it ironical that a Communist should be telling me, a Christian, about Münzer? After the war I must get hold of everything I can on him. . . .* [Freely translated and condensed from p. 104, *Tovarisija,* by Edvard Kocbek.]

Then I found and opened the bulky envelope and read Kocbek's epistles from the Liberation Front Headquarters on Mount Rog and the various dugouts in Lower Slovenia to the bishop in Ljubljana and to priests here and there, calling on them to cease collaborating with the Axis occupation and join the people in their struggle. This correspondence—so extensive it would fill a book itself—is before me and falls in the same pigeonhole in my mind as Kocbek's diary entry about Kidric and Münzer, Turjak and Jajce, and the old Serbian Orthodox priest in Nova Varos, and the frequent impressions I received of individuals and groups in New Yugoslavia (especially from June 1949 on)—that they, perhaps the whole country, were in a state of suspense, on the verge of re-thinking their upheaval.

The delayed re-attempt at Reformation in Yugoslavia, with its revolutionary economic emphases, was anti-Church less on the ground of doctrine or dogma than because the Church—closely associated with the prewar regime in Belgrade, or with Rome, or with both Rome and Belgrade, and with the whole sick situation in Europe which finally flowered in fascism—had been a mainstay of technological backwardness and had helped to put the South Slavic people into an ever deepening political-diplomatic-military hole. I don't know for sure but I think that herein is the primary significance of the Yugoslav Revolution which, under Tito's leadership, reached its climax in 1943–44.

The strictly Marxian intelligentsia among the Yugoslav revolutionaries didn't understand that climax. Circumstances hitting them in the face right and left compelled them, they felt, to embrace the Soviet system—which perhaps, too, was inceptionally a Reformation measure but which by the 1930's had become the anti-climax of the climax called the Russian Revolution. The nature of the Yugoslav Revolution, at its climax, was clearest, perhaps, in the instincts of ordinary, non-intellectual Yugoslavs, the *borci* and the people behind them: in their united multi-mindedness, their *partizanstvo*, which was still there in 1949, still vital—perhaps vital as ever, or more so—but in a pause, about to take time out to try to look at itself, to look at the rest of the world and see, if possible, what had happened, what was the matter, and why, as though beginning to perceive the inevitableness of some of the fallacies in the drives of the upheavals, as though it was on the verge of asking "And what now?"

For a while in the second half of 1950, when this aspect of the Yugoslav Revolution appeared to me, I thought—superficially—it was the height of irony that, from 1945 on, Protestant Britain and Protestant America, having grown into "giants" partly as a result of the Reformation, supported—indeed, led—Rome's Counter-Reformationary struggle against Tito; that the British and Americans, caught in and confused by the welter of problems issuing from the Industrial Revolution which followed the Reformation, became a factor in the anti-climactic period of the Yugoslav Revolution; that they gave Tito no choice but to take Yugoslavia into the Soviet orbit.

Then, gradually, I perceived that "Anglo-American" behavior in regard to Tito probably was inevitable too, part of British and American hallucinations still in process. And later still, as I played a recording of Beethoven's *Eroica,* which I had heard so often in Yugoslavia, it seemed to me that this thought was irrelevant too. It took me back to Goethe, to Shelley's translation of *Faust,* in which I came upon "Gabriel" and "Michael" saying:

> GABRIEL: . . . *Alternating Elysian brightness*
> *With deep and dreadful night—*
> MICHAEL: *And tempests in contention roar*
> *From land to sea, from sea to land;*
> *And raging, weave a chain of power*
> *Which girds the earth as with a band.*

Not to mention Britain, America had begun to weave "a chain of power" during World War II—in fact, long before the war; Protestantism and Catholicism, both nearly devoid of Münzer, had long ago been caught in this chain, perhaps Protestantism more than Catholicism; so what could you expect? Captain Ahab and his mates were on their voyage. What could you expect but insanity and tremors? Especially now—with a new "giant," calling itself the USSR, at large? . . . What chance had Njegos? His concept of a nation's, a man's self-realization in freedom? . . .

Climax was loaded with anti-climax. But perhaps the other way around was true too. Anti-climax was pregnant with a new climax. Only, this time, was it *the* Anti-Climax all around? Or would a new climax be born? Was the New Birth of Freedom possible? Hardly. That was utopianism! cried the self-styled Marxians and the hysterical "private enterprise" voices in unison. All right. But, *if* it didn't occur——

If it occurred, it would have to begin to occur everywhere: within the roaring Industrial Revolution in America, in scarcely developed Yugoslavia, in Russia too—— But how? *How?*